MW01259409

SAP® Change and Transport Management

Armin Kösegi, Rainer Nerding

SAP® Change and Transport Management

Bonn • Boston

ISBN 978-1-59229-247-9

3rd edition, updated and revised

3rd German Edition published 2008 by Galileo Press, Bonn, Germany.

Galileo Press is named after the Italian physicist, mathematician and philosopher Galileo Galilei (1564–1642). He is known as one of the founders of modern science and an advocate of our contemporary, heliocentric worldview. His words *Eppur si muove* (And yet it moves) have become legendary. The Galileo Press logo depicts Jupiter orbited by the four Galilean moons, which were discovered by Galileo in 1610.

Editor Florian Zimniak
English Edition Editor Justin Lowry
Translation Lemoine International, Inc., Salt Lake City, UT
Copy Editor Jutta VanStean
Cover Design Jill Winitzer
Photo Credit Getty Images/Rosemary Calvert
Layout Design Vera Brauner
Production Kelly O'Callaghan
Typesetting Publishers' Design and Production Services, Inc.
Printed and bound in Canada

Contents at a Glance

Contents

PART II Technical Tasks

Appendices 881

Foreword

At SAP, our first priority is to ensure that the SAP software solutions in your enterprise run successfully and at minimal cost. This "lowest cost of ownership" is achieved with fast and efficient implementation, together with optimal and dependable operation. SAP Active Global Support is actively and consistently there to help you, with the new SAP Solution Management strategy. With this strategy, throughout the entire lifecycle of a solution, SAP offers customers all necessary services, first-class support, a suitable infrastructure, and the relevant know-how. The new strategy is backed up by three powerful support programs: *Safeguarding*, or—in other words—risk management; *Solution Management Optimization*, which aims to optimize the customer's IT solution; and *Empowering*, which ensures targeted, effective transfer of knowledge from SAP to the customer.

Imparting knowledge is also one of the key goals of this book. It gives you a detailed overview of technical aspects and concepts for managing SAP software solutions.

Whether you are new to SAP system management or want to obtain further qualifications, you will benefit from the wealth of practical experience and first-hand information contained in this book. With this book, SAP also endeavors to help prepare you for qualification as "Certified Technical Consultant." Please note, however: Books can't replace — nor do they attempt to — personal experience gained from working with the various SAP solutions! Rather, the authors offer suggestions to help in your day-to-day work with the software.

Innovation in SAP solutions always brings with it new challenges and solutions for system management. The demands made on the customer's own or external support organizations also increase. The expertise and knowledge of these organizations can be a great help in avoiding problems when using the software. Therefore, one of the core tasks of this series of books is to teach problem-solving skills.

Even in this Internet age, books prove to be an ideal medium for imparting knowledge in a compact form. Furthermore, their content complements the new service and support platform SAP Solution Manager, as well as other new services offered by SAP. The book series provides background knowledge on the operation and functioning of new SAP solutions and contributes to customer satisfaction.

Gerhard Oswald
Member of the SAP executive board

Uwe Hommel
Executive Vice President, SAP AG
SAP Active Global Support

Introduction

SAP ERP 6.0 is the SAP solution around the successor of SAP R/3—SAP ECC 6.0—that provides even more functionality by using additional software components to meet the requirements of enterprises and organizations of any size. Although this functionality is built into the software, it must be configured during its implementation to meet the specific needs of an organization. This process, known as *Customizing*, uses special SAP adaptation tools. A customer's SAP adaptation may also require *development* work; that is, the customer must program new or modified functionality using SAP's ABAP programming language.

Implementation requirements

In general, SAP ERP 6.0 resembles most other business software installations in that its implementation requires the following:

- Configuration and/or development work
- A carefully planned realization of business needs in the software
- The realization of an appropriate technical infrastructure in the system landscape
- Project management that controls the scope of what is to be implemented and defines the roles and responsibilities of the people on the implementation team
- Thorough testing and validation of the changes achieved through Customizing or development
- Training for end users
- Future expansion of the software's initially implemented functionality and usage

To provide an infrastructure that fulfills these implementation needs, SAP recommends implementing the different software instances with three strictly separate environments:

- A development environment for Customizing and development work

- A quality assurance environment for testing business functionality using representative test data
- A production environment for normal business operations that is safe from changes made in other environments until the changes have been verified and are ready for transfer into the production environment

These three environments are realized through *systems* and *clients*, which are logical divisions within an SAP system. The collection of clients and systems required for an SAP implementation forms the *system landscape*.

Figure 1 shows the standard three-system landscape used to support SAP ERP 6.0 (or previous versions) and that is recommended by SAP. The development system is an SAP ERP system for Customizing and development efforts. When Customizing and development work has been completed, the quality assurance system is used to test and verify this work. After Customizing and development changes have been validated and approved, they are delivered to the production system.

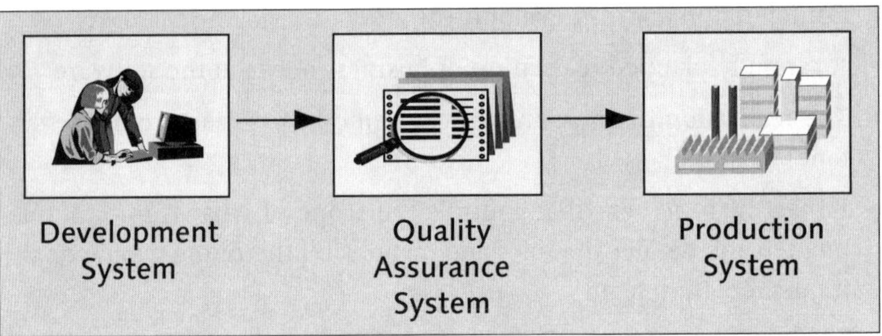

Figure 1 The Standard Three-System Landscape

To manage changes created during Customizing and development, and to ensure that applications remain consistent across multiple SAP systems, changes are recorded and organized in *change requests* and are *transported* to different clients and SAP systems within the system landscape. The process of transporting requires the *releasing* and *exporting* of the change requests from the development system and then *importing* them into another SAP system. The techniques for change and transport management are also known as software logistics—the process of moving or transporting changes made to the SAP software

Change and transport management tasks

Implementing change and transport includes the following tasks:

- Setting up a system landscape
- Regulating the systems and clients in which Customizing and development changes are made
- Recording Customizing and development changes to change requests during the initial implementation of SAP *and* during any subsequent improvement of the production environment
- Managing the transport of changes to all clients and SAP systems within the system landscape
- Testing, validating, and approving changes using the quality assurance system
- Maintaining the production system over time by applying SAP Support Packages and upgrades

Although the main goal of a particular SAP ERP 6.0 implementation is to fulfill your business requirements, this can be realized only if you ensure system stability and data validity through correct change and transport management. Beyond the implementation of the software solution, only well-conceived and proven strategies for further projects, software maintenance activities, and upgrades make it possible to keep your investments for many years and possibly even increase them.

Many aspects of change and transport management are technical in nature, but the procedures you define to implement change and transport management will affect all staff members. It is mainly the staff in the corresponding functional departments who have the business knowledge required to perform Customizing and to test SAP systems, and it is they who perform these functions. Therefore, not just technical staff, but all people involved in an SAP implementation need to understand change and transport management and the structure of the system landscape. Those who actually make the changes to the SAP system need additional expert knowledge of the relevant tools and procedures.

The information in this book is organized in three parts, each aimed at people involved in this procedure at different levels.

Part 1 Part 1, The Big Picture, provides a basic explanation of how changes are made and distributed. It enables those managing the SAP implementation to develop a valid change and transport management strategy.

Part 2 Part 2, Technical Tasks, is essential reading for technicians coordinating the setup of the technical infrastructure or performing, for example, SAP system administration tasks.

Part 3 Part 3, Tools, is the how-to section, providing detailed information on the tools described in Part 1. This part also serves as a reference for those who require in-depth knowledge. The first three chapters of Part 3 (Chapters 10 to 12) will be of particular use to anyone performing Customizing or development work during an SAP implementation. They also describe changes that can be made without modifications—enabled by the Switch and Enhancement Framework that was delivered for the first time with SAP NetWeaver 7.0.

Chapters 13 and 14 are indispensable to those responsible for importing changes and analyzing potential errors. Chapter 15 contains information about transports in Java by using the SAP NetWeaver Development Infrastructure (NWDI), which is primarily used for distributing developments with SAP Web Dynpro in the SAP NetWeaver Portal. Chapter 16 describes the options in CTS+, an enhanced transport system, to distribute ABAP and non-ABAP changes within the systems using the same procedure.

Chapters 17 and 18 contain information about maintenance and the change of release in an SAP ERP system landscape. These chapters are relevant to system administrators and technical consultants who need to perform these tasks. Project leads can also obtain an overview of necessary activities and efficient procedures for maintenance or upgrade projects. This holds particularly true for the description of Unicode conversions in the context of upgrades and for the usage of the new functions provided in SAP enhancement packages.

Chapter 19 describes new SAP Solution Manager functionality in the area of software change management. In addition to the Customizing synchronization within an SAP system landscape and its usage in the context of upgrade projects, this chapter deals with the comprehensive options in change request management in particular.

The information in this book pertains primarily to the ABAP instances of SAP NetWeaver 7.0 and the software components based on it such as SAP ERP 6.0 ECC 6.0. Other SAP products—parts of SAP ERP 6.0 as well as other SAP solutions—use the same technology because they are all based on SAP NetWeaver 7.0. There can be slight differences, however. For example, not all SAP products use the same client concept as SAP ERP 6.0 ECC 6.0, and some SAP products have extended the standard functionality for their purposes. In these cases, the menu paths shown in this book might not be directly reproducible. However, the basics of and the tools for operating these products are still of value because they will enable you to understand the principles of change and transport management. In addition, you should consult the specific product documentation.

Important notes and tips can be found in the sections indicated with this icon. **[+]**

Gray passages indicate examples.

PART I
The Big Picture

During customer activities in the SAP ERP system such as development and Customizing, changes are made to the software. Change and transport management consists of special procedures for distributing these changes across your system landscape. The need for logistics or coordination of changes arises from three main facts:

- To ensure data consistency, changes may need to be limited to some or all clients, in some or all systems. Where, how, and when these changes are introduced must be regulated.
- The customer's production system must be protected from changes that have not been fully tested. This means Customizing, development, and testing of changes should be performed in systems outside of the production system.
- Any number of people may be making different kinds of changes at the same time or at different times. This means that objects and settings must be protected, changes must be documented, and a change history must be made available.

Software logistics is the logistics of managing these changes and the corresponding requirements in the system landscape. To establish software logistics during your SAP implementation, you need to do the following:

- Set up change management
- Implement a transport strategy

- Build a system landscape that allows you to make and test all required changes while preventing inconsistencies and protecting the integrity of your production system

In Part 1, this procedure is explained in more detail, and you are encouraged to use SAP-recommended standards. The specific topics covered in Part 1 include the following:

- An introduction to the components of the system landscape
- An introduction to the realization of business requirements through Customizing and development efforts
- An explanation of clients and client roles used in an implementation
- Guidelines for setting up and maintaining a system landscape
- An introduction to the relevant SAP tools. These tools receive more extensive coverage in Part 2 and Part 3.

To understand the SAP client/server architecture and the concepts of correction and transport system based on this architecture, this chapter describes concepts such as data, Customizing, and client as well as their interdependencies.

1 SAP ERP Architecture and Data Components

SAP ERP architecture is shaped by its use of client/server technology—that is, the way the architecture distributes the software services needed by users over multiple servers. SAP ERP system administration and performance optimization require a detailed understanding of this technology. In contrast, change and transport management—which is implemented by configuring the SAP ERP system appropriately—focuses mainly on a specific element within the architecture, namely the database. Change and transport is concerned with the following:

Contents

- The role the database plays in the architecture
- The architecture of the database itself, in terms of the data components and clients

The database stores the SAP ERP software. An important part of this software is the *SAP ERP Repository*, which provides the runtime environment for the various business applications. The database also contains the various data components, such as the business data required for or generated by day-to-day business transactions.

Container

Data can be isolated by assigning it to one of several separate *containers* in the SAP ERP Repository. These containers are called *clients*. When a user logs on, they log on to a particular client and can display or change only the data that corresponds to that client. Data that can be displayed or changed from only one client is called *client-dependent* data. Data that can be accessed from all clients is called *client-independent* data or *cross-client* data.

To ensure the success of your change and transport management strategy, the people performing Customizing or development during SAP ERP system implementation need to understand the following:

- The different data components in the database
- Which data is client-dependent and which is client-independent

After a brief look at the client/server architecture, this chapter describes the SAP ERP database, clients, and the various data components. It also explains which data is client-dependent and which data can be accessed by all clients.

For information on how to create and maintain the various data components, see Chapter 2.

1.1 Client/Server Architecture in Brief

SAP recognized early on that to provide a scalable and global business software package to meet a wide range of customer needs, client/server technology was the way to go. This technology distributes different applications and system services across multiple hardware servers. Servers may contain a combination of services, and run on different hardware platforms. SAP's use of multilayer client/server computing maximizes performance and provides flexibility in management and hardware options.

Services

The client/server architecture of SAP ERP consists of three types of services:

- A database service for storing and retrieving business data
- An application service for running business processes
- A presentation service for the graphical user interface (GUI)

From a hardware perspective, these three layers—the database, application, and presentation layers—can run separately on different servers or all together on the same server. A typical installation supporting numerous SAP users uses multiple presentation servers. To increase system performance, the application layer can be distributed over multiple servers. This is shown in Figure 1.1, where a database server and multiple application and presentation servers support an SAP ERP system.

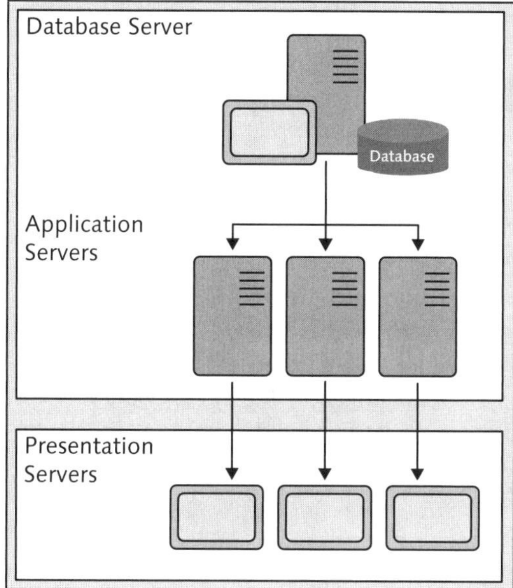

Figure 1.1 The Three-Layer Architecture of SAP ERP

Regardless of the number of application and presentation servers, each SAP ERP system has only one database. It is the number of databases (one for each SAP ERP system) in which changes originate or to which changes must be transported that is of central importance for change and transport management.

Example: SAP ERP Client/Server Technology in Practice

A medium-sized distribution firm purchases a Hewlett-Packard server for running the Windows Server 2003 operating system. An Oracle database is chosen because the company is already using Oracle for other applications. Both the Oracle database and the SAP ERP applications run on the Hewlett-Packard server.

The presentation servers are PCs using SAP's graphical user interface (SAP GUI) or a Web browser running SAP NetWeaver Portal to connect to the database and application processes of SAP ERP (see Figure 1.2).

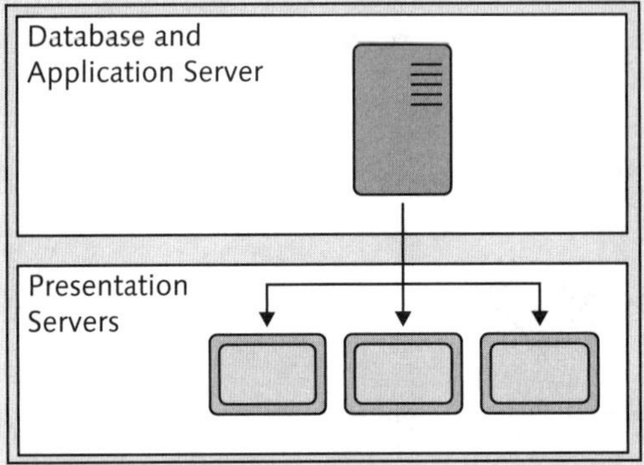

Figure 1.2 An Integrated Database and Application Server

After some time has gone by, significant growth in the data volume and the number of users reduces system performance. Therefore, two additional Hewlett-Packard servers are purchased and added to the SAP ERP system as application servers. The only service still running on the original server is the Oracle database (see Figure 1.3).

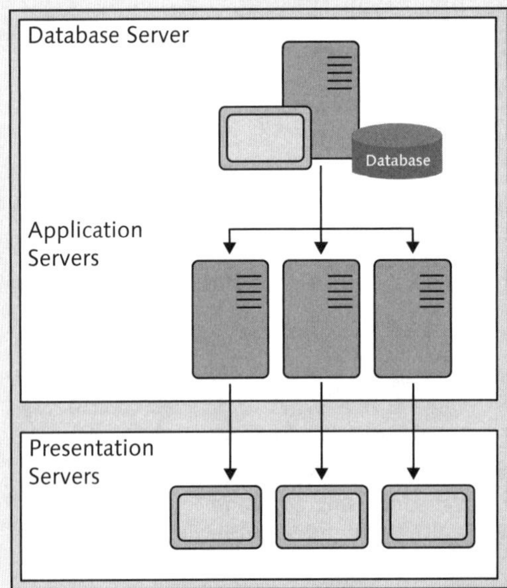

Figure 1.3 One Database Server With Additional Application Servers

Thus, an SAP ERP system may have a single server that provides both application and database services. Alternatively, the application layer can be distributed over multiple computers. In any case, the SAP ERP system has only one database.

1.2 The SAP ERP Database

In many software packages, the actual software is considered to be separate from the data that is entered or created using the software. The term *software package* is synonymous with *program* or *executable*, and the data is stored external to this software in a file. When you print a spreadsheet, for example, you require both a software executable and a spreadsheet file.

Unlike other software packages, SAP ERP software is not separate from its data. Both application functionality and business data are stored together in the database, along with SAP ERP documentation and performance statistics. The database contains almost everything users can see: transaction data, program source code, text, menu options, screens, and even printer and fax definitions. In other words, the database contains virtually all system-related components. Only a few system-related files reside outside the database—for example, the kernel.

Two components

The database can be divided into two logical components: the *Repository* and *customer data*.

1.2.1 The Repository

The Repository provides the data structures and programs you need to maintain data in the SAP ERP system.

ABAP Dictionary

The central part of the Repository is the *ABAP Dictionary*, which contains descriptions of the structure and the relationships of all data. These descriptions are used by SAP ERP to interpret and generate the application objects of the runtime environment—for example, programs or screens. Such objects are referred to as *Repository objects*.

During an SAP ERP implementation, you may want to perform development work in the system to adapt the Repository to meet specific requirements. Using the tools in the *ABAP Workbench*, you can create or modify Repository objects, thus adding or changing table structures or programs. The result of such development work is one or both of the following:

- New customer Repository objects are added to the Repository.
- Standard SAP objects in the Repository are modified.

[+] SAP recommends that you do not modify standard SAP objects in the Repository. See Chapter 2 for more information.

1.2.2 Customer Data

In addition to the Repository, the other logical component of the database is customer data. It consists of any kind of data entered into the system by the customer—the organization or company that purchased and uses the SAP software—either during SAP ERP implementation or during day-to-day business processing. Customer data includes the following:

- Customizing data
- Application data
- User master data

Customizing data is generated when SAP ERP is configured to meet the particular needs of the customer through Customizing. *Application data*, also known as *business data*, is the data required for or generated by day-to-day business processing in the system. *User master data* is the records of SAP users' passwords and authorizations.

To return to the analogy of the spreadsheet application, the data in the spreadsheet file is the equivalent of the customer data in SAP ERP. Of this data, the application data is the data entered to fill the cells of the spreadsheet. The Customizing data is the formatting data—for example, the data specifying bold characters or colored cells in the spreadsheet. The equivalent of the Repository objects is the spreadsheet application itself, with its menu options, macros, and screens.

1.2.3 Technical Implementation

SAP ERP requires a database that has a relational database management system (RDBMS) such as Oracle, MS SQL Server, MAX DB, and DB2 databases. The chosen database system is system-neutral until it is populated with the Repository during the installation process.

The name of the relational database and the name of the SAP ERP system are frequently the same, and consist of three uppercase alphanumeric characters. Examples of SAP ERP system names include DEV, P11, or ST0. Some names, such as the system identifier "SAP," are reserved by SAP and may not be used as system names. (See Chapter 7 for more information.)

The abbreviation SID, which stands for *system identification*, is often used as a placeholder for any SAP ERP system name. [+]

1.3 SAP ERP Clients

An SAP ERP system has only one Repository that provides the runtime environment where you create and maintain customer data. Within this single Repository, you can set up subdivisions called *clients* that help separate customer data into different groups.

When you log on to the system, you must log on to a specific client and can read or change only the data of that particular client. This data is client-dependent. Each client has its own data, but accesses the same Repository objects.

Most customer data is client-dependent. More precisely, application data is entirely client-dependent, while some Customizing data is shared by all clients and thus is client-independent. Figure 1.4 shows a database with multiple clients containing client-dependent data, and sharing all client-independent Customizing data and all Repository objects. These Repository objects provide the runtime environment.

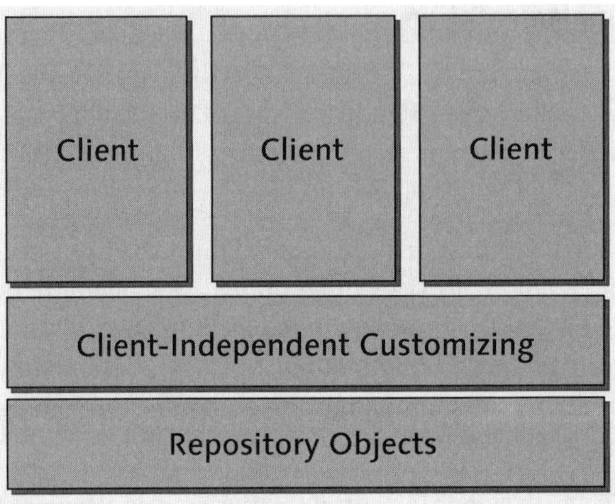

Figure 1.4 A Database Contains Separate SAP ERP Clients that Share Client-Independent Customizing Data and Repository Objects

1.3.1 Technical Implementation

To protect customer data created in different clients, when you log on to an SAP system, you must log on to a specific client within that system. The client-dependent data you can access from this client is restricted to the data assigned exclusively to that client. After you are in that client, the client-dependent data of all other clients in the SAP ERP system is inaccessible. You can still access all client-independent Customizing data and Repository objects.

Clients are technically identified by a three-digit number, the client ID. SAP uses the client ID as a key field in all tables that contain client-specific data. The data in these tables can be displayed or changed only if you log on to a specific client.

MANDT

Example: Client-Dependent Data

The clients of an SAP ERP system are logical constructs within the database of that SAP system. Tables for client-dependent data have the client ID as the first key column. This column is always called MANDT, from the German word *Mandant*, meaning "client."

An example of a client-dependent SAP table is VBAP. It contains detailed line-item information for all sales documents created in the SAP ERP system. This table contains over 200 columns, of which the first 3 are unique for each row, thus enabling the database to uniquely identify the relevant sales document item.

In table VBAP, the first three columns are MANDT (client ID), VBELN (sales document number), and POSNR (sales document item number). All other columns, for example MATNR (material number), are used to specify the details of the sales document item.

Here is an example of the kind of data stored in table VBAP:

MANDT	VBELN	POSNR	MATNR
400	0000006398	000010	C-1100
400	0000006401	000010	CCS-99
400	0000006401	000020	CCS-80
400	0000006403	000010	C900
520	0000000844	000010	C-1100
520	0000000844	000020	C-2000

Although table VBAP stores data from both client 400 and client 520, you cannot access the sales document data associated with client 520 when you are logged on in client 400. This is because table VBAP contains the column MANDT as its first key column, making the table's data client-dependent. To display or change any data in table VBAP, you must log on in the SAP ERP client indicated in the column MANDT.

1.3.2 Data Components

The data components of an SAP ERP client are the types of data a user can access after logging on to a particular client (see Figure 1.5). As mentioned previously, these include the following:

Data types

- **Customizing data**
  This is the configuration data that results from Customizing, which is a mandatory task during SAP ERP implementation. Most Customizing data is client-dependent; some is client-independent.
- **Application data**
  This is the sum of business data including *transaction data*, which is generated by individual sales or other transactions, and *master data*, which is a prerequisite for entering day-to-day transactions. Application data is the main source of database growth and eventually occu-

pies the most space in the database. All application data is client-dependent.

- **User master data**
  This is data that specifies which users can work in the system and which transactions they are authorized to use. All user master data is client-dependent.

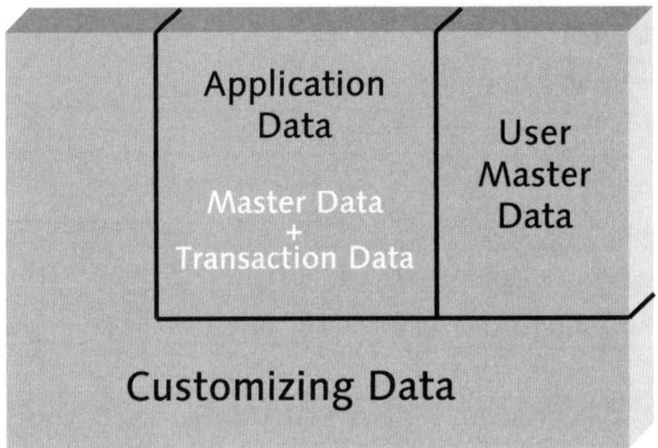

Figure 1.5 Data Components of an SAP ERP Client

Customizing Data

Customizing data is generated when the customer configures the required parameters and settings during Customizing, enabling SAP ERP to meet the customer's specific business requirements. Customizing data defines what kind of application data can be generated and how this data will look. Examples of Customizing data include the following:

- Organizational units such as companies, plants, and sales organizations
- A specific purchase order process flow
- Distribution requirements for production planning
- Multiple-language text for reports

Most Customizing is client-dependent. Some Customizing, however, is client-independent. This includes adjustments to global settings that affect all clients, as well as the creation of—or changes to—Repository objects. A global setting may be technical in nature—such as the setting defining a printer—or more business-related—such as the setting specifying a company's factory calendar. More complicated customizing efforts may require the creation of a table to house data and configuration settings. Such a table structure is client-independent because it is a Repository object. For example, to configure your pricing strategy for a given product, you are required to create a table that specifies discounting criteria and amounts. This Customizing change, unlike the definition of the sales organization, is a client-independent change.

Application Data

Application data is the sum of all SAP ERP business data, and comprises both master data and transaction data. Application data is affected by Customizing settings, which determine what kind of application data can be generated and how this data will look. Application data is client-dependent.

Master data is the prerequisite for processing day-to-day transactions, and includes lists of approved vendors, supplier addresses, materials used in production, and purchaser data. Master data

Transaction data is generated by day-to-day business operations, and includes customer orders, production orders, debits and credits, and payroll transactions. Transaction data is frequently accessed and is the fastest growing data in the SAP ERP system. Transaction data

While application data is logically a construct of both master data and transaction data within the system, there is no formal distinction between the two. In other words, it is not possible to separate master data and transaction data.

User Master Data

SAP ERP's user and authorization concept is an essential part of system security. Information about users—known as user master data—is recorded in the system to authenticate users at logon and to check their authorization for particular transactions.

When a user logs on to a client, the system authenticates whether a user ID exists in the user master data that matches the entered password.

When the user triggers a transaction they want to use in SAP ERP, the system checks whether one of the authorization profiles assigned to that user in their user master data contains the necessary authorization for that transaction.

User IDs and authorization profiles are client-dependent, and therefore are valid only in the client in which the corresponding user master data records were created. User master records contain, for example, the user's logon name, assigned authorizations, and other attributes such as address, and user type.

1.3.3 Standard SAP ERP Clients

SAP delivers SAP ERP with three standard clients:

- Client 000
- Client 001
- Client 066

Client 000

Client 000 is reserved by SAP to enable maintenance of the standard Repository objects and baseline Customizing settings in the system. For example, during upgrades, new functions are supplied to this client and subsequently transported to the other clients in the system. Client 000 contains the basic Customizing settings with organizational structures and business parameter settings that are legally required for German organizations with regard to, for example, payment and tax structures. Even if you are not implementing SAP ERP in Germany, these settings provide helpful examples for your own Customizing. Due to its special role in the system, client 000 may not be modified or deleted by the customer. It contains no application data.

Client 001

Client 001 is a copy of client 000, including the sample organizational structure and configuration. However, customers can modify Client 001. Client 001 contains no application data.

Client 066

Client 066 is reserved for SAP access to its customers' systems to perform remote services such as EarlyWatch® and GoingLive™ Check. Almost no data exists in this client; it simply serves as a mechanism to allow remote access for the purpose of system monitoring without compromising the security of your system. This client should not be modified or deleted.

New clients

To create new clients in SAP ERP, you can use the technique known as *client copy*, which creates a copy of an existing client (see Chapter 9 for more information). To perform Customizing and development in SAP ERP, you should use client 001 or create a new client with a client copy. Usually, a copy is made of client 000. This copy is then used to realize company-specific business processes.

1.4 Questions

1. **Which of the following components indicate that SAP ERP is a client/server system?**

   A. Multiple databases.

   B. A database server.

   C. Three separate hardware servers: a database server, an application server, and a presentation server.

   D. A database service, an application service, and a presentation service.

2. **Which of the following is NOT contained in the SAP ERP database?**

   A. The Repository

   B. Kernel

   C. Customer data

   D. Transaction data

   E. Customizing data

   F. ABAP Dictionary

3. **Which of the following statements is correct with regard to SAP clients?**

   A. An SAP client has its own customer data and programs, which are not accessible to other clients within the same SAP system.

   B. An SAP client shares Customizing and application data with other clients in the same SAP system.

C. An SAP client shares all Repository objects and client-independent Customizing with all other clients in the same SAP system.

D. An SAP client enables you to separate application data from Customizing data.

4. **Which of the following statements is correct with regard to SAP's client concept?**

A. All Customizing settings are client-independent.

B. A client has a unique set of application data.

C. A client has its own Repository objects.

D. All Customizing settings are client-dependent.

SAP develops standard software. However, this software provides comprehensive Customizing options to meet individual requirements. This chapter describes the different Customizing options available at the business process and program levels.

2 Realizing Business Processes in SAP ERP

The software SAP delivers to its customers is referred to as the *SAP standard*. It contains over 1,000 business process chains and their associated functions. Before working with SAP ERP, you not only have to install the software, you must also *implement* it. To meet the specific requirements of your company, you need to make decisions about *which* business processes and associated functions and settings you require, and whether you might even need to create new programs or functions. To implement these decisions, SAP ERP offers two main techniques:

- Customizing
- Development

Customizing involves using the *Implementation Guide* (IMG), and development is performed using the *ABAP Workbench*. Development is further divided into three methods:

Development methods

- Creation of new Repository objects
- Enhancements
- Modifications

Figure 2.1 shows the SAP ERP software that results from the implementation process. The software—represented by the horizontal bar—consists of the SAP ERP business applications and customer programs. The techniques used to add to, configure, and change the SAP standard are shown as arrows.

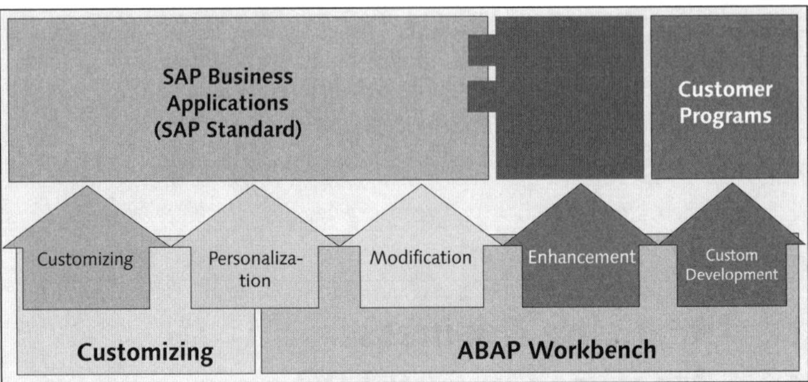

Figure 2.1 Methods of Adding and Changing the SAP Standard

2.1 Customizing

Customizing is a mandatory activity during an SAP ERP implementation. When performing Customizing, you use the IMG (Transaction SPRO) to select the SAP ERP business processes your company requires, and to adjust all associated settings, such as those used to specify units of measurement and relevant business concepts. Customizing alterations adapt the standard SAP solution for different branches of industry and company types, as well as for multiple languages and country-specific characteristics.

The Customizing procedure adds customer-specific data to the tables that correspond to standard SAP objects. Therefore, Customizing is often thought of as table maintenance. These tables are later read by the programs that comprise the different business workflows.

Example: Business Transactions That Are Set Up through Customizing

An international company that manufactures bicycles begins installing its new SAP ERP system. To meet the company's specific needs, the following business processes and features are selected and set up during Customizing:

- **Sales organizations and distribution channels:**
  To enable wholesale customers to place orders for bicycles, SAP ERP is customized to recognize the sales organization responsible for the order, and the distribution channel used in getting the order to the customer.

- **Production planning:**
  The SAP ERP application component Production Planning is customized to enable orders to be filled on time.
- **Materials management:**
  The SAP ERP application component Materials Management is customized so that all required materials—such as tires and chains—are recognized and can be made available during the manufacture of all types of bicycles.
- **Billing and cost allocation processes:**
  Customizing in this area sets up invoicing by defining pricing structures and applicable taxes.

As this simple example shows, Customizing covers numerous features of business processes. The people performing Customizing, whether they are company employees or external consultants, require a detailed understanding of the company's business processes.

2.1.1 SAP ERP Reference Model

In addition to the IMG (discussed in the next section), another SAP ERP tool that is helpful for Customizing is the *SAP ERP Reference Model*, accessed in the *Business Navigator* (Transaction SB09 in SAP ERP releases up to R/3 4.6C; later releases use, for example, Transaction SOLAR01 in the SAP Solution Manager). The Reference Model is a collection of modeling tools, and it provides configuration recommendations by offering different business scenarios to help you map out your company's business requirements.

The Reference Model enables you to model all essential elements of a company, such as organizational units, business processes, business objects, and the applications that use these business objects.

Subsections of the SAP ERP Reference Model include the following: Subsections

- SAP ERP process model
- Data model and object model
- Organization model
- Distribution model

The SAP ERP Reference Model and its various graphical tools act as a bridge between a company's everyday business needs and the actual implementation of its SAP ERP system (see Figure 2.2). Using the SAP ERP Reference Model to determine and model the scope of the SAP ERP implementation makes it easier to perform Customizing activities using the IMG.

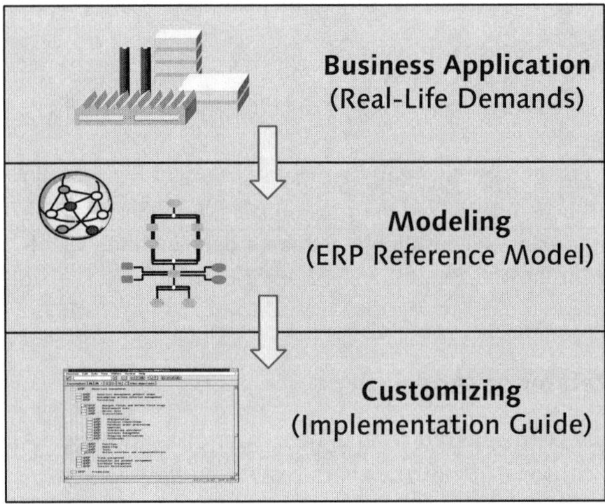

Figure 2.2 Modeling Business Needs to Facilitate Customizing

2.1.2 Implementation Guide (IMG)

To simplify Customizing, the IMG (Transaction SPRO) guides you through the various Customizing stages and procedures. In addition, the *project management* function within the IMG enables you to set up and manage Customizing projects, complete with planned and actual deadlines, resources, and activity completion status.

To start Customizing in the IMG, access the *SAP Reference IMG* (from the initial screen of Transaction SPRO, choose IMPLEMENT. PROJECTS • SAP REFERENCE IMG). The SAP Reference IMG is a tree structure in which you drill down to specific Customizing activities (see Figure 2.3). The nodes of the tree structure you see first are organized to reflect the different SAP ERP application modules such as Financial Accounting, Sales and Distribution, Materials Management, and Plant Maintenance. Drilling down within (or expanding each branch of) the tree structure ultimately reveals lists of Customizing activities that are arranged in the order these activities should be performed.

Figure 2.3 shows sample Customizing activities in the typical IMG tree structure. Clicking the icons beside each Customizing activity name enables you to access the following:

- The screen where you perform the Customizing activity
- Relevant SAP ERP documentation
- The screen where you can document why and how you perform this Customizing activity
- The relevant project management data (assuming you have chosen to set up the project management functionality)

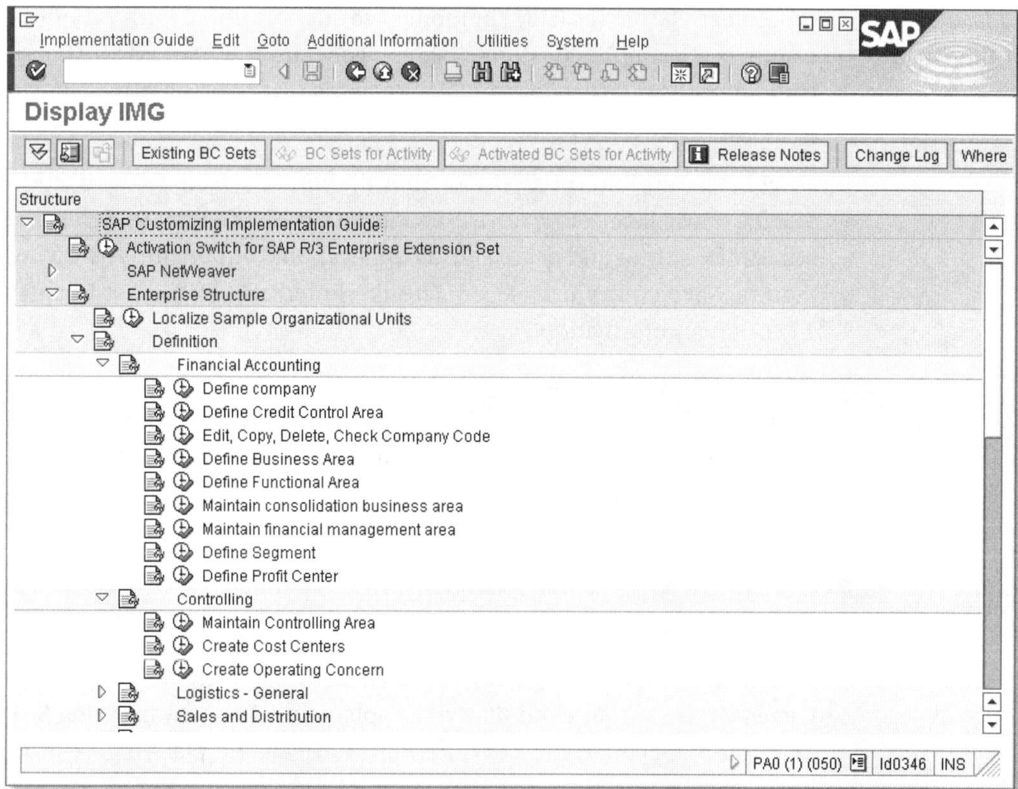

Figure 2.3 A Sample IMG Tree Structure

The preliminary task for Customizing is to filter out the parts of the SAP Reference IMG your company does not require, and save the remainder as your *Enterprise IMG*. You can then divide your Enterprise IMG into various subdivisions called *Project IMGs*, representing groups of related Customizing activities. These various IMGs are explained in more detail in the text that follows.

Enterprise IMG

The SAP Reference IMG contains the Customizing activities for all SAP ERP application modules and functions. However, many SAP ERP implementations do not need all of the available application components; in fact, they may require only specific components implemented for particular countries. For example, a company may initially want to implement the Human Resources (HR) component to support only North American countries. To simplify Customizing, you generate an Enterprise IMG that contains only the parts of the SAP Reference IMG that are relevant to your implementation.

To generate an Enterprise IMG, from the initial screen of Transaction SPRO, choose BASIC FUNCTIONS • ENTERPRISE IMG • GENERATE. Select the relevant countries and deactivate all application components you do not require. Save your work to generate the Enterprise IMG. (See Chapter 11 for more information.)

[+] One Enterprise IMG can be generated for each SAP ERP system. If you subsequently need to implement additional countries or more business application components, you can regenerate the Enterprise IMG. Regeneration does not affect the existing documentation or project management information.

[+] Since R/3 Release 4.6, the Enterprise IMG is no longer used. Instead, SAP delivers the SAP Reference IMG, and from this IMG, you create Project IMGs only.

Generally, we recommend that you implement SAP software using SAP Solution Manager. With SAP Solution Manager, the planning of processes and their implementation can be extensively supported, and, by using the data and process steps contained in the SAP Solution Manager system, a large variety of activities and their associated costs can be saved in other actions of the lifecycle of the implemented SAP software. Examples of this are the setup of system monitoring and the automatic generation of test plans.

Project IMGs

Customizing requires expertise from different areas of business. In addition, most implementations are rolled out in phases; that is, new functionality is added over time by different user groups. Therefore, while it is possible to perform Customizing from either the SAP Reference IMG or the Enterprise IMG, a useful alternative is to divide the Enterprise IMG into subsets. These subsets, called Project IMGs, reflect the various business areas and implementation stages, and make it possible to organize Customizing activities according to the different types of business expertise and project teams.

Example: Project Teams for an SAP ERP Implementation

Before starting an SAP ERP implementation at a bicycle company, the responsible manager decides to set up several teams to handle different aspects of the implementation project. Initially, two project teams are formed: one for finance and another for logistics. These teams are again subdivided into different areas of expertise. The finance team splits into one group for controlling and one for accounting. Similarly, the logistics team divides into two teams: one for production planning and another for materials management. Thus, a total of four project teams emerge. After creating an Enterprise IMG tailored to the company's needs, four Project IMGs are created. Each team can begin Customizing in the respective Project IMG.

One year later, management decides to extend its use of SAP ERP to include human resources. A new implementation phase is created. The human resources team is divided into two sections, one for payroll and one for personnel management. The Enterprise IMG is regenerated, two additional Project IMGs are created, and Customizing for human resources is started.

To coordinate the efforts of the various implementation teams, SAP recommends that you perform all Customizing activities from within a Project IMG. [+]

Since Release R/3 4.6C, you can also integrate the transport control via projects. This lets you plan and transport your developments and Customizing activities in project structures. Changes that do not depend on each other can be structured in separate projects and imported to the follow-on systems independently. This is advisable, for example, when different projects are used at different times in the production operation, or to make assignments regarding contents. For this purpose, you must first create an IMG project in the IMG project management, and then activate a related Change and Transport System (CTS) project.

Note that the settings assigned in a specific Customizing activity may affect one or more application components. Therefore, cross-application activities may appear in a Project IMG, even though the second application was not selected when the Project IMG was generated. For example, a Project IMG for production planning contains activities relating to production planning and controlling.

Project IMGs provide project management functions to enable you to:

- Maintain status and resource information
- Maintain project documentation in SAP Office folders using either a standard text editor or Microsoft Word
- Transfer data between a Project IMG and Microsoft Project

[+] The Enterprise IMG and Project IMGs are cross-client. In other words, these IMGs, and their documentation and project data, are all accessible from any client within the system.

Project views for filtering according to priority

To organize your Customizing activities more effectively, Project IMGs can be filtered into views based on priority (see Figure 2.4). This helps you decide which Customizing activities are critical or mandatory and should be tackled first, and which activities can wait until a later time. You can create the following views when generating a Project IMG:

Views

- Critical activities
- Mandatory activities
- Non-critical activities
- Optional activities

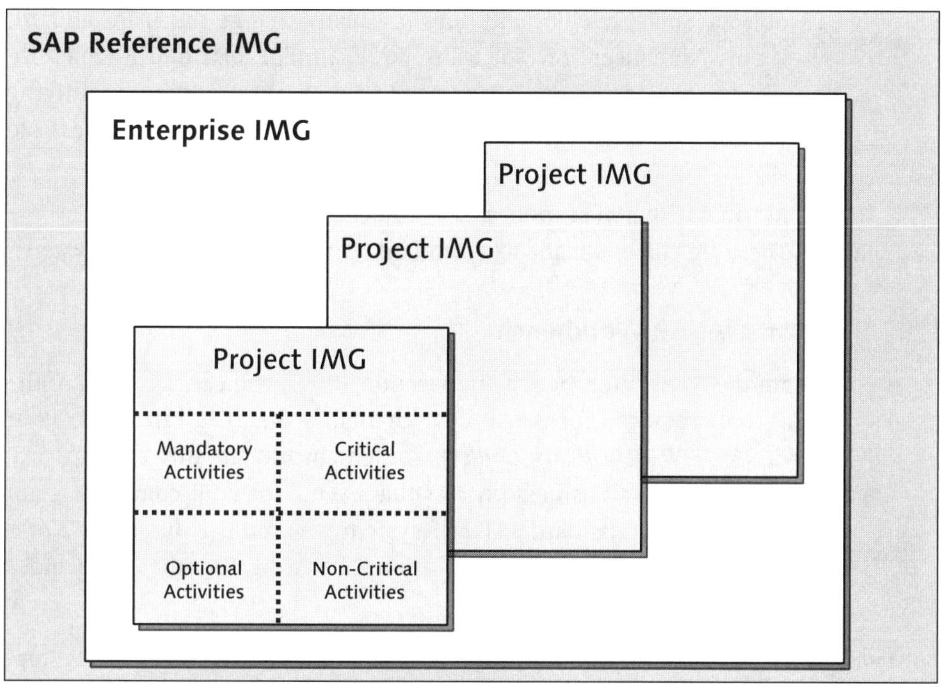

Figure 2.4 The Different Views of Customizing Activities

2.2 Development

The SAP ERP system creates the runtime environment by drawing on the Repository, which contains object definitions, user interfaces, and business transactions. These Repository objects are configured through Customizing, which normally satisfies all business requirements. When this is not the case, you can use the ABAP Workbench to develop new Repository objects or modify existing ones. Development can take the following forms:

Development forms

- **Creation of new Repository objects:**
  The customer develops new Repository objects, such as new reports, screens, and tables.
- **Enhancements:**
  These are customer-developed objects that are anticipated in the standard SAP software; that is, they are referenced by standard SAP

objects. Such development does not really change the SAP standard; it only "enhances" the software. For example, certain SAP tables are constructed so that you can append fields to them without modifying them, and some SAP programs contain built-in "branches" to possible customer programs.

- **Modifications of standard SAP objects:**
  These are changes made to a standard SAP object in a customer system.

2.2.1 ABAP Workbench

From the ABAP Workbench (Transaction S001), you can access all of the SAP tools required for ABAP development work. You can create your own SAP ERP Repository objects, and enhance or modify existing SAP objects. Thus, if a business process that is vital for your company is not contained in the standard SAP ERP system, you can use the ABAP Workbench to build an appropriate solution. The ABAP Workbench includes the following tools:

ABAP tools

- *ABAP Dictionary Maintenance* (Transaction SE11) is used for development work on table descriptions and their interrelationships.
- The *ABAP Editor* (Transaction SE38) is used to modify ABAP programs.
- The *Function Builder* (Transaction SE37) is used to develop, maintain, test, and document function modules, and contains a function library, which serves as a central storage facility for all function modules.
- The *Menu Painter* (Transaction SE41) is used to create the user interface of an ABAP program. It lets you create or modify screen titles, menu bars, the standard toolbar, the application toolbar, and function keys.
- The *Screen Painter* (Transaction SE51) is used to create dialog boxes and the underlying flow logic. The Screen Painter can be run in either graphical or alphanumeric mode.

[+] ABAP stands for Advanced Business Application Programming and is SAP's proprietary programming language. It is designed to support the development of data processing applications in distributed systems, and handles multiple currency and multilingual issues. ABAP also contains a special set of commands for database operations called *Open SQL*, which allows SAP ERP to be programmed independently of the database system and operating system.

SSCR for Developers

SAP Software Change Registration (SSCR) is a procedure that registers all developers of Repository objects. Before creating or modifying Repository objects using the ABAP Workbench, developers must register and obtain an access key from the SAP Service Marketplace. The SSCR access key for a developer needs to be entered into the SAP system only once; that is, during the developer's subsequent attempts to create or change Repository objects, the SAP system will not request the SSCR access key.

2.2.2 Customer-Developed Repository Objects

Customer-developed SAP ERP Repository objects include programs, screens, menus, function modules, and data structures. These objects are created by an SAP customer using the ABAP Workbench to satisfy business needs beyond the scope of the SAP standard.

Example: A Possible Customer Development

The head of sales at a bicycle company wishes to obtain sales order statistics based on a nonstandard type of user input, and to simplify the screens where orders are entered by end users. The order-entry screen in the SAP standard is replaced with a new screen, created by the company's developer using the SAP Screen Painter. Using the ABAP Editor, this developer then attaches the new screen to an ABAP program that reacts to user input and performs the required statistical analysis. Finally, another program is created that displays the results in multiple currencies.

Not all customer-developed objects are completely unique; that is, the new objects may have standard SAP objects incorporated in their design. A customer-developed ABAP program may include, for example, standard SAP function modules, such as user input validation routines.

Customer-developed Repository objects are not completely isolated from the existing standard SAP objects, but like the SAP standard, are contained in the SAP ERP Repository. Therefore, to distinguish standard SAP

Repository objects from customer-developed objects, SAP requires you to heed the following precautions:

Precautions

- All customer-developed Repository objects must be assigned to a customer *development class*. Development classes are used to group similar business objects, and every Repository object is assigned to a development class. All standard SAP Repository objects are assigned to SAP development classes.
- New Repository objects must be given a unique name that falls within the *customer name range*. In SAP ERP, the name range of customer-developed objects typically begins with Y or Z.
- In larger, decentralized SAP ERP implementations, Repository objects may also be assigned to a *namespace*. A namespace is a name field that provides an integrated validation that checks for allowed object names. Namespaces provide a method by which objects for specific development can be created without the risk of creating objects with the same names. All objects that belong to this namespace start with the following prefix: */CUSTOMER/*. This unique namespace must be requested from the SAP Service Marketplace. This ensures, for example, that developments from SAP software partners do not conflict with other developments, and that your own developments are not overwritten.

2.2.3 Enhancements

Standard SAP programs that have been designed to allow enhancements can call customer-developed Repository objects. Enhancements also exist for data dictionary objects. To be enhanced, SAP objects must have one of the following:

Technologies of SAP objects

- **User exits:**
  Points in an SAP program from which a customer's own program can be called.
- **Program exits (also known as function module exits):**
  Predefined function module calls in the standard system for accessing customer-developed function modules.
- **Menu exits:**
  Predefined placeholders in the graphical user interface for customer-developed menu options.

- **Dynpro exits:**
  Predefined places in dynpros where customers can insert a dialog box they have created.
- **Table appends:**
  Placeholders in ABAP Dictionary tables or structures for customer-defined fields external to the table or structure.
- **Field exits:**
  Fields on screens that trigger processing of the field contents by customer-developed function modules.
- **Text enhancements:**
  Enhancements in SAP data elements that allow customers to replace SAP-specified text with customer-defined keywords or documentation.
- **BAdIs:**
  Enhancement technique based on ABAP Objects. Provides interface definitions used for enhancing ABAP sources, screens, GUI elements, and tables without modification. Upward compatibility of the BAdI interface is ensured; registering in SSCR is not necessary.

User exits, program exits, menu exits, field exits, and screen exits enable customers to extend SAP applications by adding their own processing logic at predefined points. These types of customer exits are inactive when delivered. For the exit to call an enhancement developed by the customer using the ABAP Workbench, the exit must be activated. Customer exits provide you with a predefined interface between SAP programs and customer-developed programs.

Enhancements to tables and structures in the ABAP Dictionary are realized using append structures and text enhancements.

Appends

Appends are placeholders in standard SAP tables that refer to an append structure external to the table. By adding fields to the append structure, you are adding fields to the table without changing the table itself. After the new fields have been added and the table has been activated, these fields can be referred to in ABAP programs the same way you refer to normal table fields.

Extension index

The SAP NetWeaver 7.0 ABAP Dictionary now includes an additional enhancement option: the *extension index*. The reason for this enhancement was that the creation of a secondary index for an SAP table is a modification, even if the customer namespace is used. An extension index, on the other hand, is a modification-free option to create a secondary index. To create an extension index, refer to Section 10.4. The merit and purpose of SAP enhancements are to enable you to add functionality to SAP-standard objects by creating new objects rather than modifying standard SAP objects. Customers who avoid modifying standard SAP objects enjoy three benefits:

- They can receive customer support from SAP more easily.
- They have fewer problems applying SAP's periodic corrections to its software in the form of *Support Packages*.
- They can perform release upgrades more quickly.

SAP guarantees that when you use enhancement techniques, you will not lose the functionality provided by your enhancement when you perform a release upgrade or apply a Support Package. SAP encourages the use of enhancement techniques because they reduce the periodic effort required to update your system—a reduction that is particularly significant in the long term.

User exits do in fact change a standard SAP object—specifically, an INCLUDE module (see the example in the next section). However, SAP guarantees that functionality provided by user exits will not be lost as long as the customer performs a modification adjustment for the INCLUDE module during upgrades.

Enhancement Framework

SAP NetWeaver 7.0 now includes another framework to enable further modification-free adaptation in addition to these system enhancement options: the Enhancement Framework. This concept is particularly interesting because you can implement the available enhancements using implicit enhancement points without any preparatory work from SAP.

Not only does the Enhancement Framework provide additional enhancement options for you, but also for SAP within the SAP Enhancement Packages. For more information, refer to Sections 10.4 and 18.5.

2.2.4 Modifications

The benefit of enhancement technologies, such as program exits and append structures, is that they do not require customers to modify standard SAP objects. SAP does not recommend making modifications to standard SAP objects other than the user exit modifications described previously. Otherwise, after a release upgrade or after the application of Support Packages, you must allow for an increased support effort within the scope of modification changes. This means that your internal maintenance costs increase.

[+] SAP also recommends avoiding modifications to the standard code because this may have unwanted effects or cause errors in other parts of an application. SAP cannot ensure error-free system operation after customers make modifications.

Reasons for changes

Apart from activating user exits, customers usually perform modifications to their SAP systems for one of two reasons:

- To adjust functionality to meet a business need that SAP does not provide or provides differently.
- To manually apply a correction to fix a known programming error as described by SAP in an *SAP Note*. However, if SAP Notes are implemented using the SAP Note Assistant tool, these corrections are not marked as modifications (Chapter 15).

Instead of modifying SAP objects, SAP recommends using Customizing, customer developments, or enhancements. If modifications are unavoidable, consult SAP.

Example: The Most Common Modification: the User Exit

The Sales and Distribution application has a wide variety of user exits that can be used to enhance existing functionality. You can implement a user exit by changing the INCLUDE module `MV75AFZ1` to define a more complex sort procedure for contracts. This module is a standard SAP object, and, prior to the customer's changes, looks like this:

```
Include MV75AFZ1

form user_sort using u_rcode.
 clear u_rcode.
* Sort rules
* u_rcode = 4.
endform.

```

This INCLUDE module is called by another standard SAP program, SAPMV75A, which lists contracts:

```
Program SAPMV75A
*-----------------------------------------
* Central Report to Display Contracts
*-----------------------------------------
  :    :    :    :    :
  :    :    :    :    :
 * customer modifications
 include mv75afzl.
 include mv75afz2.
 include mv75afz3.

```

Inserting sort criteria to `MV75AFZ1` is a customer modification. SAP guarantees that it will continue to support the use of this module and its call from program `SAPMV75A` in future SAP ERP releases. Therefore, while program `SAPMV75A` may change from one SAP ERP release to another, the customer version of `MV75AFZ1` will remain effective after the modification adjustment process.

[+] During an upgrade, you can check whether you still require previously created user exits and allow exits you no longer need to be overwritten.

Modification Adjustments

An important reason for not making modifications is to avoid modification adjustments during release upgrades or when applying Support Packages, also known as *patches*, from the SAP Service Marketplace—SAP's online support services formerly known as SAP's Online Service System (OSS). Modification adjustments are adjustments to SAP objects that ensure previous modifications remain implemented in the system after an upgrade. Depending on the number and scope of modifications, the adjustment process may make a release upgrade or application of

Support Packages a complex and time-consuming process, requiring developers to have extensive application knowledge.

[+] During the import of Support Packages or release upgrades, the new modification adjustment tools provide you with information about changes SAP has implemented in objects that were modified by you. You obtain no information for custom developments you created as copies of SAP objects. You should consider this disadvantage if you think about using custom developments or modifying SAP codes.

Modification Assistant

As of SAP R/3 Release 4.5, the *Modification Assistant* tool guides you when making modifications and when subsequently performing modification adjustments. The Modification Assistant structures the way changes are made to SAP standard objects and logs all changes, providing you with a detailed overview that is easy to read and that drastically reduces the amount of effort needed to upgrade your system.

Even with the advent of the Modification Assistant, you should keep the number of modifications you make to an absolute minimum. Extensive background knowledge of application structure and process flow is indispensable for deciding whether modifications are avoidable, and if not, what kind of modifications should be made, and how they should be designed.

[+] See Chapter 17 for more information on Support Packages from the SAP Service Marketplace.

Modifications Recommended in SAP Notes

The SAP Notes in the SAP Service Marketplace provide you with a database of task- or problem-oriented recommendations regarding SAP software and the applicable hardware. These recommendations sometimes provide solutions that require the customer to perform modifications to SAP objects—for example, manual programming corrections for Repository objects.

Support Packages

To eliminate the need for manually keying in such corrections, SAP offers Support Packages, or patches, to replace the objects affected by the error with improved versions. Support Packages are not customer modifications because the objects modified by Support Packages are overwritten during a release upgrade, and there is no need to make modification adjustments.

If there is no Support Package available for solving your problem, you may have to make a manual change to the standard SAP object based on SAP Notes. Before starting work, however, you need to confirm that the SAP Note is applicable to your release, and that the symptoms it describes actually match those in your system. If you aren't sure, please contact SAP or use the SAP Note Assistant, which automatically checks these criteria before implementing SAP Notes and notifies you, if necessary, of any other dependent SAP Notes.

[+] Because modifications can subsequently entail modification adjustments during release upgrades or when applying Support Packages, you should consider the following notes to accelerate modification adjustment:

- Encapsulate your own source text into small units—for example, by calling your own function modules in the program source text—instead of integrating long passages in the code.
- Do not delete SAP source text; instead, comment it out. This is supported by the Modification Assistant.
- Do not modify any Dictionary objects of the central basis, unless you are prompted to do so by SAP support.
- Keep a central list of all modifications, including additional information, such as a reference to a transport request, information about the developer responsible, or a validity note.
- Define a company-wide standard for both the execution of modifications and for their documentation.

SSCR for Modifications

Before making a modification, you must be registered as a developer in the SSCR of the SAP Service Marketplace. In addition, you must register each standard SAP object you intend to modify. After registering a standard SAP object, you receive an SSCR access key that must be applied to that object. After the SSCR access key has been applied, it remains stored in the database so that subsequent changes to that object at the current release level do not require additional SSCR registration.

By requiring this type of registration, SAP is made aware of the frequency of changes to the different Repository objects, and can respond by creating more enhancement technologies. Knowing which objects a customer has modified also makes it easier for SAP to provide quality customer support.

Recommended Procedure for Functionality Changes

The following questions can support you in your decision on the technology to be used to modify functionality:

- Can the customer requirement be implemented via Customizing?
- If so, adapt Customizing.
- If not, is a comparable functionality available in the SAP standard?
- If not, check the availability of corresponding partner solutions, for example, via the SAP Service Marketplace (*http://www.service.sap.com/softwarepartner*) or at the start of a custom development.
- If so, can the customer requirement be implemented via an enhancement?
- If so, implement an enhancement.
- If not, start a custom development or implement a modification of the SAP standard.

2.3 Questions

1. **Which of the following strategies enables SAP customers to avoid making modifications to standard SAP objects?**

   A. Using enhancement technologies such as program exits and menu exits.

   B. Modifying SAP-delivered programs.

   C. Changing standard SAP functionality using the IMG.

   D. Performing Customizing to provide the required functionality.

2. **Which of the following statements are correct with regard to the IMG?**

   A. The IMG consists of a series of Customizing activities for defining a company's business processes.

B. The IMG is an online resource providing the necessary information and steps to help you implement SAP application modules.

C. The IMG is client-independent.

D. All of the above.

3. **Which of the following strategies enables an enterprise to meet its business needs by changing or enhancing SAP functionality?**

A. Maintaining application data using the various SAP business transactions in the SAP standard.

B. Using the ABAP Workbench to create the required Repository objects.

C. Using Customizing to modify programs after obtaining an access key from the SAP Service Marketplace.

D. Using customer exits to enhance the functionality of existing standard SAP objects.

4. **Which of the following statements are correct with regard to modifications?**

A. A modification is a change to a standard SAP object.

B. A modification must be registered through SSCR.

C. SAP recommends modifications only if the customer's business needs cannot be met by Customizing, enhancement technologies, or customer development.

D. All of the above.

5. **Which of the following statements is correct with regard to Customizing?**

A. Customizing enables SAP application processes to be set to reflect a company's business needs.

B. Customizing can be performed only from within a Project IMG.

C. Customizing is necessary because SAP ERP, for example, is delivered without business processes.

D. None of the above.

6. **Which of the following statements are correct with regard to Repository objects?**

   A. Customers can develop new Repository objects using the tools in the ABAP Workbench.

   B. Customer-developed Repository objects reside in the Repository alongside standard SAP objects.

   C. Customers can create and assign new Repository objects to a development class.

   D. All of the above.

A system landscape includes the type and structure of systems to ensure secure operation with the highest degree of flexibility for the adaptation of the relevant business processes. In the context of change management, numerous implementation options exist, depending on the scope of the changes and the project requirements.

3 The SAP ERP System Landscape

Your system landscape consists of the SAP systems and clients required to take you from the first stages of an SAP ERP installation, through the realization of your business needs within the software, to the start of production activities. When in production, your system landscape will need to support continuous changes to the software—due to corporate demands for additional business functionality as well as because of updates in the form of release upgrades or SAP Support Packages. Therefore, the objective of a system landscape is to provide an implementation environment where:

Activities in the system landscape

- You can perform Customizing and make development changes without affecting the production environment.
- You can validate business processes before using them in the production environment.
- You can simulate and test release upgrades and the application of Support Packages before they impact the production environment.
- You can work on Customizing and development to meet future business requirements without influencing the current production environment.

To meet the needs of your software implementation and to ensure smooth operation in the production environment, your system landscape must contain multiple clients and multiple systems. Clients provide isolated environments in which changes can be developed, tested, and then rolled into production. At least one client is needed for each step in this process; that is, every SAP ERP implementation requires at least three clients. In addition, due to the immediate impact of client-independent changes on all clients within the same SAP ERP system, SAP recommends that an SAP ERP implementation also have more than one SAP ERP system. Although every implementation will have a unique system landscape, SAP provides several recommended system landscapes and methods for setting up and maintaining landscapes. This chapter will present the different system landscapes and explain their advantages and disadvantages.

3.1 SAP ERP Client Roles

Access to SAP ERP is always in the context of a specific client number. In other words, when you log on to an SAP system, you log in to a specific client within that SAP system. Because different clients have different roles, your SAP ERP implementation needs several clients. For example, one client is required for Customizing and development, another for quality assurance testing, and yet another for end users to record business transactions and build production data.

Often, over time, SAP implementations acquire clients that no longer have a purpose or value for the implementation. Each client uses database space, which equates to used hardware resources. Even more costly are the organizational efforts necessary to keep and maintain the client over time. Such maintenance efforts include managing user access, and ensuring that the client receives the latest Customizing and development changes. To ensure optimal performance, your SAP implementation should have only enough clients to fulfill your specific needs.

3.1.1 Critical Client Roles

To begin SAP ERP implementation efforts, one client is required. However, as the implementation progresses, this single client will no longer suffice. Other separate clients will be necessary, each devoted to a particular task. To function properly, an implementation requires a minimum of three clients. The critical client roles needed to fulfill the basic requirements of your SAP ERP implementation include the following:

- Customizing and development
- Quality assurance
- Production

[+] Clients are technically represented in the SAP system using three digits. For example, the three standard clients delivered by SAP—and explained in Chapter 1—are client 000, client 001, and client 066. However, to promote consistency and ease of reading, three abbreviations will be used throughout this book to represent the three standard SAP ERP client roles: CUST for the Customizing-and-development client, QTST for the quality assurance client, and PROD for the production client.

The Role of CUST

In the CUST client, you adapt SAP ERP to meet your specific needs. In other words, this is where you perform Customizing and development work with the ABAP Workbench. All changes performed in this client are documented and recorded in *change requests* so that the changes can be transported to all other clients in the system landscape. A change request is an important mechanism for recording, documenting, and transporting changes throughout the system landscape (see Chapter 4).

While it is technically possible to perform Customizing in different clients and then merge these Customizing efforts in a third client using change requests, SAP does not recommend this procedure. The end result is neither predictable nor retractable. If functionality that works in the original client does not work in the merged client, you will have problems tracking down the conflict responsible for the disrupted functionality. It is much more efficient for the people customizing your SAP system to work together in one central location, the CUST client.

[+] To meet your implementation needs, Customizing of SAP ERP should be performed in and distributed from a single client.

The Roles of QTST and PROD

The QTST client provides the environment for testing and verifying new and existing Customizing settings as well as business application functionality. Application data can be added and manipulated for quality assurance testing. The PROD client is needed for all production activities; in other words, this is where your company's business is carried out. This client holds your production data.

It is important to remember that the effects of Customizing changes on application behavior are similar to those involved in changing a program: The effect is immediate and, if incorrect, may negatively impact existing data. As a result, changes should first be performed in a Customizing-and-development client. It is only after Customizing and development are carefully tested in the QTST client that the changes are transported to the PROD client. This ensures disruption-free production operation and the availability of valid functionality.

[+] SAP recommends avoiding Customizing and development work in the QTST and PROD clients.

The roles the required clients play during an SAP ERP implementation are comparable to the operation of an assembly line (see Figure 3.1). Assembly lines require a well-defined procedure with different mandatory steps performed at different, yet linear, stages to arrive at a final deliverable result. Similarly, each change made to your SAP system starts at the beginning of the implementation process (CUST), moves on to testing (QTST), and, after the change is verified, makes its way into production (PROD). Having all changes originate from a single client ensures all of the following:

Origin from one client

- The changes all follow the same testing procedures.
- The associated documentation is centralized, and is therefore easier to manage.
- Customizing settings and Repository objects in your system landscape remain consistent.

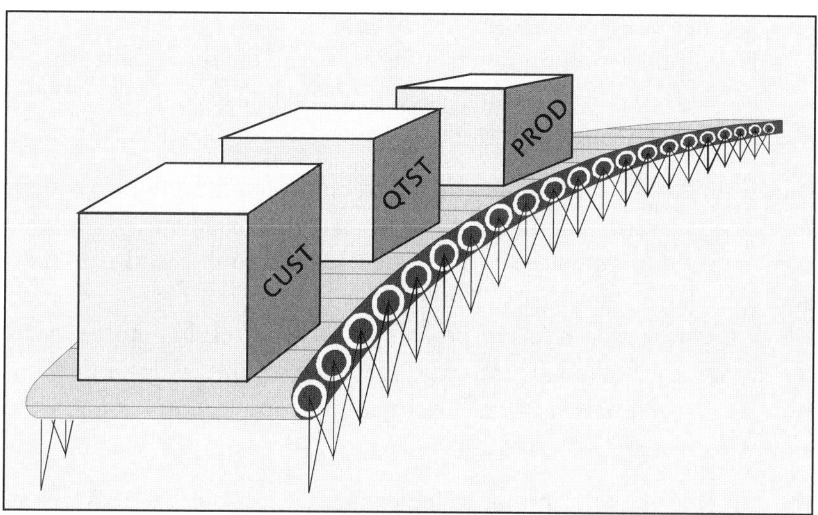

Figure 3.1 The Assembly Line for an SAP ERP Implementation

3.1.2 Additional Client Roles

To function properly, your SAP implementation requires the three standard clients mentioned previously. However, you may find it necessary to define additional clients to fulfill certain needs. These alternative client roles can include any of the following:

- Unit test client
- Specialized development client
- Sandbox client
- End-user training client

Unit Test Clients

Before you transport Customizing and developments to the quality assurance client, SAP recommends that you perform *unit testing*. Unit testing is the lowest level of testing, where the program or transaction is tested and evaluated for faults. It is usually part of the development phase, and focuses on the inner functions of the program rather than on integration. For example, after configuring a new sales document type, you should test it and see whether you can create a sales order using that document type. Or, perhaps you have written a report to analyze plant utilization. You should run this report several times to verify the results and achieve the desired layout. This requires a cyclical combination of Customizing and development and then testing to get the desired results.

Unit testing of SAP ERP functionality requires application data—more specifically, transaction data and master data. For example, to create a sales document, you need to have a customer number and materials, which are both master data. The result of the test is a new sales order, which is transaction data. To be able to provide results, most reports require some set of transaction data. Therefore, to unit test your Customizing and developments, you require sample application data and the ability to create new application data.

You can perform unit testing in the client CUST. However, SAP recommends setting up a unit test client to keep CUST free of application data. There are two reasons for this:

Setting up unit test clients

- Over time, unit testing causes a client to be cluttered with "bad" data; that is, data that is no longer suitable for unit tests. Inappropriate data does not allow for predictable test results.
- Application data is tightly coupled to Customizing settings. A Customizing change may not be possible because application data is already associated with the present Customizing settings. In fact, some settings, such as the configuration of your organization structure, cannot be changed after application data has been associated with it. To enable such a change, you would have to delete all application data associated with the original setting. This is a very tedious task.

Example: Application Data Associated with Customizing

When Customizing the application Sales and Distribution, a project team creates the required sales organizations within their company. In addition, the team configures all possible distribution channels that are used by the different sales organizations. For example, the Canadian sales organizations distribute only to retail centers, whereas the American sales organizations distribute to retail centers and wholesalers, and by mail order.

The team assigns the sales organizations to the appropriate distribution channels and verifies the combinations through testing with different types of sales orders. During the first round of user acceptance testing, it becomes obvious that the mail order business is not valid for the American sales organizations. Because mail order sales already exist for the American sales organizations, the team cannot simply delete this Customizing assignment. Before eliminating it, they must first delete all related sales orders—that is, the application data.

To avoid such complications, you can create another client that contains the necessary application data for unit testing. This unit test client provides an environment for maintaining a variety of application data separate from the Customizing environment. Here, the people who perform Customizing can test transactions and developers can test reports and programs. (See also Chapter 6.)

For the sake of consistency and ease of reading, the abbreviation TEST will represent the unit test client throughout this book. [+]

If your developers have diverse testing requirements for special programs, such as data conversion routines or interfaces to other computer systems, you may want to provide them with their own unit test client. This allows for a unique set of business data that can be manipulated by the developers without impacting Customizing tests. In more complex SAP ERP implementations, you may need a *development unit test client* to test reports, screens, and other new functionality.

CUST is the client in which all Customizing—both client-dependent and client-independent—and developments are performed. TEST enables people who perform Customizing to test the contents of their tasks and change requests. It also provides an environment for maintaining application data separate from the Customizing environment. [+]

Specialized Development Client

SAP recommends that both Customizing and development be performed in the same client. It is more efficient to have changes and documentation supporting an SAP implementation originate from a single source.

However, developers often demand a separate client in which they can develop their programs in isolation from the Customizing environment. They want a more stable client where the Customizing does not change every hour. Because each additional client in your system landscape requires increased administrative effort to ensure that all clients are updated regularly with the latest Customizing efforts, other alternatives should be tried. First, you should try a single CUST client. If that does not suffice, try using a combination of two TEST clients, one for Customizing and one for development. Only if these alternatives do not provide your developers with satisfactory results should you consider creating a unique development client.

Other Common Client Roles

In addition to the clients for Customizing and development (CUST), unit testing (TEST), quality assurance testing (QTST), and production (PROD), two other clients commonly found within a system landscape include the following:

- **Sandbox client**
  This client is a "playground" for people who are performing SAP ERP Customizing tasks and who want to test their efforts before actually impacting the Customizing-and-development client.
- **End user training client**
  This is an environment for training end users who will be using SAP ERP to supply and access production data.

[+] For the sake of consistency and ease of reading, the following abbreviations will be used throughout this book when representing the additional clients: SAND for a sandbox or playground client, and TRNG for the end user training client.

3.2 Defining an SAP Client

An SAP client is defined by its unique client settings. When you first create a client—for example, using *client maintenance* (Transaction SCC4)—you select the client's ID number and provide a short description. In addition, you make selections for all of the following parameters:

Parameters

- The client's default currency
- The client role, such as production, test, or Customizing

- The client-dependent change option
- The client-independent change option
- The client protection and restrictions—for example, protecting the client against overwriting and upgrades

The last four settings allow only approved activities to take place in that particular client. It is your responsibility to see that the correct role, restrictions, and change options have been chosen for each client in your system landscape. These settings are established when the client is created, but you can change the settings for a client at any time. For more details on creating a client and selecting the appropriate settings, see Chapter 9.

The critical client settings are the client-dependent change option and the client-independent change option. They will be explained in more detail in the next sections.

3.2.1 Client-Dependent Change Option

The most critical client setting used to define a client is its client-dependent change option. This option determines whether changes are permitted in a client, and whether the changes are going to be recorded automatically to change requests (see Figure 3.2). Because Repository objects are client-independent, they are not affected in this case. For Repository objects, the client-independent changeability discussed in the next chapter is relevant. The client change options for client-dependent attributes include:

Manual changes

- **Changes without automatic recording**
  This setting allows changes to client-dependent Customizing, but does not automatically record or include the changes in change requests. Customizing changes can be manually included in change requests for transport to other clients and systems at any time. However, because it is difficult to keep track of changes and then manually record them, SAP does not recommend this option for any client in your system landscape. This setting will be useful only if you need a client from which certain selective changes will be transported.

Automatic changes

- **Automatic recording of changes**
  This setting allows changes to client-dependent Customizing settings and automatically includes them in a change request. This enables their promotion and distribution to all other clients within your system landscape. This option should be assigned to your Customizing-and-development client (CUST).

No changes

- **No changes allowed**
  This setting prevents all users from making client-dependent Customizing changes from within the client. This option is useful for those clients in which Customizing changes do not take place—that is, clients that are used for testing and training purposes as well as production activities. Most clients in your system landscape, including TEST, QTST, TRNG, and PROD, should have this option.

No transports

- **No transports allowed**
  This setting allows client-dependent Customizing changes that will not be transported either manually or automatically to other clients. This option can be used to isolate a SAND client, where Customizing settings are sampled, but do not need to be moved to any other client.

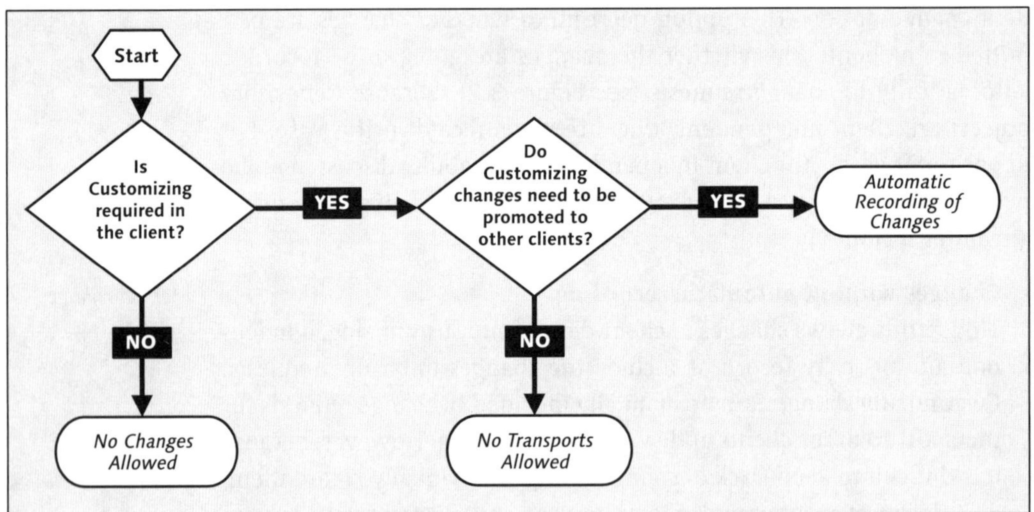

Figure 3.2 The Path for Determining the Appropriate Client-Independent Change Option

As mentioned previously, SAP recommends setting the NO CHANGES ALLOWED option for your PROD client. An alternative option for the PROD client is NO TRANSPORT ALLOWED. This option is required for the production client if you also use the CURRENT SETTINGS function. When special Customizing changes—known as data-only Customizing changes—need to be carried out in a production client without being saved to change requests, the NO CHANGES ALLOWED setting is no longer valid. An example of data involved in such a change is currency exchange rates, which may require frequent adjustment in SAP ERP. To avoid having to use change requests for these changes, SAP has introduced the CURRENT SETTINGS function (see Chapter 11).

3.2.2 Client-Independent Change Option

The client change options for client-independent attributes protect both client-independent Customizing and Repository objects (see Figure 3.3). Repository objects and cross-client Customizing are categorized separately and can therefore be protected against changes either together or individually. The client-independent change options are as follows:

Settings

- Changes to repository and client-independent Customizing allowed
- No changes to client-independent Customizing objects. (Changes to repository objects are still allowed.)
- No changes to repository objects. (Changes to client-independent Customizing are still possible.)
- No changes to repository and client-independent Customizing objects

All clients in your system landscape—except for the CUST client—should be assigned the last client-independent change option, NO CHANGES TO REPOSITORY AND CLIENT-INDEPENDENT CUSTOMIZING OBJECTS. The CUST client needs the CHANGES TO REPOSITORY AND CLIENT-INDEPENDENT CUSTOMIZING ALLOWED setting.

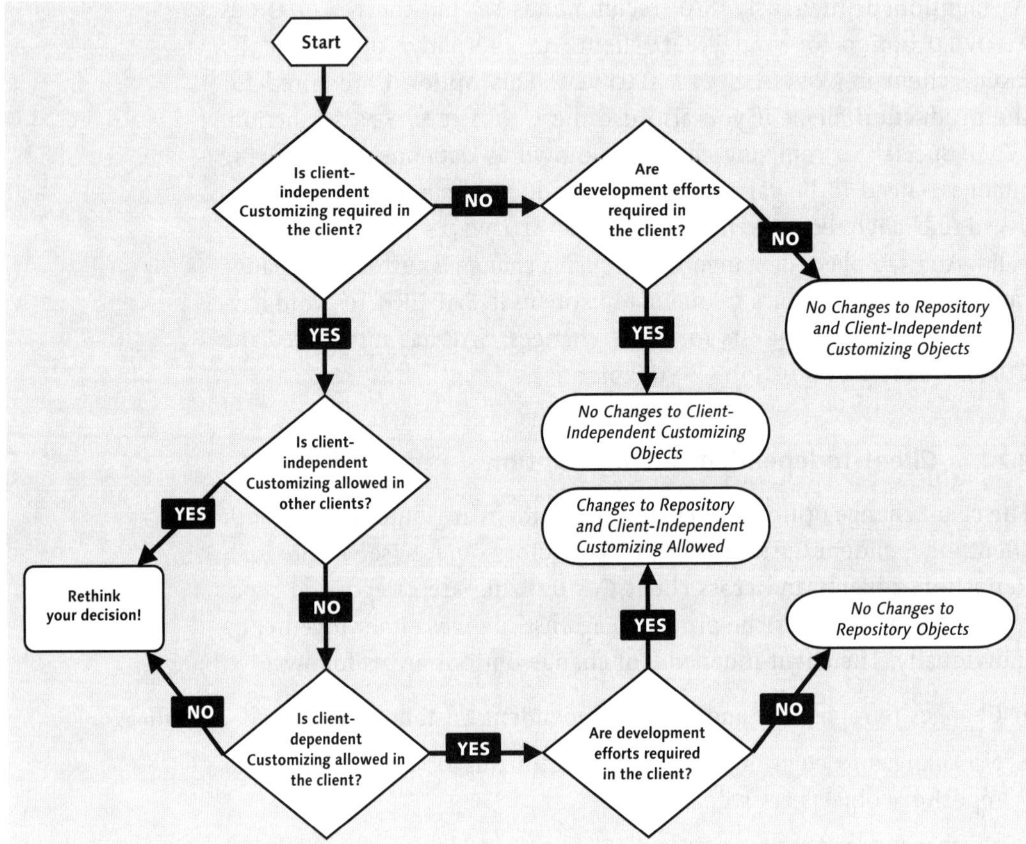

Figure 3.3 The Path for Determining the Appropriate Client-Independent Change Option

Technically, the client-dependent and client-independent change options are two different settings. Logically, the two settings are linked with regard to Customizing changes. Customizing changes rely and build upon other Customizing changes, regardless of whether they are client-dependent or client-independent. For this reason, all Customizing activities should take place in a single client, the CUST client. Although a second client such as the SAND client may allow for client-dependent Customizing changes, client-independent Customizing should not be performed in this client.

If client-independent Customizing takes place in a client, that client should also be used for client-dependent Customizing. Only one client within an SAP ERP system should allow for both client-dependent and client-independent Customizing. [+]

3.3 Multiple Clients in an SAP ERP System

A client is used to keep the application data of one client isolated and completely independent from another client. This is not, however, necessary for all SAP products. In an SAP NetWeaver Portal, for example, users log on to the portal only once and then can call any other SAP system—even with different clients—and log on to it. Systems based on SAP Business Information Warehouse (SAP BW) or SAP NetWeaver Business Intelligence (SAP NetWeaver BI) also have only one client. Because development, quality assurance, and production tasks each require different sets of application data, each area is provided with a different client. Based on the uniqueness of application data in each client, one might assume that any number of independent clients could operate in the same SAP system. With regard to hardware costs and required system maintenance, such a setup (one SAP system with all required clients) makes financial and organizational sense. The multiple-client concept for the SAP system does, however, have certain limitations that are both functional and technical in nature.

3.3.1 Functional Limitations

Standard functions of the SAP system are implemented as programs in the Repository. The client independence of the entire Repository—with all of its program and Dictionary objects—is a fundamental characteristic of the system. Customizing provides the finishing touches to the standard SAP functionality that supplies you with an operational client.

The SAP ERP system provides full multiple-client capability at the application data level; that is, all data created in a client is visible for only that one client and cannot be changed or even displayed by other clients. The vast majority of Customizing settings are also client-dependent. These *client-specific* Customizing settings are valid for only that one client.

However, some IMG Customizing activities are client-independent. They create globally valid settings (such as decimal places for currencies) or result in the generation of programs and Dictionary elements. Because client-independent Customizing and all Repository objects are always accessible from every client, they are a potential source of conflict. Customizing and Repository changes in one client could accidentally change, overwrite, or conflict with the needs of another client. An even worse scenario involves clients that do not detect changes to client-independent settings and objects that affect them.

Only one client

To deal with these functional limitations, SAP recommends that you have only one client in an SAP system where changes to client-independent Customizing and Repository objects are allowed. This helps ensure the integrity of each client in a multiple-client system. Using the appropriate client-change options ensures that client-independent changes are made only in a single client within the SAP ERP system.

Similar clients in one system

SAP also recommends that only "like" clients reside in the same SAP system. For example, test or training clients can be in the same SAP system. This does not cause problems because these clients are generated as a copy of an existing Customizing-and-development client, and are based on the same Customizing and developments. Thus, such clients are not self-sufficient Customizing environments, but rather derivatives of the Customizing client, requiring the same client-independent objects and settings.

3.3.2 Technical Limitations

At a technical level, a client ID is the primary key field in the Customizing and application tables of the database. A database can contain as many clients as you wish—up to a total of 1,000 clients. The required database resources, as well as the hardware performance, are largely a result of the number of active users, not the number of clients used.

You do, however, need to consider the influence of the number of clients in a system on system performance with regard to the following technical system concepts:

Client–performance ratio

- More clients require additional main memory for the system buffers. As a general rule, an additional 10MB is required for each client.
- Because each client occupies entries in database tables, more clients in a system may lead to higher database access times. This is especially true when accessing tables with a full table scan.
- The runtime of a release upgrade depends on the number of clients. The more clients that have been defined in a system, the greater the import effort will be, because new entries have to be distributed to all clients within the system. Although upgrade runtime will increase with each additional client, note that a large portion of the time required for an upgrade is spent delivering new Repository objects, not client-dependent data. Therefore, the increased effort in upgrading a system with more clients is not directly proportional. For example, the upgrade of a four-client system will not take twice as long as the upgrade of a two-client system.
- Only limited technical maintenance is possible due to increased availability requirements. Multiple clients within an SAP system will have different roles and therefore different end-user demands. Technical maintenance, such as reorganizing the database or making an offline backup, requires the SAP system to be down and unavailable. Scheduling of system unavailability is more difficult if the end-user audience has varying demands.

[+] For more information on the database requirements of a standard SAP client, see SAP Note 118823 in the SAP Service Marketplace.

3.3.3 Protective Measures for Multiple-Client Operations

SAP provides you with protective measures to prevent inadvertent changes being made from a client within a multiple-client system, and to ensure the successful coexistence of multiple clients in the same physical system, as follows:

- **Client-change options**
  Changes to client-independent Customizing and Repository objects can be restricted to a specific client using the appropriate client-change options.

- **User authorizations**
  Special user authorizations must be assigned for client-independent maintenance.
- **Special popups**
  Whenever you perform client-independent Customizing activities or maintain a client-independent table, a warning message informs you that the changes will affect all clients in the SAP system.

[+] For more information on the limitations of multiple clients in a single SAP system, see SAP Note 31557 in the SAP Service Marketplace.

3.4 The SAP Three-System Landscape

Clients provide an environment where application data can be isolated, while sharing a common Repository and client-independent Customizing. Because of the functional and technical limitations of multiple clients in a single SAP system—including sharing a common Repository—SAP recommends that you distribute the critical clients among several SAP systems. The three standard systems in this distribution are as follows:

Standard systems

- **Development system**
- **Quality assurance system**
  (Sometimes referred to as the *test* or *consolidation* system.)
- **Production system**

The recommendation for building a three-system landscape is not only valid for the SAP ERP system. If, for example, an SAP NetWeaver Portal has common business processes with this system, the Portal system should also use a parallel three-system landscape. Otherwise, it is not possible to build and verify sensible test cases in the quality assurance system.

3.4.1 Standard SAP Systems

Development system

Customizing and development take place in the *development system*. All changes made in the development system are recorded to change requests and then transported to quality assurance for validation. This system contains the CUST client.

Quality assurance system

In the *quality assurance system*, functionality is tested without affecting the production environment. A quality assurance system enables you to integrate Customizing and developments, and to check the validity and consistency of transported changes before moving the changes into the production environment. This system contains the QTST client.

Production system

All changes imported into the quality assurance system are then delivered to the *production system*. In this system, your business data will be collected and accessed. The system contains the PROD client.

For the sake of consistency and ease of reading, the following abbreviations will be used throughout this book to represent the different SAP systems: DEV for the Customizing-and-development system, QAS for the quality assurance system, and PRD for the production system. Each system needs a unique three-character alphanumeric system ID. For all purposes, the previously mentioned abbreviations can be considered the system IDs.

3.4.2 Distribution of Client Roles

As explained previously, each required client is housed in its own SAP system. Additional client roles should then be distributed accordingly within the system landscape:

- Sandbox client: The SAND client, where sampling of client-dependent Customizing takes place, should be in the development environment. After testing Customizing settings in the sandbox client, the person performing the Customizing can go into the CUST client and implement the changes.
- Unit test client: The TEST client must be in the same SAP system as the CUST client. Customizing changes and development changes are tested in the unit test client. After having been unit tested, changes can then be transported to the QTST client.
- End-user training client: Because the quality assurance system is more stable than the development system, the TRNG client is often found in the quality assurance system, where it will not impact the production system.

To meet the needs of your software implementation, and to ensure smooth production operation, your system landscape should therefore contain at least three systems, the required clients, and any additional clients that are necessary and advantageous for your implementation. Figure 3.4 shows the standard system landscape and the distribution of required and other commonly used client roles.

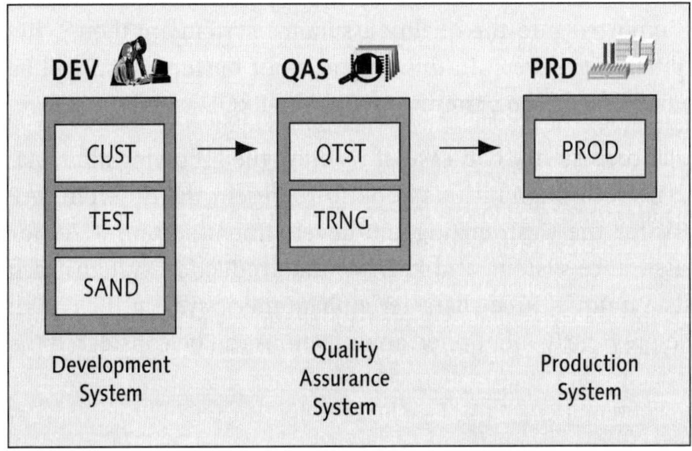

Figure 3.4 The Standard SAP Three-System Landscape with Its Client Distribution

The three distinct systems and the clients recommended by SAP benefit your implementation in the following ways:

Advantages

- All Customizing and developments are separate from production activities for testing-, security-, and system performance-related reasons.
- A quality assurance system lets you integrate Customizing and development, and also check the validity and consistency of transported changes before they are delivered to the production system.
- Upgrades as well as the application of SAP Support Packages can be simulated and tested before applying them to the production system.

Example: Adjusting the SAP-Recommended Three-System Landscape

A large chemical firm decided to implement SAP ERP with the objective to move all manufacturing and distribution processes from an existing, antiquated system to SAP ERP. This also required migrating historical data from the legacy system to SAP ERP at the start of production activities.

Initially, the company began its implementation of the three-system landscape SAP recommends with the following clients:

- CUST client 100, TEST client 200, and SAND client 400 in the development system (DDV)
- QTST client 100 and TRNG client 300 in the quality assurance system (DQA)
- PROD client 100 in the production system (DPR)

It immediately became obvious that testing data conversion routines with the legacy system was interfering with the testing of Customizing changes. To alleviate this problem, two new clients were created—client 210 in DDV for the unit testing of data conversion routines, and client 210 in the quality assurance system (DQA) to support stress testing of conversion routines.

Also, because training sessions for end users occurred on a weekly basis, a master training client 310 was created in DQA. From this master client, the training client 300 in DQA was generated each week. This ensured a base level of application data and default user accounts for the support of each training session.

The company's system landscape now looked like that shown in Figure 3.5.

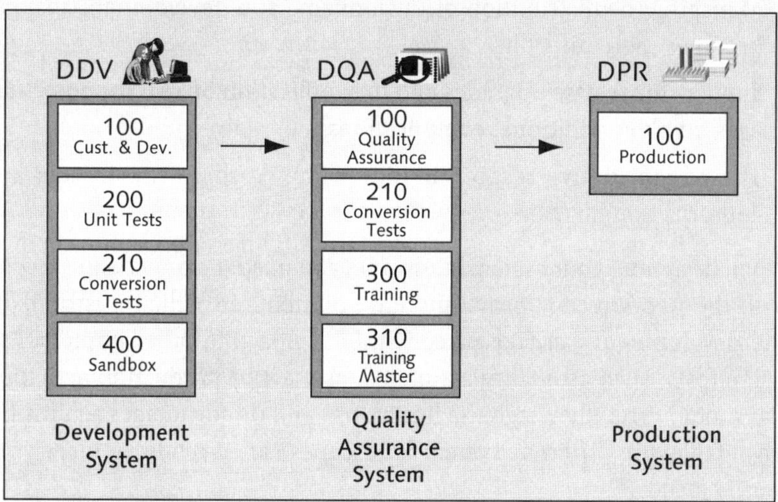

Figure 3.5 System Landscape Example

After the system was in production, and the legacy system was eliminated, the company no longer required the data conversion clients. Therefore, client 210 in DDV and client 210 in DQA were deleted.

3.5 Alternative System Landscapes

The SAP-recommended three-system landscape is simply a template from which you can build your own system landscape. Many customers have specific or temporary client needs that are added to the system landscape; other customers have a need for additional SAP systems—for example, for a system used solely for end-user training. Some customers may also have constraints that require them to implement a one-system or two-system landscape. Or, a customer may begin with the three-system implementation recommended by SAP, but over time require more SAP systems because of a need to introduce more functionality while still providing support changes to the production system.

Regardless of your environment, it is important to note that additional clients and additional SAP systems mean certain costs to your implementation, as follows:

Costs

- More hardware resources are needed.
- Managing the distribution of Customizing and development changes becomes more difficult.
- Support for release upgrades and the application of SAP Support Packages involves additional complications.
- The administrative responsibilities with regard to user access and authorization increase.

When designing your system landscape, you need to compare these costs with the necessity for providing environments in which Customizing and development can take place without impacting other implementation efforts, such as quality assurance testing and production activities. You should carefully weigh the limitations and disadvantages against the advantages the different system landscapes can provide to meet your specific needs.

3.5.1 One-System Landscape

A one-system landscape consists of a single SAP system used for Customizing and development as well as for quality assurance testing and production activities. A single SAP system implementation requires that all clients share the same hardware, the Repository, and client-independent Customizing. Sharing these resources results in the following limitations for a one-system landscape:

Limitations

- Changes to Repository objects are client-independent and immediately affect the runtime environment. Therefore, changes are tested in the runtime environment of your production system and production data loss can occur as a result of inconsistencies or incorrect changes.
- The Customizing-and-development client as well as the quality assurance client can affect production performance.
- System availability for production activities is required at all times, preventing dedicated development or meeting quality assurance demands.
- Production data security is compromised. For example, developers can create reports that access production data from another client.
- The system administrator cannot perform upgrades on a nonproduction system before upgrading the production system.

As a consequence of these limitations, no further development is possible after production work has started. Changes to Repository objects can be made only when production operations are stopped for development and testing. For these reasons, SAP does not recommend using a one-system landscape.

3.5.2 Two-System Landscape

A small, uncomplicated SAP ERP implementation may need only two systems. This two-system landscape is able to support an SAP ERP implementation with standard business functionality and limited customer development needs.

Weaknesses

A two-system landscape allows development and production to be performed in two separate environments. However, this landscape has its weaknesses. Because development and quality assurance testing both occur in the development system, the stability of central resources during actual quality assurance testing may be jeopardized. Therefore, changes to Repository objects or client-independent Customizing cannot be made while quality assurance testing is in progress.

Change management Change management also presents a problem for the two-system landscape. Complex development projects often involve transporting partial functionality, sometimes without taking dependencies into account. Change requests and the functionality in the change requests are not fully tested until after the changes have been imported. In addition, upon import, a change request may result in an error due to dependencies on other change requests or problems within the change request itself. Therefore, in a two-system landscape, the transport of a change request cannot be fully tested before it is imported into the production system. This can cause inconsistencies and affect the production system.

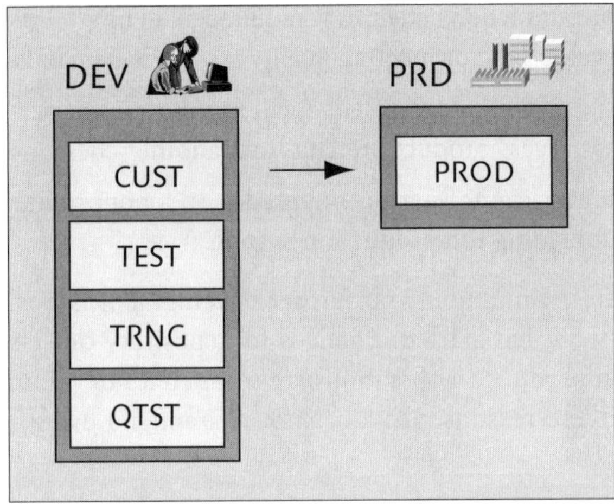

Figure 3.6 A Two-System Landscape

Figure 3.6 shows a two-system landscape. In this landscape, the development system has four different clients. Customizing and development activities occur in client CUST. Unit testing takes place in client TEST before being delivered to the QTST client. End-user training also takes place in this system in the client TRNG. The production system is reserved solely for production activities in the client PROD.

A three-system landscape provides a unique environment dedicated to quality assurance testing and, just as important, allows testing of transported change requests. The two-system landscape, in contrast, does not offer this option. This means that the two-system landscape is viable only for environments where very few complex Customizing and development changes have to be transported to production after the start of production activities.

3.5.3 Four-System Landscape

The SAP-recommended system landscape requires three SAP systems. These three systems house the critical roles for the SAP ERP implementation. However, customers frequently include more systems in their landscape to support a variety of testing demands or training needs. Noncritical clients, such as the sandbox client, training client, or an additional testing client, are then isolated in their own SAP ERP system, extending the landscape to a four-system landscape. Such a system landscape is valid as long as the additional system provides long-term value for the implementation plan. It will also require the latest copy of Customizing and development changes. An example of such a system is a training environment that is isolated from quality assurance activities (see Figure 3.7).

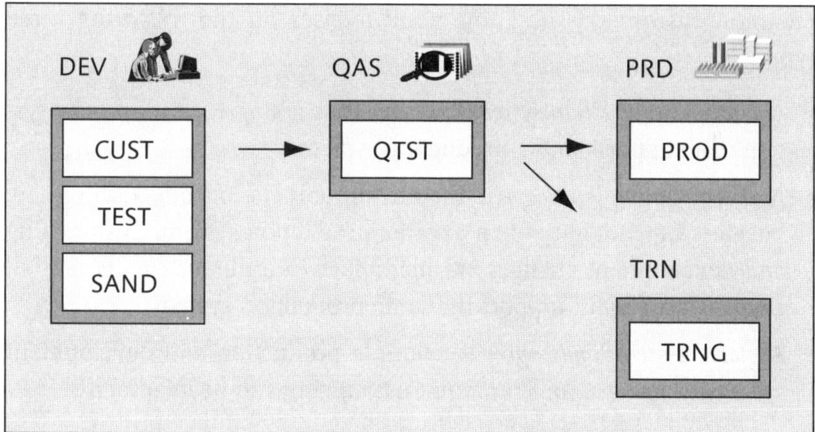

Figure 3.7 A Four-System Landscape with a Separate Training Environment

3.6 Complex System Landscapes

Some customers require implementations that go beyond the SAP-recommended system landscape—for example, a large, multinational implementation. Such customers may need a *complex system landscape*—that is, an environment that extends beyond the standard three-system landscape. More specifically, you can think of a complex system landscape as a system landscape that includes more than one client playing any one of the critical client roles. For example, a system landscape that has two different production clients or two different Customizing-and-development clients is considered complex.

SAP solution

Because of its complexity, this type of system landscape requires strong management effort and centralized coordination that still allows for localizing particular implementation tasks. It may also require using special SAP tools for the support of Customizing and development as well as the distribution and/or sharing of application data. The most important tool in this context again is SAP Solution Manager. You can use this tool for an intelligent distribution of Customizing in complex landscapes via Customizing distribution, or solely by using Business Configuration (BC) Sets in Solution Manager projects.

Several types of complex system landscapes exist. To reflect the most common customer issues, this book focuses on the following three types:

Types of complex system landscapes

- A *multiple production system landscape* has a single development system that supports many production systems.
- A *phased system landscape* is used to support the introduction of new business functionality to an existing production system. Customizing and development changes are made in two different clients, but all changes ultimately support the same production system.
- A *global system landscape* has multiple production and development systems sharing some common Customizing and developments.

3.6.1 Multiple Production System Landscape

A multiple production system landscape has multiple production data clients with similar Customizing and development needs. Such a landscape is shown in Figure 3.8. Because the multiple production systems stem from a single Customizing and development system, you may find yourself asking the following questions:

- If the data and business needs of the production environments are similar enough to share the same Customizing and developments, why isn't a single production system enough?
- When in production, what happens if the different production systems have different Customizing and development demands that can no longer be served by a single development system?
- Different production systems require multiple production data environments. How do these different production systems share business data, such as master and transaction data?

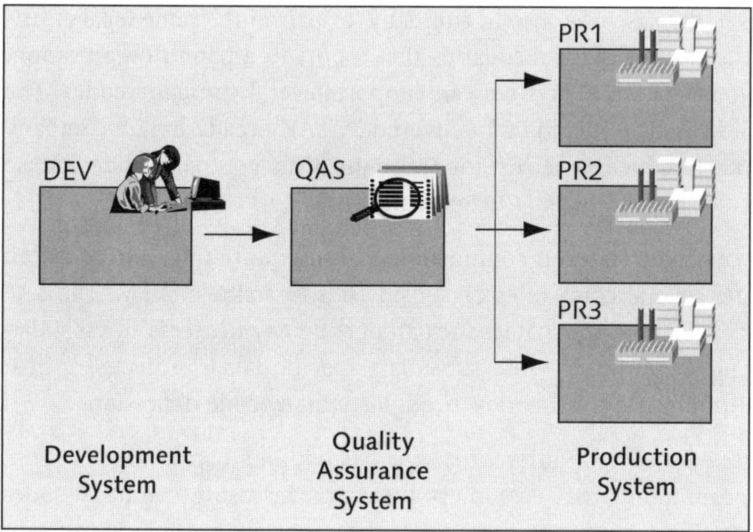

Figure 3.8 A System Landscape with Multiple Production Systems

The first two questions about the need for and support of multiple production systems are addressed in this chapter. The management of business data across multiple SAP ERP systems is discussed in Chapter 4.

Company Codes versus Multiple Production System Landscapes

Some organizations divide their SAP implementation and production data among different subsidiaries. In such organizations, one subsidiary may demand that its production data be in a separate SAP system (or even a separate client) from the production data of the other. The subsidiary could be accommodated by implementing a multiple production system landscape. However, this would impair the parent organization's ability to view all its subsidiaries' business data from within a single client.

A more fitting alternative for sharing business functionality and business data between different organizations can be provided by using *company codes*. Company codes in SAP ERP define the smallest organizational element for which a complete, self-contained set of accounts can be drawn up for external reporting. Company codes are either separate legal entities, as in the case of a second company, or part of the same legal entity, as in the case of two subsidiaries that report to a parent organization. One client in an SAP system can support several company codes. The standard clients 000 and 001 delivered by SAP already have a company code 0001, which is set up for Germany. This company code can be adapted or copied during Customizing.

Using company codes in conjunction with user authorizations, you can integrate several companies or subsidiaries in a single client. The SAP authorization concept enables the parent company to access all subsidiaries for report purposes, while subsidiary-specific data is protected against access from other subsidiaries through company code definition.

[+] To meet the needs of different companies within a parent organization, SAP recommends that customers first consider using company codes within a single production client rather than using multiple production clients.

Specific Scenarios for Multiple Production Systems

When using company codes and user authorizations does not provide a large organization with the production requirements it needs, a multiple production system landscape becomes necessary. This type of system landscape will satisfy the following requirements:

Requirements

- **Unique language demands**
  In older SAP ERP systems a single codepage such as Latin-I, for example, often proved to be sufficient. However, multinational corporate

groups needed to use multiple codepages, which was implemented primarily by using Multiple Display Multiple Processing (MDMP), a technique that allows using several non-Unicode codepages in parallel. Aside from the increased complexity of maintaining different codepages, you should also be aware of the increased effort required if you want to later migrate these systems to a Unicode-enabled system. Other problems such as risking data inconsistencies arise when using portals to access MDMP systems. In this scenario, a separation of systems by codepage will provide advantages. Aside from several systems running separate codepages, a single Unicode system that is wholly supported by SAP ERP solves all of these problems with only slightly increased hardware requirements compared with a single codepage system. Section 18.6 provides more information on Unicode and upgrades.

Example: A Multiple Production System Landscape to Meet Specific Language Requirements

A multinational distribution company has facilities spanning the globe, from its headquarters in North America to distribution centers in Eastern Europe, to subsidiaries in Korea and China. The organization uses SAP ERP to manage corporate sales and financial data. However, due to the inherent cultural differences and autonomy of many of the Asian subsidiaries, the Board decides that all business data must be maintained in its local language.

In other words, not only is the SAP GUI presentation interface for the end-user community in the local language, data is also entered in the respective languages. The language support for Korean and Chinese, or Polish and Chinese, in a single SAP system is not possible using one standard codepage. Therefore, either servers in the respective codepages or a Unicode system need to be installed. The following is a list of the required systems without Unicode support:

The respective end-user communities use production systems with the following system IDs:

- PNA supports North America by providing English.
- PEE supports Eastern Europe by providing Czech, English, Polish, and German.
- PCH supports China by providing Simplified Chinese and English.
- PKO supports Korea by providing Korean and English.

- **Performance concerns**
  The client/server technology of SAP ERP, and newer hardware technologies, let you distribute many active users across multiple application servers. This distribution of resources typically meets the needs of even the largest customers. However, some customers have performance needs, networking concerns, and varying end-user demands that go beyond what one production system can provide. These customers require a multiple production system landscape.

Customizing and Development in Multiple Production Systems

A multiple production system landscape depends on the fact that all production systems have the same Customizing settings and Repository objects. After the initial start of production activities, Customizing and development activities continue in the development system to support production activities, enhance existing functionality, and introduce new business processes. Although many of these changes are created to satisfy a specific need of one production system, the changes still have to be distributed to all clients and systems to ensure consistent Customizing and development.

However, when in production, reluctance is greater to introduce changes into the production system, especially if there is no apparent benefit for the production activities. Therefore, over time, as the multiple production systems in a multiple system landscape become more autonomous, such landscape-wide Customizing and development transports become a hindrance. In this case, the multiple production system landscape may need to expand to become more like a global system landscape, which is explained in more detail later in this chapter.

[+] Support for a multiple production system landscape requires centralized Customizing and development that are rolled out to all production systems.

3.6.2 Phased System Landscape

Customers often implement SAP ERP in different phases to meet varying business objectives within a specific time frame and to deal with management constraints and resource limitations. The first phase might be used to start up certain production plants, or to install a particular application component such as Financial Accounting. The next phase either adds plants or even a new component, such as Human Resources. Another phase could be an upgrade to the latest SAP release. (See also Chapter 6.) To support a multiple-phased implementation, and to provide an environment in which new business processes can be introduced while current production activities are supported, SAP recommends using a *phased system landscape*.

Note that the word "phase" is used to represent a customer's need for implementing new functionality in its production system. This functionality may or may not be a release upgrade. The implementation phase is often the introduction of new business processes through additional configuration. For example, phases one through three may be the rollout of all company codes, plants, and financials. Phase four may be an upgrade of the SAP software, and phase five may be the introduction of Internet functionality. The phased system landscape is designed to support the rollout of new Customizing to address business needs as well as SAP release upgrades.

Requirements of a Phased System Landscape

A phased system landscape requires resources to support production while at the same time providing an environment for new Customizing and development. To realize these goals, the following systems need to be added to the SAP-recommended three-system landscape:

Adding systems

- **Production support system**
  This is a Customizing and development environment that closely resembles the production system; that is, its Customizing data and Repository objects are identical to those in the production system. This system is used to make changes or corrections demanded by production while the next phase of the implementation is being planned and tested in the DEV and QAS systems.
- **Final quality assurance system**
  This is a quality assurance environment that closely resembles the production system and includes sample or complete production data. This system is used for testing and verifying any changes demanded

by production—that is, changes made in the production support system. This testing, also known as *regression testing*, is necessary so that the changes will not have an adverse affect on production data after import; that is, the new functionality will not negatively impact existing business functionality.

Realizing a Phased Implementation

With the addition of these two new systems, the phased system landscape recommended by SAP should have five systems. As in the case of the three-system landscape, each critical environment required for the implementation has its own SAP system.

Figure 3.9 shows the standard client roles and SAP systems for a phased system landscape. The notation PHASE N represents the phase currently in production. PHASE N+1 represents the next phase of the implementation to be brought into production at a later date and time, for example, the introduction of a new component or an SAP ERP release upgrade.

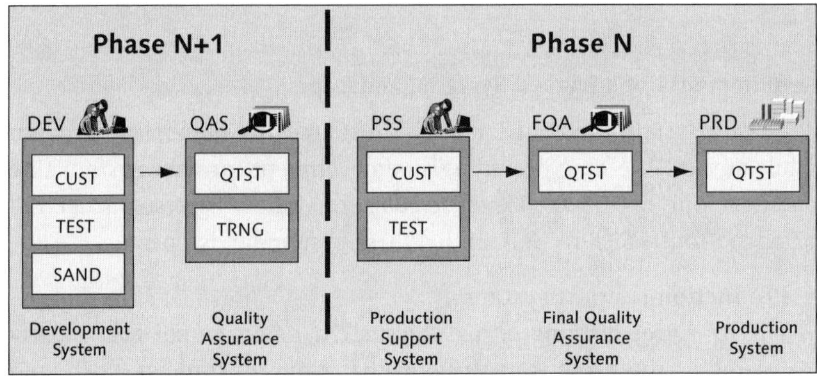

Figure 3.9 The SAP-Recommended Phased System Landscape

In a phased system landscape, Phase N changes are only the changes required to immediately support production. These take place in the production support system (in Figure 3.9, the SAP system PSS). All other Customizing and developments are part of the next phase and take place in the original development system. Phase N+1 functionality is unit tested in the development system (DEV) and then transported to the quality assurance system (QAS) for validation.

Figure 3.10 shows the next step, the promotion of PHASE N+1 functionality into production. SAP recommends first applying the changes to the final quality assurance system (in Figure 3.10, the SAP ERP System FQA). This lets you perform business integration testing on a system most similar to a production system. During this final quality assurance testing, if any changes are required for the new phase, they must originate from the development system (DEV). The production support system (PSS) then remains consistent with production and can provide any production support needed in the meantime.

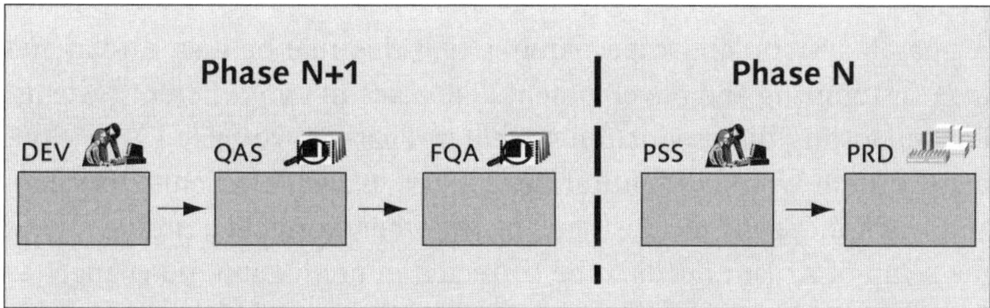

Figure 3.10 The Procedure for Promoting Changes in a Phased System Landscape

After validation of Phase N+1 on the final quality assurance system (FQA), all of these changes are applied to the production system (PRD) and eventually to the production support system (PSS). All SAP systems, including the production system, are then at Phase N+1. At this point in time, Phase N+2 changes can be transported from the development system to the quality assurance system to start preparing for the testing of the next phase, to be rolled into production at a later date.

If Phase N+1 is a new release, an upgrade of the systems to the newest release is a prerequisite for the transport of change requests. This is because change requests are release-dependent. The development and quality assurance systems are first upgraded to the new release. Changes required for the support of this release are then made in development and verified in quality assurance. Prior to promoting the changes to the final quality assurance system, that system must also be upgraded to the new release. Likewise, the production system will need to be upgraded before the change requests from Release N+1 can be applied and the production system can be moved from Release N to Release N+1.

Multiple Customizing-and-Development Clients

A basic rule with regard to client and system strategies is that Customizing and development originate from a single client. Customizing is the configuration of the SAP software and requires changes that are both client-dependent and client-independent. Customizing changes also build on one another, creating dependencies that cannot be separated and are often hidden from those performing the Customizing. Development work then depends on the Customizing settings.

Two systems

A phased system landscape requires that this rule be disregarded and that Customizing and development take place in two different systems. For supporting the production system in Phase N, you need a development system with an identical Repository, as well as client-dependent and client-independent Customizing. In other words, if a problem with the setup of a plant needs to be corrected in production, no changes to that plant or changes that may impact that plant should have been made in the production support environment.

Likewise, if a report is not working properly in production, a developer needs to modify the same version of the report in the production support environment—not a newer version of the report. Therefore, Customizing and development support for Phase N requires a constant environment, not one in which new business processes are being added. Accordingly, Phase N production support and configuration of Phase N+1 functionality must be in separate environments.

Any changes made to support Phase N production activities need to be part of the Phase N+1 rollout, and must be realized in the Phase N+1 development system, as shown in Figure 3.11. For example, if a production planning scheme is adjusted to support production needs, the required change must also be made in the development system. SAP recommends that these changes be manually applied to avoid conflicts with the current configuration in the Phase N+1 environment.

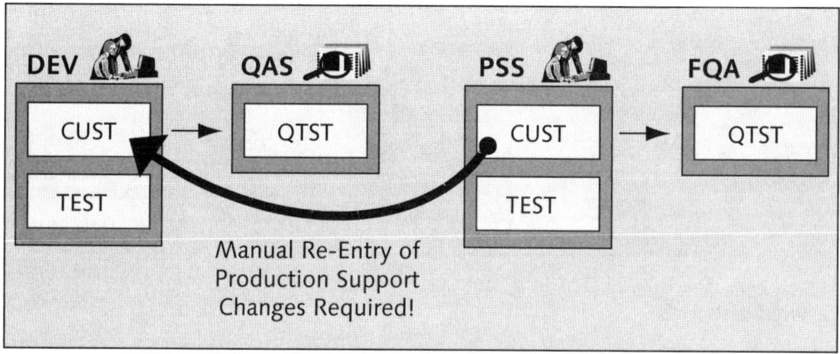

Figure 3.11 Ensuring Consistency between DEV and PSS

SAP provides several tools that help manage Customizing and development changes in multiple clients. These tools are explained in more detail in Section 3.6.3.

Alternative Phased System Landscape

Often, phased implementations that are small and uncomplicated do not require five SAP systems to maintain a stable production environment while also introducing new functionality. Based on the stability of your production system, the extent of customer developments, and the aggressiveness of your phased implementation, you may find that a four-system landscape suffices for a phased implementation. However, this option does have its limitations.

A four-system landscape functions without the final quality assurance system (FQA). The quality assurance system (QAS) is used in its place. First and foremost, the quality assurance system serves Phase N by providing immediate support for production. This is shown in Figure 3.12.

When you begin thorough testing of Phase N+1, the quality assurance system supports Phase N+1, as shown in Figure 3.13. At this time, any changes required for the support of production are made in the production support system, are unit tested there, and are then transported into the production system without true quality assurance validation. As pointed out in the section about two-landscape systems, when the transport of changes cannot be fully tested before import into the production system, inconsistencies may arise and affect production.

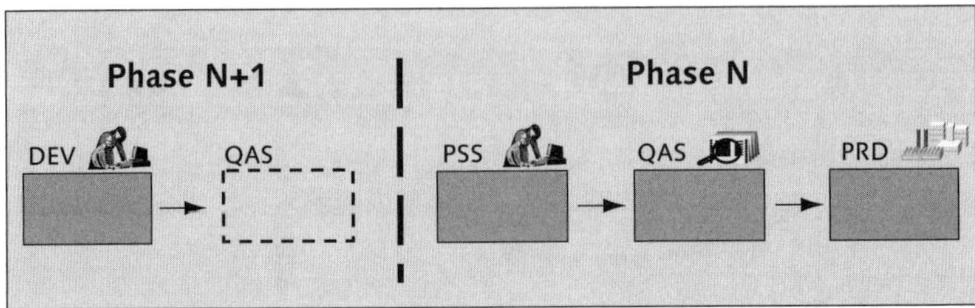

Figure 3.12 The Role of QAS in a Four-System Phased Landscape Prior to Testing Phase N+1

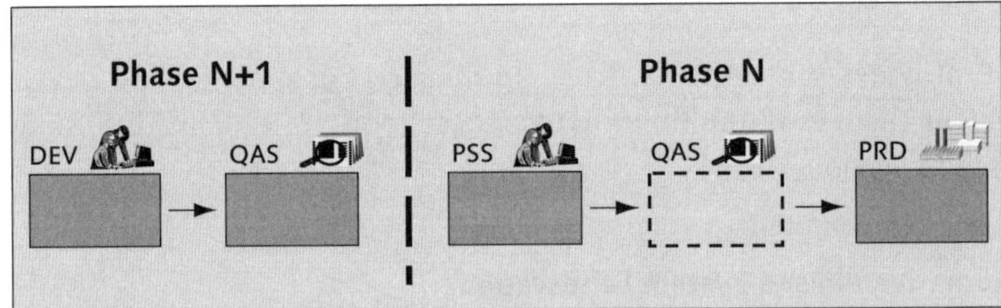

Figure 3.13 The Role of QAS in a Four-System Phased Landscape While Testing Phase N+1

Therefore, there should be a restrictive assessment of the requested changes for PRD. For important corrections necessary to solve problems that prevent production from working properly, this phase should also have an emergency plan ready to implement.

3.6.3 Global System Landscape

Many enterprises today implement SAP ERP on a worldwide scale and coordinate their efforts centrally. The demands of many subsidiaries and different legal and financial marketplaces require unique implementations. To maximize the benefits of a company's global business, such a global implementation has to provide all of the following:

- Core business processes on a global basis while coping with local and legal regulations
- Universal user access using different types of interfaces and supplying interfaces in local languages
- Global data consistency

While a global organization may want to implement SAP ERP globally from a centralized production system, or perhaps using a multiple production system landscape, local requirements may not be addressed with such approaches. Therefore, many organizations centrally define their SAP organizational standards and default business processes, and then implement unique systems worldwide. To do so, a central corporate office supplies multiple subsidiaries with a set of Customizing and developments, which the subsidiaries use as a baseline when configuring SAP ERP to meet their local requirements. This procedure is often referred to as a *rollout strategy*. The resulting environment is considered a *global system landscape*.

Realizing a Global System Landscape

Figure 3.14 shows a global system landscape where different subsidiaries accept Customizing and developments from their corporate headquarters. This Customizing and development package, referred to as the *global template*, is created in the corporate development system and tested in its quality assurance system. The global template is then passed on to the individual subsidiaries, which continue to customize and develop the SAP systems to meet their specific needs. This procedure takes place in each subsidiary's unique system landscape, which can be a standard three-system landscape or any of the alternatives mentioned previously. Ultimately, all subsidiaries are in production with similar settings and functionality, while unique requirements are fulfilled. This forms a system landscape with decentralized—yet loosely coupled—production systems.

Managing a Global Template

The difficulties managing a global rollout strategy, as shown in Figure 3.14, involve the need for a global template. Using a global template is not a one-time effort. As SAP ERP expands throughout the organization, and more and more business functionality is required, new global templates will have to be distributed on a regular basis. This sparks many concerns, particularly within the subsidiaries, and the following questions need to be addressed:

- What is considered global and what is considered localized business functionality? Can Customizing be easily divided into global and local terms?
- What assurance do subsidiaries have that new changes delivered from the corporate development system will not negatively impact local Customizing and developments? With Customizing dependencies and the coupling of SAP ERP function modules causing possible complications, how can global templates be introduced to a subsidiary over time?
- Which dependencies exist between the different products used with SAP ERP, and how can these changes be synchronized across systems?

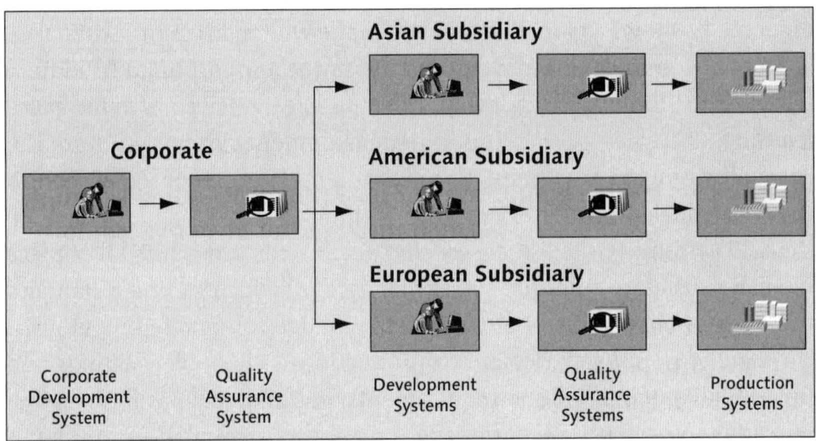

Figure 3.14 A Global System Landscape

SAP's first response to these questions is that a strong, centrally managed implementation with representative resources from all subsidiaries is needed. From a technical rather than an organizational perspective, change management in a global system landscapes requires that centrally created Customizing and development objects not be changed locally. Likewise, a global template should not change the Customizing settings or development objects of a subsidiary.

Repository objects have a sense of "ownership." An attribute for every Repository object is the SAP system from which it originated. Therefore, development objects in a global system landscape can easily be managed and protected as follows:

Protection of development objects

- Every SAP ERP system has a *system change option* (Transaction SE06; GoTo • System Change Option). Within this option, you can disallow modifications to different namespaces. This determines which Repository objects in the SAP system can be changed. If a global implementation requires a lot of central development, one namespace can be created for all global objects. This global namespace can then be protected in all local development systems, disallowing any changes to such objects.
- You can use development classes and naming conventions to prevent the creation of an object with the same name within two different SAP systems.

[+] For more information regarding the use of system change options, namespaces, and development classes for the protection of customer developments, see Chapter 10.

Customizing is more difficult to manage in a global system landscape than in the other landscapes. Unlike for Repository objects, there is no concept of ownership for Customizing settings, nor are there standard methods by which subsets of Customizing can be "locked" or protected against change. To manage a global template from a Customizing perspective, corporate standards must define which Customizing settings are part of the global template, and which can be maintained locally. Such a strategy requires detailed definitions, and the procedure must be managed not from within SAP ERP, but as project efforts. This well-defined strategy for protecting both global and local Customizing settings can be realized using one or a combination of the following methods:

Methods

- Corporate headquarters determines and documents all global Customizing settings. These global settings are then reentered manually in the local development systems. This ensures successful merging with local settings. However, in addition to the duplication of Customizing efforts, manual reentry of global settings leaves a margin for error. Changes may not be realized in the local development system, or worse, they may be realized incorrectly.

- By assigning specific user authorizations, you can prevent the person performing local Customizing from accessing Customizing activities and tables that are "owned" by the corporate system. This requires added effort to not only single out these activities, but also to develop the proper user profiles to ensure that those performing local Customizing can perform only the appropriate activities.
- *Cross-system tools*, such as the *Customizing Cross-System Viewer* and the *Transfer Assistant*, allow you to compare clients in different SAP ERP systems. Using the Cross-System Viewer (Transaction SCU0), you can identify global template settings that conflict with a subsidiary's local settings before you apply the global template to that subsidiary's local development system. The Transfer Assistant (Transaction SADJ) then uses change request functionality to transfer differences between clients (see Chapter 11).
- *Business Configuration (BC) Sets* (Transaction SCPR2) allow a local subsidiary to preserve its current Customizing settings and compare local and global settings after applying a global template. This tool provides a mechanism for detecting conflicts between global templates and local Customizing. It is therefore the most recommended of the variants introduced here, particularly because of its interaction with the SAP Solution Manager-Global Template Scenario.

[+] For more information about the use of the Customizing Cross-System Viewer, the Transfer Assistant, and Business Configuration Sets as a means to support a global system landscape, see Chapter 11.

Management of a global system landscape is difficult, more so from a business application perspective than from a change management perspective. Using a variety of the tools mentioned, you can provide a template of global Customizing and development settings while still maintaining local needs. Global settings can, for example, refer to discounts to be granted, whereas factory calendars are usually local due to regional differences. However, you will need to invest a lot of effort in testing global functionality at each of the local levels, as well as in regression testing existing local functionality. Performing valid tests for all local implementations is the ideal method of confirming any functionality—regardless of the efforts you make in advance to protect changes to Customizing and developments.

3.7 Questions

1. **Which of the following statements is correct with regard to critical client roles as recommended by SAP?**

   A. Customizing changes can be made in any client.

   B. All Customizing and development changes should be made in a single client.

   C. Repository objects should be created and changed in the quality assurance client.

   D. Unit testing should take place in the Customizing-and-development client.

2. **Which of the following activities should not be performed within a system landscape?**

   A. Customizing and development changes are transported to a quality assurance client before being delivered to production.

   B. The SAP ERP system is upgraded to new releases.

   C. Development changes are made directly in the production client.

   D. Clients are assigned a specific role.

3. **Which of the following benefits does the three-system landscape recommended by SAP have?**

   A. Customizing and development, testing, and production activities take place in separate database environments and do not affect one another.

   B. Changes are tested in the quality assurance system and imported into the production system only after verification.

   C. Client-independent changes can be made in the development system without immediately affecting the production client.

   D. All of the above.

4. **Which of the following statements is correct with regard to multiple SAP clients?**

   A. All clients in the same SAP system share the same Repository and client-independent Customizing settings.

B. No more than one client in the same SAP system should allow changes to client-independent Customizing objects.

C. If a client allows for changes to client-dependent Customizing, the client should also allow for changes to client-independent Customizing objects.

D. All of the above.

5. **Which of the following statements is correct with regard to the setup of a three-system landscape?**

   A. There is only one database for the system landscape.

   B. One client should allow for the automatic recording of client-dependent Customizing and for client-independent changes.

   C. All SAP systems have the same system ID.

   D. All clients must have unique client numbers.

6. **Which of the following statements is correct with regard to the CUST client?**

   A. It should allow changes to client-independent Customizing, but not Repository objects.

   B. It should automatically record all changes to Customizing settings.

   C. It should not allow changes to client-dependent and client-independent Customizing settings.

   D. It should allow for all changes, but not require recording of changes to change requests.

7. **Which of the following statements is correct with regard to a two-system landscape?**

   A. It is not optimal because opportunity to test the transport of changes from the development system to the production system is limited.

   B. It allows for changes to Customizing in the production system.

   C. It is recommended by SAP because Customizing and development do not impact quality assurance testing.

   D. All of the above.

8. **Which of the following statements are correct with regard to a phased implementation?**

   A. All Customizing changes made in the production support system must also be made in the development system.

   B. The system landscape requires five SAP systems.

   C. Changes in the production support system do not have to be made in the development environment.

   D. The system landscape needs an environment that supports the production system with any required changes.

9. **Which of the following statements is not valid with regard to a global system landscape?**

   A. A global template can be used for the rollout of corporate Customizing settings and development efforts.

   B. Management of different Repository objects (those developed by the corporate office versus those developed locally) can be managed using namespaces and name ranges for the Repository objects.

   C. Merging the Customizing settings delivered by the corporate office with local Customizing efforts can be accomplished easily using change requests.

   D. SAP provides different tools to aid in the rollout of a global template.

You can make different types of changes in transport management to be able to control changes in the best possible way. This is possible from the individual development level all the way to the transfer of entire clients.

4 Managing Changes and Data in an SAP ERP System Landscape

Within the SAP ERP system landscape, you need to be able to transfer Customizing or development changes, as well as business data, from one client or SAP system to another. This chapter explains the tools and strategies used to transfer these changes and data. The first half of the chapter is concerned with managing and distributing changes using the tools in the *Change and Transport System* (CTS). The second half of the chapter is concerned with the techniques used to transfer business data—master data, transaction data, and user master data—into SAP, or from one SAP system or client to another.

Starting with SAP ERP 2004, different ABAP- and Java-based systems can be installed. However, change management is not identical in all systems. This is in part the case because for some of the other products, there is no Customizing in the sense of the Customizing done in SAP ERP—partly because there is no development workbench, and partly because more contents, such as documents—rather than programs—need to be distributed, among other reasons. The following sections are therefore most applicable for using ABAP-based components such as SAP ERP. [+]

4.1 Transporting Customizing and Development Changes

The implementation of SAP ERP requires, at a bare minimum, that you customize the SAP ERP system using the IMG. Customizing is performed in a client in the development system, transferred to a client in the quality assurance system for testing, and finally made available to a client in the production system. Similarly, changes due to development in the ABAP Workbench require well-organized distribution techniques from the development system to the quality assurance system and the production system.

Although it is possible to manually reenter the changes in successive systems, this is not desirable because of the quantity and complexity of the changes required. Therefore, SAP ERP enables you to record changes to change requests, which can then be distributed to other clients in the same system, or in another system.

[+] The word "change" is used loosely. It refers to the creation or modification of a Repository object, a change in the attributes associated with Repository objects, or the addition or modification of entries in tables (as often occurs during Customizing).

4.1.1 Change Requests and Tasks

In SAP ERP, *change requests* and their constituent *tasks* provide the mechanism with which you can record the objects you have changed. When changes to either Customizing objects or Repository objects are made, the changed objects are recorded to a task. A single user owns each task, which is simply a list of objects changed by that user. Tasks are grouped together into change requests corresponding to specific project objectives.

On top of adding changed objects to a change request, the people who customize and develop record their documentation of the change and its purpose in each task. Change requests and tasks provide a complete history of all changes made during SAP ERP implementation.

Types of Change Requests

Because software changes created during SAP ERP implementation are the result of either Customizing or development, there are two types of change requests:

- Customizing change requests
- Workbench change requests

Usage

Customizing change requests are used to record only client-specific changes. Because most Customizing activities in the IMG are client-specific changes, they are recorded to Customizing change requests. All client-independent (cross-client) changes are recorded to Workbench change requests. Workbench change requests are used for the following:

- Client-independent (cross-client) Customizing objects
- All Repository objects created and maintained through the ABAP Workbench

Keep in mind that changes in application and user master data are not recorded to change requests, as shown in Figure 4.1.

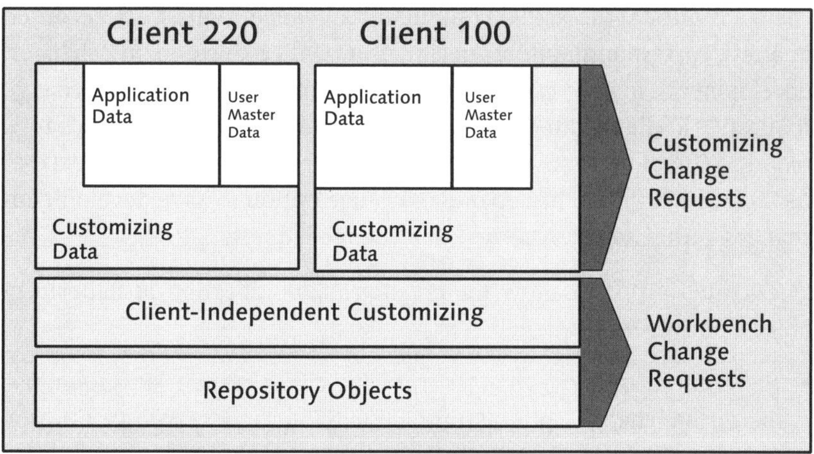

Figure 4.1 Recording Changes to Change Requests

Customizing changes

Customizing activities in the IMG must be performed in a client that permits Customizing changes. To determine whether Customizing changes are permitted in a particular client, and whether these Customizing changes are automatically recorded to a change request, set the client-dependent change option (Transaction SCC4) appropriately. (See Chapter 3.)

[+] To ensure that changes are recorded and can be distributed, SAP recommends that you set the client change option for the Customizing-and-development client so that Customizing changes are automatically recorded to change requests.

The IMG guides you through configuring business processes, recording changes, and saving changes to change requests. In the *Customizing Organizer* (Transaction SE10), you can display, create, change, document, and release change requests. The Customizing Organizer lets you see which Customizing objects have been changed, and whether they have been released (see Chapter 11).

Development changes

The *Workbench Organizer* (Transaction SE09) lets you display, create, change, document, and release Workbench change requests. When you make a client-independent change, the change is recorded to a Workbench change request for release and transport to the quality assurance system, and eventually the production system. As with Customizing change requests, the actual contents of a change request are recorded in a task corresponding to a specific user. Unlike Customizing changes, development changes can be made only in conjunction with a change request. All client-independent changes must be saved to a change request. Therefore, you do not need to specify AUTOMATIC RECORDING OF CHANGES in the client-dependent change option to have development changes automatically recorded to a change request.

You can permit or disallow the creation or modification of Repository objects on two levels:

- To permit or disallow changes from any client in the SAP system, use the system change option (Transaction SE06; GOTO • SYSTEM CHANGE OPTION). (See also Chapter 7.)
- To permit or disallow changes from within a specific client, set the appropriate client-dependent change option (Transaction SCC4).

Technical Representation of Change Requests and Tasks

The ID number for change requests or tasks begins with the three-character system ID—for example, `DEV`, followed by `K9` and a sequential five-digit number. Thus, DEVK900005 is the fifth change request or task to be created on the SAP system DEV. The next task or change request created will be DEVK900006.

A project lead who creates change request DEVK900116 assigns two users to the change request. These users are assigned by creating tasks DEVK900117 and DEVK900118. If, after other change requests are created, the project lead wants to add another user as a task to this change request, the corresponding task will receive the next available ID number—for example, DEVK900129. Figure 4.2 shows these examples as they would appear in the Customizing Organizer.

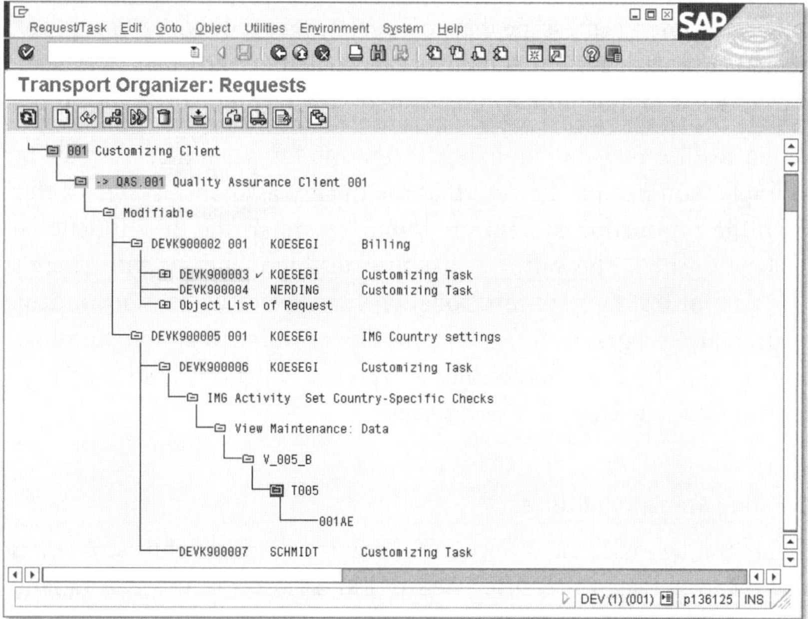

Figure 4.2 The Customizing Organizer Displays Customizing Change Requests and Tasks

The ID numbers of change requests or tasks reveal only the SAP system in which each change request or task was created, and the temporal order of creation. Therefore, it is important to maintain the associated title and documentation for later reference.

4.1.2 Preparing Changes

Change requests are a collection of tasks that list the different objects that have changed in the database. This information enables you to update any other client within the system landscape with a new copy of the changed objects. To do this, you use the technical procedure for transport, which consists of two steps: transportation and import. Transporting changes involves releasing them and then exporting them out of their SAP system and onto the operating system level; next, they are imported into another SAP system.

The value of SAP's techniques for transporting and importing changes is the way they enable a system landscape to be kept neat and orderly. It is only in an orderly landscape that you can know exactly which changes are operative in each system and client, and whether particular clients and SAP systems are functionally identical, or in which functions they differ.

When testing new functionality in the quality assurance system, for example, you need to be sure that the quality assurance system differs from the production system only with regard to the new functionality being tested. This ensures that such testing is meaningful. There is no value in testing new functionality in a system whose Customizing settings and programs differ dramatically, or differ to an indeterminate extent from those in the production system. Functionally identical systems are known as *synchronized* systems.

Defining Transport Routes

Before transportation and import can occur, you must define strict *transport routes* between the different SAP ERP systems in the system landscape. To define the routes change requests will follow, use the *Transport Management System* (TMS), which is called with Transaction STMS. The TMS is essentially the "traffic cop" of change requests: it centrally monitors the export process to ensure that changes are delivered in the correct order, and notifies you of errors during import.

Synchronization

During SAP ERP implementation, all clients and systems must be synchronized by defining appropriate and fixed transport routes. Typically, you test and verify changes from the development system in the quality assurance system before importing them to the production system. The appropriate transport routes include a transport route from the development system to the quality assurance system, and a subsequent transport route from the quality assurance system to the production system (see Figure 4.3).

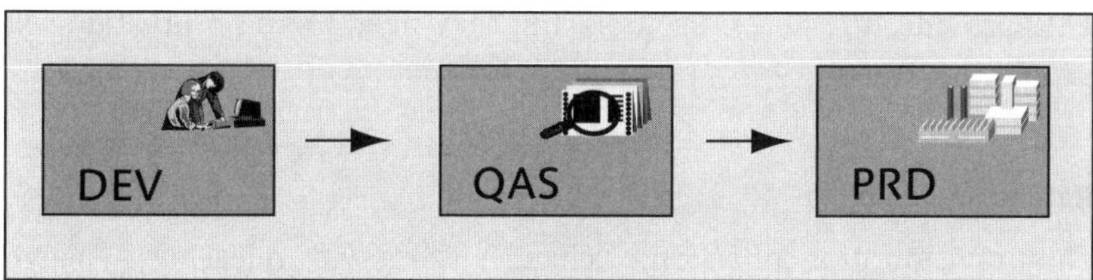

Figure 4.3 Transport Routes Defined in the TMS for a Standard System Landscape

Prior to R/3 Release 4.5, the transport routes defined in the TMS could move change requests only from one R/3 system to another, as shown in Figure 4.3. As of R/3 Release 4.5, however, a transport route can also be defined from one client to another client by activating EXTENDED TRANSPORT CONTROL. In the example shown in Figure 4.4, a change request that is released in the Customizing-and-development client is added to the import queue of both the sandbox client and the quality assurance client. After import to the quality assurance client, the change request is automatically added to the import queues of the training client and the production client.

Client-specific transport routes provided by extended transport control allow more control over the delivery of changes, ensuring that changes not only reach all the SAP systems but also all clients.

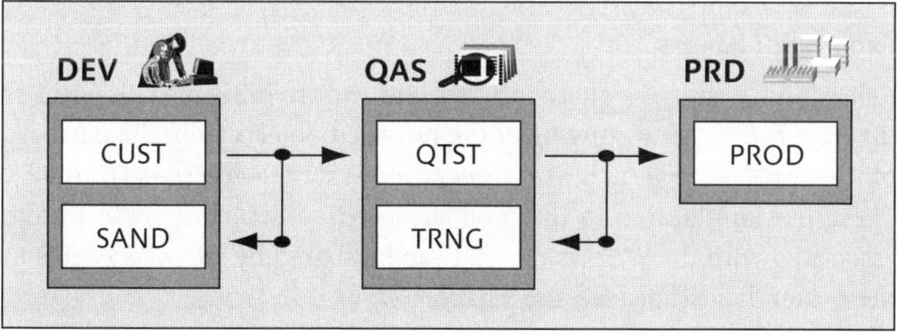

Figure 4.4 Client-Specific Transport Routes

Regardless of whether you transfer your change requests along transport routes defined in terms of clients or in terms of SAP systems, the important issue is maintaining consistency. The clients and the SAP systems in your system landscape will be synchronized only if all changes are transported in an orderly way, and the import of changes is verified. The TMS provides the necessary tools, but they need to be set up and used properly.

Releasing Changes

The provision of a collection of changes starts with releasing a change request. If you want to release a change request, either you or the developers assigned to the tasks first need to document and release all of the individual tasks contained in the change request. Aside from background information about what led to the change and the description of the correction itself, the documentation should include detailed information on how to perform the necessary tests.

Coherency and effectiveness

Before you release the objects recorded in a change request, the objects must be tested for internal coherency and effectiveness. This is known as *unit testing* and can be performed in the current client or in another client (see also Chapter 3). To perform *unit testing* in another client, you can use the *Client copy according to Transport Request* tool (Transaction SCC1) to copy the contents of a change request (released or not released) to another client within the same SAP system (see also Chapter 6).

The owner of a task should release the task as soon as it has been completed and unit tested.

Exporting Changes

Releasing a change request initiates the export process. This process involves the physical copying of the recorded objects from the database of the SAP system to files at the operating system level (see Figure 4.5). These files are located in the *transport directory*, which is a file system associated with the SAP system that can be shared by all SAP systems in the system landscape (see also Chapter 7).

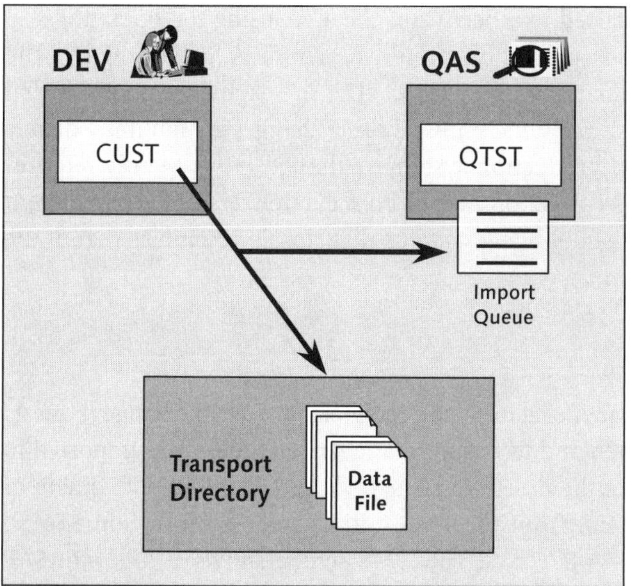

Figure 4.5 Exporting a Change Request

Import queues

A change request is transported to ensure that its objects reach other clients and systems along the transport route. When the objects in the change request are exported, the change request ID number is automatically added to the *import queue* of the next target client or system, according to the transport route set up in the TMS (see Figure 4.5). The import queue is a list of change requests that have been released and exported and are awaiting import.

4.1.3 Importing Changes

Importing is the process by which copies of the changed objects listed in a released change request are brought from the transport directory into the database of the target system and client. The import queue of the target client and system will have been notified during the export process that a request is ready for import. However, no automatic mechanism imports a change request into the target immediately after export. To trigger and monitor imports into SAP systems, use the import queue in the TMS.

[+] Imports can be started irrespective of the TMS using the operating system; however, this procedure should be considered thoroughly. The result of the automatic import to QAS after the export from DEV is that DEV and QAS have the same status. If these changes are not immediately imported into the production system—although PRD urgently requires a correction—this correction cannot be accurately tested. An intelligent test environment should have a status that closely resembles that of the production system.

The Import Queue

The TMS import queue enables you to determine which change requests have been exported and to ensure that change requests are imported in the same order as they were exported. To access the import queue of a given SAP system, from the TMS initial screen (Transaction STMS), choose OVERVIEW • IMPORTS. This TMS screen shows all relevant SAP systems. To access the import queue of a particular SAP system, double-click the system name. The import queue is displayed, listing any change requests that are awaiting import.

During an import, files in the transport directory corresponding to each change request are read and copied into the database of the target system. In Figure 4.6, the target system of the development system is the quality assurance system. To examine the various log files generated during the import process, from the import queue screen, choose GOTO • TP SYSTEM LOG, for example. The logs will show whether any errors occurred during the import (see Chapter 13). If the CCMS is set up, it can be used to elegantly monitor errors during transports.

After change requests have been imported successfully, they are deleted from the import queue, and are automatically added to the import queues of the next target clients and systems, as defined by the transport route specified in the TMS. Typically, the target SAP system after an import to the quality assurance system is the production system.

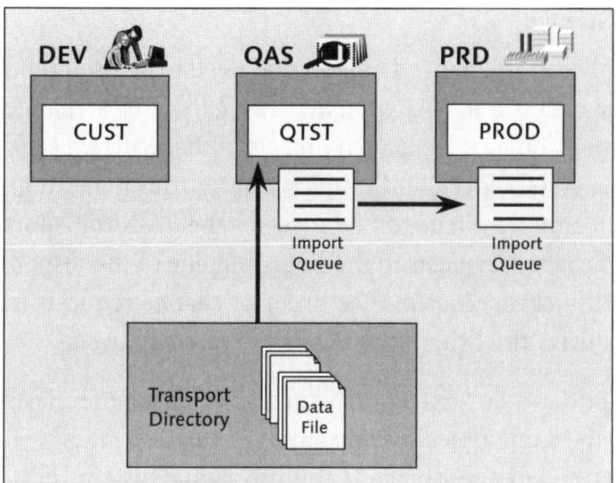

Figure 4.6 Import to the Quality Assurance System and Delivery to the Production System

Subsequent imports into SAP systems such as the production system are similarly monitored and triggered in the TMS. During these imports, the files corresponding to the change requests in the transport directory are again copied to the database of the target system. By using the same files that were originally exported from the development system and tested in the quality assurance system, the TMS ensures that the same changes are delivered to both SAP systems (see Figure 4.7).

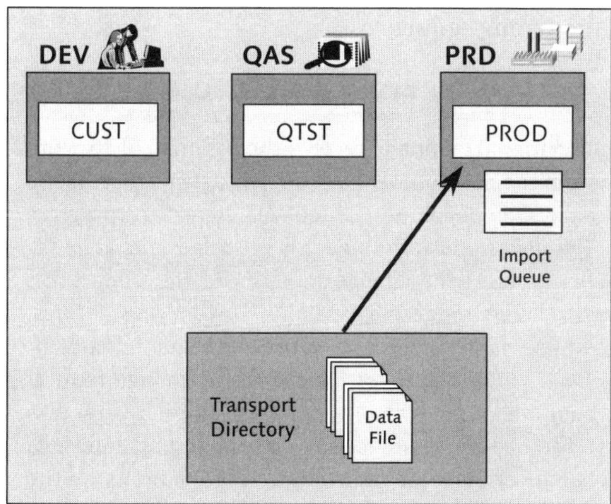

Figure 4.7 Importing the Same Files Into the Production System

Sequence in Import Queues

Change requests are only lists of changed objects that need to be promoted and imported to other clients and SAP systems. The export of a change request is the process that copies the changed objects in their current state to a file at the operating system level, and simultaneously adds the change request to the relevant import queue, as defined by the TMS transport route. The sequence of change requests in the import queue of the respective SAP system is strictly chronological. The order of change requests in the import queues is always the order in which they were exported.

This sequencing is important. For example, if successive change requests are created to change the same object, when they are released, they will each deposit new versions of the object at the operating system level. Because the change requests in the import queue are processed sequentially, the last import of the object will represent the most recent version.

The import process then ensures that defined recipient systems, such as the production system, receive the change requests in the same order in which they were imported into the quality assurance system.

Sequence

The significance of the import queues is that they control the order in which changes are imported into an SAP system. By ensuring that this order is consistent, import queues enable the various SAP systems to be functionally synchronized. Import queues track the order in which changes are imported and ensure that changes are not imported into the production system in the wrong sequence.

Example: Sequencing Change Requests in an Import Queue

Two developers at a multinational company receive the assignment to write data conversion programs in the development system—programs that will be used to convert legacy data. One developer named Miller creates a program called `ZLEGACY_DATA`. The new Repository object is recorded in change request `DEVK900834`. Miller releases the change request. At the same time, other people are releasing change requests containing Customizing settings. The second developer, whose name is Schmidt, adds additional functionality to the program `ZLEGACY_DATA` and saves his change to change request `DEVK900876`. Schmidt then releases the change request. When it is time to import the changes into the quality assurance system, the import queue of the quality assurance system contains the following change requests (in the order in which they were released):

Change Request	Owner	Description
DEVK900834	MILLER	Conversion routine
DEVK900912	HAMM	Customizing for Materials Management
DEVK900820	THOMAS	Organizational data
DEVK900876	SCHMIDT	Conversion routine with validation loop

Two change requests, DEVK900834 and DEVK900876, recorded changes to the program ZLEGACY_DATA. Therefore, the transport directory contains two different versions of the program. If change request DEVK900876 is imported before change request DEVK900834, the program ZLEGACY_DATA in the quality assurance system will not have the additional functionality programmed by Schmidt, because the version of DEVK900876 which was imported first is overwritten with the old version of DEVK900834. The program in the quality assurance system would then differ from that in the development system, and the two systems would be inconsistent.

By having the imports occur in the order indicated in the import queue, the developers ensure that DEVK900834 is imported first, because it was released before DEVK900876. Program ZLEGACY_DATA is imported twice, but the final import, which overwrites its predecessor, is the current version. This helps to ensure consistency between the different SAP systems.

As of SAP R/3 Release 4.6C, another way to group change requests is available by using *projects*. In projects, transports for specific tasks can be grouped so that a comprehensive import process can be started and the risk of using a wrong transport sequence is reduced. The procedure of a *quality system acceptance* is suitable in this respect as well. In this case, requests are placed in the import buffer of the PRD system only if this is explicitly confirmed after a successful test in the quality assurance system. The related details are described in Chapter 5, Section 5.2.3.

Manipulating Import Queues

Within the TMS, users are able to manipulate import queues to add or delete change requests, or to change the order in which they appear in the queue. However, SAP does not recommend this because these types of changes may create inconsistencies between the source and target systems.

Deleting change requests

Users often want to delete a change request because it contains incorrect information. However, deleting a change request may delete more than the incorrect data because change requests typically contain more than one change. In addition, deleting a change request may make the objects in another change request fail, due to a dependency on the objects in the deleted change request. For example, if you delete a change request that contains a new data element, all other transported objects that contain tables that refer to that data element will fail.

To avoid these inconsistencies, you are strongly advised against manipulating import queues. It is more prudent to make the necessary corrections in the development system and release a new request.

[+] SAP recommends that you do not manipulate an import queue. For example, you should not delete change requests or alter the sequence in the queue.

Technical Aspects of the Transport Process

tp

The program `tp` resides at the operating system level and controls both the export and import process. It is responsible for reading change requests in import queues and making adjustments to import queues after completion of successful imports. The TMS import functionality is the user-friendly interface that communicates from within SAP ERP with the transport control program `tp`.

R3trans

Another relevant program is `R3trans`. To accomplish an export, `tp` triggers another tool at the operating system level called `R3trans`. `R3trans` creates the operating system data file for the export. During import, `R3trans` reuses this data file. `R3trans` is used to communicate with the database to read or insert data.

4.1.4 Change and Transport System (CTS)

SAP collectively refers to the tools that support change management as the Change and Transport System (CTS). These tools include:

Tools

- **Change and Transport Organizer (CTO)**
  The CTO consists of the Customizing Organizer, the Workbench Organizer, and the Transport Organizer. The most frequently used component is the Customizing Organizer. It enables the creation, documentation, and release of change requests generated during Customizing. It also enables the people implementing SAP ERP to track their changes to change requests, view the change requests for which they are responsible, and then make the changes available to other systems by releasing the change requests. The Workbench Organizer provides similar functionality for developers using the ABAP Workbench. The Transport Organizer provides support for transports that do not fall within the realm of the Customizing Organizer and the Workbench Organizer.
- **The Transport Management System (TMS)**
  You use the TMS (Transaction STMS) to organize, monitor, and perform imports for all SAP ERP systems within a system landscape. For example, you use the TMS to import change requests into the quality assurance system for testing and verification. In addition, you use the TMS to centrally manage the setup of your transport environment by adding SAP ERP systems and defining transport routes.
- **The programs tp and R3trans**
  These programs are executables at the operating system level used to communicate with the SAP system, the database, and the files in the transport directory necessary for the export and import processes. For example, when you import the objects in a change request into the quality assurance system, `R3trans` copies the data to the database of that system.

The CTS comprises all of the tools required to support SAP change and transport management for ABAP-based products (see Figure 4.8). A similar tool exists for Java-based products, the Change Management System (CMS), which is described in more detail in Chapter 15.

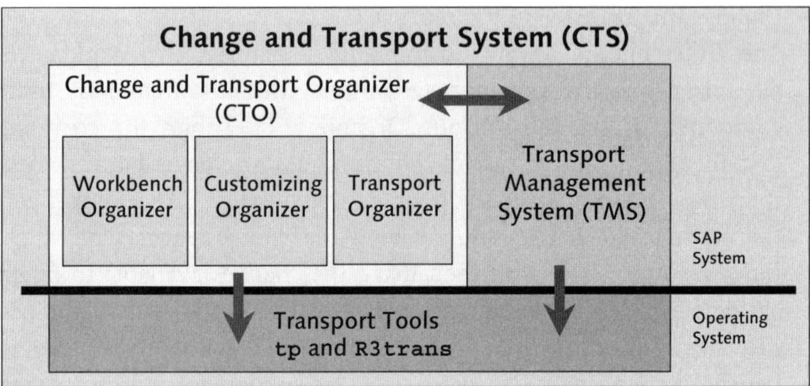

Figure 4.8 The Components of the CTS

4.2 Transferring Data

Change requests do not transport application data such as master data, transaction data, and user master data. That you would even have to distribute this type of data may surprise you. After all, this data is required for production activities, and there is only one production client in most system landscapes. However, you may need to distribute business data to perform the following:

- **Functionality testing and end-user training**
  Master data is required for both unit testing in the unit test client in the development system and testing in the quality assurance system. For example, when you test the creation of sales orders, the database needs to contain at least one specified material that a customer can purchase. Ideally, the entire material master list should be available. This is especially true for quality assurance testing and end-user training.
- **Report testing**
  To test most reports (for example, month-end closing reports), data from multiple business transactions is required—that is, data from various business processing scenarios.
- **Authorization assignment testing**
  Quality assurance testing includes testing authorization assignment for certain users and also for randomly selected users. The test system

therefore requires user master data. To avoid having to manually recreate users in the quality assurance system, you may want to transfer existing user master data from the production system.

- **Production data replication**
  Complex system landscapes, such as those found in companies with international subsidiaries, often contain more than one production SAP ERP system. To ensure the consistency of application data across such a landscape, you may need to ensure that the various production systems are synchronized with regard to master data records such as customer master data, or transaction data such as financial transaction data.

During the initial and subsequent implementation phases, you may need to transfer application data for unit testing, quality assurance testing, and training. After going live—that is, after work begins in the production system—you may need to transfer application data to synchronize multiple production environments or to share application data with other computer systems.

Transferring business data to different clients is not as straightforward as transferring changes that can be recorded to change requests. The methods used vary according to whether you want to:

- Transfer application data
- Share application data with other SAP systems or non-SAP computer systems

Whether you need to distribute application data, and the methods for its distribution, should be determined early in the SAP ERP implementation process.

4.2.1 Master Data

Master data is a type of application data that changes infrequently, but is required for the completion of most business transactions. Examples of master data include lists of customers, vendors, and materials, and even the company's chart of accounts. Master data usually exists in an organization prior to the implementation of SAP ERP. Before implementing

SAP ERP, you need to determine how to import the data into the SAP system. Ideally, the method used for the initial migration can also be used to subsequently transfer the data between clients.

Because master data changes over time, you must also consider how to provide for data transfer across all of your clients to maintain the consistency of master data within the landscape.

Importing Master Data into SAP ERP

Master data can be imported into SAP ERP from non-SAP systems using the following techniques:

Techniques

- Manually entering each data item
- Loading the data from sequential data files outside SAP ERP
- Communicating with other SAP or non-SAP systems through various interface technologies

To save time and ensure consistency, you should import master data either through data loads from external data files, or through interface technology. These techniques let you supply copies or subsets of the master data to multiple clients. Manual data entry may be more cost-effective for some implementations because data loading and interface technology can be handled only by someone with programming knowledge or SAP interface experience. However, manual entry is not an efficient way of distributing data to multiple clients.

[+] When importing data by loading it from files outside SAP ERP, SAP provides the Data Transfer Workbench and the Legacy System Migration Workbench to help you plan and develop programs to perform your data transfer. For more information on these tools, refer to SAP online documentation.

Transferring Master Data between SAP Systems

Although master data is relatively static, it will change over time. You need to determine whether changes to master data in the production system will be distributed to all clients in your system landscape. You also need to determine how frequently this synchronization process is required—that is, whether a large delay is acceptable. Master data can be transferred by the following methods:

Transfer methods

- Manually entering each data item
- Using change requests (only possible for some types of master data)
- Using interface technologies

Manual data entry may be an adequate method for transferring master data to clients other than the SAP client in the production system. It isn't necessary, for example, to make a customer's change of address known to the quality assurance client, because a change in the details of an address will not affect general business processing. However, if new customers are added to the production system, they can be manually entered into the quality assurance system to ensure their inclusion in testing.

Some master data is transferred using change requests in conjunction with special IMG activities. Examples of this type of master data include the chart of accounts, material groups, and cost accounting areas.

ALE

SAP also provides extensive interface technologies that support the transfer of master data. One such technology is *Application Link Enabling* (ALE), which lets you exchange data between different SAP ERP systems, or between SAP ERP systems and non-SAP systems. ALE is the technology that is most frequently used to support master data in an environment with multiple production clients, or where master data is required to be identical in more than one client. When you use ALE, master data can be either:

- Managed centrally and distributed to other clients when necessary (as is the case in Figure 4.9, where master data is distributed from the SAP system PR1 to clients in system QAS and PR2)
- Managed in different clients, transferred to a central client, and distributed from there to all other clients

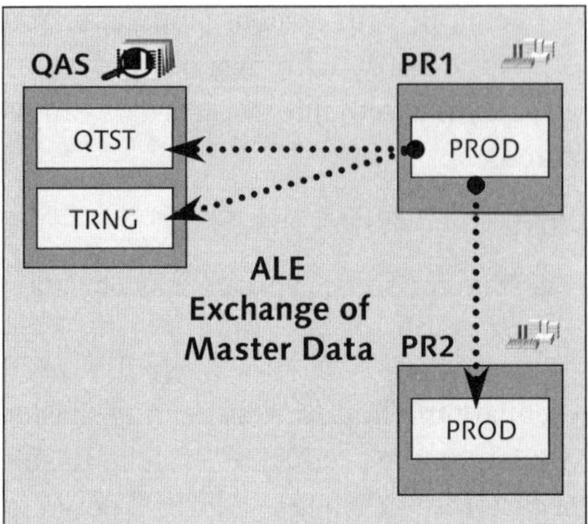

Figure 4.9 An Example of ALE Data Exchange between Different SAP Systems

To help you implement ALE, SAP provides preconfigured master data templates known as *ALE scenarios*, which you can adapt to meet your specific master data needs. Examples of ALE scenarios for master data include scenarios for materials, vendors, customers, profit centers, chart of accounts, bill of materials, and cost centers. ALE is not limited to master data—it can also be used to distribute transaction data.

In principle, you can use ALE to distribute master data freely between all SAP ERP systems. However, a certain degree of common Customizing is required in the target systems. SAP's *ALE Customizing Distribution* ensures that the Customizing settings related to ALE scenarios are identical on the different SAP ERP systems in the system landscape.

4.2.2 Transaction Data

Transaction data is shared across different computer systems—for example, for testing, training, or multiple production environments. These systems can be other SAP ERP systems or non-SAP systems. Transferring the data requires a communication link using interface technology. Transaction data distribution is complex because of transaction data's high volume, its dependency on the Customizing environment, and its need for master data. These factors mean that transaction data cannot simply be transferred from one client to another, nor is there a way to extract a subset of transaction data from one client and distribute it to another.

You must carefully consider how sample transaction data will be made available in different clients for testing and training. Because transaction data is altered during testing and training, you may need to delete and replace all transaction data for each successive test or training course.

Creating Sample Transaction Data

Sample transaction data will be required in the quality assurance and training clients in your system landscape. Users can manually create this data during testing or training. However, manual data creation is tedious if testers require many completed transactions—for example, when testing month-end financial reports. SAP recommends that you develop scripts to generate standard sets of transaction data. These scripts can evolve over time to generate data reflecting new functionalities, and can also be used to test existing business processes in *regression testing*. (See Chapter 6.)

A general example of a script is a script that creates 20 production orders for a specific plant. If necessary, this script can be copied and altered for all other plants. The data produced by the script is used for testing new versions of the production-planning functionality. During every rollout cycle for this functionality, the script and its data can be altered and used for testing how new functionality will impact production operations.

The *extended Computer Aided Test Tool* (eCATT, successor of the CATT tool as of Web Application Server 6.20) by SAP provides tools for creating scripts. eCATT allows you to combine and automate business processes as repeatable test procedures and use them to generate sample data. eCATT can also simulate transaction results, analyze the results of database updates, and monitor the impact of changes in Customizing settings. eCATT

Except eCATT, other tools for creating scripts and performing tests make up the SAP Test Workbench. Ideally, these test scripts can be controlled and managed using SAP Solution Manager as a central system, because eCATT can simulate business processes using Remote Function Calls (RFCs), even across system boundaries. [+]

Interfaces for Transaction Data

SAP's open interface provides several methods and tools for communication between different types of computer systems (see Figure 4.10). With regard to transaction data, you can create interfaces to do the following:

- Distribute transaction data from one client to another
- Import existing transaction data from a non-R/3 system into an SAP ERP system
- Distribute transaction data to non-SAP systems

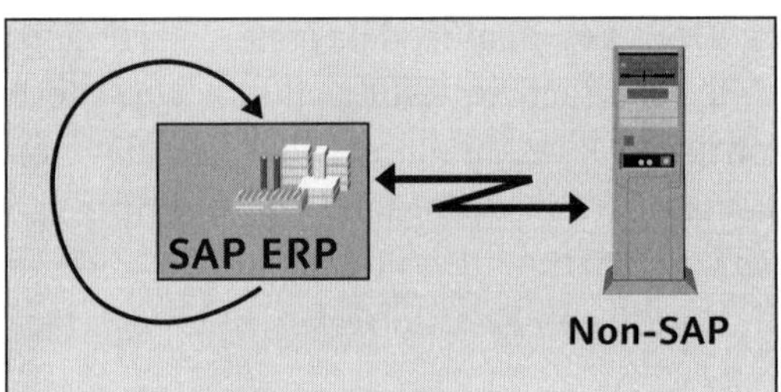

Figure 4.10 Possible Interfaces for Distributing Application Data

As an integral part of SAP ERP 6.0, SAP NetWeaver Process Integration (SAP NetWeaver PI)—the successor of SAP NetWeaver Exchange Infrastructure (SAP NetWeaver XI)—provides a particularly flexible way to exchange data, including conversion between different data types.

Example: Using ALE with Multiple Production Systems

Large organizations often require centralization of financial data. Producing millions of sales orders every day conflicts with management's need for timely reports and with the needs of the finance department. A large computer component supplier decides that while the Customizing and development of the different function modules is possible in a single development system, multiple production systems are required.

The production system SAL is used for all sales order entry and processing. A second production system, FIN, is used for financial and accounting data.

To configure SAP ERP for multiple production systems, the company must determine which master data must be shared among the different systems, and how this master data will be shared. The company decides to set up an enterprise reference data "library" to centrally manage all master data. This requires yet another production SAP ERP system, MDR, for the sole purpose of managing master data. ALE is used to transfer master data changes to FIN and SAL.

ALE is also used to share other data between the different production systems. For example, when a sales order is entered in SAL, ALE is used to make the customer's credit information from FIN available to SAL. To ensure that management reports are up to date, ALE enables sales information to be transferred from SAL to FIN, and accounting information to be transferred from FIN to SAL.

All of the production environments receive changes originating in the same Customizing and development system, DEV. The company's system landscape and ALE strategy can be represented as shown in Figure 4.11:

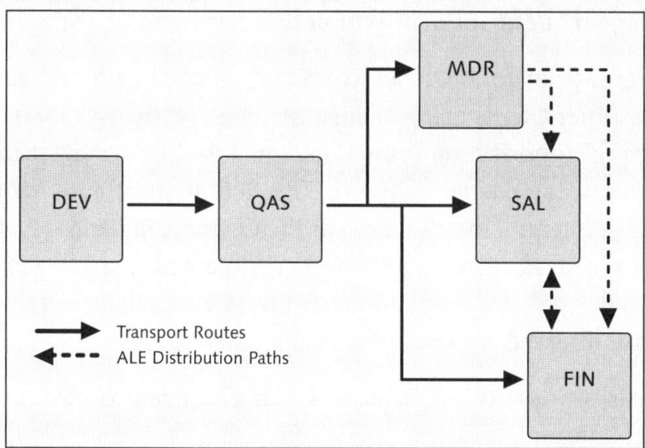

Figure 4.11 System Landscape and ALE Strategy

4.2.3 User Master Data

User master data includes the data used by the SAP system to validate a user's ID at logon, and assign user access rights based on passwords and authorization profiles. User master data also includes the user's name, phone number, as well as the default printer and the default screen the user will see after completing logon.

User master data is a type of master data—much like material master data and vendor master data. User master data is client-specific data. SAP separates user master data from other types of application data because user master data must be different in different clients, even if master data is the same. For example, in the development client, you must give extensive authorizations to your developers so that they can view tables, change programs, and test reports. However, these developers should not receive such authorizations for the production client. In fact, they may not even need a user account in the production client.

Authorization profile

Each *authorization profile* groups together different business objects and transactions that a user may access, and each user may have a number of authorization profiles assigned to their user ID. Authorization profiles are created either manually or, as recommended by SAP, using a tool called the *Profile Generator*. Regardless of how they are created, authorization profiles are technically considered Customizing data and can be recorded to change requests for distribution to other clients.

In SAP ERP releases prior to R/3 Release 4.5, authorization profiles can be distributed to other clients using change requests, while user master data—including the authorization profiles assigned to the user ID—cannot be transported using change requests. The definition of authorizations is managed in a central location such as the Customizing-and-development client. User master data is separately maintained in each client to ensure that users have different authorizations in each client and that specific clients are reserved for specific activities.

In SAP ERP releases prior to R/3 Release 4.5, if you need to have the same user master data and the same authorization profiles in two clients, you must perform a client copy that copies only user data. This procedure copies the user master data and authorization profiles from one client to another. However, this requires that all users be distributed to another client, rather than just some of the users.

As of R/3 Release 4.5, you can manage user data and authorization profiles in your system landscape centrally using *Central User Administration*. This allows you to maintain all SAP users in a single client and assign the user IDs to other clients in the system landscape with the same or different authorizations. Authorizations can be assigned either centrally or locally in each client, as required. Central User Administration simplifies user management and system security by allowing you to globally change a user's data.

[+] For more information on how to set up and use Central User Administration, refer to the SAP online documentation.

For SAP R/3 releases as of 4.6, the provided *roles* (before: activity groups) are a good alternative with their simplified assignment and grouping of authorizations to end users. In this context, we advise you to use the role maintenance functions and the Profile Generator (Transaction PFCG) to maintain your roles, authorizations, and profiles. Additionally, you can centrally maintain the roles delivered by SAP, or your own newly created roles, and assign any number of users using the Central User Administration (CUA) functions. Furthermore, the Profile Generator enables integration with HR-Org (organization management, time dependency).

Using roles, you assign users the user menu they see after their logon to the SAP system. Roles also include the authorizations users can use to access the transactions, reports, and web-based applications, for example, contained in the menu. Because the SAP standard delivery already provides many roles, you should determine whether you can use these standard roles before you start defining your own.

To obtain an overview of the delivered roles, you can do the following:

- In the SAP Easy Access menu, select TOOLS • ADMINISTRATION • USER MAINTENANCE • INFORMATION SYSTEM • ROLES • ROLES BY COMPLEX SELECTION CRITERIA and then RUN.
- Select the input help in the ROLE field of the role maintenance (TOOLS • ADMINISTRATION • USER MAINTENANCE • ROLE ADMINISTRATION • ROLES).

[+] To adapt existing roles, copy the respective standard role and modify the copy. If you don't find any suitable roles, you should define the job descriptions in writing before you start working in role maintenance (see also "First Installation Procedure" or Organizing Authorization in the SAP Online Help) (BC-SEC-USR).

4.3 Copying SAP ERP Systems and Clients

The following question is asked again and again: "Why must I record all of my changes to change requests—can't I just periodically copy the development system or the Customizing-and-development client?"

The answer to this question is that, technically, you can always copy an SAP system or even a client. However, the result may create extra work or even cause chaos in your system landscape. While copies of SAP systems and clients have their advantages, they should be used only to set up or create a system or client. A copy of a system or a client does not help you maintain your existing system landscape because it completely overwrites the target system or client, and eliminates all application data.

SAP recommends using change requests to record Customizing and development changes so that these changes can be distributed to all systems and clients without deleting existing application data.

4.3.1 System Copy

A copy of an SAP system is called a *system copy* and is used to create an identical copy of an existing SAP system. A system copy is sometimes referred to as a database copy, because you are copying the database of one system to another system. A system copy copies everything from the source database, including all clients, all Repository objects, and all data such as transaction data.

SAP does not recommend using system copies to set up critical systems, such as the quality assurance system or the production system (see Chapter 5). However, a system copy is useful when you need an exact copy of an SAP system for a limited scope and a limited time frame, or when you need to establish another noncritical SAP system in your system landscape. For example, to set up a system for training purposes, you may want to use a copy of the quality assurance system. Alternatively, you may want to make a copy of the production system to use as a temporary system for simulating data archiving routines.

Often, customers make a copy of the production system to set up a quality assurance system with good production data. They believe that a copy of production data is the easiest way to provide for a true quality assurance environment, or even to rebuild a development system. While this may be technically true, remember that because the size of the production system grows dramatically as more and more transaction data is collected, the cost of hardware required to support a copy of the production system may render such a copy unfeasible. For large production systems, consider the alternative methods of transferring business data previously discussed in this chapter.

Avoid using a copy of the production system to create the development system, because you will lose all data stored in the development system. This includes your Enterprise IMG, Project IMGs, and associated project documentation with your change history in the form of change requests and version histories of Repository objects.

Technical details about making a system copy can be found in the installation guides and in SAP Note 89188. [+]

4.3.2 Client Copy

SAP's client copy tools enable you to copy one client to another in the same or in a different SAP system. Whenever you use client copy (except when copying user master data or a single change request), the target client is deleted prior to copying the source client.

Like a system copy, a client copy is useful for creating a client, but generally cannot be used to maintain a client. Because the target client is deleted prior to copying data from the source client, a client copy does not provide a way of merging the source client with the target client. A client copy enables you to copy application data that cannot be transferred using change requests (see also Chapters 5 and 9).

4.4 Questions

1. **Which of the following statements is correct with regard to Customizing and development changes?**

   A. All changes are recorded to tasks in Customizing change requests.

   B. The changes should be recorded to tasks in change requests for transport to other clients and systems.

   C. The changes must be manually performed in every SAP system.

   D. The changes can easily be made simultaneously in multiple clients.

2. **Which of the following statements with regard to change requests is FALSE?**

   A. The Customizing Organizer and the Workbench Organizer are tools used to view, create, and manage change requests.

   B. A change request is a collection of tasks where developers and people performing Customizing record the changes they make.

   C. All changes made as a result of IMG activities are recorded to Customizing change requests.

   D. SAP recommends setting your SAP system so that Customizing changes made in the Customizing-and-development client are automatically recorded to change requests.

3. **For which of the following activities is the TMS (Transaction STMS)** *not* **designed?**

   A. Releasing change requests

   B. Viewing import queues

   C. Viewing log files generated by both the export process and the import process

   D. Initiating the import process

4. **Which of the following statements is correct after you have successfully imported change requests into the quality assurance system?**

A. The change requests must be released again to be exported to the production system.

B. The data files containing the changed objects are deleted from the transport directory.

C. The change requests need to be manually added to the import queue of the production system.

D. The change requests are automatically added to the import queue of the production system.

5. **Which of the following statements is correct with regard to the change requests in an import queue?**

A. They are sequenced according to their change request number.

B. They are sequenced in the order in which they were exported from the development system.

C. They are sequenced according to the name of the user who released the requests.

D. They are not sequenced by default, but arranged in a variety of ways using the TMS.

6. **Which of the following techniques can be used to transfer application data between two production systems?**

A. Recording transaction data to change requests

B. Using ALE to transfer application data

C. Using the client copy tool

D. All of the above.

7. **Which of the following types of data transfer are possible with an appropriate use of interface technologies?**

A. Transferring legacy data to an SAP system

B. Transferring data between clients

C. Transferring data to non-SAP systems

D. Transporting change requests to multiple SAP systems

8. **Which of the following statements is correct with regard to user master data?**

   A. User master data can be transported in a change request.

   B. User master data is unique to each SAP system, but is shared across clients in the same SAP system.

   C. A specific client copy option lets you distribute user master data together with authorization profile data.

   D. User master data includes all user logon information, including the definition of authorizations and profiles.

A secure operation of the production system also requires the configuration of the system settings with respect to their change options. This chapter describes the standard roles you can use for the different system types.

5 Setting Up a System Landscape

The strategy you use to set up your system landscape determines how all of the SAP ERP systems in your system landscape will be created and receive Customizing settings and development changes. This chapter outlines the various setup steps—taking you from the initial installation of the development system through the setup of the quality assurance system to the production system. The focus will be on how Customizing and development changes are properly transferred throughout the landscape.

Ideally, you should set up your system landscape using change requests. However, because change requests cannot always be used to support the setup of your critical clients, the client copy strategy is a viable alternative. In rare cases, using a system copy may be an appropriate method for creating your quality assurance system and possibly the production system as well. The advantages and disadvantages of these different strategies are outlined in this chapter.

5.1 Setting Up the Development System

Every SAP ERP implementation begins with the installation of one initial SAP ERP system. Because the individuals in charge of Customizing and development will be anxious to begin configuring SAP ERP to meet your company's different business needs, this first SAP ERP system is typically your development system. This is the system where all changes to the SAP software—both Customizing and development—originate.

Before you make changes to the software, you must ensure that the environment has been properly prepared and is ready for changes to take place. After you begin making changes to the SAP software, you must record them to change requests to allow for their transport.

5.1.1 Post-Installation Processing

After the installation process is complete, you may need to perform any or all of the following activities, collectively known as *post-installation processing*:

Activities

- **Languages**
  The SAP system delivered by SAP supports two languages, English and German. If your implementation requires additional languages, you need to install them at this time. A language import inserts language-specific text into the standard client 000. For example, if you import French and Spanish after installation, they will be available in client 000. To add these languages to your other clients, use the Language Transport Utility (Transaction SMLT).
- **Industry solutions**
  To fulfill the unique needs of different industries or types of businesses and to help accelerate the Customizing process, the product line of SAP ERP includes different industry solutions, such as SAP Banking and SAP Oil & Gas. These solutions provide customers with additional ERP functionality by adding special Repository objects to the SAP system.
- **Support Packages**
  SAP provides Support Packages to fix programming errors. Support Packages are bundled SAP software Repository corrections in which individual SAP Note corrections are delivered. Before you start Customizing and development activities, SAP recommends applying all available and relevant Support Packages to your development system.

You should document all post-installation activities. You will want to use the same setup procedure for the quality assurance and production systems and the documentation will assist you when you establish these critical SAP systems, or any other system in the landscape.

5.1.2 Setting Up the Transport Management System (TMS)

The Transport Management System, as its name implies, lets you manage the transport process for all ABAP-based systems within your system landscape. The TMS ensures that all SAP systems share the same transport configuration. This uniformity allows changes to be promoted and delivered to the right clients and systems in the correct order.

Without the TMS, you will not be able to save changes to change requests for transport to other SAP systems. After installing an SAP ERP system, your next task is to set up its TMS (Transaction STMS). This allows you to define the role of the system in your landscape. Because the development system is typically the first SAP system installed, it is also used to define the system landscape and the other SAP systems that will eventually be supported with the same changes and transport process.

Most important, you use the TMS to indicate which system is the target for changes transported from your development system. For example, if you have a three-system landscape, changes from the development system are transferred to the quality assurance system. The TMS helps you create the transport route between the development and quality assurance systems. In a two-system landscape, the transport route leads directly from the development system to the production system.

In many implementations, the quality assurance system is not installed—or does not even physically exist—until much later in the process. However, you still need to establish a transport route to connect it with the development system. Without this transport route, you cannot create change requests for later release to the quality assurance system. You need a placeholder for the quality assurance system. This *virtual system* is created using the TMS. This procedure requires that you provide a three-character alphanumeric system ID for the virtual system. You should also create a virtual system to represent your production system. For more details on setting up the TMS, including information on creating virtual systems and defining transport routes, see Chapter 8.

Although it is possible to change the name of the development and quality assurance systems (or of the production system) later on, SAP recommends that you maintain the same system IDs throughout your SAP implementation. It is important to keep the relationship between the development and quality assurance systems consistent and the transport route unchanged for the following reasons:

- By default, change requests for Customizing cannot export data from the development system without an established target system. The standard transport route defined for the development system determines the target system.
- Customer development objects can be created only for a particular development class. Each development class is associated with a transport layer. The transport layer in turn depends on a transport route to identify the location of the change request after release and export.

Changes are moved from one SAP system to another according to the relationships established by the transport route. Changing an SAP system name and/or transport route will therefore impact existing and future change requests.

5.1.3 Creating Clients

After you have set up the TMS, you can begin creating clients in the development system. After installation, an SAP ERP system contains the standard SAP clients 000, 001, and 066. SAP reserves clients 000 and 066 for maintenance and support, leaving client 001 for your implementation process. Client 001 can function as your Customizing-and-development client, known as CUST.

However, client 001 may not contain the settings established during post-installation processing, such as applied Support Packages or imported languages. You must integrate all additional settings into this client using tools provided by SAP. Alternatively, you can copy client 000 to create a new client that contains all of the post-installation settings. This copy will ensure consistent settings throughout the system, and allows you to preserve client 001 as it was delivered by SAP. Retaining clients 000 and 001 provides you with a reference for comparing your changes in subsequently created clients with the SAP standard.

SAP recommends that you create a new client as a copy of client 000 for Customizing and development efforts. [+]

Procedure

To create a client within SAP ERP, follow these steps:

1. Access CLIENT MAINTENANCE (Transaction SCC4).
2. Define the client with a three-digit client number and text description.
3. Select the client's role, restrictions, and client change options. After this new client has been defined, you can log on to it with the special SAP user SAP*.

Your new client does not contain the data necessary to perform Customizing. This data consists of basic Customizing settings and language data. The new client also does not have the standard SAP user authorizations needed to create additional users: standard SAP authorizations and profiles. After using client maintenance to define the new client, you need a *client copy tool* to copy the contents of client 000 into the new client. A client copy transfers the user data and Customizing data that currently exist in client 000 to the new client.

For more details on how to use client maintenance and client copy, see Chapter 9. [+]

SAP recommends including a unit test client (TEST) in your system landscape so that you can evaluate new Customizing settings and developments using sample application data. You may also consider creating a sandbox client (SAND) to allow the people performing Customizing to experiment with settings. Use client copies of client 000 to create both the unit test and the sandbox clients (see Figure 5.1).

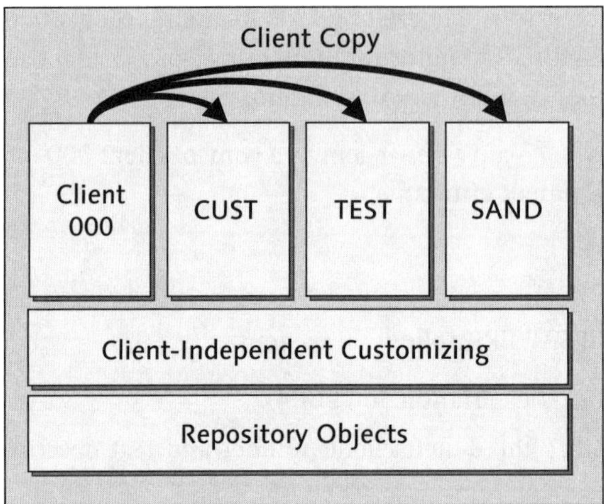

Figure 5.1 Creating New Clients in the Development System

Setting the Client Change Options

Before starting Customizing and development, you must set the client change options for the different clients you have created. For the development system, SAP recommends setting the client change options in Transaction SCC4, as outlined in Table 5.1.

Client	Client-Dependent Change Option	Client-Independent Change Option
Customizing and development (CUST)	Automatic recording of changes	Changes to Repository and client-independent Customizing allowed
Unit test (TEST)	No changes allowed	No changes to Repository and client-independent objects allowed
Sandbox (SAND)	No transports allowed	No changes to Repository and client-independent objects allowed

Table 5.1 Recommended Client Change Settings

Although you may have planned your own unique system landscape, for the following reasons SAP recommends abiding by these development system restrictions set through the client change options:

- All Customizing changes—both client-dependent and client-independent—must originate in a single client. These changes are then distributed from this client to the rest of the system landscape.
- Client change options provide a solid wall of protection—regardless of user authorizations—by restricting the changes possible within a client (see Table 5.1). You should limit the number of people with the authority to alter client settings.

Recording Changes Automatically

SAP recommends that you use automatic recording of all changes to change requests for your CUST client. Occasionally, customers question the importance of this procedure, thinking that it is tedious and slows down their Customizing work. Nonetheless, changes should be recorded to change requests consistently from the beginning of your SAP implementation. This provides the following benefits:

Advantages of recording

- A documented history of the changes made to different Customizing settings, including who made the changes and when they were made.
- A mechanism that copies changes to other clients in the same SAP system prior to the release of the change request. The contents of a change request can be unit tested, modified if necessary, and verified before the actual release of the change request (see Chapter 12).
- A method ensuring that all changes originate in one client and are systematically transported to other clients in the system landscape.
- Project management, through the allocation of change requests to teams for completing different parts of the Customizing project.

You can track Customizing changes by activating *table logging*. Table logging records the changes made to many of the tables and to Customizing settings (see Chapter 9). Table logging does not, however, provide a method to document and distribute changes. You can also successfully set up clients and systems without automatically saving all changes to change requests. However, you *cannot* maintain clients within a system landscape over time without change requests. There is no other alternative for supplying existing clients with the most recent Customizing changes.

Because all people who perform Customizing will eventually need to save changes to change requests to maintain existing clients and systems, you should train them early on in the implementation process to use change requests. Changing procedures and providing training in the middle of an implementation is awkward. At such a time, concerns will involve testing and completing business functionality and not learning to work with change requests.

[+] To obtain a complete history of all changes made and to simplify your implementation process and future client maintenance, SAP recommends recording all changes to change requests from the very beginning of your SAP implementation.

5.2 Setting Up the Quality Assurance and Production Systems

Eventually, you will be ready to test the entire SAP system with your Customizing and development changes. To run this *integration testing*, you will need to set up the quality assurance system. Keep in mind that you also need to start planning for the production system. The quality assurance system acts as your proving ground for production activities. Setting up and testing the quality assurance system ensures that subsequently, the production system—including the procedure for setting it up—will function properly.

Different methods exist to set up—that is, to transfer Customizing and development changes to—the quality assurance and production systems. SAP recommends using change requests to move Customizing and development changes from the development system to the quality assurance system. As an alternative you can use the client copy strategy. Each method has certain advantages and disadvantages.

[+] SAP recommends that you use the same techniques to set up both your quality assurance and production systems. This is a safeguard for the production system and ensures consistency between the two environments.

5.2.1 After Installing the New SAP System

Before using the change request or client copy techniques to distribute Customizing and development changes, you need to install the SAP system that will become your quality assurance or production system. Both systems will require the same post-installation support that was necessary for the development system. That is, you need to provide the systems with the necessary Support Packages, industry solutions, and languages. After completing post-installation processing, you can begin setting up the TMS and creating the required clients.

Setting Up the TMS

Regardless of how you will subsequently set up the quality assurance and production systems, after they are installed, you first need to set up the TMS. The TMS allows you to import change requests into the quality assurance system and ensures that they are also delivered to the production system.

Ideally, your quality assurance and production systems, although not physically existing until this point in time, have already been represented in the TMS by placeholders. In other words, virtual systems have been used to define the two systems. Because these virtual systems do not contain any technical details, they need to be deleted before you can continue with the TMS setup on your installed quality assurance or production systems. The TMS includes the new SAP ERP systems and their technical settings in the system landscape (see Chapter 8).

Before importing the first change request into the quality assurance system, you must represent the production system in the TMS, either as a virtual system or, if it exists, as the installed system. A transport route from the quality assurance to production system must also be active.

As changes are imported into the quality assurance system, the import queue of the production system also receives notification of the changes. The objective is to ensure that the steps used to create the quality assurance system are recorded and then replicated to create the production system— this includes the import of all change requests in the exact order in which they were applied.

Creating Required Clients

Quality assurance test client

The quality assurance system requires at least one client, the quality assurance test client (QTST). The production system, in turn, needs the production client (PROD). To import changes or clients from the development system into these clients, you must first create the QTST and PROD clients in their respective systems.

The procedure for creating the QTST and PROD clients is the same as the procedure used for creating the Customizing-and-development client. Using client maintenance, you define the client by providing it with a client number and description, and selecting its role, restrictions, and client change options. The quality assurance and production clients should both be protected against changes by setting the client change options to No changes allowed and No changes to Repository objects and client-independent Customizing. For additional protection or to use Current settings (see Chapter 11), you can assign the production client the client role Production.

Before you can supply the newly created client with the latest Customizing settings and developments using change requests, you must use the client copy tool to copy the contents of an existing client into the new one. To ensure consistency, the QTST and PROD clients are created in the same manner as you created the CUST client—that is, by making a copy of client 000.

5.2.2 Change Request Strategy

SAP recommends using change requests to set up your quality assurance system and ultimately your production system. In this way, you can ensure that only the changes transported or released from the development system are imported into the quality assurance and production systems. Change requests also provide you with a methodical process for adding business functionality to an SAP system after realizing that functionality in a development environment.

Requirements

To set up your quality assurance system using change requests, you must have saved all Customizing changes made in the development system to change requests. This is the only requirement for using this setup strategy. If you follow SAP's recommendations regarding the client-dependent change options when setting up your CUST client, your changes are automatically recorded to change requests from the beginning of your implementation. An incomplete recording of Customizing change requests results in only partial functionality in the quality assurance system. An easy method for transporting changes that were not recorded does not exist; instead, the changes have to be manually assigned to change requests through the respective IMG Customizing activity.

[+] If a large number of changes made in your Customizing-and-development client was not recorded to change requests, do not use the change request strategy to set up your quality assurance and production systems. Use a client copy.

Procedure

Before and during the installation of your quality assurance system, you record changes to change requests and unit test functionality in the development system. By releasing and exporting the change requests, you cause the changes to be copied to files at the operating system level. There, they are added to the import queue of the quality assurance system. After you have copied the contents of client 000 into the quality assurance client and selected the appropriate client change options, the changes in the import queue of the quality assurance system can be imported into the system itself.

After the change requests have been successfully imported into the quality assurance system, they continue along any other defined transport routes. The next transport route typically leads from the quality assurance system to the production system. After the changes are imported into the quality assurance system, they are also delivered to the import queue of the production system. Eventually, you will import the same changes into the production system, in the same order as they were imported into the quality assurance system.

Figure 5.2 shows the steps involved in setting up a system landscape using the change request strategy. This setup strategy is actually the same method you will use later to maintain the system landscape: Changes are released and exported from the development system, imported into the quality assurance system for verification, and then imported into the production system.

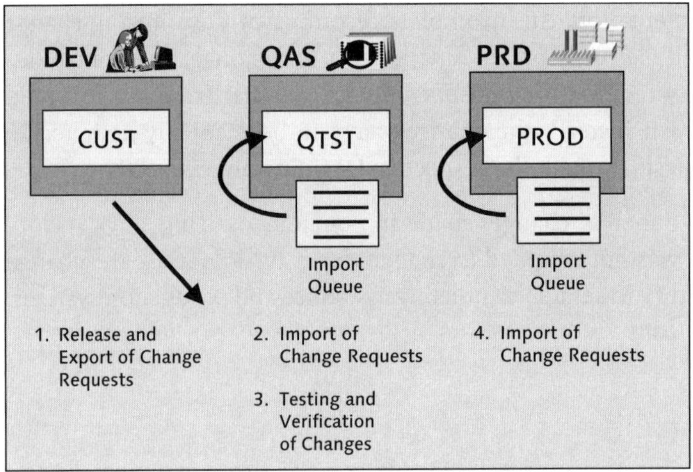

Figure 5.2 Setting up a System Landscape Using Change Requests

At this stage in the implementation procedure, your quality assurance client (and perhaps your production client) contains the latest Customizing settings and developments transported from the development. However, the client contains no application data or user data. Unless you specifically transport user data, or manually create users in the client itself, only the default SAP user is defined in this client. Your next step is to verify user accounts and authorizations. Also, because the client has no application data, it also has no master data. Master data will be needed in quality assurance for validation to take place. Ultimately, master data will be needed in the production client prior to the start of production activities.

For solutions on how to manage master data within a system landscape, see Chapter 4. [+]

Advantages

The most significant advantage of using change requests to set up your quality assurance and production systems is that this strategy is identical to the maintenance strategy. No additional training or procedures will be required before or after the start of production. The procedures defined during project preparation and system setup are valid for the entire implementation cycle, future upgrades, and the addition of any new business functionality.

The other main advantage of using change requests is that this strategy provides project control and management. It allows the project lead to improve the efficiency of the implementation project by:

Measures that improve the efficiency

- Assigning different tasks or activities to individuals
- Bundling a collection of tasks into one or several change requests
- Ensuring that Customizing and development work has been unit tested before it is released

These steps provide the project lead with an up-to-date overview of the configuration and ensure that only completed Customizing units are transported for quality assurance testing.

5.2.3 Quality Assurance Procedure of the TMS

To supplement the change request strategy, as of R/3 Release 4.6C, SAP provides the *quality assurance* (QA) *procedure* as an extension to the TMS. This procedure provides a security mechanism to balance the drawback of change requests—which is that all requests must be imported into the production system—and thus increasing the quality and availability of the production systems.

For this purpose, the QA approval procedure is activated in a system of the transport landscape. As soon as it has been activated, transports are not forwarded to the downstream recipient systems until all QA approval steps for the respective request, and the request as a whole, have been approved. If any approval step is not confirmed, the entire request cannot be approved.

[+] Rejected requests are not imported into the recipient systems of the QA system.

Prerequisites

If you want to use the quality assurance procedure within the TMS, you must use Basis Release 4.6C or higher, and have set up a system landscape that contains at least one QA system. Delivery channels to other systems must also be in place from this QA system.

Aside from the configured delivery channels, the QA approval procedure has to be set up. This includes information to identify which system is the QA system and which approval steps must be carried out during the approval procedure.

In a three-system landscape, requests are usually imported from the development system to the QA system, where the requests are verified. The verification uses a list of transport requests, which is created based on the worklist of the QA system. In the worklist, a log is generated as well, showing who approved or rejected which transport request and at what time. Approved requests are forwarded or imported to the production system according to configured transportation schedules and the import queue sequence.

Procedure

The same prerequisites and steps that apply to the regular change request strategy apply to the QA approval procedure. Changes in the system are recorded in change requests. By releasing and exporting changes from the development system, they are copied to files at the operating-system level and then automatically added to the import queue of the quality assurance system.

When importing these changes to the quality assurance system, however—contrary to the regular change request procedure—the imported request is not placed into the import queue of the production system in a way that it can be directly imported, even inadvertently. Instead, the request becomes visible to the transport tools and can be imported only after the corresponding approval steps have been carried out successfully. This ensures that no requests are imported into the production system untested.

Additionally, the QA approval procedure can support you in checking transport requests by searching for specific critical objects. Critical objects in this context are any objects, for example, Repository objects or objects that follow a specific naming convention. Objects to be considered critical can be specified in a Customizing table of the TMS. Using this information, you can carry out a preliminary check and sort the transport requests from the worklist accordingly.

As with the regular change request strategy, you should ensure that none of the requests that are referred to by subsequent requests are refused in the quality assurance procedure because the lack of objects of the refused request would lead to errors in the recipient system. Therefore, in this context, it is safer to correct a change request classified as faulty by using a subsequent transport. [+]

5.2.4 Client Copy Strategy

Although SAP recommends that you use change requests to set up your system landscape, the change request strategy can be used only when most (ideally *all*) changes made in the source client have been saved to change requests. If you are unsure whether this has been done in your implementation, SAP recommends an alternative for the setup of your quality assurance client and eventually your production client—the client copy strategy.

Requirements

Before beginning the client copy procedure, you must have installed the quality assurance or production system, completed all post-installation processing, and defined the required quality assurance or production clients. There is no need to copy the contents of client 000 into the new clients. Instead, you will transfer data into the new client using a client copy of the Customizing-and-development client, CUST.

Procedure

The setup procedure using the client copy strategy consists of the following steps:

Setup procedure

1. Import change requests that have already been released.
2. Begin a *client transport* by exporting data in the source client CUST from the database of the development system to files at the operating system level.
3. Import the files stored at the operating system level into the target client, providing the client with a copy of the data found in the original client.
4. Perform post-import activities with Transaction SCC7 (see Chapter 9).

Any change requests with new developments must be imported into the new client before starting with the client transport. A *client transport* (Transaction SCC8) is a special type of client copy used to set up your critical SAP systems. The client transport corresponds to steps 2 through 4 in the previous list. It makes use of standard transport functionality; that is, data is exported to files at the operating system level and then imported into the target client.

Several client copy tools are available, including a client transport or a *remote client copy* (Transaction SCC9). A remote client copy employs *Remote Function Calls* (RFCs) to transfer a client from one SAP system to another. A client copy using remote functionality does not provide a method to "freeze" the client; that is, the stream of data that is transferred is not stored at the operating system level (see Chapter 9). Therefore, you do not have a physical copy of the client that can be used later to set up the production system. Because your setup strategy should try to create the production system the same way the quality assurance system was created—using the same recorded changes and clients—SAP recommends using a client transport rather than a remote client copy.

[+] When you cannot use the change request strategy, SAP recommends using a client transport—not a remote client copy—to set up your quality assurance and production systems.

Importing existing change requests

Before and during the installation of your quality assurance system, you may have released change requests with unit tested changes and functionality from your development system. These change requests appear in the import queue of the quality assurance system. Although they may seem irrelevant for the client copy setup of the quality assurance system, they need special attention.

Some of these change requests contain development changes to Repository objects such as programs. Because the client copy procedure duplicates only client-dependent data and the related client-independent Customizing changes, the client-independent development changes affecting Repository objects will not be transported into the quality assurance system. For this reason SAP recommends that all change requests are transported before the start of the client transport—that is, those change requests already released and exported—should be imported into the quality assurance client.

[+] A client copy does not copy changes to Repository objects made in the ABAP Workbench. Such changes are automatically recorded to change requests and can be imported into a new client from the import queue before performing the client copy.

As the existing change requests are imported into the quality assurance system, they are also placed into the import queue of the production system. When the production system is created, the same change requests are imported into the production system in their correct order.

Exporting the client

When you export a client from an SAP ERP system with Transaction SCC8, you can specify the type of data you want to copy from the source client. Possible selections include:

Selecting the type of data

- Client-dependent Customizing data
- Client-independent Customizing data
- Application data
- User data

Although you can select different data combinations, SAP recommends that you copy only the two types of Customizing data to create the quality assurance and production clients. Avoid copying application data, because typically, the transaction and master data in the CUST client is either nonexistent or simply test data that should not be duplicated.

User data may be included in the copy, but this is potentially problematic. Current users and their authorizations will be distributed from the development system into your production client. For example, your developers will have the same user authorizations in the production system that they needed for the development system. This could lead to a possible security problem in the production system.

If you do copy application and/or user data, you will have to "clean up" the new client to remove unnecessary data and users. This clean-up process is complicated and time consuming. It also requires extensive knowledge of the data model to ensure that dependent data is eliminated in the correct sequence. Perhaps the biggest disadvantage is that you will have to repeat the clean-up procedure for the production client.

Importing the client export

The import of change requests released prior to the client transport ensures that all development changes transported from the development system exist in the quality assurance system. After you have imported these change requests, you import the exported client into the quality assurance client. This import process (using TMS) consists of the following steps:

Import process steps

1. The existing quality assurance client, QTST, and any client-dependent data in this client—including Customizing imported in change requests—are deleted.
2. The exported copy of the CUST client is imported into the new QTST client, thereby placing all Customizing data that existed in the development system in the client. This ensures consistency with the CUST client.

Example: Import Sequence for the Client Copy Strategy

Assume that your development system has been installed for three months and that you have recently installed your quality assurance system. Although you recorded all ABAP Workbench changes to change requests, you did not start recording all Customizing changes until the second month of the implementation procedure. Therefore, to set up your quality assurance system, you need to perform a client export of the CUST client from the development system.

After you export the CUST client with all of its Customizing settings, the import queue for the quality assurance system looks like this:

```
Order Change Request   Description
1     DEVK900034       Conversion routines
2     DEVK900012       Customizing for Materials Management
3     DEVK900020       Organizational data
4     DEVK900076       Sales Reports and New Routines
...   ...              ...
158   DEVK900410       Production Reports
159   DEVK000005       Client export (client-independent
                       Customizing)
160   DEVKT00005       Client export (client-dependent
                       Customizing)
161   DEVKX00005       Client export (texts)
```

The import queue contains 158 change requests released prior to the client export and three change requests containing the client copy data. Some of the 158 change requests contain reports and programs that you will need but that are not part of the client export. You must first import the 158 change requests into the quality assurance system.

When you import the client export files, both the client-dependent and client-independent Customizing imported from the 158 change requests is overwritten. This is of no consequence because the client export contains all current Customizing settings from your CUST client.

If you discarded the 158 change requests and just imported the client export, your quality assurance system would not contain the new sales reports or conversion routines. If you imported the client export before importing the other 158 change requests, some relevant Customizing settings would have been overwritten by older versions. For example, the change request DEVK900012 is second on the list in the import queue. After that change request was released, you may have modified the Materials Management settings in the CUST client.

If you then imported DEVK900012 after the client export, the settings would revert back to an older and incorrect version. The correct procedure is to import the 158 change requests prior to the client export.

To provide a consistent environment and ensure that the production system is the same as the tested and verified quality assurance system, you must set up the production system in the same way you set up the quality assurance system. The procedure is as follows:

1. All change requests in the import queue of the production system—that is, the change requests released *before* the client export—are imported into the production system.

2. The exported CUST client is imported into the system.
3. Any change requests that appear in the import queue after the client export are imported into the system.

Disadvantages

The main disadvantage of the client copy method concerns the type of Customizing settings that are copied. A client copy copies *all* Customizing settings, even if they provide only partial functionality. There is no way to filter out incomplete settings. In other words, Customizing changes that are incomplete—or perhaps even unnecessary for the start of production activities—will be transferred to the quality assurance client and eventually the production system.

5.3 System Copy Strategy

Many customers mistakenly think that a system copy is a viable method for establishing any kind of additional SAP system within a system landscape. A *system copy*, also known as a *database copy*, can be useful for creating optional systems, such as a training system or a copy of the production environment for upgrade tests. However, SAP does not recommend using a system copy to set up a critical system. This means you should not use a system copy of the development system to set up a quality assurance or production system.

Reasons against system copies

SAP has several reasons for advising against the use of system copies, and recommending either the change request or the client copy strategy, as follows:

- A system copy transfers all Customizing settings and developments, even if they are incomplete. Removing unwanted Repository objects and Customizing entries to ensure that only complete business transactions exist in the SAP system is difficult.
- A system copy transfers application data. Although SAP does provide some production start and reset routines to eliminate existing application data, these routines do not exist for all application data.
- A system copy does not provide you with true documentation on the creation of the environment. A system copy used in conjunction with manual elimination of data also eliminates the audit history and documentation provided by change requests.

5.3.1 System Copy of Quality Assurance

SAP strongly advises against using a system copy of the development system to set up your quality assurance system and ultimately your production system. However, on occasion, customers still choose to make a system copy of the quality assurance system to set up their production system. They do this for any of the following reasons:

- They believe that too much time and effort is required to apply the necessary Support Packages, languages, and change requests to the production system.
- They have made manual changes to the quality assurance system that either cannot be transported using change requests, or that were neither performed nor recorded in the development system.
- They do not have a record of the sequence in which change requests and/or a client copy were applied to the quality assurance system. In other words, the import queue of the production system does not match the list of change requests imported into the quality assurance system.
- They no longer have the data files required by the change requests. The change requests used to build the quality assurance system are no longer in the transport directory, and they cannot be located on backup devices.

The last three reasons are typically the result of poor planning and incorrect procedures. Changes in the quality assurance system should never take place, but if they do, they must always be re-created in the development system. Such manual changes should also be performed in the production system. Although it is possible to re-create an import buffer using information currently stored in the quality assurance system, missing data files cannot easily be re-created. By properly planning and structuring your implementation, you can avoid having to make a system copy for any of these reasons.

The time factor, however, may still be compelling. The initial setup of the quality assurance system is straightforward. It requires post-installation processing, possibly a client copy, and some change requests. However, over time, more and more change requests are imported into the quality assurance system. When you begin to install the production system, the list of change requests may number well over a thousand. To complicate matters, during the quality assurance testing, you may have applied additional Support Packages (see Chapter 17). Setting up the production system suddenly seems an insurmountable task. A system copy may appear to be the only solution. Keep in mind, however, that this is not a solution recommended by SAP.

[+] SAP does not recommend using a system copy to set up your quality assurance or production systems. However, this is a proven technique for creating, for example, a sandbox system for an initial upgrade test (see Chapter 18).

5.3.2 Cleaning Up after a System Copy

If you do use a system copy of the quality assurance system to set up your production system, you will have to address several issues before the start of production. You must ensure that all application data is eliminated and that the new production environment is thoroughly tested.

Initial activities

After performing the database copy, and prior to eliminating application data, you must complete the following activities:

- Reinitialize the Change and Transport Organizers (Transaction SE06) to close any open change requests that originated in the source system (see Chapter 7).
- Verify that the TMS configuration is correct and active so that change requests can be delivered to the new SAP ERP system.
- Assign the clients in the new system unique logical system names to avoid conflicts with the logical system names of other clients (see Chapter 9).
- Use authorization techniques to manage user access to the SAP system.

Eliminating application data

One of the reasons SAP advises against using a system copy is that production start programs used to remove transaction data exist only for certain functional areas. To remove the data not covered by such a program, you could use a combination of archiving, running your own deletion routines, and removing data manually—overall, a very tedious and time consuming process.

A more practical method of removing the test data copied from the quality assurance system is to use a client copy to generate a client without application data. For example, after the system copy of the quality assurance system, you can make a client copy of what was once the quality assurance client to create the production client. When you make this client copy, you allow only Customizing data to be transferred. This ensures that there will not be application data in the production client at the start of production activities. Figure 5.3 illustrates this procedure.

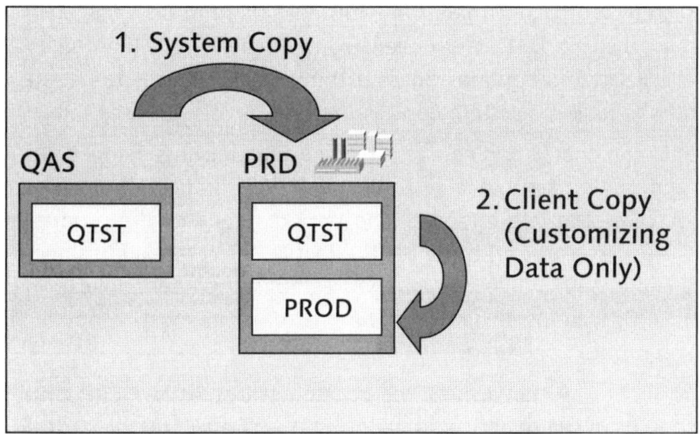

Figure 5.3 Setting up a Production Client Using a System Copy

Validating the production environment

SAP advises customers who are setting up a system landscape to always use the same method when establishing the critical SAP systems. In the system copy procedure, however, the production system—more specifically, the production client—is created in a manner different from that used to create the quality assurance system and client. This means you must verify the new production system before starting production. You should make a system copy of the new production system and use it for testing purposes. These validation tests need to be thorough and comprehensive. Remember that, as in any other step of the implementation procedure, a system copy is only as good as the tests that are performed to verify it.

Example: Using a System Copy to Set Up a Production System

An implementation team that lacked the necessary technical expertise early on in the project plan hires a woman who is an experienced technical consultant. Her first objective is to determine the best strategy for setting up the production system. Although the quality assurance system has been in place for the past two months, she is unable to determine which change requests have been successfully imported. She discovers that several Hot Packages were applied at various times. Also problematic are the client change settings, which may have allowed additional Customizing changes in the quality assurance client.

The consultant recommends setting up the production system with a system copy. She proceeds as follows:

- To support a system copy and hopefully allow for the verification of the production system setup, she creates an additional client in the quality assurance system, client 200. This is a client copy of client 100, the quality assurance test client, and contains only Customizing settings. After creating this client, she makes a system copy of the quality assurance system.
- The consultant then checks and confirms that no Customizing changes can be made in the quality assurance system. All changes imported into the quality assurance system are added to the import queue of the production system. She also works with the testing teams to migrate all business validation to client 200. While this involves establishing new application data in client 200, it helps ensure that the environment most resembles the soon-to-be production client.
- When the production system arrives, the consultant installs SAP ERP with the system copy from the quality assurance system. She deletes client 100 from the system and sets up client 200 as the production client with the appropriate settings. Any changes applied to the quality assurance system after the system copy are also applied to the production system.

5.4 Release Considerations

When selecting a method to set up your system landscape, you must also consider release levels. Ideally, the release installed within the system landscape should be the same for all systems. However, implementations frequently begin at one release and are upgraded as soon as newer releases become available.

When considering an upgrade that would take place during your implementation process, you must keep an important factor in mind: change requests and the client transport are release-dependent. This means you should not transport changes from one release to another. The change requests used to create a system must originate in a system at the same release level.

[+] Change requests and the client copy tools, such as a client transport, are release-dependent.

An upgrade delivered by SAP may contain Repository objects that differ from those in the original release. The table structures that house the Customizing data also vary in the different releases. If the data recorded in a change request originates from a system at a higher level of release, you may not be able to import the data into a system at the lower release level. For the same reason, a client transport can be imported only to an SAP system at the same level of release.

If you need to upgrade your development system prior to the installation of the quality assurance system, first check whether any change requests have been released. If there aren't any released change requests, you can upgrade the development system and install the quality assurance system at the new release level. However, if change requests have been released, you need to employ one of the following methods to ensure that these released changes are distributed to the quality assurance and production systems:

Methods to distribute changes

- Install the quality assurance and production systems at the initial release level. After the released changes are imported, upgrade the systems to the latest release.
- Upgrade the development system to the new release. The released change requests are re-recorded to a new change request at the new release level. This *bundling* of several requests *includes* the contents of the old, released change requests in a new change request (see Chapter 10). You install the quality assurance and production systems at the newer release level and then transport this single bundled change request.
- Instead of using change requests for the initial setup of the quality assurance and production systems, upgrade the development system and use the client copy strategy. All change requests released prior to the upgrade are thus discarded. After the upgrade, you release a

change request from the development system for all modified Repository objects. This is accomplished using the Transport Organizer (Transaction SE01) to create a transport of copies (see Chapter 10). It ensures that all Repository changes are transported to the quality assurance and production systems, both of which are installed at the newer release level.

Example: A Release Upgrade During Implementation

Based on needs for the latest SAP ERP functionality, a company decides in the middle of the implementation process that its development system should be upgraded from R/3 Release 4.6C to SAP ERP 6.0. The company's system administrator, a man named Frank, is concerned that the upgrade will significantly delay his plans for setting up the quality assurance system.

After some consideration, Frank decides to upgrade the development system to SAP ERP 6.0 and to install the quality assurance system at the new release level. Frank then discovers that change requests were released from the development system. Because the change requests now at the operating system level originated in release 4.6C, Frank realizes they cannot be imported into an SAP system at the SAP ERP 6.0 level.

Frank's alternative plan includes the following steps:

- Install the quality assurance system at the release 4.6C level.
- Apply the release 4.6C change requests to the quality assurance system.
- Upgrade the quality assurance system to the new release.

Import any change requests released from the SAP ERP 6.0 development system into the quality assurance system.

Frank's project lead, Barbara, is not in favor of his plan. She feels it would take too long to install and then later upgrade the quality assurance system. As an alternative, she suggests the following procedure:

- Upgrade the development system and install the quality assurance system at the SAP ERP 6.0 level.
- Include all of the released 4.6C change requests into a single change request in the upgraded development system; this single bundled change request is then at the SAP ERP 6.0 level.
- Import the bundled change request into the quality assurance system, providing the system with a copy of all Customizing and development changes released earlier.

Frank follows her suggestions. When he installs the production system at the SAP ERP 6.0 level, he imports all change requests that were imported into the quality assurance system, including the bundled change request.

5.5 Questions

1. **Which of the following clients should you copy to create new clients and ensure that all data from post-installation processing is also copied?**

   A. Client 001

   B. Client 000

   C. Client 066

2. **Which of the following is not an SAP-recommended strategy for setting up a system landscape?**

   A. Using a client copy from the development system to set up your quality assurance and production systems when the change request strategy is not an option

   B. Creating the production system as a combination of a client copy from the quality assurance system and change requests from the development system

   C. Using the same setup strategy to establish both the quality assurance and production systems

   D. Setting up the quality assurance and production systems by importing change requests transported from the development system

3. **Which of the following are correct with regard to the setup of the TMS?**

   A. The TMS should be set up when the development system is installed.

   B. The TMS should include all SAP systems in the system landscape, even if the SAP systems do not physically exist.

   C. The TMS is critical in establishing the transport route between the development and quality assurance systems.

   D. The TMS should be set up before change requests are created in the Customizing-and-development client.

4. **Which of the following is correct with regard to the system copy strategy?**

   A. SAP recommends the system copy strategy because all Customizing and development objects are transferred.

   B. SAP does not recommend the system copy strategy because there is no easy way to eliminate unwanted application data.

   C. A system copy is the easiest setup strategy recommended by SAP.

   D. A system copy eliminates the need for change requests for your entire SAP implementation.

In addition to the tools to implement changes in your SAP system, you also need the respective structures and guidelines in the project organization to efficiently maintain the software.

6 Maintaining a System Landscape

In the early phases of your implementation, to enable the systematic implementation of changes in the SAP systems, you not only need a setup strategy, but also a plan for maintaining your system landscape. This maintenance includes:

- Managing implementation projects through change requests
- Setting up a transport process that ensures that approved changes are distributed to all clients in the system landscape
- Planning and importing SAP Support Packages or SAP Support Package Stacks, and performing release changes

The responsibilities, roles, and procedures involved in recording and transporting changes must be clearly defined and documented. In addition, defined procedures are required to support the import of changes outside of the standard transport process—for example, when applying Support Packages.

This chapter focuses on these issues, and outlines the decisions you will have to make. It explains SAP's recommended system landscape maintenance strategy, as well as SAP's recommendations for testing and validating changes, which play an important role in all maintenance strategies. The maintenance strategy mapped out in this chapter is based on the standard three-system landscape recommended by SAP. The processes and procedures presented here can be adapted to cover system landscapes that differ from that standard.

6.1 Implementation Plan

A system landscape is in a continuous state of maintenance, and maintenance activities need to be coordinated. The overall maintenance process focuses on successive implementation phases—that is, phases in which new or changed SAP software will be implemented in the system landscape. To coordinate these implementation phases, you need to map them in an *implementation plan*, as shown in Figure 6.1.

The various implementation phases in the life of an SAP system can be summarized as follows:

Implementation phases

- An initial phase to configure the SAP software to meet your business needs and start production.
- A series of subsequent phases to introduce new or improved business processes and functionalities.

All implementation phases presuppose that changes to be implemented have been created through Customizing and development activities in SAP ERP, and require subsequent *production support*. This is the use of a special SAP ERP system or client to perform the Customizing and development needed to repair any errors associated with the changes already implemented in the production system.

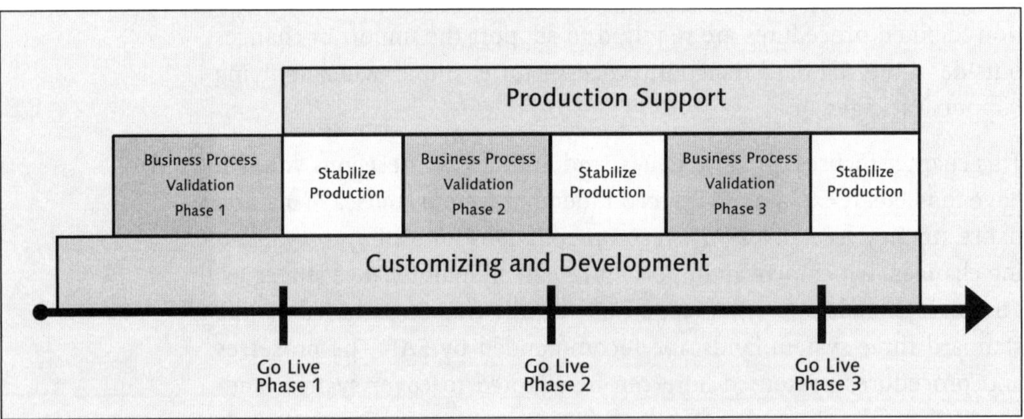

Figure 6.1 Implementation Cycles in the Implementation Plan

Time and security concerns vary depending on the maintenance activity. Both factors are particularly significant for production support. Creating new business processes is not as time-critical as production support, but results in a greater need for end user training, business process validation, and new test scenarios. Before going live with new or modified business processes, stringent testing is required in the quality assurance system.

The implementation cycle is indicated as a horizontal bar at the center of the implementation plan in Figure 6.1. It is a repeating pattern consisting of a business validation period followed by a going live date and a stabilize production period. Prior to the going live date for each bundle of development or Customizing changes, the *business validation* period consists of the following:

Tests during the business validation period

- Extensive testing in the quality assurance system of SAP ERP business processes to verify that the changes will work smoothly in the production system
- Stress tests to validate the technical environment and to ensure that the introduction of new changes will not reduce performance in the production system

After going live, the *stabilize production* period is a time set aside to allow the production system to stabilize. Any conflicts resulting from the introduction of changes in the production system should be resolved before the beginning of the business validation period of the next implementation phase.

In addition to the business validation and stabilization cycles, Figure 6.1 also shows the related, ongoing activities of production support, and Customizing and development. Customizing and development begins immediately after SAP ERP installation, whereas production support begins after the start of production.

Your implementation plan will consist of a schedule based on a diagram such as the one shown in Figure 6.1, as well as documentation that defines the business processes you intend to introduce in each implementation phase. The associated Customizing and development tasks are then assigned to particular individuals to prevent conflicts and procedure overlaps. The three main parties involved in an implementation are as follows:

Parties

- Project leads
- Members of the project teams—that is, customizers and developers
- The system administrator responsible for transports

Their roles and responsibilities will be outlined in the next section.

6.2 Managing Implementation Projects

To facilitate implementation, you should use the project management capabilities provided by change requests in SAP ERP.

Throughout the implementation process, changes made in the Customizing-and-development client must be recorded to change requests. These change requests not only provide a change history and documentation, but also a method of organizing the efforts of the people contributing to the implementation project. Most important, change requests provide a method for transporting different implementation projects—first, to the quality assurance system for testing, and then to the production system.

6.2.1 Implementation Phases

Most implementation projects introduce new SAP functionality to the production system in successive phases. Initially, one new application component is introduced to the production system, and then, after a few months of production activity, another component is introduced. Although it is possible to Customize and develop for multiple projects and phases in the development system, you want to transport only the changes relevant to a specific phase of the implementation project to the quality assurance and production systems. By using change requests, you can appropriately limit what you release and transport.

If you include all of the people working on the project as tasks in a single change request, you can then transport the project as a whole by simply releasing the change request. For larger projects, the project will need to be divided into parts using multiple change requests. For transportation to the quality assurance system, you will need to transport these change requests together.

For example, a company may choose to start production activities with the Financials applications, and a few months later, implement the Logistics applications. To save time, Customizing and development for both application areas are done simultaneously. However, change requests related to Logistics will not be released from the development system until it is time to transport them to the quality assurance system, which is after production is stabilized for Financials.

Example: Change Requests for Implementing in Phases

When implementing SAP ERP, a manufacturing firm decides to introduce the software in multiple phases. The implementation begins in May, when the firm's largest plant goes live with the Production Planning application. In July, the firm's other plants start using SAP ERP. Finally, in October, the Financials applications are added.

To coordinate the procedure, different Project IMGs are created for each phase of the project. The customizers and developers are careful to save changes to the correct change requests for each phase. Likewise, project leads release only the Customizing and development changes related to the business processes currently being tested in the quality assurance system. In other words, prior to the start of production in May, only change requests relevant to Production Planning are released.

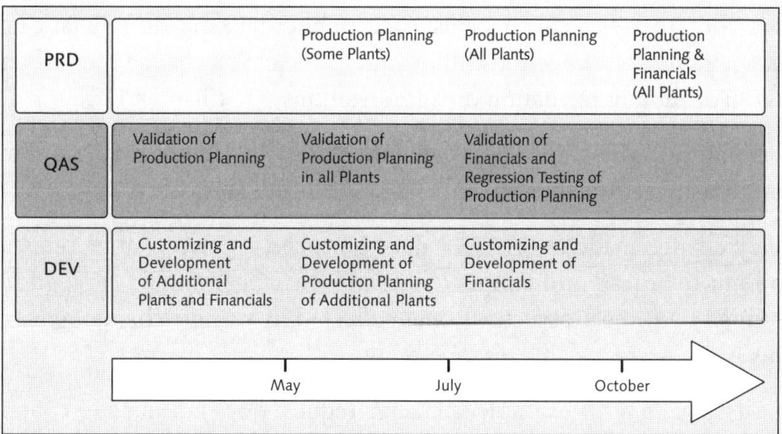

Figure 6.2 Releasing and Exporting Change Requests in Phases

After the start of production in May, only the changes required for the July implementation phase (implementing SAP ERP at the company's other plants) are released from the development system for business validation in the quality assurance system. The change requests required for testing the Financials applications are released only after the new plants are in production.

Having different change requests for the various implementation phases allows development and unit testing for all phases to occur at the same time in the development system. Only releasing and exporting change requests for a specific phase allows for complete business validation of each successive phase.

It is not always possible to separate Customizing activities and assign them to specific implementation phases. During quality assurance testing, missing Customizing due to dependencies between the implementation phases may be discovered. It may then be necessary to release the change requests of a subsequent implementation phase to supply the missing Customizing. Such dependencies between changes in different phases may not become apparent until quality assurance testing.

6.2.2 Managing Change Requests

Ideally, all changes in the implementation process are recorded to change requests. You can do this by using the appropriate client-change settings (see Chapters 3 and 9). A user working in the Customizing-and-development client is then forced to save all changes to a task in a change request. Therefore, to save a change, a user must either be assigned to a task in a change request or have the authorization to create a change request and task. (For more information on authorizations, see Chapter 11.)

[+] User authorizations and the assignment of users to change requests allow you to manage whether and when an SAP user can make changes.

Every change made in SAP ERP does not need its own change request. To limit overhead and simplify validation, changes should be logically grouped by project objectives, and collected in a single change request. This is the project lead's responsibility.

In Customizing, for example, a change request does not need to contain all changes made by an entire Customizing team over a three-month period. Ideally, a change request should be a testable unit of work. This means the objects in the change request correspond to a set of business processes that can be tested together, or to an executable program. A testable change request can more easily be unit tested prior to release, and can more easily be verified after being imported into the quality assurance system.

Responsibilities

Project leads assign project responsibilities to their team members—the people performing Customizing, and developers. These responsibilities correspond to Customizing activities or development work in SAP ERP. To manage the team, the project lead should create change requests and assign team members to them (see Figure 6.2). The project lead is responsible for the change request, and team members are responsible for their *tasks* within the change request. Team members, although they cannot create a change request or task, are able to save their changes to the task created by the project lead.

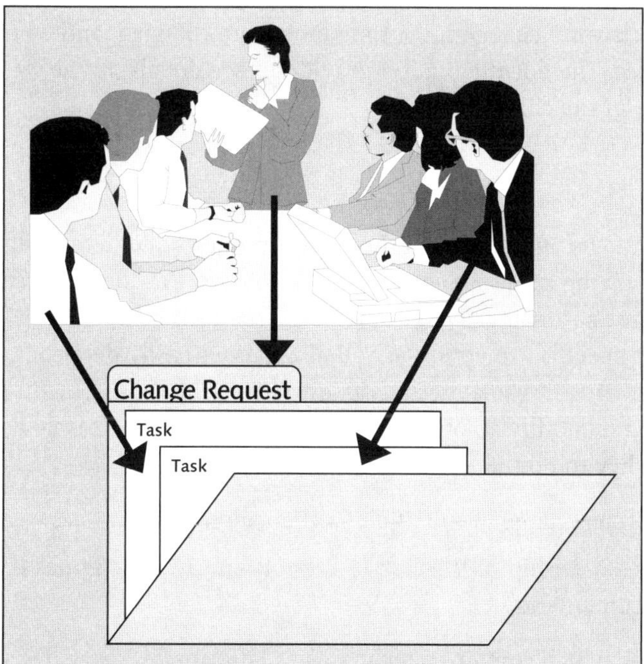

Figure 6.3 Organizing a Project Team

The Customizing Organizer (Transaction SE10) and the Workbench Organizer (Transaction SE09) enable project leads to view, create, and delete change requests. Team members can use these same tools to view any change requests in which they have a task, view the contents of any task in the change request, and record changes to their tasks.

An example of a project objective is to use Customizing to define the process chain for a sales order. After this objective has been agreed on, the project lead, using the Customizing Organizer, creates a change request and assigns each person working on the project to a separate task within the change request.

Documentation

All customizers and developers working on change requests are required to write documentation associated with a task. The documentation must be completed prior to the release of the task. The documentation should state the goals of the changes, the completion status of the task, and any special features that result from the changes. The objects in the task tell you which objects were changed, the time they were changed, and who made the changes. The documentation provides more details on the status and purpose of the changes.

Project IMGs

Ideally, you should be able to look at the change requests and determine to which Customizing project they belong. In R/3 releases before 4.6, the IMG does not automatically set up change requests that recognizably belong to a specific Project IMG. You also cannot easily determine from the Customizing Organizer (Transaction SE10) which Customizing activity was used to modify an object. Therefore, before R/3 Release 4.6, make it your policy to do the following:

Before Release 4.6

- Include the project name in the title of a change request
- Indicate the relationship of the task to the relevant IMG activities in task-level documentation

As of Release 4.6

As of Release 4.6, which contains a technology platform, SAP provides a direct link between change requests and IMG activities. By activating *CTS*

Project Management, you can set up change requests specific to a Project IMG. Then, when you perform Customizing activities from within the Project IMG, changes are recorded to change requests of the corresponding project. The project management functionality also organizes the change requests in the import queues in groups, according to project. This makes it easier to choose what to import. During import, the project management functionality also detects objects shared between different projects, and monitors such dependencies during import activities.

[+] For more information on the CTS Project Management functionality, see SAP online documentation for SAP ERP 6.0.

Example: Managing Change Requests

An international travel services group plans to implement SAP's Human Resources applications over a four-month period. During the first month of configuration, a large number of SAP users record changes to change requests, often saving a change to a new change request. At the end of the first month, over 600 change requests have been created.

Fearing that this number will only continue to grow, the system administrator realizes that a strategy for managing change requests is necessary and that users have to be informed of new procedures. Together with the project leads, the system administrator defines a change request strategy that includes the following:

- Changing most user authorizations so that only project leads can create change requests
- Educating project leads about the procedure for creating and managing change requests and properly assigning users to change requests

The development projects are made the responsibility of the developers themselves rather than the project leads. The developers are then directly responsible for their change requests.

At the end of the second month, only 120 change requests have been released and exported and are waiting for import—a much more manageable number than the 600 at the end of the first month.

6.2.3 Unit Testing

Before releasing the Customizing and development changes in a change request, you must unit test the changes. Because unit testing requires application data, SAP recommends conducting unit tests in a separate unit test client rather than in the Customizing-and-development client (see Chapter 3). Use the unit test client as follows:

Using the unit test client

- To copy the latest Customizing changes to the unit test client, use the COPY BY TRANSPORT REQUEST function (Transaction SCC1; see Figure 6.4). After performing unit testing, return to the Customizing-and-development client to make any necessary corrections. Again, test the latest changes in the unit test client. This process continues until the task required for the project has been completed and is ready for release.
- Because Repository objects are client-independent, a developer does not need to copy development changes from one client to another in the same SAP ERP system. Developers developing in one client can immediately perform unit testing in another client that has test data. After developments are completed and unit tested, they can usually be released to the quality assurance client for integration testing. However, if the development consists of SAPscript and report variants—which are types of client-dependent data—copying the development to different clients within the same SAP ERP system for testing requires special routines (see Chapter 12).

Performing unit testing in a special unit test client enables you to ensure that the objects in your change request include all of the changes they should contain and that will be required for testing in the quality assurance system.

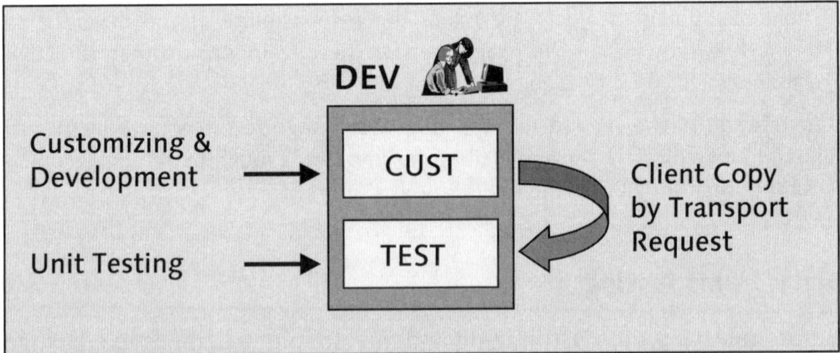

Figure 6.4 For Unit Testing, Use the Copy by Transport Request Function (in Transaction SCC1)

Responsibilities

Team members unit test the tasks for which they are responsible. After a team member has completed unit testing at the task level, the task is released.

Releasing a task to a change request indicates to the project lead that the task has been completed. However, it is not as final a step as releasing a change request. If a person performing Customizing or development realizes that additional changes are required after releasing a task, the project lead can create another task for that user.

The project lead performs unit testing of the objects listed in the change request by using the documentation and test instructions included in the transport tasks, before he releases the change requests.

6.2.4 Releasing and Exporting Change Requests

Before transporting a change request from the development system to the quality assurance system, the project lead must release the change request. In general, releasing a change request automatically initiates the export process. (For details on the release and export processes, and examples of change requests that are released but not exported, see Chapter 12.)

Releasing and exporting a change request is a significant step in the overall change management process, and achieves the following:

Export and release targets

- It indicates that the changed objects recorded in the change request have been unit tested and are ready to be transported.
- It "freezes" the objects recorded in the change request by copying them in their current state to a file external to SAP ERP.
- It places the change request in the import queue of the target system, which is typically the quality assurance system.

A change request only lists the changed objects—it does not contain the changed objects themselves. Releasing and exporting a change request causes the physical download of the changed objects and table entries—in their current state—to a file at the operating system level. The target system receives an entry in its import queue, indicating that the change request (and its collection of changes) is waiting to be imported. If a change request is not ready for promotion to the quality assurance system, it should not be released, because release and export initiates the transport process for that change request.

[+] Perform release and export only for change requests that are ready to be validated in the quality assurance system.

Repository Object Checks

Before you release a change request, you can subject the Repository objects in the request to various checks. Unit testing the change request can reveal errors. In addition, the Workbench Organizer lets you activate *object checks* for Repository objects contained in a change request (see Chapter 12). Object checks identify and display errors found in customer developments before the change request is released. These errors, such as program syntax errors, must be either corrected or verified by the developer before the change requests are actually released.

[+] SAP recommends that developers activate object checks in the development system.

Responsibilities

The person who creates a change request—also known as the *owner* of the change request—initiates the release and export process. That person is usually the project lead. Prior to releasing the change request, the owner is responsible for ensuring that the request is ready to be transported. After releasing their change requests or tasks, neither the project lead nor the team members play any further role in the transport process. Instead, the system administrator is responsible for importing and managing change requests in the import queue. However, the system administrator does not determine whether a change request is placed in the import queue. The project lead should act as a control point, and release and export only changes that are genuinely ready to be imported into the target system.

SAP recommends that only specific users, such as project leads, have the authorization to release and export change requests. Chapter 19, Section 19.2 presents additional annotations and descriptions of recommended procedures. [+]

6.3 Transport Management

The task of transporting change requests is an important responsibility in any SAP implementation. After the start of production, it becomes even more critical because you need to protect the production system from untested changes. Before beginning an SAP implementation, ensure that your system landscape maintenance strategy covers transport management in detail.

Your transport process should be based on change requests as summarized in Figure 6.5 (see also Chapter 4). To establish a transport management plan for your system landscape, focus on the critical steps of the transport process, define how each step is managed, and assign the roles and responsibilities for each.

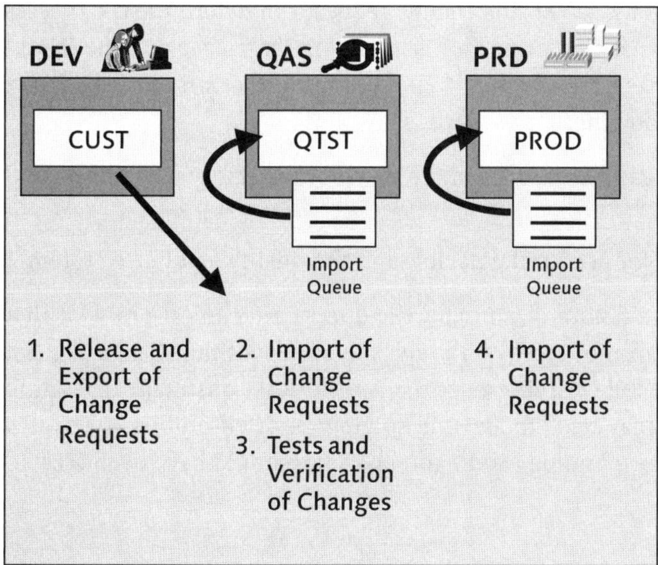

Figure 6.5 Transporting Change Requests

6.3.1 Exporting Change Requests

Releasing a change request in the development system usually automatically triggers the export process and is the first step in transporting the changed objects listed in the change request to the quality assurance system.

During the export process, the changed objects listed in the change request are copied from the database to a data file at the operating system level. The change request is automatically added to the import queue in the target system, the quality assurance system. If data from the source database cannot be exported, or if releasing the change request fails to add the change request to the import queue of the target system, the export will fail.

Responsibilities

Only responsible people such as project leads should release and export change requests in the system landscape. To limit these activities, set the user authorizations appropriately (see Chapter 12).

The person who releases the change request must also verify the success of the export. The owner of a change request can determine the success or failure of an export from the Customizing Organizer and the Workbench Organizer (see Chapter 12). Examples of errors during export include the following:

Possible export errors

- Lack of available disk space in the transport directory for the data and control files
- Inability to connect to the database of the quality assurance system

Sometimes, the failure of an export is due to a technical problem that a project lead cannot solve. Although the owner of the change request is responsible for verifying exports, a technical consultant or system administrator may need to assist in solving reported problems. For this purpose, a corresponding action and task plan should have been created beforehand.

6.3.2 Importing Change Requests

As change requests are released in the development system, they are automatically entered in the import queue of the quality assurance system. Your procedural documentation for performing imports using change requests should include the following:

Procedural documentation

- A policy of preventing users from manipulating the order of change requests in the import queue to ensure that target clients receive the released change requests in the correct sequence
- A time schedule for imports and a procedure for managing change requests that fall outside of the schedule
- A duty roster assigning responsibility for performing imports and listing who has authorization
- Procedures for verifying imports and handling errors that occur during the import

Initiating Imports

An import queue displays change requests that are awaiting import. The change requests are listed in the order of their release. The import process, however, is not initiated automatically. To initiate and control imports into SAP ERP systems, use the Transport Management System (Transaction STMS) as described in Chapter 4.

Prior to the introduction of the TMS in R/3 Release 3.1H, the only method for performing imports was to use transport commands at the operating system level. The TMS import functionality consists of a user-friendly interface in SAP ERP that communicates with the transport control program `tp` using Remote Function Calls (RFCs). Instead of using the TMS to communicate with `tp`, you can still use `tp` directly at the operating system level to perform imports. This requires the appropriate operating system commands. To automate the import process, you can also use tp commands in scripts at the operating system level (see Chapter 14).

[+] For imports, SAP recommends using the TMS or, even better, the Change Request Management, as a part of SAP Solution Manager.

Regardless of whether you use the TMS or the transport control program `tp`, when performing an import, you have the following options:

Have changes been made?

- Use IMPORT ALL to import all change requests waiting to be imported. In SAP ERP, this option is accessed with the START IMPORT menu option, and at the operating system level by using the `tp import all` command.
- Use PRELIMINARY IMPORT to import individual change requests. In SAP ERP, this option is accessed with the REQUEST • IMPORT menu option, and at the operating system level by using the `tp import <change request ID> u0` command. This so-called *U mode* 0 for `tp` ensures that the request imported beforehand continues to remain in the import queue and that an error does not occur in the order of requests.

Import all

Because an IMPORT ALL imports all change requests waiting in the import queue, the import sequence plays an important role. By importing change requests in the chronological order in which they were exported—that is, the order in which they are listed in the import queue—you ensure that during import, objects in earlier change requests are replaced by any corrections in later change requests.

[+] SAP recommends that change requests be imported in the chronological order in which they were exported—that is, the order in which they are listed in the import queue.

To help you import only the change requests you require, you can add an *end mark* to the import queue after the set of change requests you want to import. When you perform IMPORT ALL, any change requests listed in the queue after the end mark will not be imported.

To add an end mark, in the import queue screen (Transaction STMS; OVERVIEW • IMPORTS), double-click the system ID, and choose QUEUE • CLOSE. The end mark is indicated by the END OF IMPORT QUEUE statement that appears at the end of the import queue.

If necessary, you can move this statement further up the import queue to include fewer change requests in the next import. For example, let's say you want to import only the first 15 change requests in an import queue. To do this, place the cursor on the 16th change request and choose EDIT

• MOVE END MARK. This places the end mark between the 15th and 16th change requests. You can now start the import.

Preliminary import

A *preliminary import* allows you to rapidly transfer single requests through the defined transport routes. For example, you may have a production problem that needs immediate correction. The corresponding change request is released from the development system and needs to be tested immediately. Although other change requests are waiting in the import queue of the quality assurance system, you want to import only the single change request at this time. You therefore import the individual change request using a preliminary import. If the contents of the change request successfully correct the problem, you can import the change request to production immediately, using another preliminary import.

To minimize the risks associated with preliminary imports, the imported change request remains in the import queue after import and is reimported the next time the entire import queue is imported. This guarantees that export and import sequences are the same and ensures that the target system does not return to the way it was prior to the preliminary import.

To prevent inconsistencies that may result from object dependencies, SAP recommends avoiding preliminary import and using only IMPORT ALL. For example, if you import a change request with an ABAP report that refers to a table, and that table is contained in another change request that has not yet been imported, executing the report will only generate short dumps until the table is also imported.

Example: A Preliminary Import

A multinational company purchases a new facility and begins making adjustments to its SAP ERP system. After the rollout of the required accounting settings to support the new manufacturing facility, it is discovered during a month-end closing period that the real estate accounting settings are incorrect, and due to the error, month-end closing cannot be completed. The error is immediately simulated in the quality assurance environment, the problem is pinpointed, and corrections are made in the development system. A change request with the required changes is released from the development system.

The import queue of the quality assurance system looks like this:

```
Change Request   Owner   Description
DEVK901832       MARY    Plant configuration
DEVK901910       SUE     Real estate controlling
DEVK901830       ALEX    Rental accounting
DEVK901676       JON     Manufacturing
DEVK902015       BILL    FIX: month-end with new
                         facility
DEVK901703       MARY    Plant maintenance
```

The import queue of the quality assurance system already included recently released changes that support manufacturing requirements for the new facility. However, these application settings are neither ready for validation nor required in production immediately.

Change request DEVK902015 contains the changes needed to complete month-end closing. This request needs to be imported immediately. Because the other requests are not ready for validation, an import of the entire import queue is not possible. The individual request itself is imported using a preliminary import.

Importing DEVK902015 to the quality assurance system enters this change request in the import queue of the production system. After the correction contained in this change request has been validated in the quality assurance system, DEVK902015 is imported into the production system with an additional preliminary import.

During the next scheduled import into the quality assurance system, DEVK902015 is again imported, this time as part of the listed series of change requests. Because the change request is imported in sequence, changes made to solve the month-end closing problem are not overwritten by earlier requests such as DEVK901910 or DEVK901830, which may contain conflicting changes.

Import Considerations

Before importing a change request, consider the following:

- Importing to all clients in all SAP ERP systems. This ensures consistency of all clients and systems in your system landscape.
- Scheduling imports into the quality assurance system at times known to the entire implementation team. This creates transparency for project management and for the business validation team. For a larger

number of transport requests, it makes sense to import them as a group to QAS once a week, for example, and to test all of them together before they are imported into PRD.

Importing into multiple clients

Typically, a quality assurance system contains more clients than just the quality assurance client. One or two additional clients may be dedicated to end-user training, and another client may be reserved for data conversion tests. Regardless of the number of clients, your import procedure needs to ensure that all clients in the quality assurance system receive the change requests in the same order they were exported from the Customizing and development system.

To enable you to import to multiple clients, SAP introduced functionality known as EXTENDED TRANSPORT CONTROL in R/3 Release 4.5, which allows client-specific transport routes. These transport routes allow you to assign imports to multiple clients in a single SAP system at the same time or at different times. Client-specific transport routes use client-specific entries in import queues (see Figure 4.4 in Chapter 4).

If you do not use extended transport control, you have to import the change requests several times, once for each client in the system. Ensure that all change requests are imported into all clients in the same sequence so that client-independent functionality is not overwritten by older versions of the functionality delivered in earlier change requests (see Chapter 13).

[+]

When you have multiple clients in the quality assurance system, SAP recommends that you use a documented strategy to ensure that all change requests are imported to all clients in the quality assurance system.

Additional clients in the development system

While development changes automatically impact all clients in the system, Customizing changes are typically specific to the Customizing-and-development client in which they originated. You need to take certain steps to ensure that all clients in the development system are also supplied with all client-dependent changes.

Although unit testing copies the changes to the unit test client, importing released change requests into the unit test client provides a way of ensuring that all changes are entered into this client. Similarly, a sandbox client updated with the latest changes ensures that the people working in that client are working in an up-to-date environment.

You can ensure in a number of ways that the clients in the development system contain the latest client-dependent changes, as follows:

- Using the client-specific transport routes of the EXTENDED TRANSPORT CONTROL.
- Performing a COPY BY TRANSPORT REQUEST (Transaction SCC1) for all change requests released from the development system.
- Importing released Customizing change requests. To do this, you need to give the development system its own import queue (through the transport parameter TESTSYSTEMS). Released change requests are then transferred into the development import queue.

  [+] Prior to using the import queue of the development system to import to other clients in that system, you must eliminate change requests containing development work. This prevents these change requests from overwriting recent changes to client-independent objects in the development system.

- Performing periodic client copies of the Customizing-and-development client to other clients such as the sandbox client. Note that this will eliminate all data, including application data, in the target client.

Scheduling imports

Imports into the quality assurance system can be automated to occur at specific, predefined intervals. However, SAP recommends such scheduling only when responsible people such as project leads control the release process—that is, that someone makes sure that whatever is supposed to be released has been checked and is needed in the quality assurance system. If you have established no such control, you must provide some other method by which users can inform a system administrator or technical consultant that released change requests should be imported. This can be a complicated process and may cause misunderstandings.

[+] As a prerequisite for scheduling imports to the quality assurance system, import queues should contain only requests that are ready for import. Therefore, only responsible people such as project leads should be in charge of the release and export process.

You need to determine when imports should be scheduled. All imports introduce changes and thus invalidate previous test results, including test results for other areas of SAP ERP. Thorough testing is required after all imports. Because this takes time, the timing of imports is controlled by whether the business validation team is ready to perform the testing.

Fixed import intervals

Early in an implementation phase, imports are usually scheduled at regular intervals—for example, once a day; every hour; or at 9:00 A.M., noon, and 4:00 P.M. As you get closer to the going live date, business validation teams need more time for testing, and you will want to limit the import process to once a week.

[+] Define an import schedule that allows sufficient time for the testing and correction of changes prior to the next import.

Tools for scheduling imports

As of R/3 Release 4.6, the TMS contains the *Import Scheduler*, which lets you schedule change requests for immediate import, periodic import, or import at specific times. You can use the Import Scheduler to schedule TMS activities such AS IMPORT ALL, PRELIMINARY IMPORT, and to import to a specific client.

In releases prior to R/3 Release 4.6, you can perform imports at specific intervals, either manually or using scheduling programs. To manually schedule imports, the system administrator performs an IMPORT ALL in the TMS. As an alternative, scheduling programs can be used to issue the appropriate `tp` commands at the operating system level. For example, if Unix is your operating system, you can schedule `tp` commands using the Unix program `cron` (see Chapter 14).

[+] You must still monitor and verify the results of each import even if your import process is automated.

Responsibilities

Traditionally, when the import process was more technical and required access to the operating system level, it was the responsibility of the system administrator. With the introduction of the TMS, the import process is controlled from within the SAP system. This means any SAP ERP user with the correct user authorization can initiate either an IMPORT ALL or a PRELIMINARY IMPORT.

[+] To avoid errors, prevent unauthorized imports by carefully assigning and monitoring all relevant user authorizations.

6.3.3 Post-Import Issues

To complete the import procedure, you need to do the following:

- Review the relevant logs
- Resolve any errors that occurred during import
- Notify the people who will perform testing and business validation

Responsibilities

The post-import issues are the responsibility of both the technical team and the project leads (or owners of the change requests). Using a formal notification procedure, ensure that communication between the people involved happens.

Import logs

Every import activity, such as an IMPORT ALL or a PRELIMINARY IMPORT, results in a *return code* in the TMS. These logs can be viewed in the Import Monitor in Transaction STMS, as described in Chapter 13. If the return code indicates an error, it is initially the responsibility of the system administrator to evaluate the error. During import, errors can be the result of a particular change request or a problem with the target SAP system.

Transport logs

To determine whether the import of individual change requests was successful, project leads should check the logs specific to each change request. These are known as transport log files. Using either the Customizing Organizer (Transaction SE09) or the Workbench Organizer (Transaction SE10), you can access an overview of change requests that have been released, exported, and imported. Traffic-light icons on the right-hand side of the initial Organizer screens are red to indicate transport errors, yellow for warnings, and green for successful imports.

[+] The transport logs also contain transport log files that are not assigned to only one transport request (activation or conversion logs for dictionary objects such as tables). These transport log files must also be checked for potential errors.

By activating the DISPLAY TRANSPORT ERRORS AT LOGON setting in the Workbench and Customizing Organizers, a user can obtain information at logon about the status of change requests that have been transported. After this setting has been activated, whenever a user logs on and a change request import has failed since the user last logged on, a message box appears, informing the user of the failure. The user can access the transport log files and determine which import errors have occurred. You can activate this setting either for an individual user or globally for all users (see Chapter 12).

[+] SAP recommends having all users automatically informed of transport errors when they log on to both the development and quality assurance systems.

Problem resolution

The system administrator should review and evaluate the import log to check for errors after every import. Severe errors can cause the import process to stop, leaving change requests in the import queue and only partially imported into the quality assurance system. Such errors require the system administrator's immediate attention. Even when scheduling routines for import into the quality assurance system are used, a system administrator should check the import log after each import.

Errors in the import log indicate either problems with the import process or problems with specific change requests. The change request owner, usually the project lead, must resolve problems affecting specific change requests. Correcting a problem may simply require releasing additional changes from the development system. In more difficult situations, the project lead may need to consult the system administrator to understand and resolve the problem.

Problems not with specific change requests but with the import process must be resolved by having the system administrator analyze the SAP system and database (see Chapter 14 for troubleshooting tips).

Notification of imports

After the import of change requests into the quality assurance system, the people responsible for the business validation must be notified so that they can begin testing. Notification may occur informally in the early stages of implementation. As the final, more general phase of testing approaches, the business validation team requires more formal notification. Project leads should provide this notification because they are responsible for the project at the going live stage.

6.3.4 Importing into the Production System

When planning for import into the production system, your procedural documentation for performing imports using change requests should include the following:

- Procedures for signing off change requests that contain approved functionality, after testing in the quality assurance system
- A procedure and time schedule for imports of change requests required to support production problems
- Procedures for verifying imports and for the immediate handling of errors that occur during the import
- A duty roster assigning responsibility for performing the import

Imports into the production system are performed using the same tools used to import change requests into the quality assurance system (the TMS and the transport control program `tp`), but the import process itself must be more closely managed. The exact focus of this management varies depending upon whether the import is the going live step in an implementation project or is providing production support for current production activities. The support for a project go live requires more testing and business validation testing. In contrast, imports for production support require more careful management of the import queue.

Going Live at the End of an Implementation Phase

Ideally, all change requests imported into the quality assurance system are also imported into the production system in the same order. This rule applies not only for the initial setup of the production system (as described in Chapter 5), but also for going live at the conclusion of an implementation phase.

Before going live at the conclusion of an implementation phase, a formal business validation of the entire quality assurance client is necessary to ensure that the collection of imported change requests provides the expected business processes. In addition, regression testing is necessary to ensure that the new business processes do not conflict with existing business functionality. The approved collection of change requests is introduced into the production system by importing the entire import queue.

Production Support

Even after the introduction of a new implementation phase, and a period of time dedicated to stabilizing the production environment, additional changes to the production environment may be required—for example, because errors emerged or because of changed configuration requirements. These changes are the responsibility of production support, which should introduce only urgently required corrections, not new functionality. Every system landscape should include the system resources and transport processes required for production support (see Chapter 3).

Corrections made during production support must be tested in a client that is identical to the production client. This ensures that the testing is a true validation of business functionality and provides a simulation of the impact the changes will have on the existing production data. Only when a change request has been tested and verified in the quality assurance system should it be imported into the production system.

The change requests required to support production may be the responsibility of different project initiatives, with different priorities. It will not be possible to sign off and import all change requests at the same time. After the start of production activities, the import queue of the production system may contain any of the following:

Changes in the import queue

- Emergency fixes that require one or more change requests to be imported into production immediately (regardless of their position in the import queue sequence)
- Change requests that have been signed off and are ready for import into production
- Change requests that have not been signed off and are not yet ready for import into production

The START IMPORT TMS menu option, which imports all change requests waiting for import, cannot be used in this case. Instead, imports into the production system require you to check whether a change request has been signed off and to import emergency fixes separately from other signed off change requests. Thus, the import procedure involves careful manipulation of the import queue to determine the order in which change requests are imported into the production system.

Indicating sign-off after testing

After business validation testing is completed, the tested change requests are signed off; that is, they are approved for transfer to the production system. When the affected change requests were imported into the quality assurance system, they were also added to the import queue of the production system. However, in releases before R/3 Release 4.6, the import queue of the production system cannot be used to indicate whether change requests have been formally signed off.

The sign-off process is often managed as follows:

Managing the sign-off process

- SAP Business Workflow® functionality is used to send a formal sign-off email to the system administrator who will do the import.
- External to SAP, sign off is recorded using the form shown in Figure 6.6, either on sheets of paper (one for each change request) or in a spreadsheet (as in Figure 6.8 later in this chapter) in a shared file.
- Verbal notification is provided by speaking with the system administrator who will do the import.

Change and Transport Request Form			
Requestor		Date	
Source Client		Target Client(s)	
Source System		Target System	
Change Request #			
☐ Customizing	☐ Workbench	☐ Client-dependent	☐ Client-independent
Description of Contents			
Tasks/Request	☐ All tasks released ☐ Change request released ☐ To be released		
Special Requirements			
Approved by (please sign)			
IT Team USE ONLY			
Imported by		Date	
Transport Log Return Codes	☐ 0 Transport (export and import test) was successful. ☐ 4 Warning messages were generated. ☐ 8 Error messages were generated ☐ ≥ 12 Fatal error has occurred		
Comments			
Exception Handling–Corrected Change Request #		Date Reason	
Project Management Approval		Date	

Figure 6.6 Sample Production Support Change Request Form

In R/3 Release 4.6, SAP introduced the *QA Approval Process*, which provides a formal sign-off procedure for change requests waiting for import into an SAP system. The process allows you to define which users are responsible for sign-off. Although a change request may be in the import queue of the production system, it cannot be imported until the people responsible for sign-off have approved the change request. The QA Approval Process is linked with the CTS Project Management functionality in Release 4.6 so that the approval process is linked to all change requests of a project. The approval process can be unique for the change requests of different projects.

Emergency production fixes

Typically, an emergency fix to correct a production problem is performed using a PRELIMINARY IMPORT. This imports the individual change request required to correct a problem, and retains that change request in the import queue of the production system, to be reimported in sequence at a later time.

Import Queue: System PRD

Request for PRD: 10 / 10

Number	Request	Owner	Short Text
1	DEVK901532	KESTER	Condition table for pricing
2	DEVK901561	HAMM	Pricing agreements
3	DEVK901502	ROEHRS	Foreign trade data
4	DEVK901514	SMITH	Invoice lists
5	DEVK901585	SMITH	Billing types
6	DEVK901592	HAMM	Delivery scheduling
7	DEVK901633	SCHMIDT	FIX: shipping points
8	DEVK901543	KESTER	Pricing rules
9	DEVK901638	SCHMIDT	FIX: shipping determination
10	DEVK901501	JAKOBI	New matchcode for billing

Figure 6.7 A Sample Import Queue for a Production System

Figure 6.7 shows a sample import queue for a production system, PRD. The seventh and ninth change requests in the import queue have been signed off and are needed in the production system immediately. To accomplish this, preliminary imports of change requests `DEVK901633` and `DEVK901638` will be performed.

Importing signed-off change requests

After having been signed off, change requests that are not part of an emergency fix are usually imported during the next scheduled import. There is a danger of incomplete functionality being imported if change requests that depend on other change requests do not receive sign-off at the same time.

Figure 6.8 provides an example of customer documentation showing an import queue, and also displays the status of the change requests and the dependencies among them. Change requests `DEVK901633` and `DEVK901638` have already been imported, possibly to provide an emergency fix, but should be imported again with the other change requests in the correct order. As revealed by the indicated dependencies, the change requests numbered 1, 2, 6, and 8 must be imported together to provide the desired functionality. Because they have all been signed off, you can assume that the functionality that will be imported is complete and fully tested. The third change request in the list has been signed off and is ready for import. Both the fourth and fifth change requests have not been signed off. If they are not signed off before the next scheduled import, they cannot be imported.

Number	Request	Status	Dependencies
1	DEVK901532	Approved	DEVK901561, DEVK901592, DEVK901543
2	DEVK901561	Approved	DEVK901532, DEVK901592, DEVK901543
3	DEVK901502	Approved	None
4	DEVK901514		
5	DEVK901585		
6	DEVK901592	Approved	DEVK901532, DEVK901561, DEVK901543
7	DEVK901633	Already imported	
8	DEVK901543	Approved	DEVK901532, DEVK901561, DEVK901592
9	DEVK901638	Already imported	
10	DEVK901501		

Figure 6.8 Sample Import Queue Documentation with Sign-Off Status and Dependencies

In such a situation, you should not perform an IMPORT ALL of the production import queue. To import the required changes into the production system, either all change requests must be approved or the required change requests must be imported individually.

[+] To minimize the need to import change requests out of sequence, SAP recommends that you ensure all change requests receive business validation and sign-off as soon as possible.

When you need to import change requests and cannot perform an IMPORT ALL, you have the following options:

Import without "Import All"

- Set an end mark at a certain point in the import queue and IMPORT ALL change requests above the end mark
- Perform a preliminary import for each individual change request
- Perform preliminary imports for a group of individual change requests

Either one or a combination of these import options can support the import of change requests into a production environment.

[+] Support of production activities requires experienced judgment in weighing the advantages of importing change requests in their original sequence against the advantages of performing imports out of sequence to provide emergency corrections to the production system.

To ensure consistency, change requests that are imported out of sequence are always imported again with all other change requests in the sequence dictated by the import queue. For example, after importing the signed-off change requests in Figure 6.8, the import queue would look like the one shown in Figure 6.9. (Figure 6.9 no longer shows the first three change requests seen in Figure 6.8 because these were sequentially imported.) The change requests now numbered 3 through 6 (numbered 6 through 9 in Figure 6.8) will be imported again to ensure they enter the production system in the correct sequence.

Number	Request	Status	Dependencies
1	DEVK901514		
2	DEVK901585		
3	DEVK901592	Already imported	DEVK901532, DEVK901561, DEVK901543
4	DEVK901633	Already imported	
5	DEVK901543	Already imported	DEVK901532, DEVK901561, DEVK901592
6	DEVK901638	Already imported	
7	DEVK901501		

Figure 6.9 Import Queue after Import of Approved Change Requests

Scheduling Imports into the Production System

Importing change requests brings new Customizing settings and Repository object changes into the production system. These changes affect the runtime environment and have an impact on production activities. Imports into a live production system should be performed at times when online processing activity is low and scheduled background jobs have been completed. This is usually in the evening, when few or no users are in the system. For a global implementation, you can import at a time that represents the close of the business day for one region and the start of a new business day for another. The imports should not take place when the respective developers are not available to make corrections if need be.

[+] Before you perform imports, SAP recommends backing up the production system. If an import results in unexpected problems, you can restore the SAP ERP system with the data preserved in the backup. When errors occur in the conversion of table structures, or when table structures are wrongly imported with fewer fields than the target system, you can no longer revert to the original system state using the former object versions, because doing so would lead to data loss.

Responsibilities

A change request's owner is responsible for that change request from the time it is created until it has passed through the quality assurance system and has been imported into the production system.

The business evaluation team takes over responsibility for the change request after it has been imported into the quality assurance system. The business validation team provides sign-off for the change requests (or collection of change requests), which can then be imported into the production system.

The actual import of change requests into the production system is the responsibility of the system administrator. The critical nature of changing a live production environment necessitates that the person performing the import must understand the current backup strategy, know when the system is carrying a low system load, and be able to react to any issues or errors that arise due to importing.

6.4 Business Validation

A well-managed change and transport process helps ensure the success of your SAP implementation. However, thorough quality assurance testing is what guarantees the successful addition of new and modified business processes to the production environment. Testing is only as good as the testing plans you devise, so design your testing plans carefully.

Several kinds of testing are required in the quality assurance system, as follows:

- **Business validation**
  The functional verification of your business processes.
- **Technical validation**
  Performance and stress tests, to ensure that the new business processes are optimized and supported by the hardware resources.

The technical validation required for production support is not covered in this book.

6.4.1 Testing Procedures

Business validation is critical to the success of your SAP implementation. It should always be performed before you import changes into the production system. Testing for production support is not as time consuming as the testing done at the conclusion of an implementation phase, but it still requires business validation and sign-off. Standard, documented business validation procedures are required throughout the entire implementation process.

Business validation tests and verifies the following:

- New business processes and scenarios
- Existing core business processes (tested using regression testing)
- Customer developments and SAP enhancements

The focus of business validation is on the SAP ERP application processes, but it may also include technical components such as interfaces, input and output methods, and print functions.

Designing a Test Plan for Business Validation

Like all other aspects of the SAP implementation, business validation requires a defined procedure with assigned roles and responsibilities. A test plan should determine the following:

- The business scenarios and processes that require validation—for example, common business activities and core business transactions
- The testing methodology, including the different tools and user groups
- The people responsible for validating test results

The sophistication of SAP ERP ensures that there are always several ways of performing a business task. Therefore, it is not easy to define all possible scenarios. Project leads in collaboration with end user representatives can define the core business processes and common scenarios that require testing. Project leads must also define the acceptance criteria that form the objective of the tests.

Developing a test plan

Your test plans will continuously change over time, to deal with the variety of business processes being implemented. For example, your first phase of implementation may require business validation of the Financials components, a large number of data conversion routines, and interfaces to external systems. The subsequent introduction of the Logistics components does not require you to test any data conversion routines, but adds many more business processes and requires the verification of interfaces. In addition, in all testing procedures, you must test existing business processes through regression testing.

Test cycle

Business validation involves the repeated testing of business processes in the quality assurance system until the acceptance criteria have been fulfilled. If the acceptance criteria are fulfilled, the change requests are signed off and are ready for import into the production system. If not, corrections are made in the development system *only*, and then the corresponding change requests are released to the quality assurance system for renewed testing.

During this cycle of business validation, it is common to "freeze" the quality assurance system—that is, to prevent the import of any new change requests and thus ensure the testing of a finite group of changes.

Before freezing the system, you will want to create a system backup. Because numerous transactions are run during testing—possibly creating unwanted data—it may be necessary to restore the system from a backup after testing. SAP recommends backing up data so that you can restore the SAP system to its original state at any time.

Responsibilities

Business validation is process-oriented and should be set up and performed in consultation with experts from the business departments responsible for the particular process area. For the testing period, the project leads' responsibilities include the following:

The project lead

- Identifying the transactions that need testing (in conjunction with experts from the business departments)
- Defining the testing methodology that best suits the requirements
- Defining the acceptance criteria that form the objective of the tests

After the project leads have defined the relevant transactions and methodology, the business validation team begins testing and verifying those transactions. The business validation team should represent different business departments and perform quality assurance tests for their respective SAP ERP settings, reports, and transactions. To enable the business validation team to check the import status for different projects, ensure that team members have display authorization for the Workbench Organizer and Customizing Organizer.

The SAP system administrator

The SAP system administrator should participate in setting up hardware and backups, and provide technical support during the actual testing.

6.4.2 SAP Testing Tools

To achieve "perfect" business validation and performance testing, all employees would need to spend a day or more in an SAP system performing all of their typical tasks. Because this procedure is too costly and inconvenient, project leads generally use either or both of the following:

- Real users that are representative of all of the different user communities, running actual transactions
- Scripts that simulate SAP transactions and processes

The real user approach is a simulation using actual, logged-on users. Although this approach allows you to test a realistic transaction mix while operating on actual user data, coordinating such tests may be difficult when many users are involved, especially when users are scattered all over the globe. In addition, such users may not always be available to test business validation when they are needed.

Scripting tools, on the other hand, provide a flexible method for testing a specific set of transactions. These tests are much easier to control, and therefore are easy to replicate. They also let you simulate a different set of transactions and support business validation over time. To facilitate such testing, SAP provides testing tools as part of its core SAP application. These tools make up the *Test Workbench* whose primary tool is the extended Computer Aided Test Tool (eCATT).

The Test Workbench

Using the Test Workbench (Transaction S001; TEST • TEST WORKBENCH), you can specify the applications to be tested by creating a *test catalog*. Within the test catalog, a series of scenarios exist that need to be tested, also known as *test cases*. These can be performed either manually or through scripting using a tool such as eCATT.

After creating different test cases, another tool, the *Test Organizer*, records which tests are necessary for the current business validation period. As testers perform the different tests in the Test Organizer, you can use this tool to track the status and test results.

[+] For more information on the SAP Test Workbench and on how to organize your business validation testing, refer to the SAP online documentation. We recommend that you use the SAP Test Workbench via SAP Solution Manager as a central test system. Moreover, Chapter 19 describes the various options in SAP Solution Manager in the context of system changes.

extended Computer Aided Test Tool (eCATT)

eCATT is an SAP tool that is part of the ABAP Workbench and that you can use to automate repeatable transactions in SAP ERP and associated software components. You can also use this tool to record user activities for systematic tests. eCATT is the successor of Transaction CATT. Contrary to CATT, eCATT can run all SAP ABAP Transactions, even if they were developed using the Control technology. Via RFC, you can also call transactions across system boundaries in another SAP system. You can use eCATT to perform the following tasks:

Application possibilities

- Testing transactions
- Checking table values and database updates
- Setting up Customizing tables
- Testing the effect of changes to Customizing settings
- Creating test data

eCATT includes the necessary functions to create, start, maintain, and log test procedures. When an eCATT script is running, eCATT validates user authorizations and produces a detailed result log that can be automatically archived. The eCATT logs contain all information relevant to the test run and are stored centrally in the database of the executing SAP system—either the local system or the SAP Solution Manager.

[+] For more information on how to build test scenarios with eCATT, see the SAP online documentation.

SAP Change Request Management (ChaRM)

SAP Change Request Management is a tool in SAP Solution Manager that supports you in implementing changes and the necessary processes between transport and testing. You can approve changes based on the workflow and according to specific regulations, transport them to testers, and control the import into the production system via additional tasks. This establishes a direct link between the transports and tests, which can also be evaluated at a later stage. For more information on this procedure, see Chapter 19.

6.5 Support for the SAP Standard

To provide an SAP implementation with new and enhanced business functionality and to support its customers' growing business needs, SAP periodically delivers new releases. Existing SAP ERP customers obtain the new functionality in a release upgrade. An upgrade replaces the current standard SAP objects—that is, the Repository—with new objects, while preserving customer data and developments.

In addition, SAP provides Support Packages and SAP Notes, which allow customers to integrate smaller scale changes and repairs to the SAP standard. As with a release upgrade, Support Packages and SAP Notes ensure that the customer's data and Customizing and development changes will not be changed or lost. Your system landscape must be able to support all three forms of support, and your maintenance strategy should include the relevant procedures.

6.5.1 Support for an SAP Release

SAP's Support Packages and SAP Notes are release-specific. Initially, SAP announces a correction for a particular release and provides solutions in an SAP Note. Then, to assist you in maintaining your SAP system, these corrections are bundled into Support Packages. A Support Package contains changes to source code, as well as general improvements. A Support Package can in some ways be compared to a release. For example, both change the SAP standard. Each SAP system not only has a release level, but also a Support Package level that defines the status of the system's SAP standard.

To support your SAP systems at their current release level, you must closely monitor the application of SAP Notes and Support Packages and ensure that:

- You consistently transport changes that are based on SAP Notes
- All SAP systems in your system landscape have the same release level and the same Support Package level

- You do not overwrite modification adjustments that were imported to a system by subsequently applying a Support Package (see Chapter 17 and 18)

SAP Notes

The solutions provided in SAP Notes typically require you to make programming changes that modify the SAP standard, creating what is known as a *modification*. To simplify applying these changes to your SAP ERP system, the corrections in SAP Notes are bundled into Support Packages. They are available for download from SAP Service Marketplace and can be automatically incorporated into your SAP system without manual programming or creating modifications.

SAP recommends that you apply the corresponding Support Packages instead of making manual changes based on recommendations in an SAP Note. However, you may still be required to make manual modifications for any of the following reasons:

Reasons for manual modifications

- **Availability**
  A change documented in an SAP Note has not been bundled into a Support Package.
- **Urgency**
  A correction documented in an SAP Note is required as soon as possible. Rather than wait for the corresponding Support Package, you make the change in your development system according to the SAP Note. The change request containing the modified SAP object is then transported to the quality assurance system and distributed to production after thorough testing and verification.
- **Verification**
  Making a single change according to an SAP Note is much easier to verify than multiple changes. A single change requires only limited tests in contrast to the complete business validation of affected objects needed after applying a Support Package.
- **Dependencies**
  Support Packages must be applied in sequence. Because of this dependency, you cannot apply a Support Package until all of the previous Support Packages have been applied and verified. Additional depen-

dencies may also exist if, for example, you are using industry solutions. However, these dependencies are recognized by the tool used to import the Support Packages (SPAM). Missing Support Packages are requested if necessary.

Performing a modification

Before making modifications based on SAP Notes, verify that the SAP Note applies to your release and that the symptoms documented in the SAP Note correspond to the symptoms apparent in your SAP system. If you are uncertain, SAP recommends contacting SAP Support.

You should create all modifications of SAP objects in your development client. The change request containing the modification must then be transported to the quality assurance system for verification. Only after it has been thoroughly tested and signed off should you import the change request containing the modification into the production system.

For more information on the modification procedure, see Chapter 10.

Documentation requirements

For every SAP object changed by the customer, you will need to perform a modification adjustment during release upgrades, and possibly also when applying Support Packages. To help speed up the modification adjustment process, you should document modifications when making them. Your documentation should include the SAP Note number and release dependencies. This information should be recorded in task documentation as well as in the short text of each change request. When you begin a modification adjustment, you will then be able to recognize the corresponding change requests in the import queue.

Figure 6.10 shows how properly documented changes, made as a result of an SAP Note, should appear in the import queue of a target system. Note that the relevant Support Package is also specified. This enables system administrators to decide whether the change request needs to be imported—it may be preferable to simply apply the corresponding Support Package to the target system.

[+] Document all changes to standard SAP objects completely. If the change is based on an SAP Note, include the SAP Note number and relevant Support Package in the change request description.

Import Queue: System PRD			
Request for PRD: 3 / 21			
Number	Request	Owner	Short Text
1	DEVK902032	GANTS	Logistics planning requirements for new plant
2	DEVK902061	SMITH	R/3 Note 342 R40B – fixed in Hot Package 3
3	DEVK902101	HART	Human resource planning reports for QTR4

Figure 6.10 A Sample Change Request Resulting from an SAP Note is Waiting for Import

Support Packages

SAP's Support Packages enable SAP to quickly and easily repair software errors in the SAP ERP Repository that require urgent attention. By applying Support Packages, you can maintain the latest corrections in your SAP system and avoid making modifications to the SAP standard based on SAP Notes. Support Packages keep your SAP system up to date. However, you cannot apply Support Packages without considering the following:

- Possible conflicts with any modifications previously made to the SAP standard
- The impact of the corrections on your SAP ERP system, as well as the additional business validation tests required in the quality assurance system

Support Package Stacks

For many products, aside from the Support Packages, SAP delivers what are called *Support Package Stacks*. These provide Support Packages in a specific combination. This is particularly interesting for SAP products such as SAP R/3 Enterprise 4.7 or SAP ERP 6.0, for which Support Packages for all installed software components exist. For example, SAP ERP 6.0 ECC 6.0 has five SAP NetWeaver components, two ERP main software components (APPL and HR), eight software components of the Enterprise Extension category, and up to eight software components of industry solutions that have been returned to the SAP standard. To avoid problems with cross dependencies between all of these Support Packages, using the additionally validated Support Package Stacks provides increased security and simplifies the process. The SAP Maintenance Optimizer provides additional support in this context. Chapter 17 discusses this tool in detail.

When applying a Support Package, you may be asked to adjust SAP objects that you have modified manually. This is true whether the modification was made according to an SAP Note or to add customer-specific functionality. Modification adjustment involves making a choice to either retain the changes comprising the modification or to delete them to restore the original SAP objects as contained in the Support Package. Ideally, the objective of this adjustment is to return the object to the SAP standard. SAP recommends limiting modifications to the SAP standard to simplify the application of Support Packages.

Support Packages introduce new versions of standard SAP objects into an SAP system. The number of affected objects and application components impacted by the changes varies from Support Package to Support Package. However, because a considerable number of objects are changed, every Support Package (or collection of Support Packages) requires verification before being applied to the production system. Such validation testing is time consuming and may not be possible within the current implementation plan.

SAP recommends that you apply all available Support Packages during the initial installation of your SAP system or immediately following an upgrade. Subsequent Support Packages for the same release level should be applied at the beginning of a new implementation phase to ensure that they are part of the business validation cycle.

Example: Applying Support Packages

An implementation phase has been undergoing business validation for a month. Initial business validation in the quality assurance system has begun, to test newly implemented business processes. While large numbers of sales orders are being processed, a performance problem is detected. The system administrator looks for and finds a relevant SAP Note. According to the SAP Note, the solution is to either manually modify three different standard SAP objects or to apply the next available Support Package.

Because final validation of the quality assurance system as a whole has not started, the customer has a choice: make manual modifications or apply the Support Package. If, however, the performance problem had been detected in the middle of final business validation, the implementation schedule would probably have caused the customer to decide to make the necessary modifications manually and then apply the Support Package in a subsequent implementation phase.

6.5.2 Release Upgrades

Although Support Packages provide a select number of new Repository objects, a release upgrade supplies a completely new SAP Repository to provide new SAP functionality. The upgrade procedure requires a wider range of activities than those associated with Support Packages.

Release upgrades require the following:

- Downtime for each SAP system during the import of the new release
- Modification adjustment
- Customizing

The activities and tools required for a release upgrade are covered in more detail in Chapter 18.

Release Upgrade Phase

Because of the changes associated with an upgrade, SAP recommends that you dedicate an entire implementation phase to the upgrade process. A release upgrade should not be part of an existing implementation phase that is necessary to introduce changes or that creates business processes.

As with the rollout of new business processes, a release upgrade also requires additional upgrade-specific Customizing activities known as *Release Customizing*. The successful implementation of Release Customizing and the new SAP ERP Repository require the following:

- Technical changes to your SAP ERP environment, such as upgrades to operating system and database software, or to hardware
- Business validation testing
- Stable SAP ERP systems—in particular, a stable production environment

Responsibilities

Although your system administrator is responsible for production support—for example, applying SAP Notes, Support Packages, and release upgrades—the impetus for applying such changes is usually one of the following:

- A problem arises for which there is a relevant SAP Note or Support Package.
- Business departments want functionality contained in upgrades.

The decision-making process may involve people at many levels within your company.

6.6 Questions

1. **Which of the following activities is NOT necessary for releasing and exporting a change request?**

   A. Documenting every task in the change request

   B. Releasing every task in the change request

   C. Verification of the contents of the change request by the system administrator

   D. Unit testing the change request

2. **Which of the following statements is correct with regard to the tasks used in change requests that record Customizing and development changes?**

   A. Tasks belong to a change request.

   B. Tasks can be used by several SAP users.

   C. Tasks are the direct responsibility of a project lead.

   D. Tasks record only client-specific changes.

3. **Which of the following indicates that a change request has been signed off after quality assurance testing?**

   A. The change request is released after unit testing.

   B. The change request is successfully imported into the quality assurance system.

   C. The change request is added to the import queue of all other SAP systems in the system landscape.

   D. The project lead communicates their approval of the change request.

4. **Which of the following is NOT an SAP recommendation?**
   A. Imports into the quality assurance and production systems should occur in the same sequence.
   B. Even if the import process is automatically scripted, a technical consultant or system administrator should review the results of the import.
   C. Project leads should manually add change requests to the import queue of the quality assurance system.
   D. Change requests are imported in the same sequence in which they were exported from the development system.
5. **Which of the following is SAP's recommendation on how to rush an emergency correction into the production system?**
   A. Make the change directly in the production system.
   B. Transport the change from the development system to the quality assurance system and production system using a preliminary import.
   C. Make the change and use a client copy with a change request to distribute the change to production.
   D. Make the change in the quality assurance system and transport the change using a preliminary import.
6. **Which of the following transport activities is NOT typically the responsibility of the system administrator?**
   A. Importing change requests into all clients within the system landscape
   B. Verifying the success of the import process
   C. Releasing change requests
   D. Assisting in solving either export or import errors
7. **Which of the following does SAP provide as customer support?**
   A. Release upgrades to provide new functionality.
   B. Support Packages to correct identified problems in a specific release.
   C. SAP Notes to announce errors and corrections for the reported problems.
   D. All of the above.

PART II
Technical Tasks

The first six chapters of this book have provided you with an overview of the change and transport concepts as well as recommendations for the implementation and maintenance of your SAP ERP system landscape. The next part of the book expands on the introduction to the transport mechanism, and outlines the technical tasks required to realize your system landscape. These tasks include:

- Setting up a transport directory at the operating system level
- Setting up the Transport Management System (TMS)
- Creating new clients

This part will be of most interest to the person directly responsible for setting up, upgrading, or extending a system landscape. This is typically the implementation's system administrator.

During the installation of an SAP system, a system ID is assigned to the system and a transport directory is created for it at the operating system level. Chapter 7 focuses on this transport directory, its structure, and the way it is often shared by many different SAP systems. Other post-installation activities covered in Chapter 7 include:

- Configuring a Transport Profile
- Initializing the Change and Transport Organizer (CTO)
- Setting the system change option

The next step in your implementation is setting up the Transport Management System (TMS). This procedure is explained in detail in Chapter 8. Setting up the TMS is divided into two phases:

- Initializing the TMS
- Configuring the transport flow in the system landscape by defining transport routes

Although you initially install your SAP system with default clients, SAP recommends that you create new clients in the system to perform standard business processes or to perform Customizing and development. Chapter 9 outlines how to:

- Define a new SAP client
- Define client settings used to restrict the changes that can be made from within the client
- Copy a base set of data to that client
- Log Customizing changes made to a client

To ensure a simple and safe customization of the SAP systems, you must adapt the transport tools for the selected system landscape after system installation.

7 Transport Setup Activities at Installation

To set up the capability to transport SAP ERP change requests, you must perform certain activities when installing an SAP ERP system. These activities are explained in this chapter and include the following:

- Specifying the system ID
- Setting up the transport directory
- Configuring a transport profile
- Performing activities within SAP ERP such as:
  - Initializing the Change and Transport Organizer (CTO)
  - Setting the system change option
- Verifying the background jobs and background work processes required for transports

7.1 Specifying the System ID (SID)

When installing the SAP ERP system, you must determine a name for the new system. The system name is known as the *system ID* (SID). If you perform a standard installation, you must define a name for the system and the database at an early stage in the installation. If the new system is the result of a system copy, you must specify a new SID for the system and the database.

The SID of each system in the system landscape must be unique. When you specify a SID, especially when adding a system to an existing landscape, ensure that the new SID does not conflict with an existing SID.

[+] Two systems within a system landscape may not, under any circumstances, have the same SID.

Because you need to set up transport routes early in the implementation of a system landscape, when you set up the development system, a placeholder or virtual system name is assigned to, for example, the production system, despite that system not yet having been created. When you install additional systems in the system landscape, if a system has already been established within the Transport Management System (TMS) as a virtual system, use the name provided in the TMS and delete the reference to the virtual system. For more information on setting up transport routes and virtual systems, see Chapters 5 and 8.

SIDs that are reserved by SAP and that may not be used by customers when naming new SAP systems include ADD, ALL, AND, ANY, ASC, B20, B30, BCO, BIN, COM, DBA, END, EPS, FOR, GID, INT, KEY, LOG, MON, NOT, OFF, OMS, P30, RAW, ROW, SAP, SET, SGA, SHG, SID, UID, and VAR.

[+] In addition to not being able to use the SIDs reserved by SAP, you also cannot use a number as the first character of the SID.

7.2 Setting Up the Transport Directory

After starting the installation, you must specify the path to the system's *transport directory*. The transport directory is a file system located at the operating system level. This is where the objects in change requests that were released and exported from the system are physically copied so that they can subsequently be imported to a target system. The transport directory is an integral part of transporting change requests from one system to another. The transport directory allows you to perform the following tasks throughout your system landscape:

- Sharing changes, using change requests and client transports
- Applying SAP Support Packages

Because the files in the transport directory that correspond to the objects in the change request must be accessed by different systems within the system landscape, only one physical transport directory that can be shared by all other systems is usually used on a system. This single, shared transport directory is called the *common transport directory*. Every application server needs to have access to the *common transport directory*.

During installation, at least one physical transport directory has to be created in one system of your system landscape. You are asked very early in the installation process to specify where the transport directory should be created, or—if a transport directory has already been created—which host system serves as the *transport host*.

The transport host is the system that physically contains the common transport directory. [+]

All systems that share the same *transport directory* make up a *transport group* (see Chapter 8). Figure 7.1 shows an example of a common transport directory. The transport host—the system that contains the transport directory—is the development system, DEV. The quality assurance system (QAS) and the production system (PRD) share the transport directory of DEV. Together, all three systems—DEV, QAS, and PRD—are part of the same transport group.

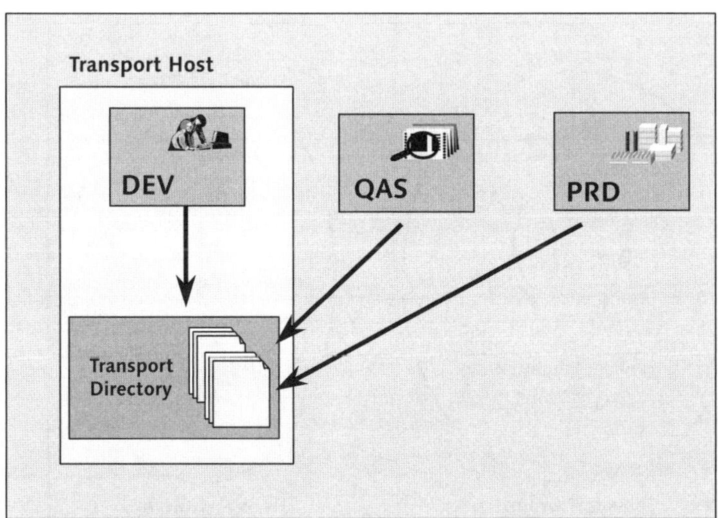

Figure 7.1 A Common Transport Directory for a Three-System Landscape

[+] All systems belonging to one transport group share the same physical transport directory, called the common transport directory.

7.2.1 One or Many Transport Directories?

Standard practice is to have one common transport directory in a system landscape. However, it may be useful to have more than one transport directory if, for example, the following is true:

More than one transport directory

- The network connection to a system is not fast enough.
- A permanent network connection between the different systems of the system landscape does not exist.
- Security reasons prevent direct access to a system.
- Different hardware platforms exist that do not allow a common transport directory.

If you require additional transport directories, you should use either additional common transport directories (if multiple systems share the directory) or a private transport directory (if only one system uses the directory). For example, you could create a transport directory in the production system. If this transport directory is not shared with other systems, it is called a *private transport directory* (see Figure 7.2).

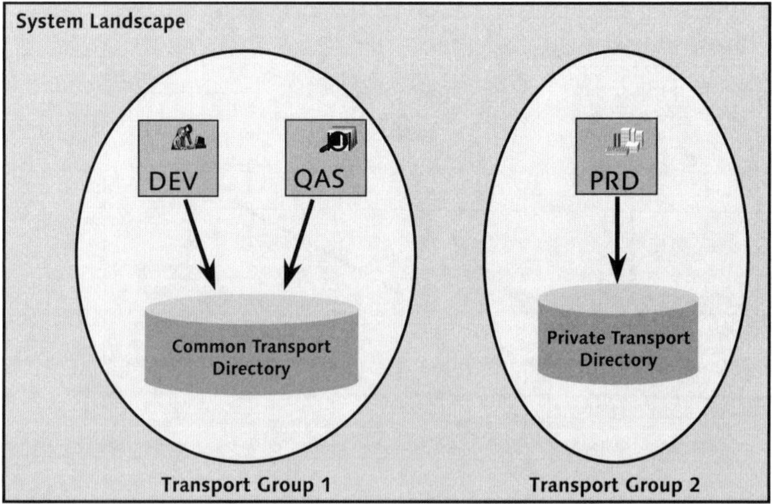

Figure 7.2 Two Transport Groups

When you create a new transport directory, an additional transport group is added to your system landscape. Customizing and development work can be transported between different transport groups (see Chapter 13). However, transporting between different transport groups requires additional steps, time, and disk space due to the indirect transport through different transport directories.

If you use several transport groups, keep the following in mind:

- Log files generated during the export process can be displayed only in systems that are in the same transport group as the source system. The source system is typically the development system.
- Log files generated during the import process can be displayed only in systems that are in the same transport group as the target system. The target system is typically the quality assurance or production system.
- You must maintain the transport profile for each transport group.

Example: System Landscape with Two Transport Groups

To provide a solid, 24-hour maintenance and support solution for a production SAP system, a company outsources its system support for the production system. The internal technology team manages support for the development system and quality assurance system, both of which physically reside at company headquarters. The production system, however, is located at a different facility across town. For this system, the external support vendor provides support.

Although the production system is physically accessible from the company's headquarters through the network and the company's firewall, it does not share the same transport directory as the development and quality assurance systems. The main reasons for having separate transport directories are: eliminating the need for an NFS (*network file system*) mount across the network and protecting the production system from non-relevant transport activities. Consequently, there are two transport groups: one for the development and quality assurance systems, and another for the production system (see Figure 7.2).

7.2.2 Transport Directory Structure

The subdirectories in the transport directory store all of the files required for transports (see Figure 7.3). To create the subdirectories, user action is not required—they are created automatically during the installation of a system.

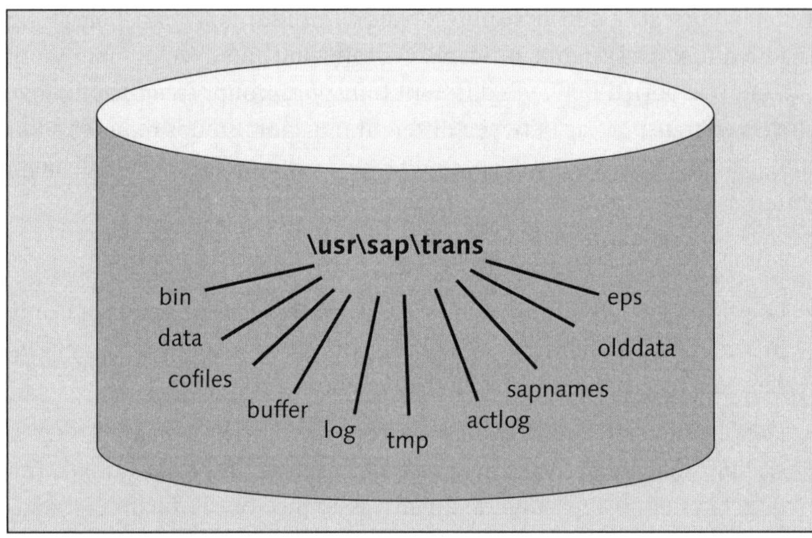

Figure 7.3 Transport Directory Structure

The subdirectories in the common transport directory include the following:

Subdirectories

- **bin**
  Contains the transport profile, called `TP_<domain>.PFL`.
- **data**
  Stores the actual data files of the related change requests with Customizing and development changes.
- **cofiles**
  Contains *control files*, or change request information files, used by the transport tools at the operating system level. The information in the files includes data about transport types, object classes, required import steps, and post-processing exit codes. These files also contain the current status of the change request in the various systems of the transport group.
- **buffer**
  Contains an import buffer for each SAP ERP system in a transport group. These buffer files indicate which change requests should be imported in the respective system. Import queues—mentioned previously in Chapters 4, 5 and 6—represent the import buffer within an

SAP system. Buffer files also provide information on the steps that must be performed for import, and the order in which requests are to be imported.

- **log**
  Includes all general log files, as well as all log files generated by the export and import of change requests or client copy activities.
- **tmp**
  Needed to temporarily store log files and semaphores during transports.
- **actlog**
  Stores the log of user actions in an SAP system for all change requests and tasks. This is the transport directory's only subdirectory that is not accessed by the operating system command `tp`. It is accessed only by the *Change and Transport Organizer* (CTO).
- **sapnames**
  Contains a file for each SAP user working with the CTS. These files log transport activities for each transport request.
- **olddata**
  Needed when you clean up the transport directory. Old exported data that should be archived or deleted is stored in this directory.
- **eps**
  Used for downloading SAP Support Packages from the SAP Service Marketplace.

For more information on the files contained in these directories, see Chapter 14.

7.2.3 Procedure

To set up the common transport directory, you must provide a file system on the system you have selected as the transport host. Many customers select the development system as the transport host because it is typically the first system to be installed. Next, you run `R3setup` from the CDs to start the actual installation. The transport directory, with its subdirectories, is automatically created.

Every computer in the transport group on which an SAP instance is installed should have read and write access to the transport directory. This is implemented through corresponding authorizations of the operating system user who owns the SAP instance—for example, <sid>adm on Unix platforms. You should ensure that network availability is sufficient between the systems that belong to the same transport group.

Configuration

To set up your transport directory, follow these steps:

1. Create the following directory on the transport host:
   - `/usr/sap/trans` on Unix and AS/400 platforms
   - `\sapmnt\trans` on Windows platforms
2. As part of the installation preparation, on the hosts that belong to the same transport group, mount this directory using operating system tools.
3. Ensure that the correct path to the transport directory is stored in the parameter `transdir` in the transport profile, and in the parameter `DIR_TRANS` in the instance profile.

Technical Requirements

The free space required in the transport directory depends greatly on the transport volume. As a rule of thumb, to estimate the amount of disk space required for your transport directory, proceed as follows:

Disk space

- Estimate 100MB per SAP instance that will be using the transport directory.
- Estimate 20MB for each user involved in Customizing and development. The minimum total amount of disk space for the transport directory derived from the two estimates should be 200MB.
- Add the estimated additional disk space needed for client exports. This depends on the data to be transported (see also Chapter 9).
- Add the estimated additional disk space needed for SAP Support Packages (see also Chapter 17). In a system where few development activities are carried out, the memory required for the SAP Support Packages can be the main factor. Therefore, at least 100MB should be reserved for this purpose.

The following sections cover how to set up the transport directory for Unix, Windows, AS/400, and a heterogeneous environment.

Transport Directory on Unix

To set up the transport directory on a Unix platform, follow these steps:

1. Log on to the transport host as user `root`.
2. Create the file system for the transport directory.
3. Mount this file system as `/usr/sap/trans` (default value). Ensure that the directory belongs to the group `sapsys` and has the permission 775. After installation, you should restrict the permission to 771.
4. Export the directory using a tool such as NFS (network file system).

Ensure that the group `sapsys` has the same *group identification number* (GID) on all computers in the network. [+]

Next, perform the following steps on all other SAP instances in the transport group:

1. Log on as user `root`.
2. Create the mount point `/usr/sap/trans`.
3. Establish a network connection to the transport directory—for example, using NFS to mount the transport directory from the transport host.

For details on the command syntax of the specific Unix derivatives, see *Installation on Unix-OS Dependencies*, one of the implementation guides accompanying the SAP installation package. [+]

Transport Directory on Windows

To share a common transport directory, all application and database servers for an SAP system must be either in the same Windows NT domain or, if the domains differ, you must specify the TRUSTED RELATIONSHIP Windows setting between them.

For Windows, you can choose any computer as the transport host. If you have chosen a computer that contains the SAP ERP central instance to be the transport host, skip the following three steps. Otherwise, if the computer chosen contains a dialog instance or no instance at all, perform the following steps before installation (that is, before running `R3setup`):

1. Create the directory `\usr\sap\trans`.
2. Set a global share `sapmnt` to point to the `usr\sap` file tree. This allows the transport directory to be accessed through path `\sapmnt\trans`.
3. Grant Windows access type FULL CONTROL for EVERYONE on this directory.

[+] The Windows access type FULL CONTROL is required for the transport directory only during SAP ERP installation. After the installation, for security reasons, you should restrict this access to write authorization for operating system users.

You must define the transport host using the alias SAPTRANSHOST. Whenever it is necessary to point to the transport host, this alias is used instead of the name of the transport host. Prior to SAP ERP installation, make this alias known to all Windows systems within the transport domain by using either of the following techniques:

SAPTRANSHOST

- On the Domain Name Server (DNS), record the alias SAPTRANSHOST for the transport host. This technique is recommended by SAP and creates what is known as the *central transport host*. Its main advantage is that you do not have to adjust the parameters of every system when moving the transport directory, but only the central record of the transport host on the DNS.
- If no DNS server is available, you can use the hosts file to record the alias SAPTRANSHOST. This file is located in the Windows default directory `<drive>:\WINNT\system32\drivers\etc`. Use an editor to add the entry `<IP_address> <hostname> SAPTRANSHOST`. Ensure that this file is identical on all hosts where an SAP instance is installed or will be installed.

[+] For more information on the configuration of a central transport host, see SAP Note 62739.

Early in the SAP ERP installation process, you are asked to name the host that contains the transport directory. For a common transport directory, enter the alias SAPTRANSHOST. For a private transport directory, enter the host name of the computer that contains the transport directory.

Transport Directory on AS/400

To enable access to a common transport directory on AS/400 systems, use the integrated file server QFileSvr.400 on the AS/400 system to provide access to other file systems on remote AS/400 systems.

[+] To avoid performance problems, use the QFileSvr.400 file server instead of NFS to connect the SAP systems on AS/400 platforms.

Perform the following steps prior to SAP installation on AS/400:

1. For each host that shares the transport directory, create a subdirectory named with the respective host name in QFileSvr.400. To create the subdirectory, execute the following command with the respective host name:
   ```
   MKDIR '/QfileSvr.400/<hostname>'
   ```
   Create the host directories with the startup program QSTRUP because these directories no longer exist after the initial program load (IPL) of AS/400 and must be recreated.
2. Create the following operating system users on all AS/400 systems in the transport group:
   - <SID><nn> (nn denotes the instance number)
   - <SID>OFR (for the SAP system superuser)
   - <SID>OPR (for the SAP system operator)

[+] These users must have the same passwords on all computers and need *write* authorization on the transport directory.

For each AS/400 SAP system in the transport group, perform the following:

1. When installing the SAP ERP software, in the `R3setup` main menu (SAP INSTALLATION), select option 3 to change the location of the transport directory `/usr/sap/trans`.

2. Specify the host name of the transport host. As a result, the transport directory can be accessed through /usr/sap/trans, which is a symbolic link that points to /QfileSvr.400/<hostname>/sapmnt/trans.

For an SAP installation with a private transport directory, perform a default installation for the transport directory. When the SAP installation program asks for the location of the transport directory, agree to the settings proposed by default. Accepting the default settings automatically creates the transport directory under /sapmnt/trans. The transport directory can be accessed through /usr/sap/trans, which is a link to the physical directory /sapmnt/trans.

[+] SAP Note 67213 provides more detail on the transport directory for AS/400 platforms.

Heterogeneous Operating Systems

It is possible to use a common transport directory in heterogeneous operating system environments. The configuration depends on the operating systems. For example, you can set up the physical transport directory on a Unix system and provide network access to AS/400 systems. You can also have the transport directory located on an AS/400 server and access it from Unix systems, although this configuration is more complex. In both cases, you must use NFS for the connection between the different platforms.

[+] For more information on setting up a central transport directory in environments with both Unix and AS/400 platforms, see SAP Note 69429.

The implementation of a common transport directory in mixed environments with Windows and Unix is more difficult. Some files in the transport directory are written in text mode. On Unix platforms, a *linefeed* is written at each line end. On Windows, the line end is indicated by a *carriage return* followed by a linefeed. All SAP systems must be configured so that the transport directory files are written only in binary mode—the line end is indicated by a linefeed on both platforms.

A hierarchical file system does not exist on Windows platforms. It is also not possible to create soft links to mount Unix file trees on Windows systems, or links that mount Windows file trees on Unix systems. To enable this access between the systems, you must install additional software such as SAMBA.

[+] For more information on setting up a central transport directory in environments with both Unix and Windows platforms, see SAP Note 28781.

7.3 Configuring a Transport Profile

For each transport group, you need to set up and maintain a transport profile. The transport profile contains the settings needed to configure the transport control program `tp` and the transport program `R3trans`. The transport profile is stored in subdirectory `bin` of the transport directory.

In the transport profile, the following parameters must be maintained:

Parameter

- Database-specific parameters:
  - `dbhost`
  - `dbname`
- Path-specific parameters:
  - `transdir`
  - `r3transpath`
- Parameters for heterogeneous environments

If you have more than one transport group, the transport profiles should all be identical. The only exception might be parameter `transdir`.

[+] As of R/3 Release 4.5, transport profile parameters are specified in uppercase—for example, `TRANSDIR`. For simplicity, the transport profile parameters in this book are written in lowercase.

7.3.1 Transport Profile as of R/3 Release 4.5

As of SAP R/3 Release 4.5, the file `TP_<domain>.PFL` is used as the transport profile. You no longer need to copy and adapt the profile at the operating system level. It is automatically generated the first time you call the Transport Management System (TMS) and contains the required transport parameter settings. This file is also stored in the transport directory's `bin` subdirectory, and is managed in the TMS.

[+] At the operating system level, you do not modify the transport profile using a text editor.

The transport profile is maintained automatically when certain TMS functions are performed, such as adding a new SAP system. If required, you can also adapt the transport profile manually. To modify the transport profile, from the SAP initial screen, perform the following steps:

Modify

1. Call Transaction STMS.
2. Select OVERVIEW • SYSTEMS.
3. Mark one system and choose SAP SYSTEM • CHANGE.
4. Select the TRANSPORT TOOL tab.

Figure 7.4 shows how the `TP_<domain>.PFL` transport profile is displayed. You may change global, system-specific, and operating system-specific parameters. Enter the changes directly in the VALUE column and choose SAVE. This creates a backup file by saving the previous version of the transport profile as `TP_<domain>.BAK` in the transport subdirectory `bin`.

In the TYPE column, the symbols indicate the origin of certain parameters. Via the icon, select LEGEND (see Figure 7.5) to access the legend of these symbols.

In Figure 7.4, the parameter `transdir` is the only parameter that is used explicitly at the operating system level. All database parameters—`dbhost`, `dbname`, and `dbtype` have been automatically generated by the TMS. The `tp_version` parameter has been added by a user when implementing a current version of `tp`. `CTC=1` indicates that the client control of transport routes is activated, and `NBUFFORM=1` allows for an import buffer format with long request names.

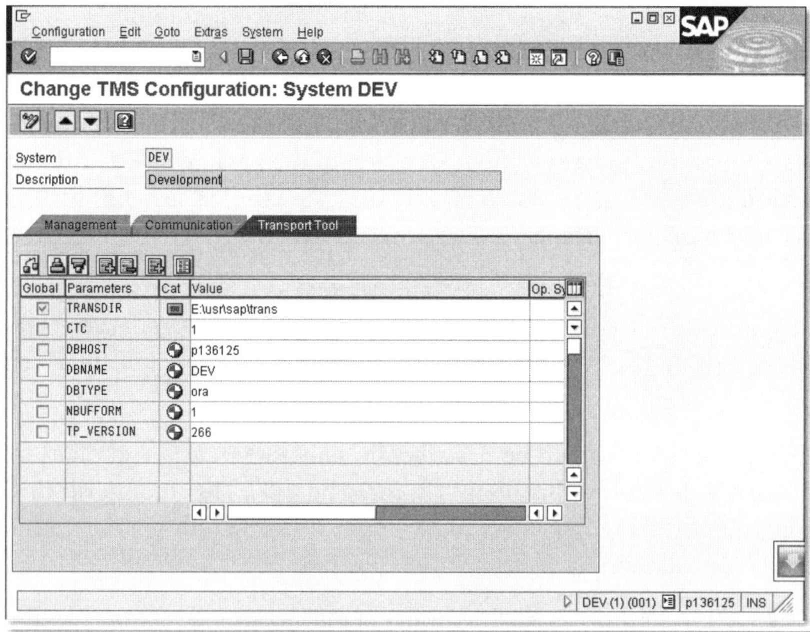

Figure 7.4 Transport Profile Parameter

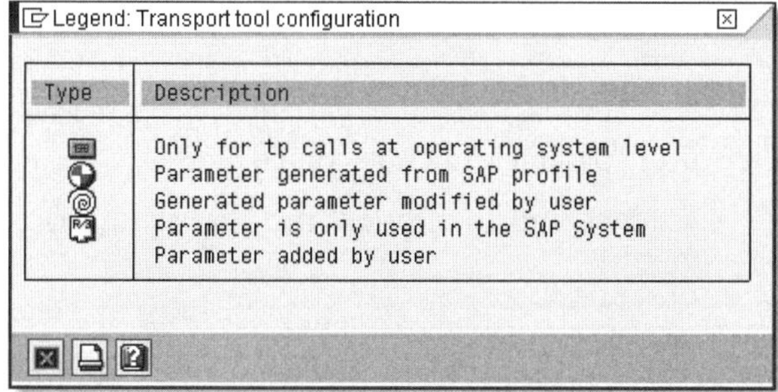

Figure 7.5 Legend for Parameter Types

To list all of the defined parameters and their values, in the DISPLAY TMS CONFIGURATION: SYSTEM <SID> screen, choose GOTO • TP PARAMETERS.

Upgrading to R/3 Release 4.5 or Higher

After an upgrade to SAP R/3 Release 4.5 or higher, your SAP system will contain two transport profiles: `TPPARAM` and `TP_<domain>.PFL`. The transport profile TP_<domain>.PFL is always used when calling tp from the SAP system. A conflict may arise when you run tp at the operating system level if the formerly used transport profile TPPARAM still exists in the subdirectory bin after the upgrade. To start tp from the operating system, you must specify the location of the parameter file with the option pf=<path of TP_<domain>.PFL>. Otherwise, tp searches for the TPPARAM transport profile.

[+] If both transport profiles TPPARAM and TP_<domain>.PFL exist, a conflict may arise when you run tp at the operating system level. Therefore, when starting tp at the operating system level, you must indicate which profile tp should use.

Each SAP system should be described in only one transport profile—as of Basis Release 4.5, this file is TP_<domain>.PFL. To accomplish this, copy the settings in TPPARAM to TP_<domain>.PFL and then delete the entries in TPPARAM.

To copy the settings from the former transport profile TPPARAM to the new transport profile TP_<domain>.PFL, proceed as follows:

1. Call Transaction STMS.
2. Select Overview • Systems.
3. From the System Overview: Domain <DOMAIN> screen, mark the system that is the source of the parameters to be copied.
4. Choose SAP System • Change and then select the Transport tool tab.
5. Choose Extras • Copy configuration from TPPARAM.
6. Choose Save and, as described in Chapter 8, distribute these changes to all systems in the transport domain.

7.3.2 Profile Syntax

The parameters specified in the transport profile and their syntax are valid for both TPPARAM and TP_<domain>.PFL. The syntax for TP__<domain>.PFL corresponds to how it is represented at the operating system level; In the SAP ERP system, the parameters are represented as shown in Figure 7.4.

As of Basis Release 4.5, the transport profile parameters are generated automatically. You do not need to set up the transport profile parameters for a minimum configuration; you can maintain and add them using TMS.

Parameter Types

Comment lines are preceded by # in the transport profile. All other lines contain parameter definitions, which can be any of the following:

- **Global**
  Valid for all SAP systems in the transport domain
- **SAP system-specific**
  Valid only for one SAP system
- **Operating system-specific**
  Valid for all systems running a specific operating system
- **Database-specific**
  Valid for all systems on a specific database platform

Table 7.1 shows the syntax for the different parameter types in the transport profile.

<table>
<tr><th>Parameter Types</th><th>Syntax</th><th>Possible Acronyms</th></tr>
<tr><td>Global</td><td><parameter>=<value></td><td></td></tr>
<tr><td>System-specific</td><td><SID>/<parameter>=<value></td><td></td></tr>
<tr><td>Operating system-specific</td><td><CPU>|<parameter>=<value></td><td>aix, axp (Open VMS), hp-ux, osf1, sinix, sunos, wnt (Windows), as4 (AS/400)</td></tr>
<tr><td>Database-specific</td><td><DB>:<parameter>=<value></td><td>ora (Oracle), inf (Informix), ada (MaxDB), mss (MS SQL Server), db2 (DB2 for OS390), db4 (DB2/400), db6 (DB2 for AIX)</td></tr>
</table>

Table 7.1 Profile Syntax

If a parameter is not specified, the default value is used. SAP recommends grouping global settings at the beginning of the transport profile, because in general, the last setting for a given SAP system, operating system, or database overrides previous settings.

Predefined variables

Predefined variables can be used as part of the parameter values of the transport profile. They have the format `$(<variable-name>)`. If required, the brackets may be masked with a backslash (\). Table 7.2 lists all possible predefined variables.

Variable	Description	Possible values
`$(cpu)`	CPU name (important in heterogeneous system landscapes)	alphaosf, hp, rm600, rs6000 sun, wnt, as4
`$(cpu2)`	Acronym for the operating system	aix, hp-ux, osf1, sinix, sunos, wnt
`$(dname)`	Abbreviation for the day of the week	SUN, MON, ...
`$(mday)`	Day of the current month	01 to 31
`$(mname)`	Abbreviation for the name of the month	JAN, FEB, ...
`$(mon)`	Month	01 to 12
`$(system)`	System identifier (SID) of the SAP system	For example, PRD
`$(wday)`	Day of the week	00 to 06 (Sunday = 00)
`$(yday)`	Day of the current year	001 to 366
`$(year)`	Year	For example, 1999
`$(syear)`	Short form of the year	For example, 99
`$(yweek)`	Calendar week	00 to 53

Table 7.2 Predefined Variables

Example: Using Predefined Variables

Transport parameter `syslog` specifies the file `SLOG` that is used to monitor the transport activities of a specific SAP system.

The file is stored in subdirectory `log` of the transport directory and contains a general overview of performed imports. The name of this log file can be set in the transport profile using `syslog` as a global parameter. The default setting for the parameter `syslog` is `SLOG<year><week>.<SID>`.

The appropriate configuration is as follows:

- The parameter type for `syslog` is set to `global`.
- The parameter is set using predefined variables to `SLOG$(syear)$(yweek).$(system)`.

In week 31 of year 2008, this configuration instructs the system to log anything written to the file `SLOG` in the SAP system QAS to a file called `SLOG0531.QAS`.

Table 7.3 contains the additional predefined variables available on Windows platforms.

Variable	Description
`$(SAPGLOBALHOST)`	Points to the host on which the central instance is installed.
`$(SAPTRANSHOST)`	Points to the transport host.

Table 7.3 Additional variables for Windows

7.3.3 Required Parameters

As of Release 4.5, the required parameters are automatically set during the setup of TMS. They are described in this section. For information on additional uses of these parameters and other transport profile parameters, see Chapter 14 and Appendix A.

Database Parameters

Database-specific parameters in the transport profile enable the transport control program `tp` to access the databases. The following parameters are required.

dbhost

For each SAP system within the transport group, configure the parameter dbhost (system-specific). This parameter specifies the host name—that is, the computer on which the database runs or, valid for Oracle and DB2 on AIX, on which the database processes run.

[+] On Windows platforms ensure that you use the TCP/IP computer host name as the value for parameter dbhost.

dbname

Parameter dbname is used to specify the name of the database instance. Typically, the parameter is realized as a global parameter, and the value is specified using the variable $(system). The transport parameter dbname passes over the name of the database, for which tp is called.

[+] Note that parameter dbname is case sensitive on Informix platforms. For SAP DB as well as for DB2, this parameter has to be changed from lowercase to uppercase after the installation.

Exceptions are DB2/400 platforms and standard SAP installations on Oracle platforms. Standard installations use the name of the system for the name of the database instance and for the logical name of the database in the network. On these platforms, you do not need to specify parameter dbname.

Additional database parameters

Depending on your database platform, you must also set additional parameters, as listed in Table 7.4.

Platform	Parameter	Value
SAP MaxDB	dbuserkey	Name of the SAP instance
DB2/400 (only if opticonnect is used)	opticonnect	1

Table 7.4 Additional Parameters for Database Platforms

[+] For information on transport profile parameters required for a DB2 database on OS/390, see SAP Note 77589.

Path-Specific Parameters

The parameters that ensure that the tools involved in the transport process use the correct paths are as follows:

- transdir
- DIR_TRANS
- r3transpath

The transport parameters transdir and r3transpath are specified in the transport profile. DIR_TRANS must be set in the instance profile.

The parameter transdir is located in the transport profile and specifies the name of the transport directory for tp as it has been mounted on all hosts of a transport group. transdir

To set this parameter in a noncomplex landscape that has no special requirements (such as special security demands), proceed as follows:

1. Set the parameter transdir as a *global* parameter. It cannot be set *system-specific* or *database-specific*, but can be set as *operating system-specific*.
2. Set transdir identical for all SAP systems within a single transport group.
3. Set the default values as listed for the respective platforms in Table 7.5.

In heterogeneous operating system environments, set the parameter transdir to operating system-specific. For example, wnt|transdir = \\trans02\trans\ specifies that for all Windows systems, the transport directory can be found on the host trans02 in the directory trans. [+]

Platform	Value for transdir
Unix	/usr/sap/trans
AS/400	/usr/sap/trans
Windows (if you have configured a central transport host with alias SAPTRANSHOST)	\\(SAPTRANSHOST)\sapmnt\trans
Windows (without a central transport host)	\\<transport host>\sapmnt\trans

Table 7.5 Operating System-Specific Values for transdir

DIR_TRANS

The parameter DIR_TRANS is located in the instance profile. As with transdir, it points to the transport directory and is used by several programs, such as the kernel. Whenever the operating system transport tool tp is called from the SAP system, the value of transdir is overridden with the value of DIR_TRANS.

[+] The transport parameters transdir and DIR_TRANS should always point to the same directory.

Example: Parameters transdir and DIR_TRANS with Unix

Figure 7.6 illustrates how the transport directory is accessed using the parameters transdir and DIR_TRANS on a Unix platform.

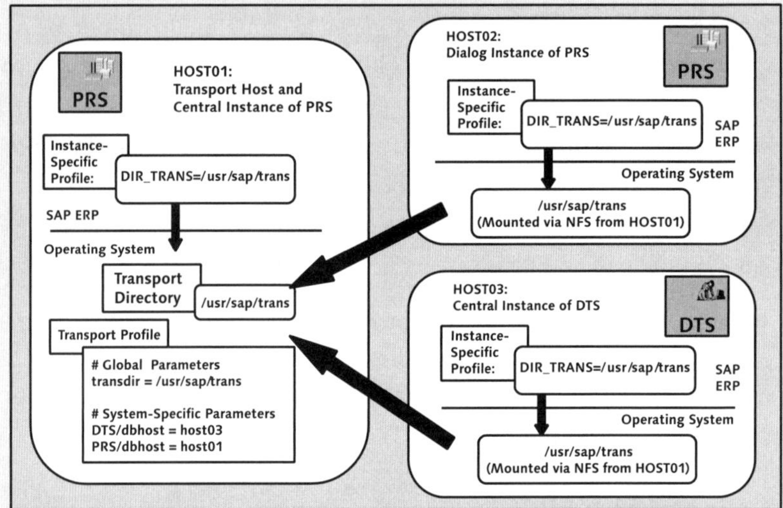

Figure 7.6 Accessing a Transport Directory for a Unix Platform with transdir and DIR_TRANS

This landscape consists of two SAP systems: the development-and-test system DTS and the production system PRS. DTS consists of a central instance (host03). PRS consists of a central instance (host01) and a dialog instance (host02). DTS and PRS share the same transport directory that is stored on host01 in the transport directory /usr/sap/trans. In the instance profiles of all instances, the parameter DIR_TRANS is set to /usr/sap/trans. This directory is mounted on host02 and host03 using NFS.

DIR_TRANS for Windows

In Windows environments, parameter DIR_TRANS points by default to directory \\$(SAPGLOBALHOST)\sapmnt\trans. If you have configured a transport host—that is, specified the alias SAPTRANSHOST on the domain name server—you must set the value of DIR_TRANS to \\(SAPTRANSHOST)\sapmnt\trans.

If you have chosen a path that is different from the one specified by the share \sapmnt\trans, you must set parameter DIR_TRANS explicitly using the alias $(SAPTRANSHOST). For example:

```
DIR_TRANS = \\$(SAPTRANSHOST)\transport
```

Another way of defining the access path to the transport directory is to set the transport host specified in the domain name server to be overridden locally. This is recommended if all systems require a private transport directory. To cause the transport path stored in the domain name server to be overridden, add the following line to the directory Winnt\system32\drivers\etc\hosts:

```
<IP address of private transport host> <TCP/IP name of private
transport host> SAPTRANSHOST
```

For example:

```
10.16.162.61      twdfmx05      SAPTRANSHOST
```

The entry in the file hosts has to end with a blank line. Keep in mind that the hierarchy governing which parameter value is determinant is as follows:

1. DIR_TRANS in the instance profile
2. Value of SAPTRANSHOST of the local hosts file
3. Value of SAPTRANSHOST of the domain name server

For example, DIR_TRANS will override SAPTRANSHOST.

[+]

When maintaining DIR_TRANS in the instance profile, you can also maintain parameter DIR_EPS_ROOT. This parameter points to transport directory's eps subdirectory, which is used to deliver SAP Support Packages (see Chapter 17).

Example: Parameters transdir and DIR_TRANS with Windows

Figure 7.7 shows an example of how the transport directory is accessed in a three-system landscape on Windows.

The landscape consists of the development system DEV on host01, the quality assurance system QAS on host02, and the production system PRD on host03. DEV and QAS share the same transport directory, whereas PRD has its own private transport directory due to special security demands.

Host01 is the physical location of the transport directory (`c:\usr\sap\trans`) shared by system DEV with system QAS. Directory `c:\usr\sap` on host01 is shared as `sapmnt`. DEV is also the domain name server of the Window domain, on which alias SAPTRANSHOST is set to host01.

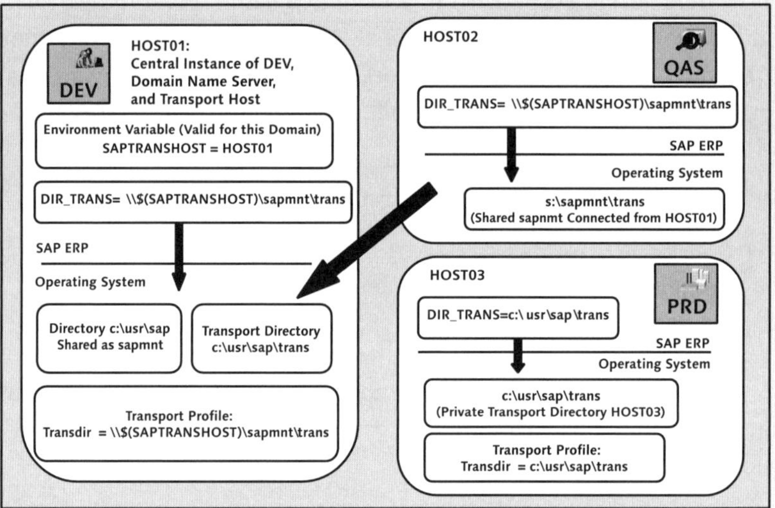

Figure 7.7 Accessing a Transport Directory in a Three-System Landscape on Windows

The instance profiles of DEV and QAS contain parameter `DIR_TRANS`, which is set to `\\$(SAPTRANSHOST)\sapmnt\trans`. Therefore, for both DEV and QAS, the parameters `DIR_TRANS` and `transdir` point to directory `c:\usr\sap\trans` on host01. Because PRD has its own private transport directory, both `DIR_TRANS` and `transdir` point to the private transport directory `c:\usr\sap\trans` on host03.

r3transpath Parameter `r3transpath` specifies which platform-specific version of `R3trans` is used by `tp`. The default value—`R3trans` for Unix and AS/400 platforms and R3trans.exe for Windows platforms—usually works. No explicit path is given. The path relies on the correct path definition of the user starting tp. If problems arise, and for heterogeneous environments, make sure the specification is correct. Set the value for parameter r3transpath as described in Table 7.6.

If the system landscape consists of SAP systems running on different database platforms, you must set the parameter to *system-specific* or *operating system-specific* to use different platform-specific versions of R3trans.

Platform	Parameter Specification	Value
Unix, AS/400	r3transpath	R3trans
Windows	Wnt|r3transpath	R3trans.exe

Table 7.6 Specification of r3transpath

[+] See SAP Note 83327 for more information on transporting in a heterogeneous environment.

Parameters for a Heterogeneous Environment with both Windows and Unix

If a transport group includes systems running on Windows and systems running on Unix, additional settings are required.

For systems running on Windows, perform the following steps:

1. Set binary mode as the default mode for opening a file for tp.exe and R3trans.exe:
   - Set the parameter ababntfmode in the transport profile to b.
   - Set the instance profile parameter bap/Ntfmode to b.
2. Make the following entries to the transport profile. Note that all of these entries are platform-specific for Windows and, with the exception of parameter transdir, are also specific to a certain SAP ERP system:
   - wnt|transdir = <path to the transport directory>
   - wnt|<SID>/r3transpath=\\<WINDOWSHOST>\sapmnt\<SID>\sys\exe\run\R3trans.exe

- wnt|<SID>/sapevtpath=\\<WINDOWSHOST>\sapmnt\<SID>\sys\exe\run\sapevt.exe
- wnt|<SID>/system_pf=\\<WINDOWSHOST>\sapmnt\<SID>\sys\profile\default.pfl

3. Maintain parameter DIR_TRANS (and also DIR_EPS_ROOT) correctly in all instance profiles.

[+] On Windows platforms, the transport profile TPPARAM is edited with SAP's editor SAPPAD, which is stored as sappad.exe in the SAP executable directory \usr\sap\<SID>\SYS\exe\run. SAPPAD lets you save the settings using the Unix formatting option.

7.4 Activities within SAP ERP

After installation, the following activities from within SAP ERP are required to set up transport capabilities:

- Initializing the Change and Transport Organizer (CTO)
- Setting the system change option
- Verifying the background jobs and background work processes required for transports

Keep in mind that there are different types of "SAP installations," and that how you perform the transport-related tasks described in this section will vary according to which type of SAP installation you are working on. These installation types include:

Installation types

- **Standard SAP installation**
  A standard SAP installation is installed from the SAP CDs using the program R3setup.
- **System upgrade**
  A system upgrade uses SAP CDs and the program R3up to upgrade an existing system release to a higher system release—for example, from SAP R/3 Release 4.6C to SAP ERP 6.0. (See Chapter 18.)
- **System copy**
  A *system copy* or *database copy* as a method for creating a new system was discussed in Chapter 5. The tools for creating system copies

depend on the database and the operating system platform, as well as the demand for migrating the system from one platform to another.

Unlike a standard SAP installation or a release upgrade, a system copy requires you to manage entities carried over from the source system, such as:

- Clients
- Customizing data, application data, and user master data
- Open tasks or change requests
- The system name (SID) for customer-developed Repository objects that remain owned by the source system

7.4.1 Initializing the Change and Transport Organizer (CTO)

After an installation by system copy, you must manually initialize the Change and Transport Organizer (CTO) with Transaction SE06. This causes the SID of the system to be stored in the appropriate database table, and establishes the initial value of the serial ID-number for change requests. This initialization is not required for a standard SAP installation, because when configuring TMS (see Chapter 8), it automatically checks whether the CTO has been initialized, and, if not, initializes it.

To initialize the CTO manually, perform the following steps:

Manually initializing CTO

1. Log on to your system.
2. Call Transaction SE06.
3. Select DATABASE COPY OR MIGRATION if the SAP ERP system is the result of a system copy.
4. To initialize the CTO, select EXECUTE.

[+] To use Transaction SE06, you need the administration authorization S_CTS_ADMIN that is found in the authorization profile S_A.SYSTEM.

When initializing the CTO using Transaction SE06 and selecting DATABASE COPY OR MIGRATION, Transaction SE06 not only initializes the CTO, it also provides functionality to handle change requests that have been copied into the new system. (Such change requests are not an issue for standard installations, because the SAP-delivered system contains no carryover change requests.) Change requests that have been copied into the new system may cause problems when you upgrade or modify objects. The following activities take place:

- Initializing the control tables for change requests and the release upgrade process.
- Detecting and listing all open tasks and change requests that existed in the originating system—including modifications—that are changes to the SAP standard. You will want to release these open tasks and change requests to delete the locks on the corresponding objects. For documentation purposes, these change requests remain recorded in the new system with the status RELEASED.
- Enabling you to decide whether the customer-developed Repository objects belonging to open change requests should be made original objects in the target system. If so, the original system for these objects, which are still "owned" by the source system after a system copy, is changed to the current system (see Chapter 10).

[+] For information on Repository object locks after a system copy, see SAP Note 62519.

7.4.2 Setting the Global System Change Option

The global system change option for each SAP system determines whether Repository objects and client-independent (cross-client) Customizing objects can be changed. To set the system change option, follow these steps:

1. Call Transaction SE06 and choose SYSTEM CHANGE OPTION.
2. In the SYSTEM CHANGE OPTION screen, choose GLOBAL SETTING.
3. In the dialog box, choose either MODIFIABLE or NOT MODIFIABLE.

The development system should be the only system within your system landscape in which changes to objects are allowed. From the development system, you can transport the changes into the other systems of your landscape.

[+] For the quality assurance system and the production system, SAP strongly recommends setting the global system change option to NOT MODIFIABLE.

After setting the system change option to MODIFIABLE, from the SYSTEM CHANGE OPTION screen, you can determine which specific namespaces and name ranges can be modified. After selecting or deselecting for specific namespaces or name ranges, select MODIFIABLE, RESTRICTED MODIFIABLE, or NOT MODIFIABLE.

[+] If you set the option for a namespace or name range to NOT MODIFIABLE, you cannot change the objects in this namespace or name range, even if the global system change option is set to MODIFIABLE.

Figure 7.8 shows the system change settings for a development system DEV. The global system change option is set to MODIFIABLE — this is indicated by the GLOBAL SETTING message: REPOSITORY AND CLIENT-INDEPENDENT CUSTOMIZING CAN BE CHANGED. Below this message, the column MODIFIABLE indicates the objects in certain namespaces and name ranges that can be changed.

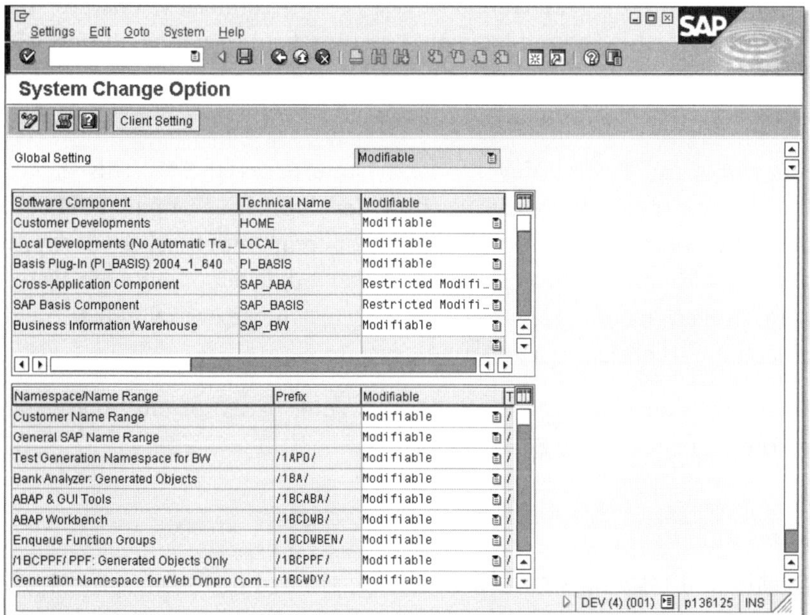

Figure 7.8 Global System Change Option and Namespace and Name Range Change Option

[+] Resetting MODIFIABLE for a namespace or a name range prevents changes in a specific namespace or name range, even though changes are permitted globally.

When you save your changes to these settings, the new setting, date, time, and responsible user are logged. To display the log file, from the SYSTEM CHANGE OPTION screen, choose LOG.

In addition to the global change option and the change option for namespaces and name ranges, you can also set change options on a client basis (see Chapter 9).

Namespaces

A *namespace* is specified by a character set and a permitted name length. All names that match these criteria belong to the corresponding namespace. For example, the namespace for programs covers all strings with up to 30 alphanumeric characters. Technically, a namespace is implemented by a template—that is, by a field in which all possible names can be entered. This field has a defined length and an integrated validation to check for allowed characters.

Customers can reserve development namespaces at SAP. This makes sense for customers who have a central development group that delivers developments to subsidiaries, as well as for companies that commercially develop add-ons for SAP customers. A reserved development namespace helps prevent naming clashes that can occur when externally developed objects are imported to a given SAP system.

[+] For more information on development namespaces for customers and partners, see SAP Note 84282.

Name Ranges

A *name range* is a subset—that is, an interval within a namespace. Each object type in the repository has both an SAP name range and a customer name range. The SAP name range is reserved for objects delivered by SAP. Within the customer name range, customers can create and develop their own objects. The names reserved for customer objects typically start with "Y" or "Z."

[+] For more information on the customer name range, see SAP Note 16466.

All customer developments must be made in the customer name range or in a customer namespace. This prevents customer developments from being overwritten during a release upgrade. Objects in the SAP name range should not be changed unless to apply corrections of known errors in accordance with SAP Notes if a corresponding SAP Support Package is not yet available (see Chapter 17).

Example: Namespaces and Name Ranges

Software object names such as program names are assigned to a namespace when preceded by a prefix placed between slashes: `/<prefix>/<object name>`. This makes it possible to have objects with the same name belong to different namespaces. Consider, for example, the object name `ZABAP`. The "Z" indicates that it belongs to the customer name range. Within the SAP training organization's namespace, there is another ZABAP program, which is distinguished from the customer report by being called /SAPTRAIN/ZABAP.

7.4.3 Verifying Required Background Jobs

To control the transport process, the transport control program `tp` requires various operating system programs and SAP programs to run in the background. To run these programs in the background, the *transport dispatcher* `RDDIMPDP` must be scheduled as a periodic background job in each respective client. These jobs are named `RDDIMPDP_CLIENT_<nnn>`, where `nnn` specifies the client. They are automatically scheduled for all delivered standard clients or after a client copy for customer-created clients. The background jobs are scheduled *event-periodic*. They start to run as soon as they receive a certain event.

RDDIMPDP jobs correct?

To help avoid transport problems, check whether the `RDDIMPDP` jobs are running by using the following procedure:

1. Use Transaction code SM37. Alternatively, from the SAP ERP initial screen, choose TOOLS • CCMS • JOBS • MAINTENANCE.
2. In the SELECT BACKGROUND JOBS screen, enter "RDDIMPDP*" in the JOB NAME field. Enter "*" in the USER field and in the OR START AFTER EVENT field.

3. To display a list of the jobs that match the search criteria, press Enter. The RDDIMPDP jobs should appear in the list.

An alternative way of checking whether the RDDIMPDP jobs are running is to call tp at the operating system level with the following command:

```
tp checkimpdp <SID of the SAP system>
```

If, for any reason, you must schedule RDDIMPDP manually, you can do so by running program RDDNEWPP. To run this program, log on to the system using the DDIC user or another user with the same authorizations, and call the ABAP Editor in the respective client using Transaction code SE38. Or, in the SAP ERP initial screen, in the SAP Easy Access menu, select Tools • ABAP Workbench • ABAP Editor. In the field program, enter "RDDNEWPP" and choose Execute.

[+] For more information on the transport dispatcher RDDIMPDP, see Chapter 14.

7.4.4 Verifying Background Work Processes

All systems from which data will be exported and/or imported require at least two background work processes to support the RDDIMPDP jobs. When importing changes into an SAP system, the import dispatcher RDDIMPDP is triggered by tp and occupies one background work process. Depending on the type of objects to be imported, other background jobs need to run and are scheduled by the dispatcher. To guarantee that RDDIMPDP can monitor the status of the specific job runs, at least two free background work processes are needed.

7.5 Questions

1. **The SAP system ID (SID):**
   A. Must be unique for each system sharing the same transport directory
   B. Must be unique for each system in the system landscape
   C. Can start with a number
   D. Can consist of any three-character combination

2. **Which of the following statements is correct with regard to the transport directory?**
   A. There can be only one transport directory in a system landscape.
   B. All SAP systems within a transport group share a common transport directory.
   C. In system landscapes using heterogeneous platforms, it is not possible to have a common transport directory.
   D. Only the production system can contain the transport directory.
3. **Which of the following statements are correct with regard to the transport control program `tp`?**
   A. It is stored in subdirectory `bin` of the transport directory.
   B. It uses program `R3trans` to access the databases when transporting changes.
   C. It cannot be used directly at the operating system level.
   D. It depends on the settings of the transport profile.
4. **The transport profile:**
   A. Is stored in subdirectory `bin` of the transport directory
   B. Contains comments and parameter settings that configure the transport control program `tp`
   C. Is managed from within TMS as of R/3 Release 4.5, but is modified with operating system text editors in earlier releases
   D. Contains only settings that are valid for all SAP systems in the system landscape
5. **The initialization procedure of the CTO:**
   A. Is especially required after a system copy
   B. Establishes the initial value for change request IDs
   C. Is not mandatory to enable transports
   D. Is performed automatically during SAP installation by program `R3setup`

6. **Which of the following statements is correct with regard to the settings governing changes to Repository objects?**

   A. Only the customer name range should be modifiable in production systems.

   B. Developments are possible in an SAP system only if you have applied for a development namespace.

   C. If the global change option is set to NOT MODIFIABLE, it is nevertheless possible to make changes in certain name spaces or clients that have their change option set to MODIFIABLE.

   D. The global change option should always be set to NOT MODIFIABLE for the quality assurance system and the production system.

To facilitate work in change management, SAP has developed its own Transport Management System. It includes comprehensive adaptation options with regard to customer requirements to provide the desired changes for the system landscape.

8 Setting Up the TMS

After installing SAP ERP, to enable change requests to be transported in your system landscape, you need to configure the Transport Management System (TMS). This chapter introduces the setup of the TMS and describes how to configure it using the following steps:

- Creating the transport domain
- Configuring transport routes
- Verifying the system landscape setup

This chapter also explains how to change the TMS configuration when adding more SAP systems, changing the role of an SAP system, or upgrading to a new release. It is targeted at people looking for general information about the TMS, as well as system administrators and technical consultants responsible for setting up the system landscape. If you are involved in development and Customizing, you will also want to familiarize yourself with TMS concepts and terminology.

This chapter does not outline the TMS functionality for performing transport activities, such as importing change requests. If you are responsible for transporting change requests, you should refer to Part 3 of this book.

8.1 TMS Terminology and Concepts

The TMS lets system administrators and technical consultants centrally manage the transport configuration of multiple SAP systems by using a transport domain and defining transport routes. The TMS offers easy to use configuration tools to set up a transport domain and to set up and maintain transport routes.

[+] Aside from enabling global transport maintenance and configuration, the TMS also provides a user interface for the transport tools at the operating system level. It allows you to view change requests for ABAP that are waiting for import and to perform and monitor the respective imports from within the SAP system (see also Chapter 13).

SAP introduced the TMS in SAP ERP Release 3.1H, and its use became mandatory for ABAP-based SAP systems as of R/3 Release 4.0.

8.1.1 Transport Domain

All SAP systems you plan to manage centrally using the TMS form a *transport domain*. Within a transport domain, all SAP systems must have unique system IDs, and the transport routes and associated settings are identical for all SAP ERP systems.

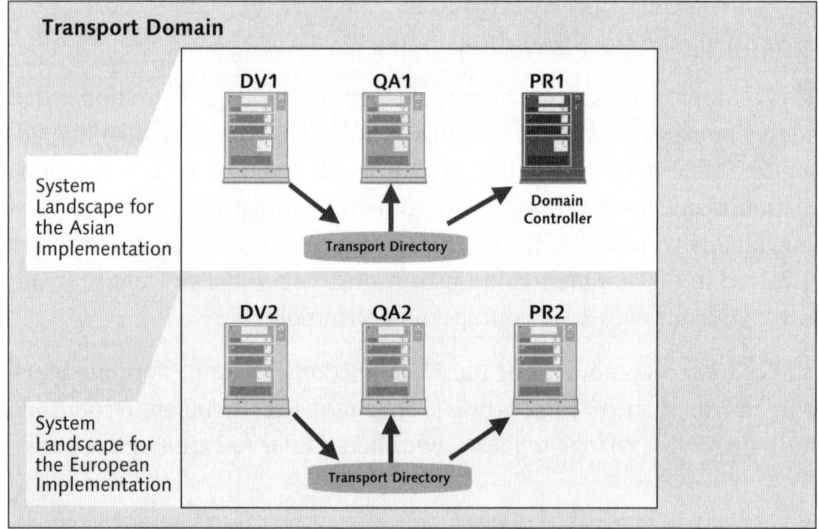

Figure 8.1 Transport Domain Including Two System Landscapes

The system landscape is the set of all SAP systems required to take your implementation from the development stages through to production.

Typically, your system landscape and your transport domain will contain the same SAP systems. However, you can have several system landscapes in one transport domain—centrally managed using the TMS. Figure 8.1 shows the transport domain of a multinational company that consists of two separate three-system landscapes, one for Asia and one for Europe. Both are managed centrally by system PR1.

Transport Domain Controller

One of the great benefits of the TMS is the centralized configuration of the entire transport environment. One of the SAP systems in the transport domain holds the reference configuration, and all of the other SAP systems hold copies of this configuration. The SAP system with the reference configuration is called the *transport domain controller*— in Figure 8.1, for example, this is system PR1.

From the transport domain controller, you can manage the entire TMS configuration—that is, the configuration of all included SAP ERP systems, their roles, and their interrelationships. The centralized administration of the TMS ensures consistency throughout the transport domain.

Within a transport domain, each SAP system can communicate with all other SAP systems through RFC connections that are generated when the TMS is configured. The transport domain controller, for example, uses RFC connections to distribute configuration changes to all other SAP systems in the transport domain.

Backup Domain Controller

To manage SAP systems and transport routes, every system landscape requires a transport domain controller. In addition, another SAP ERP system in the transport domain should be designated as the *backup domain controller* (see Figure 8.2). The backup domain controller lets you perform necessary configuration changes to the transport domain when the transport domain controller is unavailable—for example, when that SAP system is not running. In such cases, the backup domain controller can take over the role of the domain controller, and configuration changes to the transport domain can be made.

However, even if the transport domain controller is unavailable, you can use RFC links to perform transport activities such as viewing import queues and initiating imports from any SAP system in the transport domain. The domain controller is required only for configuration changes to the transport domain.

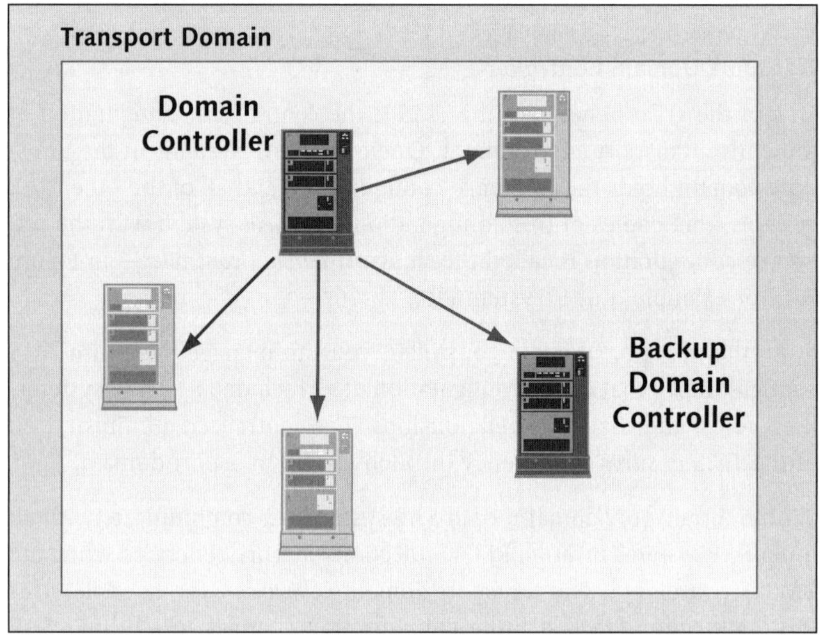

Figure 8.2 Central Administration from the Transport Domain Controller or the Backup Domain Controller

Transport Groups and Transport Domains

A transport group is a collection of SAP systems that share the same transport directory (see Chapter 7). It is a technical and physical setup because the involved SAP systems access a common transport directory. Rather than being a physical unit, a transport domain is purely an administrative unit for the TMS.

A transport domain may consist of several transport groups. However, it typically consists of only one transport group and involves only one common transport directory. Even when multiple transport groups are required (see Chapter 7), all SAP systems in the transport domain are managed centrally, regardless of whether they share the same transport directory.

Figure 8.3 shows a more complicated transport domain composed of five SAP systems and two different transport groups. The transport domain controller manages the transport configuration of all five SAP systems. The transport routes that determine the flow of change requests are not shown in Figure 8.3. All SAP systems that regularly need to share change requests must be part of the same transport domain (but not necessarily the same transport group). To define transport routes, you first must establish the transport domain and transport groups.

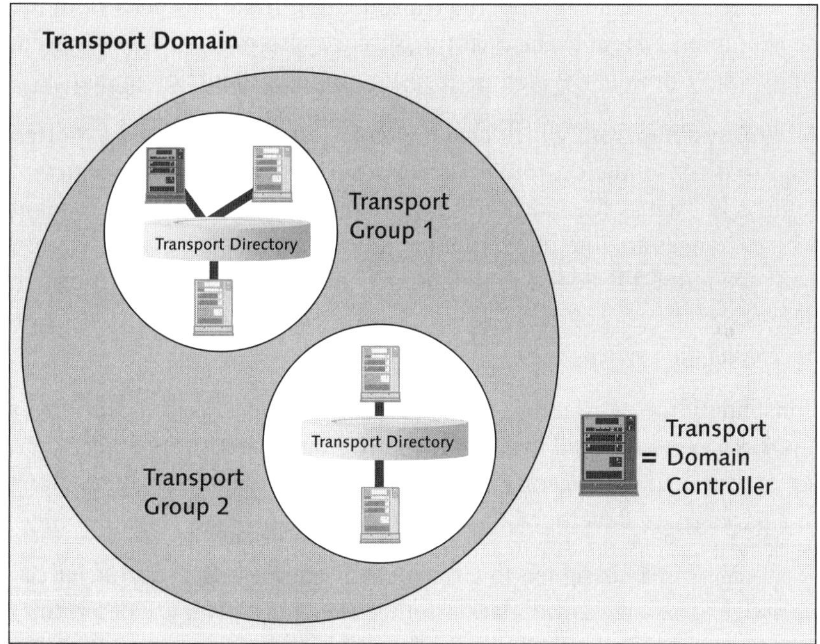

Figure 8.3 A Transport Domain with Two Transport Groups

8.1.2 Transport Routes

The terms *transport domain*, *domain controller*, and *transport group* concern only the physical environment. They do not include the transport relationship between the SAP systems, which is defined by transport routes. Transport routes are used to indicate the role of each system and the flow of change requests. SAP distinguishes between two types of transport routes:

- Consolidation route
- Delivery route

Consolidation Route

A consolidation route defines the path (the successive SAP systems or clients) that is followed by change requests immediately after their release. The consolidation route is used to accumulate the customer changes that have been integrated with the standard software. Typically, in a standard three-system landscape, the consolidation route proceeds from the development system to the quality assurance system, or, in a two-system landscape, from the development system to the production system.

All SAP systems from which change requests are released and exported require a consolidation route. Such a source system in a consolidation route is known as the *integration system* because it provides the point at which changes are integrated into the SAP system. At the time of export, a change request is added to the import queue of the target SAP system defined by the consolidation route. The target system assumes the role of *consolidation system*.

Packages and transport layers

Consolidation routes are closely associated with *packages* and *transport layers*. Packages are used to group logically related Repository objects, and act as containers to organize development work. All objects that belong to a package are developed, maintained, and transported together.

A package can be assigned to a transport layer. Each transport layer can be assigned to one consolidation route. The transport layer determines which consolidation route is valid for all objects of a package. Packages and transport layers let you specify a consolidation route for each Repository object. A consolidation route is defined by an integration system and a consolidation system and is associated with a specific transport layer.

[+] For information on using packages and transport layers, see Chapter 10.

Standard transport layer

Because all Customizing changes must follow the same consolidation route, a *standard transport layer* is specified for each integration system. The standard transport layer is used to transport changes that have no concept of a transport layer, unlike Repository objects that belong to a package. Assigning a standard transport layer to a consolidation route enables all Customizing changes made in the development system to be transported to the quality assurance system. A standard transport layer is a system attribute of integration systems.

[+]

Transport routes can include not just SAP systems but also clients. Client-dependent changes do not always need to be transported using the standard transport layer, but can be transported using a client-specific transport route (see Section 8.3.3) if the respective transport layer has been assigned to the client.

For each integration system, at least two transport layers are defined: the standard transport layer and the SAP transport layer (see below). There may also be several other transport layers. Each transport layer may have several development classes assigned to it. Although an integration system can be the source system for several consolidation routes, each consolidation route has exactly one transport layer assigned to it.

SAP transport layer

The SAP transport layer is the predefined transport layer for the packages of all standard SAP objects. To modify standard objects in the SAP ERP system and then transport them along the same routes as development and Customizing changes, a consolidation route is assigned to the SAP transport layer. When setting up transport routes using the standard transport route configuration options, the consolidation route is generated automatically (see Section 8.3.1, Standard Configurations).

Delivery Route

Delivery routes are used to transport changes from the consolidation system to additional SAP systems. They are required only in a system landscape that consists of more than two SAP systems. In the standard three-system landscape, for example, a delivery route is specified between the quality assurance system and the production system. This enables changes to be transported to the production system after they have been tested and verified in the quality assurance system.

After change requests have been imported to the quality assurance system, a defined delivery route causes the change requests to be added to the import queue of the next SAP system in the system landscape, the production system. While consolidation routes dictate which SAP system receives the change request at export, a delivery route determines which SAP system receives the change request after successful import. The definition of a delivery route specifies a source system and a target system.

8.2 Setting Up the Transport Domain

To set up a transport domain, first determine which systems should be included in the transport domain. This domain should contain all systems in your system landscape and any other SAP systems that will be managed centrally using the TMS. One of these systems must be designated as the transport domain controller. You may later switch the role of domain controller to a different system, but during the implementation process, the first SAP system for which the TMS is initialized is automatically designated as the transport domain controller.

[+] To set up the transport domain, you require the S_A.SYSTEM authorization profile.

Figure 8.4 shows the components of a standard configuration. The transport domain includes system DEV as the development system, system QAS as the quality assurance system, and system PRD as the production system. DEV is designated as the transport domain controller. All systems use a common transport directory and thus form a single transport group.

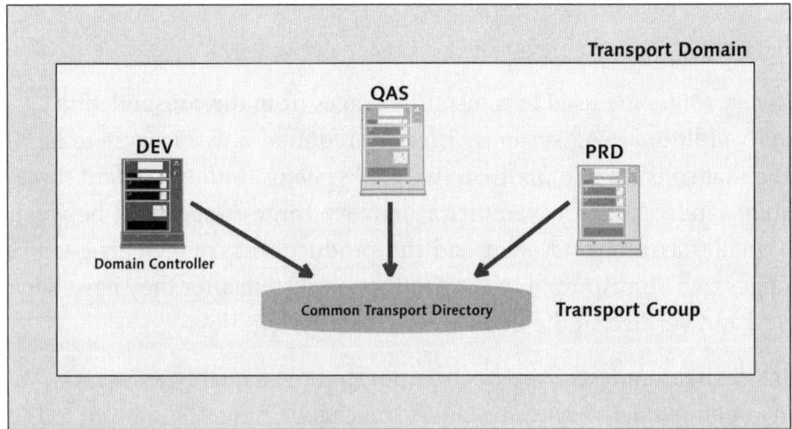

Figure 8.4 Example of a Transport Domain

8.2.1 Setting Up the Domain Controller

Within a transport domain, the transport domain configuration—that is, the included systems, their roles, and the configured transport routes—is identical for all systems. The transport domain controller stores the reference domain configuration. All other systems in the transport domain have copies of this configuration. The advantage of the centralized administration of the transport domain is that it ensures consistency.

The development system is often initially designated as the transport domain controller, because the TMS must be set up to store the released development and Customizing requests in the import queues of the other systems that have not yet been installed.

Because the transport domain controller must provide high levels of system availability, security precautions, and maintenance, it is often subsequently moved to the production or quality assurance system. The system load generated by TMS configuration activities on a domain controller is very low. The system load increases only briefly when the TMS configuration is changed.

Initializing the TMS

When using the TMS for the first time after system installation, you are automatically prompted to initialize it. To initialize the TMS for an SAP system, proceed as follows:

1. Log on to the SAP system you have designated as the transport domain controller in client 000 with a user ID that possesses transport authorization profile S_A.SYSTEM, such as user SAP*.
2. Use Transaction code STMS or, from the SAP Easy Access menu, choose TOOLS • ADMINISTRATION • TRANSPORTS • TRANSPORT MANAGEMENT SYSTEM.
3. When starting the TMS for the first time, the dialog box shown in Figure 8.5 appears and prompts you for values to create the new domain. For example, because the development system DEV is declared the transport domain controller in Figure 8.5, DOMAIN_DEV is suggested as the transport domain name.

4. You can accept the proposed name or enter a different name. Type a short description and choose ENTER. Subsequently changing the name of a transport domain requires deleting the TMS configuration and reconfiguring it—for all SAP systems in the transport domain. Only the short description can be easily changed at any time.

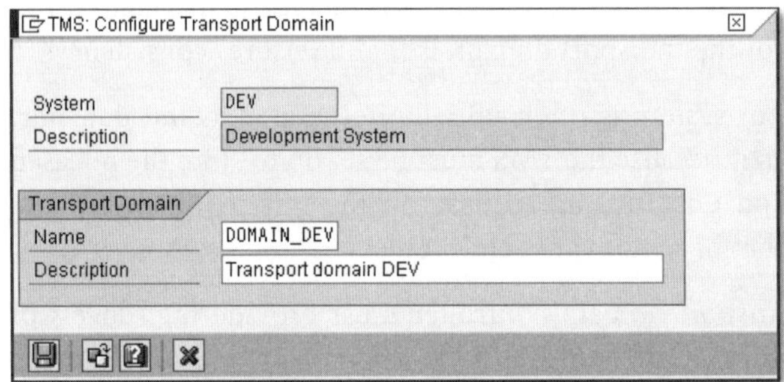

Figure 8.5 The Dialog Box that Appears When You First Use the TMS in a Transport Domain

[+] The first system of a transport group from which the TMS is called is automatically designated as the transport domain controller.

Initializing the TMS has several effects on an SAP system (see Section 8.2.5, Technical Aspects of the Configuration Process). During initialization, the basic settings of the TMS configuration are stored in file `DOMAIN.CFG` in subdirectory `bin` of the transport directory on the transport domain controller. These settings include the transport domain name, the transport domain description, and the system IDs (SIDs) of all SAP systems in the transport domain. After you install an additional SAP system that shares the same transport directory as the domain controller, the new SAP system reads the already established configuration out of file `DOMAIN.CFG` and automatically recognizes to which domain the new system belongs.

After initializing the TMS, the TMS initial screen indicates which transport domain contains the transport domain controller. Assuming your system landscape consists of only one SAP system at this point, if you now choose OVERVIEW • SYSTEMS from the TMS initial screen, you will see that the transport domain controller is currently the only system belonging to the transport domain.

To obtain detailed information on an SAP system, proceed as follows:

Information via the system

1. From the TMS initial screen, choose SYSTEMS.
2. Input a system name and choose ENTER.
3. The DISPLAY THE TMS CONFIGURATION: SYSTEM <SID> screen appears, providing you with details about the selected system. For example, on the COMMUNICATION DATA tab, you can see that the system is not only assigned to the transport domain, but also to a transport group with the default name `GROUP.<domain controller SID>`. The screen also shows the generated address information used for communication between the different SAP systems in the transport domain (see Section 8.2.5).

8.2.2 Extending the Transport Domain

When other SAP systems that will be part of an existing domain are ready for inclusion in the transport domain, you can extend the transport domain by adding these SAP systems.

Extending a transport domain is not restricted to physically installed SAP systems. Virtual systems are often included as placeholders for planned systems and are replaced by the planned systems after they are implemented. In addition, you can extend the transport domain to include external systems—for example, an SAP system from another transport domain.

New SAP Systems

To add new systems to a transport domain, you must perform configuration activities on both the new SAP system and the transport domain controller. After you add systems to a transport domain, you should designate one SAP system as the backup domain controller.

Requesting the inclusion of an SAP system of an existing transport group

To add a new SAP system to a transport domain from within the same transport group, you must perform the TMS initialization process on the new system. Proceed as follows:

1. Log on to the new SAP system in client 000 using user identification with full transport authorization.

2. To access the TMS, use Transaction code STMS or, from the SAP Easy Access menu, choose TOOLS • ADMINISTRATION • TRANSPORTS • TRANSPORT MANAGEMENT SYSTEM.

3. If the new system uses the same transport directory as the transport domain controller, the new system will read file `DOMAIN.CFG` in subdirectory `bin` of the transport directory and recognize the existence of a transport domain. When you initialize the TMS on a new SAP system, the dialog box shown in Figure 8.6 appears. The example in this figure shows the quality assurance system QAS, which shares a transport directory with system DEV. Choose SAVE.

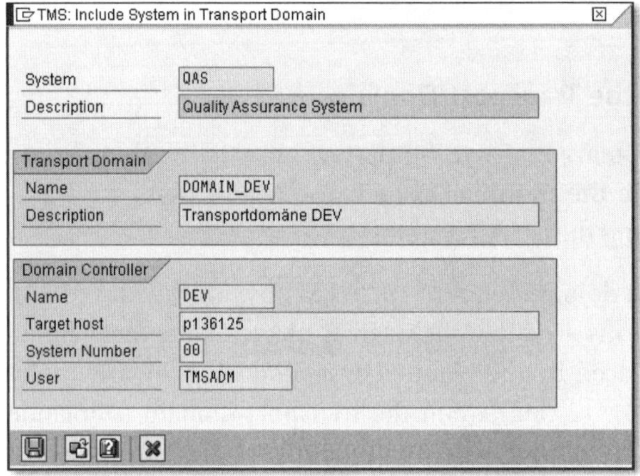

Figure 8.6 Including an SAP System in an Existing Transport Domain

Requesting the inclusion of a new transport group's SAP system

If the new SAP system is the first system in a new transport group, and therefore does not share a transport directory with another SAP system that is already part of the transport domain, the new SAP system cannot recognize the transport domain in which it should be included. In this case, the TMS automatically tries to configure a new transport domain (see Figure 8.5 earlier in this chapter).

To add an SAP system to an existing domain from a different transport group, you must proceed as follows:

1. Log on to the new SAP system in client 000 using user identification with full transport authorization.

2. To access the TMS, use Transaction code STMS or, from the SAP Easy Access menu, choose TOOLS • ADMINISTRATION • TRANSPORTS • TRANSPORT MANAGEMENT SYSTEM.
3. Because the new system has not been connected to the TMS yet, a dialog box is displayed for admission to the detected domain. Because this is not what we want here, you must open the TMS CONFIGURATION dialog box via the OTHER CONFIGURATION icon and select INCLUDE SYSTEM IN DOMAIN. If the first dialog box is not displayed automatically, it can also be opened using SYSTEM OVERVIEW.
4. Specify the transport domain controller of the transport domain in which the system should be included. Enter the TARGET HOST and the SYSTEM NUMBER of the transport domain controller.
5. Choose SAVE. Using RFC technology, the transport domain controller is automatically contacted for transport domain data from the file `DOMAIN.CFG` at the operating system level. The SAP system to be included is now waiting for the transport domain controller to accept it into the transport domain.

If the SAP system consists of more than one application server, you can select one server as the target host. In the TMS: INCLUDE SYSTEM IN TRANSPORT DOMAIN dialog box, you can specify to list all possible servers. The suggested target host is the central instance. Ideally, you should select the host system with the highest availability.

Accepting new SAP systems

You must explicitly accept new SAP systems into the transport domain controller. Prior to this, the new system is waiting for inclusion into the transport domain. As long as a system waits for inclusion, the SYSTEM OVERVIEW screen of the TMS on this SAP system displays only this system and the transport domain.

To accept an SAP system that is waiting for inclusion, proceed as follows:

1. In the SAP system that is the transport domain controller, from the TMS initial screen, choose OVERVIEW • SYSTEMS. The SYSTEM OVERVIEW screen appears. Position the cursor on the SAP system that is waiting for inclusion and choose SAP SYSTEM • ACCEPT. The ACCEPT SYSTEM dialog box appears.

2. When asked to include the new system, click on YES. Please note that when you accept this dialog, the TMS configuration is changed. This change must always be distributed to all other systems in the transport domain. The DISTRIBUTE THE TMS CONFIGURATION dialog box appears and asks if you want to distribute the new configuration immediately. You have two options:
   - If you choose YES, the configuration is distributed immediately, and the TMS status of the new SAP system is set to ACTIVE.
   - If you decide to distribute the configuration later, you must distribute it explicitly. As long as the new configuration is not distributed, the TMS status of the new SAP system remains OBSOLETE. To distribute the new configuration explicitly and change the TMS status of the new system to ACCEPTED, from the SYSTEM OVERVIEW screen in the domain controller, choose EXTRAS • DISTRIBUTE AND ACTIVATE CONFIGURATION.

By default, whenever you change the TMS configuration, the DISTRIBUTE THE TMS CONFIGURATION dialog box appears to ask if you require immediate distribution. To change this default setting, from the TMS initial screen, choose EXTRAS • SETTINGS • SYSTEM OVERVIEW (or, from the SYSTEM OVERVIEW screen, choose EXTRAS • PERSONAL SETTINGS). You can change the default setting to EITHER AUTOMATIC DISTRIBUTION AFTER CHANGE or to DO NOT DISTRIBUTE AUTOMATICALLY. These options are shown in Figure 8.7.

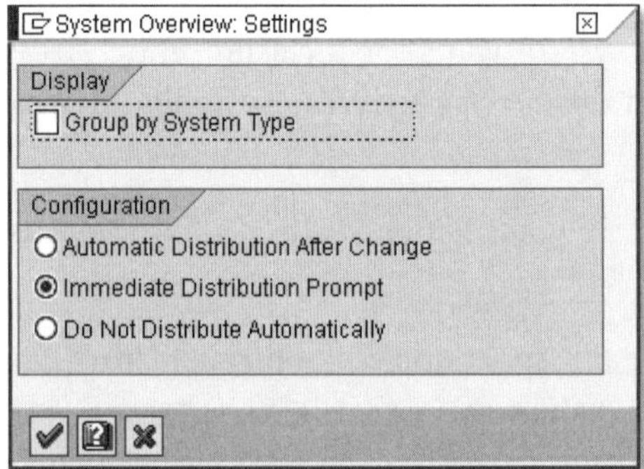

Figure 8.7 Settings for the Distribution Process

Virtual Systems

The TMS allows you to create—that is, enter in the list of SAP systems known to the TMS—SAP systems that are planned but not yet physically installed. These systems are referred to as *virtual systems*.

[+] To allow a virtual system to be replaced by an installed SAP system, the virtual SAP system must have the same SID as the subsequently installed SAP system.

By creating virtual systems, you can model the transport routes of the planned system landscape and ensure that the import queues of subsequent systems already exist. In the initial phase of an SAP implementation, customers frequently have only the development system physically installed, and store the development and Customizing work in the import queues of the respective planned systems.

To create a virtual system, proceed as follows:

Creating a virtual system

1. Log on to the transport domain controller, with a user ID that has complete transport authorization.
2. From the TMS initial screen, choose OVERVIEW • SYSTEMS. The SYSTEM OVERVIEW screen appears. Choose SAP SYSTEM • CREATE • VIRTUAL SYSTEM.
3. In the TMS: CONFIGURE VIRTUAL SYSTEM dialog box, enter the name of the SAP system and description text. You must also specify an SAP system as the COMMUNICATIONS SYSTEM for the virtual system. This system must be a system that is already part of the transport domain. It cannot be a virtual or external system. Choose SAVE.
4. Distribute the configuration change.
5. The default setting in the transport profile for the parameter `dummy`, which is the correct setting for this system, is `TRUE`.

Because an RFC address cannot be created for virtual systems, RFCs are accessed using the transport directory of an already existing SAP system. This system acts as the *communications system*. A virtual system always belongs to the same transport group as the associated communications system. In the TMS: CONFIGURE VIRTUAL SYSTEM dialog box, the communications system proposed by default is the transport domain controller.

Replacing a virtual SAP system with a real SAP system

You can replace a virtual system when the corresponding planned system is realized—that is, it is either physically installed or has been upgraded to a release with TMS functionality. In this context, this realized system is what is meant when referring to the *real* SAP system. On the transport domain controller, proceed as follows:

1. Delete the virtual system from the transport domain:
   - From the TMS initial screen, choose OVERVIEW • SYSTEMS. The SYSTEM OVERVIEW screen appears. Position the cursor on the virtual system you want to delete.
   - Choose SAP SYSTEM • DELETE. Confirm.
   - Distribute the configuration change.

   As soon as the configuration change is distributed, the virtual system is deleted. In the TMS, the import queue for this system disappears. However, the import buffer at the operating system level remains unchanged.
2. Add the real SAP system to the transport domain:
   - Initialize the TMS on the real SAP system and request the inclusion of that system in the transport domain.
   - On the transport domain controller, accept the system.

   The existing import buffer at the operating system level is assigned to the real system. No change requests will be lost.
3. Distribute the configuration change.

[+] After replacing a virtual system with the installed SAP system, ensure the consistency of transport routes between all SAP systems in the transport domain.

External Systems

You can also add external systems to the transport domain that are not physically part of it. Like virtual systems, they are accessed using a communications system—a real SAP system already included in the transport domain. Unlike virtual systems, external systems have their own transport directory. This transport directory, which must be explicitly defined, resides on a disk partition, is accessed by an SAP system in another transport domain, or resides on an exchangeable data medium such as a CD-ROM. External systems are used for the following reasons:

Use of external systems

- To write transport requests to exchangeable data media
- To read transport requests from exchangeable data media
- To provide an intermediate directory to let you send transports to other transport domains (see Chapter 13)

To add an external system, proceed as follows:

Creating external systems

1. From the TMS initial screen, choose Overview • SYSTEMS and then SAP SYSTEMS • CREATE • EXTERNAL SYSTEM. The TMS: CONFIGURE EXTERNAL SYSTEM dialog box (shown in Figure 8.8) is displayed.
2. Enter the path to the transport directory of the external system, relative to the communications system (this is the path used by the communications system). The communications system proposed by default is the transport domain controller. In the example in Figure 8.8, the external system is DE2 (the development system of DOMAIN_DE2), and system DEV from DOMAIN_DEV is the communications system enabling transports between the two domains.

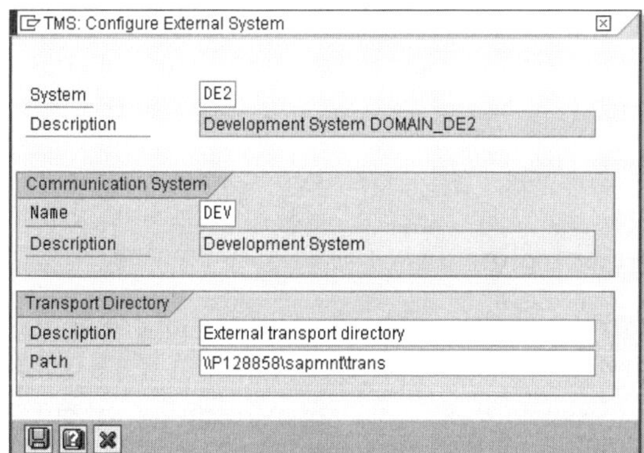

Figure 8.8 Adding an External SAP System to the Transport Domain

The default setting in the transport profile for the parameter `dummy`, which is the correct setting for this system, is `TRUE`. Also note that you must create the subdirectories of the external transport directory, which are not created automatically in the specified transport directory.

Unlike virtual systems, external systems do not belong to an existing transport group in the transport domain, but are assigned to a new transport domain which has a default name of `EXTGRP_<transport domain controller SID>`.

Changes to the Transport Domain

Changes to the TMS configuration correspond to changes to the transport domain—for example, when you:

- Move an SAP system to another host
- Delete an SAP system from the transport domain
- Cause an SAP system to use another transport directory
- Change the transport profile settings

Such changes to the configuration of the transport domain can be performed only on the transport domain controller and must be immediately or subsequently distributed to the other SAP systems in the transport domain. If you decide to distribute a configuration change later, you must do so explicitly, using the following procedure:

1. From the TMS initial screen, choose OVERVIEW • SYSTEMS. The SYSTEM OVERVIEW screen appears. Choose EXTRAS • DISTRIBUTE THE TMS CONFIGURATION AND ACTIVATE.
2. In the resulting dialog box, choose YES.

8.2.3 Backup Domain Controller

The transport domain controller is the source system for all configuration data. It is important to designate another SAP system as the backup domain controller because this gives you a way of performing configuration changes when the transport domain controller is not available. After an SAP system has been defined as the backup domain controller, you can activate that system as the transport domain controller.

[+] The system selected as the backup domain controller must be an existing SAP system that is part of the transport domain. It cannot be a virtual or an external SAP system.

Defining a Backup Domain Controller

To define an SAP system in the transport domain as the backup domain controller, proceed as follows:

1. Log on to the SAP system that is the transport domain controller. From the TMS initial screen, choose OVERVIEW • SYSTEMS. The SYSTEM OVERVIEW screen appears.
2. Position the cursor on a system that is neither a virtual nor an external system and select SAP SYSTEM CHANGE. The CHANGE TMS CONFIGURATION screen is displayed.
3. In the BACKUP field on the COMMUNICATION DATA tab, choose the SID of the SAP system you want to designate as the backup domain controller.
4. Choose SAVE. Distribute the configuration change either immediately or subsequently.

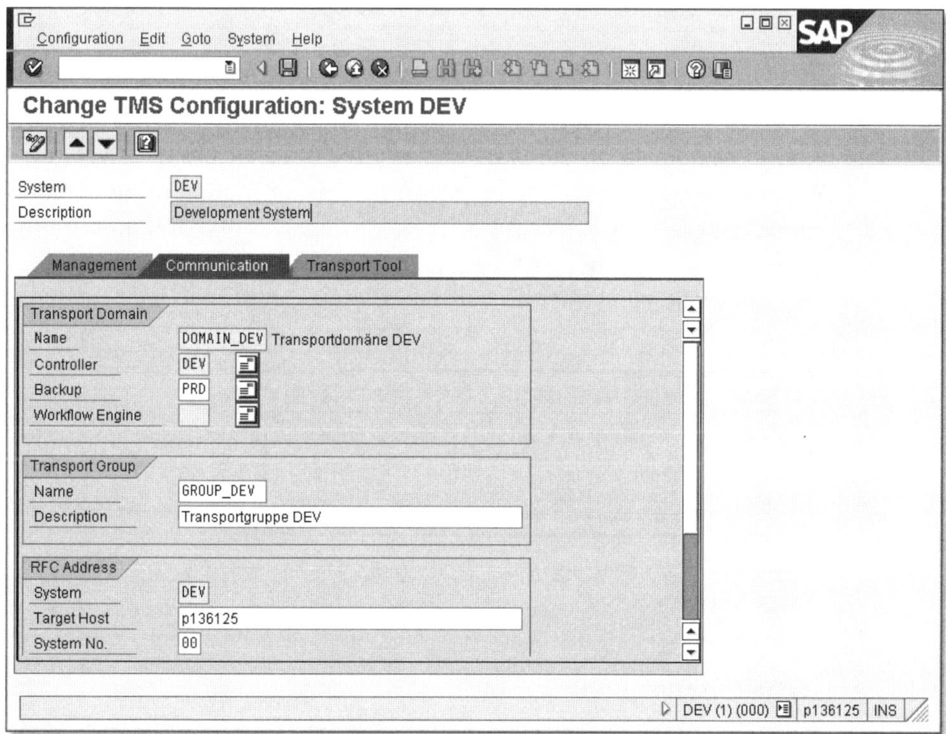

Figure 8.9 Designating a Backup Domain Controller in SAP ERP 6.0

Figure 8.9 shows the Change TMS Configuration screen for SAP ERP 6.0. In this screen, the system PRD has been entered as the backup domain controller.

Activating a Backup Domain Controller

To use a backup domain controller to change transport domain configuration, you must activate it as the domain controller. Proceed as follows:

1. Log on to the backup domain controller with a user ID that has complete transport authorizations.
2. From the TMS initial screen, choose Overview • Systems. The System Overview screen appears.
3. Choose Extras • Activate backup controller.

If the SAP system that was previously the domain controller is available, it is automatically designated as the new backup domain controller.

8.2.4 Verifying the Transport Domain

System roles

You can view a variety of information about the SAP systems in the transport domain on the System Overview screen (from the TMS initial screen, choose Overview • Systems). For an explanation of the symbols used, choose Extras • Legend. The icons next to the SIDs indicate the roles of the respective SAP systems. These icons and their descriptions are shown in Figure 8.10.

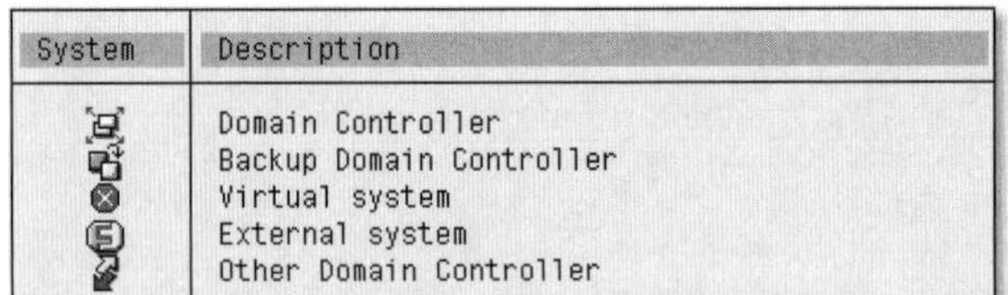

System	Description
	Domain Controller
	Backup Domain Controller
	Virtual system
	External system
	Other Domain Controller

Figure 8.10 The Key to the Icons for System Roles in the System Overview Screen

System Status

The icons in the Status column of the System Overview screen indicate the status of each SAP system (see Figure 8.11).

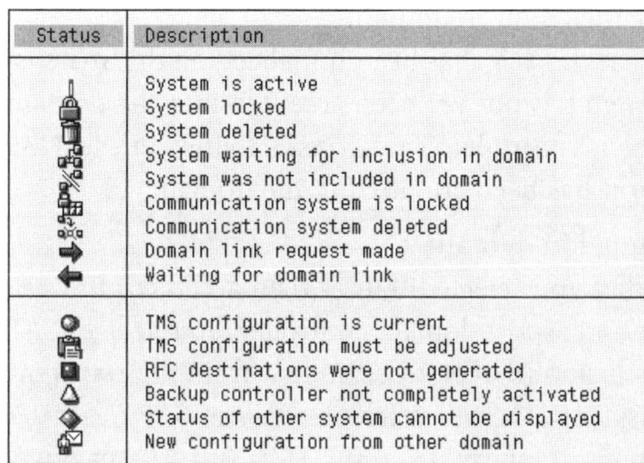

Status	Description
	System is active
	System locked
	System deleted
	System waiting for inclusion in domain
	System was not included in domain
	Communication system is locked
	Communication system deleted
	Domain link request made
	Waiting for domain link
	TMS configuration is current
	TMS configuration must be adjusted
	RFC destinations were not generated
	Backup controller not completely activated
	Status of other system cannot be displayed
	New configuration from other domain

Figure 8.11 The Key to the Icons for System Status in the System Overview Screen

The various system statuses indicated in the SYSTEM OVERVIEW screen can be explained in more detail as follows:

Various system statuses

- **System is active**
  This status means that the TMS has been initialized on this system, and that the system has been successfully included in the transport domain. A system must have this status to be integrated into the transport route configuration and included in the transport flow.
- **System is locked**
  From the domain controller, you can lock an SAP system, thus preventing any TMS activity within the domain from accessing this system. You can do this, for example, to perform hardware maintenance. The TMS transport functionality is deactivated for a system with this status. To lock a system, position the cursor on the SAP system in the TMS SYSTEM OVERVIEW screen and choose SAP SYSTEM • LOCK. To unlock this system, position the cursor on the locked SAP system and choose SAP SYSTEM • UNLOCK.
- **System was deleted**
  This status indicates that the system has been deleted from the TMS domain configuration and that transports via TMS cannot be performed anymore for this SAP system. Note that the import buffer file of a deleted system is not deleted. Accessing the TMS on a system with this status displays a dialog box requesting the renewed inclusion of the system.

- **System is waiting for inclusion in domain**
  This status indicates that the TMS has been initialized on the SAP system, and that this system has not yet been accepted into the domain by the transport domain controller. Therefore, activities in the TMS are possible only after it has been admitted to the domain.

- **System was not included in domain**
  This status indicates that you rejected (rather than accepted) the system in the TMS on the transport domain controller. To reject an SAP system waiting for inclusion (that is, to exclude it from the transport domain), from the SYSTEM OVERVIEW screen, choose SAP SYSTEM • DELETE. The SAP system disappears from the TMS SYSTEM OVERVIEW screen as soon as the deletion has been distributed to all SAP systems in the transport domain. If you restart Transaction STMS on this SAP system, you can again request acceptance into the transport domain.

- **Communications system is locked**
  This status means that the system is a virtual system and that the associated communications system has been manually locked, thus blocking access by the TMS of any other system in the transport domain.

- **Communications system deleted**
  This status means that the system is a virtual system and that the associated communications system has been deleted in the TMS on the domain controller.

- **Domain link was requested**
  This status indicates that you requested the connection of this domain with another domain at the remote domain controller. For the SAP systems of this domain to communicate with the systems of the other domain, you must confirm the link between the domains with the remote domain controller.

- **Waiting for domain link**
  This status indicates that a remote domain controller has requested the connection between this domain and the remote domain. If you confirm the connection between the domains, all SAP systems in both domains can communicate with each other. You can then, for example, carry out transports between systems from different domains.

Distribution Status

The icons in the STATUS column on the SYSTEM OVERVIEW screen indicate whether the distributed configuration data for the transport domain, as recorded locally on the respective system, is up to date. The options are as follows:

Background colors

- **TMS configuration is current**
  This means that the configuration data in the system is up to date, that is, the configuration recorded in the system is identical to the reference configuration on the domain controller.
- **TMS configuration must be adjusted**
  This means that the configuration data recorded in the TMS of an SAP system is obsolete, that is, it differs from the reference configuration stored on the domain controller. This may be the case if the TMS configuration has been changed on the transport domain controller but has not yet been distributed, or if the specific system was not available when configuration changes were distributed. If the status of a system is obsolete, you must distribute the transport domain configuration from the domain controller.
- **RFC destinations were not generated**
  This means that errors occurred while the RFC destinations were generated during the TMS initialization. If a system shows this status, use the Alert Monitor (see the text that follows) to identify and eliminate the error. Then, redistribute the TMS configuration, or from the TMS system overview, select EXTRAS • GENERATE RFC DESTINATIONS to recreate the RFC destinations.
- **Backup controller not completely activated**
  This means that errors occurred when the backup domain controller was activated as the domain controller. Use the Alert Monitor (see the text that follows) to identify and eliminate this error. Then, restart the activation process.
- **Status of other system cannot be displayed**
  You cannot display the status of the TMS configuration for systems of a remote domain, except for the domain controller.

- **New configuration from other domain**
  This means that the TMS configuration of the remote domain has been changed. You can now distribute this configuration change to the systems in the local domain. This happens implicitly when you distribute a change made to the local configuration. You can also distribute the changes explicitly (see the section on distributing a transport domain configuration).

If the TMS configuration has not yet been distributed to all SAP systems in the transport domain, a warning is displayed on the TMS initial screen in the SAP system that is the transport domain controller.

8.2.5 Technical Aspects of the Configuration Process

Whenever you initialize the TMS on an SAP system, several steps are automatically performed on that system:

Automatic steps

- In client 000, CPIC user TMSADM is created.
- The RFC destinations required for the TMS connections are generated.

If the system you are initializing is the domain controller, the following additional steps are automatically performed:

- Certain basic settings for the TMS domain configuration are stored in the file `DOMAIN.CFG` in subdirectory `bin` of the transport directory. These settings include, for example, the transport domain's name and description, as well as the transport domain controller's host name, instance number, SID, and transport group.
- The transport profile for the transport control program `tp` is generated (see Chapter 7).

If the system you are initializing is not the domain controller, the following additional steps are automatically performed:

- The address data of the system is sent to the transport domain controller, as part of the request for membership in the transport domain.
- The profile parameter for configuring the transport control program `tp` is sent to the transport domain. If there are several transport groups in the transport domain, transport profiles are generated in the transport directory of every group.

RFC Connections

RFC connections are used for communication between the SAP systems in a transport domain. When you initialize the TMS on an SAP ERP system, RFC destinations are generated to enable access between all involved SAP systems. There are two distinct types of access. One type is for *read* access and any *write* access that is not critical to security—for example, distributing the TMS configuration after a virtual system has been added from the domain controller to all SAP systems in the transport domain. The other type is any write access that is critical to security—for example, starting an import. This section explains the underlying techniques of the RFC connections used by the TMS.

Read access and noncritical write access

To set up the RFC destinations, user TMSADM of user type CPIC is generated in client 000 during TMS initialization. By default, TMSADM authorizations are limited to *read* and *write* authorization in the common transport directory, RFC authorization in the TMS, and display authorization in the CTS. This user is required to display import queues and to distribute the basic TMS configuration settings from the transport domain controller to all systems in the transport domain. For all SAP systems, to enable accesses that are not critical to security, the RFC connection `TMSADM@<SID>.<domainname>` is generated. Figure 8.12 shows the RFC destinations that are generated during TMS initialization.

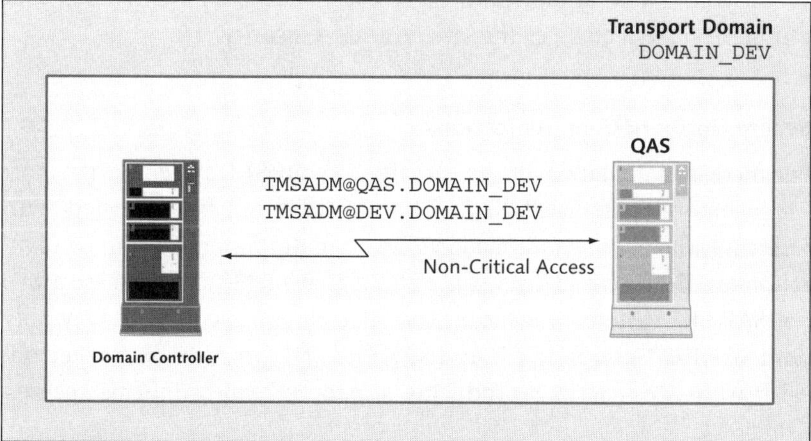

Figure 8.12 RFC Connections Required for TMS Read Access and Non-Critical Write Access

Critical Write Access

Because *write* accesses can cause changes in the target system—for example, changes to the import queue—the authorizations of user TMSADM are not sufficient to enable write accesses for certain activities. To execute a function that will result in a critical change in the target system—for example, starting an import into an SAP system or changing transport routes—you must log on to this target system and have sufficient authorization in the target system. The username and password for this RFC link should not be stored in the source system.

The destination for critical accesses is calculated at runtime, based on the address information stored in the TMS configuration. This concept avoids creating destinations for all targets, which—due to the new functionality for creating client-specific transport routes—may be numerous.

The TMSADM connection is initially used for all accesses. If the authorizations of TMSADM do not suffice, a logon screen is automatically triggered for the target system, and a user with the proper authorizations must log on. If this procedure is too time consuming—for example, if there are a large number of SAP systems—you may provide user TMSADM with the required authorizations through profile S_A.TMSCFG. If an SAP system where the user TMSADM has sufficient authorization is accessed, the logon procedure is suppressed.

[+] When you extend authorizations for user TMSADM, an anonymous user can make system changes that are critical to security.

Secure Network Communications

For increased demands on the security of your SAP systems, Transport Management System (TMS) RFC connections can be protected with *Secure Network Communication (SNC)*. Automatic support of the configuration for SNC-secured TMS connections is available as of Release 4.6D. For SAP ERP systems this means that SNC can be used in this way only with SAP R/3 Enterprise 4.7 und SAP ERP SNC. In addition, for technical reasons, connections producing a logon screen cannot be secured using SNC.

Detailed information about SNC can be found in the SAP Service Marketplace under *http://service.sap.com/SECURITY-Security in Detail-Secure System Management*. [+]

If you are using SNC for RFC connections between SAP systems, you must be aware of the following restrictions:

- The transport workflow cannot trigger imports to these systems.
- The synchronization of import queues for these systems is possible only via a direct logon.
- For importing transports, you need to log on to these systems directly.

At first, the transport domain's SAP systems should be set according to the SNC manual so that the systems involved can communicate via SNC-secured RFC connections. You don't need to carry out the reconfiguration of the entire system landscape at once; you can do it step by step.

Note that you should not disallow insecure RFC access to the systems until all systems in the TMS domain have been reconfigured to SNC. Also, if you activate the RFC communication over SNC, consider the previously mentioned restrictions in the TMS. [+]

As soon as the SNC communication works, adapt the TMS settings as follows:

1. Log on to the SAP system acting as domain controller.
2. Call Transaction STMS.
3. Select OVERVIEW • SYSTEMS. You are now in the system overview.
4. Select GOTO • TRANSPORT DOMAIN. The DISPLAY TMS CONFIGURATION: DOMAIN <DOMAIN> screen is shown.
5. Select the MANAGEMENT tab.
6. Switch to change mode.
7. Under SECURITY OPTIONS, mark the SNC PROTECTION option as ACTIVE.
8. Save your changes and distribute the configuration.

To use SNC, the TMS domain controller must receive SNC-specific information about the systems it maintains. Determine this information via COPY SNC INFORMATION, and apply and distribute it. The RFC connections between the systems of the current transport domain are secured using SNC. If a domain link exists, the communication with remote systems also occurs via SNC-secured connections.

TMS Trusted Services

Apart from using RFC connections for communication and synchronization between systems, when working with the Transport Management System (TMS), it is also necessary to log on to all systems you want to change—for example, by activating transport routes or performing imports—with your user name and your password. This can be inconvenient, particularly in larger system landscapes. With *TMS Trusted Services*, you can set your transport domain so that these logon procedures are omitted if you have the corresponding authorization on the target system. TMS Trusted Services are available as of R/3 Release 4.6C.

[+] Note that TMS Trusted Services apply to the systems of only one domain.

Before implementing TMS Trusted Services, you should check whether they comply with your security concept. You should only implement TMS Trusted Services if the same security measures apply to all of your systems because the most *insecure* system of the transport domain defines the security of all systems in the transport domain.

[+] Activate TMS Trusted Services only if the user names are unique to all systems and clients of your transport domain.

For later evaluation, the TMS records—for all actions—which user started an action and from which system. This information can be analyzed in the TMS Alert Viewer.

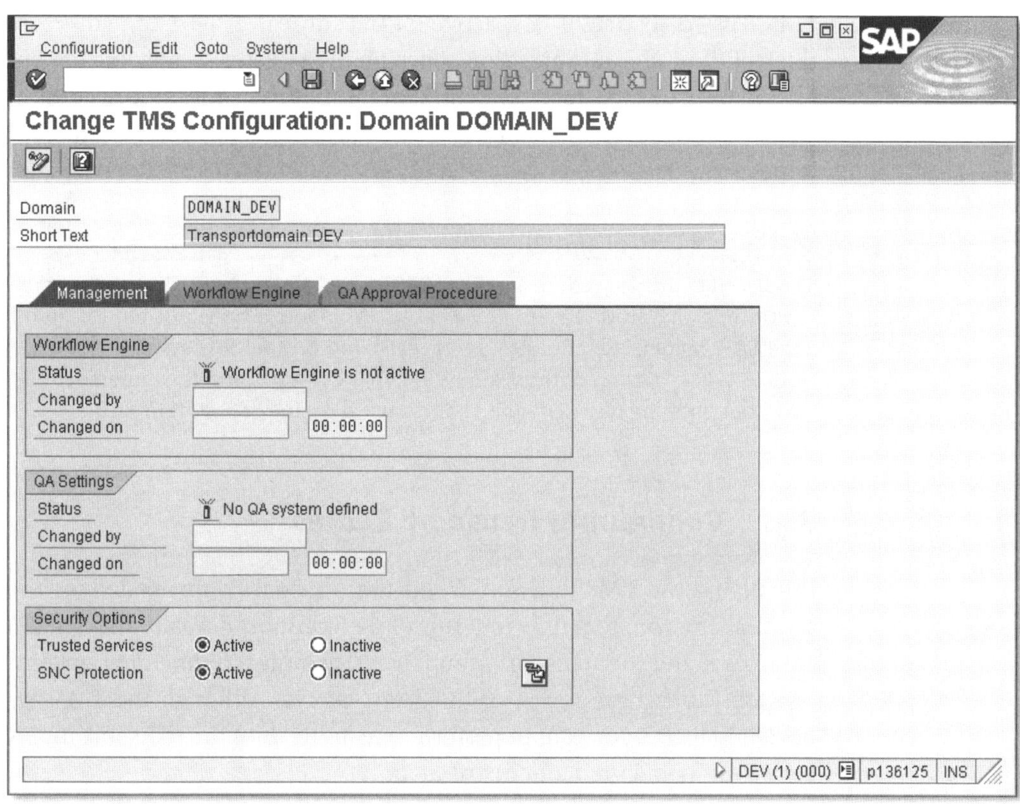

Figure 8.13 Extending the Security Options in the TMS with Trusted Services and SNC

The TMS Trusted Services are configured as follows:

1. Log on to the SAP system acting as transport domain controller.
2. Call Transaction STMS.
3. Select OVERVIEW • SYSTEMS. You are now in the system overview.
4. Select GOTO • TRANSPORT DOMAIN. The DISPLAY TMS CONFIGURATION: DOMAIN <DOMAIN> screen is shown.
5. Select the MANAGEMENT tab.
6. Switch to change mode.
7. Under SECURITY OPTIONS, mark the TRUSTED SERVICES option as ACTIVE.
8. Save your changes and distribute the configuration.

TMS Trusted Services is now active for the entire transport domain. From this point on, the authorization check on the target system is carried out for the user of the source system. Only if that user does not have sufficient authorization on client 000 of the target system—for example, for importing a request—does the target system send a logon screen.

Example: Usage of TMS Trusted Services

User MILLER is logged on to client 010 on the SAP system DEV and works with the TMS on that system. He wants to import a transport request into the SAP system PRD. Because he is registered on the PRD system on client 000 as a user with all authorizations in CTS, he can perform the import action without entering his username and password on the SAP system PRD.

8.3 Configuring Transport Routes

Initializing the TMS and setting up the transport domain defines the physical environment only in terms of the transport domain, the domain controller, and the transport group. Next, you must define the transport relationship between each of the SAP systems. Although the TMS has been initialized, you cannot perform transports until the transport routes have been configured and distributed.

Transport routes indicate the role of each system and the flow of change requests. They are what actually define your system landscape. The prerequisites for configuring transport routes are setting up the transport domain—including all involved systems—and configuring the transport control program `tp`. Configuring a transport route involves the following:

Transport route configuration

- Consolidation routes
- Delivery routes
- Target groups

8.3.1 Procedure

To ensure consistency, transport routes can be configured only on the transport domain controller. To help define a transport route, the TMS provides a graphical editor and a hierarchical list editor, which can be used interchangeably. After you define a transport route, you must distribute it to all SAP systems in the transport domain and activate it.

SAP recommends creating transport routes as follows:

Creating transport routes

1. Use one of the standard installation options in the TMS editors. You can choose from a single-, two-, or three-system landscape. If your system landscape extends beyond a three-system landscape, begin with a three-system landscape and extend the setup using one of the TMS editors.
2. Distribute and activate the transport route configuration to all SAP systems in the system landscape.

[+]

When you are using TMS, Transaction SE06 is no longer used to configure transport routes, and the tables used to store the transport route configuration are no longer TSYST, TASYS, and TWSYS.

Standard Configurations

The easiest way to create transport routes and thereby define a system landscape is to use one of the standard configuration options provided by both the hierarchical list editor and the graphical editor. The following standard configurations are possible:

- **Single system**
  The option used for a single-system landscape.
- **Development and production system**
  The option used for a two-system landscape.
- **Three system group**
  The option used for a three-system landscape.

After you enter the names of the SAP systems that will form the system landscape, the SAP system automatically generates the necessary transport routes and transport layers. To create a more complex environment, use a three-system landscape initially and extend it later. To implement one of the standard configuration options, proceed as follows:

Implement standard configurations

1. Log on to the transport domain controller with a user ID that has complete transport authorization.

2. To access one of the TMS editors, from the TMS initial screen (Transaction STMS), choose OVERVIEW • TRANSPORT ROUTES.
3. Switch into change mode using CONFIGURATION • DISPLAY ↔ CHANGE.
4. Regardless of which editor you are using, choose CONFIGURATION • STANDARD CONFIGURATION and select one of the three standard configurations.

[+] By selecting one of the standard configurations, all existing transport routes are deleted. Existing transport layers and packages are retained.

After selecting one of the three standard configurations, proceed as follows.

One-system landscape

For a single-system landscape, specify the SID of the SAP system that will be the single system in the system landscape. You also may specify a transport layer for local developments. For a single-system landscape, you do not need to define transport routes. (Imports can still be performed if necessary.) All object changes you make in a single SAP system are recorded in change requests of type LOCAL (see Chapter 10).

Two-system landscape

For a two-system landscape, enter the SIDs of the development-and-test system and the production system. Choose SAVE. The following steps are performed automatically:

- The transport layer Z<DEVELOPMENT-AND-TEST SYSTEM SID> becomes the standard transport layer.
- A consolidation route is created from the development-and-test system to the production system through the transport layer Z<DEVELOPMENT-AND-TEST SYSTEM SID>.
- A consolidation route is created from the development-and-test system to the production system through the transport layer SAP.

As a result, all Customizing changes, all developments in packages assigned to the standard transport layer, and all changes to standard SAP objects are recorded in change requests for transport to the production system.

Figure 8.14 shows a standard configuration of a two-system landscape with DTS as the development-and-test system and PRS as the production system. The standard transport layer ZDTS is automatically generated, as well as the two consolidation routes: one for customer-developed objects belonging to the transport layer ZDTS and one for standard SAP objects.

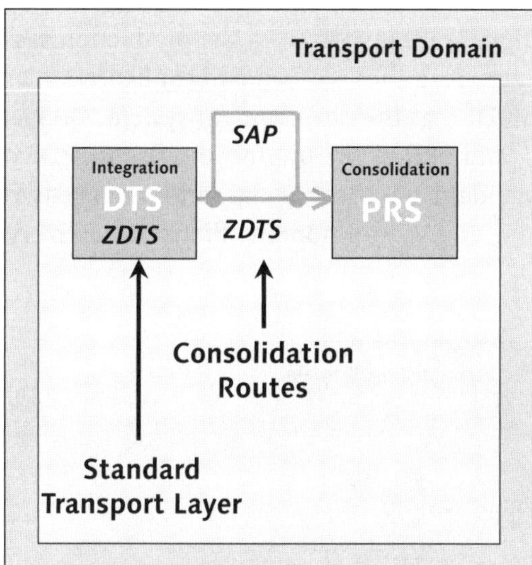

Figure 8.14 Components of the Standard Transport Route Configuration for a Two-System Landscape

Three-system landscape

For a three-system landscape, assign SIDs to the development system, the quality assurance system, and the production system. Choose SAVE. The following steps are performed automatically:

- The transport layer Z<DEVELOPMENT SYSTEM SID> becomes the standard transport layer.
- A consolidation route is created from the development system to the quality assurance system through the transport layer Z<DEVELOPMENT SYSTEM SID>.
- To transport standard SAP objects, a consolidation route is created from the development system to the quality assurance system through the transport layer SAP.
- A delivery route is created from the quality assurance system to the production system. The production system is the recipient system for the consolidated changes.

As a result, all Customizing changes, all developments in packages that are assigned to the standard transport layer, and all changes to standard SAP objects are recorded in change requests for transport to the quality assurance system for consolidation.

After consolidation, the changes are transported to the production system via the delivery route. Figure 8.15 shows a standard configuration of a three-system landscape with DEV as the development system, QAS as the quality assurance system, and PRD as the production system. ZDEV has been generated as the standard transport layer, and there are two consolidation routes, SAP and ZDEV. Additionally, there is a delivery route between QAS and PRD.

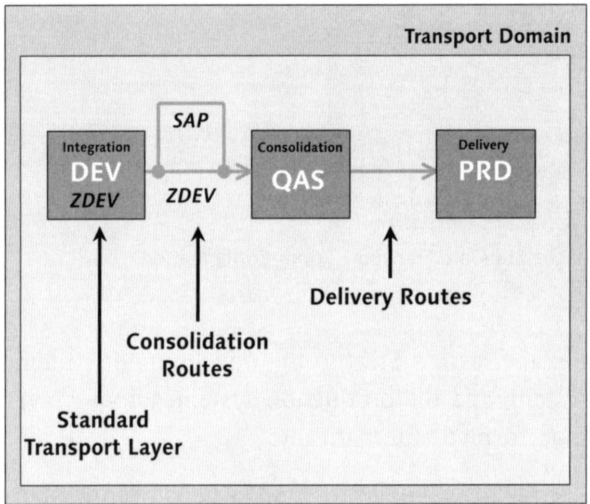

Figure 8.15 Components of the Standard Transport Route Configuration for a Three-System Landscape

Distributing and Activating a Standard Configuration

Changes in configuration are not valid until manually distributed and activated. To distribute and activate the changes, from either the hierarchical list editor or the graphical editor, choose CONFIGURATION • DISTRIBUTE AND ACTIVATE.

8.3.2 Extending and Changing a Transport Route Configuration

You can extend and change a transport domain's transport route configuration at any time using either of the TMS editors: the graphical editor or the hierarchical editor. The graphical editor is often easier to use for this purpose, because it provides a diagram of the existing environment into which you can "draw" your additions to the landscape.

The transport route configuration can be changed on the transport domain controller only with a user ID that has complete transport authorization. In either editor, to change the transport route configuration—that is, to add, delete, or modify transport routes—you must be in change mode. After making changes, always distribute and activate the changes by choosing CONFIGURATION • DISTRIBUTE AND ACTIVATE. When activating a transport route configuration, you are prompted to log on to all involved SAP systems. To do this, you need a user ID that has complete transport authorization in each of the SAP systems.

Using the TMS Editors

Either editor can be used to add consolidation routes or delivery routes. To call an editor, from the TMS initial screen, choose OVERVIEW • TRANSPORT ROUTES. The default editor appears.

Changing the default editor

To change the default editor, proceed as follows:

1. From the TMS initial screen (Transaction STMS), choose EXTRAS • SETTINGS • TRANSPORT ROUTES.
2. Select either the graphical or the hierarchical list editor.
3. Press [Enter].

The hierarchical list editor

The *hierarchical list editor* lists all SAP systems, transport layers, and target groups in the transport domain in a tree structure. For example, Figure 8.16 shows the tree structure of the hierarchical editor for the transport domain DOMAIN_DEV.

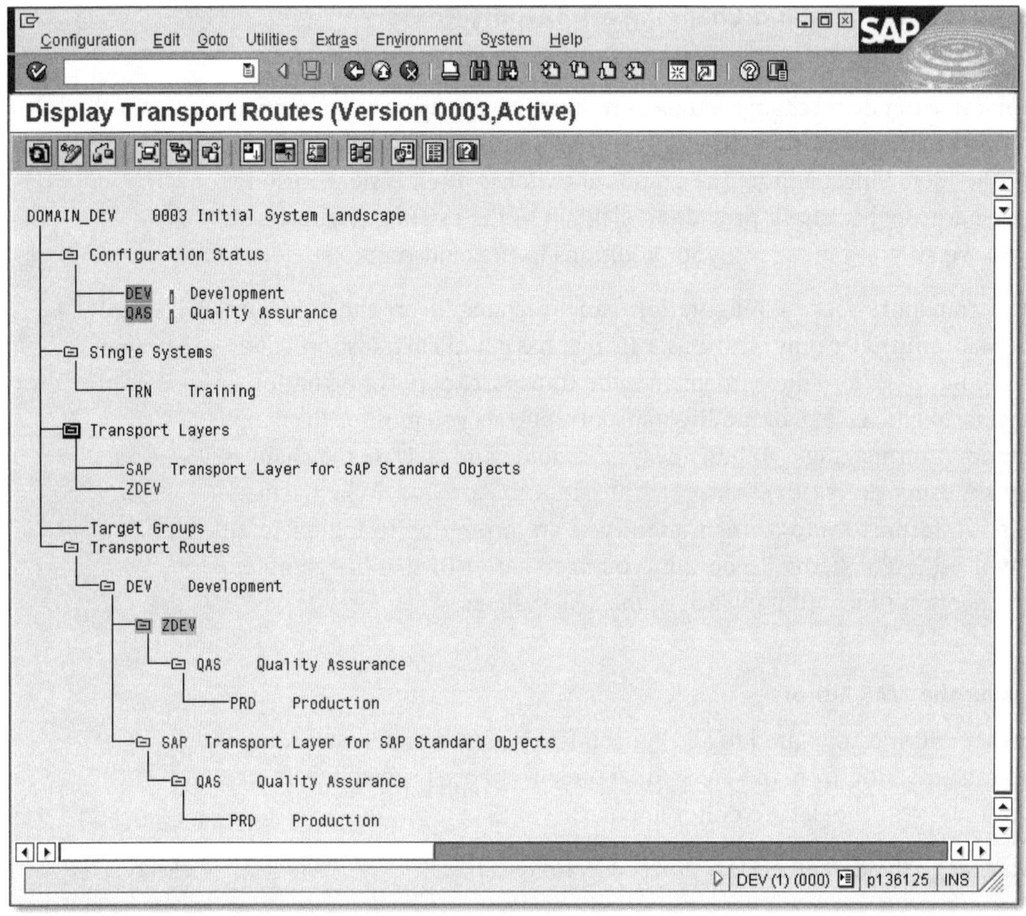

Figure 8.16 The Hierarchical List Editor

The system landscape shown in Figure 8.16 consists of two "real" SAP systems (the development system DEV and the quality assurance system QAS) as listed under the node CONFIGURATION STATUS. The production system PRD has not yet been installed, but has already been configured as a virtual system for integration into the transport route configuration. The SINGLE SYSTEMS node lists the training system TRN, which has not yet been integrated into the transport route configuration. DEV, QAS, and PRD form a standard three-system landscape for which standard transport routes have been configured: two consolidation routes between DEV and QAS, one associated with transport layer SAP for standard SAP objects, and one associated with the generated standard transport layer ZDEV for customer objects.

Adding transport routes using the list editor

To add a new transport route using the hierarchical list editor, proceed as follows:

1. Log on to the transport domain controller with a user ID that has complete transport authorization.
2. From the TMS initial screen (Transaction STMS), choose OVERVIEW • TRANSPORT ROUTES.
3. Switch into change mode using CONFIGURATION • DISPLAY • CHANGE.
4. Choose EDIT • TRANSPORT ROUTE • CREATE.
5. In the resulting dialog box (shown in Figure 8.17), select the type of transport route you require: either CONSOLIDATION or DELIVERY.
   - For a consolidation route, you must specify an integration system, a transport layer, and a consolidation system. When a transport layer is assigned to a consolidation route, all objects belonging to the transport layer are assigned to this consolidation route.
   - For a delivery route, you must specify a source system and a recipient system.

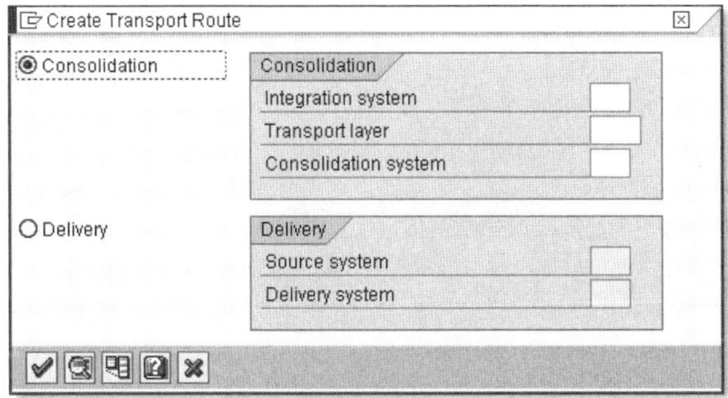

Figure 8.17 Adding a New Transport Route

6. Choose CONTINUE to confirm the settings and save the new transport route.

Graphical editor

The display of the *graphical editor* is divided into three areas, as seen in Figure 8.18. The left-hand area at the top of the screen displays all objects that can be connected via transport routes. These objects include all real, virtual, or external SAP systems in the transport domain that have not yet been integrated into transport routes. The objects in this area are called *insertable objects*. Its objects can be inserted in the area below—the biggest portion of the screen, called the *display area*—containing a graphical representation of current transport routes between SAP systems. This area also contains a legend (not shown in Figure 8.18). The right-hand area at the top is the *navigation area*, which contains a simplified representation of the display area. In the navigation area, by using your mouse to drag, you can determine the part of the landscape that is shown in the display area.

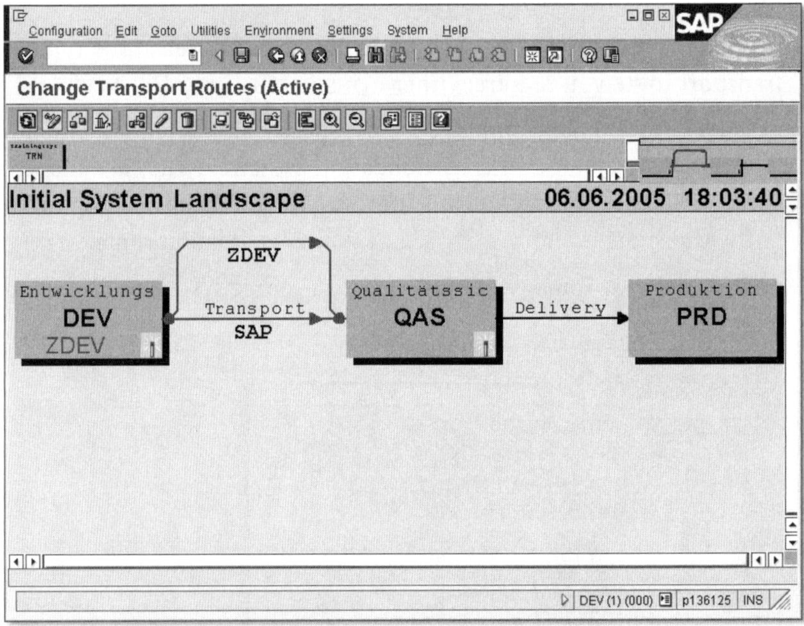

Figure 8.18 The Graphical Editor

Adding transport routes using the graphical editor

To add a transport route using the graphical editor, proceed as follows:

1. Log on to the transport domain controller with a user ID that has complete transport authorization.
2. From the TMS initial screen (Transaction STMS), choose Overview • Transport routes. If necessary, switch to the graphical editor using menu option GoTo • Graphical Editor.

3. Switch into change mode using CONFIGURATION • DISPLAY ↔ CHANGE.
4. If a new SAP system (or target group) needs to be added to the transport route configuration, use the mouse to drag the SAP system (or target group) out of the insertable objects area and drop it into the display area.
5. Choose EDIT • TRANSPORT ROUTE • CREATE.
6. The mouse becomes a stylus you can use to draw a transport route—a line from one SAP system (or target group) to another.
7. After you draw a transport route, a dialog box similar to the one shown in Figure 8.17 appears. After you select either CONSOLIDATION ROUTE or DELIVERY ROUTE, the graphical editor—unlike the hierarchical list editor—automatically enters some of the required information:
    - For a consolidation route, you need to specify only a transport layer.
    - For a delivery route, after selecting DELIVERY, additional entries are not required.
8. Press Enter.

Additional Consolidation Routes

It is sometimes useful to consolidate specific Repository objects to an SAP system outside of the standard transport routes by creating an additional transport layer. Development projects that require this technique are called *multi-layered development projects*.

Example: Multi-Layered Development Project

A training system TRN is needed. This system should be identical to the production system, but also requires special programs such as reset routines to return sample data to its original state. These programs only need to be consolidated to TRN, and should never be transported into the production system.

To implement this, all training objects are assigned to a package whose transport layer differs from the standard transport layer. It must be assigned to a consolidation route with TRN as the consolidation system.

Additional Delivery Routes

Parallel forwarding

One technique for setting up additional delivery routes is known as using *multiple delivery routes*. This technique is frequently used by customers who have more than one recipient system. Multiple delivery routes have the same source system but different target systems. The concept of multiple delivery routes is also called *parallel forwarding*. The import queues of the target systems receive change requests in parallel as soon as the change requests have been imported into the source system of the delivery route.

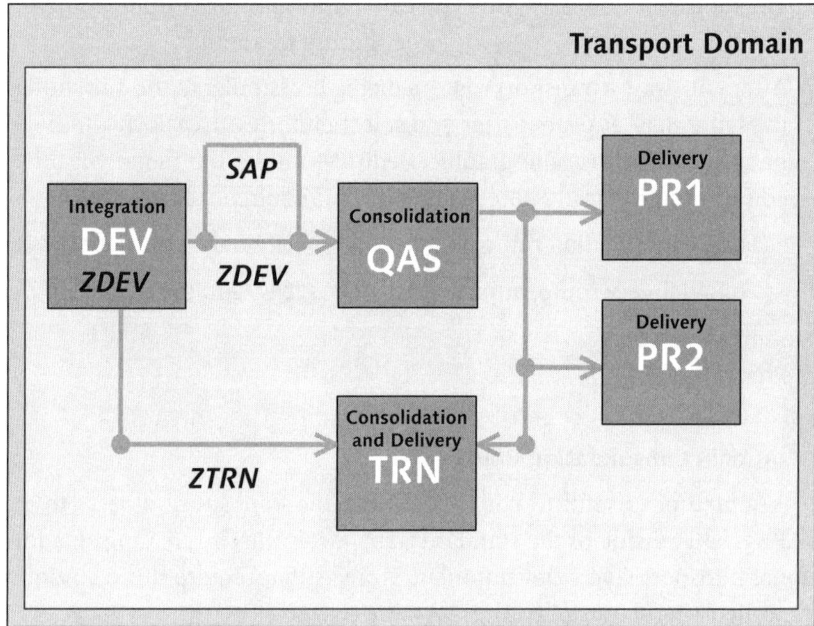

Figure 8.19 Multi-Layered Development and Multiple Target Systems

Example: Multiple Delivery Routes

If you have a separate training SAP system, TRN, which is used to train users working in the production system PR1, it makes sense to set up TRN in the same way as PR1 (see Figure 8.19). Both the training and production systems should receive the same changes in parallel after they have been verified by quality assurance testing in system QAS.

After a standard transport configuration has been created with DEV as the development system, QAS as the quality assurance system, and PRD as the production system, an additional delivery route may be created in the TMS editor with QAS as the source system and TRN as the target system.

Figure 8.19 combines the multi-layered development and multiple target system examples. In addition, Figure 8.19 shows that a second production system, PR2, is delivered in parallel to PR1.

Multi-level forwarding

Another way of configuring more than one recipient system—not shown in the diagram in Figure 8.19—is to use *multi-level delivery* or *multi-level forwarding*, which arranges the delivery routes in sequence. This is implemented by defining a target system for a target system—that is, defining a target system of a delivery route as the source system for an additional delivery route.

An example of multi-level delivery for the complex system landscape of an international company is shown in Figure 8.20. In this example, a standard transport flow exists between the global development system DEG, where global Customizing and development occur, and a global consolidation system QAG. After testing and verification in QAG, changes are delivered in parallel to the development systems of the two regional development systems, DEU for the U.S. and DEE for Europe.

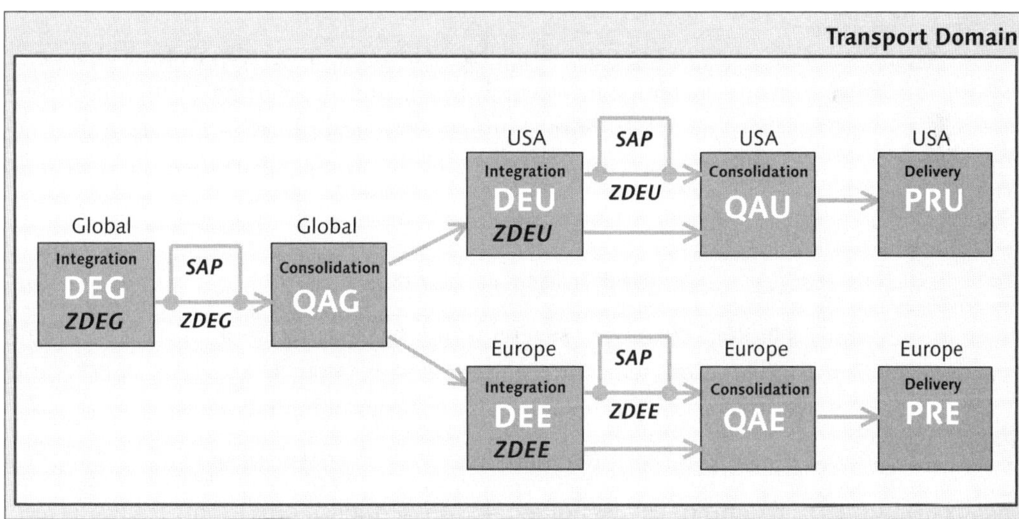

Figure 8.20 A Complex System Landscape

Because each region requires its own specific Customizing and development, each has its own development, quality assurance, and production system. Global changes are delivered to the regional quality assurance systems and then to the regional production systems. The concept of multi-level delivery here means that three transport routes exist between the regional development and quality assurance systems: one consolidation route for regional changes, one consolidation route for SAP objects, and one delivery route for global changes

Version Control

The TMS provides a "version control" function for transport route configurations. Each activated configuration is stored with a sequential number and can be reactivated if needed. To reactivate a former configuration version from within the TMS editor, proceed as follows:

Activating a former configuration version

1. From the transport routes initial screen, choose CONFIGURATION • GET OTHER CONFIGURATION.
2. Select the version from the list of displayed versions. In this case, it is helpful if the short description contains a friendly name, or if you logged the changes you had carried out on a specific date.
3. Press [Enter]. The selected version displays.
4. If you want to use the selected old version—as a basis for a change or in its current state—switch to change mode using CONFIGURATION • CHANGE and adapt the configuration accordingly. Then, save the new configuration with a meaningful short text and activate and distribute it.

8.3.3 Extended Transport Control

As of R/3 Release 4.5, several additional features exist for transport route configuration, which are summarized as EXTENDED TRANSPORT CONTROL. Extended transport enables you to assign the following:

- Clients to transport routes
- Groups of clients (known as *target groups*) to transport routes
- Clients to transport layers

To take advantage of this functionality, in the transport profile, you must explicitly set parameter CTC to TRUE. The default value for this parameter is FALSE, which deactivates extended transport control. Ideally, before using extended transport control, you should globally set parameter CTC to TRUE. After activating extended transport control, you can use the normal, system-to-system transport routes or client-specific routes. You cannot, however, use a mixture of both types of connections in the same system landscape. If you are using a client-specific transport route, you must specify the clients when defining the source and target.

[+] All SAP ERP systems that are linked by transport routes must have either client-specific or client-independent source and target specifications, but not a mixture of both.

[+] When you switch to extended transport control, if any change requests are present in any of the import queues, they will be highlighted in red in the new CLIENT column in the appropriate import queue, and cannot be transported until you specify a client for them (see Chapter 13).

Client-Specific Transport Routes

Extended transport control enables you to include clients in both consolidation and delivery routes (see Figure 8.21). To create a client-specific transport route, proceed as follows:

Creating client-specific transport routes

1. Create an SAP system-specific transport route as described previously in the section "Using the TMS Editors." In the CREATE TRANSPORT ROUTE dialog box, choose EXTENDED TRANSPORT CONTROL.
2. Select either CONSOLIDATION or DELIVERY.
   - For a consolidation route, enter the integration system and transport layer. In the TARGET SYSTEM/CLIENT field, enter the SID of either an SAP system and a client, or an existing target group.
   - For a delivery route, enter a delivery source and a recipient system/delivery client. The latter can be either a SID and a client, or an existing target group.
3. Press Enter.
4. Choose SAVE.
5. Distribute and activate the new configuration.

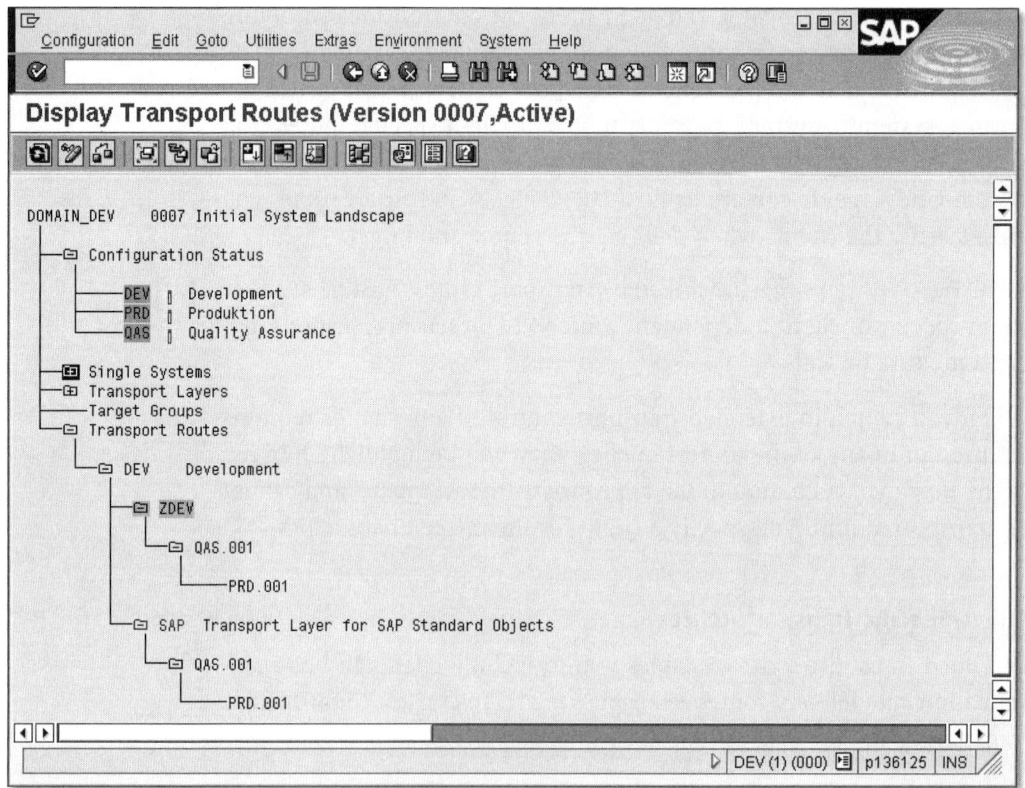

Figure 8.21 Client-Specific Transport Routes

Figure 8.21 shows a three-system landscape with client-specific transport routes as displayed in the hierarchical list editor. Changes in the development system DEV are transported to client 100 of the quality assurance system QAS. The target of the client-specific consolidation route is `QAS.001`. The delivery route from QAS to the production system PRD must also be client-specific. Client 001 of PRD is the production client, so the target of the client-specific delivery route is `PRD.001`.

Target Groups

Extended transport control enables you to create *target groups* for consolidations and deliveries. A target group is a group of target clients. Each target client is specified in terms of an SAP system and a client within that system. When you release a change request from the source system of a target group, the change request is automatically added to the import buffers of all targets in the target group. To define a target group, proceed as follows:

Defining a target group

1. Access the initial screen of either the graphical or the hierarchical editor in change mode.
2. Choose CONFIGURATION • TARGET GROUP • CREATE.
3. In the CREATE TARGET GROUP dialog box (shown in Figure 8.22), enter a name for the target group and a description. The name must begin and end with a forward slash (/).

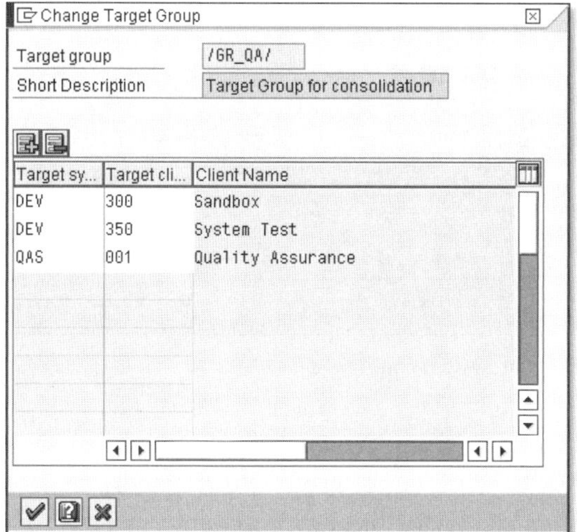

Figure 8.22 Creating Target Groups

4. Choose INSERT LINE. Enter the required target system client combinations. Use a separate line for each client.
5. Choose COPY. If you use the graphical editor, the created target group is displayed in the insertable objects area.
6. You can now use the target groups when defining transport routes in the TMS editors. After using a target group as part of a transport route, distribute and activate the changes as usual by choosing CONFIGURATION • DISTRIBUTE AND ACTIVATE.

The use of target groups in a three-system landscape is shown in Figure 8.23. In this example, Customizing and development changes are made in client 100 in the development system DEV. Target group /GR_QA/ has been specified as the consolidation target for the consolidation route from the integration system DEV. Changes are added in parallel to the respective import buffers for client 100 of the quality assurance system QAS, and for clients 300 and 320 of system DEV. Target group /GR_PR/ has been specified as the delivery target of client 100 in system QAS. After change requests are validated in QAS, they are transported into client 100 of the production system PRD as well as into training client 300 of QAS.

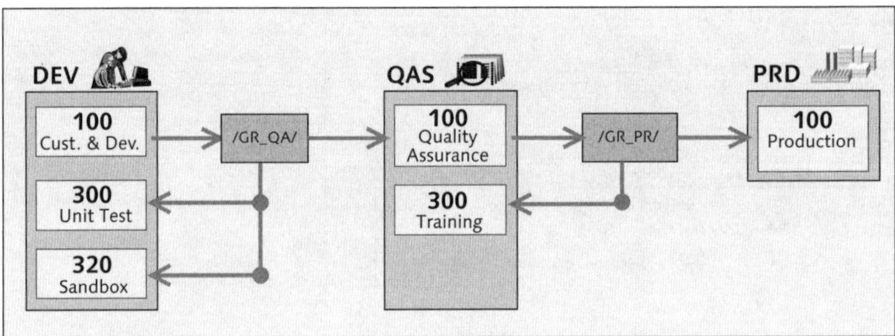

Figure 8.23 Target Groups in a Three-System Landscape

[+] After you export change requests from the Customizing-and-development client, SAP recommends using target groups to transport change requests back into the other clients in the development system. This ensures consistency among the clients in the development system.

Client-Specific Transport Layers

Extended transport control also lets you give a client its own client-specific standard transport layer for client-dependent changes. Client-specific transport layers do not affect Repository objects. If no client-specific transport layer is created, each client uses the standard transport layer of the SAP system to which it belongs.

With client-specific transport layers, the client in which a Customizing change is released determines the consolidation route. If a standard transport layer is defined for this client, the associated consolidation route is used. If no standard transport layer is defined for this client, the consolidation route is determined by the standard transport layer of the SAP system.

To assign clients to transport layers, proceed as follows:

Assigning clients

1. Access either the graphical or the hierarchical editor in change mode.
2. Position the cursor on the SAP system in which the client resides.
3. For the hierarchical editor, choose CONFIGURATION • SYSTEM • CHANGE.
4. For the graphical editor, choose CONFIGURATION • SYSTEM REPORTS • CHANGE.
   - In the resulting CHANGE SYSTEM ATTRIBUTES dialog box: To change the standard transport layer for the whole SAP system—that is, for all clients—enter the name of the new standard transport layer.
   - To assign clients to a transport layer, choose CLIENT ASSIGNMENT. Choose INSERT LINE and enter the required client and the transport layer combinations.
5. Choose COPY.
6. Choose SAVE.
7. Distribute and activate the new transport route configuration.

Figure 8.24 shows a system landscape with client-specific transport layers using the graphical editor. This example has a three-system landscape with a development system (DEV), a quality assurance system (QAS), and a production system (PRD). The SAP ERP application component for Financial Accounting (FI) is configured separately in client 100 in DEV and has its own, separate SAP ERP systems for quality assurance and production (QA2 and PR2). To consolidate all Customizing changes made for FI to QA2, these changes are made in client 100 in DEV (rather than in client 001), for which a client-specific standard transport layer (ZFI) has been defined.

Transport layer ZFI is assigned to a consolidation route with DEV as the integration system and client 100 in system QA2 as the consolidation target. This ensures that all client-dependent Customizing changes made in client 100 of DEV are consolidated to client 100 in QA2. To consolidate Repository objects to QA2, these objects must be created in packages assigned to transport layer ZFI. Finally, all changes that have been imported into QA2 are delivered to PR2, the production system for FI.

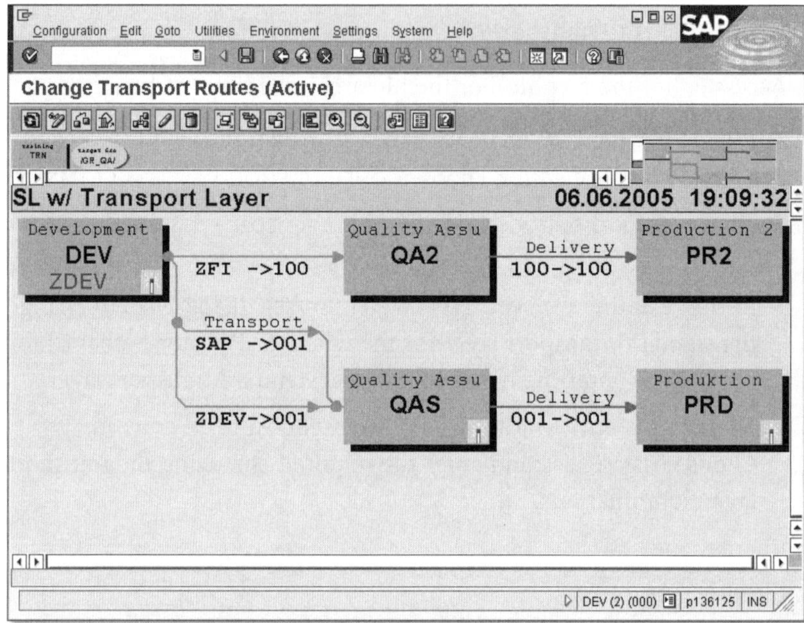

Figure 8.24 Creating Client-Specific Standard Transport Layers

[+] Although client-specific transport layers allow for the consolidation of client-dependent Customizing efforts to different target systems and clients, client-independent Customizing changes will follow only a single transport layer.

8.4 Verifying the System Landscape Setup

The TMS provides the following checks and monitor functions to help ensure that your system landscape is set up correctly:

Checks and monitor functions

- TMS checks
- Transport route configuration checks
- The Alert Monitor

You should use these tools to verify your transport configuration and to perform troubleshooting.

[+] For information on troubleshooting procedures and additional checks for TMS import functionality, see Chapters 13 and 14.

All checks can be performed on any SAP system in the transport domain, not only the domain controller.

8.4.1 Verifying the TMS Setup

To verify whether the TMS has been set up correctly, enter the SYSTEM OVERVIEW screen (from the TMS initial screen, choose OVERVIEW • SYSTEMS). Choose SAP SYSTEM • CHECK. The check is performed on all SAP systems unless you select a particular SAP system by positioning the cursor on it. Choose one of the following checks:

- Connection test
- Transport directory
- Transport tool

During a connection test, the TMS tries to establish the RFC connection for the target hosts of all active SAP systems in the transport domain. The results list indicates whether the individual connections were successfully established and the time that was required to establish the respective connection, in milliseconds. A "backward check" is also performed to verify whether each target host can establish a connection back to the source system. To display details on a particular RFC connection, click the STATUS field for a specific system.

When checking the transport directory, the TMS tries to create, read, and delete test files in all transport directories of the transport domain, including the transport directories of its external systems. The following subdirectories are covered in the check: `bin`, `buffer`, `cofiles`, `data`, `log`, `sapnames`, and `tmp`. From the results screen of this transport-directory check, you can run another check that tests whether a system is correctly assigned to a transport group. To run this check, choose GOTO • TRANSPORT GROUPS.

The transport tool check provides an overview of the availability of the transport tools. This check may take some time to complete. The check covers the tp interface, the transport profile, and the RFC destinations. It tests a tp call to every SAP system of the transport domain. The tp call includes an RFC call, a database connect, and an offline call.

8.4.2 Verifying the Transport Route Configuration

To verify whether you have used TMS correctly to set up your system landscape, access one of the TMS editors. Unless you decide to run the check on a particular SAP system (by positioning the cursor on it), the check is performed on all SAP systems in your system landscape. To start the check, choose CONFIGURATION • CHECK. Choose one of the following checks:

- Transport routes
- Request consistency

A *transport routes check* investigates three things. First, it checks whether the transport flow provides deliveries from at least one consolidation system. Second, it checks whether the delivery is multi-level. If so, the check verifies that the parameter multileveldelivery is set in the transport profile for any SAP systems in the transport domain with an SAP Release before 4.0. Third, if extended transport control is activated (that is, if parameter CTC is set to 1 in the transport profile and an SAP R/3 Release is 4.5 or higher), the check also verifies that the client-specific transport routes are not mixed with system-to-system transport routes for the same system landscape.

Request consistency check

Request consistency check can be run either for the local system or for all systems. It checks whether transport routes associated with open tasks and requests are consistent with the current transport route configuration. If inconsistencies are found, it may be necessary to change the TYPE of open requests—that is, either from LOCAL to TRANSPORTABLE or vice versa, or from REPAIR to CORRECTION or vice versa.

Open requests may also need a new transport destination if the original target system for these change requests does not correspond to the new configuration of the transport routes, and does not provide a valid target system. This check also locates inconsistent change requests—requests that contain invalid object combinations and make release impossible. After running the request consistency check, a list of all inconsistent change requests is displayed. To display details on the type of inconsistency and the required actions, position the cursor on a specific request and choose EDIT • DISPLAY LONG TEXT.

8.4.3 The Alert Monitor

The *TMS alert monitor* enables you to monitor all actions that have been performed with the TMS. Highlighting is used to draw your attention to critical information. To access the alert monitor from the TMS initial screen, choose MONITOR • TMS-ALERTS • TMS-ALERT VIEWER.

You can display either all messages or just warnings and error messages. The information is SAP system-specific. To display information that corresponds to a different SAP system, choose TMS LOG • OTHER SYSTEM in the TMS-Alert Viewer. In the resulting dialog box, enter the appropriate SID in the SYS. NAME field and press [Enter]. To display the full text of a message, click the respective line.

Information

The information provided by the alert monitor includes:

- Date and time of the activity
- Name of the user who performed the activity
- Related TMS function
- TMS messages, including error messages and warnings
- SAP system and client where the TMS function was triggered

Alert monitor

You should check the alert monitor in case of transport or TMS configuration problems, or to get detailed information to help you solve these problems.

Besides the display options of the TMS alerts in the TMS, you can also transfer information from the TMS to the standard SAP tool for system monitoring, the *Computing Center Management System* (CCMS). It is built automatically during the TMS configuration. The CCMS alert monitor can be opened by selecting MONITOR • TMS ALERTS • CCMS ALERT MONITOR in the TMS initial screen.

Basic information about Alert Monitor can be found in the *Computing Center Management System* area of the online help.

The *CCMS Alert Monitor* provides the following functions:

- Display of error alerts that occur in the TMS or during the export of requests—clearly grouped in a tree structure by subjects
- Analysis method for every alert
- Option to set alerts to the DONE status
- Visibility of alerts as long as they are not completed (completed alerts are visible in the history)

All systems in the current system landscape are added to the CCMS alert monitor. When new systems are added to the system landscape, they also show up in the monitor, and when systems are deleted from the system landscape, they disappear from the monitor. Note that open (i.e., not completed) alerts might be deleted as well.

Often, problems that occur locally on a system are reported, that is, problems the system has with itself or via contact with other systems. At the same time, these alerts are sent to the TMS controller. If you are logged on to the controller, you can view and edit all alerts that occurred in the domain.

[+] Note that errors that occurred when writing the CCMS alerts are written to the TMS Alert Viewer. Therefore, you should check the entries in the TMS Alert Viewer on a regular basis.

To open the TMS Alert Viewer or the CCMS alert monitor of the TMS from other areas of the TMS, select GoTo or Environment from the respective menu and then select the corresponding option.

8.5 Questions

1. **Which of the following statements is correct with regard to the SAP systems belonging to a transport domain?**

   A. They all share the same transport directory.

   B. They are managed centrally using TMS.

C. They belong to the same transport group.

D. They must run on the same operating system and database platform.

2. **Which of the following statements is correct with regard to the domain controller?**

   A. It must be the production system.

   B. It occurs once in a transport domain.

   C. It occurs in each transport group.

   D. It can only be the SAP system that was originally designated as the transport domain controller.

   E. It should never be the production system due to the high system load caused by the domain controller.

3. **Which of the following statements are correct with regard to the TMS?**

   A. It needs to be initialized only on the transport domain controller.

   B. It needs to be initialized only on the transport domain controller and the backup domain controller.

   C. It must be initialized on every SAP system.

   D. It must be set up before you can set up transport routes.

4. **Which of the following statements are correct with regard to the RFC destinations for TMS connections?**

   A. They are generated automatically when a transport route is created.

   B. They are generated between the domain controller and each SAP system in the transport domain.

   C. They must be established manually before you can use the TMS.

   D. They are generated during the TMS initialization process.

   E. They are only needed for importing change requests.

5. **How is the actual system landscape, including SAP system roles and relationships, defined using the TMS?**
   A. By including all SAP systems in the transport domain
   B. By configuring transport routes
   C. By assigning a role to each SAP system during the TMS initialization process
   D. By designating real, virtual, and external SAP systems
6. **Which of the following statements is correct with regard to a consolidation route?**
   A. It is defined by an integration system and a consolidation system, and is associated with a transport layer.
   B. It is created in the TMS by defining only an integration system and a consolidation system.
   C. It is not necessarily required in a two-system landscape.
   D. It can be defined only once in a transport group.
7. **Which of the following statements are correct with regard to client-specific transport routes?**
   A. For security reasons, client-independent objects such as programs can no longer be transported.
   B. They can only be used if the extended transport control is activated and `tp` includes a minimum version status.
   C. They are only allowed for target groups.
   D. They may not be used in conjunction with client-independent transport routes.

In the SAP system, using clients enables clear allocation of customer data to different groups. This approach can be used in production, as well as in the context of development, training; and test activities. This chapter describes the tools you can use for this purpose.

9 Client Tools

After installing SAP ERP, you need to set up clients so that users can log on to the system and perform Customizing and other tasks. Setting up the different clients for the SAP systems in your system landscape involves the following tasks:

Setup tasks

- Defining the purpose of each client.
- Enabling the appropriate users to access the client through user administration and authorization.
- Preventing unwanted changes to Customizing settings and Repository objects in a client.
- Providing all clients other than the source client CUST with the latest Customizing and developments in an organized and timely manner.
- Populating a client with the necessary application data.

To perform these tasks, or subsequently modify clients to match your changing business needs, SAP provides the tools discussed in this chapter:

- Client maintenance tools (used to define a client and maintain its settings)
- Client copy tools (used to provide a client with the necessary data)
- Client delete tool (used to remove unwanted clients)

This chapter also explains the logging of Customizing changes that affect tables (table logging). Table logging is activated at the client level and needs to be considered when clients are set up.

9.1 Creating Clients

Table T000

To create a client, you need to make an entry in table T000. Without this entry, you will not be able to log on to the client, import change requests into the client, or copy another client into the client. After creating the client entry, adjust the client settings to define the role of the client within the SAP system landscape.

Please note that not all SAP systems support several clients. SAP NetWeaver BI systems, for example, support only one client. Therefore, the majority of the information in this chapter is not applicable for these systems.

The newly created client is empty—it contains no client-dependent data. You must provide the client with the necessary user master data, application data, and Customizing data so that users can log on to the client and perform, for example, Customizing activities or business transactions.

9.1.1 Client Entries

You can create, display, and change entries in table T000 using client maintenance (Transaction SCC4).

Creating a Client Entry

To create an entry in table T000 and thus create a new client, proceed as follows:

1. Access client maintenance by calling Transaction SCC4, or, from the SAP Easy Access menu, choose Tools • Administration • Administration • Client administration • Client maintenance.
2. The Display View "Clients": Overview screen appears. You are in display mode. Switch to change mode by selecting Table view • Display ↔ Change.

3. A message box appears: THE TABLE IS CLIENT-INDEPENDENT (SEE HELP FOR FURTHER INFO). Choose CONTINUE—you are now in change mode.
4. Click on the NEW ENTRIES button or use the EDIT • NEW ENTRIES menu option to reach the NEW ENTRIES: DETAILS OF ADDED ENTRIES screen (see Figure 9.1).
5. Enter a three-digit client ID in the CLIENT field. For example, to create client 145, enter "145" in this field. If this client ID is already in use, the message AN ENTRY ALREADY EXISTS WITH THE SAME KEY will appear in the status bar. Provide a new and unique ID number.
6. Save your entry.

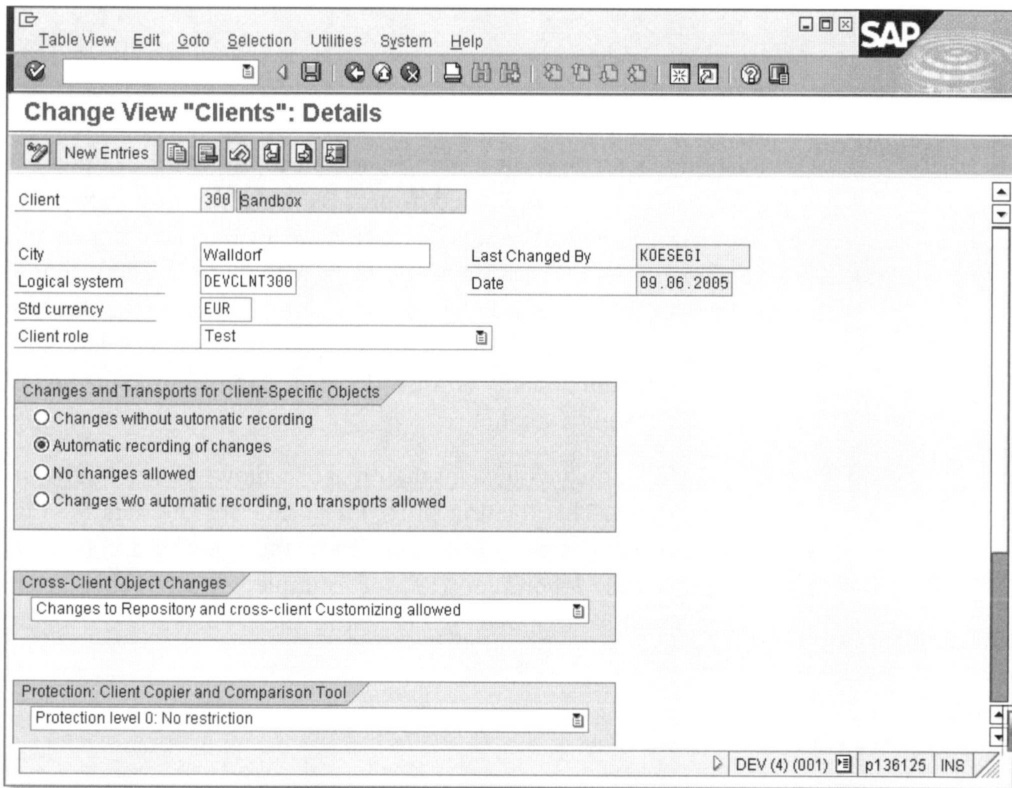

Figure 9.1 The Client Maintenance Screen

Maintaining a Client Entry

You can use client maintenance (Transaction SCC4) to view and change the settings for a client. From the DISPLAY VIEW "CLIENTS": OVERVIEW screen, you can do any of the following:

- Display the settings for a client by double-clicking the client ID
- Change client settings by choosing DISPLAY • CHANGE to switch into change mode, then double-clicking the client ID
- Delete a client by selecting the client entry and then choosing EDIT • DELETE

[+] You should avoid deleting a client entry from within client maintenance. Instead, use Transaction SCC5.

Deleting a Client Entry

When you delete a client entry from table T000 using client maintenance (Transaction SCC4), you can no longer log on to the client or update it using change requests. The deletion process, however, does not eliminate the data belonging to that client. This means the client-dependent data remains in your SAP system—possibly without your knowledge—occupying valuable space in the database. To eliminate a client entirely—that is, to delete both the client entry and the client-dependent data—use the client delete functionality (Transaction SCC5), which is explained in Section 9.3, Deleting a Client.

Locking

Deleting a client entry with client maintenance allows you to temporarily lock the client. The deletion procedure preserves the data for that client, but prevents users from logging on to the client or accessing its data. By preventing logon, you can, for example, ensure that no users make changes during a client copy. To restore the client and allow logon, re-create the client entry using client maintenance.

9.1.2 Client Settings

When you create a client entry, the only required input is a three-digit client ID. You can also make selections for the client settings or change previously selected settings. These settings are very important, because they further define and restrict the way the client is used. The different client settings include:

- Client name
- Client city
- Logical system name
- Standard currency
- Client role
- Client-dependent change option
- Client-independent change option
- Client protection against a client copy and client compare
- Restrictions

Assigning a name to a client lets you provide a description that complements the client ID. The CLIENT CITY field is used to identify the physical location of the hardware for the SAP system or the implementation team that is responsible for the client. Both the client name and city are optional. The other seven client settings provide more critical functions and deserve a more detailed explanation.

Logical System Name

You define a client within an SAP system by creating an appropriate client ID. You may, however, have other clients with the same client ID in your other SAP systems. For example, you may have a client 145 in both your development and quality assurance systems. To differentiate these two clients, you can provide them with unique 10-character logical system names. Logical system names are crucial for:

Consequences of the logical system names

- **Application Link Enabling (ALE)**
  ALE is based on a distribution model that defines the message flow (or data exchange) between different logical systems (see Chapter 4).
- **SAP Business Workflow**
  SAP Business Workflow, often simply referred to as *Workflow*, allows you to automatically control and execute cross-application processes within SAP ERP. To define the steps and events in these processes, you need to know the logical system names of the clients where the events are initiated and performed.

ALE and SAP Business Workflow recognize only logical system names, not client numbers or system IDs. These logical systems can be clients in the same or different SAP systems.

When creating a logical system name, follow these guidelines:

Creating logical system names

- Use a logical system name only once—each logical system name must be unique within your system landscape.
- Do not change a logical system name after it has been established or used by ALE or SAP Business Workflow.

[+] Avoid changing a logical system name. Such a change could result in the loss of ALE or SAP Business Workflow documents.

Standard Currency

The standard currency is the default currency used for that client. It is entered as a three-letter code, such as USD for U.S. dollars or EUR for the Euro. For example, if you assign EUR as the client standard currency, whenever you enter a monetary value in that client, SAP ERP will assume that the currency is Euro unless you specify something different.

To be able to select a default currency for a client, currencies must be defined within the client or copied into the client from a standard SAP client. The standard SAP clients recognize over 100 different currencies.

Other currencies can be defined using an IMG client-dependent Customizing activity.

Client Role

When you create a client, you typically assign a predefined role to it. The role reflects the purpose the client serves, and can prevent or limit certain activities. The possible client roles include:

- **Production**
  A client with this role will not be deleted by a mistakenly initiated client delete or client copy. No client-independent changes can be imported into this client or into its SAP system as part of a client copy. This prevents possible inconsistencies from occurring that could affect production. In addition, changing certain Customizing settings in a production client, such as currency exchange rates and posting periods, can be allowed in this client—despite the standard client-dependent change option used to prevent Customizing changes in a production client. These *current settings* (see Chapter 11) can be maintained in a production client without being recorded to a change request.
- **Test**
  A client with this role is protected against a release upgrade by the appropriate client restriction (see the section "Client Restrictions").
- **Customizing**
  The factory calendar can only be maintained in and transported from a client with this role.
- **Demonstration**
  Setting up a demonstration client allows you to have a separate client for demonstration purposes.
- **Training/Education**
  Setting up a training client allows you to have a separate client for training purposes.

In future SAP software releases, SAP plans to link additional functionality to the client roles to increase the scope of protection they provide.

Client Change Options

The client change options control the types of changes that can be made in the client and determine whether Customizing changes are recorded to change requests. The default change options for a client are as follows:

- Automatic recording of changes
- Changes to Repository and client-independent Customizing allowed

Because of the significance of these settings, the client change options were outlined in detail in Chapter 3.

Client Protection

When you select this client option—PROTECTION: CLIENT COPIER AND COMPARISON TOOL—on the client maintenance screen (see Figure 9.1 earlier in this chapter), the client is protected against being overwritten by a client copy. This option also ensures that sensitive data cannot be viewed from another client during client compares—an activity performed using the Customizing Cross-System Viewer (Transaction SCU0; see Chapter 11). The levels of overwrite-protection you can select are as follows:

Protection levels

- **Protection level 0:**
  No restrictions.
- **Protection level 1:**
  No overwriting. This ensures that the client will not be overwritten by the client copy program. It also protects the client from the adjustment activities of the Customizing Cross-System Viewer. Use this setting for your Customizing-and-development client, as well as for clients that contain critical settings or data that should not be overwritten, such as your quality assurance client.
- **Protection level 2:**
  No overwriting and no external availability. This protects a client

against being overwritten by a client copy, and also against *read* access from another client using the Cross-System Viewer tools. Protection level 2 should be used for clients that contain sensitive data, such as your production client.

Client Restrictions

The following options enable you to restrict activities in clients:

- **Start of CATT and eCATT processes allowed**
  Select this option for a client, such as the quality assurance test client, if you want to run the Computer Aided Test Tool (CATT) or the extended Computer Aided Test Tool (eCATT) to perform scripted validity tests of application functionality. Because CATT scripts generate application data, they should not be run in every client.
- **Currently locked due to client copy**
  This option is automatically set by the SAP system when you use the client copy tool. You cannot select it manually.
- **Protection against SAP upgrade**
  You can assign this option only to a client whose role is set to TEST. This option prevents the introduction of new client-dependent Customizing changes into a client during a release upgrade, preserving the settings that existed prior to the upgrade. After an upgrade, the test client can be used together with the Cross-System Viewer to compare the client-dependent differences between the two releases.

9.2 Providing a Client with Data

After you create a client, it will not contain any data: not Customizing data, application data, or user master records. You must copy data into the new client to provide an environment where users can customize, develop, test, or train, depending on the client's purpose. A client copy is used to initially populate a client with base data from either the standard SAP client 000 or an existing customer client (see Chapter 5). Change requests are then used to distribute the latest Customizing and developments to the different clients.

Tools The client copy tools you can use to initially populate a client with data include:

- Local client copy
- Remote client copy
- Client transport

9.2.1 Selecting a Client Copy Tool

To select the most suitable client copy tool in a given situation, you must consider the locations of both the source client and the target client, and the type of data to be copied. To copy a client in an SAP system to another client in the same system, use a local client copy. You can use either a remote client copy or a client transport to copy a client from one SAP system to another (see Figure 9.2).

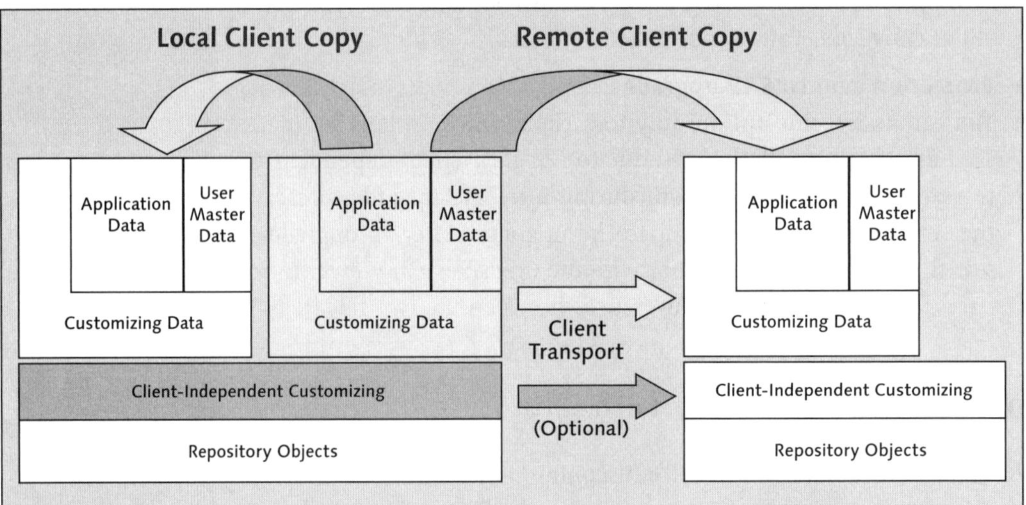

Figure 9.2 The Three Client Copy Tools

Advantages of a Client Transport

When you copy a client from one SAP system to another, you can use a client transport to:

- Preserve a copy of the client outside SAP ERP in files at the operating system level. A client transport involves writing a client to the transport directory (similar to the export process for a change request). This provides you with a copy of the client you can use later, for example, to help create multiple clients based on one client.
- Copy client-independent Customizing. As of R/3 Release 4.6, this can also be done with a remote client copy.
- Schedule the two steps—data export and import—independently.

For these reasons, SAP recommends using a client transport when you cannot use change requests to build a new SAP system (see Chapter 5). A client transport also provides a newly installed target system with the necessary client-independent and client-dependent data.

Note that you should not use a client transport to copy client-independent Customizing to a target system that already contains such Customizing, because the client transport will overwrite the existing client-independent Customizing objects in the target system. This causes inconsistencies when client-dependent data in other clients within the target system depends on the entries that were overwritten.

[+] Importing client-independent Customizing into an SAP system that already contains such Customizing may affect the data and functionality of other clients in the system.

Advantages of a Remote Client Copy

If you do not need client-independent Customizing in your new client, SAP recommends using a remote client copy to provide the client with data. For example, a remote client copy is ideal if you want to copy the user data from a unit test client in the development system to the training client in the quality assurance system. A remote client copy transfers data to another SAP system using RFC technology. The client copy tool has the following advantages:

- It can prevent data loss. During a remote client copy, an automatic Repository consistency check is performed. The structure of each table to be copied is checked and compared with tables in the target system. If inconsistencies are detected—for example, tables are missing in the target system or fields are missing in the tables—the client copy is canceled, and an error message is displayed. This kind of check is not performed automatically during a client transport.

- It is faster than a client transport, because it can copy data in parallel rather than sequentially.
- It does not require the multiple export and import steps required by a client transport.
- It does not generate files at the operating system level and therefore does not take up disk space in the transport directory. In contrast, the client transport of a production client may generate files larger than the available disk space, or reach file size limitations set by the operating system.

9.2.2 Using Client Copy Profiles to Select Data

Types of data

Regardless of the client copy tool you select, you must determine the type of data you want to copy from a source client to a target client. A client copy profile determines the data to be copied. The data that can be copied includes:

- Client-dependent customizing data
- Client-independent customizing data
- Application data—both master data and transaction data
- User data, which is a combination of user master data and authorization profiles (see Chapter 4)
- Variants, which are sets of input values saved for programs you use often

When you begin the client copy procedure, you select a particular client copy profile (see sections 9.2.3, Local and Remote Client Copy, and 9.2.4, Client Transport). The profiles delivered by SAP are displayed in Table 9.1 (for SAP ERP 6.0). Note that you can copy application data only when you also copy Customizing data because application data depends on the Customizing settings of the client, and is of no value without those settings.

[+] General information about the client copy and about the differences in copy profiles between different releases can also be found in SAP Note 24853.

[+] Before data is copied from the source client, the contents of the target client are deleted. This is true for all client copy profiles *except* the SAP_USER profile. In addition, if Central User Administration is active, you will not be able to copy user data, regardless of the client copy profile you select.

Copy Profile	Client-Dependent Customizing Data	Application Data	User Data	Variants	Client-Independent Customizing Data
SAP_ALL	X	X	X	X	
SAP_APPL	X	X		X	
SAP_CUST	X				
SAP_CUSV	X			X	
SAP_EXBC*	X		X	X	X
SAP_RMBC**	X		X	X	X
SAP_EXPA*	X	X	X	X	X
SAP_RMPA**	X	X	X	X	X
SAP_EXPC*	X			X	X
SAP_RMPC**	X			X	X
SAP_UCUS	X		X		
SAP_UCSV	X		X	X	
SAP_USER			X		

* These profiles can only be selected for a client transport (SCC8).

** These profiles can only be selected for a remote client copy (SCC9).

Table 9.1 Client Copy Profiles for Selecting Data

Example: Using Client Copy Tools to Support Training Needs

A company whose SAP ERP system has been in production for over a year decides to roll out additional business processes in the production system. This requires training for new users as well as those unfamiliar with the new business functionality.

To provide a training environment, a new client—client 300—is created in the quality assurance system. Client 300 is created as a client copy of the quality assurance client using a local client copy and the SAP_ALL client copy profile. The training staff cleans up client 300 by removing unnecessary data and providing base data for the business transactions the users need to learn. Client 300 thus provides a basis that instructors can use to develop training materials.

Prior to the start of training classes, client 400 is created using a local client copy of client 300 with the SAP_ALL client copy profile. To verify profiles and help users feel comfortable in their accounts, user data is copied from the production client into client 400 on the quality assurance system. This is done using a remote client copy with the SAP_USER client copy profile. The training then begins in client 400.

Displaying Client Copy Profiles

You can display the client copy profiles from within the different client copy tools. For example, to display the SAP_UCUS client copy profile from within the local client copy tool, proceed as follows:

1. Use Transaction code SCCL or, from the SAP Easy Access menu, choose TOOLS • ADMINISTRATION • ADMINISTRATION • CLIENT ADMINISTRATION • CLIENT COPY • LOCAL COPY.
2. Use the F4 help to get a list of the different profiles.
3. Select the SAP_UCUS profile.
4. Display the profile using PROFILE • DISPLAY PROFILE.

Figure 9.3 shows the screen that appears. When you select this profile, Customizing and user data—but not application data—will be copied. This client copy profile also initializes and recreates the target client—it deletes the target client prior to copying in data. It does not copy variants. This profile is valid for all client copy tools.

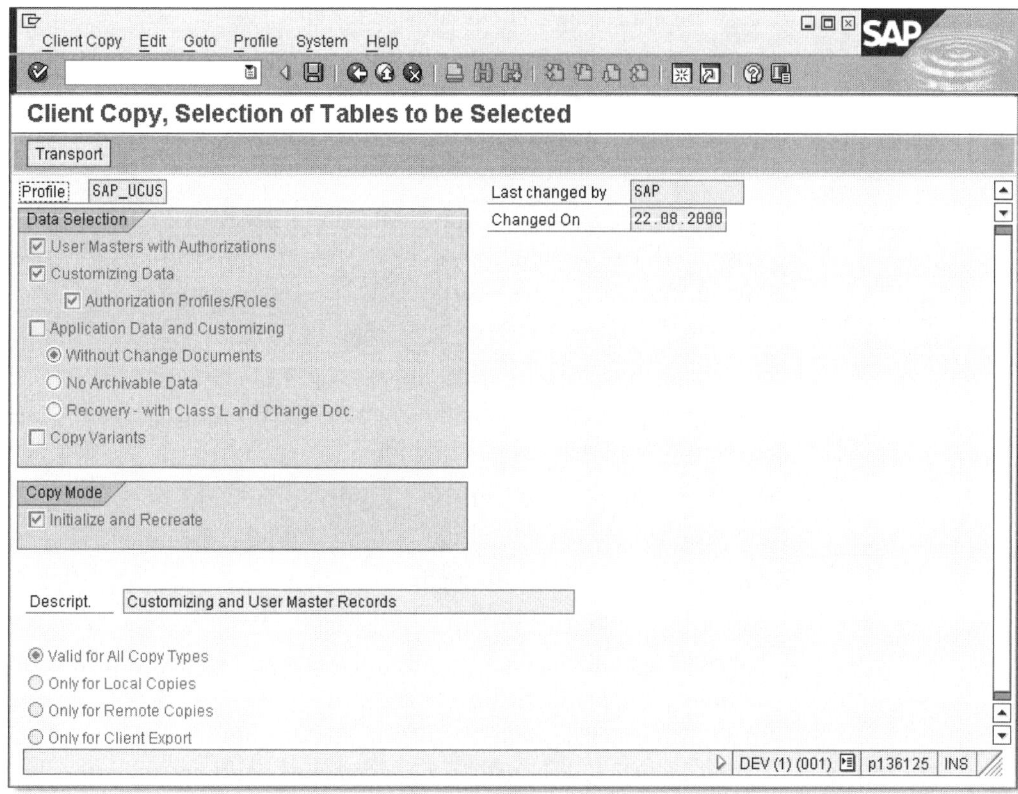

Figure 9.3 Displaying Client Copy Profile SAP_UCUS

9.2.3 Local and Remote Client Copy

To perform a local or remote client copy, proceed as follows:

1. Use client maintenance (Transaction SCC4) to ensure that the target client is defined in table T000.
2. Log on to the SAP system in the target client.
   - If the target client is new and has no defined users, log on with the user SAP* and the password PASS.
   - If users are defined in the target client, log on with a user that has authorization to perform a client copy, such as the user SAP*.

3. Access the appropriate client copy activity.
    - To copy a client from the same SAP system, access the local client copy tool. Use Transaction code SCCL or, from the SAP Easy Access menu, choose TOOLS • ADMINISTRATION • ADMINISTRATION • CLIENT ADMINISTRATION • CLIENT COPY • LOCAL COPY.
    - To copy a client from another SAP system, access the remote client copy tool. Use Transaction code SCC9 or, from the SAP Easy Access menu, choose TOOLS • ADMINISTRATION • ADMINISTRATION • CLIENT ADMINISTRATION • CLIENT COPY • REMOTE COPY.

    If a message box appears with the message THE CLIENT IS LOCKED FOR DATA IMPORT BY CLIENT COPY, the client protection setting for the target client does not allow overwriting.
4. Select the appropriate client copy profile. To view the possible client copy profiles, use the F4 help for the SELECTED PROFILE field.
5. Enter the source client information.
    - For a local client copy, provide the client ID of the source client whose Customizing data, application data, and variant information should be copied. In the SOURCE CLIENT USER MASTERS field, you may also enter a client ID for the source client whose user data should be copied. Usually the two source clients are the same, but you may want to copy user data from a different client.
    - For a remote client copy, you must provide an RFC DESTINATION. (maintained with Transaction SM59). It is used to communicate with a client in another SAP ERP system to share data. Using the F4 help for the SOURCE DESTINATION field, select the appropriate RFC destination. The name of the source SAP system and the client ID of the source client are entered automatically.

    If a message box appears with the message SOURCE CLIENT IS PROTECTED AGAINST DATA EXPORT BY CLIENT COPY, the client protection setting for the source client does not allow external access and cannot be copied.
6. Choose EXECUTE or EXECUTE IN BACKGROUND to start the client copy. Because a client copy is often very time-consuming, SAP recommends performing your client copy as a background job.

7. A VERIFICATION dialog box appears, which allows you to check and confirm the profile and source information. If everything is correct, choose YES to start the client copy. Select NO to cancel the procedure.

9.2.4 Client Transport

You can think of a client transport as a very large change request that contains the contents of an entire client. The multi-step process requires, first, a client export from the source client to files at the operating system level, and then the import of these data files into the target client. In addition, post-import processing is required to complete the procedure.

RFC System Check

Consistency check

Before data is copied with a remote client copy, an SAP system consistency check is automatically performed. With a client transport, this check is not automatic but you can opt to perform it. The initial screen of the client transport tool (Transaction SCC8) has an RFC SYSTEM CHECK button to initiate the check.

The check program first determines what data should be copied based on the selected client copy profile. RFCs are then used to locate the target system and client, and check whether all ABAP Dictionary definitions exist in both, and are identical. The check report usually confirms that all structures are consistent. If that is not the case, a list of the ABAP Dictionary table definitions missing in the target system is generated. This will help you recognize in advance problems that may occur during the import of the source data.

[+] To ensure the consistency of the ABAP Dictionary in the source and target SAP systems, SAP recommends performing an RFC system check before starting a client transport.

Client Export

A client export writes data files at the operating system level. These data files, unlike the data files that result from a standard change request, may be rather large. For this reason alone, SAP does not recommend copying large production clients using the client copy tools. A system copy may be more appropriate. In any case, prior to using a client transport, you should verify that enough disk space is available in the transport directory using operating system tools.

[+] For information on how to copy large production clients, see SAP Note 67205.

To perform a client export, follow these steps:

1. Log on to the SAP system in the source client. Do not log on as user SAP*.

[+] Because user SAP* cannot create a change request, it cannot perform the client export step in a client transport.

2. Access the client export tool using Transaction code SCC8 or, from the SAP Easy Access menu, choose TOOLS • ADMINISTRATION • ADMINISTRATION • CLIENT ADMINISTRATION • CLIENT TRANSPORT • CLIENT EXPORT.
3. Select the appropriate client copy profile. To view the possible client copy profiles, use the F4 help for the SELECTED PROFILE field.
4. Enter the system ID of the target system. The exported files will be imported into this SAP system. It must differ from the SAP system in which you are initiating the client export. Only SAP systems defined in your transport domain may be selected. Proceed as follows in these special situations:
   - If the target SAP system is not part of your transport domain, prior to the client export, use the TMS (Transaction STMS) to define the SAP system as either a virtual or an external system.
   - If the TMS is set up with extended transport control, you may provide a SID, a combination of a SID and a client, or a target transport group in the field for the target system.
5. Choose EXECUTE or EXECUTE IN BACKGROUND to start the client export. Because this process can take a long time to complete, SAP recommends performing the client export as a background job.
6. A VERIFICATION dialog box appears, which allows you to check and confirm the profile and source information. If everything is correct, choose YES to start the client export. Choose NO to cancel the procedure.

7. An INFO CLIENT EXPORT message box appears. This displays any change requests that may be generated as a result of the client export. Choose CONTINUE to begin the client export.

Client Import

Three change requests

A client export generates up to three change requests for import into the target SAP system. Table 9.2 displays the change requests for a sample client export. These change requests and files will be found in the transport directory for the 15th client export from the development system DEV. Because this sample client export uses the SAP_EXPA client copy profile, which includes all client-dependent and client-independent data from the source client, three change requests were generated. If the SAP_USER client copy profile, which selects only user data for export, had been selected for the sample client export, the DEVKO00015 change request would not have been created.

Note that the client export files have a naming convention distinct from Customizing and Workbench change requests. Like these change requests, the ID number for client export files begins with the system ID of the source system (here, DEV), and ends with a sequential five-digit number. In the middle, however, a combination of the letters K and O (for client-independent data), T (for client-dependent data), or X (for client-dependent texts) is used. These letters allow you to quickly distinguish a client export change request from standard change requests when viewing an import queue.

Change Request	Data Contents	Data File	Command File
DEVKO00015	Client-independent data	RO00015.DEV	KO00015.DEV
DEVKT00015	Client-dependent data	RT00015.DEV	KT00015.DEV
DEVKX00015	Client-dependent text, such as SAPscripts	RX00015.DEV	KX00015.DEV

Table 9.2 Sample Change Requests from a Client Export

As a result of the client export, the change requests are added to the import queue of the target system. To view the import queue of a system, call Transaction STMS and choose OVERVIEW • IMPORTS; then double-click the system ID.

Import queue Figure 9.4 shows a sample import queue. A total of six change requests are waiting for import, three of which resulted from a client export initiated by user KOESEGI. Because client export change requests are special requests that, in most cases, delete and recreate a client, as well as provide a client with new data, they cannot be imported using standard import commands (in Transaction STMS: START IMPORT or PRELIMINARY IMPORT). They must be imported as individual change requests. Such change requests are highlighted in a different color to indicate that they will not be imported. To determine the meaning of the different icons and colors, use the LEGEND button on the import queue screen.

All change requests, including those released as a result of a client export, should be imported in their correct order—the order in which they appear in the import queue (see Chapter 5). Before you import change requests as part of your client export process, import the change requests higher up in the import queue. For example, in Figure 9.4, the first two change requests should be imported before the client export.

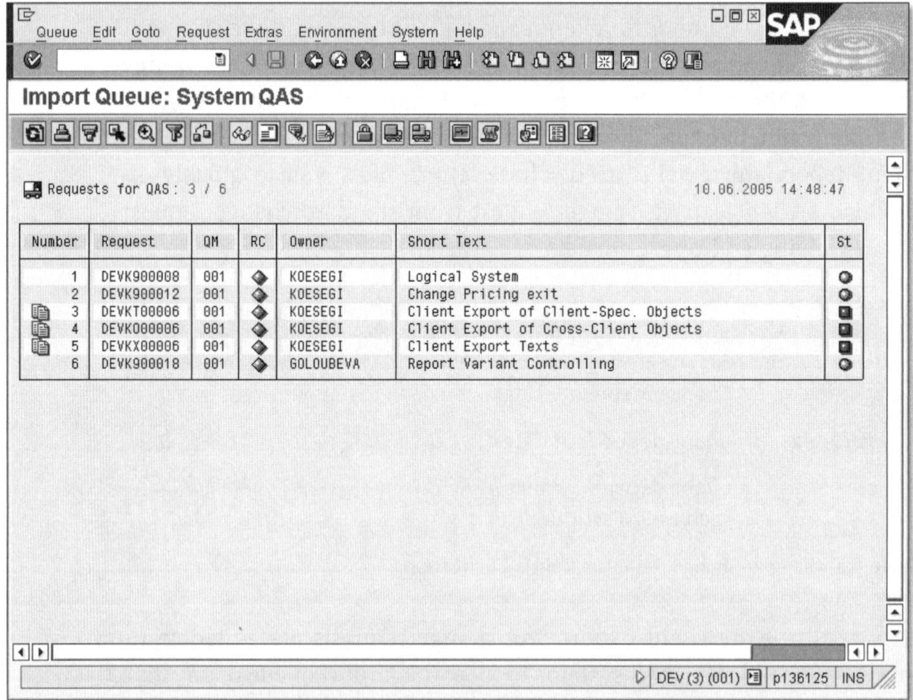

Figure 9.4 Sample Import Queue with Client Export Change Requests

Follow these steps to import the client data that has been exported and is waiting in the import queue:

Data import

1. Call Transaction STMS and then choose Overview • Import. Double-click the target SAP system of the client export to display its import queue.
2. Select the first client export change request waiting for import and choose Request • Import. By selecting this change request, you initiate the import for all of the client export change requests.
3. The Client Import screen, as shown in Figure 9.5, appears. It lists the names of the change requests to be imported. Enter the client ID of the target client.
4. Execute the import by clicking on the Import button. The change request import takes place as a background job.

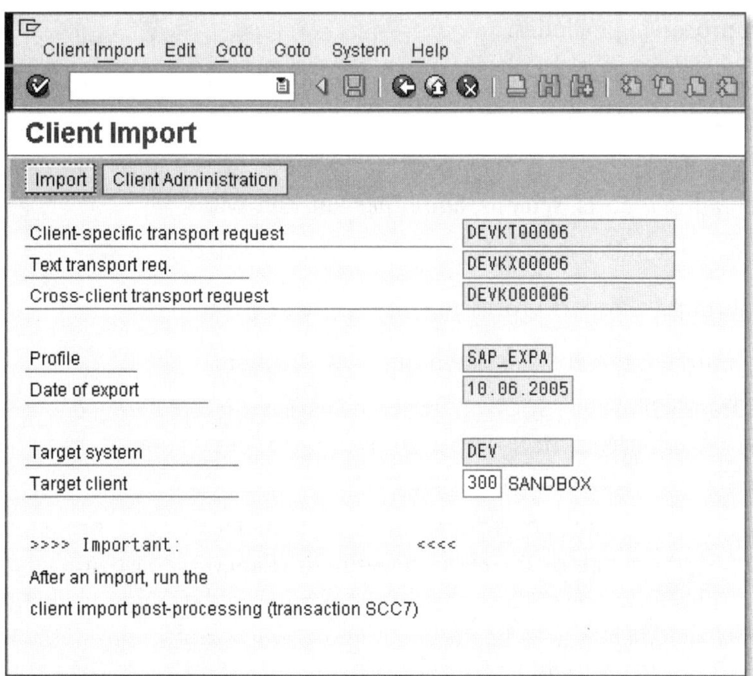

Figure 9.5 The Client Import Screen

Post-Import Considerations

For all SAP releases, after successful import, the client export change requests remain in the import queue of the target system. You should delete them by individually by selecting each change request in the import queue and choosing REQUEST • DELETE.

Client export change requests do not continue along the standard transport routes. In other words, if you import a client into the quality assurance system, the change requests will not be added to the import queue of the production system. If the client export should be imported into other SAP systems or clients, you must add the change requests to the import queues accordingly.

No one should work in the client until the necessary post-import activities have been performed successfully. The only exception to this is when you perform a client import that contains only user data. Post-import processing includes:

- Deleting data from certain imported tables, including tables with delivery class "L" (explained in more detail in the section "Table Delivery Classes")
- Generating reports, screens, and other Repository objects
- Adjusting number ranges

Post-import processing

To perform post-import processing, follow these steps:

1. Log on to the target SAP system in the target client.
2. Use Transaction code SCC7 or, from the SAP Easy Access menu, choose TOOLS • ADMINISTRATION • ADMINISTRATION • CLIENT ADMINISTRATION • CLIENT TRANSPORT • POST-PROCESS IMPORT.
3. The CLIENT IMPORT - POSTPROCESSING screen appears (see Figure 9.6). It shows the name of the client-dependent change request from the client import process. The name of the profile used during the client export also displays. To begin post-import processing, choose either EXECUTE or EXECUTE IN BACKGROUND.
4. If client-independent Customizing objects were copied, you will be prompted to process the cross-client Customizing changes. If the SAP system contains none of its own unique client-independent Customizing, choose YES.

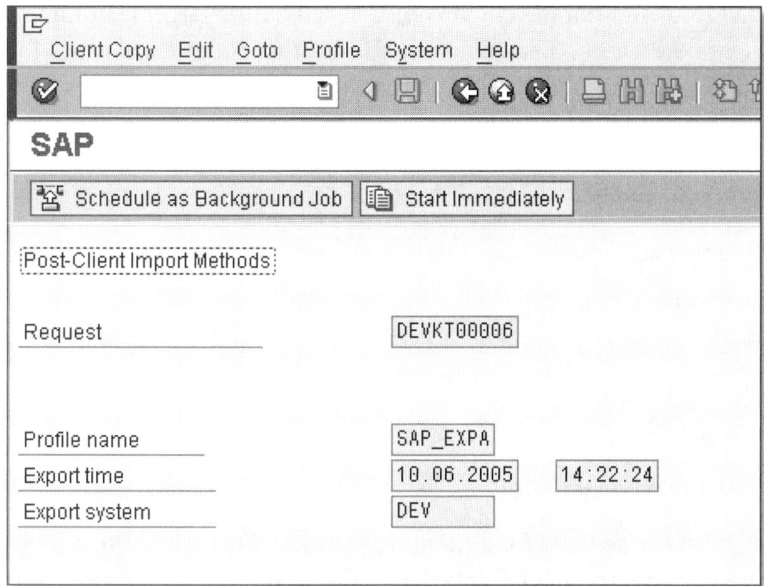

Figure 9.6 Client Import Post-Processing Screen

Post-import processing needs to be performed only once. If you try to restart post-import processing, one of the following messages will appear in the status bar:

- A PHYSICAL CLIENT TRANSPORT WITH TP HAS NOT TAKEN PLACE. This message appears when post-import processing has been completed.
- CLIENT HAS NOT YET BEEN GENERATED BY A DATA IMPORT. This message appears when a client import has not occurred or the import of the client data did not complete successfully.

9.2.5 Monitoring and Verifying a Client Copy

While a client copy is running, throughout the rather long procedure, you can view the status in the CLIENT COPY LOG. After the procedure is complete, you can also use the log to check whether the client copy was a success or failure before you begin working in the target client.

To access the client copy log, use Transaction code SCC3 or, from the SAP Easy Access menu, choose TOOLS • ADMINISTRATION • ADMINISTRATION • CLIENT ADMINISTRATION • COPY LOGS. The screen displays the current status of all local and remote client copies, listed by the target client number. Figure 9.7 shows a sample screen indicating client export logs for three different target clients. The NUMBER RUNS column indicates how many client copy log files exist for the target client. The most important column, STATUS TEXT, displays the status of the last client copy. Possible status texts include:

Status texts

- INITIALIZING ...
- PROCESSING ...
- EXPORTED SUCCESSFULLY
- ENDED WITH ERRORS
- CANCELED
- R3TRANS EXPORT (SEE SE01)

These texts are also valid for a client transport. In fact, the last text is client transport-specific and is explained in the section "Special Transaction for Client Transports."

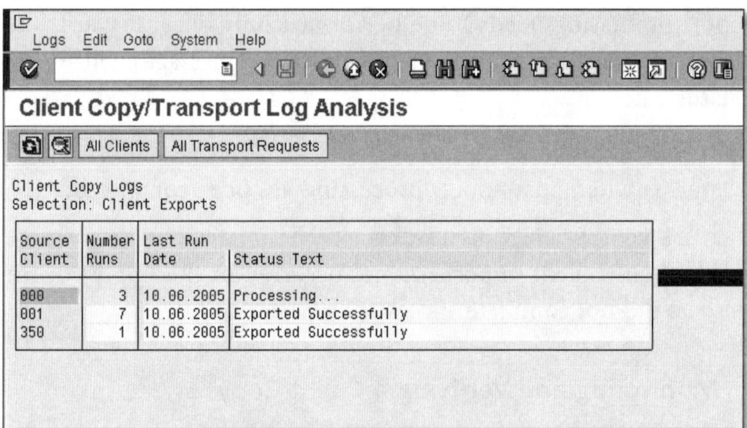

Figure 9.7 Client Copy/Transport Log Analysis Screen

With Transaction SCC3, you can also monitor the client export and import activities that make up a client transport. To view import logs, from the initial screen of Transaction SCC3, you can choose either CLIENT EXPORTS or CLIENT IMPORTS.

Copy logs

To access the logs for a particular target client, double-click that client ID. A list of all available log files for that client will be displayed. A sample screen is shown in Figure 9.8. The table in this screen contains a variety of information, including the client copy profile (PROFILE column) and the CLIENT COPY type (MODE column). In the TEST column, the entry "R" indicates that a resource check was run, and "X" refers to a simulation (explained in section "System Resources"). By double-clicking a particular log file, you can obtain the following information:

- For client copy logs resulting from a test run (an entry in the TEST column), you have detailed access to the tables impacted by the copy as well as an estimated resource analysis.
- For client copies with status PROCESSING, you can see the table whose data is currently being processed and the number of tables still to be copied.
- For client copies with status EXPORTED SUCCESSFULLY, you can verify the tables that were copied and the number of table inserts and deletes.
- For client copies with status CANCELED or ENDED WITH ERRORS, to determine the cause of the error, you can view the log files.

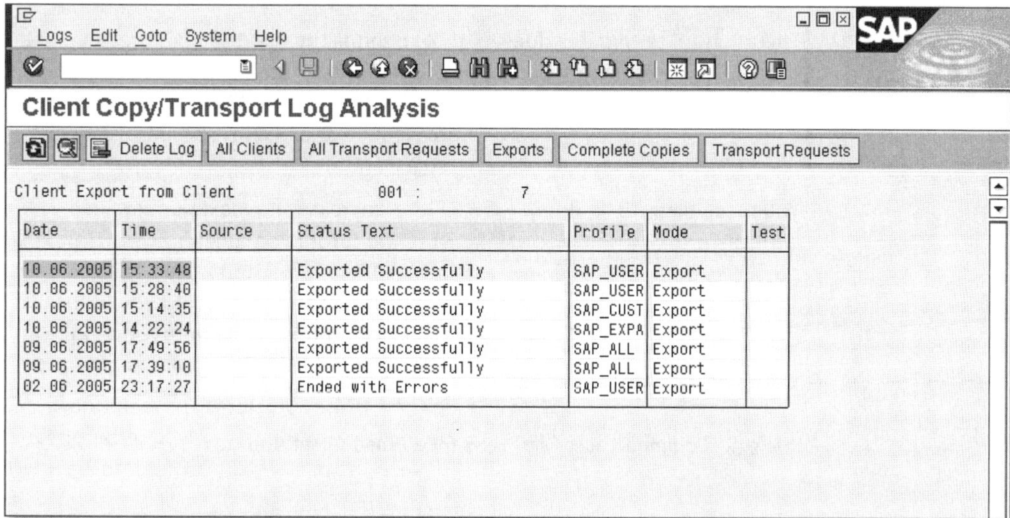

Date	Time	Source	Status Text	Profile	Mode	Test
10.06.2005	15:33:48		Exported Successfully	SAP_USER	Export	
10.06.2005	15:28:40		Exported Successfully	SAP_USER	Export	
10.06.2005	15:14:35		Exported Successfully	SAP_CUST	Export	
10.06.2005	14:22:24		Exported Successfully	SAP_EXPA	Export	
09.06.2005	17:49:56		Exported Successfully	SAP_ALL	Export	
09.06.2005	17:39:10		Exported Successfully	SAP_ALL	Export	
02.06.2005	23:17:27		Ended with Errors	SAP_USER	Export	

Figure 9.8 Client Copy Logs for a Single Client

Special Transaction for Client Transports

When data is being extracted for a client export, the status for the client copy log in this transaction will read R3TRANS EXPORT (SEE SE01). Because client transports use `R3trans`, a database tool external to R/3 (see Chapter 7), you can view only limited log files within Transaction SCC3.

To see all of the export and import log files generated during a client transport process, access the Transport Organizer by calling Transaction SE01. From the initial screen, select CLIENT TRANSPORTS as the request type, and click CHOOSE. This displays client transport change requests in the same hierarchical manner used for standard change requests in the Customizing Organizer or Workbench Organizer.

Restarting a Canceled Client Copy

Table 9.3 lists the most common reasons why a client copy is terminated, and presents possible solutions.

Cause of Termination	Solution
A user stops the program.	Restart the client copy.
A user shuts down the SAP ERP system, or the system fails.	Restart the client copy.
The program terminates due to inadequate storage space in the database.	To monitor the database fill level and size of objects such as tablespaces or tables, use Transaction DB02. Using database tools such as SAPDBA, increase available space and restart the client copy.
You receive an ABAP dump with the error cause TIMEOUT.	Either increase the maximum online runtime (profile parameter `rdisp/max_wprun_time`) and restart the client copy, or perform the client copy in the background (discussed in the section "Background Scheduling of a Client Copy").

Table 9.3 Common Causes and Fixes for a Failed Client Copy

Cause of Termination	Solution
The program terminates due to an error in an EXIT module. You receive an ABAP dump.	Review the copy logs to determine which program failed. Using SAP Service Marketplace, search for SAP Notes related to the failed program to find a correction. Correct the problem or contact SAP for further support.
An inconsistency occurs between the database and the SAP system. You receive an ABAP error message noting a database inconsistency.	Data cannot be copied properly because table structures in the source and target systems differ. Correct the inconsistencies and restart the client copy. (Refer back to the section "RFC System Check.")

Table 9.3 Common Causes and Fixes for a Failed Client Copy (Cont.)

Restart

After correcting the problem, restart the client copy by again calling the appropriate client copy transaction (Transaction SCCL, SCC9, or SCC8). Because the initial client copy failed, the RESTART option will be suggested by default. For example, if a local client copy failed because of inadequate tablespace, you would remedy the problem and then call Transaction SCCL. The parameters you initially used for the canceled client copy would still be present, and the RESTART MODE ACTIVE field would be selected. To run the client copy from the point of failure—that is, to begin copying the table where the failure occurred—choose either EXECUTE or EXECUTE IN BACKGROUND. To perform a completely new client copy, choose RESTART • NEW START.

[+]

If a terminated client copy was a recent run—which will be indicated in the status line—SAP recommends restarting the client copy from the time of termination. This will save the time required for recopying data that has already been successfully copied.

Additional Tools

In addition to reviewing the client copy logs, you can also monitor and verify a client copy with the following tools:

- Analyze a client copy error by calling Transaction SM21 (SYSTEM LOG) and checking the system log. This indicates whether database problems are responsible for the client copy error. Correct any database problems and then restart the client copy.

- Check the status of a client copy started as a background job by calling Transaction SM37 (Background Job Overview). This indicates whether a background client copy job has started, is active, or has been completed.
- Monitor the progress of a particular client copy by using Transaction SM30 (View Maintenance) to access view V_CCCFLOW. This view contains, for example, the runtime and processing status of a local client copy, the number of tables already copied, and the name of the table currently being copied.
- View the log files physically stored in the transport directory at the operating system level. Log files are named `CC<number>.<SID>`, where `<number>` is the six-digit serial client copy number and `<SID>` is the source system ID. For example, the 21st client copy on the development system will generate the log file `CC000021.DEV`.

9.2.6 Considerations for a Client Copy

The client copy process impacts not only the performance, memory, and database resources of the involved SAP system (or systems), but also the availability of the source and target clients. Before starting a client copy, you must evaluate the system resources and client availability in your system landscape. In addition to technical issues, you must also consider the impact a client copy has on certain data, including number ranges and address data.

Client Impact

Unless you are copying only user data, a client copy or client import reinitializes the target client by deleting it. The key entries of the tables corresponding to the target client are deleted.

To ensure data consistency in the target client during the client copy or client import, the target client's restriction Currently locked due to client copy is activated automatically, and only the users DDIC and SAP* can log on to the target client.

No user should work in the source client during the copy procedure. This prevents possible inconsistencies from occurring—particularly in the number ranges—that result from changes in tables that are being copied. You should schedule a client copy for a time when the source system's usage is minimal—for example, in the evening.

[+] Users should not make changes in a source client while it is being copied.

Background Scheduling of a Client Copy

The client copy program has a long runtime. Therefore, it should always be started in the background. This has the following advantages:

Advantages of background scheduling

- The client copy will not use or block work processes required for online processing.
- The client copy will not be terminated if it exceeds the allowed execution time. This is important when very large tables are involved in the copy. Although the maximum execution time for online work processes (profile parameter `rdisp/max_wprun_time`) is usually too short to allow a complete client to be copied, this runtime restriction does not apply to background processing.
- Changes to tables during online processing are not blocked. (While the client copy is in progress, to prevent possible inconsistencies, no changes can be made to tables in the source client.)

To perform a client copy as a background job, choose EXECUTE IN BACKGROUND when initiating the client copy. Next, schedule the job as immediate, or specify a start time—preferably a time when the system is not being used. Provide the print parameters for the spool output. After you save these parameters, the client copy is scheduled for background processing.

System Resources

As pointed out in Chapter 3, every client requires both hardware and administrative resources. To copy a client, you must ensure that adequate space is available in the target SAP system. In other words, the target SAP system database must have enough free storage space available in existing tables for the client copy to succeed. In addition, you need enough system memory to process the copying of data. Without the required system resources, the client copy will fail.

Tablespace requirements For an SAP system whose database management system (DBMS) is Oracle, Informix, MaxDB (formerly known as SAP DB), or DB2/CS you can determine whether the database space for each table is sufficient by performing a test run of the proposed client copy. After the test run, you receive a list of all database areas (tablespaces) that will be extended during the copy. In addition, because these test runs are logged, you can use the log to check how much space the entries require.

Test run To perform a client copy as a test run, simply execute the client copy with the TEST RUN option selected. A test run can be executed either online or, more appropriately, as a background job. To start the test run, choose either RESOURCE CHECK or SIMULATION. These two types of test runs differ as follows:

- A resource check estimates the required database space by counting the records to be copied. It is faster than a simulation.
- A simulation estimates the required database space by reading all records to be copied without updating them in the database.

There is no way to exactly determine the range of free storage space available in existing tables. For every table copied, the number of required inserts is calculated. However, because database deletions are not possible in some databases until after reorganization, these deletions are not taken into account. This means that the forecasted database requirements may be considerably larger than the actual requirements. If a resource check or a simulation indicates that you have enough tablespace to perform a client copy, you can be certain the client copy will not fail because of a lack of tablespace.

[+] Note that the space requirements can only be estimated because space that is reserved but not yet occupied is not taken into account. A client without application data requires roughly 500MB of storage space in the database. Additionally, you must consider that in most databases, the space that is freed by deleting data becomes available only after reorganization. For pool tables, the estimate is very imprecise because their extent sizes are very substantial. Nevertheless, you have to assume that a new extent is required for every pool table, which increases the estimated value. For more information, refer to SAP Note 118823.

A client copy requires a great deal of system memory. If your system memory is limited, you should not perform any other activities in the system during the copy procedure. In this case, SAP recommends running the client copy as a background job at a time when regular system activity is greatly reduced.

Memory requirements

Table Delivery Classes

By selecting a particular client copy profile, you determine which data is copied in a client copy. In turn, the SAP system uses table delivery classes to determine which data corresponds to the client copy profile.

A table delivery class indicates the type of data housed in a table—application data, Customizing data, or some type of system data. Every table in the ABAP Dictionary is assigned a table delivery class. Release upgrades and the client copy tools use this information to determine which table data to copy to target clients.

Table 9.4 lists the different table delivery classes and indicates when the different classes are copied. For example, if you select the client copy profile for client-dependent Customizing data only, the client copy will select the client-dependent data from tables with delivery class "C." In addition, the client copy selects the client-dependent data from system tables with delivery classes "G," "E," and "S."

Table Delivery Class	Type of Table	Copied* When?
A	Application data	When selected
C	Customizing data	When selected
L	Temporary table	Never
G	Customizing table protected during an upgrade	Always
E	Control table	Always
S	System table that you cannot maintain	Always
W	System table	Never

* It is assumed that the copy mode is set to INITIALIZE AND RECREATE.

Table 9.4 The Role of Table Delivery Classes in a Client Copy

You do not need to select particular delivery classes because they are tied to the client copy profile. However, when you are debugging, the table delivery class may help you discover why a certain data type was not included in a client copy. For example, if data is stored in a table with the table delivery class "W," you know it will not be part of any client copy. However, if you selected a profile that includes application data, and the data from a table with delivery class "A" was not included in the copy procedure, one of the following has occurred:

Problems

- The data was entered into the source table after the client copy.
- The data was deleted from the target client after the client copy was completed.
- The table containing the data is assigned to the temporary development class $tmp. Data in tables that are assigned to a temporary development class is not copied during a client copy.
- A programming problem exists. In this case, check the SAP Service Marketplace for a specific SAP Note or report the problem to SAP Support.

To view the delivery class of a table, use Transaction code SE11 or, from the SAP Easy Access menu, use TOOLS • ABAP WORKBENCH • DEVELOPMENT • DICTIONARY. Enter the name of the table and select DISPLAY.

Number Ranges

When performing Customizing activities within the IMG, you often adjust *number* ranges. A number range is the set of consecutive numbers that can be assigned to business objects—or their sub-objects—of the same type. Examples of such objects include addresses, business partners, general ledger accounts, orders, posting documents, and materials. Number ranges are assigned to application data—master data in the case of business partners or transaction data for orders. When working with multiple clients and using client copies to create new clients, you should evaluate the status of your number ranges. For example, if you want to, for the purpose of testing, use different number ranges in different clients, or use the same number ranges for certain master data but not necessarily for transaction data.

If you copy only Customizing data, the target client will not contain any application data after the completion of the client copy. In this case, the number ranges will be automatically reset to default values during the copy procedure. In all other cases, the number range status remains unchanged or is copied from the source client.

After a client copy, SAP recommends that you evaluate number ranges in the target client and reset them when necessary. [+]

Address number ranges can be problematic when information is shared between clients. For more details on avoiding possible address inconsistencies in your system landscape, see SAP Note 25182. [+]

9.3 Deleting a Client

When you delete a client from your system landscape, you have to remove:

- All of its associated client-dependent data
- Its entry in table T000

Deleting a client is irreversible. The client can be reinstated only by restoring the entire database of the SAP system from a backup.

After you have deleted a client, you cannot simply undo the procedure. A restore of the SAP system database is the only way to restore a client. [+]

To delete a client's data and its entry in table T000:

1. Log on to the SAP client you want to delete.
2. To access the client delete tool, use Transaction code SCC5 or, from the SAP Easy Access menu, choose TOOLS • ADMINISTRATION • ADMINISTRATION • CLIENT ADMINISTRATION • SPECIAL FUNCTIONS • DELETE CLIENT.
3. Select a client delete option. Choose from either:
   - TEST RUN: To simulate the deletion process and see what table entries will be deleted.
   - DELETE ENTRY FROM T000: To delete the client ID from client maintenance.
4. Click on the DELETE ONLINE or BACKGROUND button to start the procedure.

9.4 Table Logging for a Client

Table logging is different from recording changes to change requests. Logging table changes made in a client provides an audit trail that allows you to verify who made exactly what change to the data and when. For example, if a user changes the company name associated with a company code:

- A change request records that the key value—in this case, the company code—has been changed by a particular user.
- Table logging indicates the actual field that changed in a table and stores the original company name. It records who made the change and when.

When you log table changes made as a result of Customizing activities, you can pinpoint the actual change. For example, you can determine whether data in a particular field was changed or whether a new record was added to a table. You can also display table logs at the Customizing-activity level. To activate table logging, see the text that follows.

9.4.1 Resource Constraints

Table logging saves a "before image" by documenting the complete set of table entries before a change is made. Each time a Customizing change is made, a new before image is created. Therefore, table logging will constrain your system resources in the following way:

- Each before image requires storage space in the database of your SAP system. Table logging is not suitable for recording or managing large quantities of data.
- Activating table logging causes twice as many database updates as before, resulting in a higher database memory load and reduced system performance. However, as long as table logging is restricted to Customizing tables (not application data tables), performance should not be greatly reduced.

Large quantities of data

This tool has the potential to produce large amounts of data, more than you may actually be able to review and evaluate. For all of these reasons,

SAP recommends using table logging only in clients where Customizing changes must be closely monitored. Most Customizing changes occur in the Customizing-and-development client. However, it should suffice to rely on the information provided by change requests in this client. Table logging is more appropriate in the production client, providing you with a complete audit of any immediate changes to Customizing settings or changes that usually occur in the production client, such as adjustments to currency exchange rates.

9.4.2 Activating Table Logging

To activate the logging of table changes for Customizing, the SAP system profile parameter must be set to `rec/client = <client ID>`. To change the SAP system profile, use Transaction code RZ10 (Maintenance of Profile Parameters) or, from the SAP Easy Access menu, choose Tools • CCMS • Configuration • Profile Maintenance.

For example, to activate the recording of table changes in the production client 400, the profile for the production system requires the entry `rec/client = 400`. Possible variations of the profile parameter include the following:

- `rec/client = 300, 400` activates logging in two clients, 300 and 400.
- `rec/client = OFF` deactivates logging for all clients.
- `rec/client = ALL` activates logging in all clients within the SAP system.

For changes in the SAP system profile to take effect, the SAP system must be restarted. [+]

Activating Logging during Imports

When you activate table logging using the `rec/client` profile parameter, you ensure that table changes made within the client or clients will be logged. However, because Customizing changes may also be imported into the client, you can set the recclient = <client ID> transport parameter in the transport profile to record them (see Chapter 7).

The transport parameter should have the same setting as the `rec/client` parameter in the SAP system profile. In other words, if you have activated table logging for client 300 and client 400 by setting the profile parameter (`rec/client = 300,400`), the transport profile should be identical (`recclient = 300,400`).

Logging imported change requests as well as using table logging in the SAP system provides a comprehensive, collective audit of all Customizing changes. If you do not have logging turned on during import, you can always use change requests in conjunction with table logging to get a similar audit history. In fact, this may be a more viable alternative because logging imported changes can negatively impact system resources and unnecessarily inflate the amount of data collected.

The Log Data Changes Option

SAP has preset the tables that are logged. They contain Customizing settings and were chosen because of their significance to the flow of business processes within SAP ERP. When you activate table logging for a client, a history of changes will be collected for the tables in the ABAP Dictionary selected by SAP. Technically, they are the tables for which SAP has activated the LOG DATA CHANGES option in the ABAP Dictionary. To check whether a specific table will be logged when you activate table logging, display the table in the ABAP Dictionary Maintenance (Transaction SE11) and choose TECHNICAL SETTINGS to see if LOG DATA CHANGES is selected for the table.

Logging has advanced beyond the table level to the Customizing-activity level. Technically, logging still occurs at the table level using the LOG DATA CHANGES option in the ABAP Dictionary. However, from within each IMG Customizing activity, you can view the associated tables and learn which have table logging activated.

Using Table Maintenance (Transaction SE13), you can change the technical settings for a specific table, including the LOG DATA CHANGES option. However, SAP does not recommend altering this setting. If you deactivate logging for an object, an analysis of changes will result in inconsistencies. Activating table logging for a table may also negatively affect system performance. This is particularly true for application tables, due to the frequent changes to application data.

9.4.3 Viewing Table Logs

After you have activated table logging in a client, changes to tables are saved to *change documents*, often referred to as *change logs*. Using the tools provided by SAP, you can view change documents in detail and compare older change documents with present table entries to obtain a before and after picture of your Customizing settings.

Table Log Analysis

To view the audit history for tables, use Transaction code SE38 (ABAP Editor) and execute the ABAP program RSTBHIST. Or, from the SAP ERP initial screen, choose TOOLS • BUSINESS ENGINEER • CUSTOMIZING • TOOLS • TABLE HISTORY. From the resulting screen, you can do any of the following:

- List all logged Customizing changes that occurred on the current day.
- List all logged changes that occurred during a given time period (for example, over the last 15 days) or only those in a specific table.
- List all tables for which table logging is active.
- Compare the present contents of a table (for which logging is active) with its contents at a previous date and time.

Execution

For example, to compare the current exchange rates (table TCURR) in an SAP ERP system with the values on June 13, 1999, you would do the following:

1. Log on to the client whose data you want to analyze.
2. Access the table history tool by using Transaction code SE38 and executing program RSTBHIST. Or, from the SAP ERP initial screen, choose TOOLS • BUSINESS ENGINEER • CUSTOMIZING • TOOLS • TABLE HISTORY.
3. To compare the current values of the table with its contents in the past:

   Select COMPARISON: HISTORY ↔ CURRENT, and choose FUNCTION • ANALYZE CHANGE DOCUMENTS.
4. Provide the name of the table whose values you want to compare—in our example, table TCURR. Enter the date (June 13, 1999) and, if you wish, a time.
5. Choose COMPARE to begin the comparison.

In the screen that displays, the first column, STATUS, is particularly interesting. This column permits the following entries:

Status

- **Status "M"**
  The current value and the past value are different.
- **Status "C"**
  A current table entry did not exist in the table on the past date.
- **Status "S"**
  A table entry on the past date no longer exists in the current table.
- **No status**
  The values for the table entries are identical.

Customizing Activity Logging

You can also analyze table logs from within a Customizing activity. This lets you see changes to tables that are part of a Customizing activity without knowing the specific names of the tables involved. Using Customizing activity logs from within an IMG activity, you can do the following:

- Examine the tables involved in the current Customizing activity and determine which have table logging activated.
- View the current changes that have been logged for the Customizing activity.

Execution

If you want to see, for example, which tables are affected by the Customizing activity for CURRENCIES EXCHANGE RATES and which are logged, proceed as follows (this example refers to SAP ERP 6.0):

1. Access the IMG (Transaction SPRO) and select IMPLEMENTATION PROJECTS • DISPLAY SAP REFERENCE IMG. In the tree structure, select SAP NETWEAVER • GENERAL SETTINGS • CURRENCIES • ENTER EXCHANGE RATES.
2. Select GOTO • CHANGE LOG to display information about table logging with regard to the activity.
3. Click on the LOGGING: DISPLAY STATUS button to display the logging status of the current client and the tables that are being logged in the current Customizing activity.

The results of this analysis are shown in Figure 9.9. The table involved in this activity is TCURR.

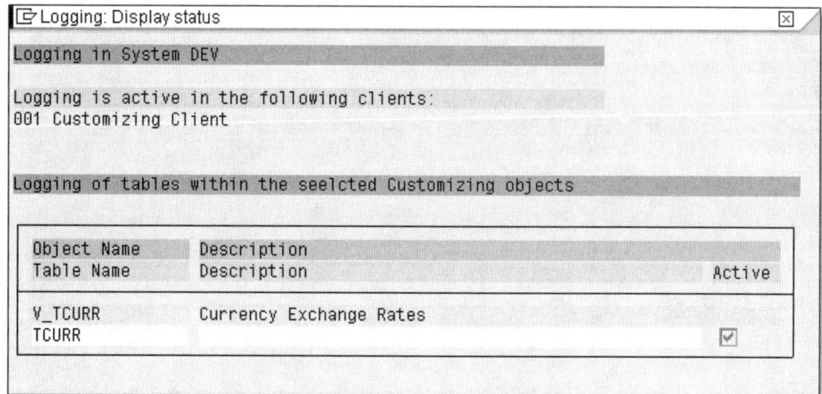
Logging: Display status

Logging in System DEV

Logging is active in the following clients:
001 Customizing Client

Logging of tables within the seelcted Customizing objects

Object Name Table Name	Description Description	Active
V_TCURR TCURR	Currency Exchange Rates	☑

Figure 9.9 Customizing Activity Logging Status

You can also view the actual changes that have been recorded for a particular IMG Customizing activity. To do this, begin the Customizing activity and then choose UTILITIES • CHANGE LOGS. For example, to view the changes made in a production system for the Customizing activity to change currency exchange rates, proceed as follows:

1. Access the IMG (Transaction SPRO) and select IMPLEMENTATION PROJECTS • DISPLAY SAP REFERENCE IMG. In the tree structure, select SAP NETWEAVER • GENERAL SETTINGS • CURRENCIES • ENTER EXCHANGE RATES.
2. Select GOTO • CHANGE LOGS to display information about table logging with regard to the activity.
3. Enter the time frame you want to view.
4. Click on the EXECUTE button to display the information logged during the specified time frame for the current Customizing activity.

Figure 9.10 displays the results of this analysis. The KEY FIELDS column shows the table entries that were adjusted. The actual changes are shown in the second column, FUNCTION FIELDS, CHANGED. Here, you can see whether the entry was changed, deleted, or newly created.

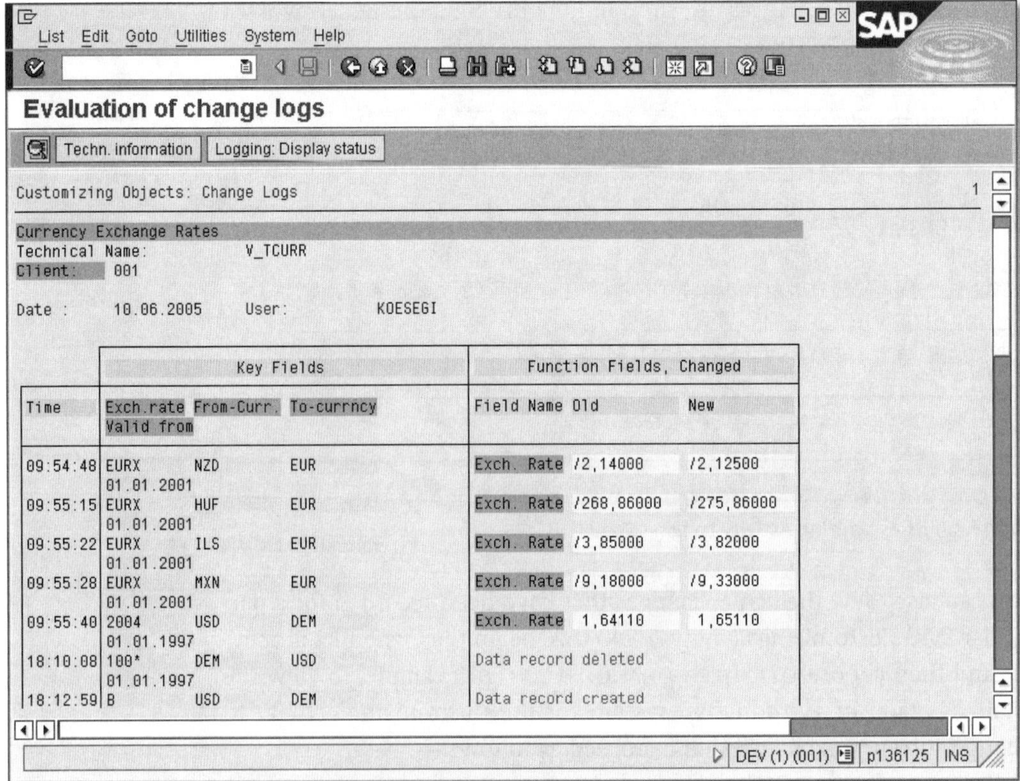

Figure 9.10 Change Documents for a Customizing Activity

9.4.4 Removing Change Documents

As more and more Customizing changes impact different tables, the number of change documents increases over time and occupies valuable space in the database. Therefore, it is important for you to manage the growth of change documents. SAP ERP provides you with two alternatives: You can either delete change documents that contain table logging data or archive the documents for later retrieval and analysis. Archiving is the ideal method for preserving a complete audit history.

Deleting change requests

To delete unnecessary change documents, proceed as follows:

1. Log on to the client where you want to delete change documents.

2. Access the table history tool by using Transaction code SE38 and executing program RSTBHIST; or, from the SAP Easy Access menu, choose TOOLS • CUSTOMIZING • IMG • IMG LOGGING.
3. To delete the change requests, select EDIT • CHANGE DOCS • DELETE.
4. Enter a date. All change documents prior to and including that date will be deleted.
5. Provide the name of the table or tables for which change documents should be deleted. To delete all change documents regardless of the table name, leave this field blank.
6. Choose EXECUTE or PROGRAM • EXECUTE IN BACKGROUND to delete the selected change documents.

Archiving

Change documents are archived using the archive administration (Transaction SARA) or by jumping from the table history tool via the SAP Easy Access menu TOOLS • CUSTOMIZING • IMG • IMG LOGGING to EDIT • LOGS • ARCHIVE. To archive change management documents that resulted from table logging, use the archive object for database log files, BC_DBLOGS. You can also select archived change documents for inclusion in a Customizing activity log analysis.

9.5 Authorization Profiles for Client Tools

To provide a method for controlling access to the different client tools, SAP delivers its software with standard authorization objects. In addition to these objects, you can rely on the client protection setting defined for each client to protect its data from being overwritten or accessed externally. When a client has this setting, no matter how many authorizations a user has, that person cannot overwrite the data in the protected client by performing a local client copy.

Authorization objects

Table 9.5 provides a list of the SAP-delivered authorizations relevant for the client copy tools. It also specifies whether that authorization is required for the user account in the target client and/or the source client. For example, in a remote client copy, the source client's user is defined by the RFC destination used during the client copy. To perform a remote client copy, the user referenced in the RFC destination must at least have the authorization S_ TABU_RFC.

Authorization Object	Description of Permitted Activities	Local Client Copy	Remote Client Copy	Client Transport
S_TABU_CLI	Maintenance of client-independent tables	Target	Target	Source and target
S_TABU_DIS	Maintenance of the client copy control table CCCFLOW	Target	Target	Source and target
S_DATASET	Writing log files to the operating system level	Target	Target	Source and target
S_CLNT_IMP	Importing data into a client	Target	Target	Source and target
S_TABU_RFC	Performing a remote client copy		Source	
S_CTS_ADMI with TTYPE 'CLCP', ACTVT '01'	Creating object lists for client transport and copying them to another client			Source and target
S_USER_PRO	Copying user profiles	Target	Source and target	Source
S_USER_GRP	Copying user data	Target	Source and target	Source
S_USER_AGR	Copying roles	Target	Source and target	Source

Table 9.5 Authorization Objects Needed in Source/Target Clients when Using Client Copy Tools

A client entry and its settings are stored in table T000. Because this is a client-independent table, a user needs the authorization object S_TABU_CLI to maintain client entries using Transaction SCC4. To delete a client, you must have three authorization objects: S_TABU_CLI, S_TABU_DIS, and S_DATASET. Analyzing table logs and Customizing activities requires two authorization objects: S_TABU_CLI and S_TABU_DIS.

[+] User SAP* has complete authorization to use all client tools. However, because this user cannot create a change request, it cannot perform the client export step in a client transport.

9.6 Questions

1. **After you create a new client entry in table T000, which of the following activities lets you provide the client with data?**

   A. A remote client copy to populate the client with data from a client in another SAP system

   B. A client transport to import data from a client in another SAP system

   C. A local client copy to import data from a client within the same SAP system

   D. All of the above

2. **Which of the following *cannot* be used to restrict a client from certain activities?**

   A. The client role

   B. The client-dependent change option

   C. The client ID-number

   D. A client restriction

   E. The client-independent change option

3. **Which of the following tasks can be performed using the client copy tools?**

   A. Merging application data from one client into another

   B. Copying only application data from one client to another

   C. Copying only Customizing data from one client to another

   D. All of the above

4. **Which of the following tasks can be performed using client copy profiles?**

   A. Scheduling a client copy to occur at a time when system use is low

   B. Selecting the subset of application data that will be copied when a client copy is executed

   C. Providing required user authorization for the use of client tools

   D. Determining the data that will be copied when a client copy is executed

5. **Which of the following statements is correct with regard to table logging?**

   A. Table logging should be used instead of change requests whenever possible.

   B. Table logging provides an audit history of who made what changes and when.

   C. Table logging does not negatively impact system resources.

   D. All of the above.

PART III
Tools

Part 1 of this book provided you with an overview of the change and transport concepts and recommendations for your SAP system landscape. Part 2 covered the technical requirements as well as the setup of these tools. Part 3 explains in detail how to use the following change and transport tools:

- Transport Organizer (Chapters 10 and 11)
- Transport Management System (TMS) (Chapters 12 and 13)
- Transport control program `tp` (Chapter 14)
- Tools for transport management on Java (Chapter 15)
- Enhanced transport system for ABAP and non-ABAP objects (Chapter 16)
- Methods and tools for SAP system maintenance (Chapter 17)
- Tools for upgrades and modification adjustment (Chapter 18)
- SAP Solution Manager (Chapter 19)

The first four chapters of Part 3, Chapters 10 to 13, will be of most interest for those directly involved in making changes to the SAP system—the people who participate in Customizing or development projects.

Chapter 14 contains detailed information on the import process, which is particularly helpful when it comes to troubleshooting. In most cases, these tasks are handled by system administrators and technical consultants.

Chapter 15 provides insight into the transport tools and concepts on Java in general. Chapter 16 deals with the enhanced transport system CTS+ and details the options for distributing changes within the system landscape.

Chapters 17 and 18 deal with maintaining and upgrading the SAP system landscape. These chapters are of interest for system administrators who are responsible for these tasks. Project leads, however, are also invited to get an overview of the necessary activities and efficient approaches in maintaining and upgrading projects.

Chapter 19 describes new functionalities of SAP Solution Manager in the area of software change management. It focuses on Customizing Synchronization in a system landscape and on managing change requests.

To implement developments in SAP systems, the system provides you with numerous development tools. These are directly connected with the various transport tools to ensure error-free distribution of system adjustments.

10 Managing Development Changes

Technically, development changes in an SAP ERP system are changes made to Repository objects using the tools of the ABAP Workbench. These changes are recorded to Workbench change requests, which are then managed using the Workbench Organizer. Development changes include creating and changing customer-developed or SAP-delivered objects.

Proper management of development changes, which ultimately ensures that all changes can be validated and distributed to all SAP ERP systems in the system landscape, can be divided into the following areas:

- Development prerequisites
- Change requests and tasks
- Repairs and modifications
- The Object Directory

10.1 Development Prerequisites

The following are prerequisites for performing development:

- The client-independent change option and the system change option allow changes to Repository objects.

- Each developer has the appropriate authorizations and has obtained an SAP Software Change Registration (SSCR) key.
- Development classes and object names that enable the transport of new Repository objects are used.

A user with developer authorizations can perform development work only if the current SAP client allows for client-independent changes—changes to Repository objects. In addition, the system change option must allow the relevant types of objects to be changed—for example, local objects, customer-developed objects, or SAP-developed objects.

[+] See Chapter 11 for more information on developer authorizations, Chapter 9 for information on client-independent changes, and Chapter 7 for information on the system change option.

10.1.1 SSCR Registration of Developers

SSCR key

Any user who wants to use the ABAP Workbench to create, change, or delete Repository objects (including customer-developed objects) in the SAP system must be registered using the *SAP Software Change Registration* (SSCR) key. Such users are often referred to as *development users* or *developers*.

The first time development users attempt to create or change an object, the system displays the ADD DEVELOPER dialog box, which asks for their access key (see Figure 10.1). To obtain this access key, enter the developer's user ID and the system's installation number in the SAP Service Marketplace under *http://service.sap.com/sscr*. Copy the resulting 20-digit key into the appropriate field in the ADD DEVELOPER dialog box.

After a developer has been registered through SSCR, the system will not request an SSCR key for any subsequent attempts by that developer to create or change Repository objects.

[+] For more information on SSCR, see SAP Note 86161 in the SAP Service Marketplace.

Figure 10.1 SSCR Key Request for a Developer

10.1.2 Packages

Today, SAP ERP consists of more than one million development objects (programs, tables, dynpros, BAPIs, function modules, types, etc.). These objects are grouped in more than 10,000 development classes at the same level.

In general, every developer can use every development object. Therefore, it is almost impossible for a developer to protect against the use of his development objects. Similarly, it is almost impossible to identify the development objects that should be made available to others. In addition, the possibilities of a technical modularization, for example, via module pools, function groups, or classes, are very limited. Thus, appropriate mechanisms for technical modularization are missing on both a large and small scale.

This is where packages come in. They are an enhancement of the previously used development classes with new additional semantics and serve to split, encapsulate, and decouple SAP ERP on a large and small scale.

Package Concept

Development classes—being simple containers for development objects—have a transport layer that specifies the transport route. As an extension of development classes, packages are characterized by the basic properties of nesting, visibility and interfaces, as well as use access, as follows:

Basic properties

- *Nesting* is the ability of packages to embed other packages.
- *Visibility* is a property of package elements. An element can be visible outside of its package. It is always visible within its package, but never within embedded packages. If an element is visible from the outside, it is placed in at least one *package interface*.
- A *use access* is associated with a package's one-sided right to use the visible elements of another package's interface.

Figure 10.2 illustrates the basic properties of packages in a graphical way.

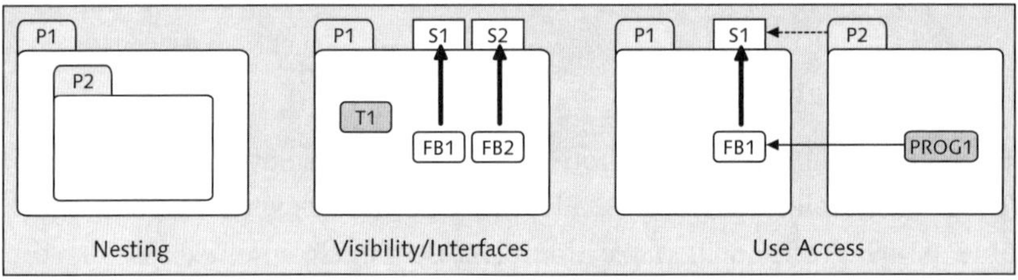

Figure 10.2 Package Concept

Using interfaces and visibility, a package can identify its range of services. All visible elements can potentially be used by other packages. Elements that are not visible cannot be used by other packages. Therefore, a package can protect its elements from any foreign use and encapsulate its contents.

Use access limits the use of foreign interfaces' visible elements. Not all visible elements can be used either. Only if a use access for a foreign package's interface exists, can a package use the visible elements of this package.

Nesting allows for a hierarchical organization of larger units in SAP ERP. Through the combination of interfaces and use access, package elements can be hidden easily and thus be protected from unauthorized use.

The highest level of the package hierarchy consists of structure packages, which usually comprise several main packages. Inside the main packages, standard packages are created which can contain development objects.

Structure packages

This package concept lets you split and encapsulate the SAP ERP system into technical units in the form of packages to reduce the large number of dependencies, and to therefore decouple the system on both a large and small scale.

Creating a Customer Package

By default, package validation is deactivated in the customer system. This means that packages have the same properties as the previously used development classes. In this case, packages are simply a container for SAP objects that logically belong together.

Package Builder: Create Package

Package	ZSALESREPORTS
Short Description	Sales Reports, Screens and Menus
Appl. component	
Software Component	HOME
Transport Layer	ZDEV
Package Type	Not a Main Package

Figure 10.3 Creating a Customer Package

If you want to create new programs, screens, or tables for transport to other SAP systems, you need at least one customer package. To create a customer package for your development environment, proceed as follows:

1. Access the Repository Browser using Transaction code SE80 or, in the initial screen, select TOOLS • ABAP WORKBENCH • OVERVIEW • OBJECT NAVIGATOR.
2. In the screen OBJECT NAVIGATOR: INITIAL SCREEN, select PACKAGE.
3. Enter a name for the new package. The name can be up to 30 characters long and must be within the customer namespace or name range.

For example, use a name such as Y<Name> or Z<Name>, where <Name> should be a short description of the package.

4. Choose DISPLAY. The system checks whether the package exists. If it does not, the CREATE OBJECT dialog box is displayed, where you can specify whether the package should be created. Select YES.
5. The CREATE PACKAGE dialog box is displayed (see Figure 10.3). Enter/assign the following:
   - A short description of the new package.
   - An application component, if all objects to be secured in the package are intended for the same application component.
   - A software component—usually, the HOME software component.
   - A transport layer—typically, you should use the standard transport layer suggested by default.
   - A package type. If you do not use package validation, you can keep the suggested standard package type.
6. Select SAVE. The SAP system prompts you for a change request identification. You have the following two options:
   - Enter the change request identification of an existing change request.
   - Select CREATE REQUEST to create a new change request. The system displays the CREATE REQUEST screen (see Figure 10.8). Enter a descriptive name for the change request.

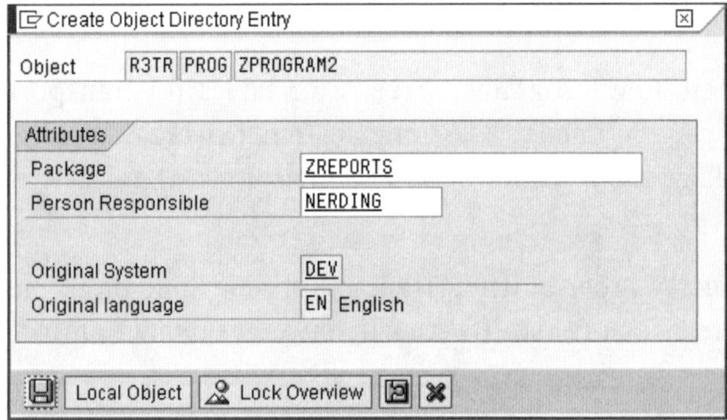

Figure 10.4 The Creation of a New Repository Object Requires the Assignment of a Package

7. Select SAVE. The REPOSITORY BROWSER: PACKAGE <PACKAGE> screen is displayed, showing your new package at the top of the package list. Because the package is new, it has not yet been assigned any Repository objects.

Naming Conventions for Packages

Packages from the SAP namespace

Packages starting with the letters [A–S] or [U–X] are reserved from the SAP name range for the standard SAP version's objects. Customer-specific objects or objects from prefix namespaces cannot be created in these packages.

Note that a package name can consist of a maximum of 30 characters. Furthermore, the package semantics should be reflected in the name. For *neighboring* packages, we advise you to use similar names.

Changes to these packages' objects are recorded by the Transport Organizer and can therefore be transported. The packages belong to the SAP transport layer and are assigned to an SAP software component (e.g., SAP_BASIS, SAP_APPL).

Packages from the customer namespace

In packages starting with Y or Z, you can create customer-specific objects from the customer name range. Changes to these packages' objects are recorded by the Transport Organizer and can be transported if the SAP system has been configured accordingly.

These packages are assigned to the HOME software component.

Private test packages

In a package starting with a T, you can create customer-specific objects from the customer name range, or objects from a prefix namespace that has been installed in your SAP system using the producer role.

When creating such a package, you can specify whether the package should be connected to the Transport Organizer. If this is what you want, objects being edited are recorded by the Transport Organizer in local requests that are not transported. Thc package does not belong to any transport layer. This package's objects can be transported to other SAP systems only by using special transport requests (transports of copies or relocation transports).

Newly installed SAP systems include the private test package TEST, which is not connected to the Transport Organizer. These packages are assigned to the LOCAL software component.

Local packages

In a package starting with a $, you can create customer-specific objects from the customer name range, or objects from a prefix namespace that has been installed to your SAP system using the producer role. Changes to objects of this package are not recorded by the Transport Organizer. The package does not belong to any transport layer. The objects cannot be transported.

Newly installed SAP systems contain the local $TMP package.

Packages in a prefix namespace

Like other Repository objects, packages can belong to a prefix namespace if the corresponding namespace is installed in the SAP system. The package name starts with a namespace prefix enclosed by slashes (/).

The prefix namespace has the following effects: In such a package, you can only create objects belonging to the same prefix namespace. Changes to objects of these packages are recorded by the Transport Organizer and can be transported if the SAP system has been configured accordingly.

Package Architecture as of SAP R/3 Enterprise 4.7

The design of the package architecture in SAP R/3 Enterprise 4.7 is based on the following objectives:

- Structure the software in a better way
- Encapsulate the functionality more strongly
- Provide well-defined interfaces throughout the environment
- Provide greater transparency of responsibilities

For SAP R/3 Enterprise 4.7 in particular, applying the package concept should ensure that the SAP R/3 Enterprise Core and the extensions are developed individually, with the goal of installing and maintaining them separately. The package concept can thus be used both within the SAP R/3 Enterprise Core and between the individual extensions for structuring and encapsulating.

Because software components combine packages that are always delivered together, they form the basis of the new package architecture of SAP R/3 Enterprise 4.7. Every software component is directly identified with one structure package each.

How are structure packages and software components connected?

Therefore, the structure packages BASIS, ABA, HR and APPL originate from the software components SAP_BASIS, SAP_ABA, SAP_HR, and SAP_APPL as shown in Table 10.1.

Software Component	Description
SAP_BASIS	SAP NetWeaver Application Server (before: SAP Basis or SAP Web AS)
SAP_ABA	Cross-application component
SAP_HR	Human Resources Management
SAP_APPL	Logistics and accounting
HOME	This software component contains packages with non-local objects that are not delivered to customers.
LOCAL	Comprises packages with only local objects.

Table 10.1 Software Components in SAP ERP (as of SAP R/3 Enterprise)

Creating packages in Enterprise Extensions

Several extensions are grouped in an Enterprise add-on and delivered together. The individual extensions are not dependent on each other. They represent decoupled software units and are implemented using one structure package each. The SAP R/3 Enterprise add-on is used as a container for the extensions and also corresponds to a software component. Examples of extensions include EA_HR, EA_FIN, EA_TRAVEL, and EA_RETAIL.

The upgrade or installation of SAP R/3 Enterprise always includes the SAP R/3 Enterprise Core, the SAP ERP plug-in, and several extensions that are grouped together in an SAP R/3 Enterprise add-on. To be able to use the extensions, they must be activated first.

Hierarchy of software components

The software components are hierarchically structured. Using the hierarchy (see Figure 10.5), you can see which dependencies are caused by using a software component. For example, EA_HR uses objects from the SAP_HR component which, in turn, is dependent on SAP_ABA and SAP_BASIS. This nesting is also relevant for using SAP Enhancement Packages, which are described in detail in Chapter 18.

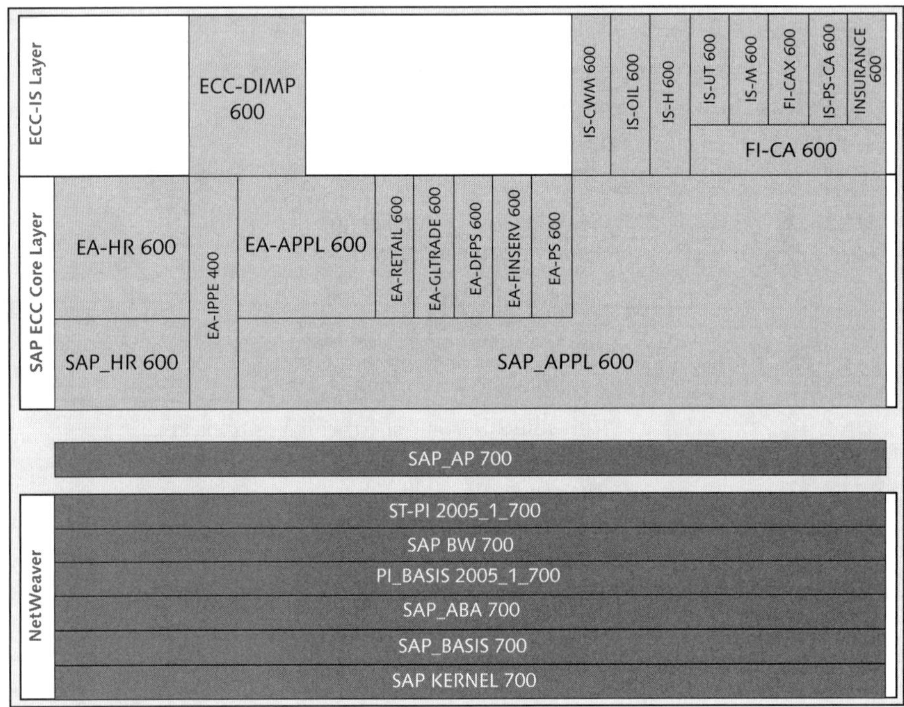

Figure 10.5 Software Components in SAP ERP 6.0

Creating Packages in Customer Scenarios

In certain customer scenarios, it is beneficial to activate package validation. To do so, the global package validation switch needs to be activated. The corresponding procedure is described in SAP Note 648898.

Scenario 1

Scenario 1: Being an SAP customer, you install SAP ERP 6.0 but also want to start with your own development and to deliver your own tools, not only to SAP ERP but also to other products such as SAP Supply Chain Management (SAP SCM) or SAP Customer Relationship Management (SAP CRM). You make your applications dependent only on the structure packages BASIS and ABA. How can you proceed in this case to effectively implement the package concept?

1. Create a structure package that will comprise all customer-specific developments.
2. Create main packages within the new structure package. The main packages are used for further structuring within the customer structure package and represent disjointed technical areas.
3. Define the usage relationships for the new structure package. Considering the fact that your own structure package is dependent on only the two SAP NetWeaver components BASIS and ABA, the usage relationship of the new structure package needs to be defined accordingly:
   - Define the usage relationship at the structure package level. This means you need to create the use access of the new structure package to the virtual package interface of BASIS and of ABA. In addition, the use access needs to be created to the respective filter package interface of BASIS and ABA.
   - Create the use access for all inner packages of the customer structure package that are affected by the usage to the virtual package interface of BASIS and ABA.
4. Activate package validation using the global package check switch.
5. To continue modularizing your customer developments, you make the package check stricter, step-by-step. In particular, you can set the PACKAGE CHECK AS CLIENT and PACKAGE CHECK AS SERVER flags for the new structure package.
6. You import a copy of your customer development into the SAP SCM and SAP CRM systems to make it available there.

Scenario 2

Scenario 2: Being an SAP customer, you already have many customer-specific developments and perform an upgrade to SAP ERP 6.0. How can you proceed to structure your own developments?

Prerequisites:

- Determine all development classes for the customer-specific development.
- Determine the packages on which the customer-specific developments should depend.
- Merge all of your own developments in a structure package.

Procedure:

1. Create a structure package for all customer-specific developments.
2. Create main packages within the new structure package.
3. Assign all of the customer-specific packages to the new structure package. You can assign packages to the structure package in a single step by using report `RS_ASSIGN_TO_STRUCTURE_PACKAGE`.
4. Determine the dependencies of these packages on SAP NetWeaver and SAP ERP structure packages BASIS, ABA, HR, APPL, and APPL_TOOLS.
5. Create use access in the customer structure package to the interfaces of corresponding SAP structure packages (use access at the structure package level).
6. Create the corresponding use access for all packages contained in the customer structure package.
7. Activate package validation using the global package check switch.

Scenario 3

Scenario 3: Being an SAP customer, you have merged your own developments in a structure package and then want to further promote the decoupling in certain areas. You can proceed as follows:

1. Another modularization can be made by creating additional structure packages. In this case, however, the dependencies among the structure packages need to be considered. If such dependencies exist, you need to create the corresponding package interfaces (for providers) or the use access (for users).
2. The decoupling can be further promoted by preassigning a specific error severity to a use access. Thus, the degree of the access permission is specified and existing uses can be gradually reduced by increasing the error severity.

Restricting Customer Object Names

To ensure that your objects are not overwritten by SAP-delivered objects during the import of Support Packages or during an upgrade, SAP has reserved name ranges for customer-developed and SAP-delivered objects. When creating a new Repository object, SAP developers must use the SAP name range, and you must use the customer name range.

For more information on customer name ranges, naming conventions, and examples of names, refer to the online documentation. [+]

SAP does deliver a few system objects with names that fall within the customer name range. To avoid using these names, consult the list in table TDKZ. [+]

Most SAP ERP implementations feature a single development system in which all customer developments are created. Performing all development work in a single SAP ERP system ensures that each object name can be used only once for a program, table, or other object type.

Naming conflicts

Performing development efforts in multiple systems may cause difficulties if objects are created with the same name in several systems. This can happen, for example, when development changes are made centrally at a company's headquarters and then delivered to its subsidiaries. An attempt to import an object into a development system that already contains an object with the same name will fail, because, by default, objects in their original systems cannot be overwritten. If the target system is not a development system, the imported object will overwrite an object that has the same name in the target system. This may cause inconsistencies if the objects were originally developed in different systems.

You may not notice that a naming conflict exists until you transport your development work. At this late stage, resolving the conflict requires renaming the objects and all references to them. To avoid this type of conflict:

- Define naming conventions in view V_TRESN (as described in the text that follows) in all systems. The ABAP Workbench will prevent you from creating objects with the same names in different systems.
- Register a namespace with SAP through the SAP Service Marketplace. Large corporate implementations or development partners may require a unique namespace to use for developing objects. This ensures that centrally developed objects delivered to other systems will not conflict with locally developed objects.

Define a Naming Convention

The first characters in the name of an object correspond to a naming convention in the ABAP Workbench. You can define a naming convention for a development class. The Workbench Organizer will not allow the creation of an object if the developer tries to assign it to a development class other than the one dictated by the naming convention. This ensures, for example, that all Repository objects beginning with the naming convention ZSALES are assigned to the development class ZSALESREPORTS. Naming conventions are stored in view V_TRESN.

To define a naming convention for a development class:

Procedure

1. Use the CALL VIEW MAINTENANCE screen (Transaction SM30). Enter the view name "V_TRESN." Choose MAINTAIN. The CHANGE VIEW "NAMING CONVENTIONS IN THE ABAP WORKBENCH": OVERVIEW screen appears.
2. Choose NEW ENTRIES. The NEW ENTRIES: DETAILS OF ADDED ENTRIES screen appears.
3. Enter data in the respective fields as shown in Table 10.2:

Field	User Entry
Program ID	R3TR or R3OB.
Object Type	To select the object type for which the naming convention applies, position the cursor in the field and use the possible entries arrow.
Name range (generic)	Enter the naming convention to be used—that is, specify the first characters of all object names that should correspond to the development class.
Development class	Enter the development class that should correspond to the naming convention.
Reservation type	Retain the default value D, which indicates a standard name range reservation.
Person responsible for object	Enter the name of the person responsible for reserving the name range.
Short description	Enter a short text to describe why the naming convention was assigned to a particular development class.

Table 10.2 Fields of the New Entries: Details of Added Entries Screen

4. Choose SAVE.

For consistent naming protection, view V_TRESN must be the same in all systems in the system landscape. New entries to V_TRESN should be recorded to a change request and distributed to all systems in the system landscape.

Example: Naming Conventions for Development Classes

In a system landscape that connects company subsidiaries in several countries, the corporate headquarters creates a standardized package of Customizing settings and development objects such as reports in the development system COR.

The two regional headquarters that receive the package, Asia and Europe, each have their own development systems. The Asian development system is ADV, and the European development system is EDV.

To avoid having Repository objects with the same name in the different development systems (COR, ADV, and EDV), the following entries are added to view V_TRESN in the development system COR and transported to all other systems in the system landscape:

```
PgId Obj   Name Range  Type  Dev. Class  Descriptions
R3TR PROG  Y           D     ZCORPORATE  Programs
R3TR TABL  Y           D     ZCORPORATE  Tables
R3TR DOMA  Y           D     ZCORPORATE  Domains
R3TR PROG  ZA          D     ZASIA
R3TR PROG  ZE          D     ZEURO
```

These entries ensure that centrally developed programs, tables, and data domains beginning with a Y belong to the development class ZCORPORATE. Programs for the Asian region will begin with ZA and receive the development class ZASIA; programs for the European region will begin with ZE and receive the development class ZEURO.

10.2 Workbench Change Requests

When you create or change a nonlocal Repository object, the object is recorded to a *Workbench change request*. To manage Workbench change requests, use the Workbench Organizer (Transaction SE09).

Unlike Customizing change requests, Workbench change requests are divided into the following types:

Types

- Transportable
- Local
- Unclassified

Unless specified, a change request is created as an unclassified change request. When a Repository object has been recorded to a task in a change request, the change request becomes either a transportable or local change request. The development classes of objects recorded to tasks in the change request determine the type. For example, any object whose development class indicates that it is local is not recorded to a change request, or any object whose development class uses a transport layer that does not have an associated transport route in TMS is recorded to a local change request.

10.2.1 Transportable Change Request

Because most changes are created with the goal of transporting them to other systems, the transportable change request is the most commonly used type of Workbench change request.

A transportable change request can be released and exported for transport to other systems. It contains Repository objects that can be transported—that is, Repository objects with a development class that is assigned to a valid transport layer. A transport layer is considered valid by the TMS if the SAP ERP system in which the object is created or changed is the source system of a designated consolidation route. For example, in Figure 8.19 (see Chapter 8), the training transport layer ZTRN is the consolidation route from the development system to the training system TRN. If the TMS is set up according to Figure 8.19, all Repository objects with a development class whose transport layer is ZDEV, SAP, or ZTRN can be recorded to transportable change requests.

[+] Repository objects that are supposed to be consolidated to different systems must be recorded to different change requests. For example, an object with the transport layer ZTRN cannot be recorded to the same change request as an object with the transport layer ZDEV. The export cannot occur because the target systems differ; the same change request cannot be simultaneously consolidated to both the training and quality assurance system (see also Chapter 8).

10.2.2 Local Change Request

Changes to Repository objects whose transport layer is invalid are automatically recorded to local change requests. A transport layer is invalid if it is not assigned to a consolidation route that includes the current system as the source system. For example, the TMS typically does not list a consolidation system for the quality assurance and production systems. Therefore, there is no valid transport layer for these systems. A change to a Repository object in a quality assurance or production system is not transportable and will be recorded to a local change request.

Transporting objects in the change request

A local change request can be released, but not transported. To transport the objects in a local change request, release the change request and then either:

- Create an appropriate transport layer for the object's development class. For example, to transport a change made to an SAP-delivered object in the quality assurance system to the production system, use the TMS to add the consolidation route from the quality assurance system to the production system for the SAP transport layer.
- Using Transaction SE80 (see Section 10.4.2), assign the object to another development class, or change the development class for the object and assign it to a valid transport layer for the current system.

10.2.3 Tasks

As long as no changes have been recorded to a task, its status in the Workbench Organizer (see the text that follows) is NOT ASSIGNED. This status is sometimes also referred to as *unclassified*. When a Repository object is first recorded to a task in a change request , the task is classified as one of the following:

- Development/correction
- Repair

Most changes are recorded to *development/correction* tasks, which contain changes to objects that originated in the current system.

Defining repair

A *repair* is a change to a Repository object that originated in a system other than the current system. The object can be an SAP-delivered or customer-developed object. For example, because all SAP-delivered objects are defined as belonging to the original SAP system, if you change such an object, the change is regarded as a repair. As another example, consider a customer-developed program, ZPROGRAM, created in the development system DEV. If you try to change this program in the training system TRN, you are automatically required to save the change to a task of REPAIR type because the object does not originate in TRN.

[+] Changing an object in a system other than the system in which it was originally created will be recorded in a task of type REPAIR.

To complete your development activities, you may need to include both types of tasks—*development/correction* tasks and *repair* tasks—in a change request. For example, after creating a new Repository object and saving it to a task in a change request, if you try to add a repair to the same change request, a CREATE TASK dialog box automatically appears to indicate that a new task must be created in the change request.

10.2.4 Viewing Workbench Change Requests

Workbench Organizer

To view Workbench change requests and their associated tasks, access the Workbench Organizer by using Transaction code SE09 or, from the initial screen, by choosing TOOLS • ABAP WORKBENCH • OVERVIEW • TRANSPORT ORGANIZER. Figure 10.6 shows the initial screen of the Transport Organizer. Enter your selection criteria to determine which change requests will be displayed. These selection criteria include the user who created the change request and its type. The default selections are as follows: transportable change requests, and local change requests that are modifiable (that is, not released). Under LAST CHANGED, you can enter dates to limit the change requests that display to those that were last changed in a certain period.

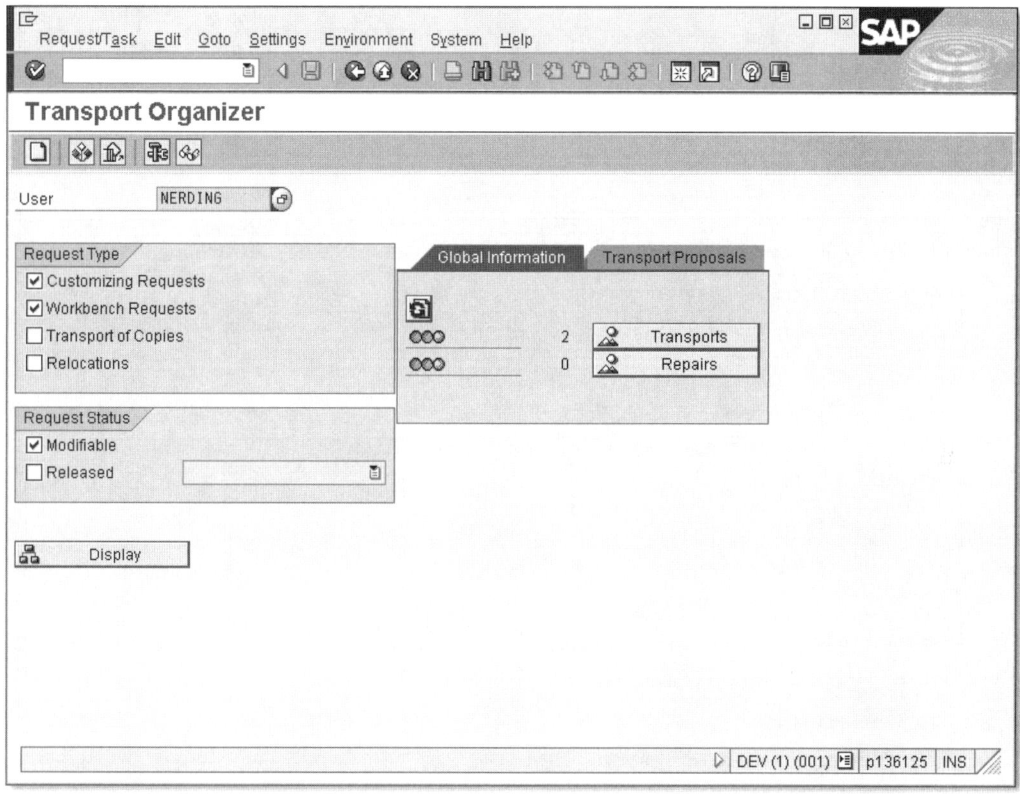

Figure 10.6 Initial Screen of the Transport Organizer

To accept the selection criteria and display the corresponding change requests, choose DISPLAY. The TRANSPORT ORGANIZER: REQUESTS screen appears, showing a tree structure that contains change requests and tasks (see Figure 10.7). The change requests listed include those created by the user whose name you entered on the initial screen and those in which that user is assigned to a task.

To see the tasks associated with a particular change request, expand the list using the + sign next to the ID number of the change request.

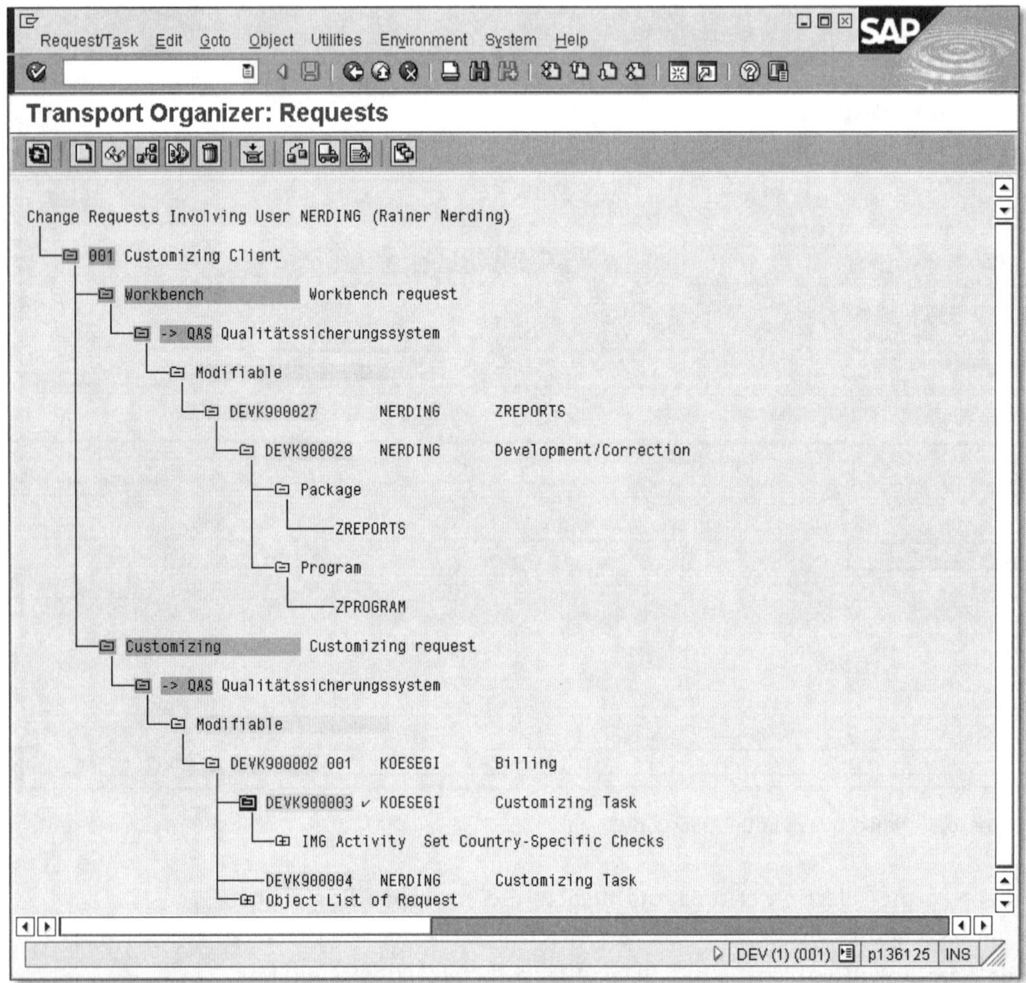

Figure 10.7 Hierarchical Display in the Transport Organizer

The example in Figure 10.7 shows all change requests of user NERDING. The list specifies that both `DEVK900027` and `DEVK900002` are transportable change requests. In change request `DEVK900027`, user NERDING has the task `DEVK900028` that records two changed Repository objects, the development class ZREPORTS, and the program ZPROGRAM. User KOESEGI is the owner of change request DEVK900002. User NERDING also has a task in this change request, but has not yet recorded any changes in it.

10.2.5 Creating a Workbench Change Request

A Workbench change request can be created either prior to or during development work. To simplify project management, SAP recommends creating change requests before starting development work. This makes it easier for developers from the same development project to record their changes to a single change request that can be released and exported as a testable unit. A project lead or development manager should be responsible for creating the change request and assigning the various developers to it. To create a change request, you need authorization profile S_A.CUSTOMIZ (see also Chapter 11).

Procedure

To create a transportable Workbench change request in the Transport Organizer (Transaction SE09), proceed as follows:

1. In the TRANSPORT ORGANIZER: REQUESTS screen, choose REQUEST/TASK • CREATE.
2. In the resulting dialog box, select WORKBENCH REQUEST. Choose ENTER.
3. The CREATE REQUEST dialog box appears (as shown in Figure 10.8):
   - In the SHORT DESCRIPTION field, enter a short text to identify the development project, describe the functionality, indicate the urgency of the change, or indicate whether the change is a modification.
   - In the fields under TASKS, enter all users who will be contributing development changes to this change request. For each user listed, a task will be created in the new change request.
4. Choose SAVE.

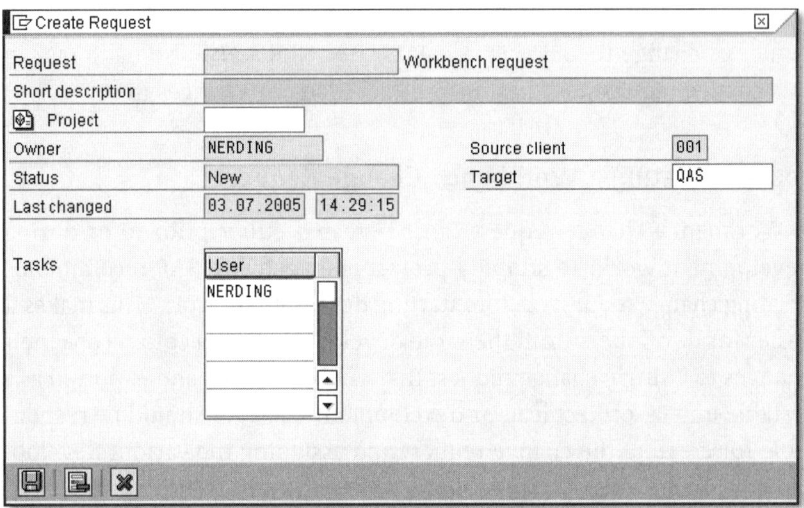

Figure 10.8 Creating a Change Request and Assigning Initial Tasks

Default settings

When creating a Workbench change request, there are some default settings you cannot change. These include the following:

- The name of the user who created the change request
- The status
- The date and time stamp
- The category
- The source client in which the change request was created

The change request category is always SYST, indicating that this change request is a Workbench change request.

The source client is always the client in which the change request was created. Only from within this client can you perform the following activities:

- Recording changes to the change request
- Changing the owner of the change request or of its tasks
- Adding additional tasks to the change request
- Releasing the change request

Adding Users to a Workbench Change Request

To add users to a Workbench change request you previously created, proceed as follows:

1. In the TRANSPORT ORGANIZER: REQUESTS screen, position the cursor on the appropriate change request ID.
2. In the menu, select REQUEST/TASK • REQUEST • ADD USER. The ADD USER dialog box appears. Enter the name of the user for whom you want to create a task. To find a user, you can use the possible entries arrow (or place the cursor in the username field and press [F4]).
3. Press [Enter].

[+] You can only add users to a change request that has not yet been released. A change request or task cannot be changed after it has been released.

Changing the Owner of Change Requests and Tasks

Every change request and task is owned by a user. When a user creates a change request, that user automatically receives ownership of the change request and a task in the change request. The owners of all other tasks in the change request are the people assigned to a task by the change request owner. Only the change request owner can perform the following activities for either change requests or tasks:

Activities of the owner

- Deleting tasks in the change request
- Changing the object list
- Releasing (exception: a user with the authorization profile SAP_ALL)
- Changing attributes, such as the short description
- Changing the owner

The owner of a change request can specify another person as the owner of the change request or the tasks it contains. To do this, proceed as follows:

1. In the WORKBENCH ORGANIZER: REQUEST screen, position the cursor on the ID of the change request or task whose ownership you want to change. Choose REQUEST/TASK • CHANGE OWNER.

2. In the CHANGE OWNER dialog box, enter the username of the new owner, or use the possible entries arrow to select a user.
3. Choose ENTER.

Protecting a Workbench Change Request

You can protect a Workbench change request to ensure that only the creator of the change request can add users to the change request. This even prevents users with the authorization profile S_A.CUSTOMIZ from adding users to the change request (see also Chapter 11).

To protect a change request you have created, in the WORKBENCH ORGANIZER: REQUEST screen, position the cursor on the ID number of the change request you want to protect, and choose REQUEST/TASK • REQUEST • PROTECT.

Remove protection

To remove this protection from the change request, choose REQUEST/TASK • REQUEST • REMOVE PROTECTION.

10.2.6 Recording Repository Objects to Change Requests

When creating or changing a Repository object, you will be required to specify the Workbench change request to which the object can be recorded unless:

- The object is already recorded in a change request that has not yet been released.
- The object is assigned to a local development class, such as $TMP, whose objects are not recorded in a change request.

Figure 10.9 shows the dialog box that appears to record a new or changed object to a change request. You can specify the change request ID in one of three ways:

- Manually enter your change request ID.
- Choose OWN REQUESTS. From the list, double-click the change request to which you want to record the object. The list will display only change requests to which this object can be saved.

- Choose CREATE REQUEST. (You require the appropriate authorization to do this.) In the CREATE REQUEST screen, enter the required data (see Figure 10.8).

After specifying a change request, choose CONTINUE. The object is recorded to the change request.

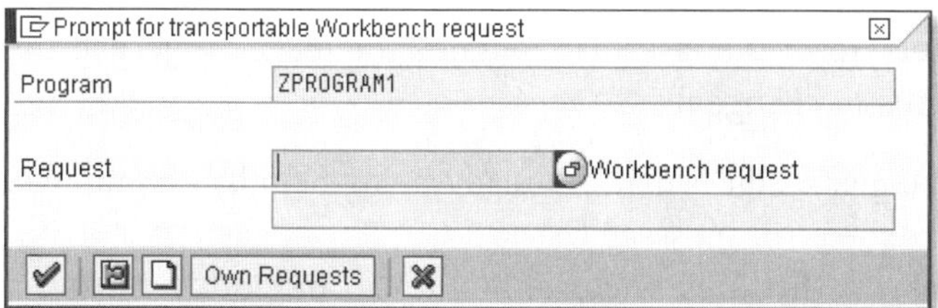

Figure 10.9 Recording a Repository Object to a Change Request

Recording development changes

When recording a development change to a Workbench change request, you must select a change request:

- In which you have a task or the authorization to create a task
- With the correct type, either transportable or local

You must save the change to a transportable change request if the object's development class is associated with a defined transport route. Otherwise, you should record the change to a local change request. The correct type of change request for development work matches the Repository object's defined transport layer and the associated transport routes for the current system as defined in the TMS.

Object Locking

When you record a new or changed Repository object to a task, the Workbench Organizer locks the object so that only the users who have tasks in the change request can modify the object. Another kind of locking—through an SAP ERP enqueue—ensures that only one user can change an object at any one time.

When the Workbench Organizer locks an object, users outside of the development team cannot change any of the objects in the change request. For example, if a user does not own a task in change request

DEVK900586, but tries to edit program ZABAP using the ABAP Editor, that person receives the error message OBJECT ZABAP LOCKED BY REQUEST/TASK DEVK900586. This user can do only one of three things:

- Display the object, but not make changes to it
- Have a new task created for the user in change request DEVK900586 by someone with authorization to create tasks
- Change ownership of the task that contains the locked object to the user who wants to change it

If you try to change an object that is already being held by an enqueue lock, you receive the error message USER ARCHER IS CURRENTLY EDITING ZABAP. This ensures that only one user at a time can modify an object in the system.

10.2.7 Object List of Change Requests and Tasks

An object list records objects that have been changed and shows what will be transported when the change request is released and exported. Each changed object has an entry in the object list. A change request's object list is filled after the tasks in the change request have been released (see also Chapter 12). The entries in the object list correspond to the entries in the *Object Directory* described later in this chapter.

The ABAP Workbench tools that record your changes to tasks automatically include the corresponding objects in the object list. Workbench Organizer tools also enable you to manually include or delete objects in the object list. In certain situations, you may want to manipulate an object list by, for example, removing the only listed object that is not ready to be released. When you remove an object, it is no longer in a change request. It is not locked by the Workbench Organizer and will not be transported. In addition, the Workbench Organizer no longer indicates that this object has been changed. Therefore, manual changes to the object list should only be made with caution.

[+] Use caution when making manual changes to the object list.

Display object list

To display the object list, in the TRANSPORT ORGANIZER: REQUEST screen, double-click the change request or task ID. In the sample object list shown in Figure 10.10, each object that has been recorded in the task is represented by a combination of entries in the columns PGMID (program identification), OBJ (object type), and OBJECT NAME. The object represented in row `R3TR DEVC ZREPORTS` is the package `ZREPORTS`. The ABAP program `ZPROGRAM` is represented in row `R3TR PROG ZPROGRAM`.

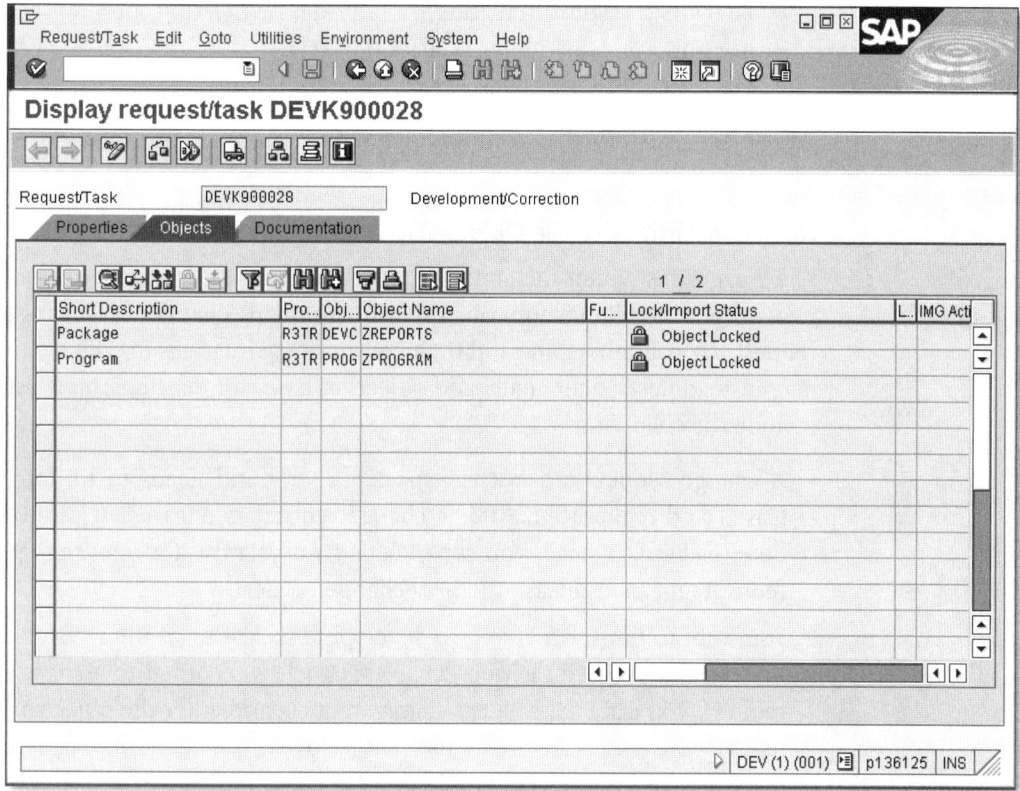

Figure 10.10 Object List

For every object in the object list shown in Figure 10.10, the entry in the OBJSTATUS column is LOCKED. These are Workbench Organizer locks. In other words, the program ZPROGRAM and the development class ZREPORTS can be changed only by the users who are specified in change request DEVK900027. The Workbench Organizer locks the objects in the request until the entire change request has been released.

The change request or task does *not* contain the actual table entries or the object content that has changed. A change request or task does *not* even record whether the change was an addition, modification, or deletion. It only *lists* the changed objects. Each row in the object list is a pointer to the actual objects—programs, tables, data domains, views, and so on—that are physically located in the Repository. As an example, task `DEVK900028` is a result of creating, modifying, or deleting the program `ZPROGRAM` and the development class `ZREPORTS`.

[+] A change request or task only *lists*—it does not actually contain objects. The objects exist outside of the change request in the Repository.

Manual Additions to the Object List

There are times when the standard, automatic procedure for recording new or modified Repository objects or Customizing changes to a change request is too cumbersome and time-consuming. Situations in which you may instead need to manually add objects to a new or existing object list include the following:

- A change request did not transport properly and needs to be rereleased and reexported. After a change request is released, it cannot be rereleased. Instead, you can include its object list in a new change request and then release the new change request.
- You want to transport an entire development class to another system. Instead of changing each object so that each is recorded to a change request, you can create a new change request and enter the objects in its object list. (See the procedure that follows.)
- You would like to combine several change requests to form a single new change request—for example, to bundle change requests that were imported into the development system or that need to be copied to another client within the current system using the CLIENT COPY BY TRANSPORT REQUEST function (Transaction SCC1). (See the procedure that follows.)
- Objects may need to be added to special change requests such as RELOCATION TRANSPORTS.

To transport some or all objects of a particular development class, proceed as follows:

Transport all objects of a development class into a change request

1. Create a transportable change request. In the TRANSPORT ORGANIZER: REQUEST screen (in Transaction SE09), choose REQUEST/TASK • CREATE. In the resulting dialog box, choose WORKBENCH REQUEST and then press Enter. A second dialog box appears—enter a short description and press Enter.
2. Position the cursor on the newly created change request and choose REQUEST/TASK • OBJECT LIST • INCLUDE OBJECTS. Select FREELY SELECTED OBJECTS. Press Enter.
3. The ADD OBJECTS TO REQUEST <CHANGE REQUEST ID> screen displays. Enter the name of the development class for which you would like to display the object list. After making your selections, choose EXECUTE.
4. A tree structure displays, showing all objects that belong to the development class. Position the cursor on individual objects or collections of objects and choose SELECT/DESELECT.
5. When all of the required objects have been selected, choose SAVE IN REQUEST. All selected objects are added to the object list of the new change request.

[+] You can include objects in the object list of a change request, but not a task, using the INCLUDE OBJECTS functionality.

To merge a copy of an existing object list from one or several change requests into a new change request, proceed as follows:

Merging multiple object lists into a single change request

1. Create a transportable change request. In the TRANSPORT ORGANIZER: REQUEST screen (in Transaction SE09), choose REQUEST/TASK • CREATE. In the resulting dialog box, choose WORKBENCH REQUEST and then press Enter. A second dialog box appears. Provide a short description and press Enter.
2. Position the cursor on the newly created change request and choose REQUEST/TASK • OBJECT LIST • INCLUDE OBJECTS. Select OBJECT LIST FROM MULTIPLE REQUESTS. Press Enter.
3. The MERGE OBJECT LISTS IN REQUEST <CHANGE REQUEST ID> screen appears. Enter selection criteria for the change requests and tasks

whose object lists should be included in the new change request. Examples of selection criteria include:

Field	User Entry
Owner	Name of a particular user or users.
Date	Begin dates and end dates. This entry selects all change requests that were last modified during a specified time period or periods.
Request type	Use the possible entries arrow to specify the type of change requests and tasks to be included—for example, *transportable change request*.

Table 10.3 Selection Criteria

4. In the same screen, select the status of the change requests and tasks to be included from the following options:
   - MODIFIABLE
   - OPEN (FAULTY STATUS)
   - RELEASED
5. Choose EXECUTE.
6. A list of all change requests matching the selection criteria is displayed. Select the individual requests or collections of change requests you need by choosing SELECT/DESELECT (or press [F7]).
7. Once you have selected the required objects, choose MERGE OBJECT LISTS. A dialog box appears asking HOW SHOULD ACTION BE PERFORMED? Proceed as follows:
   - To combine a small number of change requests, choose ONLINE.
   - To combine a large number of change requests, choose IN BACKGROUND. You are automatically asked to schedule the merger as a background job.
8. Press [Enter]. All selected objects are added to the object list of the new change request.

Changing an existing object list

You can manually change the object lists of change requests or tasks by adding or deleting objects. Users should not need this function often, because almost all changes to objects are automatically recorded to change requests. Occasionally, expert users with detailed knowledge of the respective objects may add or remove them manually.

If you want to change an existing object list, in the TRANSPORT ORGANIZER: REQUESTS screen (in Transaction SE09) move the cursor over the task or change request to be modified and select REQUEST/TASK • DISPLAY. The object list is displayed. Switch to change mode. You have the following options:

- To add entries to the object list, choose INSERT LINE. Enter the program name, object name, and object type. To make manual additions to the CHANGE OBJECT LIST option, you must be familiar with certain technical data for an object, including the program ID, object type, and other objects that may be affected. You may prefer the procedure described previously under "Including All Objects of a Development Class" to add individual objects to the object list.
- To delete objects in the object list, choose DELETE LINE. Before deleting entries from the object list, use your knowledge of the objects to ensure that the deletion does not jeopardize dependent objects.

[+] SAP does not recommend deleting objects from an object list, because it may jeopardize consistency between your systems.

Locking and Unlocking Objects in Object Lists

Adding an object manually to the object list does not automatically lock the object. Any user can record this object to a change request and perform changes on it. To prevent this, after adding objects to an object list, you are advised to manually set a lock on the objects. Proceed as follows:

1. In the TRANSPORT ORGANIZER: REQUESTS screen (in Transaction SE09), position the cursor on the change request you want to lock.
2. Choose REQUEST/TASK • OBJECT LIST • LOCK OBJECTS.

You may receive an error message indicating that one or more objects are already locked in another change request or task. If the objects are locked, you may need to release the change request that contains the locked objects.

Manual unlock

To manually unlock an object in a change request, you need the authorization S_CTS_ADMIN, which is provided in the authorization profile S_A. SYSTEM. When you have this authorization, you can unlock an object in a change request using the Organizer Tool (Transaction SE03). In the tree structure under OBJECTS IN REQUESTS, access the UNLOCK OBJECTS function. Enter the request or task you want to unlock and choose EXECUTE.

10.3 Repairs and Modifications

Every Repository object has an *original system*, which is the SAP ERP system in which the object was created and where it should be edited. If you change an object in a system that is not the original system, you are changing a *copy* of the object rather than the original; this is called a *repair*. In the production system, for example, if you change a copy of a program that originated in the development system, the changed object is considered a repair.

The original system for all SAP-delivered objects is defined as SAP. A change to an SAP-delivered object is a special type of repair known as a *modification*.

Risks

Certain risks are associated with repairs and modifications. For example:

- If you did not create the original object, you may not be able to guarantee application functionality after changing the object.
- If it has been confirmed (and therefore the repair flag is no longer set), the repair can be overwritten by imports.
- Performing an upgrade is more complex modifications exist in the pre-upgrade system.

Making a repair requires two steps that are not required when changing an object in the original system:

- Setting the repair flag for the object
- Monitoring and controlling the changes made to the Repository object with the *Modification Assistant*

10.3.1 Setting the Repair Flag

When you change a Repository object in a system that is not its original system, regardless of whether it is an SAP-delivered object or a customer-developed object, the SET REPAIR FLAG dialog box will appear. To continue, you must choose OBJECT FOR REPAIR. This sets the repair flag for this object.

The repair flag protects a Repository object from being overwritten if it is subsequently reimported from the source system. When the repair flag is set, an error message appears during import which indicates that the object has not been imported because it was repaired in the target system. By default, the repair flag is deleted when the transport request is exported.

In Transaction SE03, Transport Organizer Tools, you can display the list of all repaired objects and remove the repair flag manually, if necessary.

10.3.2 Modification Assistant

The ABAP Editor includes the Modification Assistant to guide you during repairs to objects that are not in their original system. Although the name *Modification Assistant* may imply that it is used only to make modifications, this tool is designed to help manage the repair of any object, whether it is SAP-delivered or customer-developed.

The Modification Assistant ensures that repairs to an object outside of its original system are made using only the options, INSERT, REPLACE, and DELETE. This preserves a record of the original form of objects, and indicates the change request that is used to make the change. For example, using the Modification Assistant, you can no longer simply change an existing line of code in a program. You must use the REPLACE option. This option inserts an asterisk to preserve the original line of code as a commentary (as in line 444 in Figure 10.11). The MODIFICATION UNDO option simplifies undoing all changes made during the repair.

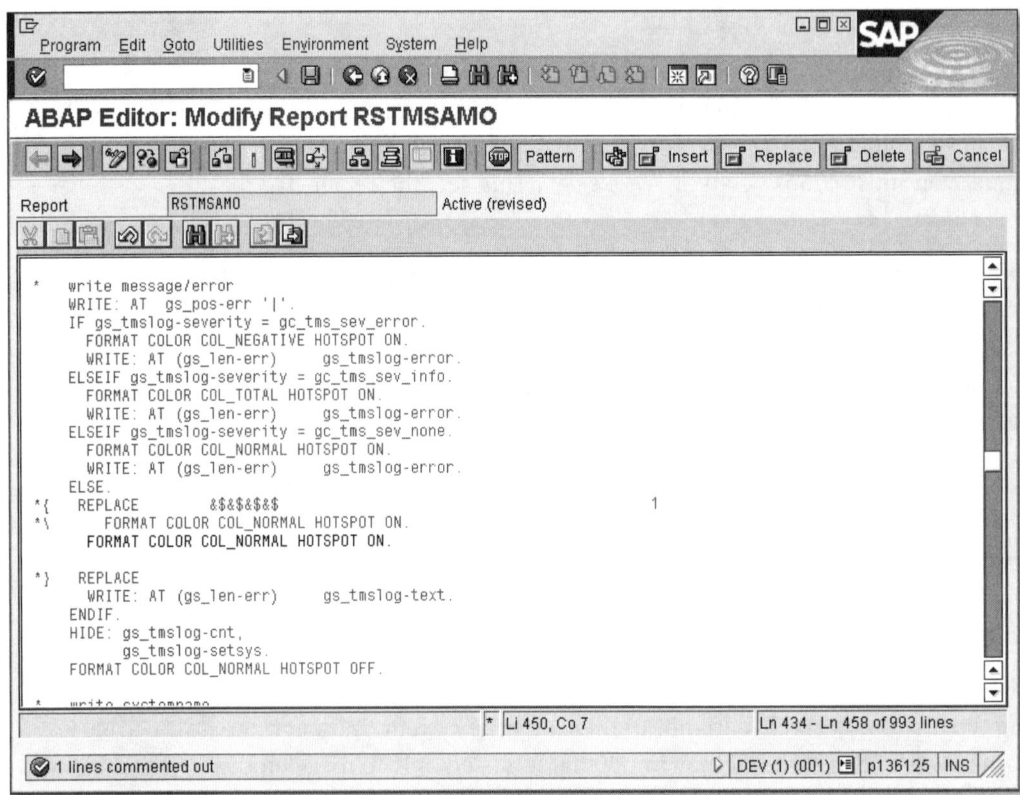

Figure 10.11 The ABAP Editor When Used with the Modification Assistant

[+] The Modification Assistant preserves a copy of the part of an object that was changed in a repair or modification.

This detailed documentation provided by the Modification Assistant in the ABAP Editor helps to dramatically reduce the amount of effort needed to apply Support Packages and upgrade your SAP ERP system.

Disabling the Modification Assistant

Occasionally, you will have to disable the Modification Assistant—for example, to upload a program into the ABAP Editor. To disable the Modification Assistant, before making changes, from within the ABAP Editor choose Edit • Modifications • Disable assistant. Repairs and modifications made when the Modification Assistant is deactivated will still be registered as repairs in the Workbench Organizer. However, you lose the pre-change documentation provided by the Modification Assistant.

When performing modification adjustments during an upgrade or when applying a Support Package, to gain insight into changes that were made without the Modification Assistant, you will have to use the version management functionality of the ABAP Workbench (see Chapter 12).

[+] To simplify future upgrades, SAP recommends having the Modification Assistant activated at all times.

10.3.3 Modification Browser

To display a tree structure listing all repairs and modifications in the Modification Browser, use Transaction code SE95 or, from the SAP ERP initial screen, choose Tools • ABAP Workbench • Overview • Modification Browser. The selection screen of the Modification Browser appears. Here, you can specify the criteria for the repairs and modifications to be displayed. For example, you can select the following:

Selecting criteria

- All repairs, or only the repairs for a specific development class and/or time period.
- Repairs made with and/or without the Modification Assistant.
- Modifications to SAP objects that may subsequently need to be adjusted during an upgrade or Support Package application (see Chapter 18).

In the Modification Browser, to access the ABAP Workbench tool relevant to a particular object type (such as the ABAP Editor for a program), position the cursor on a specific object and choose Display or Change.

Undoing repairs

To undo repairs made with the help of the Modification Assistant, in the Modification Browser, place your cursor on an object and choose Reset to original. Using this function returns the object to its original state and causes the object to be deleted from the Modification Browser.

10.3.4 Modifications

Modifications are a specific type of repair—they are changes to the SAP standard. Modifications may be made in the following ways:

- By applying the corrective coding provided to customers in an SAP Note
- By adapting the SAP ERP system to your specific business needs

[+] A modification is a change that is more serious than a repair. Making a modification changes the functionality delivered by SAP and may negatively impact the performance and functionality of the SAP ERP system.

Prior to making modifications based on SAP Notes, ensure that the SAP Note is applicable to your SAP ERP release and that the symptoms in the SAP Note are the symptoms apparent in your SAP ERP system. If you are uncertain, contact SAP.

Before making modifications with the goal of adapting the SAP ERP system to your specific business needs, you should be well acquainted with the existing construction and flow logic of the application component. This knowledge will help you evaluate modification possibilities and enable you to decide on a sensible modification design. This knowledge will also help you determine when the SAP enhancement concept provides a better alternative to performing a modification.

Prerequisites

When you make a modification, you need to set a repair flag. In addition you need the following:

- An SSCR key so that the SAP-delivered object can be modified.
- Documentation in change requests and attached to the affected objects, to assist the modification adjustment process during the application of future Support Packages or SAP ERP release upgrades.
- Correct timing for transporting the modification in relation to the point in time when Support Packages are applied (see Chapter 17).

[+] SAP recommends that you perform all modifications to SAP-delivered objects in the Customizing-and-development client.

SSCR Key for Modifications

The first time an SAP-delivered Repository object is changed, the ABAP Workbench prompts the developer for an object-specific SAP Software Change Registration (SSCR) key, using the dialog box shown in Figure 10.12. You can obtain the key from the SAP Service Marketplace (using the procedure described in Section 10.1.1, SSCR Registration of Developers).

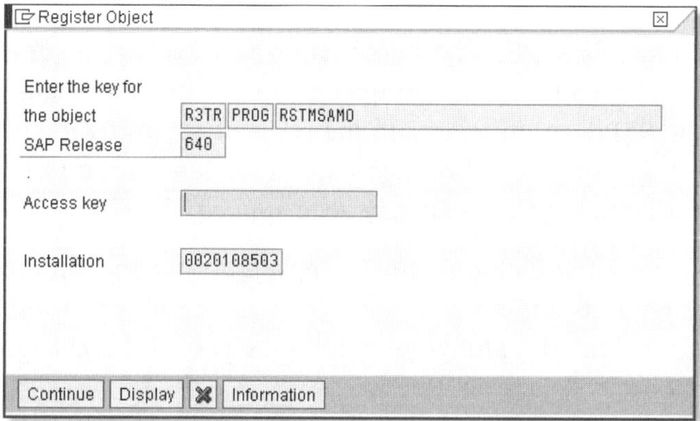

Figure 10.12 The ABAP Workbench Requests an SSCR Key When You Try to Modify SAP Objects

After you enter the key in the dialog box, it is automatically added to the table ADIRACCESS in the current system. The SSCR key is specific to the program ID and object type of the Repository object, as well as to the installation number and SAP ERP release of the SAP ERP system. Therefore, you have to register the Repository object you want to modify only once per system and SAP ERP release level.

[+] Repository objects that do not require SSCR registration include matchcodes, database indexes, buffer settings, customer objects, and objects generated through IMG Customizing activities.

Documentation Requirements

Creating modifications makes SAP ERP release upgrades or the application of Support Packages more complex due to the need for a modification review and possible adjustments during upgrade. To simplify decision making during this review process, when creating modifications, you should thoroughly document all changes in both the change request and the documentation attached to the object.

Include the SAP Note number and SAP ERP release dependencies in the SHORT DESCRIPTION field when you create the relevant change request and in the task-specific documentation (under GOTO • DOCUMENTATION in the Workbench Organizer). The change request description, for example, will then inform the person performing the upgrade that the modification was made as a result of an SAP Note and can be safely overwritten by the new SAP ERP release. The short description of the change request will also be recognizable in the import queue. This is shown in Figure 10.13, where the SAP Note number and the relevant Support Package number indicate that the second change request does not have to be imported if Support Package 3 has already been applied.

[+] All changes to standard SAP objects should be well documented in the relevant change requests and tasks. If the change is a result of an SAP Note, be sure to include the SAP Note number as part of the change request description.

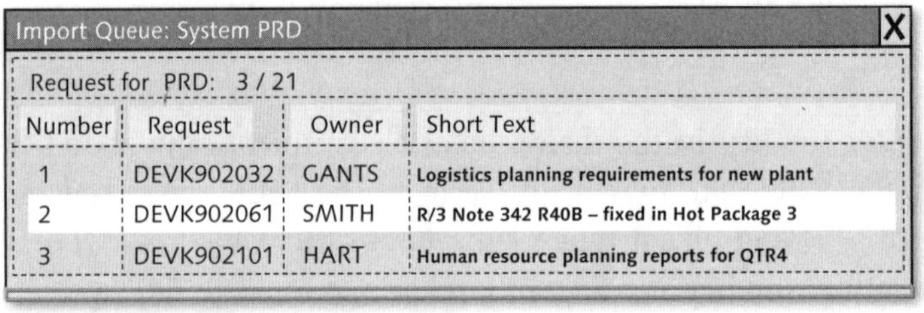

Import Queue: System PRD

Request for PRD: 3 / 21

Number	Request	Owner	Short Text
1	DEVK902032	GANTS	Logistics planning requirements for new plant
2	DEVK902061	SMITH	R/3 Note 342 R40B – fixed in Hot Package 3
3	DEVK902101	HART	Human resource planning reports for QTR4

Figure 10.13 A Sample Import Queue With a Change Request that is the Result of an SAP Note

10.4 SAP Enhancement Concept

For SAP NetWeaver 7.0 and products based on this product, for example, SAP ERP 6.0, SAP has supplemented the enhancement options with new technologies within the Enhancement Framework. Modification-free enhancements can be implemented using the following technologies:

- Implicit enhancement points
- Explicit enhancement points
- Explicit enhancement sections
- New BAdIs

Implicit enhancement points

In contrast to the already existing enhancement for which SAP has to provide specific jumps, implicit enhancement points require no preparation by SAP. Implicit enhancement points are automatically provided at specific points in SAP codes and can be used by implementing the enhancement. For example, these points can be found:

- At the beginning and end of subroutines, function modules, and methods of local/global classes, to add functionality, for example
- At the end of includes, to implement additional functionality, for example.
- At the end of a structure/structure type declaration prior to `END OF ...` to add fields
- In interface definitions of function modules and methods of global classes, to add interface parameters, for example

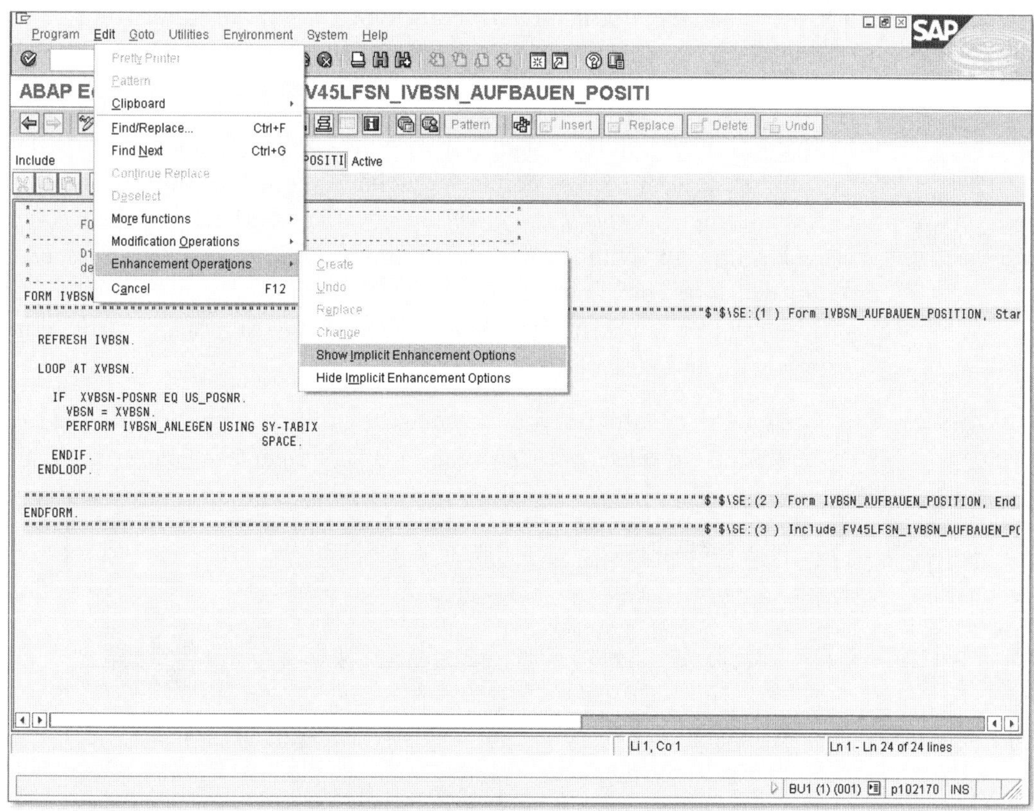

Figure 10.14 Displaying Implicit Enhancement Options

To use implicit enhancement points for inserting source text, proceed as follows:

1. In the appropriate ABAP Workbench tool, display the corresponding SAP object, for example, a program, function module, or method.
2. In the GUI status, click the ENHANCEMENTS button or select EDIT •·ENHANCEMENT OPERATIONS • SHOW IMPLICIT ENHANCEMENT OPTIONS to display the implicit enhancement options on the screen.
3. Create the enhancement implementation via the editor's context menu.
4. Insert your source text.
5. Click the ACTIVATE ENHANCEMENTS button in the GUI status.

[+] For enhancing a structure/structure type declaration directly prior to `END OF ...` you must use the syntax `DATA <additional field> TYPE <additional type>`.

Explicit enhancements

In contrast to implicit enhancement points, explicit enhancements can only be used at certain points, predefined by SAP. Similar to implicit enhancements, *explicit enhancement points* are options to enhance the SAP source text without any modifications. *Explicit enhancement sections*, for which no comparable implicit enhancements exist, allow for a modification-free replacement of SAP source text in SAP programs, function modules, and methods.

Enhancement spots

For semantic bundling, you can combine explicit enhancements and the new BAdIs in *enhancement spots* and manage them (see Figure 10.15).

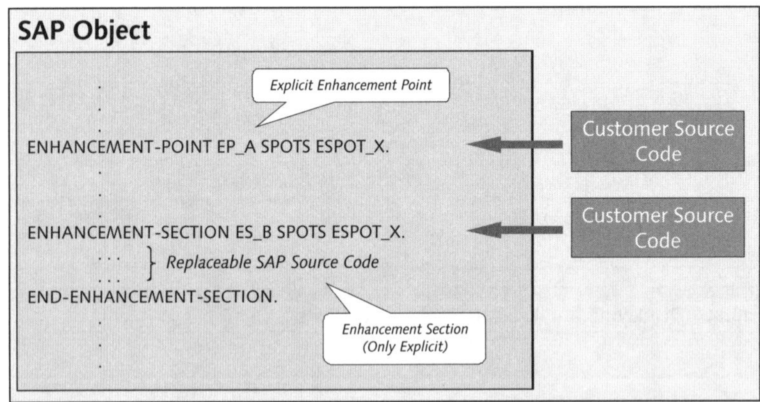

Figure 10.15 Programming Principle for Explicit Enhancement Points

To use explicit enhancement points and sections, proceed as follows:

Procedure

1. Display the corresponding SAP object, for example, a program, a function module, or a method, in the appropriate ABAP Workbench tool.
2. Search for the desired enhancement points/section.
3. Click the Enhancements button in the GUI status.
4. Create the enhancement implementation of the enhancement points/section via the editor's context menu.
5. Enter the name of the enhancement implementation (you can use the customer namespace Y*/Z*).
6. Insert your source text.
7. Then click the Activate Enhancements button in the GUI status.

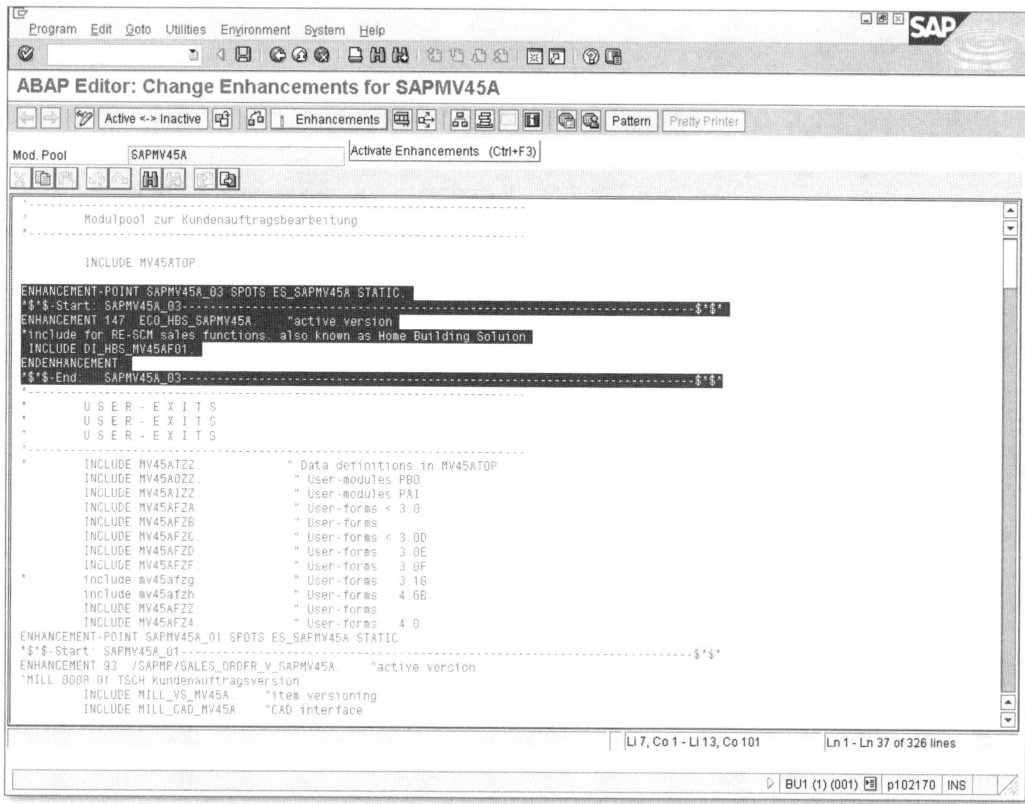

Figure 10.16 Programming an Explicit Enhancement Point

New BAdIs

Business Add-ins have been available since SAP R/3 Release 4.6 and offer an enhancement option for SAP developers who want to provide branch options to customer functions in their programs. In SAP NetWeaver 7.0, SAP has introduced the *new BAdI technology* which will implement SAP enhancements in the future. The new BAdI technology provides the following benefits:

- Increased performance
- An extended filter concept
- The option to inherit sample implementation classes
- Integration with the Enhancement Framework through management via enhancement spots

Figure 10.17 provides an overview of the new BAdI architecture.

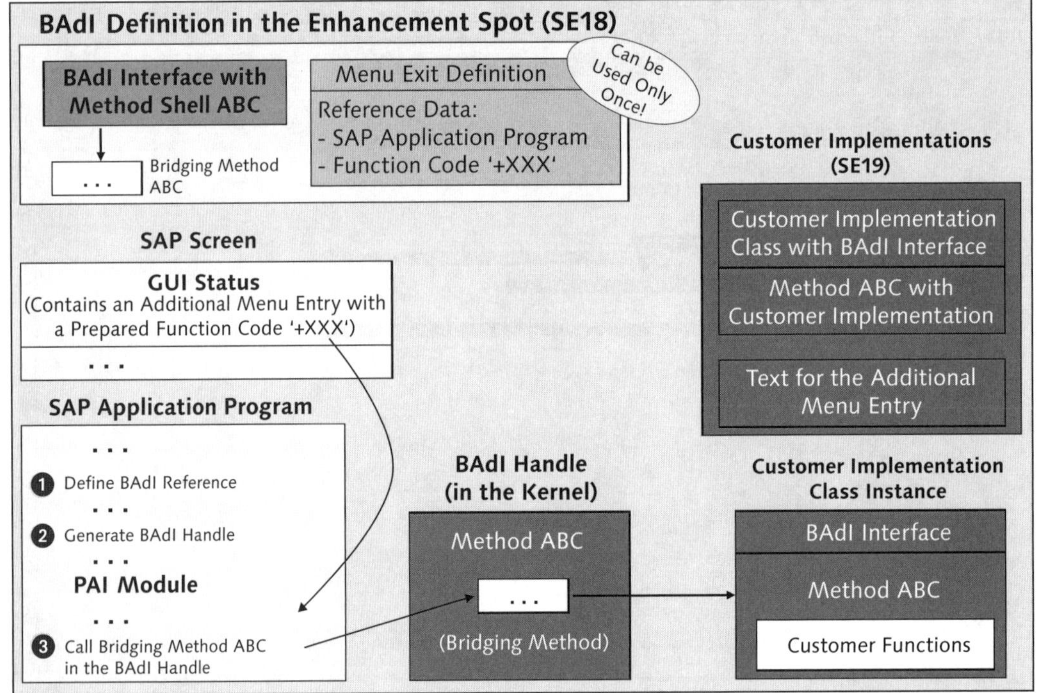

Figure 10.17 Interaction of the Individual Parts of the BAdI Architecture

To use the new BAdI program exits, proceed as follows:

1. Display the corresponding enhancement spot.
2. To create an enhancement implementation, select CREATE ENHANCEMENT IMPLEMENTATION (F6).
3. Enter a name for the enhancement implementation.
4. Enter a name for the BAdI implementation(s).
5. Maintain the properties of the BAdI implementation(s).
6. In the navigation area, select the IMPLEMENTING CLASS component for the desired BAdI.
7. Enter the name of the implementing class, and click the CHANGE BUTTON.
8. Double-click to implement the method.
9. Activate the method and all associated objects including the enhancement implementation.

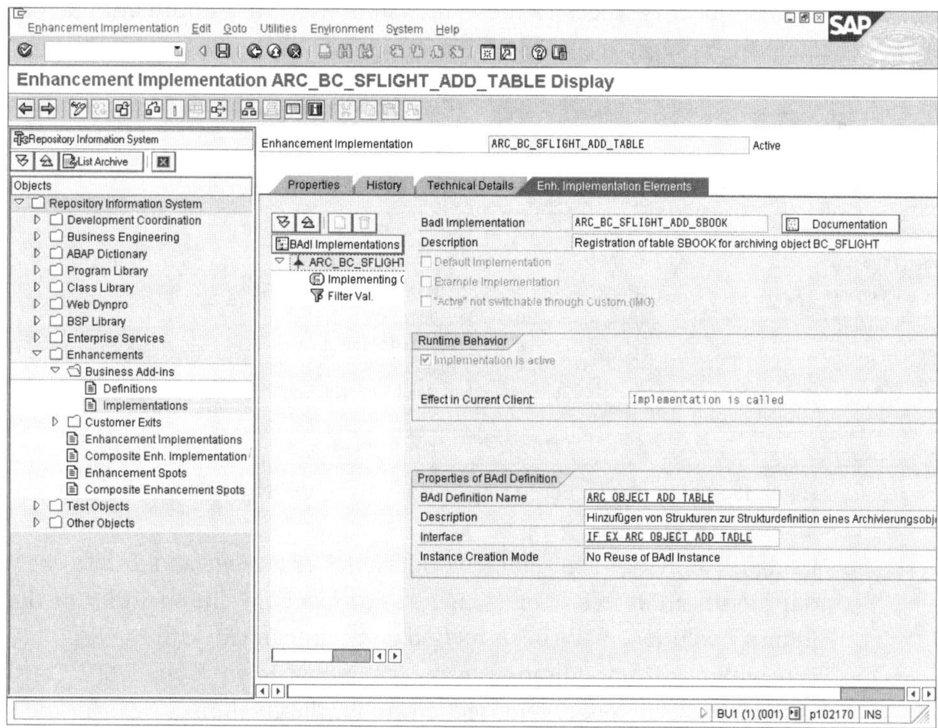

Figure 10.18 Options for Using New BAdIs

The previously used, classic BAdIs still exist in the system. In the future, however, SAP will implement BAdIs using only the new technology. Elements of the central basis cannot be extended with classic or new BAdIs.

Using the Enhancement Framework is also integrated with the system change option settings. In the transaction for the system change option, you can now make changes using general enhancements or additional enhancements for each software component (see Figure 10.19).

Industry solution retrofit

During the development of industry solutions (IS), SAP implemented special requirements of customers from different industries in the form of additionally installable add-ons. In this context, modifications to the core SAP ERP functions were frequently required. Corrections to the objects of the core ERP system involve additional adaptations to the IS modifications which are delivered in the form of Conflict Resolution Transports (CRTs). As a result, customers must wait until the CRTs are created for their specific add-on before they can import them together with Support Packages to the core system (for more information about Support Packages see Chapter 17).

Global Setting: Modifiable

Software Component	Technical Name	Modifiable
Cross-Application Component	SAP_ABA	Restricted Modifiability
SAP Application Platform	SAP_AP	Modifiable
Logistics and Accounting	SAP_APPL	Restricted Modifiability
SAP Basis Component	SAP_BASIS	Modifiable
SAP NetWeaver BI 7.0	SAP_BW	Restricted Modifiability
Human Resources	SAP_HR	Not Modifiable; Enhanceable Only
SEM-BW 600 : Add-On Installation	SEM-BW	Not Modifiable; Not Enhanceable

Figure 10.19 Options for Controlling Changes Across the System

Using the Enhancement Framework enables customers and SAP to carry out modification-free enhancements. For example, the majority of the industry solutions have been revised and reintegrated with the SAP ERP core without any modifications using the Enhancement Framework. Thus, customers are no longer required to wait for the creation of CRTs for their IS if they want to import corrections into the core SAP ERP system.

Switch Framework

Business functions

The retrofit included not only the integration of one industry solution into the SAP ERP core, but also the simultaneous reintegration of all industry solutions that have been processed this way into the ERP core. To select one industry solution out of many, the enhancements were connected with switches. Using these switches, you can activate encapsulated program lines as required. For this purpose, larger units are set that belong together technically and semantically. These units are called *business functions*. Using the switches assigned to business functions, you can set all packages belonging together at the same time. This ensures that these developments always change their status simultaneously.

Figure 10.20 shows the relationships of the different levels of this Switch Framework.

Not only can you switch on the business functions, you can also switch them off. This does not refer to the enhancements of the data dictionary objects which you can't reset because data loss might occur. For this reason, most SAP business functions cannot be switched off once they have been activated. This also applies to the larger activation units of the industry solutions mentioned earlier, for which multiple business functions are combined into *business function sets*.

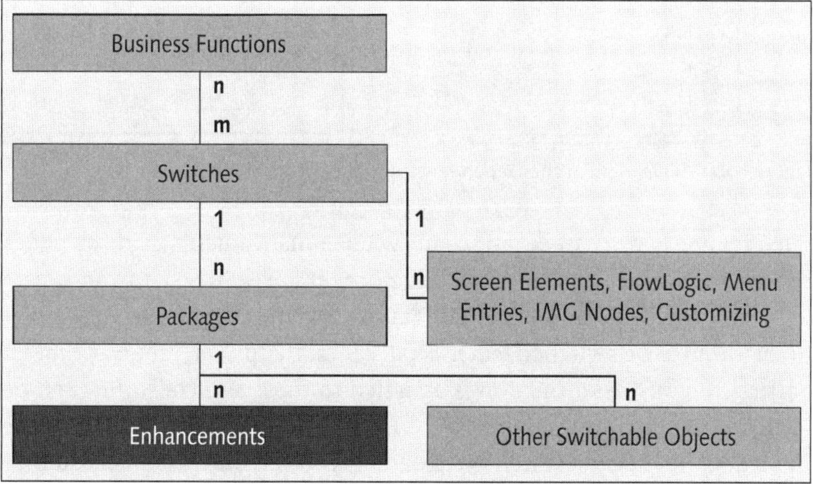

Figure 10.20 Relationships of the Individual Switch Framework Elements

[+] If you are not sure whether to use certain business functions, you should check them in a sandbox system. If you then decide not to use a business function, it is not activated permanently in the development system.

In addition, you can activate only one industry solution per system. However, the existing business functions cannot be assigned directly and completely to only one industry solution. For example, the Retail business functions can also be used for IS Oil & Gas. Switching is done using Transaction SFW5. You can switch on an entire business function set, or switch on or off individual business functions. The prerequisite for switching off is that the business functions are defined as reversible and that the package does not contain any DDIC objects.

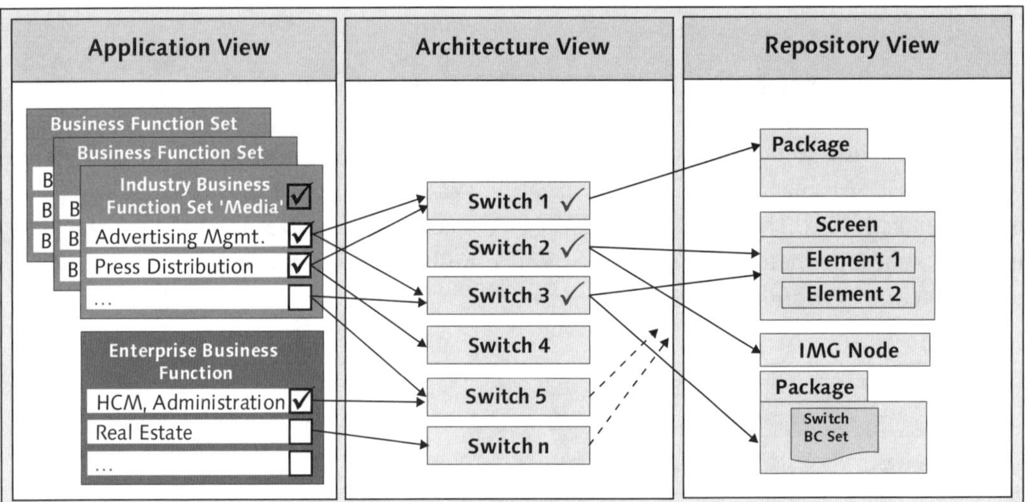

Figure 10.21 Overview of the Dependencies of the Switch Framework

The previously discussed options to switch enhancements using switches can also be used for your own developments. That is, you can create your own switches in the Switch Framework and assign to them implementations to be switched, such as packages, dynpro elements, or menu entries. If a business function is assigned to these switches, they can be switched using Transaction SFW5. Figures 10.22 and 10.23 illustrate these dependencies; as mentioned earlier, you can only use the customer namespace for your objects.

To define a switch, you use Transaction SFW1. You then assign the switch to a package via the DETAIL button (see Figure 10.22). Initially, the switch is in the state OFF. It changes to STANDBY or ON AFTER ACTIVATION.

Defining switches

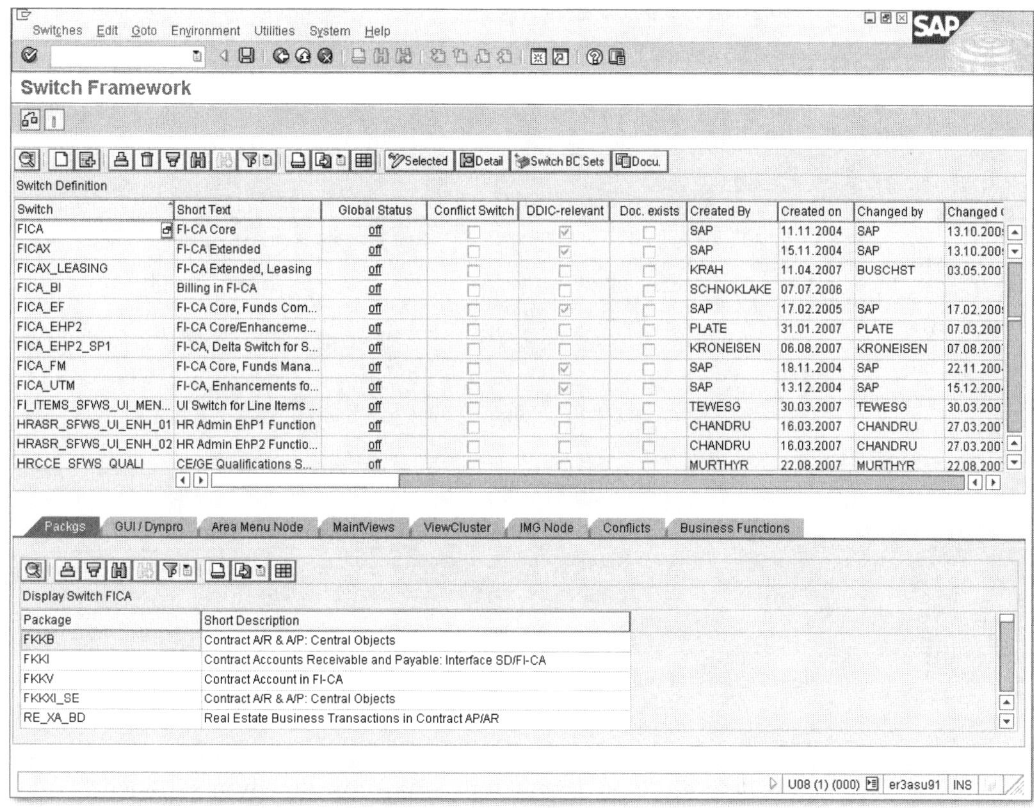

Figure 10.22 SFW1—Switch Definition with Package Assignment

In Transaction SFW2, you define the business function and create the category as an enterprise enhancement, enterprise business function, or industry business function. It is important that you determine the assignment category during the assignment of the business function to the previously defined switch. Possible values are ACTIVATION and STANDBY. STANDBY results in only the assignment of DDIC objects. ACTIVATION causes the assignment of all objects. You should therefore always select ACTIVATION. A business function represents a portion of the application functionality virtually, and establishes the connection to the enhancement switches (see Figure 10.23).

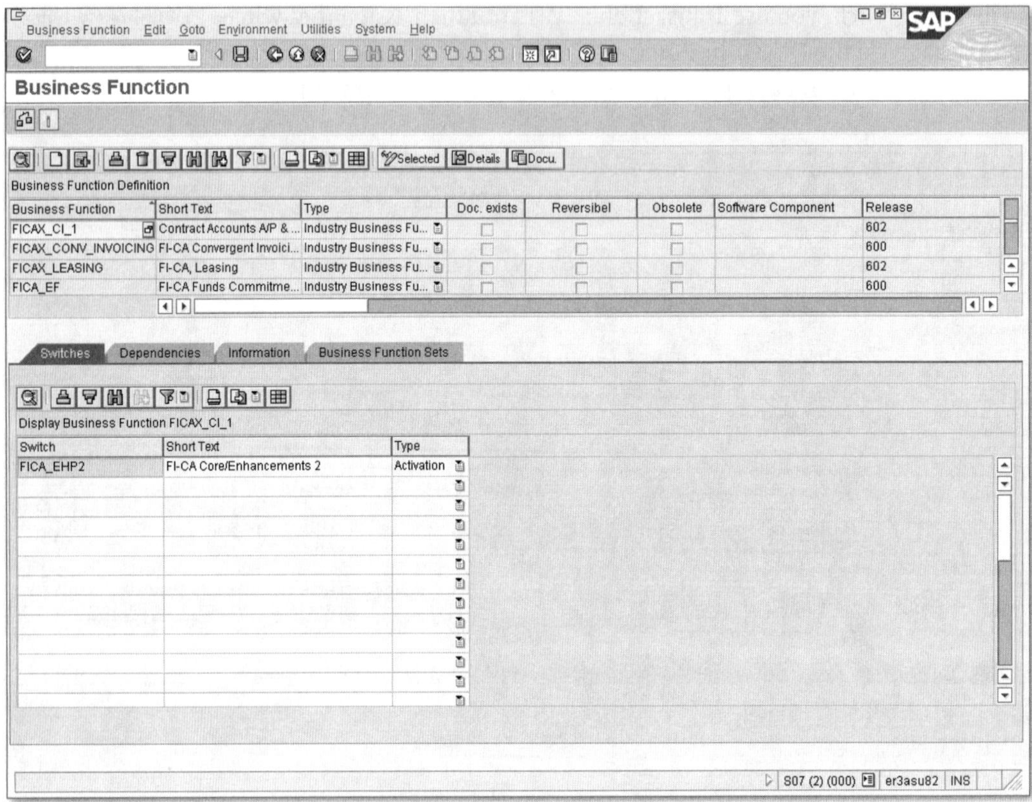

Figure 10.23 SFW2—Business Function Definition with Switch Assignment

If you want to group your switches using a business function set, you must define this in Transaction SFW3. As already mentioned for the assignment options, you can implement a hierarchical structure by grouping additional business functions, or other business function sets, using a business function set. For example, in SAP business function sets, enhancements are grouped within an industry solution (see Figure 10.24).

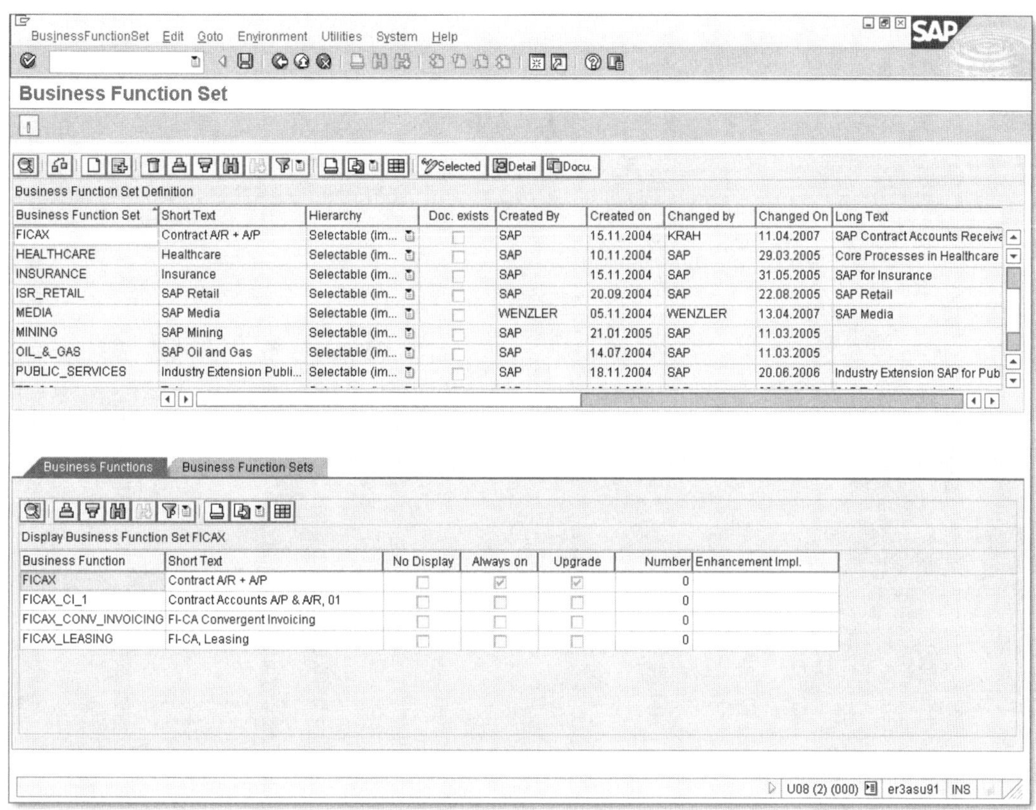

Figure 10.24 SFW3—Definition of Business Function Sets With Assignment of Business Functions

Finally, you can activate the switches using Transaction SFW5 (see Figure 10.25).

Although you can extend the SAP system via the Enhancement Framework without any modifications, you still have to implement a modification adjustment during a release update or when importing Support Packages. If the enhancement itself is changed through SAP changes, or if the including object can be affected through a semantic change, this also necessitates a modification adjustment. However, this adjustment is easier to implement than is the case for regular modifications because not all changes directly influence the enhanced objects.

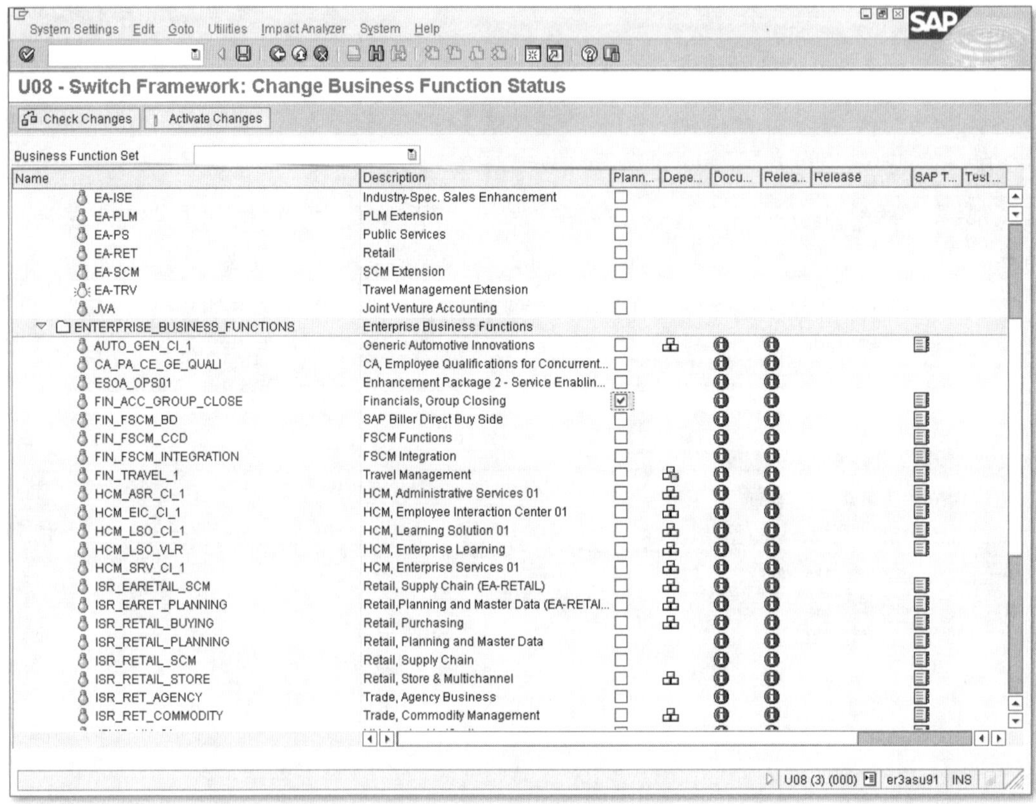

Figure 10.25 SFW5—Activation of Business Functions via Previously Defined Switches

Conflicts

If, for example, the import of Support Packages results in conflicts, you can find out in different ways. In the import log, conflicts are displayed as a warning stating PLEASE CALL TRANSACTION SPAU_ENH. Or, if you want to process an enhancement with a conflict that has not yet been resolved, you cannot switch to the enhancement mode and will instead see a message that states that you must first adjust the enhancement. The easiest way to view objects is to use Transaction SE80 via ENHANCEMENT ADAPTATIONS or, you can view them directly via Transaction SPAU_ENH.

The transaction shows a hierarchical tree structure of the objects that require adaptation. The traffic lights in the tree structure forward the highest status to the respective next higher level. To make an adaptation, proceed as follows:

1. Double-click the enhancement implementation you want to adapt.
2. Switch to CHANGE MODE and select the ADAPTATION TAB.
3. The list contains entries with yellow and red traffic lights for adaptation. Double-click the list entry you want to adapt.
4. In the split-screen editor, carry out the enhancement adaptation, for example.
5. After you have completed the adaptations, manually set the status to "done" (green checkmark).
6. Now, click the ADJUST ENHANCEMENT IMPLEMENTATION BUTTON.
7. Activate the enhancement.

After the enhancement has been activated, the object no longer appears in the tree of Transaction SPAU_ENH.

Extension Index

Aside from the previously described enhancement options, the ABAP Dictionary also includes two new types: Fixed value appends and the extension index. Only the extension index is described here as an example.

The creation of a secondary index—even if it takes places in the customer name range—is a modification that must be processed during updates, such as during upgrades or during the application of Support Packages—in the modification adjustment SPDD. The creation of an extension index is as easy as the creation of a regular index. To do so, proceed as follows:

1. Call Transaction SE11 and, in the selection field, enter the table for which you want to create an index.
2. Switch to CHANGE MODE.
3. Choose the INDICES button.
4. Click the CREATE INDEX button and then select CREATE EXTENSION INDEX.

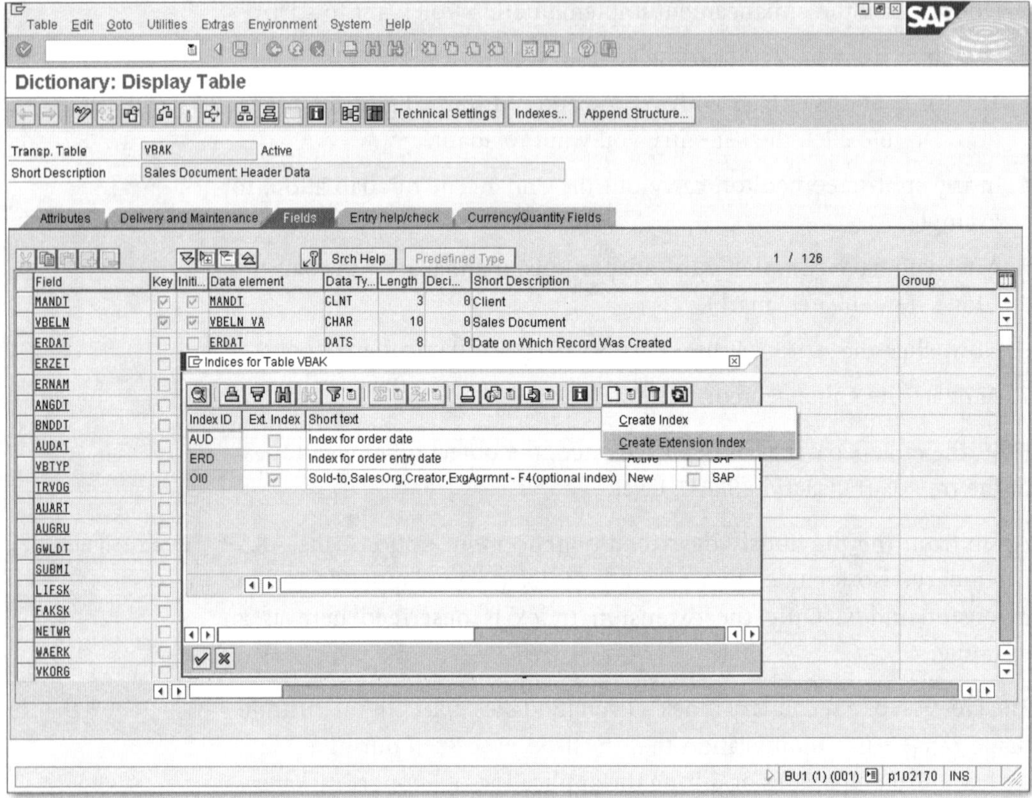

Figure 10.26 Creating an Extension Index

For comprehensive documentation on the new SAP NetWeaver 7.0 enhancement concept, refer to the SAP help. Or, in the system, click the INFO button in ABAP Editor and enter "enhancement concept" as the search term to navigate to ENHANCEMENT CONCEPT • MORE.

10.5 The Object Directory

When you create an object, a corresponding Object Directory entry is also created. The key data for this entry is visible in the object list for each change request or task. Although this information is created automatically, there may be situations in which it is useful to display and possibly change the Object Directory entry for a particular object.

The Object Directory in table TADIR is a catalog of all Repository objects in the SAP ERP system, including the standard SAP objects delivered with systems, and all objects you create using ABAP Workbench tools. These objects include ABAP programs, module pools, function groups, and ABAP Dictionary objects (domains, data elements, and tables).

Primary key of table TADIR

The primary key of table TADIR comprises the following fields:

- Program identification (PgmID)
- Object type (Obj.)
- Object name

For the majority of Repository objects, the PgmID is R3TR. The object type classifies the object—for example, PROG denotes an ABAP program, and TABL denotes a dictionary table structure. Examples of common object entries are listed in Table 10.4.

PgmID	Object Type	Description
R3TR	PROG	ABAP program
R3TR	DEVC	Development class
R3TR	VIEW	Table view
R3TR	FORM	ABAP form
R3TR	CMOD	Customer enhancement
R3TR	TABL	Table structure
R3TR	DTEL	Data element
R3TR	DOMA	Domain
R3TR	TRAN	Transaction
R3TR	FUGR	Function group

Table 10.4 Table 10.4 Sample Object Entries

When reviewing the object list of a task or change request, you may see the entry LIMU in the PGMID column. LIMU indicates that the object is a sub-object of either an R3TR or an R3OB object. These sub-objects do not have their own Object Directory entry; instead, they are included in the entry for the respective object. Sub-objects can be transported separately so that the entire Repository object does not have to be transported every time a change is made.

When, for example, the ABAP program `ZPROGRAM` is created, the corresponding Object Directory entry `R3TR PROG ZPROGRAM` is automatically created. This entry is then used in the object list of the task and, when the task is released, in the object list of the change request. After an object is initially created, all of its components are transported. Subsequent changes to the object transport only the changed sub-objects. Sample sub-objects for an ABAP program are listed in Table 10.5.

PgmID	Object Type	Description
LIMU	REPS	Program source
LIMU	DOCU	Documentation
LIMU	REPT	Text elements of the report
LIMU	VARI	Program variants
LIMU	ADIR	Object directory entry

Table 10.5 Typical Sub-Objects for ABAP Programs

10.5.1 Object Attributes

The Object Directory also contains the *object attributes* of each Repository object. You can display these attributes as described in the next section. They include:

- Development class
- Original system
- Person responsible for object
- Original language
- Generation flag
- Repair flag

You can change the ORIGINAL SYSTEM attribute—the system in which the object was created—by making a *relocation transport* in Transaction SE01 (described in the text that follows). In general, if problems exist with a particular object, consult the person indicated in the attribute PERSON RESPONSIBLE FOR OBJECT.

The ORIGINAL LANGUAGE attribute is an attribute for the language-specific components of each object, such as text elements, and is equivalent to the logon language in which the object was created. If you are developing in more than one language, when you log on in another language and proceed to edit the object, the system asks you whether you want to change the original language.

If an object is flagged as GENERATED, it was automatically created as an indirect result of other user activities, such as particular Customizing transactions (see Chapter 11, Section 11.3.1).

10.5.2 Displaying or Changing an Object Directory Entry

Repository Browser

You can display Object Directory entries in several ways. The most common is to use the Repository Browser, which lets you display and change the Object Directory entries for Repository objects in the current SAP ERP system. To display objects in the Repository Browser, proceed as follows:

1. Use Transaction code SE80 or, from the SAP ERP initial screen, choose TOOLS • ABAP WORKBENCH • OVERVIEW • OBJECT NAVIGATOR.
2. In the resulting selection screen, the upper and lower screen areas let you make a selection in two different ways:
   - In the top half of the screen, you can generate an object list and then select the object you want to display. To do this, mark one of the radio buttons and, in the adjacent field, enter the corresponding development class, program, function group, or user. Choose DISPLAY. Expand the object list if necessary, and position the cursor on a Repository object.
   - The lower half of the screen lets you display an individual object. Select the type of object and choose EDIT. A new selection screen appears. Enter the object name and choose EXECUTE.
3. To display the object's directory entry, select EDIT • OBJECT DIRECTORY ENTRY. The CHANGE OBJECT DIRECTORY ENTRY dialog box appears (see Figure 10.27), enabling you to view the Object Directory entry, or to change the development class or person responsible.

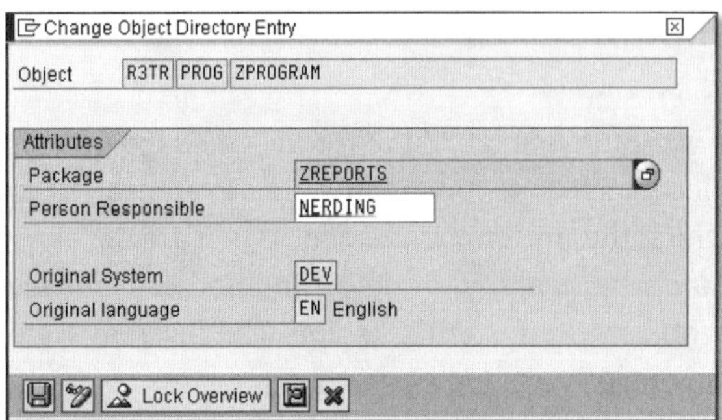

Figure 10.27 Displaying or Changing an Object Directory Entry

For example, when you want to transport an object with development class $TMP, you would use this dialog box to change the development class to a customer development class. You can also change the owner of an object—for example, if a developer has left the project and all of his objects need to be assigned to another developer.

Some attributes cannot be changed from this dialog box in the Repository Browser. For example, if you need to assign the current SAP ERP system as the original system of an object, use Transaction SE03. A tree structure is displayed listing several tools. Choose OBJECT DIRECTORY, and double-click an entry to perform the respective Object Directory task.

No matter which method you use to change Object Directory entries, keep the following points in mind:

- With authorization profile S_A.SYSTEM and using Transaction SE03, you can modify all attributes except ORIGINAL LANGUAGE.
- After changing the development class, responsible person, generation flag, or repair flag for an object, you must save your changes to a change request. Exceptions include objects local to the current system such as those assigned to the development class $TMP.
- When changing the development class of an object that has already been released and exported, the new development class ideally has the same transport layer as the previous one. This helps ensure that the affected objects continue to be transported along the same transport route.

10.5.3 Transporting Objects Using the Transport Organizer (Extended View)

The *Transport Organizer* (Extended View, Transaction SE01), is used for all nonstandard transports—that is, for transports that are not performed using the Workbench Organizer or the Customizing Organizer. In particular, the Transport Organizer lets you create change requests to perform the following kinds of transports:

Types of transports

- **Transports of copies**
  Used to transport a collection of Repository objects and Customizing objects to a specified system. The Object Directory entry of the objects remains unchanged in both the source and target system.
- **Relocations without development class change**
  Used to change collections of objects in another system on a temporary basis—for example, to create special developments that do not interfere with the normal development environment. The original system of the objects becomes the target system. The same type of relocation transport is later used to return the objects back to the source system.
- **Relocations with development class change**
  Used to permanently change the development system of individual objects. The objects' original system becomes the target system. Assign a development class that ensures that the objects will be associated with the right transport route after import into the target system. After the objects have been imported into the target system, you can record them to a transportable change request without making any further changes to their Object Directory entry.
- **Relocations of complete development classes**
  Used to permanently change the transport layer of a development class and the objects' original systems. The change request's object list for this transport is set up automatically and contains all objects in the development class.

Performing transports

To perform any of these four types of Transport Organizer transports, proceed as follows:

1. Enter Transaction code SE01 or, from the SAP ERP initial screen, choose TOOLS • ADMINISTRATION • TRANSPORTS • TRANSPORT ORGANIZER.
2. Select TRANSPORT OF COPIES, RELOCATION and click CHOOSE.

3. Choose CREATE. In the resulting dialog box, select one of the following:
   - TRANSPORT OF COPIES
   - RELOCATION OF OBJECTS W/O DEV. CLASS CHANGE
   - RELOCATION OF OBJECTS WITH DEV. CLASS CHANGE
   - RELOCATION OF A COMPLETE DEVELOPMENT CLASS
4. Press [Enter]. The CREATE REQUEST dialog box appears, enabling you to create an appropriate change request as explained in Table 10.6:

Field	User Entry
Short description:	Enter a short text describing the change request.
Target:	Enter the name of the target system (or, if extended transport management is active, the target system and client). The target system must have been defined in the TMS.
Target dev. Class:	This field appears if you selected RELOCATION WITH DEV. CLASS CHANGE. Enter the name of the target development class for the Repository objects. The development class must be defined in the current SAP ERP system and assigned to a transport layer specific to the target SAP ERP system.
Development class and Target transp. layer:	These fields appear if you selected RELOCATIONS OF A COMPLETE DEVELOPMENT CLASS. Enter the name of the development class for the objects to be copied, and the target transport layer for the development class.

Table 10.6 Creating a Change Request

5. After completing the required entries, choose SAVE.
6. The DISPLAY REQUEST screen appears, showing the newly created change request. To modify the details you entered in the previous dialog boxes, position the cursor on the change request and choose REQUEST/TASK • DISPLAY/CHANGE.

Adding objects

Unless the change request is a relocation for an entire development class, the newly created change request does not contain any Repository objects. To add objects to the change request, in the DISPLAY REQUEST screen, select the change request and choose REQUEST/TASK • OBJECT LIST • INCLUDE OBJECTS. Then, proceed as described in Section 10.2.7. After adding objects to the change request, you can release and export it.

Example: Using Relocation of a Complete Development Class

A large pharmaceutical company implementing SAP ERP initially wants a standard three-system landscape (DEV, QAS, and PRD). Due to the development and testing requirements of Internet interoperability, however, the company decides to create a second development system, NET, to be used solely for the development needs of the SAP Internet Transaction Server. DEV will still be used for traditional forms of development work such as the creation of special reports and legacy conversion routines.

The system NET is created as a system copy of the current development system. The TMS and transport routes for NET are configured as shown in Figure 10.28:

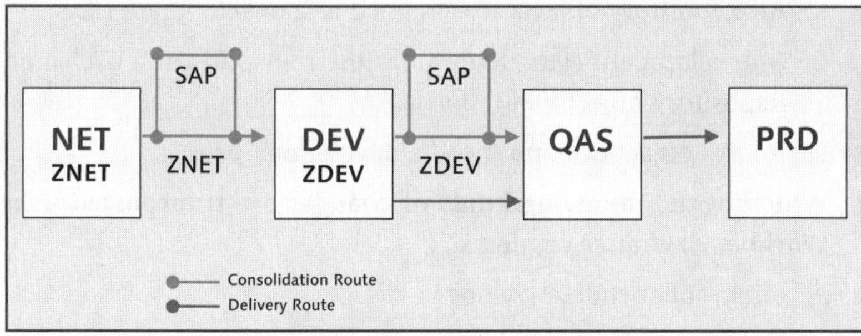

Figure 10.28 Configuration of TMS and Transport Routes for System NET

New Repository objects that support Internet activities are created in NET and assigned to the development class `ZINTERNET`, whose transport layer is ZNET. These objects are recorded to change requests and transported to DEV. The delivery route between DEV and QAS ensures that changes from NET are subsequently delivered to the quality assurance system and ultimately to the production system.

To ensure that objects created in NET and DEV have unique names, naming convention entries are added to view V_TRESN. Only an object whose name begins with "ZNET" should receive the development class `ZINTERNET`. New objects on DEV cannot be named using "ZNET."

The system NET helps bring Internet transactions to the production environment. Over time, the need for NET disappears, and all Internet development will be concentrated in DEV. To support the switch from NET to DEV, all Repository objects created on NET (objects with the development class ZINTERNET) are copied from NET to DEV by relocating the entire development class. The development class is assigned the new transport layer ZDEV. DEV then solely supports all development efforts, including those required for Internet functionality.

10.6 Questions

1. **Which of the following statements is *false* with regard to development classes?**
   A. Development classes facilitate project management by grouping similar Repository objects.
   B. All Repository objects are assigned to a development class.
   C. A development class determines the transport route a changed Repository object will follow.
   D. A local object does not need a development class.
2. **Which of the following kinds of changes are transported using Workbench change requests?**
   A. Client-independent changes.
   B. Modifications to SAP-delivered objects.
   C. Changes made using the ABAP Editor and ABAP Dictionary.
   D. Repairs to Repository objects that originated in another SAP ERP system.
   E. All of the above.
3. **Which of the following data is *not* contained in the object list of a task?**
   A. The actual change made to the objects listed in the task
   B. The list of changed objects recorded to the task
   C. Whether the objects recorded to the task are locked
   D. The complete Object Directory entry for the object

4. **Which of the following statements are correct with regard to repairs and modifications?**

   A. Repairs are changes to SAP-delivered objects; modifications are changes to any object that originated in an SAP ERP system other than the current SAP ERP system.

   B. A repair flag protects a Repository object against being overwritten by an import.

   C. All repairs are saved to Workbench change requests.

   D. A modification is a change to a standard SAP object.

   E. All of the above.

5. **Which additional enhancement options does the Enhancement Framework provide as of SAP NetWeaver 7.0?**

   A. Implicit enhancement points

   B. Implicit enhancement sections

   C. Explicit enhancement points

   D. Explicit enhancement sections

6. **Which of the following statements are correct with regard to the Switch Framework?**

   A. The Switch Framework is only available for the activation of SAP industry solutions.

   B. Business functions can be switched on and off.

   C. Business function sets group several business functions into semantic units to enable switching the business functions together.

   D. All of the above.

Customizing the SAP software with regard to the individual business processes ensures that the system meets your specific requirements. This chapter describes the tools you can use for special Customizing or for error analyses.

11 Managing Customizing Changes

This chapter explains the tools you can use to perform Customizing and manage change requests containing Customizing changes. Proper management of Customizing changes can be divided into the following areas:

- Customizing prerequisites
- Customizing change requests
- Nonstandard Customizing activities
- Support tools for Customizing

11.1 Customizing Prerequisites

To enable Customizing activities in SAP systems, do the following:

- Ensure that Customizing changes occur only in a single SAP client in your system landscape.
- Ensure that Customizing changes are recorded to change requests.
- Assign user authorizations to the Customizing team.
- Set up the necessary Project IMGs.

To ensure that Customizing changes occur only in a specific SAP client, use the client and system change settings to allow or disallow Customizing in each SAP system and client. As described in Chapter 3, to enable

Customizing changes in a specific client, the client settings in Transaction SCC4 for that client should be as follows:

- The client-dependent change option allows changes and is preferably set to AUTOMATIC RECORDING OF CHANGES.
- The client-independent change option allows changes to client-independent Customizing objects.
- The client's role is not PRODUCTION.

In addition to providing the client settings, to enable Customizing, you must set the system change option for the SAP system to MODIFIABLE, to support client-independent Customizing (see Chapter 7).

To limit who can create and release change requests and tasks, assign user authorizations based on the following authorization profiles:

- S_A.CUSTOMIZ
  This profile is for project leads and enables them to create and release change requests, and to assign tasks to team members.
- S_A.DEVELOP
  This profile is for team members and enables them to perform Customizing and development activities, and to work with the Customizing and Workbench Organizers. Team members can release their tasks after unit testing, but they cannot release the change request.

You can use SAP-delivered authorization profiles as templates for creating your own authorizations.

[+] For information on the authorization objects and authorizations related to the profiles S_A.CUSTOMIZ and S_A.DEVELOP, see SAP ERP online documentation.

Setting Up Project IMGs

Customizing management during implementation is best realized using Project IMGs (introduced in Chapter 2). Project IMGs subdivide the functionality of your SAP ERP application components, enabling you to focus your Customizing on particular areas. Project IMGs also provide project management capabilities that allow project leads to monitor the status of their project and review relevant documentation. After you have generated Project IMGs, the Customizing team can begin its work.

Enterprise IMG

To create Project IMGs, you must first generate the Enterprise IMG by selecting the desired application components and compiling the list of required Customizing for the selected components. To generate the Enterprise IMG, proceed as follows:

1. Use Transaction code SPRO or, from the SAP ERP initial screen, choose TOOLS • BUSINESS ENGINEER • CUSTOMIZING.
2. Choose BASIC FUNCTIONS • ENTERPRISE IMG • GENERATE. Enter a distinctive title for the Enterprise IMG and choose CONTINUE.
3. Choose ALL COUNTRIES or, to focus on country-specific activities, only the countries relevant for your company. Press Enter.
4. A tree structure displays, showing SAP's entire application components list (the SAP Reference IMG). Select the SAP ERP components your company requires. Choose GENERATE.

Project IMG

After generating the Enterprise IMG, you are ready to create the various Project IMGs by dividing the Enterprise IMG into several parts, as well as filter the Project IMGs to create different views based on task priority. To create a Project IMG and the associated views, proceed as follows:

1. Use Transaction code SPRO_ADMIN or, from the SAP ERP initial screen, choose TOOLS • CUSTOMIZING • IMG. Choose PROJECT ADMINISTRATION. The PROJECT ADMINISTRATION screen appears.
2. Choose PROJECT • CREATE. Enter a unique number for the new project and choose CONTINUE. The CREATE PROJECT screen appears (see Figure 11.1). When accessing existing projects, select PROJECT • CHANGE. The CHANGE PROJECT screen appears.
3. Enter a descriptive name, a default project language, a project owner, a start date, and an end date. Select the desired project management and documentation options. Choose GENERATE PROJECT IMG. The GENERATE PROJECT IMG dialog box appears.

4. Choose SELECT COUNTRIES AND APPLICATION COMPONENTS and select CONTINUE.

[+] Avoid selecting the USE WHOLE ENTERPRISE IMG option, because this does not reduce the Project IMG to a subset of the Enterprise IMG.

5. In the resulting dialog box, choose all countries or only the countries relevant for your project. Choose CONTINUE. The SELECT BUSINESS APPLICATION COMPONENTS screen appears, showing the list of application components in the Enterprise IMG.
6. Select the application components you want to include in the Project IMG. Choose GENERATE. The dialog box GENERATE VIEWS OF THE PROJECT is displayed.
7. Select the project views to be created and choose GENERATE.

Project IMGs provide project management capabilities that are not available in the Enterprise IMG. These include time scheduling, status maintenance, documentation, and Customizing task priority. The project lead should create Project IMGs for the various implementation phases (see Figure 11.1).

You can subsequently extend the Enterprise IMG and regenerate it without losing the originally selected components. This is necessary, for example, after release upgrades, because new releases include new application components and new Customizing activities. To recreate the Enterprise IMG, repeat the procedure for creating the Enterprise IMG. Then, regenerate each Project IMG as follows:

1. Use Transaction code SPRO_ADMIN or, from the SAP ERP initial screen, choose TOOLS • CUSTOMIZING • IMG. Choose PROJECT ADMINISTRATION. The PROJECT ADMINISTRATION screen appears.
2. To regenerate a single Project IMG, select the project ID and choose PROJECT • CHANGE. Choose GENERATE PROJECT IMG.

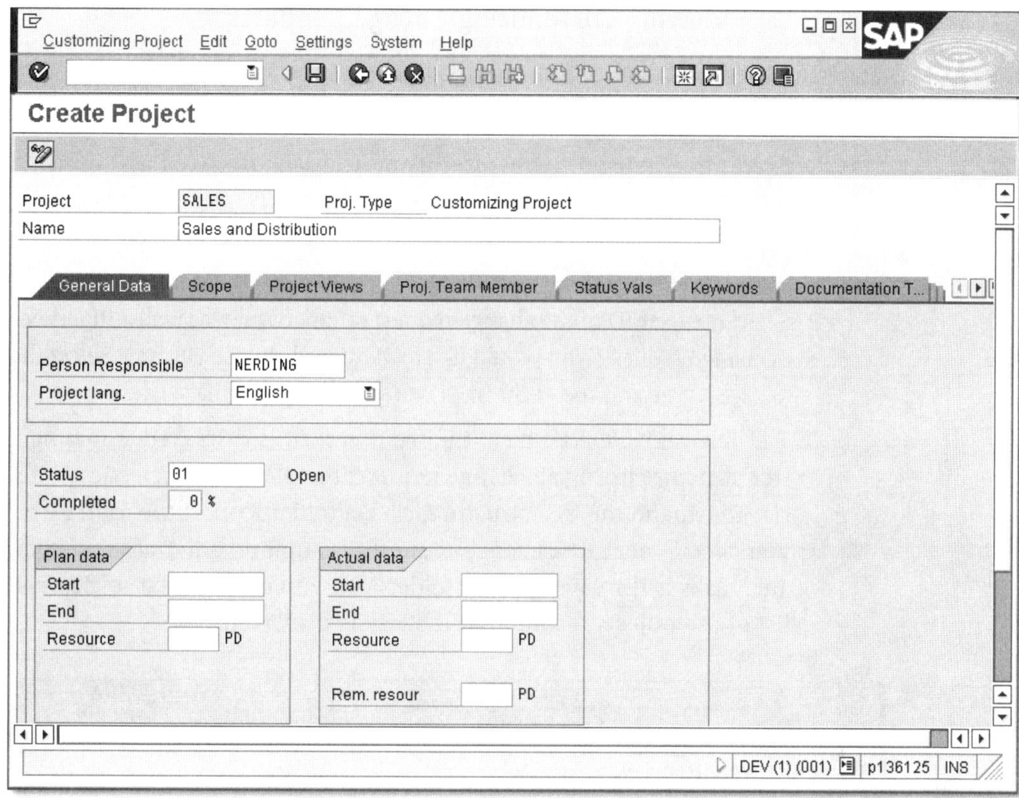

Figure 11.1 Creating a Project IMG

11.2 Customizing Change Requests

Customizing is performed in the activities specified in a Project IMG. After an activity has been completed, the changes should be recorded to change requests so they can be transported to other systems and clients. Most IMG Customizing activities are client-dependent and affect only the current client. These changes are recorded in a Customizing change request. Client-independent Customizing changes require Workbench change requests.

Project leads are responsible for creating Customizing change requests and assigning tasks within these requests to Customizing team members (see Chapter 6).

11.2.1 Viewing Customizing Change Requests

To view the Customizing change requests a user owns, as well as the Customizing change requests in which the user owns a task, proceed as follows:

1. Access the Transport Organizer using Transaction code SE10 or, from the SAP ERP initial screen, choose TOOLS • CUSTOMIZING • IMG • TRANSPORT ORGANIZER (EXTENDED VIEW). The initial selection screen of the Customizing Organizer appears (see Figure 11.2).
2. Select the user ID of the change request or task owner, as well as the types of change requests you would like to view, and choose DISPLAY. Select the REQUEST TYPE and the REQUEST STATUS and then select DISPLAY.
3. The TRANSPORT ORGANIZER: REQUESTS screen is displayed, showing a tree structure listing all change requests that match the selection criteria. To expand the tree structure, click a folder icon. If the folder icon you click is next to a change request ID number, a list of the associated tasks is displayed. If the folder icon you click is next to a task, a list of the objects recorded in the task is displayed.

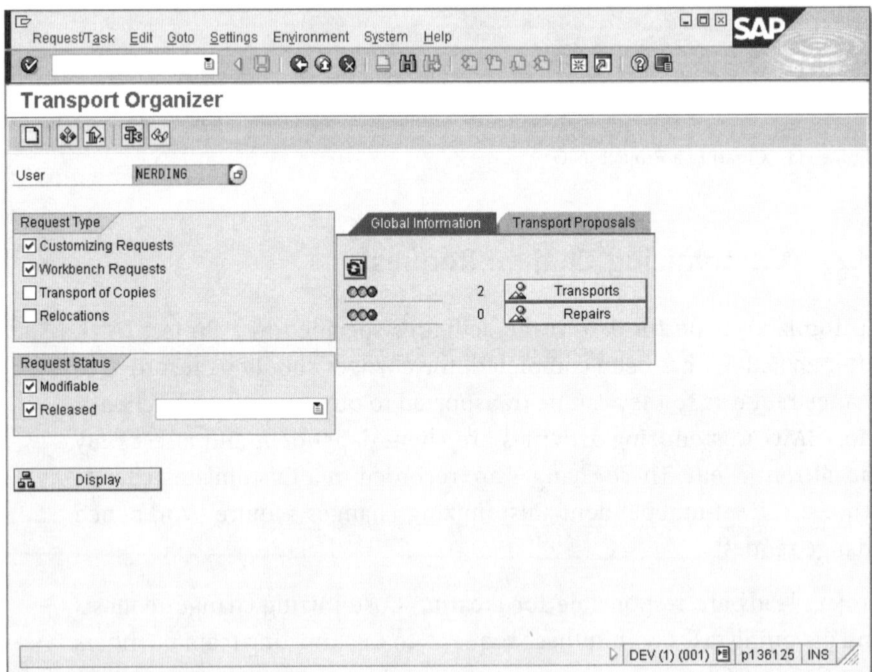

Figure 11.2 The Initial Screen of the Transport Organizer

Figure 11.3 shows an example of the tree structure with all modifiable Customizing requests in which the user KOESEGI is involved. KOESEGI is the owner of requests DEVK900002 and DEVK900005, in which the users NERDING, KOESEGI, and SCHMIDT own tasks. The task DEVK900006 of KOESEGI contains changes to view V_005_B, which consists of table T005.

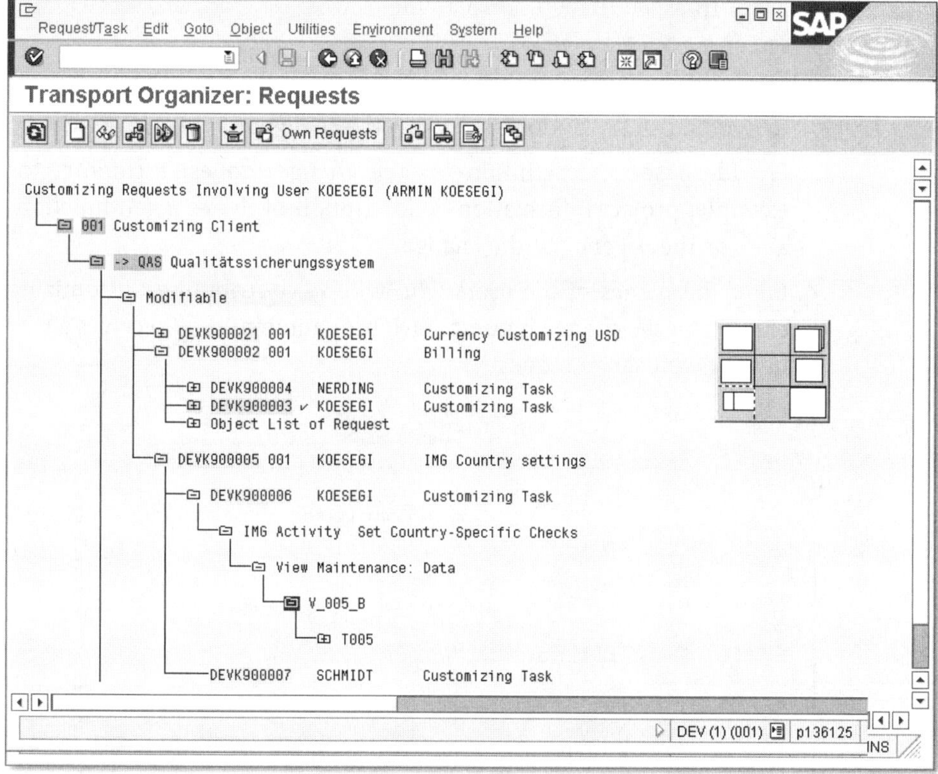

Figure 11.3 Tree Structure in the Transport Organizer Listing Change Requests and Tasks

11.2.2 Creating Customizing Change Requests

The project lead uses the Customizing Organizer to obtain an overview of all Customizing changes in their respective tasks and is responsible for releasing change requests. Therefore, the project lead should be the person to create change requests and assign project team members to the requests.

Ideally, this should be completed well before project team members begin performing Customizing activities. SAP recommends recording all Customizing activities for a particular project objective to a single change request, enabling their subsequent release and export as a testable unit.

Assigning tasks

To create a Customizing change request and assign tasks to project team members, proceed as follows:

1. From Transaction SE10, display the TRANSPORT ORGANIZER: REQUESTS screen.
2. To create a new change request, choose REQUEST/TASK • CREATE. The CREATE REQUEST window is displayed (see Figure 11.4).
3. Provide a short description for the change request including, for example, project information, a description of the changed functionality, or the urgency of the change.
4. Enter the names of the users who will be contributing Customizing changes to the change request. Each user automatically receives a task in the new change request.
5. Choose SAVE.

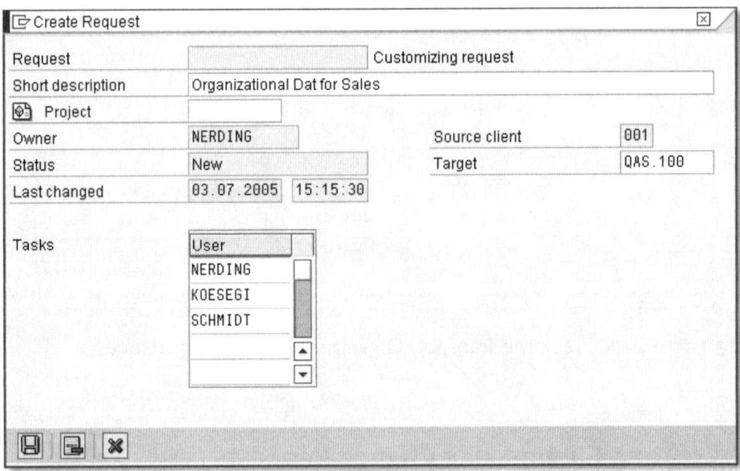

Figure 11.4 Creating a Customizing Change Request

Non-modifiable default settings

When creating a Customizing change request, you cannot change the following default settings:

- The name of the SAP ERP user who created the change request
- The status
- The date and time stamp
- The source client in which the change request was created
- The change request category

The source client is always the client in which the change request was created. You can perform the following activities only from within this client:

- Recording changes to the change request
- Changing the owner of the change request or of its tasks
- Adding tasks to the change request
- Releasing the change request

The change request category is always CUST, indicating that the request is a Customizing change request and can record only client-dependent changes.

Adding Users to a Change Request

You can add users to a change request at any time in the interval between creating and releasing the request. Proceed as follows:

1. From Transaction SE10, display the TRANSPORT ORGANIZER: REQUESTS screen.
2. Position the cursor on the change request ID to which you want to add a user. Choose REQUEST/TASK • CREATE. The ADD USER dialog box is displayed.
3. Enter the name of the user, or use the possible entries button to select a user.
4. Choose COPY.

[+] After it is released, a change request or task cannot be changed. For example, you cannot add a user to a released change request.

Changing the Owner of Change Requests and Tasks

Each change request and each task have an SAP ERP user defined as its owner. By default, the user who creates a change request becomes its owner, and a task is automatically created for that user. If other users are assigned to the change request, tasks are automatically created for those users.

If you want to change the owner of a change request or task—for example, to reassign it to another user, or to become its owner so that you can change its attributes or delete an empty task, proceed as follows:

1. In Transaction SE10, access the TRANSPORT ORGANIZER: REQUESTS screen.
2. Position the cursor on the ID of the appropriate change request or task. Choose REQUEST/TASK • CHANGE OWNER.
3. Enter the name of the user, or use the possible entries button to select a user.
4. Select CONFIRM. The new user now owns the change request or task.

11.2.3 Customizing in Project IMGs

To perform Customizing as a member of the project team, proceed as follows:

1. Use Transaction code SPRO or, from the SAP ERP initial screen, choose TOOLS • CUSTOMIZING • IMG • EXECUTE PROJECT. The CUSTOMIZING: EXECUTE PROJECT screen is displayed, listing the project IMGs that have been created.
2. Choose the project you need to customize by double-clicking the Project ID. The Project IMG tree structure is displayed.
3. To display Customizing activities for the Project IMG, expand the tree structure (see Figure 11.5).

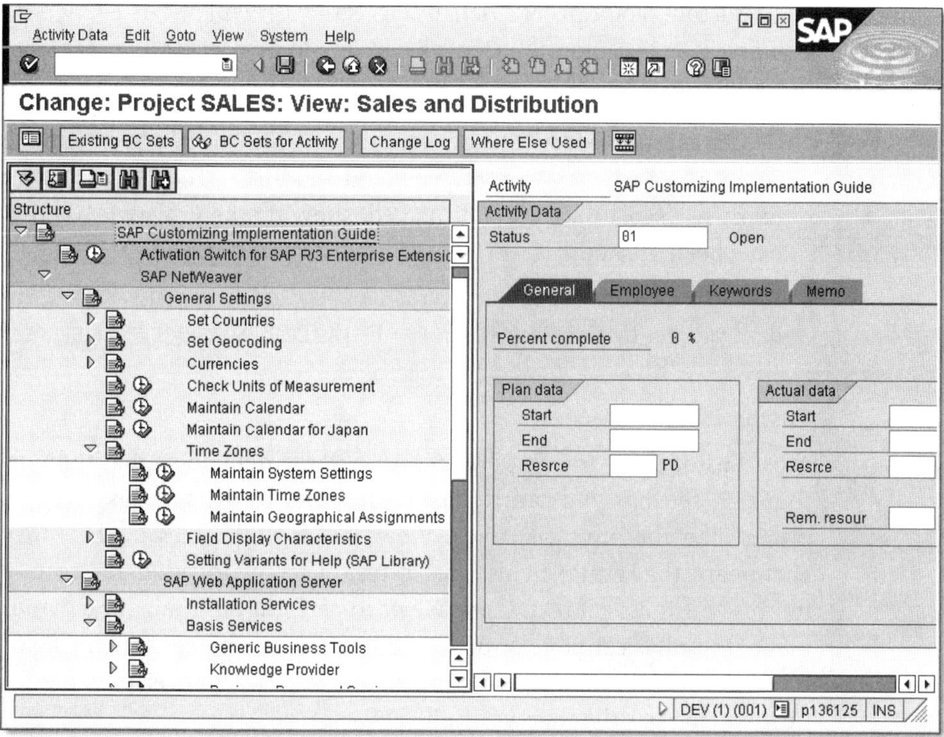

Figure 11.5 Project IMG Tree Structure

Double-clicking the appropriate icon to the left of the description of each Customizing activity takes you to various related tasks:

- The large check mark takes you to the documentation of the relevant Customizing activity.
- The pencil-and-paper icon takes you to the relevant Customizing transaction.

[+] Customizing activities are performed in the Project IMG tree structure. These activities include maintaining project status information, project documentation, and Customizing settings.

Setting a Default Project IMG

Customizers usually work in a single Project IMG, over a period of time. To eliminate the need for selecting the Project ID to access the relevant tree structure, you can set a default Project IMG that appears every time you access Transaction SPRO. To set a default Project IMG, proceed as follows:

1. Use Transaction code SPRO or, from the SAP ERP initial screen, choose TOOLS • CUSTOMIZING • IMG • EXECUTE PROJECT. The CUSTOMIZING: EXECUTE PROJECT screen is displayed, showing the Project IMGs that have been created.
2. Place the cursor over the Project IMG you want to specify as the standard project IMG and select EDIT • DEFAULT PROJECT/VIEW • DEFINE.

Customizing Using Views

Most Customizing transactions in SAP ERP are defined so that the Customizing settings you can change correspond to the settings in views rather than the physical tables. Views are logical tables in the ABAP Dictionary that group fields from physical tables together to create a uniform business context. Using views to perform Customizing activities masks the physical table structures and presents the constituent fields in a meaningful arrangement. Using table views wherever possible for Customizing has the following advantages:

Advantages

- You need only one view to customize several tables.
- You see only the fields from the physical tables that are relevant to the business object.
- The presentation and your processing of Customizing data are standardized.

Some business objects, such as material types and document types, cannot be represented in a view. Rather than having standardized maintenance transactions, these objects are maintained using special transactions. These can differ from object to object and, instead of views, use object-specific screen sequences.

[+] Customizing objects, whether simple or complex, are defined by SAP and can be viewed using Transaction SOBJ.

11.2.4 Recording Customizing Changes

Customizing changes performed in the respective Customizing transactions can be either automatically or manually saved to a change request for transport to other clients and systems.

SAP recommends that the client in which you make Customizing changes has its client-dependent change option set to AUTOMATIC RECORDING OF CHANGES. For example, when you create a new controlling area and save the change, you will automatically be required to save it to a change request.

If the client in which you are performing Customizing changes is not set to AUTOMATIC RECORDING OF CHANGES, you can manually record the change to a change request, either after saving the change or at a later time.

Certain Customizing activities, referred to in this chapter as *manual transport* Customizing activities, are not automatically recorded to a change request, even if the client is set to automatic recording. These Customizing activities are transported using a method that varies depending on the activity. [+]

Automatically Recording Changes to Change Requests

If the setting for client-dependent changes in your Customizing-and-development client is set to AUTOMATIC RECORDING OF CHANGES, when you save a Customizing change, you must indicate a change request to which the change can be recorded. The PROMPT FOR CHANGE REQUEST dialog box is displayed (see Figure 11.6).

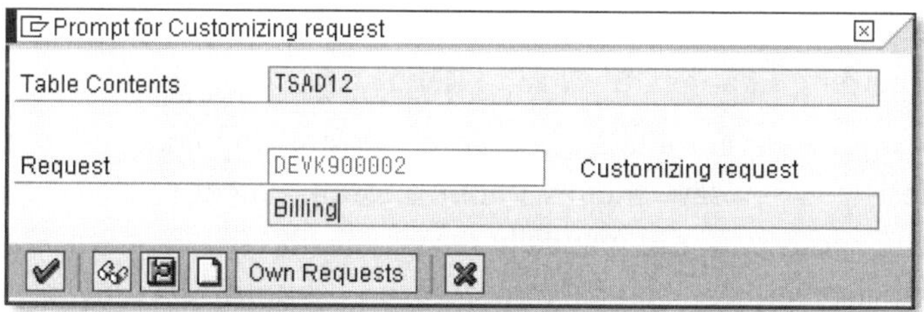

Figure 11.6 Recording a Change to a Change Request

In this dialog box, you can do one of the following:

- Enter the ID of a change request in which you have a task.
- Choose OWN REQUESTS and select a change request from the change requests offered (see Figure 11.7).
- Choose CREATE REQUEST and (assuming you have the appropriate authorization) create a new change request in which you then automatically also have a task.
- Choose CANCEL and thereby not save your Customizing changes.

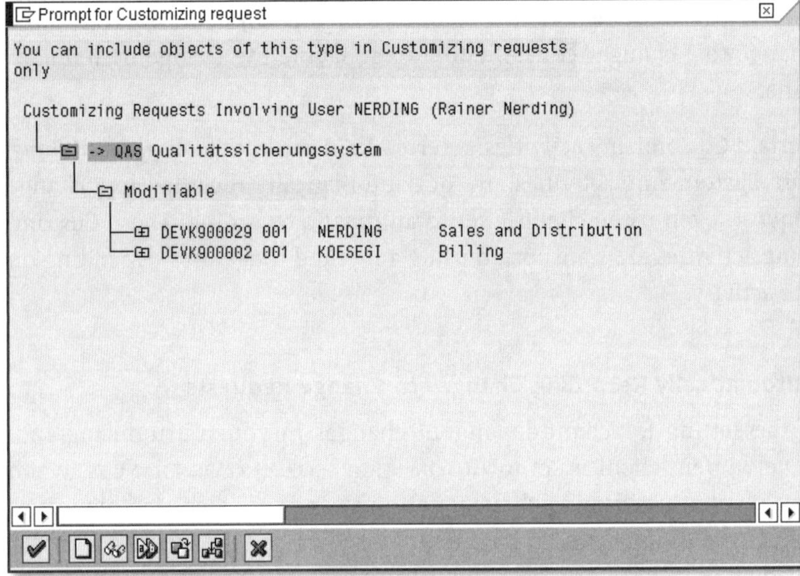

Figure 11.7 Selecting from a List of Available Change Requests

Manually Recording Changes to Change Requests

If a client is not set to automatically record Customizing changes to a change request, you can save them without recording them to a change request. Subsequently, you can manually record the existing Customizing changes to a change request. Manual recording of Customizing settings can also be used to record existing entries that, while they may already be in a change request, should be transported together in a single change request. To manually record existing Customizing entries, proceed as follows:

1. Use the IMG (Transaction SPRO) to access the Customizing activity. Click the large check mark to display the existing Customizing data you want to manually record to a change request.
2. Select the Customizing entries to be recorded to the change request. To do this, select all entries using EDIT • SELECTIONS • SELECT ALL, and then deselect individual entries by clicking the adjacent selection buttons.
3. Choose TABLE VIEW • TRANSPORT. The PROMPT FOR CHANGE REQUEST dialog box is displayed.
4. Enter the ID number of the change request to which the selected entries will be recorded. Choose CONTINUE. You return to the screen displaying the Customizing data.
5. Choose INCLUDE IN REQUEST. This records all of the Customizing entries you selected to the defined change request. Choose SAVE.

Not all Customizing activities allow changes to be manually recorded to a change request. When you display such Customizing settings, the TABLE VIEW • TRANSPORT menu option is not available. To transport such Customizing, you may need to activate automatic recording of changes and edit the existing entries to force them to be recorded to a change request.

Setting Your Default Change Request

When using automatic recording of change requests, you can set a default Customizing change request to eliminate the need to specify the change request. As a result, whenever you save a client-dependent Customizing change, it is recorded to your default change request. To set a default change request, proceed as follows:

1. In Transaction SE10, access the TRANSPORT ORGANIZER: REQUESTS screen.

2. Position the cursor on the change request you want as your default change request and choose Utilities • Standard request • Set. The change request appears in the Transport Organizer: Requests screen in a different color.

Validity period

When you have a default change request and try to save your Customizing changes, you are not prompted to specify a change request. Your default change request is valid for one week unless you change the validity period. To change the validity period, choose Utilities • Standard request • Set validity period.

If you no longer want a particular change request to be the default change request, from the Transport Organizer: Requests screen, position the cursor on the default change request and choose Utilities • Standard request • Reset.

11.2.5 Object Lists for Customizing Change Requests

The object list shows objects that have been changed, and will be transported when the change request is released and exported. Each changed object has an entry in the object list. The object list of a change request is filled only after the tasks in the change request have been released (see also Chapter 12).

By expanding the hierarchical structure of a Customizing change request, you can display the list of objects recorded in the change request. For example, Figure 11.8 shows the Customizing objects (values in tables) that were changed in task `DEVK900022`. The owner of this task is user KOESEGI. The figure shows that changes have been made to the V_TCURF and V_TCURR views. The views have been expanded so that you can see the tables (TCURF and TCURR) on which these views are based, as well as the primary keys of the table entries changed during Customizing. For table TCURF, for example, this change request recorded the primary key `001B USD DEM 80029898`.

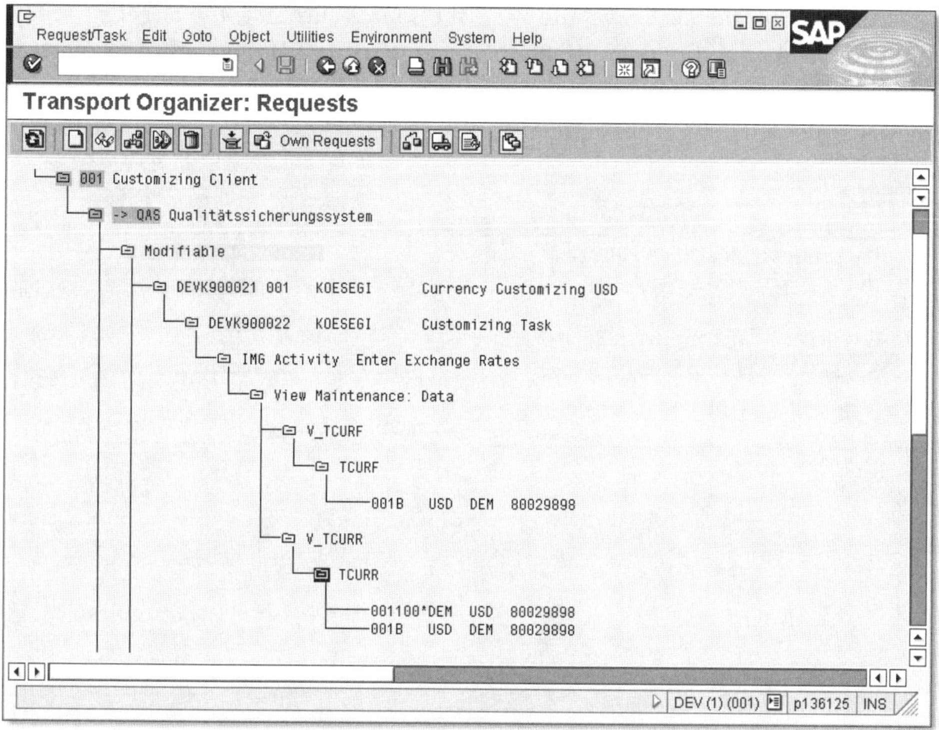

Figure 11.8 Objects in the Tree Structure for Customizing Change Requests

Primary key

You can view more information on these objects if you display the object list by double-clicking the request identification. The object list of task DEVK900022 is shown in Figure 11.9. The program identification (Pgmid) and the object description (Obj) specify the type of objects that have been changed. R3TR VDAT specifies view data. Note that a key symbol is shown in the Funct. column for the entries V_TCURF and V_TCURR. This symbol shows that a primary key has been recorded for these specific objects. If a primary key is recorded, not all of the rows of the specified table or view need to be transported. Instead, only the individual rows that match the key definition are transported.

To get a better understanding of the primary key that has been recorded for the changed Customizing entry, double-click on the key symbol in the object list and then double-click on the primary key value. A screen like the one shown in Figure 11.10 appears, displaying the key data of the table TCURR. Figure 11.10 shows that the primary key consists of the client, the exchange rate type, the source currency, the target currency, and a validity date. When this change request is released and exported, the current table entries are extracted to this primary key.

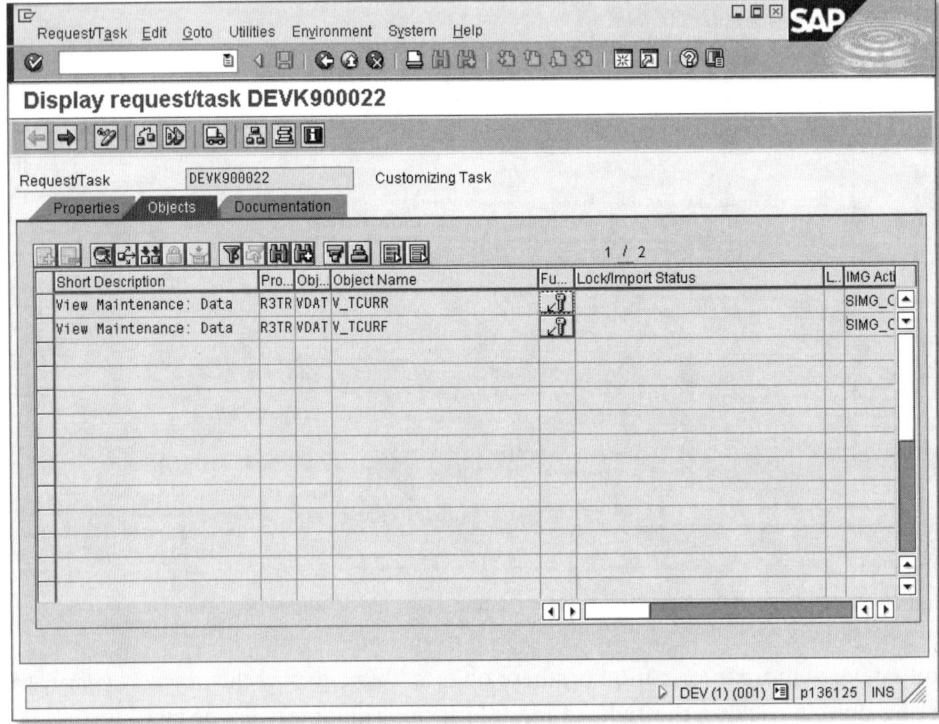

Figure 11.9 Object List for a Customizing Task

Display Key for Table TCURR

Med.field label	Field Name	Ty..	Lngth	Key Value
Client	MANDT	C	3	001
Exch.rate type	KURST	C	4	100*
From currency	FCURR	C	5	DEM
To-currency	TCURR	C	5	USD
Valid from	GDATU	C	8	80029898

Figure 11.10 Details of a Primary Key for a Recorded Customizing Change

Customizing change requests contain only client-dependent Customizing objects. For changes recorded in a Customizing change request, the client ID number is included in the primary key value. At the time of release and export, the primary key is used in an SQL `SELECT` statement to access the changed table entry.

A change request does *not* contain the actual table entries or the object that has changed. A change request does not even record whether the change was an addition, modification, or deletion. All that is recorded in a change request is the list of the objects (views, tables, and/or key values) that have changed. The objects in task `DEVK900022` shown in Figure 11.9 can be the result of creating, deleting, or changing entries in the currency table, for example.

A Customizing change request records, but does *not* contain, the actual table entries that have changed. [+]

Unlike in Workbench requests, in Customizing requests changed objects are not locked. For example, if user KOESEGI makes a change to the sales organization PRNT, the Customizing Organizer does not prevent other users from also modifying this Customizing setting while it is in an unreleased change request. Because Customizing objects in the SAP system are shared between different application components, it is important that the Customizing Organizer cannot lock entire tables or single table entries. Otherwise, Customizing could not be performed by more than one user in a client.

Changes recorded to a Customizing change request are not locked by the change request and can be changed and recorded to other change requests. [+]

11.2.6 Identifying Change Requests with the Same Object

As mentioned previously, unlike Workbench change requests, Customizing change requests do not lock objects. It is therefore possible for more than one person to change the same Customizing settings. If this shared access to Customizing objects creates a misunderstanding among project team members, it may be necessary to see which users are changing the same Customizing object.

Displaying tasks and requests

To view all tasks or change requests that include the same Customizing object, proceed as follows:

1. Access the Transport Organizer tools by using Transaction SE10 and choosing GoTo • Transport Organizer • Tools.
2. The Transport Organizer: Tools screen will appear, listing the available tools in a tree structure. Expand the Objects in requests node.
3. Double-click the Search for objects in requests/tasks option. The Search for Objects in Requests/Tasks screen appears (see Figure 11.11). This is a selection screen where you can define the object for which you are searching.

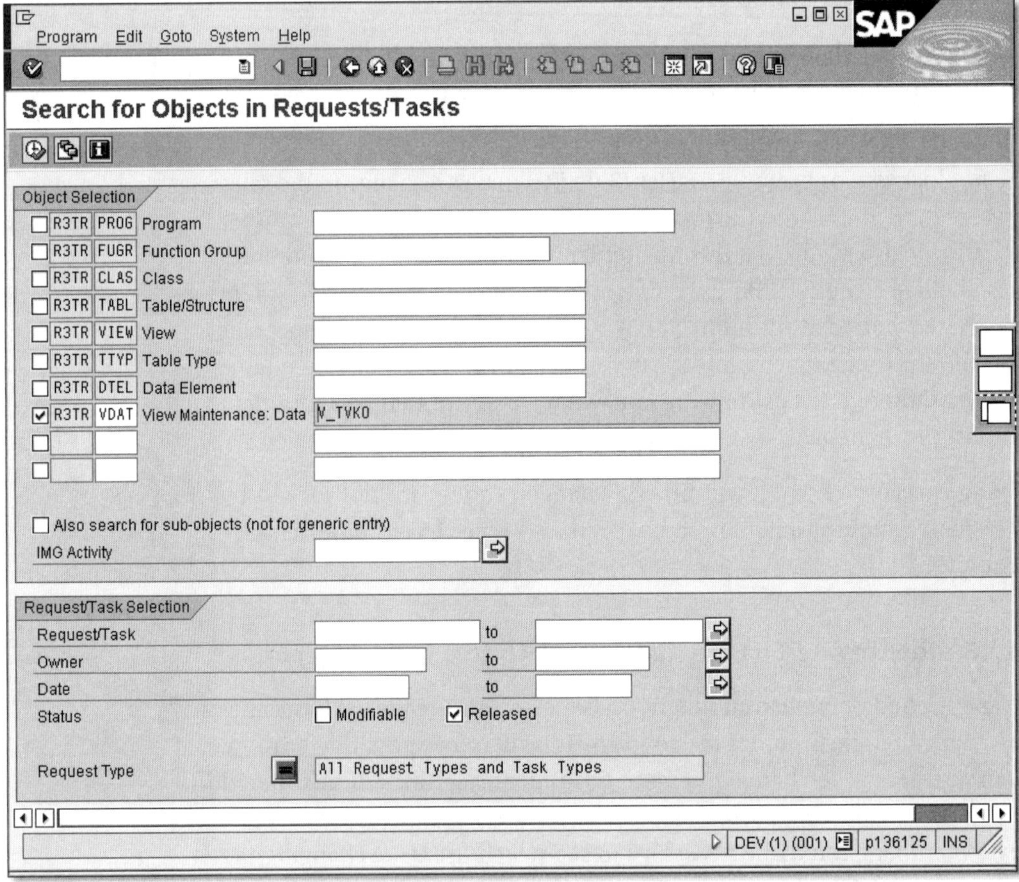

Figure 11.11 Searching for Change Requests or Tasks with Common Objects

4. Select the appropriate object type and then, in the adjacent field, enter the name of the object. For example, if the object is in a view, enter the object type VDAT and then enter the name of the view.
5. Other selection criteria include the type of change requests, whether the change requests have been released, the owners of the change requests, and a time period during which the objects were last modified. If you are searching for Repository objects, the ALSO SEARCH FOR SUB-OBJECTS option will display tasks and change requests containing LIMU entries (see Chapter 10).
6. After making your selection, choose EXECUTE. A list of change requests and tasks containing the object is displayed.

11.3 Nonstandard Customizing Activities

Customizing activities are typically client-dependent changes to views and tables that are made by a user through IMG activities. However, an implementation phase usually includes other Customizing activities that are considered nonstandard because they have one or more of the following characteristics:

- They are client-independent and, therefore, affect not only the current SAP client but all clients within the SAP system.
- They require a manual method for transport instead of being automatically recorded to a change request.
- They can be performed both in the IMG and by alternative means (because they commonly need to be performed in the production client).

11.3.1 Client-Independent Customizing Activities

Although most Customizing objects of type CUST are client-dependent and are recorded in Customizing change requests, client-independent Customizing objects are of type SYST and are recorded in Workbench Organizer change requests. Changes to client-independent Customizing settings can also create ABAP Workbench objects (known as *generated objects*).

Determining whether a Customizing Activity Is Client-Independent

To determine which Customizing activities are client-independent (or *cross-client*), proceed as follows:

1. Display either the Enterprise IMG or a Project IMG tree structure.
2. Select ADDITIONAL INFORMATION • TECHNICAL DATA • CLIENT DEPENDENCY.

Figure 11.12 shows the resulting screen. Cross-client IMG activities are indicated on the right-hand side of the screen. In the example in Figure 11.12, the maintenance of calendars is client-independent and requires a Workbench change request to be transported. The activity CHECK UNITS OF MEASUREMENT is client-dependent.

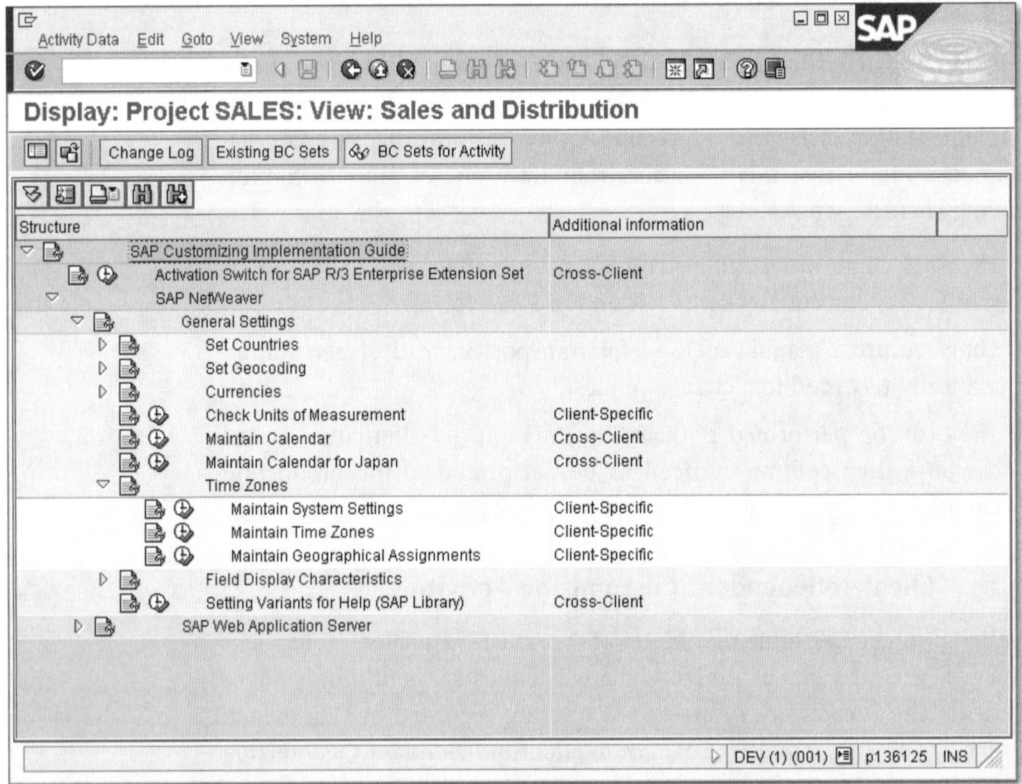

Figure 11.12 Displaying Cross-Client Customizing Activities in the IMG

Recording Client-Independent Customizing Changes

When you save changed Customizing settings that are client-independent, a dialog box always appears, prompting you to record your change to a Workbench change request, regardless of the client settings. You can either select a Workbench change request from a list after choosing OWN REQUESTS or create a new Workbench change request with CREATE REQUEST.

Assigning Generated Customizing Objects to a Development Class

Cross-client Customizing activities sometimes result in the automatic generation of new SAP ERP Repository objects. Before these are generated, in the relevant Customizing transaction, you have to provide a name for the new object. Next, a dialog box appears prompting you for a development class. Finally, a dialog box appears prompting you for a change request of type Workbench. The development class determines whether the objects can be transported. Most likely, you will want to transport all Customizing changes that trigger the creation of new SAP ERP Repository objects, and will therefore need to assign a customer development class with a valid transport layer (see Chapter 10).

Example: Objects Generated Automatically during Customizing

An example of a client-independent Customizing activity that results in the creation of new Repository objects is defining pricing condition tables. To access this Customizing activity in the IMG, choose SALES AND DISTRIBUTION • BASIC FUNCTIONS • PRICING • PRICING CONTROL • DEFINE CONDITION TABLES. Performing this Customizing activity automatically generates a pricing table, which stores various pricing criteria. After specifying the object name (such as 601, which automatically generates the object name A601) and defining pricing criteria in the relevant dialog boxes, you must assign a development class and save the object to a Workbench change request.

After saving the generated object to a Workbench change request, if you access the object list corresponding to the change request, it will show the objects recorded to the change request as the result of creating the pricing condition table A601, as shown in Figure 11.13.

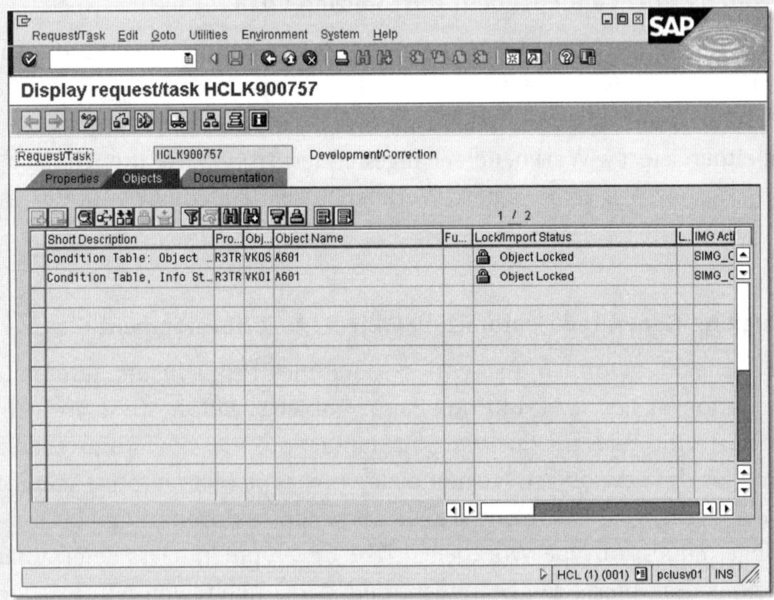

Figure 11.13 Object List Corresponding to Change Request

The two objects in the object list are not the pricing condition table A601, but rather the information required to generate that table. The definition of the object to be generated and not the object itself is recorded in the change request and subsequently transported. After export and during import into the quality assurance and production systems, the definition information is used to generate the required object.

Display Object Directory Entry

Object R3TR TABL A601

Attributes

Package VKOK

Person Responsible NERDING

Original System SAP

Original language DE German

Object generated

Lock Overview

Figure 11.14 Object Directory Entry

To check whether the object has been generated, use Transaction SE11, enter "A601" next to DATABASE TABLE, and choose EDIT • OBJECT DIRECTORY ENTRY. The screen that displays is shown in Figure 11.14.

This screen shows A601 flagged as a generated object whose original system is SAP. Because its development class does not begin with a Y or a Z, it is an SAP-delivered development class. The GENERATION FLAG field contains an X; therefore, the object was generated by SAP.

The objects defining the generated pricing condition table that are recorded in the change request are assigned to a customer development class. They do not appear as generated objects, and their original system is the customer's development system. To verify this, use Transaction SE11 to display the objects in the change request.

Often, generated Customizing objects are not transported. Instead, the definitions and instructions for the creation of the required Customizing object are transported.

11.3.2 Manual Transports and Other Transport Types

For most IMG Customizing changes, if the client setting specifies automatic recording of changes, the changes are automatically saved to a change request. However, there are some Customizing activities for which automatic recording to a change request is not possible. Such activities are considered *manual transport* Customizing activities.

Automatic recording to a change request is generally not possible when the entries for a Customizing object cannot be transported individually—the entire object (all of its entries) must be transported as a unit. Changes to such critical Customizing settings require a manual method of transport when the project lead recognizes that the entire object is ready for transport.

In the tree structure of the Enterprise IMG or of a Project IMG, select ADDITIONAL INFORMATION • TECHNICAL DATA • TRANSPORT TYPE to determine which Customizing activities require manual transport. A screen like the one shown in Figure 11.15 is displayed. The right-hand side of the screen indicates the transport method for each Customizing activity. The transport methods can include:

Transport methods

- **Automatic transport**
  If the client is set to automatic recording of changes, the client-dependent changes to the Customizing activity will be recorded to a change request when saved.
- **Manual transport**
  Individual changes to the Customizing activity will not be recorded to a change request. To transport the Customizing settings, the changes must be transported using a special menu option found in the Customizing transaction.
- **No transport**
  Changes to the Customizing activity cannot be transported. This often applies to SAP system-specific changes that are of a technical nature and not related to Customizing. It also applies when the IMG activity is a check routine that lets you verify settings and data in the current SAP client. These IMG activities are not changes to Customizing settings and therefore do not require transport.

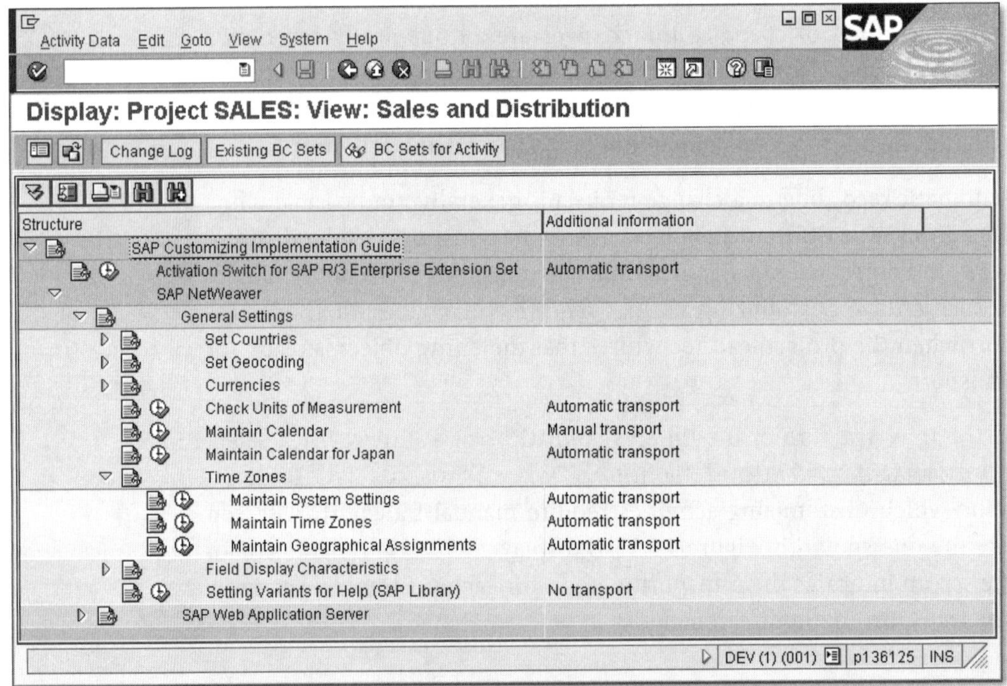

Figure 11.15 Displaying Transportability in the IMG

In Figure 11.15, the transport method AUTOMATIC TRANSPORT is assigned to the Customizing tasks for checking the units of measurement and maintaining the calendar for Japan. The Customizing activity MAINTAIN CALENDAR requires a manual transport. To transport changes to the calendar, use the TRANSPORT button in the Customizing transaction, which will transport not just the most recent change but the entire calendar.

11.3.3 Customizing in a Production Client

For your production client, SAP recommends setting the client-dependent change option to NO CHANGES ALLOWED, to ensure that all Customizing and development occur in the development system. However, some Customizing activities in the IMG concern minor changes a customer may need to make on a regular basis. Examples of these changes include interest rates, health insurance premiums, pension schemes, tax schemes, and currency exchange rates. These types of changes are known as *data-only* Customizing changes.

Current settings

Making such changes in the development system and transporting them to the production system on a regular basis is tedious and increases the amount of work necessary to maintain import queues and monitor import logs. To avoid having to use change requests for these changes, SAP introduced the CURRENT SETTINGS function. This function enables Customizing in a production client for client-dependent changes that do not impact the business flow.

Activating Current Settings

As a prerequisite for using the CURRENT SETTINGS function, the following settings must be configured in Transaction SCC4 for the production client:

- The client role is PRODUCTION.
- The client-dependent change option is NO TRANSPORTS ALLOWED.

[+] For more information on using CURRENT SETTINGS in a production client, see SAP Note 77430.

Customizing Activities in Current Settings

The Customizing activities that can be performed in a production client using the CURRENT SETTINGS function are listed in the database table CUSAMEN.

You can add Customizing activities to this table, allowing you to perform them in the production client with the CURRENT SETTINGS function. SAP recommends that you add Customizing activities to table CUSAMEN only if it is necessary and only if the changes resulting from these activities are data changes that:

- Are required on a regular basis
- Do not require a formal quality assurance sign-off
- Are not required in the other clients within the system landscape to maintain consistent Customizing environments

Adding an entry to table CUSAMEN results in a modification (see Chapter 10).

[+] For more information on adding Customizing activities to table CUSAMEN so that they can be performed using the CURRENT SETTINGS function, see SAP Note 135028.

An alternative to adding Customizing activities to table CUSAMEN is using ALE to distribute Customizing data. ALE lets you distribute a change to all SAP clients without requiring a change request. This necessitates ALE development, because SAP does not provide ALE scenarios for Customizing activities (see also Section 4.2.1, Transferring Master Data between SAP Systems).

11.4 Support Tools for Customizing

So that you can compare Customizing settings in different clients, SAP provides the following tools:

- Customizing Cross-System Viewer
- View/Table Comparison
- Business Configuration Sets
- Customizing Transfer Assistant

To use any of these tools, you must:

Usage

- Have a user authorization that includes authorization S_CUS_CMP in both the logon and comparison clients. To compare client-independent objects, you also need authorization S_TABU_CLI.
- Create an RFC connection between the logon client (RFC target client) and the comparison client (RFC source client). When you create the RFC connection, the user you have to define should be one whose authorization in the target client does not exceed the authorization required to use these tools. For example, you can define a CPIC user who only has authorization S_CUS_CMP.
- Set client protection in the comparison client to either PROTECTION LEVEL 0 or PROTECTION LEVEL 1 (see section "Client Protection" in Chapter 9.)
- To transfer Customizing settings from a comparison client, set client protection in the logon client to PROTECTION LEVEL 0.

11.4.1 Comparing Customizing in Two Clients

To compare the Customizing settings of two clients, use the Customizing Cross-System Viewer.

This tool allows you to compare Customizing objects and tables in an SAP client (comparison client) against the settings in the current client (logon client). The result is an overview screen, showing the differences between the two clients. In this screen, you can drill down the listed items to display the corresponding Customizing entries. To change these entries, you can use direct links to the corresponding IMG activity or a function that allows you to adjust the differences between the entries.

During implementation, you often need to compare the contents of tables or views located in the same SAP system or in different SAP systems. Comparing clients can help you do the following:

- Identify the differences between the Customizing settings of two SAP clients, or verify that both clients have consistent Customizing settings.
- Compare current Customizing settings to those of a reference client such as client 000.

- Compare Customizing settings delivered from a central corporate development system with local Customizing settings.

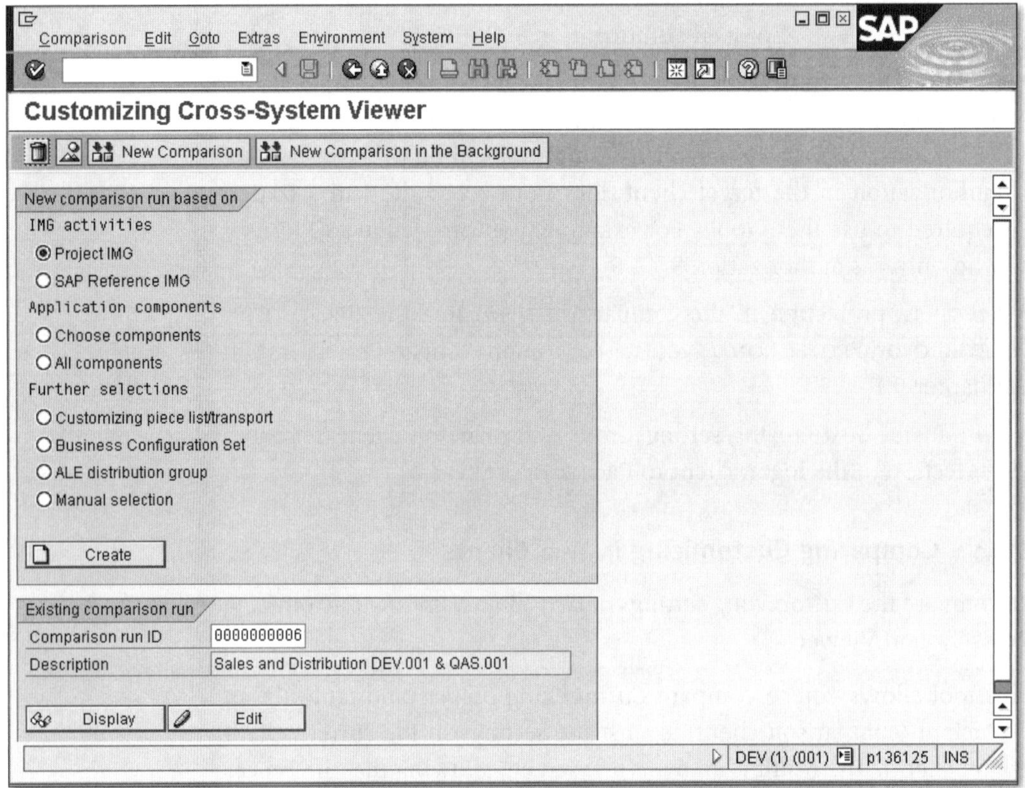

Figure 11.16 Selection Screen of the Cross-System Viewer

When you access the Customizing Cross-System Viewer using Transaction SCU0, a selection screen like the one shown in Figure 11.16 appears. This screen shows the types of objects you can compare. It contains the following selection options:

Selection options

- **IMG activities**
  This option selects Customizing objects related to an entire Project IMG or SAP Reference IMG.
- **Application components**
  This option selects Customizing objects related to one or more branches of a business application component.

- **Customizing piece list/transport**
  This option selects all Customizing objects recorded in an object list or a change request.
- **Business Configuration Set**
  This option is available only in the Cross-System Viewer. It selects all objects recorded in the Customizing snapshot known as a Business Configuration Set.
- **ALE distribution group**
  This options selects all objects belonging to an ALE distribution group.
- **Manual selection**
  This option selects the Customizing objects and ABAP Dictionary tables you specify.

The Customizing Cross-System Viewer

Comparing clients

To perform a client comparison, proceed as follows:

1. Access the Customizing Cross-System Viewer. To do so, use Transaction code SCU0 or, from the SAP ERP initial screen, choose TOOLS • CUSTOMIZING • IMG • CUSTOMIZING • CROSS-SYSTEM VIEWER.
2. The selection screen for the Cross-System Viewer is displayed. Select the criteria for comparison and choose CREATE. You may need to indicate, for example, the Project IMG, the different application components, or a change request ID.
3. After you choose CREATE, a COMPARISON RUN ID (a sequential value also referred to as the *worklist ID*) is automatically generated. A SELECTION BY: screen appears:
   - Enter a description for the comparison. The description should enable you to remember what selection criteria you are using. Note that to subsequently display the results of the comparison, you will need the comparison run ID.
   - To include client-dependent Customizing objects, select CLIENT-SPECIFIC.
   - To include client-independent Customizing objects, select CROSS-CLIENT.
   - Provide the RFC connection to the comparison client.

4. To schedule the comparison as a background job, choose NEW COMPARISON IN BACKGROUND. To begin the comparison immediately (if the comparison involves only a few objects), choose NEW COMPARISON. Alternatively, to get a list of Customizing objects that can be compared so that you can limit the comparison, choose OBJECT OVERVIEW.

Displaying the Results of a Client Comparison

The results of the comparison are the starting point for the display and subsequent adjustment of the differences between the logon client and the comparison client.

To display the results of a client comparison, proceed as follows:

1. Use Transaction SCU0.
2. In the EXISTING COMPARISON RUN field, enter the worklist ID (the comparison run ID) for the client comparison you want to display.
3. Choose DISPLAY.

The results screen shows the differences for each compared object, a description of the object, and the COMPARISON STATUS in the COMP column. The comparison status indicates the equivalence or nonequivalence of the object in the respective clients. The comparison results of the Cross-System Viewer are known as a *worklist*. You can use the worklist to review completed comparisons and maintain status information. The worklist also uses traffic-light icons to indicate processing status information—whether you are still analyzing or have already corrected differences that were found.

Figure 11.17 displays sample differences between the logon client, client 001 of system DEV, and the comparison client, client 001 of system QAS. The Customizing in the views V_T005K, V_T005_BAS, V_TCURF, and V_TCURR differs in the two clients. The Customizing in view T_005S is the same. The right-hand side of the screen compares the number of entries of this object in the two clients.

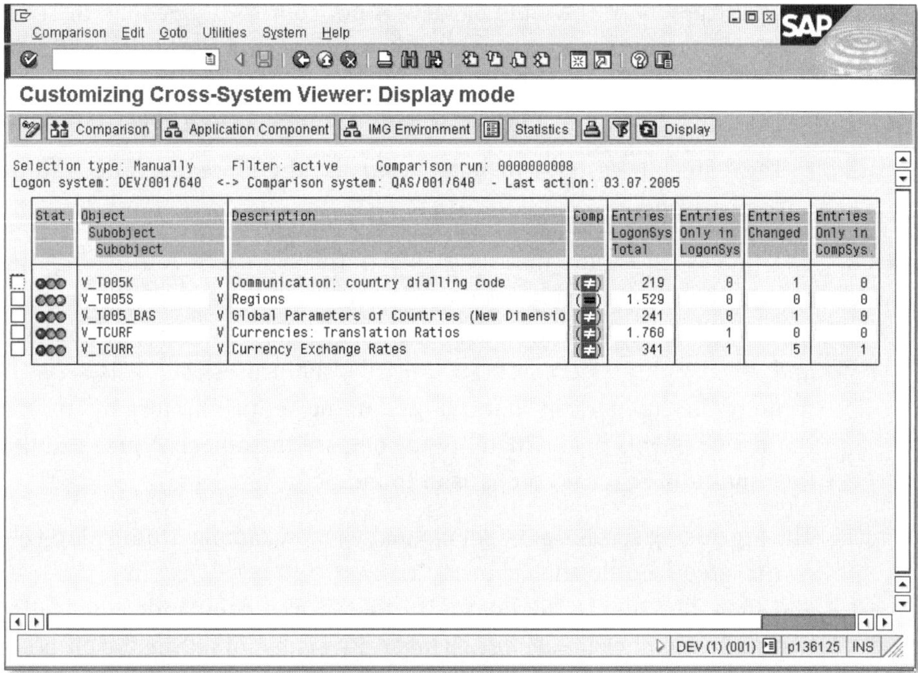

Figure 11.17 The Results of Comparing Two SAP Clients

Comparison status

The column showing the comparison status, COMP, can indicate the following:

- Contents are identical.
- Contents are not identical.
- Contents are identical, but the ABAP Dictionary structure of the object differs.
- Contents are not identical, and the ABAP Dictionary structure of the object differs.
- Contents could not be compared.

There are several reasons why a comparison may not be possible. For example:

- The table or view does not exist in a local or a remote client.
- The sum of the length of all fields in the table or view exceeds the byte limitations of the standard compare tool (this is very rare).

- The structure of the table or view is not consistent between the two clients. For example, the primary key differs, or a field is defined as a character field in one client and as a numeric field in the other client. This can occur when the clients have different release levels.
- The table is a system table and is therefore excluded from comparison.

Processing status

The processing status indicated as a traffic light lets you distinguish objects that have already been processed from those that still need to be processed. Red indicates NOT PROCESSED, yellow indicates IN PROCESS, and green indicates COMPLETED. Initially, the process status is set as a result of the comparison so that all red traffic lights indicate a difference in the two clients or the inability to compare the object. A green traffic light indicates that the comparison found no differences.

The processing status can be set manually—for example, from red to yellow to green. To do this, choose COMPARISON RUN • DISPLAY • CHANGE and then click the traffic light until the desired color indicator is displayed. Remember to save the changes. By manually setting the processing status, you can track your progress as you analyze and possibly adjust the differences for each object.

For example, in Figure 11.17, during the review of table V_T005K, the status for this object can be changed to yellow to indicate to other members of the Customizing project that the difference is currently being analyzed. During your analysis, you may discover that the reason for the difference is simply that a change request has not yet been transported from client 001 of DEV into the quality assurance system. In this case, the difference will be resolved when that change request is imported, and no adjustment is required in the comparison results screen. You can change the processing status from red to green.

Analyzing differences

To analyze the differences between two clients, you can do the following:

- Filter the comparison results screen according to various criteria for processing status, comparison status, and object type.
- Display a statistical overview showing differences and object types.

- Display the relevant IMG activity for particular objects.
- Display the application component for a particular object in the application component hierarchy.
- Perform a single comparison, as described in the text that follows.

Performing a Single Comparison

To view the corresponding records of the table or view, display the comparison results list, position the cursor on an object, and choose SINGLE COMPARISON. The OVERVIEW COMPARISON screen is displayed. To make the differences easy to identify, the entries of the respective views of each object are shown consecutively. The results of the comparison are color-coded. For an explanation of the colors, choose LEGEND. The different comparison statuses are shown in Table 11.1.

Status	Description
<blank>	The listed entry is identical in both clients.
ML	The entries are not identical; the listed entry is the logon client entry.
MR	The entries are not identical; the listed entry is the comparison client entry.
L	The entry exists only in the logon client.
R	The entry exists only in the comparison client.
(M) or (E)	Differences exist only in fields you have hidden from the comparison (for example, if you want to exclude a noncritical field such as LASTCHANGEDAT from the comparison).

Table 11.1 Single Comparison Status Indicators

An example of the results of a single comparison of object V_T005K is shown in Figure 11.18. The view includes telephone area codes to call from or to a country. The entry for country AZ is different. On the logon client, the TEL. FROM field contains "00." On the comparison client, this field is empty.

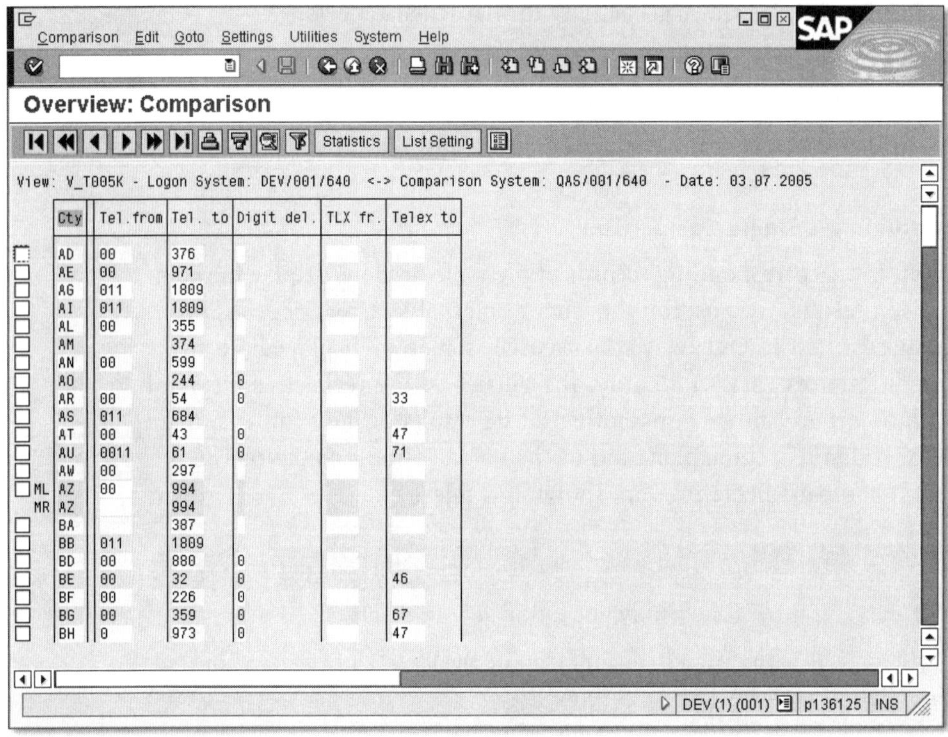

	Cty	Tel.from	Tel. to	Digit del.	TLX fr.	Telex to
	AD	00	376			
	AE	00	971			
	AG	011	1809			
	AI	011	1809			
	AL	00	355			
	AM		374			
	AN	00	599			
	AO		244	0		
	AR	00	54	0		33
	AS	011	684			
	AT	00	43	0		47
	AU	0011	61	0		71
	AW	00	297			
ML	AZ	00	994			
MR	AZ		994			
	BA		387			
	BB	011	1809			
	BD	00	880	0		
	BE	00	32	0		46
	BF	00	226	0		
	BG	00	359	0		67
	BH	0	973	0		47

Figure 11.18 Single Comparison for a View

Performance note

When you analyze a particular Customizing object by performing a single comparison, the RESTRICT SELECTION SET window appears, asking whether you would like to compare all values or restrict the comparison. To optimize performance, you will want to restrict the comparison. If the object to be detailed does not contain a lot of table entries—for example, fewer than 500—you do not need to restrict the comparison.

Adjusting the Customizing Differences between Clients

To adjust the Customizing differences between clients, you need to transfer view and table entries or the contents of individual fields from a comparison client to the logon client as described in the procedure that follows. Keep the following points in mind:

- Table and view entries can be changed only in the logon client, not in the comparison client.

- The adjustment can be performed for only one object at a time.
- The adjustment can be performed for only the tables and views that can be maintained using Table Maintenance (Transaction SM30). Other objects can be compared, but not adjusted.
- The data transferred to the logon client is subjected to the standard validation checks, which may prevent you from saving the transferred data. This can occur, for example, if you transfer a row and part of the data comprising the primary key is missing in the logon client.
- Customizing objects cannot be adjusted for Business Configuration Sets.

[+] For technical reasons, not all differences that result from a comparison can be adjusted.

You can transfer the following kinds of data from the comparison client to the logon client:

- An entire row in a view or table. If the entry is present only in the comparison client, it is added to the logon client. If the row is present, but different in the two clients, it is copied into the logon client.
- A specific field in a row. Only the contents of the field you select are copied. The contents of all other fields are not affected.
- All entries of a table or view in the comparison client.
- An entire column of data. This way, values are only added, not replaced.

In addition, you can delete entries in the logon client to resolve a difference.

Adjusting the Customizing differences between clients

The tools for performing adjustments are contained in the Cross-System Viewer. To perform an adjustment, from within the client you want to adjust, proceed as follows:

1. In Transaction SCU0, access the worklist for which you want to initiate a transfer by providing the worklist ID and choosing DISPLAY.
2. The CUSTOMIZING OBJECTS: DIFFERENCE LIST screen (see Figure 11.17 earlier in the chapter) appears. In this screen, to switch to change mode, choose DISPLAY • CHANGE.

3. Position the cursor on the Customizing object to be adjusted and choose EDIT • INTERACT. COPY.
4. The OVERVIEW: COMPARISON screen appears. Position the cursor on the entry you want to adjust and choose ADJUST.
5. The DETAIL VIEW: ADJUST screen appears. Choose the type of adjustment to be made. For example, to copy an entry from the comparison client to the current client, choose ENTRY.
6. At this stage, the data has been transferred but not saved (entered into the database). Choose BACK to leave the adjustment tool. You will be prompted to save your changes. Choose YES to save the changes. Choosing NO returns the table or view to its original state.
7. If automatic recording of changes is active, you are prompted for a change request.

11.4.2 Single comparison with Transaction SCMP

The Customizing Cross-System Viewer is useful for comparing many objects at once—for example, when comparing objects from a project or application perspective. However, you may want to simply compare a single Customizing object or table. Because the Customizing Cross-System Viewer is specifically designed for Customizing objects, you cannot use it to compare tables that are not considered Customizing objects. Such non-Customizing objects include, for example, tables that contain application data.

[+] Single comparisons read the view or table contents into memory before performing a comparison. Therefore, views or tables with a lot of entries, such as an application table, will negatively impact system performance.

To compare a single SAP ERP object or a non-Customizing object, it is easiest to use Transaction SCMP. To do so, proceed as follows:

1. Use Transaction code SCMP.
2. The VIEW/TABLE COMPARISON screen appears (see Figure 11.19). Enter the name of the view or table to be compared and the name of the RFC destination (SAP ERP connection).

- To limit the comparison to specific key values, select ENTER SELECTION REQUIREMENTS.
- To see only entries that differ between the two clients, select DISPLAY DIFFERENCES ONLY.
- To schedule the comparison as a background job, select BACKGROUND EXECUTION—the results will be available as spool output only.
- To limit the CPU resources required for the comparison, select RESTRICT FIELDS TO BE COMPARED.

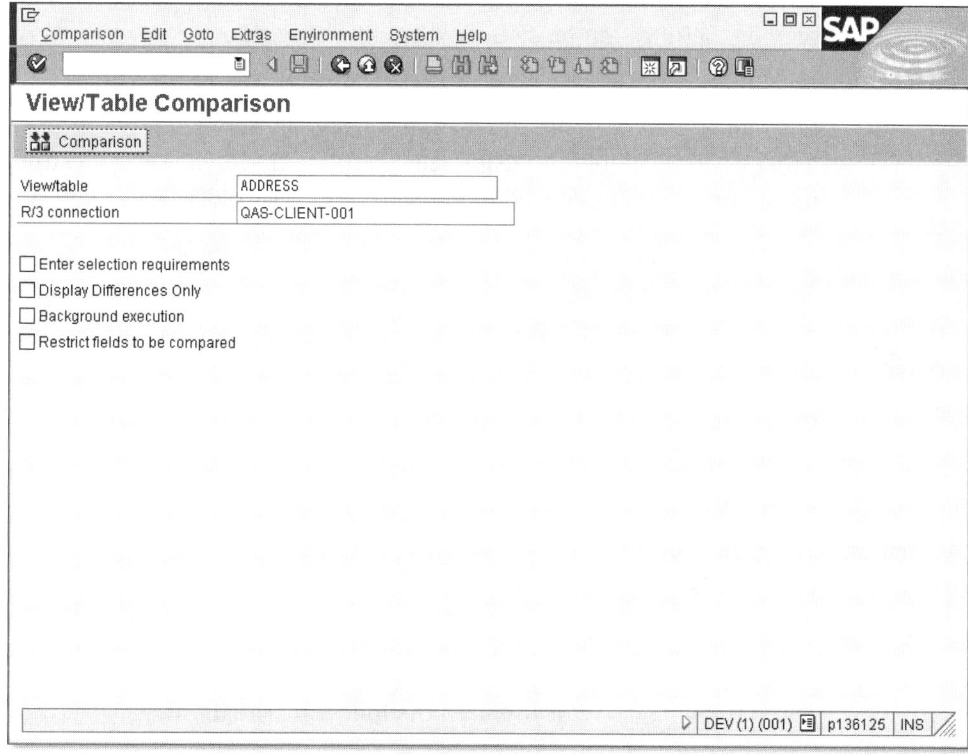

Figure 11.19 Single Comparison with Transaction SCMP

3. To run the comparison, choose COMPARISON. Depending on what you selected in the previous step, you may be prompted for information about selection requirements or the restriction of the number of fields that will be compared.

4. The comparison list is displayed. The results are identical to those of a single comparison from within the Cross-System Viewer. For example, the L status indicates that the entry exists only in the current logon client and not in the comparison client.

[+] In single comparisons using Transaction SCMP, restrict the number of fields to be compared if more than 500 entries are involved.

11.4.3 Business Configuration Sets

Business Configuration Sets (BC Sets) are containers in which you can store Customizing settings. They are transportable and versionable. Thus, previous settings can be compared to current settings.

BC Sets are for documenting and analyzing Customizing settings to make Customizing more transparent. Additionally, BC Sets can be used for a global rollout where the Customizing settings are forwarded as a structured bundle from a consolidation parent to its subsidiaries.

BC Sets are delivered by SAP to selected industries and can also be created by the customer.

Creation

When creating a BC Set, values and value combinations are copied from the original Customizing tables to the BC Set and can be imported into the tables, views, and view clusters of the customer system. On the customer side, BC Sets are always transported to the system where Customizing takes place.

Import

The import of BC Sets is logged by the system, that is, it records which BC Set was copied to the system and when, and whether this process was completed without errors. This information is significant both to a continuous change and to an upgrade.

For example, a BC Set is useful in the following situations:

- When testing a new implementation phase, a BC Set of the previous implementation phase can be compared to the current settings to highlight differences and to identify the Customizing settings that could affect existing processes in the production operation.
- Customizing standards that were specified in an enterprise development system are often delivered to subsidiaries, using change

requests. Because Customizing can neither be locked nor protected, a subsidiary can change the delivered enterprise standards. Furthermore, by using a BC Set delivered by the enterprise system, subsidiaries can compare their current Customizing settings to the enterprise standards recorded in the BC Set on a regular basis. All discovered deviations must be solved both locally in the subsidiary and in the development system of the enterprise.

- After a system upgrade, BC Set settings can be compared to system data using the Customizing Cross-System Viewer to ensure data consistency.
- Industry systems are easier to create and to maintain.
- To a great extent, Customizing can be carried out on a business level.
- Change Management can be handled faster and more securely.

Use Transaction SCPR3 to edit BC Sets in the system. Using Transaction SCPR20, you can activate BC Sets in the system and view activation logs using Transaction SCPR20PR.

More information on BC Sets can be found in the online documentation and in SAP Note 669542.

11.4.4 Customizing Transfer Assistant

Transaction SADJ

The Customizing Transfer Assistant (Transaction SADJ) lets you compare client-dependent changes that have been imported by a change request with the settings of the current client. The Customizing Transfer Assistant imports changes into a temporary "holding" client and allows you to avoid importing individual changes you may not want in the current client. This is useful in the following situations:

- An international implementation often involves the delivery of changes from a central development system to each of the subsidiaries. Because Customizing settings are not protected against overwriting during import, a subsidiary may choose to import the changes from the central development system to a holding client and check the new settings against the client-dependent settings in the subsidiary's Customizing-and-development client. If the changes do not conflict with local settings, they are transferred to the local Customizing-and-development client.

- Customizing for a new implementation phase has been done in another SAP system, such as a predevelopment system. To eliminate the need to redo these changes in the Customizing-and-development client in the development system, the Customizing changes from the predevelopment system are imported into a holding client, and the Customizing Transfer Assistant is used to adjust the settings in the Customizing-and-development client.
- During production support, emergency changes are made in the production system. These changes need to be made in the development system to ensure consistency. To avoid overwriting the changes currently being created in the development system for the next implementation phase, the production system changes can be imported into a holding client and checked with the Customizing Transfer Assistant.

[+] When importing changes to the holding client, ensure that you do not overwrite client-independent changes that apply to the entire SAP system.

Worklist

Before using the Customizing Transfer Assistant, set up an appropriate holding client. The Customizing Transfer Assistant creates a *worklist* to allow you to compare the Customizing objects in a change request of type Customizing that has been successfully imported into the holding client and therefore has the status of RELEASED.

After importing the change request to the holding client, to create the worklist, proceed as follows:

1. Log on to the client into which you will transfer Customizing changes.
2. Start the Customizing Transfer Assistant using Transaction code SADJ.
3. Provide the change request ID that will be used to create the worklist. This ID must be a change request that has already been imported into the SAP system in the comparison/holding client.
4. Choose CREATE to create the worklist.

5. The CREATE NEW WORKLIST FOR REQUEST TO BE IMPORTED screen appears, indicating the worklist ID (which you need, for example, to obtain the comparison results when the worklist is generated as a background job).
   - Provide a description for the worklist.
   - Provide the RFC connection to the comparison client.
6. To display the differences between the changes imported into the holding client and the corresponding Customizing entries in the logon client, choose DETERMINE STATUS. If the change request contains a large number of Customizing objects and will therefore require a lot of processing time, choose DETERMINE STATUS IN BACKGROUND. Alternatively, to display a list of objects that will be compared so that you can selectively initiate the comparison for particular objects, choose OBJECT LIST.

Displaying and Transferring Differences

If not scheduled as a background job, the worklist is displayed immediately following the execution of the comparison. If the comparison has been scheduled in the background, to subsequently display the worklist, enter the worklist number in the Customizing Transfer Assistant (Transaction SADJ) and choose DISPLAY.

Copy status

As is the case when using the Customizing Cross-System Viewer, you can display additional details by choosing SINGLE COMPARISON. You can also display statistics and you can filter the list. The first column of the resulting worklist, STAT., indicates the *copy status* for each Customizing object. The copy status shows whether the object can be automatically transferred or, if the transfer is complete, whether it was successful. For an explanation of copy statuses, choose LEGEND.

By switching into change mode using DISPLAY • CHANGE, you can copy entries from the comparison client to the current client. Copy options available from the menu using EDIT • COPY include:

- **Interactive**
  You perform the adjustment of single entries manually as described previously in the section "Adjusting the Customizing Differences between Clients."

- **Automatic direct**
  All differences are automatically transferred.
- **Autom. Background**
  Automatic adjustment is performed as a background job.

11.5 Questions

1. **Which of the following requirements must be met before you can change both client-dependent and client-independent Customizing settings in a client?**
   A. The client settings must allow for changes to client-independent Customizing objects.
   B. The client role must be PRODUCTION.
   C. The system change option must be set to MODIFIABLE.
   D. The client settings must allow for changes to client-dependent Customizing.
2. **Which of the following statements are correct when project leads and project team members receive only the recommended authorizations?**
   A. Only developers can create change requests.
   B. Only project leads can create change requests and are therefore responsible for assigning project team members to change requests.
   C. Project team members can create and release change requests.
   D. Project leads can release change requests.
3. **Which of the following statements are correct with regard to Project IMGs?**
   A. The Project IMG provides access to the Customizing activities defined for a particular project.
   B. Customizing is performed in the Project IMG tree structure.
   C. The Project IMG lets you display project status information and document Customizing activities.
   D. All of the above.

4. **Which of the following activities are performed using the Customizing Organizer?**

   A. Viewing all Customizing change requests related to a particular user

   B. Viewing all Workbench change requests related to a particular user

   C. Viewing all change requests related to a particular user

   D. Managing change requests you own or reviewing change requests in which you have assigned tasks

5. **Which of the following statements is correct with regard to Customizing?**

   A. All Customizing activities in the IMG are client-dependent.

   B. All changes resulting from IMG activities can be transported.

   C. All Customizing changes are automatically recorded to a change request if the client change option is set to AUTOMATIC RECORDING OF CHANGES.

   D. A Customizing activity may involve the creation of client-independent objects and therefore requires a Workbench change request.

6. **Which of the following activities are performed using client comparison tools?**

   A. Comparing the Customizing settings of two SAP clients in the same SAP system or in a different SAP system

   B. Adjusting the Customizing differences between two different SAP clients

   C. Transporting Customizing settings into the production client

   D. Comparing the objects listed in the object list of a change request with an SAP client

After having collected the changed objects in a transport request, the transport request must be exported from the SAP system. For this purpose, a file that contains all changes is created in the transport directory and can be imported to another SAP system. This chapter describes how you can export a transport request into a transport file.

12 Releasing and Exporting Change Requests

When you *promote* a change request, you release and export it. Often, the words *export* and *release* are used interchangeably. Technically, however, they are two different processes:

- The *release* process acts as a sign-off for the development or Customizing work in the task or change request. This process verifies ownership and user authorization for the respective changes—first at the task level, and then at the change request level. It also causes the respective Repository objects to be released by the Workbench Organizer and copies a version history of them to the version database. You can release a change request only if all tasks belonging to the request have been documented and released. Before releasing the change request, ensure that the changes it records have been unit tested and verified.
- The *export* process physically copies the objects and tables referred to in the change request from the SAP ERP database of the development system to a file in the transport directory at the operating system level. In addition, this process adds the change request to the import buffer of the target system defined by the relevant transport route.

This chapter covers the release and export processes, as well as documentation, unit testing, and version management. The topics are covered in the order in which the activities are performed.

12.1 Documenting Change Requests and Tasks

SAP recommends that you write thorough documentation for all tasks in a change request while performing customizing and development. This makes it easier to reconstruct the configuration process if necessary. The documentation is transported with the changes, thus becoming available in the quality assurance system, and is also a requirement for releasing the change request in the development system. In your documentation for change requests and tasks, you should include the following information:

Necessary information

- The purpose of the development or Customizing project
- The current status of the project (IMG status information is maintained within the Project IMG, not within change request documentation)
- Areas of responsibility and the people responsible, as well as contacts
- Sources of other documentation or instructions
- The expected impact of the changes on the implementation
- Interdependencies between this and other projects

The object lists of change requests and tasks indicate the objects that have changed. Action logs recorded by the SAP system provide you with information on various activities, such as who created, released, or changed the ownership of a change request or task. Together with the action logs, the object list and documentation provide a detailed audit history of all changes made.

12.1.1 Creating and Changing Documentation

To create or change documentation for a task or change request, proceed as follows:

1. In the Transport Organizer (Transaction codes SE09 or SE10), choose DISPLAY. The TRANSPORT ORGANIZER: REQUESTS screen is displayed, listing the change requests and tasks related to your user ID.
2. Double-click on the task or the change request for which you want to write documentation. Change to the DOCUMENTATION tab and switch to change mode.

3. Enter the detailed documentation and choose SAVE.
4. Choose BACK to return to the change request hierarchy.

You can release a task only if it has been documented. Before a task or change request is released, you can add documentation to it at any time. After the task or change request has been released, documentation cannot be changed.

When the task is released, the associated documentation is copied to the documentation of the change request containing the task. The documentation of the change request then contains its own documentation and the documentation of any of its released tasks. For example, suppose that there are two tasks in a change request, and both have been documented and released. Until the change request is released, the documentation for both tasks can be viewed and changed within the documentation of the change request.

12.1.2 Action Logs for Change Requests

In the ACTION LOG of each change request, the SAP system automatically logs the time of occurrence and user responsible for the following actions with regard to that change request or any of its tasks:

- Creation
- Ownership change
- Deletion
- Release

Display logs

To see the action log for a particular change request, position the cursor on the change request in the TRANSPORT ORGANIZER: REQUESTS screen and choose GOTO • ACTION LOG.

The action log of each change request is physically located—as a separate log file—in the *actlog* transport directory. The name of this file is *<SID>Z<change request ID number>.<SID>*, where *SID* is the system ID of the system on which the change request was created. The change request ID number is a six-digit number beginning with 9. For example, the log file for change request DEVK900747 is DEVZ900747.DEV. This log file is located at the operating system level and can be accessed from any SAP system within the same transport group.

12.2 Unit Testing

Before releasing a change request or task, it should be unit tested as described in Chapter 6. For a change request, this means unit testing the combined contents of all tasks as a unit.

If unit testing will take place in a unit test client, before performing testing, you must copy the client-dependent changes to the unit test client. Client-independent changes automatically impact all clients within the SAP system and therefore can be verified by simply logging on to the unit test client and performing verification. As explained in the text that follows, client-dependent changes may be of the following types:

- Client-dependent Customizing
- SAPscript styles and forms
- Report variants

12.2.1 Client-Dependent Customizing

Transaction SCC1

To unit test client-dependent Customizing changes in a client other than the one in which the changes were originally recorded to change requests, copy the changes into the applicable client using the COPY BY TRANSPORT REQUEST (Transaction SCC1). This transaction lets you verify the contents of your tasks before release. The owner of a change request can also use this transaction to verify the contents of the change request and all of its tasks before release.

You can only use Transaction SCC1 to copy the changed objects recorded in a change request or task from one client to another client in the same SAP system.

Although Transaction SCC1 can be used to copy objects recorded in tasks and change requests that have been released, you should not release the respective change requests and tasks before using the transaction to perform unit testing. If unit testing reveals missing or incorrect Customizing settings, you can still record additional changes to the unreleased task or change request.

Copying Changes with Transaction SCC1

To use Transaction SCC1 to copy changes, you need the necessary authorizations in the unit test client for testing the relevant business processes, as well as the user authorization S_CLNT_IMP. When you have the proper authorizations, log on to the unit test client—the client into which you want to copy the recorded changes of a particular change request or task—and proceed as follows:

1. Use Transaction code SCC1 or, from the initial screen, choose TOOLS • ADMINISTRATION • ADMINISTRATION • CLIENT ADMINISTRATION • SPECIAL FUNCTIONS • COPY TRANSPORT REQUEST. The COPY BY TRANSPORT REQUEST screen is displayed (see Figure 12.1).

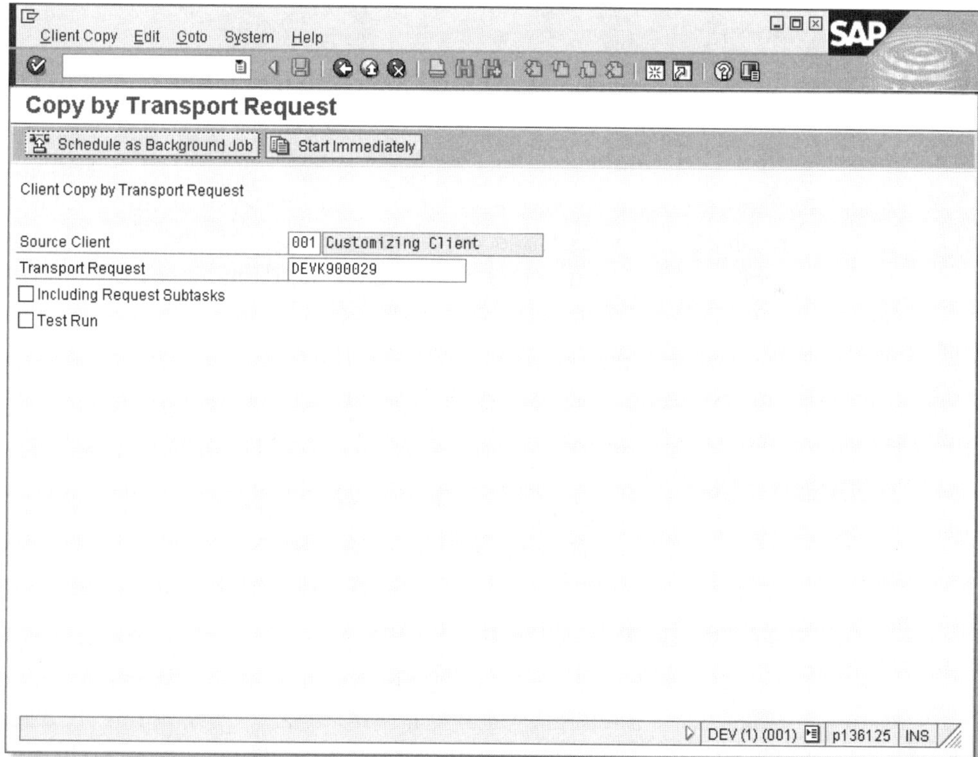

Figure 12.1 Copy by Transport Request (Transaction SCC1)

2. Enter the SOURCE CLIENT ID number, as well as the ID of the change request or task to be copied.

3. If copying a change request, select the INCLUDING REQUEST SUBTASKS option to ensure that changes recorded in unreleased tasks are also copied.
4. To start copying the change request, choose either START IMMEDIATELY or SCHEDULE AS BACKGROUND JOB.
5. If you choose START IMMEDIATELY, a dialog box appears that indicates the number of objects to be copied. If this number is zero, no changes will be copied. In that case, choose CANCEL and retry this procedure using a different change request or task ID.

Reviewing the Log Files for Transaction SCC1

To review the log files generated by Transaction SCC1, proceed as follows:

1. Access the Client Copy Log using Transaction code SCC3 or, from the SAP ERP initial screen, choose TOOLS • ADMINISTRATION • ADMINISTRATION • CLIENT ADMINISTRATION • COPY LOGS.
2. Choose TRANSPORT REQUESTS. The screen displays the current status of all client copies based on a transport request (that is, a change request). The client copies are listed by the ID number of the target client.
3. Double-click the ID number of the client into which you copied changes using Transaction SCC1. The log files for the copied change requests are displayed. The TRANSPORT column indicates the change request or task IDs.
4. To see more information on a client copy based on a change request, double-click the related change request or task ID.

12.2.2 SAPscript Styles and Forms

SAPscript is the word processing functionality of SAP systems. At its core are *forms* (often referred to as *layout sets*) and *styles*. Forms are used to control page layouts. Styles are format definitions for paragraphs and characters that can be used to format the text itself. Although SAPscript styles and forms are client-dependent, when they are created or changed, they are recorded to a Workbench change request. To unit test styles and forms as of Release 4.0, you should use Transaction SCC1 to copy the styles and forms in the Workbench change request.

Copying styles and forms

However, for copying SAPscript styles and forms from one client to another in the same SAP system, you can also use the COPY FROM CLIENT SAPscript functionality. Choose TOOLS • SAPSCRIPT • FORM • UTILITIES • COPY FROM CLIENT. COPY FROM CLIENT works only if the objects to be copied are not locked in a change request. By default, all Repository objects in a change request are locked. Before using COPY FROM CLIENT, you must either unlock the recorded objects or release the change request containing the objects. However, unlocking the recorded objects is time-consuming, and releasing the relevant change request prevents you from adding corrections to the change requests.

12.2.3 Report Variants

Although SAP ERP programs (often referred to as *reports*) are client-independent, *report variants* are client-dependent. Report variants are used to record data that is supplied to an ABAP program so that you do not need to enter the same selections repeatedly. When report variants are created or changed, by default, they are not recorded to a change request. Because they are usually localized to the current environment and have little value for other clients, report variants are not usually transported. If needed, variants can be copied to other clients. In some cases, the variants must then be added to a change request for transport.

To copy variants to a unit test client, use one of the following techniques:

- From the unit test client, execute the program RSDBVCOP. This program copies variants from another client within the same SAP system.
- In the client in which the variant was created, manually add the variant to a change request by creating the object-list entry *LIMU VARX <program name><variant name>*. Then, use Transaction SCC1 to copy the recorded variants in the change request to the unit test client.

[+] For more information on how to transport variants, see SAP Note 128908.

12.3 Releasing a Task

Promoting changes recorded in a change request begins with releasing the relevant tasks. Releasing a task indicates that the owner of the task has completed his Customizing or development work, that unit testing was successful, and that the appropriate documentation is complete. The technical requirements for releasing a task are as follows:

Technical requirements

- The task contains a recorded object.
- The task has been documented.
- You own the task (or you have authorization S_A.SYSTEM).

To release a task, proceed as follows:

1. To list the change requests you are working on, in either the Workbench Organizer (Transaction code SE09) or the Customizing Organizer (Transaction code SE10), choose DISPLAY. The request overview is displayed.
2. To view all of the tasks assigned to a particular change request, expand the tree structure. Position the cursor on the task you want to release and choose RELEASE.
3. If you have not yet entered documentation for the task, the documentation maintenance screen appears. Document your changes, save the documentation, and choose BACK. (For more information on providing documentation, see Section 12.1.1) If the task is successfully released, you will see the message "Task <task ID> has been released to request <change request ID>" in the status bar.
4. Released tasks are highlighted with a particular color in the request overview. To see the color key, choose UTILITIES • KEY.

12.3.1 Release Errors

If the task cannot be released, an error message appears in the status bar to indicate, for example, that:

- The task can be released only by the owner of the task (or a user with the authorization profile SAP_ALL).
- The task cannot be released because it contains no recorded objects and has been classified as NOT ASSIGNED (as opposed to DEVELOPMENT/CORRECTION or REPAIR).

In the event of a more serious error, the status bar will not contain a message. Instead, the LIST OF ENTRIES CANNOT BE LOCKED screen is displayed. Severe errors may occur with development work in tasks belonging to Workbench change requests. Examples include:

Severe errors

Errors

- **Object locked in another request/task**
  Prior to release, all Repository objects in a task or change request require a Workbench Organizer lock. This message indicates that the Workbench Organizer cannot lock (and therefore cannot release) objects in the task because the objects are already locked in another task or change request.
- **Transport object to target system <SID> only**
  The development class and its transport layer for objects in the task do not consolidate to the target system that was defined when the change request was created. For example, this applies if an object has a development class that consolidates to the quality assurance system, but the target for the change request is the training system. This means that, after the object was recorded to a task, someone manually changed the target system for the change request, or changed the transport routes for the development system using the TMS.

Correcting these errors may require you to:

Correcting the errors

- Modify the object list of a change request to acquire proper Workbench Organizer locks
- Change the target system for the change request
- Change the transport routes defined within the TMS

To solve a problem, the owner of the task may need assistance from the system administrator.

12.3.2 Impact on the Change Request

When you release a task, the task object list and the relevant locks and documentation are automatically copied to the object list of the change request that contains the task. Before a task is released, the object list of a change request is empty (unless objects have been added manually).

Figure 12.2 demonstrates this process. Task DEVK900003 in Customizing change request DEVK900002 has been released. Prior to its release, no objects were listed at the change request level. After the release of the task, a *comment* is added to the request overview, which, when the relevant node is expanded, indicates when the task was released.

This information can also be displayed in the object list of the change request. In Figure 12.3, for example, the object list entry *CORR RELE DEVK900003 20050608* 215306 indicates that the task was released on June 8, 2005. The other entry—the contents of view V_005_B—constitutes the contents of this task. This object was transferred from the task to the request.

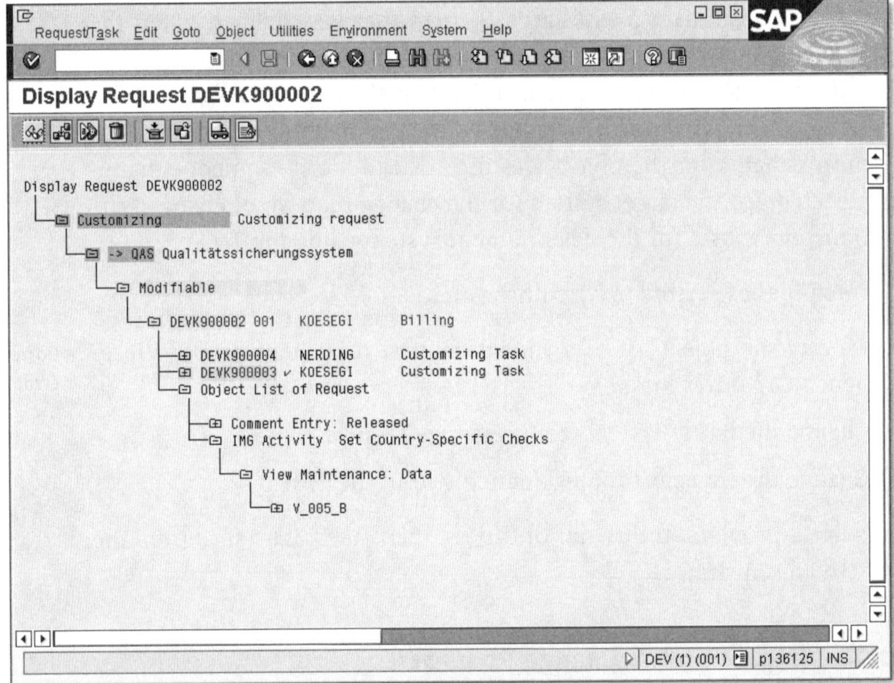

Figure 12.2 Upon Release, the Object List of a Task is Copied to the Object List of its Change Request

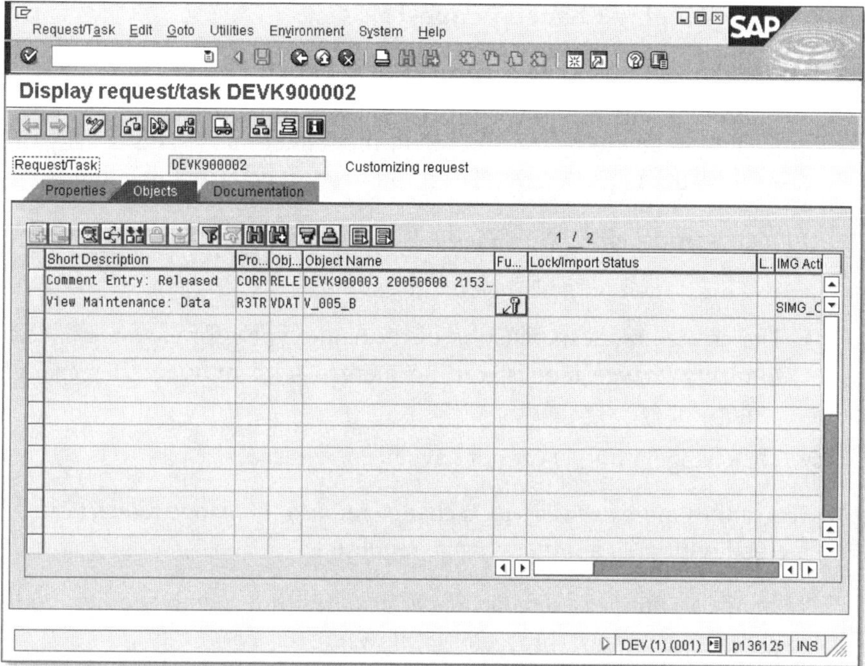

Figure 12.3 Object List of a Change Request Showing the Released Task and Locked Repository Objects

12.4 Releasing a Change Request

By releasing a change request, you indicate that it has sufficient documentation, that the changes recorded in the request have been unit tested, and that they are ready to be transported using the TMS transport routes. During the export process triggered by the release, the objects recorded in the change request are copied from the SAP ERP database to a file external to SAP ERP. This copy "freezes" the objects in their present state. In addition, a record of the change request is automatically added to the import queue of the defined consolidation system.

Releasing and exporting a single change request generates export and import logs. Testing in the quality assurance system and sign-off are necessary before import into the production system. To support the validation process and limit the technical and administrative overhead, SAP recommends merging the change requests of a project prior to export.

12.4.1 Merging Change Requests

Combining multiple change requests into a single change request to create a testable unit is useful only if the change requests for a particular project are ready to be transported at the same time. This is usually the case when the requests are related and need to be tested together.

To merge two change requests, the following requirements must be met:

Requirements

- You must own both change requests.
- The change requests must be of the same type—for example, a Customizing change request can be merged with only another change request of type *Customizing*.
- The change requests cannot have been released.

[+] You cannot merge a task with a change request. A change request can be merged with only another change request.

To merge an unreleased or *modifiable* change request with another modifiable change request, proceed as follows:

1. In the Transport Organizer (Transaction code SE09), choose DISPLAY. The request overview is displayed, showing the change requests and tasks related to your user ID.
2. Position the cursor on the change request you want to include in another change request. Select UTILITIES • REORGANIZE • MERGE REQUESTS. The Merge Requests screen is displayed (see Figure 12.4).
3. Enter the change request ID of a second change request in the second REQUEST field. At the end of the merging process, this request will contain both merged change requests. Choose CONTINUE.

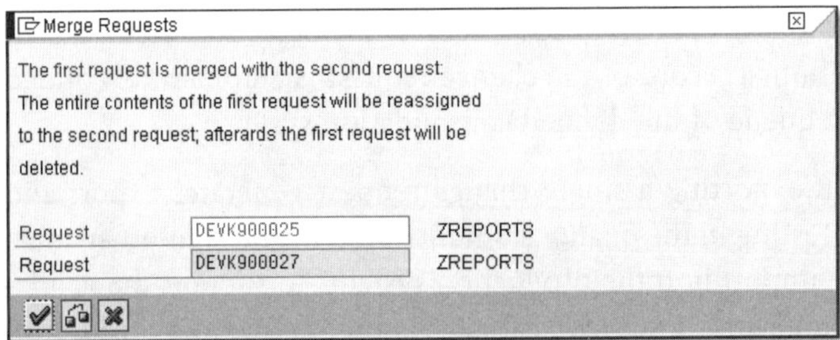

Figure 12.4 Merging Two Change Requests

Only change requests of the same type can be merged using this procedure. However, you can also combine a Customizing change request with a Workbench change request of type TRANSPORTABLE.

12.4.2 Procedure for Releasing a Change Request

To release a change request you own, proceed as follows:

1. In the Transport Organizer (Transaction code SE09), choose DISPLAY. The request overview is displayed, showing the change requests and tasks related to your user ID.
2. Position the cursor on the change request you want to release and choose RELEASE. Depending on the type of change request, this results in the following:
   - For a transportable change request, if the release is successful, this automatically starts the export process.
   - For a local change request, if the release is successful, this automatically results in the following message in the status bar: Local request released (objects no longer locked).
3. When the export process starts, the OVERVIEW OF TRANSPORT LOGS screen appears, showing the transport logs specific to the change request. The export process has the status IN PROCESS. You can wait for the export to complete or choose BACK to return to either the Customizing Organizer or the Workbench Organizer. (Reviewing the transport logs to verify the success of an export process is explained in Section 12.5).

Release Errors

If a change request cannot be released, an error message appears in the status bar indicating, for example, one of the following situations:

- There are tasks in the change request that have not been released. Before the change request can be released, all tasks in the change request must be released.
- The change request can be released only by the owner of the change request (or a user with the authorization profile SAP_ALL).
- Not all Repository objects in the request could be locked. The Workbench Organizer cannot lock an object that is already locked in another

task or change request. Before the change request can be released, all SAP ERP Repository objects in the change request must have a Workbench Organizer lock.

- The transport routes defined from within TMS have changed since the change request was created. The target system for the change request is not defined in the TMS as a consolidation system; therefore, the change request cannot be released. To change the target system for the change request, in the request overview, position the cursor on the change request and choose REQUEST/TASK • DISPLAY/CHANGE.
- The development class and its transport layer for an object listed in a transportable change request no longer consolidate to the target system that was defined when the change request was created. To solve this problem, change the development class of the object, change the target system defined for the change request, or delete the object in the object list of the change request.
- A system administrator has disallowed release from the SAP system. If you create the file `T_OFF.ALL` or `T_OFF.<SID>` in the *bin* transport directory, the release of change requests for either all SAP systems in the transport group or a specific SAP system can be prevented. This option is useful when the target SAP ERP system is being upgraded or problems at the operating system level have been reported. If the export of change requests has been disallowed, the change request will not be released and exported, and the owner will need to release and export the request later.

Object Checks

When you release either a transportable or a local Workbench change request, you can activate object checks that identify and display errors such as program syntax errors. This reduces the risk of importing "bad" Repository objects that you will be unable to activate or generate in the target systems.

If activated, these checks automatically run when you release a Workbench change request. They include a program check with Transaction SLIN, as well as an ABAP Dictionary check to verify that all ABAP Dictionary objects in the request have the status ACTIVE.

Activating Object Checks

As a user with the CTS administration authorization (S_CTS_ADMIN), you can either:

- Activate or deactivate the object checks for all users
- Leave it up to the user to decide whether to activate or deactivate the checks

To activate or deactivate the object checks, proceed as follows:

1. Use Transaction code SE03.
2. Expand the ADMINISTRATION hierarchy and double-click GLOBAL CUSTOMIZING TRANSPORT ORGANIZER. The GLOBAL CUSTOMIZING (TRANSPORT ORGANIZER) screen is displayed (see Figure 12.5).

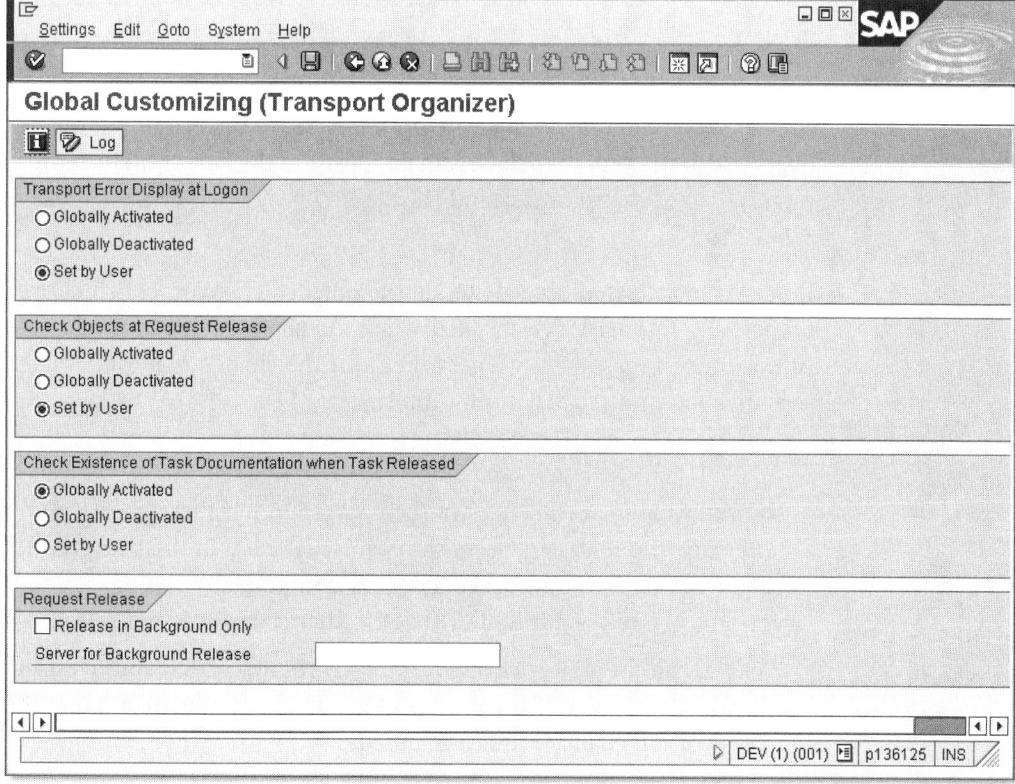

Figure 12.5 Global Activation of Transport Error Display and Object Checks in Transaction SE03

3. Under CHECK OBJECTS AT REQUEST RELEASE, select one of the following:
   - GLOBALLY ACTIVATED: This activates automatic checking of all objects before release.
   - GLOBALLY DEACTIVATED: This deactivates automatic checking of all objects before release. A user cannot set the automatic checking of objects before release as an individual default.
   - SET BY USER: This enables a user to use Transaction SE09 to set automatic object checking as their user default.
4. To save your settings, choose CONTINUE.

If the global option SET BY USER is set, individual users can activate or deactivate the checks. To do so, from the initial screen of the Transport Organizer (Transaction SE09 or SE10), the user needs to choose UTILITIES • SETTINGS • TRANSPORT ORGANIZER and select CHECK OBJECTS AT REQUEST RELEASE.

[+] Regardless of whether object checks are activated globally, you can check the objects in a change request at any time. To do this, from the request overview of the Workbench Organizer, position the cursor on the appropriate change request or task and choose REQUEST/TASK • OVERALL CHECKS • OBJECTS (SYNTAX CHECK).

If you have activated object checks, the objects in a Workbench change request are automatically checked when the change request is released. At this time, if no previous object check for the change request has been run, the OBJECT CHECKS window appears (see Figure 12.6).

You have the following options:

- You can run the object check in the background. If the objects contain no errors, the release process starts automatically in the background. When the background processing has completed, a dialog box tells you that errors were found or that the change request was released.
- You can run the object check in the foreground, which automatically displays the results of the checks. After this, you must complete the release of the change request manually.
- You can cancel the object check and do not release the change request.

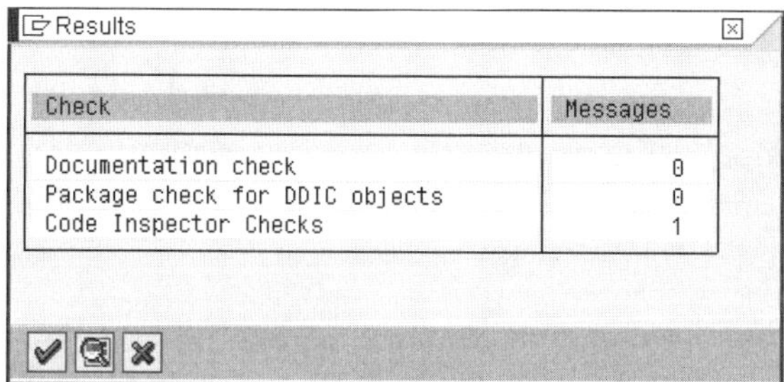
Results

Check	Messages
Documentation check	0
Package check for DDIC objects	0
Code Inspector Checks	1

Figure 12.6 Automatic Object Check Prompt when Releasing Workbench Change Request

When the object check has finished, a RESULTS dialog box informs you of any errors that were found. You can then:

- Continue the release process despite the errors
- Display the errors by double-clicking the specific check that generated the error
- Cancel the release process

The Sort and Compress Function

When a change request is released, its object list is automatically sorted and compressed to remove duplicate entries. This process does not delete objects that were changed; it simply deletes redundant listings. Often, different users of a change request record the same objects in their object lists because they are pursuing overlapping objectives within the same Customizing or development project. Suppose, for example, that two tasks of a change request contain the *R3TR TABL ZNEWTABLE* object entry. When the tasks are released, the object list of the change request shows the entry twice. After the change request has been released, thanks to the SORT AND COMPRESS function, the object occurs in the object list only once.

Starting manually

You can also manually initiate a SORT AND COMPRESS at any time. If you do this prior to releasing the change request, it may speed up the release process or prevent release failure due to a long runtime. To manually initiate a SORT AND COMPRESS, from the request overview in either the Customizing Organizer or the Workbench Organizer, choose REQUEST/TASK • OBJECT LIST • SORT AND COMPRESS.

12.4.3 The Export Process

Releasing either a Customizing change request or a transportable change request automatically initiates the export process. Understanding what happens during export highlights its significance and aids in troubleshooting. During export, the following processes occur:

1. The changes recorded in the change request are copied from the database to a data file in the transport directory at the operating system level. In addition, a control file and an export log file are created and written to the transport directory (see Table 12.1).
2. The change request is added to the import queue of the target system, which typically is the quality assurance system.
3. By default, a "test import" is performed in the target system. This import verifies the connection to the target system's database and checks the objects to be imported.
4. The Workbench Organizer lock is removed for the objects in the object list of the exported change request, allowing them to be included in other change requests.

Table 12.1 provides details on the three files created in the transport directory: the data file, the control file, and the export log file.

Naming Convention	Transport Sub-Directory	Contents	Example: Files Created for Request DEVK900747
R<request #>.<SID>	data	Data file containing exported data	R900747.DEV
K<request #>.<SID>	cofiles	Control file with instructions for import and import history for the change request	K900747.DEV
<SID>E<request #>.<SID>	log	Log file with details about the success of the export process	DEVE900747.DEV
* The *request* # is the six-digit request number from the change request ID. By default, it begins with the number 9.			
** The SID is the system ID for the source SAP ERP system from which the change request is released.			

Table 12.1 Transport Directory Files Created during the Export of a Change Request

tp and R3trans

The programs tp and R3trans are used during the export process. The program tp manages the export of a change request and issues calls to R3trans. R3trans physically extracts the recorded changes from the database of the source SAP ERP system and writes the data file and the control file. Because the data files written to the transport directory are in R3trans format rather than a database-specific format, the data file can be imported into any other SAP system regardless of its database platform.

After writing the data file and the control file for a change request to the transport directory, the transport control program tp adds the change request to the end of the import buffer—to the file <SID> in the transport subdirectory buffer, where SID is the system ID of the target system. The target system is the consolidation system defined for the change request (typically, the quality assurance system).

Exported Data

Change requests record only what has changed and do not contain actual changed objects. The export of a change request physically copies the changed objects in their current state to a file in the transport directory at the operating system level. The data can be either an SAP ERP Repository object or table entries associated with Customizing.

To return to the example in Figure 11.8 (see Chapter 11), one of the Customizing changes recorded in the change request was a change to the exchange rates. Exactly which table entries are copied by the export is determined by the primary key values recorded in the change request. The primary key of table TCURR consists of the client and the sales organization. The primary key values recorded in this change request are 001100*DEM USD80029898. These values identify the table row that will be extracted during export.

Customizing change requests record table entries rather than entire tables. Because table entries are not locked, two users may change the same table entry. Regardless of whether the change was a creation or an edit, the primary key and the object list in each of the change requests will be identical. When the change requests are released and exported, the table row corresponding to the primary key will be extracted from the database. The data from this row as it appears at the time of export is saved to the transport directory and eventually imported into the downstream system. This is illustrated in the following example.

Example: Exporting Customizing Changes with the Same Primary Key

The user THOMAS creates a new plant called PHL1 with the description PHILADELPHIA. Later, the user JANE decides to change the description of the plant PHL1 to PHILADELPHIA WEST. The users have saved their changes to different change requests.

What happens when user THOMAS releases and exports his change request depends on whether he releases and exports his change request before JANE makes her change.

- If the change request of THOMAS is released and exported before JANE makes her change, the data file in the transport directory will contain the description PHILADELPHIA for plant PHL1.
- If THOMAS releases and exports after JANE has made her change, the data file in the transport directory will contain the description PHILADELPHIA WEST for the plant PHL1.

Test Imports

In addition to entering the exported change request in the import buffer of the target system, by default, the transport program `tp` initiates a test import in the target system. The test import is not an attempted import so much as a screening of the objects to be imported. The test import process connects to the database of the target SAP ER system and reviews the objects listed in the object directory. An error is indicated in the transport log file for the change request if (for any Repository object):

- The target system is the original system.
- A repair flag is set in the target system.
- The table into which data will be imported does not exist in the target system.

If the error occurs because the target system is the original system, you may need to perform a nonstandard import or choose not to import the object to prevent overwriting the corresponding object. If a repair flag is the source of the error, this can be corrected by confirming the repair prior to importing the change request. A missing table in the target system is a serious problem and will require the transport of the table from the development system before the import of the change request that contains data for that table.

To perform a test import, the transport program `tp` must be able to connect to the target system's database. This is not possible if, for example, the target system has not been installed and is simply a virtual system, or if the target system is in a different network for security purposes. In these situations, you may want to deactivate the test import functionality.

Deactivating

To deactivate the test import as the default setting, set the transport profile parameter `testimport` to FALSE. This parameter can be set either globally—for all SAP systems in the transport domain—or for a specific SAP system. When setting the parameter for a specific system, set it in the source SAP ERP system and not in the target SAP ERP system. For example, to deactivate test imports into the quality assurance system, proceed as follows:

Use the TMS to set `testimport` in the transport parameter to FALSE for the development system (Transaction STMS; choose OVERVIEW • SYSTEMS).

12.4.4 Authorizations

The release and export process is critical because it initiates the transport process for changed objects. Therefore, SAP recommends that only specific users be authorized to release change requests. As explained in Chapter 11, the relevant user authorization profiles are S_A.CUSTOMIZ (for the project team lead) and S_A.DEVELOP (for project team members). These authorizations allow a project lead to create and release change requests, and team members to change and release only their own tasks.

Example: Using Authorizations to Control the Release and Export Process

A company initially allows all users in the development system to create and release change requests. Users inform the system administrator when a released change request is ready for import. The sequence in which change requests were imported is not taken into account.

During an important testing period, the quality assurance validation team reports several consistency problems with regard to the organization and functionality of basic business processes. After analyzing several problems, they discover that—because change requests are being imported on demand, out of sequence, and partly not imported—the quality assurance system has older versions of settings and is missing Customizing. Everyone agrees that the change requests need better management. The idea of restricting the creation and release of change requests to the project lead is regarded as unrealistic. For this SAP ERP implementation, project leads are focused on planning and are unavailable to handle the day-to-day activities of creating change requests. It is decided that all users should be able to create change requests. However, only specific users receive the authorization to release change requests or change the ownership of a change request and then release it. To release a change request, other users contact a power user, define the purpose of the change, and ask the power user to release the change request.

As a result of this new procedure, change requests are imported into the quality assurance system in the same order in which they are released—not simply whenever someone asks for a change request to be imported. This prevents older versions of settings from replacing the latest versions.

12.5 Transport Logs

The release and export of a change request is the beginning of its transport process, which is when the first transport log file—the export log file—is automatically generated. Transport log files reside in the transport directory and can be displayed within the SAP system as follows:

- A system administrator can view all transport log files for a change request in an import queue. To do so, display the import queue of a particular SAP system (Transaction STMS; Overview • Imports • Import Queue • Display). Position the cursor on the change request and choose Request • Display • Logs.
- Any user can view all transport log files related to a specific user. To do so, access the Transport Organizer (Transaction SE09 or SE10). Enter the relevant user ID and, under Global information, choose Transports.
- Any user can view all transport logs for a particular change request. To do so, call the Organizer Tools (Transaction SE03), drill down under Request/task, and choose Display transport logs. Enter a change request ID and press Enter.

Overview

After you use any of these methods, the OVERVIEW OF ALL TRANSPORT LOGS screen is displayed (see Figure 12.7). This screen shows a tree structure of released change requests and the respective export and import processing steps, grouped according to target systems. The success of individual steps is indicated by the highlight color, comment, and return code. (For more information on return codes for exports and imports, see Chapter 14.) If the change request was imported, the import log files for the various SAP systems are displayed.

Figure 12.7 shows the export steps for change request `DEVK900032`. The operating system check finished without errors (return code 0), as did the export of changes. In the quality assurance system, however, the test import was cancelled by the transport control program `tp` (return code 8) and therefore was not successful.

To see more information about the failure of a processing step, you can drill down to the associated error message or warning.

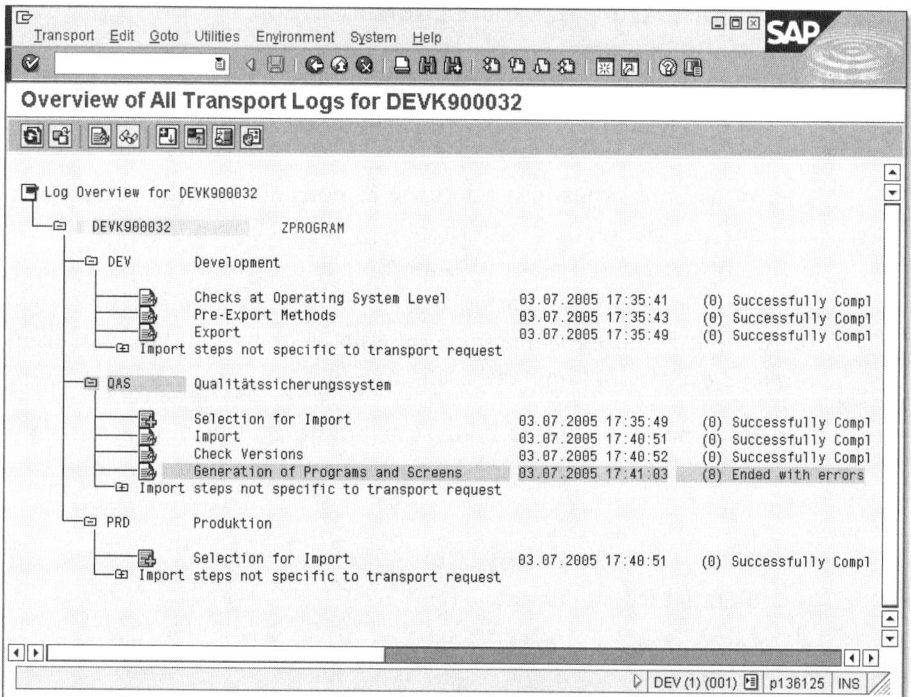

Figure 12.7 Transport Logs Displayed in the SAP System

12.5.1 Managing Transport Logs

Managing the transport logs involves reviewing errors and possibly marking them as corrected, as well as deleting unnecessary transport logs

If an error occurs with regard to either export or import, the corresponding change request receives the transport log status INCORRECT. Incorrect change requests can be easily identified when you look at the overview of your transport logs—incorrect change requests are flagged in red and appear at the top of the hierarchical list.

Over time, the number of transport logs associated with the various change request owners will increase. The only transport logs of interest are the most recent logs, not the logs either of the last implementation phase or that have received quality assurance sign-off. To facilitate your transport log analysis, you can delete old change requests from a user's list of transport logs.

12.5.2 Displaying Transport Errors at Logon

By changing a default setting, you can cause transport errors to be automatically displayed when you log on to an SAP system within the transport domain.

The release and export process is the responsibility of the person who released the change request. Therefore, it is the responsibility of the owner of the change request to monitor and correct transport errors, even if this requires the assistance of a system administrator. SAP recommends that you use the default setting that automatically informs users of failed exports and imports at logon.

The dialog box that appears at logon to indicate transport errors is shown in Figure 12.8. In this dialog box, you can select from the following options:

- CONTINUE or CANCEL to bypass viewing the errors and access the SAP ERP initial screen instead
- DISPLAY to see a list of transport logs for the affected change requests

- TRANSPORT ORGANIZER to go directly to the Transport Organizer (Transaction SE09)
- NEVER DISPLAY AGAIN to prevent the respective tasks from being displayed in this list.

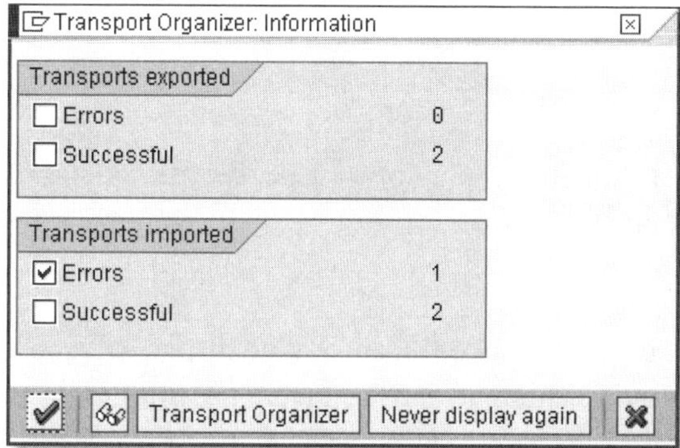

Figure 12.8 Transport Error Notification at Logon

Activating the Automatic Display of Transport Logs at Logon

By default, errors during export or import are not displayed when a user logs on to an SAP system. You can globally activate or deactivate the automatic display of transport errors at logon for all users, or you can allow users to make the automatic display one of their individual default settings.

If you are the system administrator (a user with the CTS administration authorization S_CTS_ADMIN) and you want to globally activate or deactivate the transport logs at logon, proceed as follows:

1. Use Transaction code SE03.
2. Drill down in the tree structure at ADMINISTRATION and double-click GLOBAL CUSTOMIZING TRANSPORT ORGANIZER.
3. The GLOBAL CUSTOMIZING (TRANSPORT ORGANIZER) screen appears (see Figure 12.5 earlier in this chapter). Choose one of the following options under TRANSPORT ERROR DISPLAY AT LOGON:

- GLOBALLY ACTIVATED
  Transport errors will be automatically displayed at logon for all users.
- GLOBALLY DEACTIVATED
  The automatic display of transport errors is deactivated. A user cannot set the automatic display of transport logs as an individual default.
- SET BY USER
  Users can select the automatic display of transport errors as one of their individual default settings.

4. To save your settings, choose CONTINUE.

If the SET BY USER option is set, to make the automatic display of transport errors one of your individual default settings, from the initial screen of the Transport Organizer (Transaction SE09 or SE10), choose SETTINGS • CHANGE & TRANSPORT ORGANIZER. Select DISPLAY TRANSPORT ERRORS AT LOGON and press Enter.

12.6 Versioning for Repository Objects

When a change request is released, a version of each SAP ERP Repository object in the change request is added to the version database. This enables the release process to provide a complete change history for all Repository objects. Another automatically created version is the *active* version, which displays the current state of all active objects in the SAP system. In addition to the automatically created versions, you can also create versions at any time, which are known as *temporary* versions.

The different types of versions are stored in two different sets of tables (two different databases) in the SAP system database:

- The *version database*, which stores versions saved as a result of a released change request and temporary versions
- The *development database*, which stores the active version of an object (its current state in the SAP system)

Both the development and version database are maintained in the development system, because this system is where SAP ERP Repository objects are created, changed, and released. If you discontinue a development system, you will lose all version history for all customer developments and modifications to SAP objects made in that system.

12.6.1 Version Management

You can access version management for a particular Repository object using any of the following tools:

Tools

- Repository Browser (Transaction SE80)
- Transport Organizer (Transaction SE09)
- Display and maintenance transactions for Repository objects, such as the ABAP Editor for ABAP programs and the ABAP Dictionary for tables, domains, and data elements

For example, to view the versions maintained for the ABAP program ZPROGRAM, proceed as follows:

1. Access the ABAP Editor using Transaction code SE38 or, from the SAP ERP initial screen, choose TOOLS • DEVELOPMENT • ABAP WORKBENCH • ABAP EDITOR.
2. Enter the name of the ABAP program whose versions you want to view.
3. Choose UTILITIES • VERSION MANAGEMENT. The versions stored for the ABAP program are displayed (see Figure 12.9).

The display of versions for a Repository object includes both the version in the development database and the versions in the version database. If, as in Figure 12.9, a change request ID is indicated for the active version, the object is currently locked by the change request and was changed by the indicated user. If no change request ID appears for the active version, the object is currently not recorded to a change request and not locked by the Workbench Organizer.

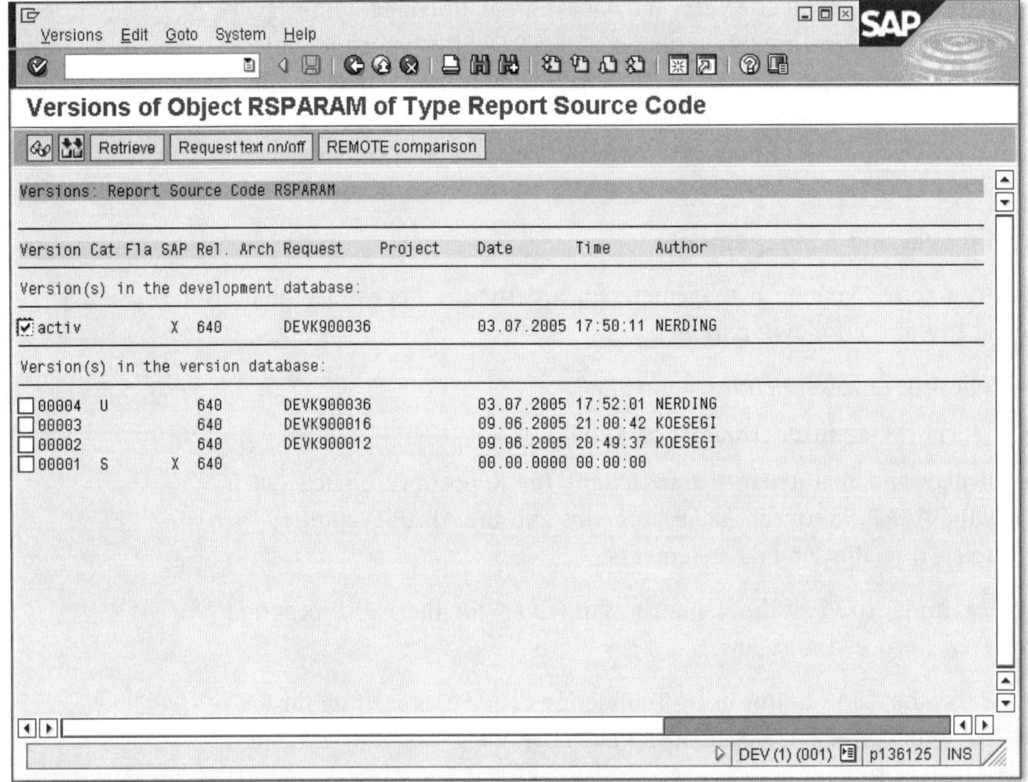

Figure 12.9 Versions of an ABAP Program

Versions in the version database are numbered starting with 0001. The first version for a customer object will always be of type S, indicating that it is the original version from when the object was created. Because most versions in the version database are the result of a released change request, the change request number and owner of the change request are also provided.

Temporary versions

Temporary versions are indicated as type U. These versions are created if, when maintaining an object, you use the Generate version option. In the ABAP Editor, for example, you would choose Program • Generate Version. Temporary versions are deleted when a change request is released, because doing so writes a permanent version to the version database.

From the display of versions for an SAP ERP Repository object, you can:

- Display a particular version by selecting the version and choosing DISPLAY.
- Compare two different versions by selecting the two versions and choosing COMPARE. A split screen will show the differences between the two versions.
- Restore a version by selecting the version and choosing RETRIEVE. This causes the currently active version to be overwritten by the older version you select. If the object has not already been recorded to a change request, you must record the change to a change request. To use RETRIEVE, the Repository object's maintenance screen must be in change mode.

12.6.2 Versions in Nondevelopment Systems

By default, SAP ERP Repository objects are not versioned upon import. This restricts version histories to the development system. The quality assurance and production systems have only the currently active version for each Repository object. This version indicates the change request that caused the import of the object, but cannot be used to display or compare older versions.

Versions cannot be transported between SAP systems. Because versions reside only in the development system, if the development system is removed from the system landscape, all versions in the version database are lost.

You can create versions at import, enabling you to preserve your version history for all Repository objects if the development system is removed from the system landscape or overwritten with a database copy. If versioning upon import is activated, when you import change requests into a system, versions of the imported objects are added to the version database of that system. [+]

Versioning at import is achieved by setting the transport parameter `vers_at_imp` to either C_ONLY or ALWAYS. The value C_ONLY causes only relocation transports (see Chapter 10) to create versions in the target system. The value ALWAYS forces all imports to create versions. This transport parameter can be set for a specific SAP system or globally for all systems.

[+] Activating versioning at import increases the number of import processing steps during the import of a change request. To minimize the amount of time required for import into the production system, you may want to avoid activating versioning at import for that system.

12.7 Questions

1. **Which of the following is a prerequisite for copying client-dependent changes to a unit test client using** CLIENT COPY ACCORDING TO TRANSPORT REQUEST **(Transaction SCC1)?**

   A. The change request has been released.

   B. The tasks have been released, but the change request has not.

   C. The tasks have been released after successful unit testing by the owner of the task.

   D. The change request has not been released.

2. **Which of the following are the result of releasing a task?**

   A. A data file is created in the transport directory and contains the objects recorded in the change request.

   B. The object list and documentation for the task are copied to the change request.

   C. All objects recorded in the task are locked.

   D. You can no longer save changes to that task.

3. **Which of the following are the result of releasing and exporting a change request?**

   A. A data file is created in the transport directory to contain copies of the objects recorded in the change request.

   B. Versions are created in the version database for all SAP ERP Repository objects in the object list of the change request.

   C. All repairs recorded in the change request are confirmed.

   D. You can no longer save changes to that change request.

4. **When you release a Customizing change request, you can do which of the following?**
   A. Release the change request to another Customizing change request.
   B. Schedule the release of the change request for a later time.
   C. Release the change request to a transportable change request.
   D. Initiate immediate release and export.

5. **Which of the following is a prerequisite for releasing a transportable change request?**
   A. There are no syntax errors in the ABAP programs recorded to the change request.
   B. You must own the tasks in the change request.
   C. All Repository objects in the change request are locked by the change request.
   D. The change request has documentation.

6. **The export process initiates which of the following activities?**
   A. The creation of files in the transport directory
   B. The automatic import of change requests into the target system—for example, the quality assurance system
   C. The addition of the exported change request to the import buffer of the target system
   D. The deletion of the change request within the SAP system

7. **Which of the following activities result in a version history for all Repository objects?**
   A. A Repository object is recorded to a change request.
   B. Change requests are imported into an SAP system, and the transport parameter `vers_at_imp` is activated.
   C. A task containing a Repository object is released.
   D. A change request containing a Repository object is released.

The SAP Transport Management System provides comprehensive support for importing change requests into SAP systems, ensuring that the requests are imported in the correct sequence. Moreover, it enables you to monitor the import process and track already imported requests.

13 Importing Change Requests

The Transport Management System (TMS) provides customers with a tool to import change requests from within the SAP system. In older releases, using operating system tools could not always be avoided; this need, however, has now been almost entirely eliminated.

The information in this chapter prepares you to:

- Understand import queues
- Perform imports
- Manage import queues
- Schedule imports
- Monitor imports
- Transport between transport groups and transport domains

Before reading this chapter, you may want to reread the sections related to imports in Chapters 6 and 8. [+]

13.1 Understanding Import Queues

The most important tools for performing imports using the TMS are *import queues*. They reflect the same information in the SAP system as do system-specific *import buffers* at the operating system level. (For more information on import buffers, see Chapter 14.) An import queue displays, in the order of their export, the change requests that should be imported.

TMS In the TMS (Transaction STMS), you will find two screens that are relevant to import queues: IMPORT OVERVIEW and IMPORT QUEUE.

13.1.1 Import Overview

The IMPORT OVERVIEW screen shows the import queues of all SAP systems in the transport domain (see Figure 13.1). To access the import overview, from the TMS initial screen (Transaction STMS), choose OVERVIEW • IMPORTS.

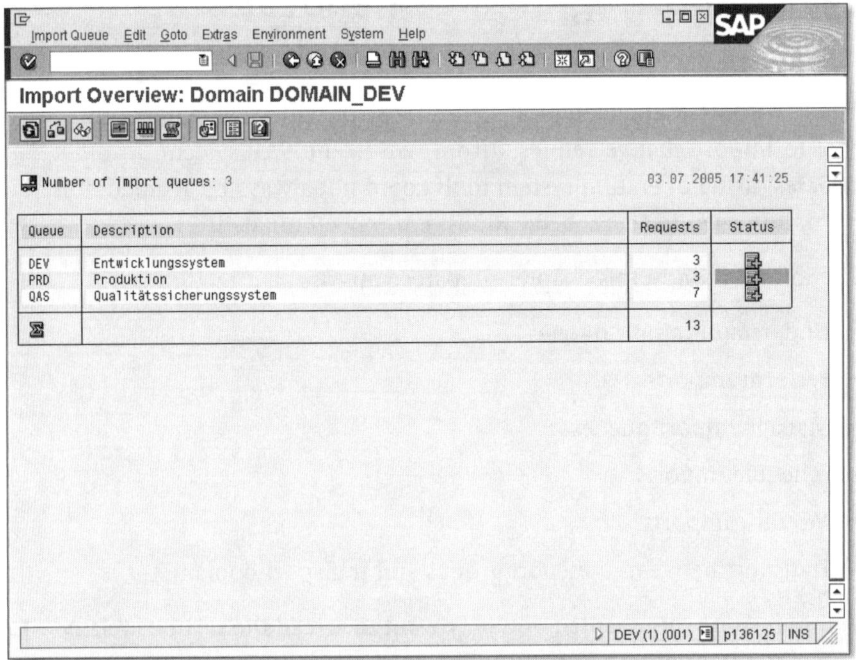

Figure 13.1 The Import Overview

In the import overview, the REQUESTS column contains the number of change requests ready to be imported. This number may differ from the total number of requests listed in the import queue for the following reasons:

- The change requests occur after an end mark in the import queue. The system administrator can set an end mark to separate change requests that will be transported in the next import from those that will not be included in the next import.

- The change requests are excluded from being imported due to certain parameter settings in the transport profile; for example, the `source-systems` parameter in the transport profile for the target system does not include the source system for some of the change requests in the import queue. (See Appendix A for more information on the `source-systems` transport parameter.)
- The change requests have already been imported—for example, change requests that belong to a client copy—and have not yet been deleted from the import queue.

Status

The STATUS column in the IMPORT OVERVIEW screen indicates the current status of each import queue in the transport domain. For an explanation of the colors and symbols indicating the status, from the IMPORT OVERVIEW screen, choose EXTRAS • LEGEND. Each combination of colors and symbols is also explained in Table 13.1.

Symbol	Color	Status	Explanation
	Green	Import queue is open	New change requests can be added and will be imported during the next import if they are located before the end mark.
	Green	Import queue is closed	The import queue is closed, and the system has set an end mark. All change requests before the end mark will be imported during the next import.
	Green	Import is running	All change requests before the end mark are currently being imported.
	Yellow	Errors occurred during import	Errors occurred during import, but the import did not terminate.
	Red	The transport was terminated	Serious errors occurred during import, and the import terminated.
	Red	Import queue could not be read	To determine why an import queue could not be read, click the symbol. One reason may be that certain files could not be accessed at the operating system level.

Table 13.1 Status Information of Import Queues

13.1.2 Import Queue

To display the import queue of an SAP system, in the IMPORT OVERVIEW screen, position the cursor on the SAP system and choose IMPORT QUEUE • DISPLAY. The import queue lists the change requests in the order in which they will be imported; as a rule, this is the order in which they were exported. The owner and the related short text are also indicated for each change request (see Figure 13.2).

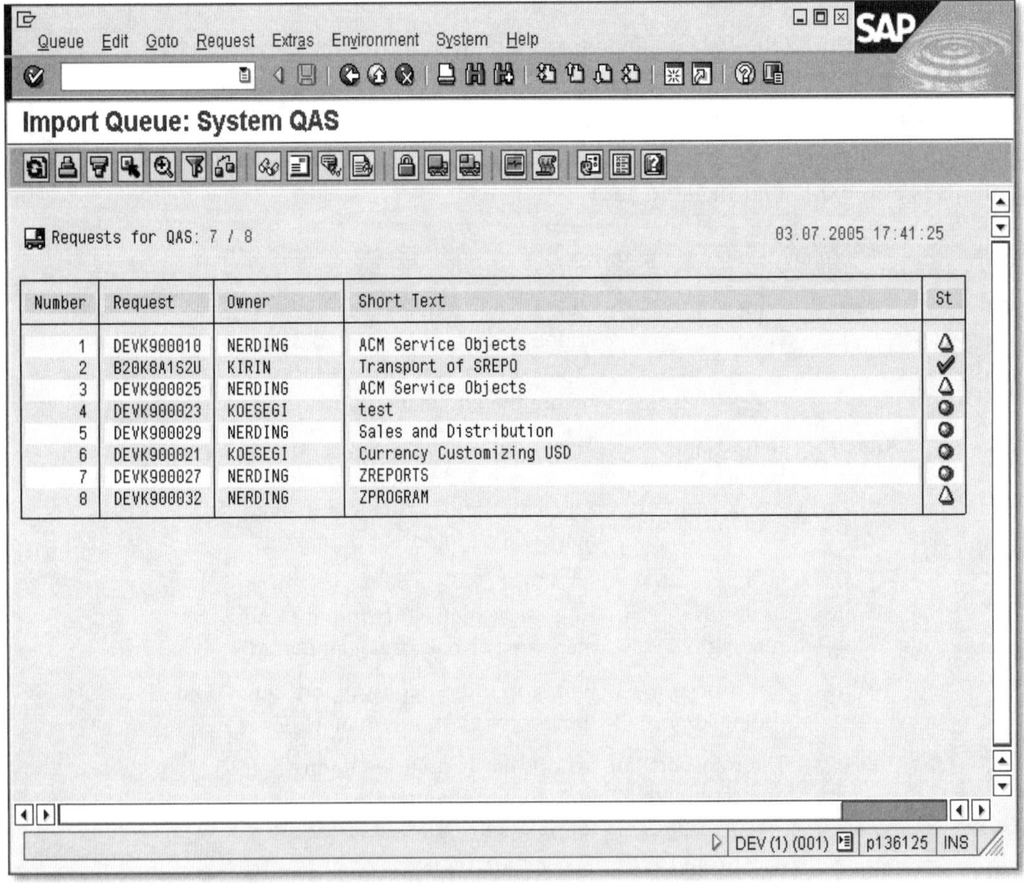

Figure 13.2 Import Queue for a Particular SAP System

The colors and symbols used in the IMPORT QUEUE screen indicate the status and type of change request. For an explanation of these colors and symbols, choose EXTRAS • LEGEND (see Table 13.2).

Status	Explanation
Request waiting to be imported	The change request will be imported during the next import.
Request was already imported	The change request is displayed in the import queue but will not be imported with the next import—for example, because it was already imported with a client transport or as an individual import with the preliminary import option deselected (see the section "Preliminary Imports").
Request was already transported	The change request was already transported as a preliminary import. To ensure consistency, it will be imported again during the next import of the entire queue.
Request will not be imported	The settings for specific transport profile parameters prevent import of the change request. For example, if the transport profile parameter `k_import` is set to FALSE, all Workbench change requests are excluded from the import, but will still be displayed in the import queue. Another example is a change request whose source system is not defined in the transport profile parameter `sourcesystems` as described earlier in this chapter. Note that these excluded change requests are not common and are only a result of special transport profile parameters that have been added to the transport profile for the target system.
Request after end mark	The change request is after the end mark. Therefore, the change request will not be imported during the next import.
Client transport	The change request results from a client transport and must be imported individually (see Chapter 9).

Table 13.2 Status Possibilities for Change Requests in an Import Queue

Additional Display Options

For additional information about the import settings for change requests, in the IMPORT QUEUE screen, choose EDIT • DISPLAY MORE. The screen displays six additional columns (see Figure 13.3 later in this section):

- T, which specifies the transport request type
- QM, which specifies the source client
- RC, which specifies the maximum return code of the import
- I, which specifies the `tp` import indicator of this change request
- UMO, which specifies the import options of this change request
- PROJECT, which specifies the CTS project to which the transport belongs

The T column shows the transport request type. The most common values are "K" for a Workbench request, "W" for a Customizing request, "T" for a transport of copies, and "M" for a client transport.

In column I, the value of the `tp` import flag (also known as the `tp` import indicator) is specified. It reflects the type of change request and under what conditions a change request is or is not imported. To display a short description of the various import flags, position the cursor in column I and press F4. The most common import flags are "W," indicating a Customizing change request, and "K," representing a Workbench change request. If either of these letters is capitalized, it indicates that the change request is excluded from transport.

Preventing imports

To prevent the import of Workbench change requests into an SAP system—for example, to supply client-dependent changes back to a client in the development system without impacting client-independent efforts—you would set the transport profile parameter `k_import` to FALSE. All Workbench change requests added to the import queue for the development system would then have the W import flag. (See Appendix A for more information on the k_import transport profile parameter.)

At the operating system level and in TMS, you can assign IMPORT OPTIONS to your imports to override specific Change and Transport System (CTS) rules. These import options are also known as *unconditional modes*. You can access these import options in the TMS through the EXPERT MODE (see Section 13.2.3). In Figure 13.3 (later in this section), the single character in the U MODES column denotes the import option assigned to a change request. For details on import options at the operating system level, see Chapter 14.

Projects

Transport requests can be combined in projects. This lets you filter and import all transport requests belonging to the same project. This functionality was introduced in Release 4.6 and meets the common practice of carrying out imports into the production system by project.

The result of an import for a change request is indicated by the *maximum return code*, as shown in column RC in the IMPORT QUEUE screen (see Figure 13.3). Every import activity results in a return code in the TMS. The return code may warn you about problems with the target SAP ERP system or about an error that has occurred during import. The system collects all return codes and displays the *maximum* return code—the code with the highest numerical value. For example, the return code 0004 represents a warning, whereas 0000 indicates that the import was successful. If you import the entire queue and these two return codes are collected, 0004 will be displayed to alert you of the warning (see Chapter 14).

To display the source client in column QM of a change request, from the IMPORT QUEUE screen, choose EXTRAS • SETTINGS • DISPLAY SOURCE CLIENT.

If the transport domain is running with extended transport control in Release 4.5, the IMPORT QUEUE screen also shows the target client in the CLT column.

In addition, if you position the cursor on a change request and choose REQUEST • DISPLAY in the IMPORT QUEUE screen, you can display additional details about the import queue, such as the following:

- Object list
- Owner
- Documentation
- Logs (export and import log files)

Keep in mind that not all log files can be displayed when you are dealing with different transport groups (see Chapter 7). See also section 13.6, Transporting between Transport Groups, later in this chapter.

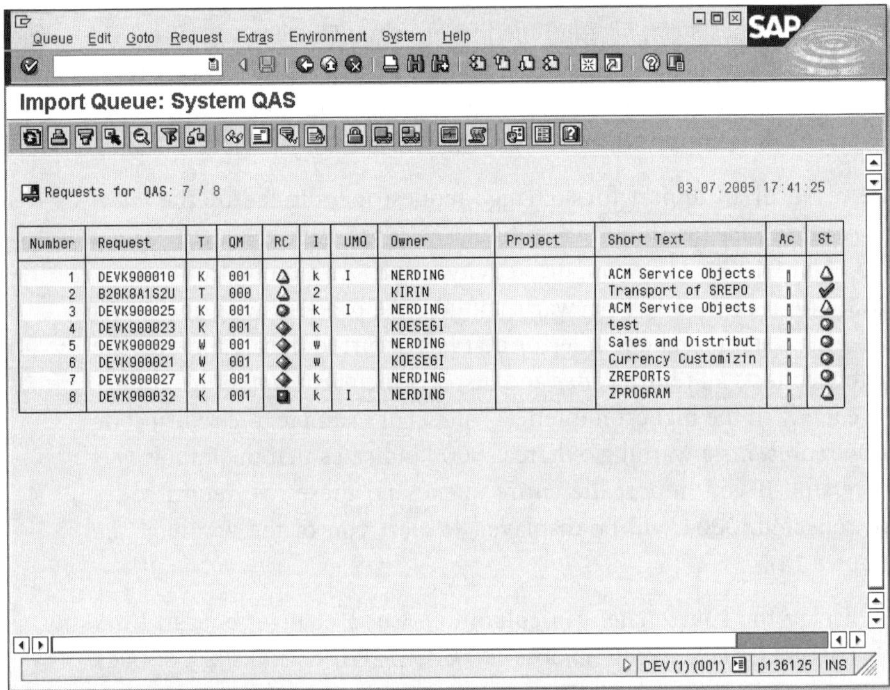

Figure 13.3 Additional Display Options in the Import Queue

Refreshing the Import Queue

To improve performance, data is read from the transport directory only the first time you access the TMS. After that, the data in the import overview and import queue is buffered in the SAP system database. The time stamp in the screen indicates how recent the data is. The internal buffers of the TMS become invalid each day at 0:00.

To refresh the data in the display, from either screen, choose EDIT • REFRESH. It may be more convenient to have the data refreshed periodically in the background. To do this, schedule the RSTMSCOL report to run at regular intervals in the SAP systems in which you frequently use the TMS. SAP recommends scheduling RSTMSCOL to run hourly.

13.2 Performing Imports

Importing is bringing exported changes into another SAP system. Because an automatic mechanism for importing a change request into a target system does not exist, you have to use the tools provided in the TMS or at the operating system level. The procedure for using the TMS is covered in this chapter. For information on performing imports at the operating system level, see Chapter 14.

13.2.1 Before Performing Imports

Before starting an import, you should ensure that the transport environment is set up to correctly address your particular import needs. By taking certain precautions, you can facilitate the import procedures and avoid unnecessary work.

Checking the queue

You should always check the import queue for SAP Support Packages and change requests resulting from client transports. The changes included in a Support Package and client transport depend on their sequence in the import queue and should be imported accordingly. However, they are not imported using the standard options, IMPORT ALL or PRELIMINARY IMPORT. For example, Support Packages have to be imported using the SAP Package Manager (Transaction SPAM) as described in Chapter 17. Change requests resulting from a client transport are imported together and should always be imported before you import the change requests that follow in the import queue (see Chapter 9).

Setting a Target Client

During import, change requests are by default imported into the client that has the same client ID as the source client. For example, change requests released from client 110 in the development system are by default imported into client 110 in the quality assurance system. If this does not satisfy your import needs, you must specify the required target client number during the initial steps of an import. At that time, a dialog box appears—either IMPORT TRANSPORT REQUEST for individual requests or START IMPORT for imports of entire queues—allowing you to enter a target client number.

[+] If you have not set the target client, the change requests will be imported into the client that has the same number as the source client.

Target Clients with Extended Transport Control

When extended transport control is activated, there is no need to specify the target client's number in the IMPORT TRANSPORT REQUEST and START IMPORT dialog boxes. Extended transport control from Release 4.5 onwards requires that transport routes specify client and system combinations; therefore, every change request in the import queue will have the client number into which it needs to be imported associated with it. You do not have to provide a target client. Figure 13.3 (earlier in the chapter) displays an import queue for the QAS system. When extended transport control is activated, it is possible that change requests in an import queue do not have a target client specified. For example, if you activate the extended transport control while change requests are still in any of the import queues, the requests will not have a target client specified. The CLT column will be highlighted in red. You cannot perform any operations on the import queue until you specify a target client for these old requests.

Specifying a target client

To set a target client for a change request:

1. From the IMPORT QUEUE screen, mark the respective change request.
2. Choose REQUEST • TARGET CLIENT • SET.
3. Enter the target client number and press [Enter].

Changing the target client

To change a specified target client before starting an import, proceed as follows:

1. From the IMPORT QUEUE screen, mark the respective change request.
2. Choose REQUEST • TARGET CLIENT • CHANGE.
3. Enter the target client number and press [Enter].

The advantage of extended transport control is that you can ensure that change requests are delivered to all clients in your system landscape in their correct sequence. Because change requests now have an additional indicator in the import queue—the target client—you can choose to specifically import only the change requests destined for a particular target client by setting a *target client filter*.

Setting the target client

To set a target client filter, follow these steps:

1. From the IMPORT QUEUE screen, choose EDIT • TARGET CLIENT FILTER.
2. Enter the target client number and press [Enter].

Closing the Import Queue by Setting an End Mark

You close an import queue and set an end mark at the end of the import queue: All change requests that are released after the import queue is closed are added to the end of the import queue in their correct sequence—but after the end mark. This will prevent the recently released change requests from being imported during the next import activity. When an import of all waiting requests is started, all of the change requests before the end mark will be imported. SAP recommends freezing certain states of development and Customizing using this closing technique.

To close the import queue, from the IMPORT QUEUE screen, choose QUEUE • CLOSE. Similarly, to open an import queue, choose QUEUE • OPEN. This removes the end mark.

If you do not close the import queue manually, the initial step in the import procedure is to close the import queue. The transport control program will automatically close the import queue and set the end mark. After the import, the queue is automatically opened again, and the end mark is removed. Setting an end mark at the end of the import queue is necessary to protect the import process from additional change requests while in the middle of performing different import steps.

13.2.2 Import All

Starting the import

After you have verified the target client settings and have closed the import queue, you are ready to start your import. To initiate an import, use the START IMPORT TMS option (explained in the text that follows), which is also referred to as IMPORT ALL because it imports all change requests waiting to be imported. Importing a collection of change requests waiting to be imported ensures that the objects are imported in their correct sequence—the sequence in which they were released and exported from the development system. (See the sections "Sequence in Import Queues" in Chapter 4 and "Importing Change Requests" in Chapter 6.)

Imports can be started from any SAP system in the transport domain. If you start the import from an SAP system other than the target system, you will be required to log on to the target system. Following logon, the TMS starts the transport control program `tp` in the target system. For the duration of the import, `tp` continues to run in the background so that the user session is not blocked. After the import, the queue is automatically opened again, and the end mark is removed.

To import all change requests waiting to be imported in the import queue of an SAP system, perform the following steps:

1. From the TMS initial screen (Transaction STMS), choose OVERVIEW • IMPORTS.
2. Mark the system into which you want to import, and choose IMPORT QUEUE • DISPLAY.
3. From the IMPORT QUEUE screen, choose QUEUE • START IMPORT.
4. The START IMPORT dialog box appears. If necessary, enter the target client number.
5. If special import options are required, choose the EXPERT MODE icon (see the text that follows on this topic).
6. Choose CONTINUE to initiate the import.

After change requests have been imported successfully into a system defined as the source system of a delivery route, they are automatically added to the import queues of the respective target SAP systems. The transport route configuration specifies which change requests are automatically delivered to which target systems.

Expert mode

The *expert mode* for an import allows you to handle special import requirements, such as reimporting change requests and overwriting objects. To use this mode, select one of the following required import options in the START IMPORT dialog box (mentioned previously) and then choose CONTINUE:

- **Select all requests for new import**
  When you select this option, after the import all imported change requests are kept in the import queue instead of being deleted immediately. This way, they can be imported into additional clients in the SAP system (see Sections 13.4.1 to 13.4.3). This import option is similar to the preliminary import option when importing single change requests (see Section 13.2.3).
- **Overwrite originals**
  If a change request contains objects that originate in the target system, the import overwrites the existing original in the target system.
- **Overwrite objects in unconfirmed repairs**
  If a change request contains objects that are currently being repaired in the target system and that are not yet confirmed, the import ignores the repair and overwrites the object in the target system.

SAP recommends using export mode options only when necessary. They should not be used during every import of an import queue. [+]

13.2.3 Preliminary Imports

As an alternative to importing entire import queues, you can also import single change requests. This is called a preliminary import because it lets you send one change request as a preliminary import through the defined transport route. To minimize the risks associated with preliminary imports, the request remains in the import queue and is reimported the next time the entire import queue is imported. This helps ensure that export and import sequences are always the same.

To ensure object dependencies and consistency, SAP strongly recommends importing all or a collection of sequenced change requests. You should limit your use of preliminary imports to exceptional situations. [+]

As of Release 4.5, the default setting for importing individual change requests is to perform preliminary imports—although you can also deselect this function in expert mode (see the text that follows on this topic).

To import a single change request, perform the following steps:

1. From the IMPORT QUEUE screen, select the change request to be imported.
2. Choose REQUEST • IMPORT.
3. The IMPORT TRANSPORT REQUEST dialog box appears. If necessary, enter the target client number.
4. If you want to select special options, choose the EXPERT MODE icon (see the text that follows on this topic).
5. Choose CONTINUE.

Multiple Change Requests

You can select multiple change requests to be imported using a preliminary import. Select the change requests you want to import by positioning your cursor on the change requests and choose EDIT • SELECT • SELECT REQUEST or press [F9]. After the change requests have been selected, perform a preliminary import as described previously. Each highlighted change request is imported one after the other—they are not imported as a collection of change requests as is the case with IMPORT ALL (see Chapter 14, Section 14.1.5).

Expert Mode

If you have special import requirements for your preliminary import, use expert mode. Expert mode for preliminary imports allows you to specify the following:

- Import options
- Execution type

[+] Setting import options during the import of change requests should be done in exceptional situations only.

In expert mode, you can select the following IMPORT OPTIONS:

Import options

- **Preliminary import of transport request**
  When performing a preliminary import, the default setting is that the change request remains in the import queue and is reimported when you import the entire queue. This option is selected by default. As of Release 4.5, you are able to deselect this option. If you do, the change request remains in the import queue, but is not imported again with the next import of all waiting requests. To remove such a change request, you have to manually delete the change request from the import queue.

  [+] To ensure consistency and object dependencies, SAP strongly recommends that you do not deselect the preliminary import option.

- **Ignore that the transport request was already imported**
  If a change request has already been imported into the target system, this option allows you to import it again without error.

- **Overwrite originals**
  If a change request contains objects that originate in the target system, the import overwrites the existing original in the target system.

- **Overwrite objects in unconfirmed repairs**
  The import ignores any repairs and overwrites the unconfirmed object in the target system (see Section 13.2.2, Import All).

- **Ignore invalid transport type**
  This option overrides the transport profile parameters that exclude a transport type. For example, if the transport profile parameter `k_import` is set to FALSE, Workbench change requests (type K) are excluded from being imported. If this option is selected, transport profile parameters restricting the type of imports will be ignored, and, in this case, imports of Workbench change requests will be possible.

Execution types

In the expert mode for preliminary imports from within TMS, two selections for the execution of the import are available, as follows:

- Start import in foreground
- Start import in background

By default, individual imports are set to start in the foreground. It is unlikely that performing an import in the foreground will exceed the dialog work process runtime (300 seconds) because work process time is consumed only for receiving and displaying `tp` status messages, not for the time `tp` is actually running. Therefore, starting the import in the background makes sense only if you do not want to have the user session locked.

13.3 Managing Import Queues

To help manage single and multiple change requests, additional functionality is provided from within the IMPORT QUEUE screen. To use the selection option, choose EDIT • SELECT. You can use the following functionalities:

- Forwarding a change request
- Deleting a change request from an import queue
- Adding a change request to an import queue
- Moving the end mark in an import queue
- Performing checks on the import queue

[+] You can select multiple change requests in an import queue prior to performing different functions on those change requests. In earlier releases, only a single change request could be selected.

13.3.1 Forwarding a Change Request

The TMS enables you to manually forward a change request. When you *forward* a change request, you add it to the import queue of a selected SAP system. The target of a forwarded change request can be an SAP system or—with extended transport control in Release 4.5—a specific client within an SAP system. Forwarding of a change request is used to add a change request to an import queue outside of predefined transport routes and therefore should be used only in exceptional cases.

To forward a change request to a target system outside of predefined transport routes, proceed as follows:

1. From the IMPORT QUEUE screen, mark the respective change request.
2. Choose REQUEST • FORWARD • SYSTEM. Provide the name of the SAP system to which the change request should be forwarded. If extended transport control is active, you will be required to forward the change request to a client and system combination.

With extended transport control, you can forward a request into a specific client of the same system. To do this, from the IMPORT QUEUE screen, choose REQUEST • FORWARD • CLIENT.

If the source and the target systems belong to different transport groups, you must adjust the import queue of the target system. For more details on adjusting import queues, see Section 13.6.

Example: Forwarding a Change Request

A company has a four-system landscape that consists of the systems development, quality assurance, production, and training. The development system consolidates to the quality assurance system. A delivery route is specified between the quality assurance system and the production system, and then between the production system and the training system.

A program included in a change request is imported into the quality assurance system. It is urgently needed in the training system, but an import into the production system is not possible at this time. A manual forward of the change request that contains the respective program is performed to rush it to the training system before it has been imported into the production system.

13.3.2 Deleting a Change Request from an Import Queue

To delete a change request from an import queue, mark the change request in the IMPORT QUEUE screen and choose REQUEST • DELETE.

Object dependencies may cause inconsistencies in the target system after the next import. For example, if you delete a request containing a new data element, all other requests containing tables that depend on that data element will fail.

[+] To avoid inconsistencies, you are strongly advised not to delete individual change requests. Make your corrections in the development system and release a new request instead.

In some situations, deleting change requests from an import queue is necessary, as follows:

- Change requests from a client transport. After successful import of a client transport, the change requests for that client transport still remain in the import queue and will need to be deleted (see Chapter 9).
- If you have deselected the preliminary import option when importing a single change request, the change request will remain in the import queue and will need to be manually deleted after import. To do so, from the IMPORT QUEUE screen, select the change request with status REQUEST WAS ALREADY IMPORTED and choose EXTRAS • DELETE IMPORTED REQUESTS.

13.3.3 Adding a Change Request to an Import Queue

If you have manually copied a change request to the transport directory or if you want to reimport a change request that is no longer in the import queue, you have to manually add the change request to the respective import queue. To do this, choose EXTRAS • OTHER REQUESTS • ADD. Provide the change request ID for the change request to be added and press `Enter`. Note that if extended transport control is active, you will also have to enter a value for the target client.

13.3.4 Moving an End Mark

When an import queue is closed, an end mark is added at the very end of the import queue. To move the end mark to another position within the import queue, position the cursor on a change request and choose EDIT • MOVE END MARK. The end mark will then be positioned above the selected change request. For example, Figure 13.4 shows the result of selecting change request `DEVK900021` and then using the MOVE END MARK option.

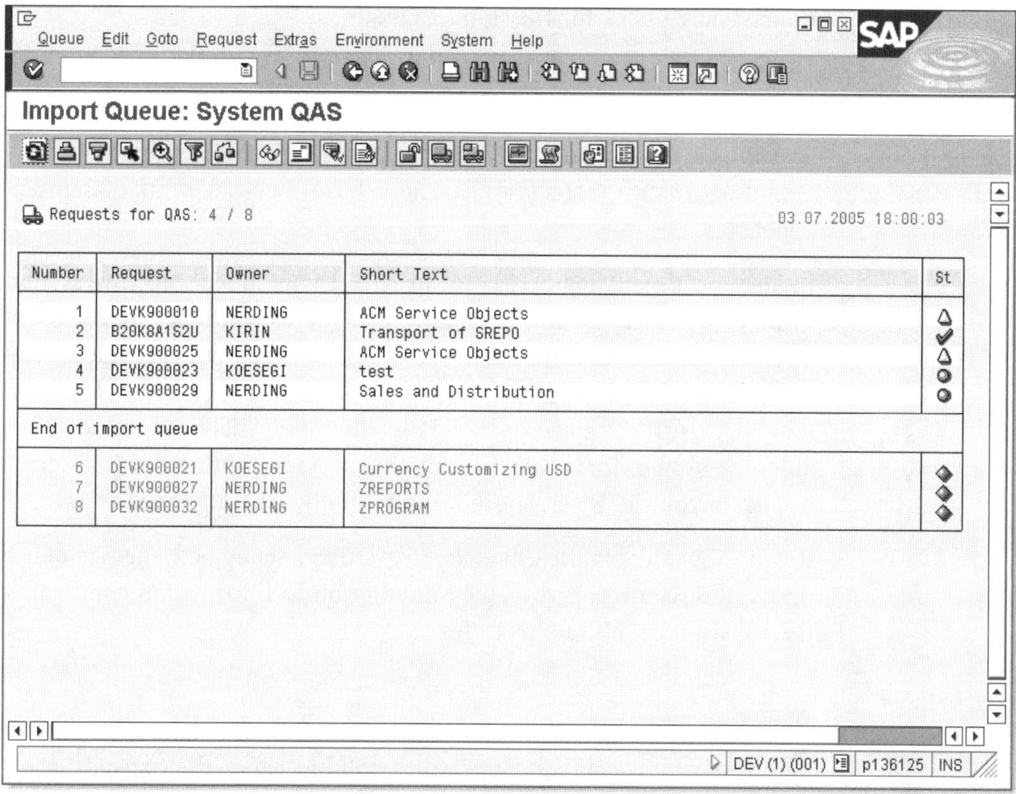

Figure 13.4 Moving an End Mark

13.3.5 Performing Checks

To ensure that your import runs smoothly, you should run checks on the import queue before performing the import. To start these checks, from the IMPORT QUEUE screen, choose QUEUE • CHECK. Then, choose one of the following checks:

- Consistency
- Transport tool
- Critical objects

Consistency Check for the Import Queue

This check function verifies that all data files and control files that belong to a change request exist in the transport directory and can be read.

Starting the check

To run this check, from the IMPORT OVERVIEW screen, choose IMPORT QUEUE • CHECK • CONSISTENCY. The CHECK IMPORT QUEUE dialog box appears.

By default, this dialog box is set to NO. If you choose NO, the system displays whether the corresponding files are available in the transport directory and whether they are readable. Consistent files are indicated by a check mark on the right side of the TMS: IMPORT QUEUE CHECK screen that appears. If the corresponding files are not available or are not readable, the system marks the files or the directory with an x. If an error occurred, you can access more information by clicking the x.

If you choose YES in the CHECK IMPORT QUEUE dialog box, the size of the files and directories is displayed in addition to information concerning the consistency of the directories.

Transport Tool Check

Before starting an import, it is also helpful to check the transport tools to ensure that they can function and have the appropriate settings for performing imports. You can check the transport tools for one or all SAP systems within a transport domain (except for virtual and external systems). The check examines the following:

- **tp interface**
  The status of the transport control program.
- **Transport profile**
  The readability of the transport profile at the operating system level.
- **RFC destination**
  The status and success of required RFC calls to the transport control program.
- **tp call**
  The status of the communication link between the transport control program and the database of the SAP system.

To perform a transport tool check, from the IMPORT QUEUE screen for an SAP system, choose QUEUE • CHECK • TRANSPORT TOOL. The TMS: CHECK TRANSPORT TOOL screen appears and indicates whether the transport tools have the appropriate settings for performing imports. To display more information about the individual tools and potential errors, expand the tree structure. A green check mark indicates a successful test. If a particular check is marked with an X, its check was not successful, indicating either an error at the operating system level or a problem with the current transport profile parameters.

Critical Objects

The TMS can search for objects that you have defined as critical. A *critical object* is an object that you expect to cause problems during import or an object that is critical for security. By defining critical objects, you can help protect against the import of objects into certain SAP systems that may cause serious errors or damage settings in the SAP system.

Authorization profiles

An example of a critical object is authorization profiles created in the development system that, for security reasons, you do not want to transport into the production system. You can define authorization profiles as critical objects in the production system. (The critical object list is specific to each SAP system in the system landscape—you have to define the critical objects for each target system within your landscape.) After the authorization profiles are defined in the critical object list, to ensure that change requests including authorization profiles are not accidentally imported, you need to perform a check for critical objects prior to each import.

To define critical objects, proceed as follows:

1. From the IMPORT OVERVIEW screen, choose EXTRAS • CRITICAL TRANSPORT OBJECTS.
2. Select YES.
3. To add an object to the table, switch to change mode by choosing TABLE VIEW • DISPLAY • CHANGE.
4. Choose EDIT • NEW ENTRIES.

5. Specify the critical objects. You can define an object as critical only if its object directory entry has a program ID of *R3TR* (see Chapter 10).
6. Save your entries.

[+] If you have defined critical objects for a system, you should always run the critical objects check on the import queue of that system before importing.

To start the check for critical objects in the import queue, from the IMPORT QUEUE screen, choose QUEUE • CHECK • CRITICAL OBJECTS. The system searches the import queue's object list for critical objects in the table of critical objects (see Figure 13.5). The results of the search are displayed in the TMS: CRITICAL OBJECTS IN REQUESTS screen.

Keep in mind that this check offers only a display function. Neither the check nor the definition of critical objects automatically prevents you from importing change requests that include critical objects. It is the responsibility of the system administrator to ensure that the respective change requests are not imported. He must also re-export any noncritical objects that are contained in the list of change requests into another change request from the source system. This must be done in a way that preserves the original sequence of the change requests.

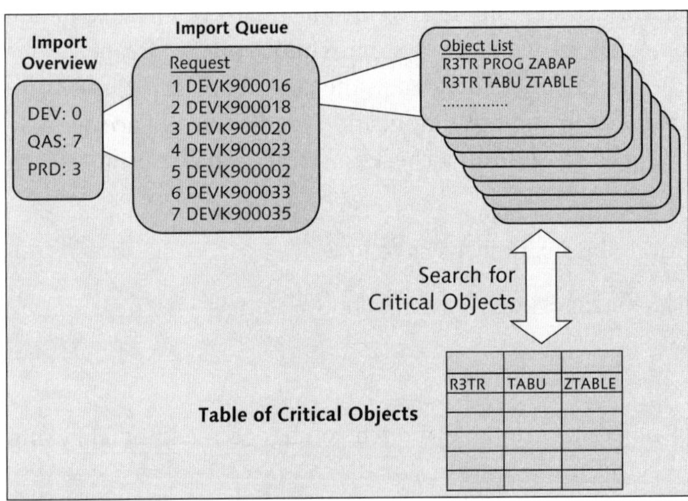

Figure 13.5 Scanning for Critical Objects

The critical objects check is only a display function. It is the responsibility of the person performing imports to manage critical objects that are identified during a critical object check. [+]

13.4 Scheduling Imports

After export, a change request is not automatically imported. To import the change requests, you have two options: You can perform a manual import, or schedule it as a job on the target system.

Even when scheduling a background job, you need to check the import results for problems. [+]

When planning imports, ensure that you include enough time to accommodate post-import tasks such as quality assurance testing. SAP recommends performing imports of entire import queues (*import all*) at regular intervals—for example, monthly, weekly, or daily. A more frequent import rate is not advisable. The import rate depends on how soon the changes are required in the production system.

Because imports into a production system affect the runtime environment, you should schedule them for times when they are least likely to affect running transactions and programs (see Chapter 14). This is especially important when you import data into a production system, because an import can invalidate certain SAP ERP buffer contents, forcing them to be reloaded and, as a result, reducing performance. Furthermore, inconsistencies may affect running programs and their environment. You should schedule imports into production systems to run at night and in the background, or perform a detailed check on the jobs that would be running at the same time and monitor the effects carefully. Before importing into a production system, perform a complete SAP system backup.

Ideally, no users should be working in an SAP system when change requests are imported. This is particularly important when importing into the production system. For this reason, you should make sure that you choose appropriate times and send a system message telling users to log off.

13.4.1 Importing into Multiple Clients

Often, customers want to import change requests into multiple clients throughout the system landscape—a procedure that poses certain problems. These problems and their possible solutions are outlined in more detail in this section.

Figure 13.6 shows an example of transport route requirements for imports into multiple clients. After the release of change requests from the CUST client, the changes are to be imported into not only the TEST and SAND clients in the development system, but also into the QTST and TRNG clients in the quality assurance system. After the change requests are imported into the QTST client, they will be transported to the TRNG client in the quality assurance system and the PROD client in the production system.

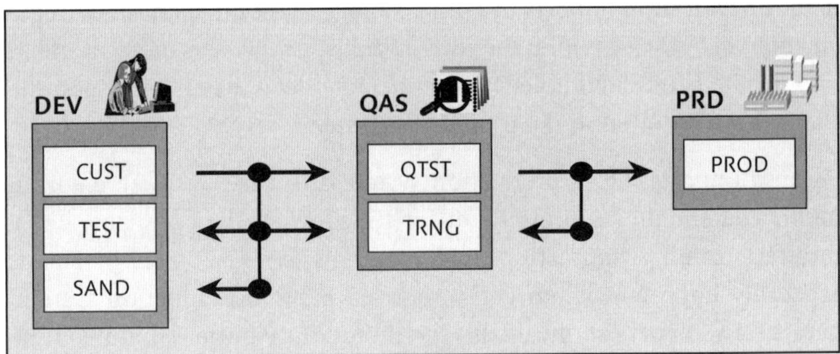

Figure 13.6 Transporting into Multiple Clients

Extended transport control

You can rely on extended transport control to ensure that all clients in the system landscape contain the latest changes that originate in client CUST. The change requests are automatically placed in the import queues of specified SAP systems and clients. Extended transport control also ensures that client-independent objects in a change request are imported into an SAP system only once, protecting newer versions of objects from being overwritten. For example, if a change request that contains an ABAP program is released from the CUST client, the program itself is imported into the quality assurance system only once, while the change request may be in the import queue for multiple clients. On the other hand, client-specific changes are imported into each client.

As of Release 4.5, you can use extended transport control to set up client-specific transport routes, which allows you to import into multiple clients in a single system at the same or different times (see Chapter 8). [+]

13.4.2 Importing into Multiple Clients without Extended Transport Control

If extended transport control is not available or if it is not activated, you cannot take advantage of client-specific transport routes. Instead, you must manually import the change requests that originate in client CUST to all of the clients in the system landscape. Although it is possible to import change requests into the quality assurance client and then wait to import them into the other clients in the same system at a later time, this requires complex management of change requests and import queues.

Without client-specific transport routes defined using extended transport control, you have to manually import the change requests several times, once for each client in the system. [+]

The standard is that at the end of an import of the entire queue, the imported change requests are removed from the import queue of the target system. If you want to import change requests into another client, you will want to import the change requests and keep them in the import queue in their prescribed order. This can be accomplished by using the preliminary import option during import.

Importing change requests using the preliminary import option requires that you decide the next client to which the change request should be imported. You also have to ensure that the change requests are imported into all of the different clients in the system. Managing imports into multiple clients at different times requires that you track change requests outside of the SAP system and the SAP ERP transport tools.

Sequential import process

SAP recommends that you import change requests into multiple clients in a sequential process. This ensures consistency in the import queues. It also ensures that all clients have received the latest change requests. If this is not possible, use client copy tools to assist in maintaining the consistency of different clients in the target system. For example, a data conversion test client could be re-created periodically as a copy of the quality assurance test client. Or, the training client could receive the latest Customizing changes on a weekly basis through *Client Copy according to Transport Request.*

The easiest way to support imports into multiple clients is to schedule them for a time when a group of change requests are sequentially imported into all clients within the quality assurance system, starting with the quality assurance client. This way, the change requests are first imported into the quality assurance client—the other clients wait until their scheduled times to receive the import.

13.4.3 Importing an Import Queue into Multiple Clients

To manually perform the import of a collection of change requests into multiple clients, first close the import queue of the target system. Then, to keep the change requests in the import queue in their correct order for import into other clients, import the import queue into all of the target clients except the last target client, using a special import option. When you perform the import into the last target client, perform an import with no import option.

To perform a preliminary import into multiple clients, proceed as follows:

1. From the IMPORT QUEUE screen, choose QUEUE • START IMPORT.
2. In the START IMPORT dialog box, enter the respective target client.
3. To perform preliminary imports of the entire queue, choose EXPERT MODE and select the SELECT ALL REQUESTS FOR NEW IMPORT import option.
4. Choose CONTINUE.

For the last client to receive changes, you should perform the import without selecting the expert mode option for a preliminary import. This final import removes the change requests from the target system's import queue.

Importing single change requests into multiple clients

For all of the target clients except the last target client, to transport a single change request originating in client CUST to all other clients within the system landscape, follow these steps:

1. From the IMPORT QUEUE screen, select the change request to be imported.
2. Choose REQUEST • IMPORT.
3. In the IMPORT TRANSPORT REQUEST dialog box that appears, enter the respective target client number.
4. Choose CONTINUE to initiate the import.

Remember that by default, single imports are set to PRELIM. IMPORT OF TRANSPORT REQ in the expert mode. Therefore, you do not need to specify the expert mode. For the last client to receive changes, you will have to change the expert mode. To do so, and to thus remove the change request from the import queue of the quality assurance system, follow these steps:

1. From the IMPORT QUEUE screen, select the change request to be imported.
2. Choose REQUEST • IMPORT.
3. In the IMPORT TRANSPORT REQUEST dialog box that appears, enter the respective target client number.
4. Choose EXPERT MODE. Deselect the PRELIM. IMPORT OF TRANSPORT REQ import option.
5. Choose CONTINUE to initiate the import.

13.5 Monitoring Imports

The TMS provides you with several tools for monitoring transport activities in your transport domain. Keep in mind that to open these tools, you have to drill down into them successively from the previous tool.

Additional information on TMS activities is provided by the Alert Monitor, which was discussed in Chapter 8. For details on monitoring and troubleshooting, see Chapter 14.

13.5.1 Import Monitor

To display status information about currently running and completed imports, start the *import monitor*. To access the import monitor for a specific SAP system, from the IMPORT OVERVIEW screen, position the cursor on the system and choose GOTO • IMPORT MONITOR. The import monitor displays information for each `tp` import command, regardless of whether it imported a single change request or the entire queue. The information includes:

Information

- `tp` command
- Start mode (online or offline)
- Start time (date and time)
- `tp` process ID
- Last change (date and time)
- `tp` status (current status of the `tp` command)
- Maximum return code
- `tp` message

In the TMS IMPORT MONITOR screen, to update the display of a currently running import in the import monitor, choose EDIT • REFRESH. If you notice that the last change date of an import has not changed in a long time and the status of the `tp` command is STILL RUNNING, it may be due to one of the following reasons:

- The data volume of the change request(s) is large.
- An error has occurred that is shown in the `tp` system log.
- `tp` has been terminated with operating system tools.

The `tp` message indicates the step currently being processed and then either the successful completion of the import or the error that last occurred.

13.5.2 tp System Log

The `tp` system log displays an overview of the transport activities for the current SAP system—for example, all `tp` calls and errors, as well as the return codes (which indicate the success of each import). To drill down to the tp system log, from the TMS IMPORT MONITOR screen, choose GOTO • TP SYSTEM LOG. The TP SYSTEM LOG screen appears. The file is stored at the operating system level in the transport directory's `log` subdirectory. This file is also known as the *SLOG*.

13.5.3 Action Log File

The *action log* contains the transport activities and return codes for all transport activities. Each transport group has its own action log file. To drill down to the action log, from the TP SYSTEM LOG screen, choose GOTO • TRANSPORT STEPS. The TRANSPORT STEP MONITOR screen appears. This file is stored at the operating system level in the transport directory's `log` subdirectory. This file is also known as the ALOG.

13.5.4 Single Step Log Files

For each transport activity, the system writes a log file called the *single step log file*. If an error is indicated in the import monitor, you can drill down to the `tp` system log and to the action log. From the TRANSPORT STEP MONITOR screen, you can open the single log file to analyze the error. To open the single log files, in the action log file screen, position the cursor on a change request and choose REQUEST • LOGS.

13.6 Transporting between Transport Groups

Multiple transport directories

Usually, all SAP systems in a transport domain share a common transport directory. In certain situations, however, multiple transport directories may be required (see Chapters 7 and 8), and the transport domain will consist of multiple transport groups, one for each transport directory used. The TMS supports transports between transport groups. Each transport group reflects the configuration of the transport domain; that is, each transport group includes import queues for all SAP systems belonging to the transport domain. Nevertheless, change requests can be imported into a target system only if they exist in the import queue of the transport group to which the target system belongs.

[+] If more than one transport group exists, each transport group contains a local import queue for each SAP system belonging to the transport domain.

After a change request has been released, it is stored in the transport directory of the source system and recorded in the local import queue of the target system, where *local* means that this import queue belongs to the transport group of the source system.

If the source and the target system belong to different transport groups, the import queue of the target transport group has to be adjusted. Figure 13.7 shows a simplified example of this process, based on the sample systems DEV and QAS.

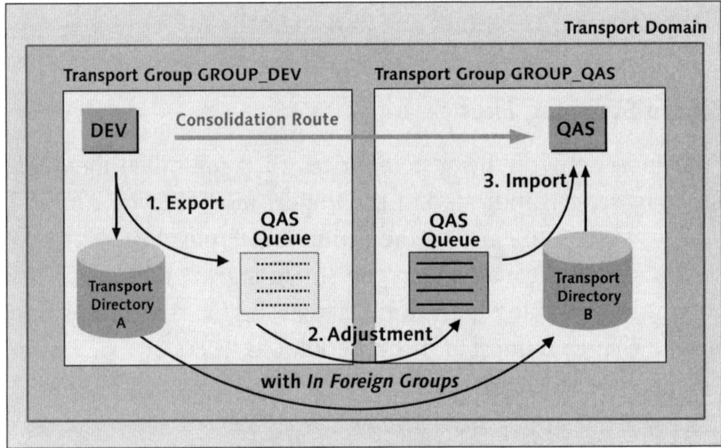

Figure 13.7 Transport Between Transport Groups

Figure 13.7 shows a system landscape with two transport groups: GROUP_DEV and GROUP_QAS. Customizing and development changes are performed in the development system DEV. A consolidation route is defined between DEV and the quality assurance system QAS. When a change request is released and exported from DEV, the data file and control file are created on the transport directory local to DEV—the transport directory for GROUP_DEV. Also, the change request is added to the import queue of QAS—the import queue that is local to the development system. For an import of the change request to take place, the data file and control file as well as the import queue entry need to be local to the quality assurance system. In other words, the files need be adjusted from the transport group GROUP_DEV to GROUP_QAS. The process for moving the required files and entries from one transport group to another is known as *adjusting*.

Adjusting Transports

Before change requests can be imported into a system whose transport group is different from its delivering system, the different transport groups need to be adjusted. The TMS adjusts the import queue in the target system's transport group to search for change requests waiting for import into the target SAP ERP system that are stored in transport directories belonging to other transport groups, and to add these change requests to the transport directory of the target system's transport group.

Procedure

You have to perform three steps when transporting between SAP systems that belong to different transport groups (as shown previously in Figure 13.7):

1. The user releases and exports a change request.
2. The person responsible for imports adjusts the import queue.
3. The user imports the change request into the target system.

To perform this adjustment, from the IMPORT QUEUE screen of the target system, choose EXTRAS • OTHER REQUESTS • IN FOREIGN GROUPS. Similarly, to adjust an import queue with requests originating in an external group, choose EXTRAS • OTHER REQUESTS • IN EXTERNAL GROUPS. When you confirm the transfer of the change requests, the TMS will transfer them to the import queue of the target system (QAS). The corresponding data files and control files are also transferred. If an error occurs, you can still restart the adjustment despite a message that appears saying that the import queue is locked. In this situation, you can ignore the message.

13.7 Transporting between Transport Domains

A transport domain is an administrative unit. Generally, all SAP systems that are connected by transport routes and that have a regular transport flow belong to the same transport domain. Even if you are forced to use more than one transport directory, by taking advantage of the concept of transport groups, all SAP systems can be kept in one domain and administered centrally by the domain controller.

Configuring multiple domains

Occasionally, there may be reason to have more than one transport domain. For example, global companies or groups may configure one domain for the headquarters and one domain for each subsidiary. Possible reasons for multiple transport domains are as follows:

- For organizational or political reasons you must have separate administrative units.
- The number of SAP systems (50 to 100) is too high to be administered within one transport domain.
- Because of certain network limitations or considerations it is advantageous from a technical perspective to have separately administered transport domains.

Before configuring several transport domains, determine whether this is really necessary. Transports between SAP systems in different transport domains are possible, but increase the administrative workload.

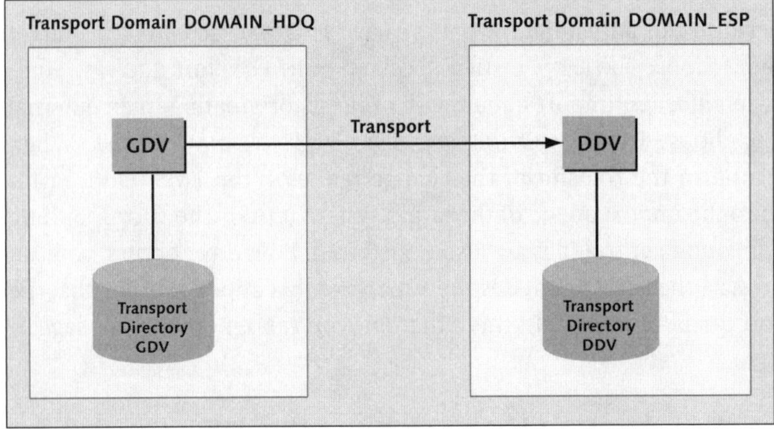

Figure 13.8 Logical Transport Flow between Two Transport Domains

Figure 13.8 shows the simplified representation of two SAP systems—GDV and DDV—that belong to different transport domains: DOMAIN_HDQ and DOMAIN_ESP. GDV is the SAP system for the headquarters of a multinational organization, and DDV is the SAP system of a subsidiary in Spain belonging to the organization. Only the involved systems are shown in this example. The system administrator wants to transport from the SAP system GDV into DDV.

13.7.1 Configuration

External transport directory

To implement the transport route shown in Figure 13.8, the system administrator has to create an external system DDV in DOMAIN_HDQ and an external system GDV in DOMAIN_ESP. The external systems are placeholders for the real systems. For both external systems, a transport directory—called the *external transport directory*— that is accessible from both transport domains must be defined. Within each domain, one available SAP system has to be defined as the *communications system* for the respective external system and must have access to the external transport directory. Figure 13.9 shows that GDV serves as the communications system for the external system DDV in DOMAIN_HDQ, and DDV serves as the communications system for the external system GDV in DOMAIN_ESP.

To configure the transports between two domains, follow these steps:

1. Manually create the external transport directory (see Chapters 7 and 8). Ensure that all transport subdirectories exist.
2. To ensure access to the external transport directory, check whether the communications systems in both transport domains have read and write authorizations on all subdirectories. In the example in Figure 13.9, all files that are written by user GDVADM from DOMAIN_HDQ into the external transport directory have to be readable and replaceable by user DDVADM (the reverse must also be possible).
3. Create an external system in both transport domains (see Chapter 8). Ensure that the SID of the external system in one transport domain is identical to the SID of the SAP system in the other domain, and vice versa.
4. To check the access authorizations in both transport domains, from the initial SYSTEMS OVERVIEW screen, choose SAP SYSTEM • CHECK • TRANSPORT DIRECTORY (see Chapter 8). The CHECK TRANSPORT DIRECTORY screen appears.
5. To check whether discrepancies exist between the transport group configuration of the TMS and the configuration of the transport directories at the operating system level in both transport domains, from the CHECK TRANSPORT DIRECTORY screen mentioned in step 4, choose GOTO • TRANSPORT GROUPS.

6. Configure a transport route from the available SAP system GDV to the external system DDV in DOMAIN_HDQ. The transport route can be a consolidation route or a delivery route.

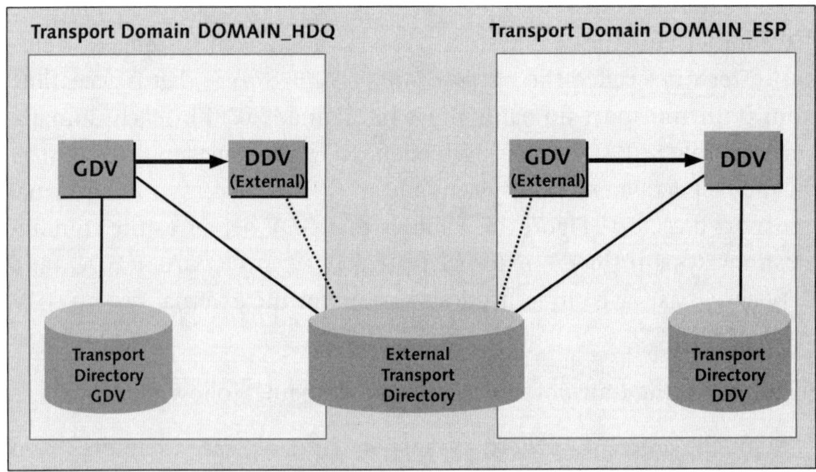

Figure 13.9 Configuration of the Transport Domains

13.7.2 Transport

Transporting change requests between transport domains—in the previous example, from GDV in DOMAIN_HDQ to DDV in DOMAIN_ESP—uses the external transport directory. In general, two adjustment steps are required (see Figure 13.10):

- On the source transport domain (DOMAIN_HDQ), all transport files such as data files and control files that belong to change requests that are waiting for import into the external system (DDV) must be copied into the external transport directory.
- On the target transport domain (DOMAIN_ESP), the files from the external transport directory must be copied into the target transport directory, that is, the transport directory of the target system DDV in DOMAIN_ESP.

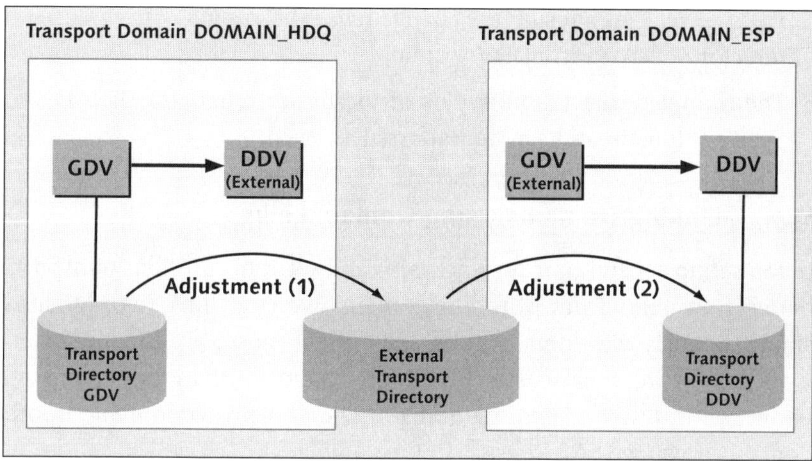

Figure 13.10 Adjusting Import Queues

To transport a change request as shown in the example in Figure 13.10—that is, from GDV in DOMAIN_HDQ to DDV in DOMAIN_ESP—proceed as follows.

In the transport domain for the headquarters:

1. Release the change request in the "real" GDV system. As a result, the corresponding files are written to the transport directory of GDV. Because of the configured consolidation route in this example, DDV is specified as the target system of the change request. If the configured transport route is a delivery route, the change request would have to be imported into GDV instead of being released.
2. For the first adjustment step, use the TMS to search for the change request. To do this, from the IMPORT QUEUE screen of the external system DDV, choose EXTRAS • OTHER REQUESTS • IN FOREIGN GROUPS.

In the transport domain for Spain:

1. For the second adjustment step, use the TMS to search for the change request. To do this, from the IMPORT QUEUE screen of the "real" DDV system, choose EXTRAS • OTHER REQUESTS • IN EXTERNAL GROUPS.

2. Press [Enter]. As a result, the change request is copied to the transport directory of the "real" DDV system.
3. The change request is now part of the import queue of DDV in the Spanish domain and can be imported as usual.

13.7.3 Linking Domains Using Domain Links

If you set up several transport domains and want to carry out transports between systems from different domains, you can link two domains simultaneously via domain links. For this purpose, a permanent network connection must exist between the systems, such as the connection between the systems within a domain. The domain controllers of both domains must use SAP Release 4.6C or higher.

To link two domains via a domain link, the connection between the domains must be requested and confirmed.

Requesting a Link Between Two Domains

To request a link between two domains, proceed as follows:

1. Log on to one of the two domain controllers.
2. Call Transaction STMS.
3. Select OVERVIEW • SYSTEMS. You are now in the system overview.
4. Select SAP SYSTEM • CREATE • DOMAIN LINK. The REQUEST DOMAIN LINK dialog box opens.
5. Enter the system name, host name, and system number of the domain controller for which you want to request the domain link, and confirm your entries.

Your SAP system automatically performs the following actions:

- The required RFC destinations are generated.
- The address data of the controller is sent to the external domain controller.

The system overview now shows that the domain link to the external domain has been requested.

Confirming a Link Between Two Domains

For security reasons you must confirm the link between the two domains with the external domain controller. Proceed as follows:

1. Log on to the external domain controller.
2. Call Transaction STMS.
3. Select OVERVIEW • SYSTEMS. You are now in the system overview.
4. Place the cursor on the domain controller that has requested the domain link, and select SAP SYSTEM • ACCEPT.
5. Confirm the security prompt and distribute the configuration.

The two domain controllers now exchange all of the required system information for the two domains. This information is distributed to all systems of the domain you are currently logged on to, and a transport profile is generated that contains all systems of both domains.

Distributing the configuration

The information on the systems of the external domain is not automatically distributed to the systems of the domain in which you requested the domain link. You must therefore distribute the new configuration to those systems.

Result

A domain link has now been established between the two transport domains. The system overview and import overview now display all systems from both domains and you can carry out transports between systems from different domains. Note that only systems from Release 4.6C onwards can be displayed.

13.8 TMS Authorization

The TMS uses RFCs for the connections between the SAP systems in a transport domain (see Chapter 8). Performing imports is not restricted to the domain controller. With proper authorizations, you can initiate imports into any SAP system from each SAP system within the domain. When using the TMS, a user's authorization is checked twice during the import process:

1. To initiate an import in the TMS, the system validates the user's authorization in the current client.
2. The TMS makes a remote function call to the target system. The user must log on to the target system with a username and password. After the user's authorization is validated in the target system, the import process begins in this target system.

Authorizations

To perform imports using the TMS, a user requires authorization in the client from which the import command will be issued as well as in the target system. This authorization concept allows you to specify from which client and into which target SAP systems a user may perform imports.

SAP provides the authorization S_CTS_ADMIN for importing change requests using the TMS. This authorization is required to confirm that imports into the target system are allowed.

No SAP profile exists to simply allow import functionality. You can assign the authorization profile S_A.SYSTEM to users who need to perform CTS administrative activities, including the initialization of the Change and Transport Organizer as well as all TMS functions—for example, setting up the TMS to perform imports. As an alternative, you may want to give a user the ability to perform imports without the ability to initialize or set up any portion of the CTS. Rather than assigning the profile S_A.SYSTEM, you can restrict this user to performing imports by creating a new authorization profile for the authorization object S_CTS_ADMI and assigning the user the new profile. This authorization profile then prevents the user from accessing administrative functions.

13.9 Questions

1. **Which of the following statements are correct with regard to import queues?**

   A. Import queues are the TMS representation of the import buffer at the operating system level.

   B. You have to manipulate import queues to transport change requests.

C. Import queues should be closed before starting an import using TMS.

D. You can import only an entire import queue.

2. **Which of the following statements are correct with regard to preliminary imports?**

A. SAP recommends using preliminary imports rather than imports of entire queues.

B. Preliminary imports should be performed only in exceptional cases.

C. Change requests imported as preliminary imports remain in the import queue.

D. Change requests are deleted from the import queue after preliminary imports. This prevents them from being imported again with the next import of the entire import queue.

3. **Which of the following statements is correct with regard to imports into an SAP system?**

A. Imports can be performed only by using the START IMPORT functionality in the TMS.

B. Imports can be performed only by using `tp` commands at the operating system level to prepare the import queue and then using the START IMPORT functionality in the TMS.

C. Imports can be performed only by using `tp` commands at the operating system level.

D. Imports can be performed by using either a `tp` command at the operating system level or the TMS import functionality.

4. **Which of the following statements is correct with regard to transports between different transport groups?**

A. They are not possible.

B. They can be performed only by using `tp` at the operating system level with special options.

C. They can be performed using the TMS with special options provided by the expert mode.

D. They require you to adjust the corresponding import queues.

5. **Which of the following statements are correct with regard to transports between different transport domains?**

   A. They are not possible.

   B. They require you to create a virtual system and a virtual transport directory.

   C. They require you to configure identical transport groups within the different transport domains.

   D. They require you to create an external system and an external transport directory.

   E. They require you to adjust the corresponding import queues.

This chapter provides basic information about the tools that perform changes to the system in the background, while you are using administrative interfaces such as the TMS. You also learn how these can be used for special tasks and how important log files are used for error analysis.

14 Technical Insight into the Import Process

The previous chapter described how imports are performed using the Transport Management System (TMS). However, when you use the TMS interface, you are not aware of the activities that take place at the operating system level during imports, such as calls for the transport control program `tp`. This chapter provides you with insight into the technical side of the import process at the operating system level. You will learn the following:

- How to perform imports at the operating system level using `tp`.
- About the `tp` processing sequence and the import steps.
- How to use log files and return codes for troubleshooting.
- How buffer synchronization affects transports.
- How to identify file naming conventions in the transport directory.
- About the different transport tools, their activities, and the way they communicate.

By covering these issues, this chapter provides system administrators with the background knowledge needed to use `tp` at the operating system level and to perform successful troubleshooting. This chapter is also of interest to project leads because learning details about what happens beyond the TMS—for example, the `tp` processing sequence and the buffer synchronization—enables a better understanding of the concepts and strategies that were introduced in Part 1 of this book.

14.1 The Transport Control Program tp

The transport control program `tp` is a tool at the operating system level that uses special programs (such as C programs), operating system commands, and ABAP programs in SAP systems to control transports between SAP systems. Accordingly, `tp` stands for "transports and programs."

Functionality `tp` controls the exports and imports of objects between SAP systems by ensuring that the steps for exporting and importing are performed in the correct order and that the change requests are exported and imported in the same order.

As a rule, it is not necessary to call `tp` directly because you can perform most transport activities using the TMS. Nevertheless, you may occasionally need to use `tp` commands at the operating system level instead of the TMS, or in conjunction with the TMS. With each new release, SAP offers more advanced transport functionality through the TMS. Although the TMS provides a wide range of functions, to perform certain tasks, such as cleaning up the transport directory, you must still call `tp` directly.

14.1.1 Prerequisites

To use `tp`, the following prerequisites must be fulfilled (for details, see Chapter 7):

- All SAP systems in the transport domain must have a unique system name (SID).
- Each SAP system involved must have access to a correctly installed transport directory.
- The transport profile must be maintained correctly. The transport profile configures the transport control program `tp`.
- Each source system and each target system must have at least two background work processes.
- The transport dispatcher `RDDIMPDP` must be scheduled as an event-periodic background job in each SAP system that acts as a source system for exports or a target system for imports.

Authorizations for Using tp

Because tp is an operating system level command, you require operating system level authorization to access it. To call tp, you have to log on to the operating system of the computer that houses the transport directory of the target system as one of the following users:

- <sid>adm on Unix and Windows
- <SID>OPR on AS/400 platforms

Typically, only technical consultants and system administrators have access to the operating system level and therefore are responsible for issuing tp commands. If necessary, you can write scripts to allow users to perform imports without logging on as user <sid>adm or <SID>OPR.

14.1.2 Command Syntax

To call tp directly at the operating system level, follow these steps:

1. Log on to the operating system.
2. Change to subdirectory bin in the transport directory.
3. Execute a tp command with the following syntax:

```
tp <command> [argument(s)] [option(s)]
```

tp commands

Table 14.1 contains a list of tp commands that may be helpful for troubleshooting or for everyday operations.

tp Command	Function
tp help	Provides general information about tp functionality—for example, about syntax and available tp commands.
tp <command>	Describes the syntax and function of the specified command.
tp go <SID>	Checks the database destination by displaying the environmental variables required for accessing the database of a specific SAP system. To do this, tp checks the values in the transport profile. Note that this command does not actually establish a database connection.

Table 14.1 Helpful tp Commands

tp Command	Function
tp connect <SID>	Checks whether a connection to the database of the specified system can be established.
tp showinfo <change request>	Displays information about a specific change request, including the owner and the type of request.
tp count <SID>	Displays the number of change requests waiting to be imported into the specified SAP system.
tp checkimpdp <SID>	Displays how the transport dispatcher RDDIMPDP is scheduled for the specified SAP system.
tp showparams <SID>	Displays all current transport profile parameter settings for the specified SAP system.

Table 14.1 Helpful tp Commands (Cont.)

14.1.3 Import Queues and Import Buffers

Transport directory buffer

In the previous chapter, you learned how to use the import queue in TMS to manage and import change requests. At the operating system level, the same change requests are contained in the import buffer. The transport directory's `buffer` subdirectory contains an import buffer for each system in the transport group. The buffer file is named after the corresponding system ID and contains transport control information such as the following:

Control information for transports

- Which change requests should be imported
- The order to follow when importing the change request
- The possible import options (explained in the section "Import Options")
- The import steps (explained in the section "Import Steps")

Import queues are the TMS representation in the SAP system of the buffer files located at the operating system level. Import queues show all change requests listed in the corresponding import buffer.

When an end mark is set in the TMS, the change requests that will not be included in the next import are grayed out in the import queue. By definition, these change requests no longer belong to the import queue. As a result, more change requests may belong to the import buffer than to the import queue. For example, in Figure 14.1, the import queue displays the four change requests before the end mark as included in the next import, whereas the three change requests after the end mark would be grayed out—that is, they are not included in the next import.

End marks

In an import queue, an end mark is indicated by the END OF IMPORT QUEUE statement. At the operating system level, the import buffer shows the term STOPMARK (see Figure 14.1) to indicate the end mark. Regardless of where the marker is created, it is always set in both the import buffer and the import queue. Only one end marker or stopmark can exist in an import queue or buffer.

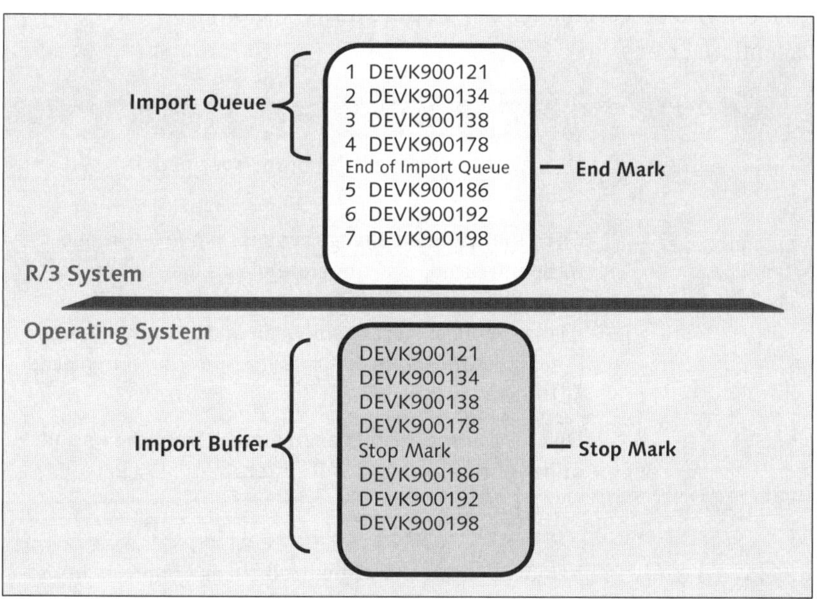

Figure 14.1 Import Queue and Import Buffer

To set an end mark, and therefore simultaneously set the stopmark, close the IMPORT QUEUE by choosing QUEUE • CLOSE from the TMS import queue screen. The operating system level equivalent is the command `tp setstopmark <SID>`. If you have not set the end mark/stopmark before starting an import, `tp` will automatically execute this command and place a stopmark at the end of the existing import queue, immediately after the import command has been issued.

Remove marks

To manually remove an end mark/stopmark, open the import queue from the TMS import screen by choosing QUEUE • OPEN. The operating system equivalent is the command `tp delstopmark <SID>`. This command is usually not needed because `tp` will automatically remove the marker after an import process has been successfully completed.

tp Commands for Import Buffers

In addition to the `tp` commands already mentioned, you can use the `tp` commands listed in Table 14.2 to access and maintain import buffers.

[+] When you access import buffers, it results mostly in mixing up the correct order of the change requests and thus may cause serious inconsistencies. The `tp` commands for import buffers should be used only in exceptional cases.

Command	Description
`tp showbuffer <SID>`	Displays the buffer entries of the specified SAP system.
`tp addtobuffer <change request> <SID>`	Adds the specified change request as the last request to be imported, and therefore places it at the end of the import buffer of the specified SAP system. If the change request has already been added to this buffer, it will be removed from its current position and placed at the end of the buffer.
`tp delfrombuffer <change request> <SID>`	Deletes the specified change request from the import buffer of the specified SAP system.
`tp cleanbuffer <SID>`	Removes successfully imported change requests from the import buffer of the specified SAP system. If you perform an import of an entire queue (that is, an *import all*), `tp` automatically executes this command at the end of the import.

Table 14.2 Commands Affecting Import Buffers

All commands listed in Table 14.2 affect both the import buffer and the related import queue. If you execute any of these `tp` commands at the operating system level, you must refresh the import queue display in the TMS to see the results.

The import buffer is the basis of all operations, regardless of whether `tp` is called through the TMS or at the operating system level. [+]

14.1.4 Performing Imports Using tp

Although SAP recommends that you use the TMS to perform imports, you may need to use `tp` commands for the following reasons:

- To script the import process so that it can be automated and scheduled
- If you use third-party tools

The `tp` commands allow you to perform imports of all change requests (*import all*) as well as imports of single change requests (PRELIMINARY IMPORTS).

Importing All Change Requests in the Import Buffer

To import all of the change requests in the import buffer, execute the `tp` command `tp import all <target SID> [client=<target client number>`.

If you are using the TMS to import an entire queue, the TMS will automatically trigger this `tp` command at the operating system level. The command imports all change requests before the end mark/stopmark in their export sequence into the target system and specified target client number. If no target client number is provided, the change requests are imported into a target client with the same client ID as the source client.

As already mentioned in Chapter 6, if change requests near the start of the import and change requests near the end of the import affect the same object, the version of the object at the end of the import will overwrite the earlier versions with the latest changes. This ensures that incorrect object versions that have been corrected will not affect your production environment (see also Section 14.1.5, "tp Processing Sequence", later in this chapter).

The command `tp import` is reentrant. If an error occurs during import, after you have eliminated the cause of the error and restarted `tp`, `tp` will automatically restart the import at the point where it was interrupted. [+]

Importing Individual Change Requests

To import a single change request, execute the `tp` command `tp import <change request> <target SID> client=<target client number> u0`. This is the operating system equivalent of the TMS function PRELIMINARY IMPORT.

[+] To ensure object dependencies and consistency, SAP strongly recommends using the IMPORT ALL function.

To ensure that objects that were imported individually are not overwritten by an older version, always use the preliminary import option `u0` (see the following section "Import Options") to import individual change requests. If you use this import option, the change request will remain in the import queue. When the entire import queue is later imported, the request will automatically be imported again in the correct export sequence.

SAP recommends avoiding the import of individual requests without this import option, because the export sequence will not be maintained. Consequently, newer versions of objects may be overwritten by older versions when the entire import queue is imported.

Import Options

Unconditional modes

When performing imports in the TMS, you can select import options using expert mode (see Chapter 13). Import options are also referred to as *unconditional modes*. At the operating system level, unconditional modes are options you can assign to `tp` commands to override specific rules of the Change and Transport System (CTS).

Each unconditional mode is represented by a digit. To use an unconditional mode, add a leading `u` followed by a concatenated list of single digits representing the different unconditional modes that should affect the `tp` command. For example, if you want to import a change request that should be kept in the import queue after the import, add `u0`. If you also want to ignore that originals in the target system are overwritten by imported objects, you can specify `u02` as follows: `tp import <change request> <SID> u02`.

Use unconditional modes carefully. SAP recommends transporting according to the rules of the Change and Transport System (CTS). [+]

Table 14.3 lists the unconditional modes you can use together with `tp` commands for performing imports.

In the UMODE column of the import buffer and also in the UMODES column of the import queue in the TMS, you may find a character that indicates certain conditions for the next `import all` caused by a previous import with the overtaker option (`u0`). Table 14.4 lists the possible letters and the corresponding conditions for the next import of all change requests waiting for import.

Unconditional Modes	Description
0	This option is used to perform a preliminary import of a change request. After import, the change request remains in the import buffer and is marked to be imported again. This import option is also called *overtaker*.
1	Although the change request has already been imported, `tp` will import it again when the entire import queue is imported.
2	Objects in change requests will overwrite the original objects in the target system.
6	Objects in change requests will overwrite objects that are currently being repaired in the target system and that have not yet been confirmed.
8	This option will ignore transport restrictions for table delivery classes.
9	This option will override certain transport profile settings that otherwise would have prevented the change request from being imported. For example, although the transport profile parameter `t_import` has been set to FALSE, change requests resulting from a transport of copies (type T) will be imported.

Table 14.3 Unconditional Modes

Indicator	Description
I	The import of the change request will be repeated from the beginning.
J	The import of the change request into the respective client will be repeated from the beginning, but client-independent objects will not be imported again.
F	The buffer entry is in the wrong position. `tp` will resolve this problem by implicitly executing the command `tp addtobuffer`.

Table 14.4 Indicators in the Import Buffer

Importing into Multiple Clients

To perform imports into multiple clients, you can use the TMS and its import options and the extended transport control (see Chapter 13). If you do not use the extended transport control, you must carry out imports at the operating-system level using `tp` with specific information.

To import change requests into the client with the same number as the source client, execute a regular `tp` command without any import options: `tp import all <target SID>`. This can be bypassed by specifying the client name as follows: `tp import all <target SID> client=<target client number>`.

These commands will ensure that a single client receives all client-dependent changes recorded in the change requests and that the SAP system will receive all client-independent changes. However, if several target clients exist, you encounter problems because:

Problems with multiple target clients

- Only one target client can be specified.
- The change request will be deleted from the import buffer after a successful import and therefore cannot be imported into other clients. This will result in problems if other clients are waiting to receive the changes.

One solution is to specify the preliminary import option `u0`. This import option will keep the change request in the buffer so that it can be imported again when the entire import queue is imported.

Example: Importing into Multiple Clients

A company's quality assurance system has three clients:

- Client 100 for business integration validation
- Client 200 for testing data migration routines
- Client 300 for user training

Because the company is using Release 4.0B, they cannot use the extended transport control with its client-specific transport routes. Therefore, the import queue of the quality assurance system contains a list of change requests that need to be imported into all three clients. To import into the three clients, the system administrator needs to execute the following tp commands:

```
tp import all QAS client=100 u0
tp import all QAS client=200 u0
tp import all QAS client=300
```

The last command is the import command for the last remaining client. At this point, all clients have been delivered with the changes—the change requests are no longer needed in the import queue. To delete the change requests from the import buffer after the import, the system administrator can leave out the import option u0.

Setting a Stopmark

A stopmark prevents all change requests that are positioned after the stopmark in the queue from being imported. This also applies to change requests that are released during a running import, because they are placed after the stopmark in the import queue.

tp automatically sets a stopmark at the beginning of an import and removes it at the end of the import. This removal is a problem when importing into multiple clients, because subsequent imports will include change requests that were located after the stopmark in the previous imports.

As a solution, tp does not remove the stopmark after import when the overtaker option (u0) is used.

If you have an earlier version of tp, you can still perform imports into multiple clients. In this case, before starting the first import, you have to explicitly add one stopmark for each client into which you will import to ensure that all clients receive the same change requests. These additional stopmarks prevent change requests from being added to the import buffer between the import processes. Although this option will technically work, SAP recommends that you use the latest version of tp for your release, as listed previously.

14.1.5 tp Processing Sequence

The contents of the import buffer are organized as a table. Each column represents an import phase, except the last one, which specifies the import option (UMODE). The numbers in the columns indicate whether the import step is necessary or the number of objects in the request that require the step. Figure 14.2 shows an example of an import buffer. The transport control program `tp` does not process all import steps for one request before proceeding to the next change request. Instead, `tp` collectively processes each import step for all change requests in an import queue before proceeding with the next import step.

Import phases

During an import, a change request passes through nine *import phases*. These phases are shown in Figure 14.2. The import phases are the technical names for the *import steps* in the `tp` processing sequence. Only the import phase ACTIV contains more than one import step (see Table 14.5 in the next subsection).

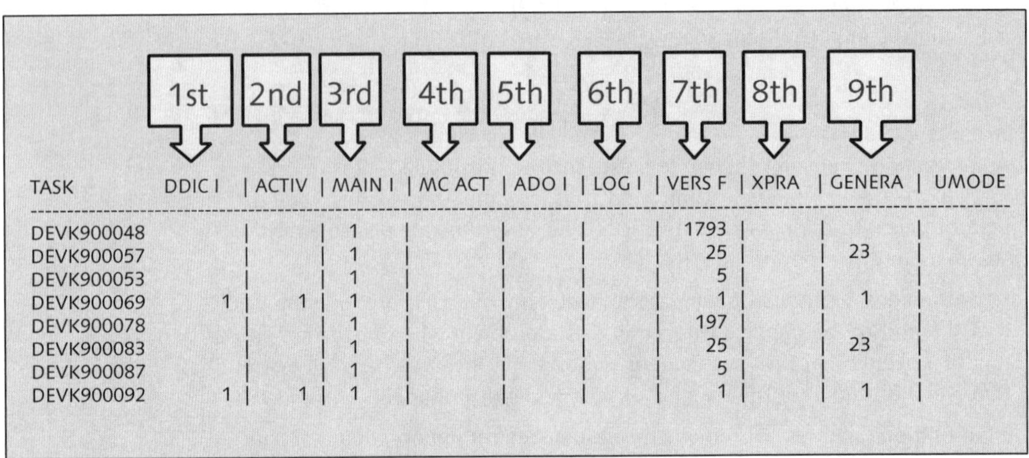

TASK	DDIC I	ACTIV	MAIN I	MC ACT	ADO I	LOG I	VERS F	XPRA	GENERA	UMODE
DEVK900048			1				1793			
DEVK900057			1				25		23	
DEVK900053			1				5			
DEVK900069	1	1	1				1		1	
DEVK900078			1				197			
DEVK900083			1				25		23	
DEVK900087			1				5			
DEVK900092	1	1	1				1		1	

Figure 14.2 tp Processing Sequence For Imports

During an import all, `tp` first processes any change requests containing changes to the ABAP Dictionary—that is, `tp` first imports these objects. This occurs during the *ABAP Dictionary import* phase (DDIC). In Figure 14.2, the change requests `DEVK900069` and `DEVK900092` contain such changes and are therefore processed by `tp` in the first phase. In the second phase (ACTIV), `tp` activates any objects that have been imported in phase DDIC. In Figure 14.2, this again affects change requests `DEVK900069` and `DEVK900092`. In the third phase, `tp` returns to the first request in the list, and performs the main import (MAIN I) for that change request and then all subsequent change requests in the buffer. This continues until each phase has been completed for all requests in the import queue. The required steps for each change request are listed in the import buffer.

Processing the import buffer in a particular sequence of phases technically and logically allows the import of multiple change requests for the following reasons:

- Dictionary structures (such as table structures) are imported and activated prior to the main import phase. The current structures are thereby able to "receive" new data (such as table entries) that may be imported in the same or another change request during the main import phase.
- The Repository objects with the fewest dependencies (the ABAP Dictionary objects) are imported and checked for consistency before ABAP programs and screen definitions are imported. This is important because these objects often depend highly on proper ABAP Dictionary settings.
- Because ABAP program generation takes place after the main import process, only the last imported version of the programs and screens is activated. Consider this situation: A "bad" version of a program is released and exported, and then corrected in a change request released later. Even though the bad version was imported, it is quickly overwritten during the main import phase with the "good" version of the program that is contained in the latest change. When the generation phase eventually takes place, only the correct version of the program is generated.
- The amount of import time required for importing multiple change requests is less than that needed for individual requests imported one at a time. Time is saved because standard activities and generic import steps (such as post-activation conversions) take place collectively for all change requests in the queue and not for each individual change request.

[+] The processing sequence ensures that if you detect an error in a change request that has already been released, you can correct the object in a new change request. After releasing and exporting the change request, the next *import all* command imports the entire import buffer in the sequence of export, and the faulty object is overwritten and does not affect your production system.

Example: Advantages of the tp Processing Sequence

Change requests DEVK900069 and DEVK900092 (see Figure 14.2 earlier in this section) both contain changes to the same table structure. By mistake, DEVK900069 contains a "bad" change that deletes a very important field from a table containing critical data. Through testing in the quality assurance system, the error is detected before DEVK90069 is imported into the production system. Change request DEVK900092 is released from the development system to correct the problem by redefining the field in its original state. Because the change requests are imported in the proper sequence, as is the case with tp processing, the bad change does not affect the production system, and the data in the important field is not deleted. Although the bad table structure is imported in the first phase during the ABAP Dictionary import, the corrected version of the table structure is then imported and overwrites what is faulty.

The table structure activated during import is the table structure imported in change request DEVK900092. The table structure in change request DEVK900069 is never activated in the production system.

Import Steps

The import process includes several import steps (see Table 14.5) that are performed by different transport tools. All of these steps are coordinated by tp. Phase ACTIV is the only phase that contains more than one import step. In addition to the activation of ABAP Dictionary objects, this phase includes the following generic import steps: distribution, structure conversion, and moving nametabs. Generic steps are not related to certain change requests, but are performed for all change requests in one step. Another generic step is the enqueue conversion, which is performed in phase MC CONV. Note that you cannot display the log files related to generic steps using the TMS. However, you can view them at the operating system level.

Table 14.5 lists, for each import step, the character (a letter or number) that is used to represent the step in the different log files and a description that includes the transport tool involved.

Import Phase	Import Step	Char.	Description	Supporting Transport Tool
DDIC I	Import of ABAP Dictionary objects	H	To enable imports into production systems, the transport program R3trans imports the ABAP Dictionary structures inactively.	R3trans
ACTIV	Activation of ABAP Dictionary objects	A	Runtime descriptions (nametabs) are written inactively, but during this phase, the steps required for activation are initiated.	RDDMASGL
ACTIV	Distribution of ABAP Dictionary objects	S	Logical checks decide what additional actions are required to bring the new ABAP Dictionary objects into the running system.	RDDGENBB (job name: RDDDISOL)
ACTIV	Structure conversion	N	ABAP Dictionary structural changes are made.	RDDGENBB (job name: RDDGENOL)
ACTIV	Move nametabs	6	The new ABAP runtime objects are put into the active runtime environment.	pgmvntabs
MAIN I	Main import	I	Import of all data including table entries.	R3trans
MC ACT	Activation and conversion of enqueue objects	M	Enqueue objects such as matchcodes that were not previously activated are now activated. These objects are immediately used in the running system.	RDDGENBB

Table 14.5 Import Steps

Import Phase	Import Step	Char.	Description	Supporting Transport Tool
ADO I	Import of application defined objects (ADOs)	D	Import of additional objects, including SAPscript forms and styles, and printer definitions.	RDDDIC1L
LOG I	Logical import	U	This phase is currently not active and is ignored during the import process.	
VERS F	Version management	V	Versions of Repository objects are created in the SAP ERP system from which the objects were exported. The import process modifies the object's *Version counter*, which is incremented during this step for all Repository objects imported.	RDDVERSL
XPRA	Execution of post-import methods	R	Post-import methods are required activities (such as the execution of an ABAP program) that rely on transported data.	RDDEXECL
GENERA	Generation of ABAP programs and screens	G	Generation of imported objects	RDDDIC03L

Table 14.5 Import Steps (Cont.)

From the beginning of the step that moves nametabs, until the end of the main import, inconsistencies may occur in the SAP system. After the main import phase, these inconsistencies will be removed because the SAP system returns to a consistent state. However, it is not until after the generation of ABAP programs and screens at the end of the import process that you can be assured that business activities in the SAP system will be unaffected (see Section 14.3 for more details).

14.2 Using Log Files for Troubleshooting

Occasionally, you will encounter problems during import. The information provided in the following areas will help you solve these problems:

- Log files stored in the transport subdirectory `log`
  - Generic log files
  - Single step log files
- Return codes

In addition to this information, certain troubleshooting techniques will prove beneficial in resolving errors to ensure a successful import.

14.2.1 Generic Log Files

The transport control program `tp` creates and writes three *generic log files*: the SLOG file (more commonly known as the `TP` System Log), the ALOG file (referred to as the Transport Step Monitor), and the ULOG file.

tp System Log

The `tp` system log that reports the contents of the SLOG file is accessed from within TMS (Transaction STMS) using the menu option OVERVIEW • IMPORTS • GOTO • TP SYSTEM LOG (see Chapter 13). The `tp` system log contains a general overview of performed imports, including the respective return code, and thus indicates the success of each import. You can use the `tp` system log to monitor the transport activities of a specific SAP system. To set the name of the SLOG file in the transport profile, use the global transport parameter `syslog`. The default naming convention is `SLOG($syear)($yweek).($system)`, where `($syear)` represents the calendar year, `($yweek)` is the week of the year, and `($system)` is the system ID for the SAP system.

Transport Step Monitor

The Transport Step Monitor, which reports the contents of the ALOG file, is accessed from within TMS (Transaction STMS) using the menu option OVERVIEW • IMPORTS • GOTO • TP SYSTEM LOG • GOTO • TRANSPORT STEP (see Chapter 13). The Transport Step Monitor records the return codes for all transport steps handled in the common transport directory. To set the name of the ALOG file in the transport profile, use the global transport parameter `alllog`. The default value is `ALOG($syear)($yweek)`, where `($syear)` represents the calendar year and `($yweek)` is the week of the year. Each entry in the ALOG file represents a single step log file from within the Transport Step Monitor.

ULOG

The ULOG file records all `tp` commands that have been executed and are free of syntax errors. This log uses the naming convention `ULOG($syear)_<one digit>`, where `($syear)` represents the current calendar year and the single digit represents the quarter of the year. For example, `ULOG08_4` specifies the log for the fourth quarter—October, November, and December—of the year 2008. The file contents are organized as a table consisting of a row for each tp command and three columns containing the following information:

- The operating system user who issued the `tp` command
- A time stamp
- The complete `tp` command executed at the operating system level, including all options and paths

[+] The `ULOG` file is not available from within TMS, but can be viewed at the operating system level in the transport directory `log`.

14.2.2 Single Step Log Files

For each import step, the respective transport tool—either `R3trans` or one of the ABAP programs involved (whose names all begin with "RDD")—writes a log file to the transport directory. The log files are written to the subdirectory `tmp`. At the end of an import, `tp` moves all log files contained in subdirectory `tmp` to subdirectory `log` (see Figure 14.3).

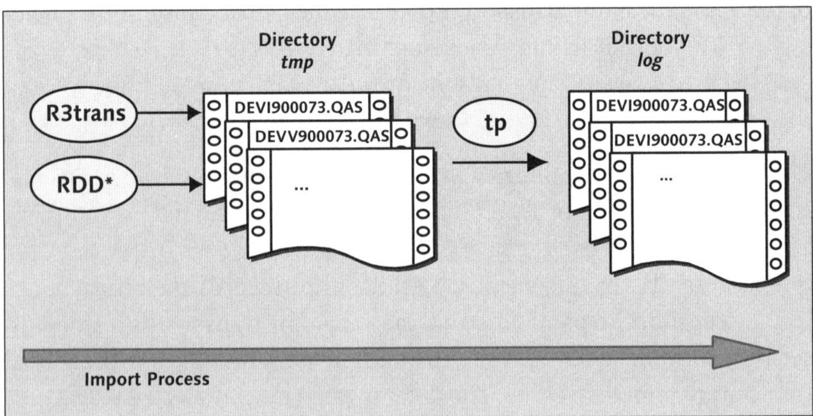

Figure 14.3 Single Step Log Files

Each log file contains a list of message texts containing information, warnings, or errors that reflect the results of the respective import step. At the end of the log file, the exit or return code of the transport tool is specified. This code indicates the overall success of the import step.

Table 14.6 lists log files for the sample change request `DEVK900021` after all import steps have been performed. The naming convention for single step log files is `<source SID><import step><6 digits>.<target SID>`. The import step is represented by a single character (see Table 14.5 earlier in this chapter). The six digits following the import step denote the corresponding change request.

Unlike the other steps, the generic import steps—distribution, structure conversion, move nametabs, and enqueue conversion—are not related to certain change requests. These log files cannot be displayed in the TMS. Their naming convention is `<import step><year><month><day>.<target SID>`.

Log File	Import Step	Import Phase
DEVH900021.QAS	Dictionary import	DDIC I
DEVA900021.QAS	Dictionary activation	ACTIV
DS991005.QAS	Distribution	ACTIV
N991005.QAS	Structure conversion	ACTIV
P991005.QAS	Move nametabs	ACTIV
DEVI900021.QAS	Main import	MAIN I
DEVMS900021.QAS	Activation of the enqueue definitions	MC ACT
N991005.QAS	Enqueue conversion	MC CONV
DEVD900021.QAS	ADO import	ADO I
DEVV900021.QAS	Version management	VERS F
DEVR900021.QAS	XPRA execution	XPRA
DEVG900021.QAS	Generation of ABAP programs and screens	GENERA

Table 14.6 Possible Import Log Files Generated For Sample Change Request DEVK900021

14.2.3 Return Codes

Each transport tool involved in the import process exits with a *return code* to `tp` that is also recorded in the respective log file. In addition, `tp` may receive signals and messages from the operating system or the database. `tp` interprets the return codes and calculates its own return code, which indicates the result of the entire import process (see Figure 14.4).

Typically, `tp` receives return codes only from the transport tools that have a value between zero and 16 (see Table 14.7). The overall success of the import then depends on the highest return code that has occurred in an import step. If no other problems occurred, `tp` will display the return code with the highest value received from a transport tool. This is called the *maximum return code*.

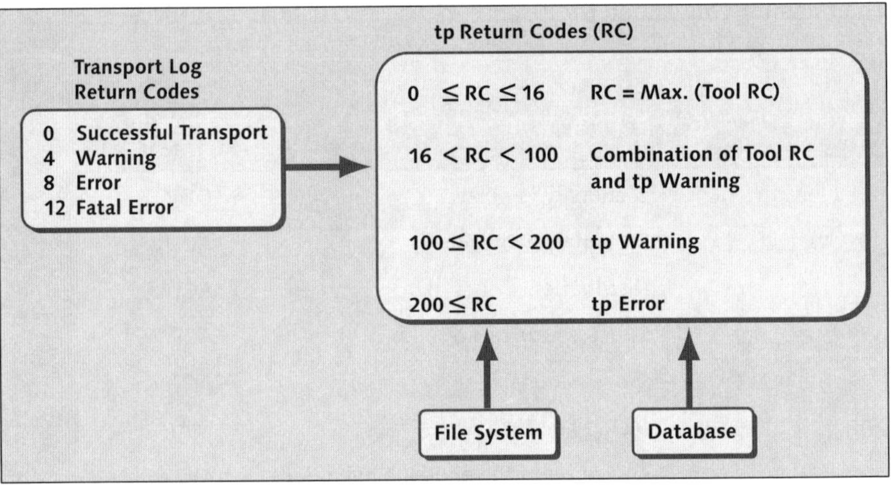

Figure 14.4 Return Codes

Abort By default, if `tp` receives a return code higher than 8 during an import phase, it will abort the import process. The transport profile parameter `stoponerror` defines which return code value will cause `tp` to abort.

Return Code	Description	Example
0	The transport activities were successful.	
4	Warnings occurred during the transport. All objects were transported successfully, but irregularities occurred.	A change request contains an object deletion.
8	The transport was carried out with errors; at least one object could not be transported successfully.	An ABAP program had a syntax error and, while being imported, was not able to be generated because of the error.
12	The transport was terminated. A serious error occurred, but was not caused by the contents of a change request.	During the import process, the database of the SAP system was unavailable for import—for example, because of a lack of tablespace.
13	The transport tool was terminated by a signal from the operating system.	`R3trans` contains a serious error.
16	The transport tool terminated due to an internal error.	There is a possible development error in `tp` or `R3trans` for which you will need to contact SAP Support for assistance.

Table 14.7 Examples of tp return codes

A return code of 17 to 99 is a combination of the return codes from the different transport tools. This results in a `tp` warning, such as a warning indicating that the import buffer of the target system has no write permission.

A return code of 100 to 199 displays a `tp` warning. `tp` has calculated the return code by adding 100 to the original return code value. There are two groups of return codes resulting in `tp` warnings:

Return code groups

- Return codes from 100 to 149 indicate "normal" `tp` warnings—that is, `tp` could not perform all tasks. For example, RDDIMPDP could not be triggered by program `sapevt`. To evaluate this kind of return code, refer to its last two digits.

- Return codes of 150 to 199 are rare and indicate incorrect user operation. For example, if `tp` tries to import a change request that is not included in the import buffer, return code 152 will be displayed. To evaluate the return code, refer to its last two digits.

A return code of 200 or more indicates a `tp` error. For example, if `tp` could not access a file as required by the import process, return code 212 will be displayed.

[+] To display the text of a specific `tp` return code, use the `tp` command `tp explainrc <value of return code>`.

14.2.4 Troubleshooting Techniques

At the beginning of the implementation phase of an SAP system landscape or after TMS configuration changes, SAP recommends using the Alert Monitor—which records all TMS transport activities—to eliminate the obvious TMS setup issues. To call the Alert Monitor, use Transaction STMS and choose MONITOR • ALERT MONITOR. The following information is displayed for each TMS function:

Information on TMS functions

- Date and time
- Username
- TMS status message
- Target system

To display the full text of an error message, double-click the message. The Alert Monitor primarily reveals TMS configuration and TMS connection errors. When your TMS configuration is stable, you can detect the cause of errors and problems in the related log files.

When your TMS configuration is stable, always use the import monitor in the TMS to ensure that imports run smoothly. If the import monitor indicates problems and errors, SAP recommends performing the following steps:

Procedure in case of errors in the import monitor

1. Use the `tp` system log in TMS (or the `SLOG` file at the operating system level) to monitor the transport activities of an SAP system and determine the results of an import.

2. If import failures are recorded in the tp system log, drill down to the Transport Step Monitor in TMS (or the ALOG file at the operating system level) and locate the import step that sent the return code listed in the tp system log.
3. From the Transport Step Monitor, locate the log file for the specific change request that produced the error and evaluate the cause of the problem. Note that although all transport log files for a specific change request can be viewed from within TMS (see Chapter 12 and Chapter 13), single log files of generic import steps cannot be displayed using the TMS.

These steps can be performed either with the TMS or at the operating system level. The procedure for using the TMS is described in the example in the box.

Example: Troubleshooting an Import Problem

As shown in the Figure 14.5, four change requests are in the import queue of system PRD.

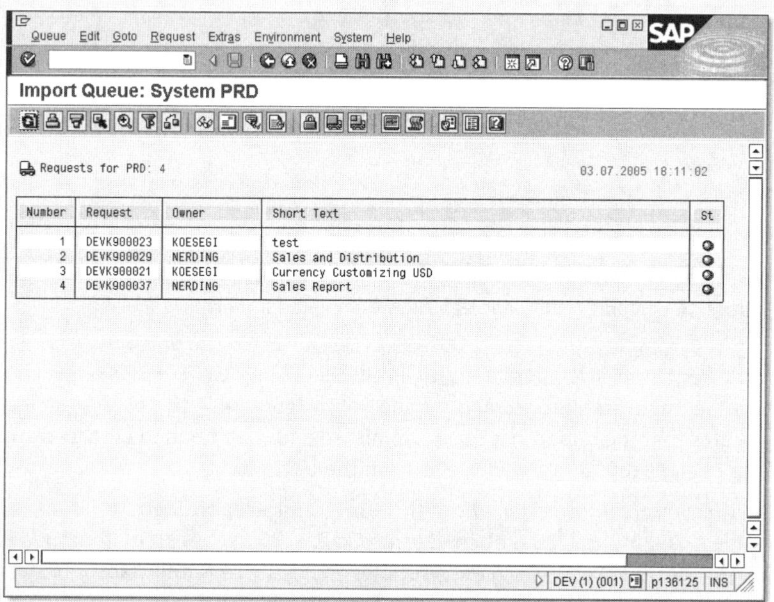

Figure 14.5 Change Requests In The Import Queue Of System PRD

From the import queue screen of PRD, the import is started using QUEUE • START IMPORT.

The import process is monitored by choosing GOTO • IMPORT MONITOR. The display is refreshed using REFRESH. Figure 14.5 shows the import monitor when the import is finished (TP FINISHED status). It shows that the import process resulted in a maximum return code of 0008. The return code indicates that errors occurred during the import process by tp, but no other details are provided. Therefore, you have to check where and why errors occurred.

To check whether the errors originated from setup errors, from the TMS menu, choose MONITOR • ALERT MONITOR. In this example, the Alert Monitor has not recorded any errors for the time frame of this import (screen not shown).

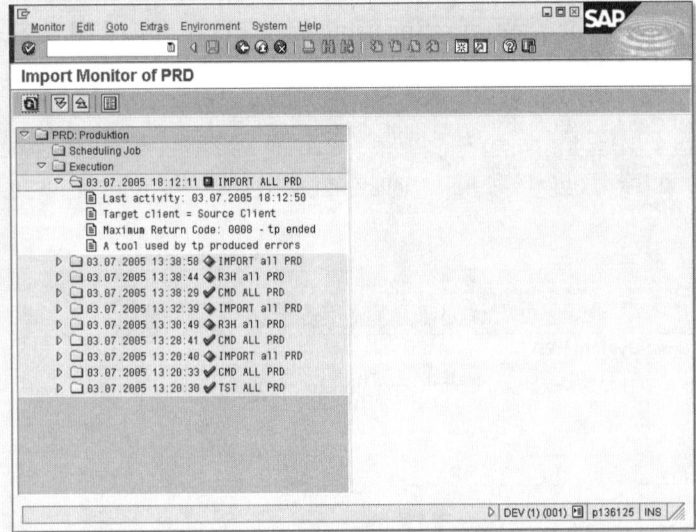

Figure 14.6 Import Monitor Screen After Completed Import

In the next step, the `tp` system log is checked using GOTO • TP SYSTEM LOG from the import monitor screen. As shown in Figure 14.7, the `tp` system log indicates that the import has been completed and that it ended with a return code of eight (0008 in the fifth row from the bottom).

To display more information about the error, the Transport Step Monitor (the log file `ALOG`) in the TMS is opened using GOTO • TRANSPORT STEPS from the TP SYSTEM LOG: SYSTEM QAS screen. As shown in Figure 14.8, the Transport Step Monitor indicates that when change request `DEVK900037` was processed, return code 0008 (R column) was sent during the import step G (S column). This import step is the GENERATION OF PROGRAMS AND DYNPROS.

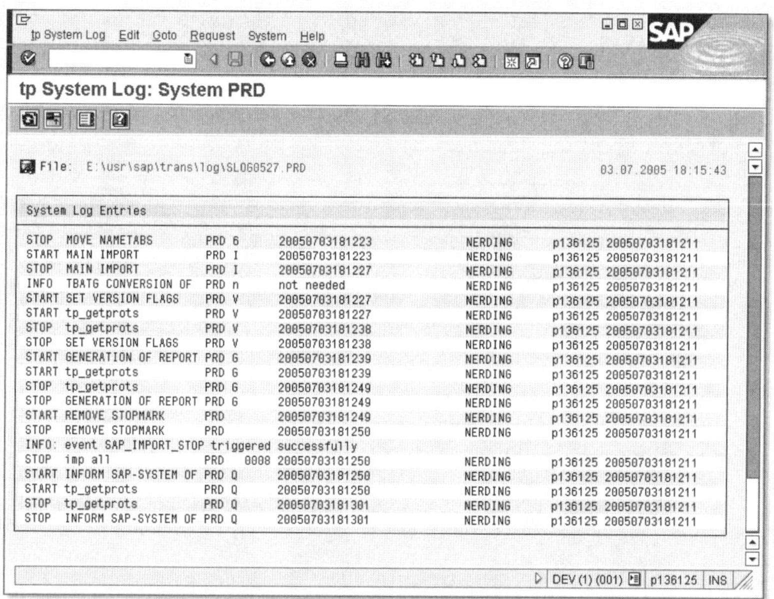

Figure 14.7 tp System Log

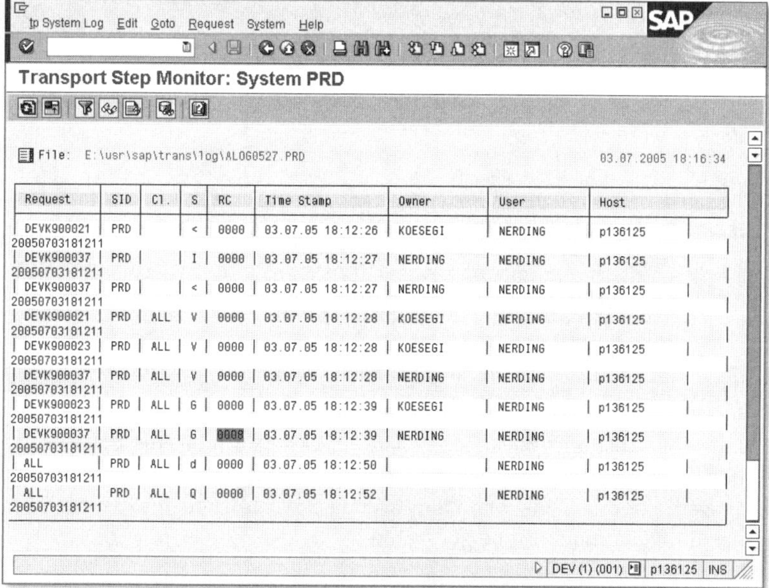

Figure 14.8 Transport Step Monitor

Now that the change request that caused the error has been located, the respective single log file is accessed. To do so, the cursor is positioned on change request DEVK900037. Then, REQUEST • LOGS is chosen from the TRANSPORT STEP MONITOR: SYSTEM PRD screen. As shown in Figure 14.9, an overview of all transport logs is given.

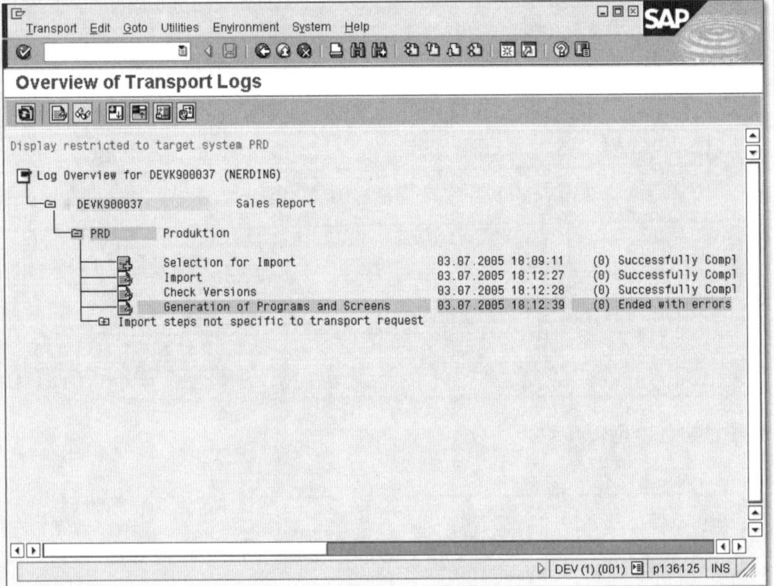

Figure 14.9 Overview of Transport Logs

In the OVERVIEW OF TRANSPORT LOGS screen, the log file for the import step GENERATION OF PROGRAMS AND DYNPROS is highlighted and listed with a return code of 8.

To display the log file for this import step, the highlighted line is double-clicked.

As shown in Figure 14.10, the single step log file for the GENERATION OF PROGRAMS AND DYNPROS import step is displayed.

The previous section from log file DEVG900037.PRD indicates that change request DEVK900037 includes program ZPROGRAM. The program could not be activated because line 9 contains a syntax error. Although the report was implemented, it could not be generated.

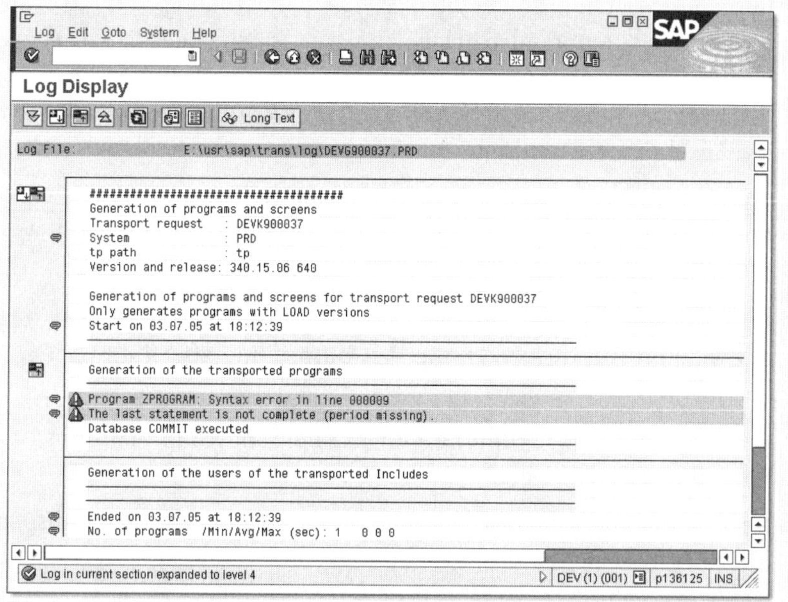

Figure 14.10 Single Step Log File

To eliminate this error, you must log on to the development system and correct the syntax error in Transaction SE38. Then, the correction can be imported along with the faulty request.

Additional Troubleshooting Hints

Detecting error sources

To detect other typical error sources, use any of the following methods:

- In the SAP system, use the job overview (Transaction SM37) to monitor the results of all related background processes (RDD* jobs).
- At the operating system level, check the import buffer. This provides information about the progress and success of imports. Use the following command: `tp showbuffer <target SID>`.
- In the SAP system, check the entries in tables TRBAT and TRJOB (see the section "Communication Between `tp` and ABAP Programs"). You should also compare them with the log file and import buffer entries at the operating system level.

- In the SAP system, use the job overview (Transaction SM37) to check whether the import dispatcher `RDDIMPDP` is scheduled as an event-periodic background job. The related event has to be SAP_TRIGGER_RDDIMPDP. You can also perform this check at the operating system level using the following `tp` command: `tp checkimp <target SID>`.
- Check whether `RDDIMPDP` is executed when the event SAP_TRIGGER_RDDIMPDP is triggered. In the SAP system, use Transaction SM64; at the operating system level, use the SAP ERP executable `sapevt`.
- If necessary, verify the version of the transport tools `tp` and `R3trans`. The version is indicated in the first output line after calling any `tp` command.
- Check whether `tp` is running—for example, on Unix platforms, use the following tp command: `ps -ef | grep tp`.
- Check whether permission or share problems exist with the transport directory.
- Check whether enough free disk space is available in the transport directory.

14.3 Buffer Synchronization

To reduce database accesses and network load, as well as improve system performance, frequently used data in an SAP system is stored in buffers. These buffers are located in the shared memory of an application server. Every work process in an instance accesses these buffers. Data stored in the buffers includes ABAP programs, screens, ABAP Dictionary data, and company-specific data, which normally remains unchanged during system operation.

If an SAP system consists of several instances on multiple application servers, changes to data stored in the local buffers of the application servers must be updated at regular intervals. This prevents inconsistencies between the local buffers on each instance. The synchronization process is asynchronous to minimize network load. Imports into an SAP system may also affect buffers, because imported objects can be objects that are stored in one of the buffers. Therefore, central systems with only one instance should also be synchronized.

Due to the required amount of network and database accesses, updating SAP ERP buffers places a high load on the system. In large systems, it may take two to three hours for performance to stabilize again after a complete buffer reset. You must take this into consideration when importing change requests.

[+] Importing data into a production system can significantly impact performance.

Inconsistencies

Data inconsistencies can occur if an application server reads data from its buffer between two synchronization procedures. If, at the time of access, the data is being processed by another server or is in the process of being imported, it will not be up to date. The examples in the boxes illustrate the risk of temporary and permanent inconsistencies when importing changes into production systems.

Example: Temporary Inconsistencies

A change to the structure of a table—that is, a Dictionary change—has been entered by an import into an SAP system. Before the buffers are synchronized, a dependent program is loaded. The program is generated with the old structure and saved with a time stamp indicating a time after the new structure was imported and activated. After the subsequent buffer synchronization, the program retains the incorrect structure. This is an inconsistency that cannot be easily detected. When this dependent program runs, the work area of the table will no longer match the structure used when the work area was generated. When the program is executed, it will terminate with the runtime error GETWA_CANT_CLEAR. To correct the inconsistency, you must manually regenerate all of the related programs that are listed in the short dump.

Example: Permanent Inconsistencies

Program A is being generated in the production system, thus, the database sets a lock on the program data. While program A is being generated, `tp` imports an include program on which both programs A and B depend. During buffer synchronization, the system tries to set a new change time stamp for programs A and B. Although the time stamp is specified, it cannot be set because program A is still being generated and is thus locked by the database.

After program A has been generated, the system sets a generation time stamp for program A, and the database lock is removed. The program then tries to set the change time stamp for programs A and B. Program B is regenerated because its last generation time stamp was set before the change time stamp. Program A, however, will not be regenerated because its most recent generation time stamp was set after the change time stamp was determined. The program retains the old structure. As a result, this inconsistency will remain in the SAP system until program A is changed.

Temporary inconsistencies are less critical than permanent inconsistencies because temporary inconsistencies exist only until the transaction is restarted. Restarting the transaction causes the buffers to be synchronized, which restores the consistency between the object and the buffers.

[+] Transporting programs and ABAP Dictionary data can cause both temporary and permanent inconsistencies if they affect running programs and their environment. SAP recommends scheduling imports into production systems to run at night in the background when system load is low. Alternatively, you can perform a detailed check on the jobs that are running and monitor the effects carefully.

14.4 Naming Conventions in the Transport Directory

Chapter 7 introduced the transport directory and its subdirectories. Because the transport control program `tp` runs on many different operating systems, the files of the transport directory use restrictive naming conventions. The naming conventions are applied to the files automatically and can help you with troubleshooting. After you have identified a change request that caused errors, you can use the naming conventions to access the related log files and find out how to resolve the errors.

Figure 14.11 illustrates the file naming conventions for the subdirectory files related to a specific change request. The sample change request `DEVK900073` serves as the basis for the subdirectory files. User SMITH created the change request in the development system DEV. A consolidation route exists between DEV and the quality assurance system QAS. QAS is the first system into which the change request will be imported. Therefore, DEV is the source SID of this change request; QAS is the target SID.

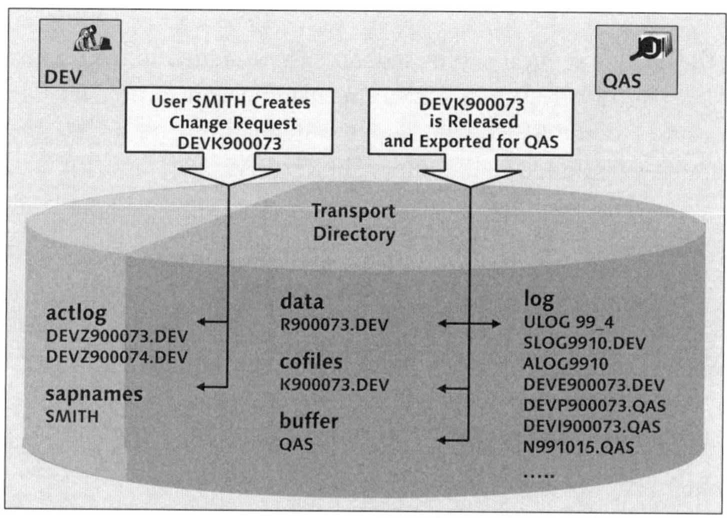

Figure 14.11 Transport Directory Naming Convention

As mentioned in Chapter 4, change requests are named following this convention: `<source SID>K9<5 digits>`. `K9` indicates that this is a customer change request. The subsequent five digits are a serial number. The naming convention for the subdirectories in the transport directory follows these rules:

Subdirectory naming convention

- **actlog**
  For each change request and also for each task, a file named `<source SID>Z9<5 digits>.<source SID>` is written. The file records each user action on the request or task—for example, creation, release, or change of ownership. In Figure 14.11, file `DEVZ900073.DEV` for the change request and file `DEVZ900074.DEV` for the only related task have been stored. If, for example, the owner of the task is changed, a new entry containing this action will be added to `DEVZ900074.DEV`.
- **sapnames**
  A file is automatically created for each user who performs transport activities on a change request. This file is updated when the user releases a request. The naming convention is the user's logon name. In Figure 14.11, this file is named `SMITH`.

- **buffer**
  When the change request is released, an entry is added to the import buffer for the target system QAS. The naming convention for the import buffer is the SID of the target system. In Figure 14.11, the change request is added to the import buffer QAS.

- **data**
  As the change request is exported, the contained objects are stored to files named according to the following naming convention: `R9<5 digits >.<source SID>`. In Figure 14.11, the corresponding file is named `R900073.DEV`. If application defined objects (ADOs) are contained in the change request, another file is created, which begins with `D9` instead of `R9`.

- **cofiles**
  When exporting, a control file named `K9<5 digits>.<source SID>` is stored. This control file contains, for example, the import steps that have to be performed. The control file in Figure 14.11 is named `K900073.DEV`.

- **log**
  Various log files are contained in this subdirectory. The generic log files, `ULOG`, `ALOG`, and `SLOG`, either get new entries or are created if they did not previously exist. The change request in Figure 14.11 was transported in October 1999. Thus, the generic log files are ULOG 99_4, SLOG9910.DEV, and ALOG9910. (For information on the naming convention of these files, see Section 14.2.1.) For each executed transport step, a single step log file is stored. Some sample log files related to the change request include `DEVE900073.DEV`, `DEVP900073.DEV`, `DEVI900073.QAS`, and `N991015.QAS`. (For information on the naming convention of these files, see Section 14.2.2.)

Cleaning up the Transport Directory

Over time, many large files may accumulate in your transport directories. These files will eventually become obsolete. Depending on your transport activities and the amount of free disk space, you should occasionally clean up the transport directory. This activity can be performed only at the operating system level using the appropriate `tp` commands. To clean up the transport directory, proceed as follows (see also Figure 14.12):

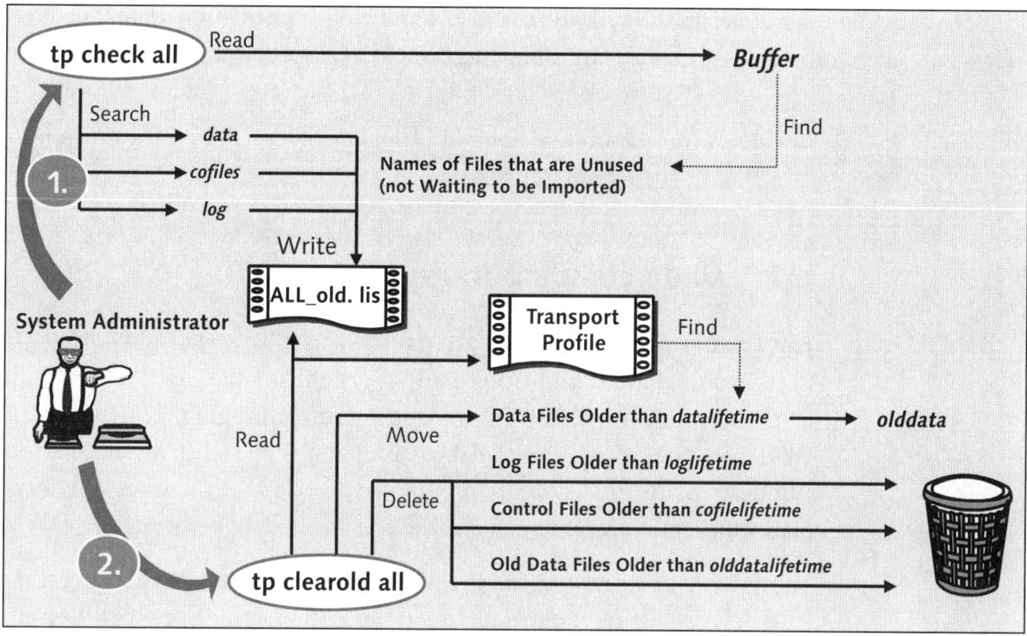

Figure 14.12 Cleaning up the Transport Directory

1. Execute the following command:

   `tp check all`

   This command reads all import buffers and searches in subdirectories `data`, `cofiles`, and `log` of the transport directory for files that are no longer needed. Such files refer to change requests that are no longer contained in any import buffer. The file names are listed in the file `ALL_OLD.LIS` in the transport subdirectory `tmp`.

2. Execute the following command:

   `tp clearold all`

   `tp` checks each file listed in `ALL_OLD.LIS` to determine whether it has exceeded a maximum age. The maximum age is specified in days by the transport profile parameters `datalifetime` (default 200), `olddatalifetime` (default 365), `cofilelifetime` (default 365), and `loglifetime` (default 200). `tp` then processes the files as follows:

   - Data files in the transport subdirectory `data` that are older than the value specified in the parameter `datalifetime` are moved by `tp` to the transport subdirectory `olddata`.

- Files in the subdirectories `log` and `cofiles` are immediately deleted by tp if they are older than the value specified by the parameter `loglifetime` or `cofilelifetime`.
- Files in `olddata` are deleted if they are older than the value specified in the parameter `olddatalifetime`.

14.5 Understanding Transport Tools

The Change and Transport System (CTS) uses several transport tools to transport data to and from an SAP system. At the operating system level, these tools include the transport control program `tp` (`tp.exe` on Windows platforms), the transport program `R3trans` (`R3trans.exe` on Windows platforms), and the program `sapevt` (`sapevt.exe` on Windows platforms).

These tools are automatically installed as executables at the operating system level during the installation of an SAP system. Note that they are not stored in the subdirectory `bin` of the transport directory, but in the following directory, which houses most executables:

- `/usr/sap/<SID>/SYS/exe/run` on Unix and AS/400 platforms
- `\usr\sap\<SID>\SYS\exe\run` on Windows platforms

[+] After a release upgrade, check the transport directory `bin`. If you find variants of the programs `tp` and `R3trans` that have been stored by a former release, delete the programs to ensure that the correct transport programs are used from the executable directory.

Several components are involved in performing transports. These include the transport dispatcher `RDDIMPDP` and several ABAP programs that carry out various steps required in the transport process—for example, generating imported reports. (See Table 14.8 later in this chapter in the ABAP PROGRAMS column.)

14.5.1 The Transport Program R3trans

`R3trans` is the transport tool at the operating system level that transports data between SAP systems. `R3trans` exports objects from the source database and stores them in data files at the operating system level. During import, R3trans reuses the data files and imports the objects into the target database.

R3trans format

The format of the data files written by R3trans is also known as R3trans format and is platform-independent. Thus, you can transport data between different databases or operating systems. In addition, upward compatibility is guaranteed; that is, you can export data with an old R3trans version and import the data with a newer version.

Although exports and imports are independent of the R3trans version, the database platform, or the operating system, due to logical dependencies, SAP does not support using tp or R3trans for transports between different releases.

R3trans is called by other programs, such as tp and the upgrade control program R3up. Because R3trans is not the only tool needed to perform a complete and correct import of change requests, SAP does not recommend calling R3trans directly. Always use tp to ensure that all export and import steps, including R3trans activities, are completed successfully.

Transport Tool Interaction at the Operating System Level

At the operating system level, tp interacts with R3trans. In the import process, tp tracks the extracted objects, ensuring that they are added to the database of the target system. The interaction between tp and R3trans is illustrated in Figure 14.13.

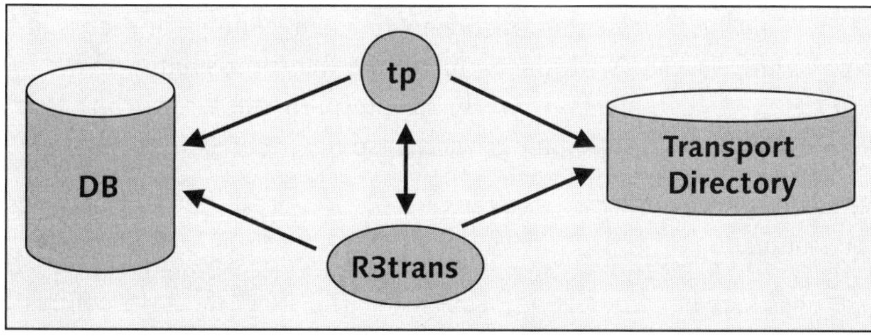

Figure 14.13 Transport Tool Interaction at the Operating System Level

tp always reads the transport profile in the transport directory that determines how tp should behave. This transport file also specifies the host, database, and path information through certain parameter settings.

When starting an import, tp sets a stopmark at the end of the import buffer of the target system and reads the import buffer to determine which change requests have to be imported and which import steps have to be performed for which change request. In addition, tp reads the corresponding control file in the subdirectory cofiles for details on the steps to be performed.

tp passes a control file to the transport subdirectory tmp for use by R3trans. tp then calls R3trans by initiating a new process using the following operating system commands:

- fork() on Unix platforms
- CreateProcess() on Windows platforms
- spawn() on AS/400 platforms

R3trans reads the control file in subdirectory tmp. This control file determines what activities R3trans should perform. R3trans reuses the data files it stored to the subdirectory data during exports and connects to the database of the target system to import the objects. When importing objects to the target database, R3trans updates, inserts, and deletes data in the database.

R3trans is responsible for the import steps DDIC (ABAP dictionary import) for the import of ABAP Dictionary definitions and MAIN I (main import) for the import of table contents (see the section "Import Steps").

R3trans always passes a return code to tp when exiting. For each transport action, R3trans writes a log file in the transport subdirectory tmp. After R3trans completes its work, tp interprets the return code from R3trans and moves its log file to the transport subdirectory log.

After the import process, tp cleans up the import buffer and removes the stopmark.

R3trans does not interact with the other transport tools. In contrast, tp communicates extensively with ABAP programs within the SAP system when performing certain steps in the target system (see the section "Communication Between tp and ABAP Programs").

14.5.2 ABAP Programs

Importing change requests involves different ABAP programs within the SAP system, depending on the import steps that have to be performed—for example, activating the ABAP Dictionary, converting structures, or generating reports and screens. The ABAP programs are executed as background jobs.

[+] Because the ABAP programs are executed as background jobs, there must be at least two background work processes running in the target system.

Control tables

To execute the necessary transport steps, tp uses the control tables TRBAT and TRJOB to communicate with the various ABAP programs. TRBAT and TRJOB are control tables that contain temporary data. After reading the control file (subdirectory cofiles) for the import of a change request, tp writes entries to the control table TRBAT, specifying the steps to be performed for the respective request. Table 14.8 lists the ABAP programs, the related job name, a description of the function, and the function code specifying the function to be performed in table TRBAT.

Function Code	Job Name	ABAP Program	Description
X	RDDDICOL	RDDDICOL	ADO export
J	RDDMASGL	RDDMASGL	Mass activator (new)
B	RDDTACOL	RDDTACOL	TACOB activator
S	RDDDISOL	RDDGENBB	Distributor
N	RDDGENOL	RDDGENBB	Import converter
M	RDDMASGL	RDDMASGL	Mass activator (enqueue)
Y(n)	RDDGENOL	RDDGENBB	Matchcode converter
O	RDDGENOL	RDDGENBB	Batch converter (not in upgrade)
D	RDDDIC1L	RDDDIC1L	ADO import
V	RDDVERSL	RDDVERSL	Create version
R	RDDEXECL	RDDEXECL	XPRA execution
G	RDDDIC3L	RDDDIC3L	Generation

Table 14.8 Functions of ABAP Programs during Change Request Import

RDDIMPDP

The interaction between tp and the ABAP programs is illustrated in Figure 14.14. After making the required entries in table TRBAT, tp triggers the import dispatcher RDDIMPDP.

As a prerequisite, RDDIMPDP must be scheduled as an event-periodic background job in client 000 of the target system. Additionally, a similar background job must be scheduled in every target client. This background job is called RDDIMPDP_CLIENT_<nnn>, where <nnn> represents the client ID. Typically, these jobs are automatically scheduled after a client copy. You can also schedule them manually by running program RDDNEWPP in the respective client (see Chapter 7).

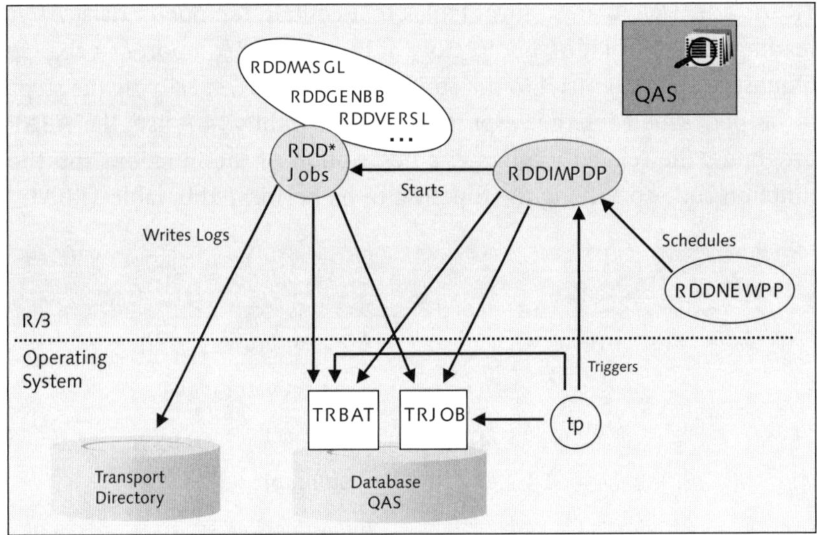

Figure 14.14 Interaction of tp and ABAP Programs

RDDIMPDP reads the information on import steps that tp writes to the control table TRBAT and then starts the corresponding programs as background jobs. The names of these programs and jobs all start with "RDD"—for example, RDDMASGL is for mass activation, RDDGENDB is for conversion, and RDDVERSL is for versioning. Each RDD* job (as they are commonly referred to) collectively receives a job number, which is recorded in table TRJOB. The jobs report their status and final return code back to table TRBAT and delete the corresponding TRJOB entry just before they finish.

They also write log files into the transport directory in the subdirectory `tmp`. At the end of an import, `tp` moves these log files to the subdirectory `log`.

Communication Between tp and ABAP Programs

This section focuses on how `tp` communicates with the ABAP programs involved in the import process. The main components for performing an import are illustrated in Figure 14.15. The figure is divided into three parts: the operating system (OS) level, the database, and the ABAP programs within the SAP system.

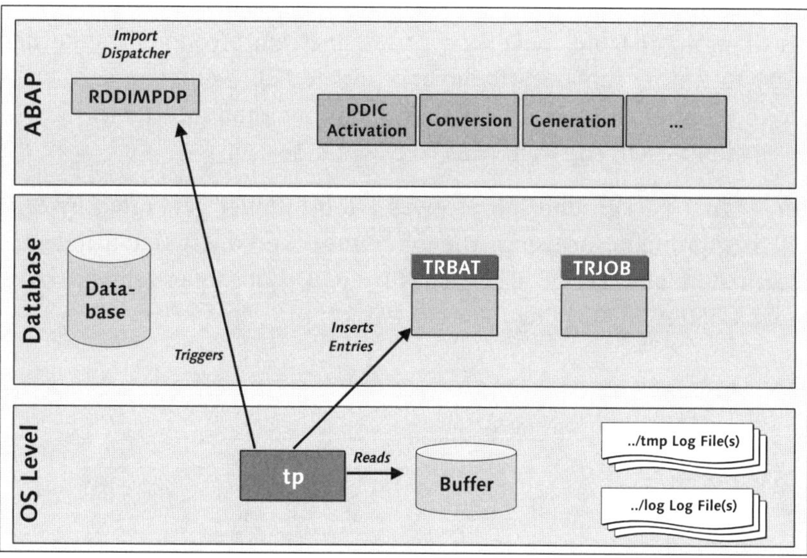

Figure 14.15 tp Starts the Import Process

When you perform an import, `tp` reads the import buffer and then writes an entry to the control table TRBAT for every change request in the import buffer. `tp` groups the change requests according to the import step to be performed. The entry in table TRBAT contains the name of the change request, the function performed during the import step, the return code, and the time stamp. The import function is represented by a character. For example, J indicates that the mass *activator* is performing the import step ABAP DICTIONARY ACTIVATION. For a list of TRBAT function codes, refer back to Table 14.8. As a signal to `RDDIMPDP` to start processing, tp writes a *header entry* after every group of change requests that have the same function code.

[+] For generic import steps that are independent of certain change requests, such as distribution and structure conversion, tp only writes a header entry in table TRBAT.

To trigger the import dispatcher RDDIMPDP, tp calls the operating system tool sapevt, which sends the event SAP_TRIGGER_RDDIMPDP to the SAP system.

When RDDIMPDP starts processing, it checks table TRBAT to find out whether an import step needs to be performed, such as mass activation, distribution, or table conversion. It sets the return code of the header entry to R (for "run"), starts the appropriate RDD* program as a background job, enters the job number of the new job into table TRJOB, reschedules itself, and then exits (see Figure 14.16).

Job Number

Each RDD* background job receives a job number generated by SAP ERP background processing. The job number and the function code are recorded in table TRJOB. The respective RDD* jobs indicate their status in table TRBAT by logging their current return code.

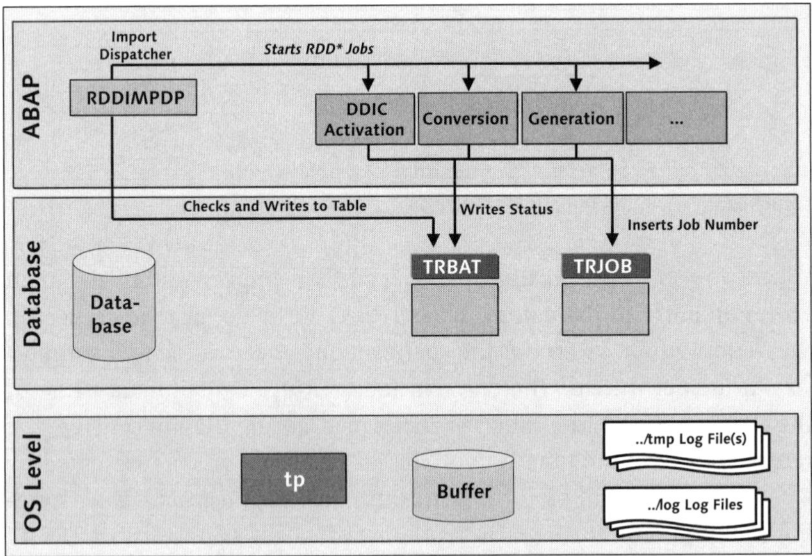

Figure 14.16 The ABAP Programs Access the Database Tables

When the background jobs exit, they write their final status as return codes in Table TRBAT and delete the corresponding job number in Table TRJOB. Return codes other than 9999 and 8888 indicate that the import step is complete. In Table TRBAT, the TIMESTAMP column contains the time of completion. When all of the necessary actions have been performed for all change requests, the respective RDD* job sets the header entry to F (for "finished") (see Figure 14.17).

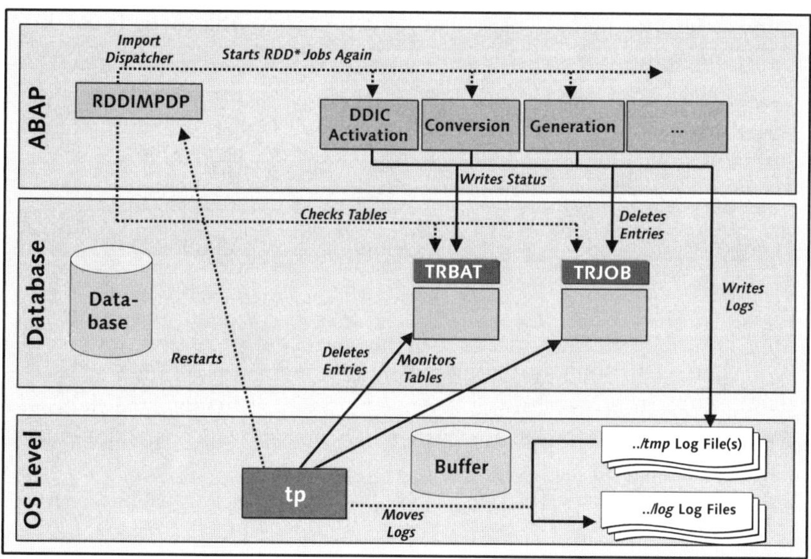

Figure 14.17 RDD* Job Exits

All background jobs log the steps they perform in either the database or in the transport subdirectory `tmp`. `tp` monitors the entries in the tables TRBAT and TRJOB. When an entry that is not a header entry has a return code other than 8888 or 9999, the job is considered finished. `tp` then copies the log file from the subdirectory `tmp` to the subdirectory `log` and deletes the corresponding TRBAT entry. When the header entry in TRBAT is set to F and TRJOB is empty, the ABAP programs have completed their role in the import steps. Log

If `tp` detects problems when monitoring the tables TRBAT and TRJOB, `tp` retriggers `RDDIMPDP` using `sapevt`. `RDDIMPDP` automatically recognizes whether an import step is still active or has been aborted by checking tables TRJOB and TRBAT. If a step was aborted, `RDDIMPDP` will restart this step.

Example: TRBAT Entries during an Import

When tp reads the import buffer of the target system, it notices that three of the change requests require the import step ABAP DICTIONARY ACTIVATION.

Therefore, tp writes the three change requests to table TRBAT, and assigns the function code J to the change requests. This indicates that ABAP DICTIONARY ACTIVATION has to be performed.

tp then writes a header entry to tell RDDIMPDP to start processing. Return code 9999 indicates that the step is waiting to be performed. For the header entry, tp inserts a B (for ""begin") as the return code. The contents of table TRBAT are as follows:

Request	Function Code	Return Code	Time stamp
DEVK904711	J	9999	00000001
DEVK904712	J	9999	00000002
DEVK904713	J	9999	00000003
HEADER	J	B	19983103143701

After RDDIMPDP sets the return code of the header entry to R, it activates program RDDMASGL. This program is the *mass activator* and performs the import step ABAP DICTIONARY ACTIVATION. While RDDMASGL is running, the status of the first entry in table TRBAT is changed to "active," which is indicated by the return code 8888.

Request	Function Code	Return Code	Time Stamp
DEVK904711	J	8888	00000001
DEVK904712	J	9999	00000002
DEVK904713	J	9999	00000003
HEADER	J	R	19983103143903

When program RDDMASGL (the mass activator) has completed the import step ABAP DICTIONARY ACTIVATION, it enters the return codes for each change request in table TRBAT and changes the status of the header entry to F. This way, RDDIMPDP will recognize that the import step ABAP DICTIONARY ACTIVATION has been completed.

Request	Function Code	Return Code	Time Stamp
DEVK904711	J	4	19983103144202
DEVK904712	J	0	19983103144357
DEVK904713	J	0	19983103144512
HEADER	J	F	19983103144512

14.6 Questions

1. **Which of the following statements are correct with regard to the transport control program `tp`?**
   A. To perform imports, `tp` must always be used directly at the operating system level.
   B. SAP recommends that you use the TMS instead of `tp` to perform imports.
   C. `tp` is responsible for exporting and importing objects from and to SAP systems.
   D. `tp` does not observe the sequence of change requests in the import queue when performing imports.
2. **Which of the following statements are correct with regard to import queues and import buffers?**
   A. Import queues are the TMS representation in SAP systems of the import buffer files at the operating system level.
   B. Import queues and import buffers are completely independent of each other.
   C. Import buffers have to be manipulated before imports can be performed at the operating system level.
   D. Manipulating import buffers may cause serious inconsistencies and should be performed only in exceptional cases.

3. **Which of the following statements are correct with regard to the import options formerly known as *unconditional modes*?**

   A. Import options cannot be used when imports are performed at the operating system level using `tp`.

   B. Import options are used to cause specific rules of the Change and Transport System (CTS) to be ignored.

   C. Import options must be used when importing into multiple clients using `tp`.

   D. Import options can be selected in the TMS using the expert mode.

4. **Which of the following statements are correct with regard to the sequence of processing steps `tp` follows when performing imports?**

   A. `tp` collectively processes each import step for all change requests in an import queue before proceeding with the next import step.

   B. `tp` processes all import steps for a single request before proceeding to the next change request.

   C. The processing sequence followed by `tp` ensures that when a change request with a faulty object is followed in the import queue by a change request with the corrected object, the faulty object will not affect the runtime environment of the target system.

   D. `tp` imports and activates ABAP Dictionary structures prior to the main import phase to ensure that the current structures can receive new data during the main import phase.

5. **Which of the following statements are correct with regard to troubleshooting imports?**

   A. In the SAP ERP system, you cannot display log files that do not depend on a specific request. For example, you cannot display log files related to generic import steps, such as structure conversion.

   B. SAP recommends that you check the SLOG file and the ALOG file before checking the single step log files.

C. By default, all return codes greater than 8 cause `tp` to abort a running import.

D. `tp` is the only transport tool that uses return codes.

6. **Which of the following statements are correct with regard to buffer synchronization?**

   A. Transport activities do not affect buffer synchronization.

   B. Imports affect buffer synchronization even in central SAP systems.

   C. `R3trans` can invalidate buffer content.

   D. Importing data into a production system can significantly impact performance because some buffer content may be invalidated and reloaded. This causes high system load.

   E. Importing programs and ABAP Dictionary data cannot cause inconsistencies in the target system, even if the programs or data affect running programs and their environment.

7. **Which of the following statements are correct with regard to the interaction between transport tools?**

   A. During exports, `tp` calls `R3trans` to access the database of the source system and extract the objects to be transported.

   B. `tp` triggers the transport daemon `RDDIMPDP` in the SAP system using the operating system tool `sapevt`.

   C. Using the tables TRBAT and TRJOB, `tp` communicates with ABAP programs involved in the transport process.

   D. `tp` communicates with only `RDDIMPD`.

The SAP NetWeaver Application Server is the first product that also provides a J2EE instance in addition to an ABAP instance. With the ABAP transport system, SAP provides support for developments; the Java standard, however, does not include this type of support. However, the SAP NetWeaver Development Infrastructure, which is based on the Eclipse development platform, establishes a connection to SAP systems to enable controlled deployment with ABAP-comparable functions.

15 SAP NetWeaver Development Infrastructure

The SAP NetWeaver Development Infrastructure (NWDI) is the environment specifically created by SAP for developing software projects in Java for the SAP NetWeaver Application Server (SAP NetWeaver AS). The NWDI supports the development process in many ways to create user-friendly and stable projects similar to what you are familiar with from the ABAP development environment. However, you cannot directly compare these two environments because their architectures are distinctly different. Nevertheless, the following sections compare the ABAP development environment with the NWDI environment wherever possible to gain better insight into the workings of the NetWeaver Development Infrastructure.

15.1 The SAP NetWeaver Application Server Structure

Runtime environment for ABAP and Java

SAP NetWeaver AS provides the runtime environment for both ABAP- and Java-based applications in SAP NetWeaver. Thus, both server- and client-based web applications can be implemented. Depending on its installation, SAP NetWeaver AS can run ABAP or Java programs, or both. Thus, both ABAP-based Business Server Pages (BSPs)—ABAP programs with embedded HTML code for presenting the pages on the web—and Java-based Java Server Pages (JSPs) can be used when creating web applications.

SAP NetWeaver AS Java

During the installation, SAP NetWeaver AS Java can be installed as either a standalone version or as an add-in of SAP NetWeaver AS ABAP. Therefore, the scalability known from ABAP-based systems can be easily created for Java as well, using a corresponding number of application servers. With the platform independence inherent as in SAP NetWeaver AS ABAP, and additional components such as the User Management Engine (UME), and the connection to other SAP systems via the proven RFC technology—using the Java Connector (JCo)—the NWDI, and many other features, SAP NetWeaver AS Java meets the operation requirements for stability, scalability, and security.

SAP J2EE Engine

SAP NetWeaver AS Java consists primarily of the SAP J2EE Engine (Java Enterprise Edition), which allows the execution of applications created according to the J2EE 1.3 standard. The SAP J2EE Engine supports all of the technologies that became popular with this standard such as JSPs, servlets, and Enterprise Java Beans (EJBs).

The SAP J2EE Engine is composed of three logical layers (see Figure 15.1):

1. The Java Enterprise Runtime, which consists of several low-level subsystems (called *managers*) and provides different kinds of basic functions.
2. The J2EE Engine components. These are based on the runtime, communicate with it, and use its functions. Three types of components exist: interfaces, libraries, and services.
3. The applications themselves. The border between the applications and the J2EE Engine components are defined in the Application Programming Interfaces (APIs) of J2EE 1.3, along with several SAP-proprietary APIs.

Architecture of the J2EE Engine

The architecture of the J2EE Engine is based on the following general rule: Higher level components can use lower level components. However, lower level components do not know the interfaces of the components above them and therefore cannot use them. This rule is also reflected in the order in which the modules are started: The runtime is started first, then the services and libraries are started; and, at the end, the application itself is started.

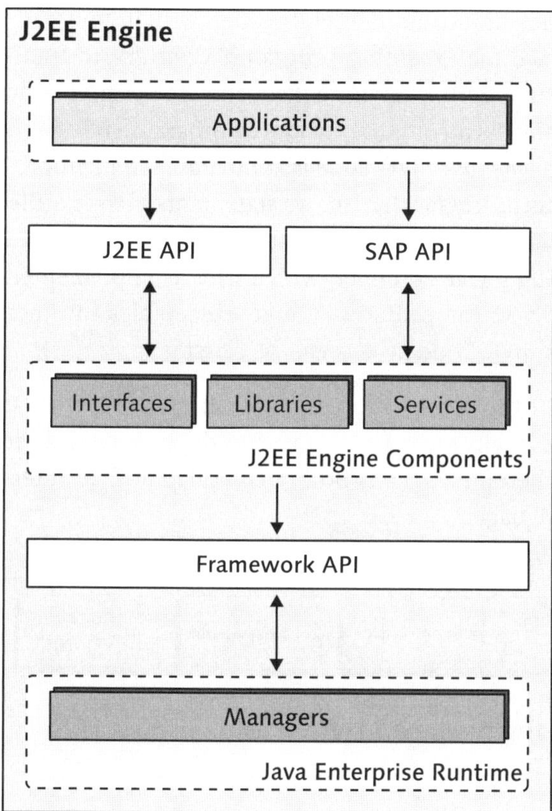

Figure 15.1 Structure of the J2EE Engine

15.2 Overview of the Java Development Process

In this context, we will first answer the question: What is Java?

Java was developed in 1991 by Sun Microsystems for domestic appliances. The primary intention was to create a language that is small and fast and can easily be ported to very different hardware platforms. Thus, Java was ideally suited as a powerful language for programs to be executed online over the Internet. Java is an object-oriented programming language with many similarities to C or C++. The entire Java code is organized in methods of classes, and all states are represented as attributes of classes. Java has a comprehensive library of classes, some of which facilitate the work with TCP/IP-based protocols such as HTTP or FTP.

Byte code Furthermore, Java has moved into a different direction with its approach of platform independence for executing programs. Contrary to traditional translators of a programming language that generate machine code for a certain platform, the Java compiler produces program code for a virtual machine, called a *byte code*. Byte code is comparable to microprocessor code for a fictitious processor that knows statements such as arithmetic operations, skips, and more. The byte code is generated by a Java compiler, for example Sun's Java compiler, which itself is implemented in Java. In Figure 15.2, you can see how, unlike executables in other programming languages, byte code in Java can be classified.

Java Virtual Machine (JVM) For the program code of the virtual processor to run, the Java Virtual Machine (JVM) runtime environment must execute the byte code after the translation phase. Therefore, Java is both a compiled and an interpreted programming language.

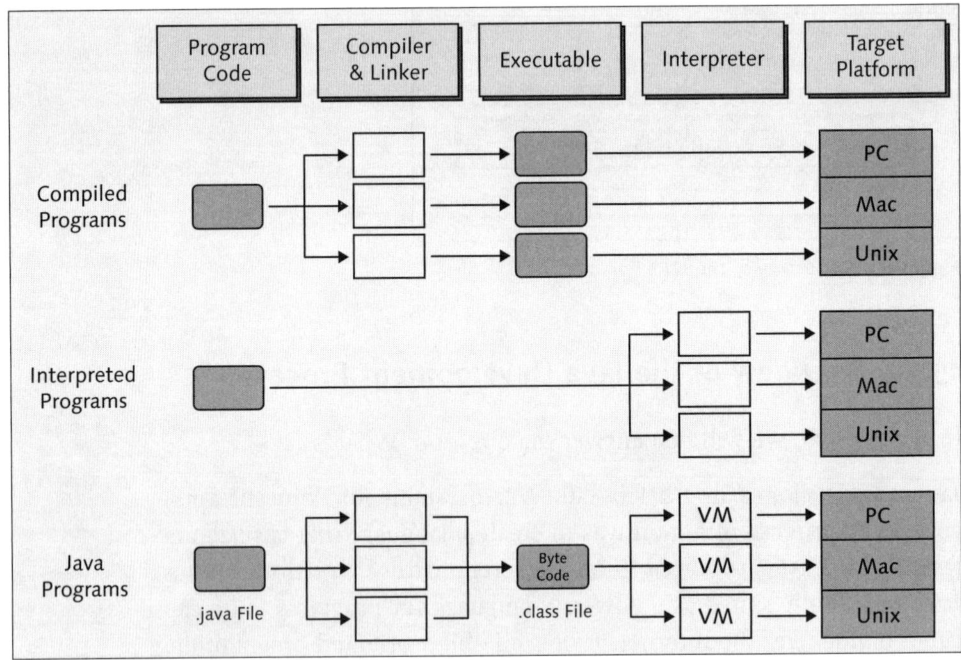

Figure 15.2 Platform Differences of Programming Languages

JVM must be developed individually by platform. In this respect, JVM is a standalone runtime environment that forms the interface between

Java programs and the operating system. Aside from Sun and IBM, other operating system vendors for JVM provide this virtual machine for their platforms. The SAP J2EE Engine is then executed within this JVM, and the corresponding applications run within the engine, as mentioned previously.

J2EE Engine components

J2EE applications consist of individual components. A J2EE component is a complete and functional software unit forming a J2EE application along with associated classes and other files (assembly), which can also communicate with other components via interfaces. The J2EE specification distinguishes between the following J2EE components:

- Java applets—presentation parts running on the client
- Java servlets and Java Server Pages—presentation parts or J2EE web components running on the server
- Enterprise Java Beans (EJBs)—components with the business process control running on the server

The communication between the J2EE server and the user is based on the Internet standards HTML, HTTP, or XML. The J2EE server can create HTML pages or XML files via JSPs or Java servlets running in a *container* for J2EE web applications within the J2EE server. Java applets can make up parts of the HTML pages sent to the browser. These are small Java applications running on the client JVM; naturally, this requires that JVM is installed on the client computer as a part of the J2SE (the Java Standard Edition, the less complex version for PCs which—in contrast to J2EE—does not support server functions). According to the J2EE application architecture, the application logic (EJBs) and the presentation layer (JSPs, and servlets) are also separated in the development phase.

Java development

The activities during Java development are divided into different roles. When developing application logic, the developer creates his own Enterprise Java Beans. For this purpose, the developer can use classes that are contained in the standard Java libraries or in Java classes of other developers. These are all included or imported, for example, by inserting the following lines in the source code:

```
import java.awt.Toolkit;
import java.awt.event.ActionEvent;
import java.io.FileInputStream;
```

Deployment descriptor

The structure and runtime behavior of the application are described in the context of an XML file called the deployment descriptor. The descriptor lists the transactional behavior as well as the persistence and security settings. To a certain extent, this permits setting and reusing the applications without changing the source code.

Build process

When the development is completed, the developer uses standard Java programs to merge the EJBs, classes used, and deployment descriptors in a Java archive (.jar). This process is called the *build process*. When creating the presentation logic, JSPs or Java servlets and HTML pages are assembled into web archives (.war) in the same way, and thus also creating a deployment descriptor.

At the end of the entire development process, these archives can be bundled with new deployment descriptors into enterprise archives (.ear). This assembly process is carried out by the Application Assembler.

Finally, the platform-independent enterprise archive must be installed on the individual J2EE servers. This deployment step is usually performed by an expert of the respective operating system environment. During this step, the tools analyze the different deployment descriptors and assign the application specific database resources or security settings, for example. Figure 15.3 shows these process steps in graphical way.

Development environment

This summarizes the individual steps for creating a Java application. Everything that is required for this process is included in the Java Software Development Kit (J2SDK). Nevertheless, this environment is not feasible for creating larger developments or for working with larger development teams. Therefore, an Integrated Development Infrastructure (IDE) is used for a more suitable development environment. However, even with an IDE, you can still encounter challenges and problems stemming from individual developers developing locally in their own runtime environment. This localized development often results in errors due to lack of consistency between local and central system environments (see also Figure 15.4).

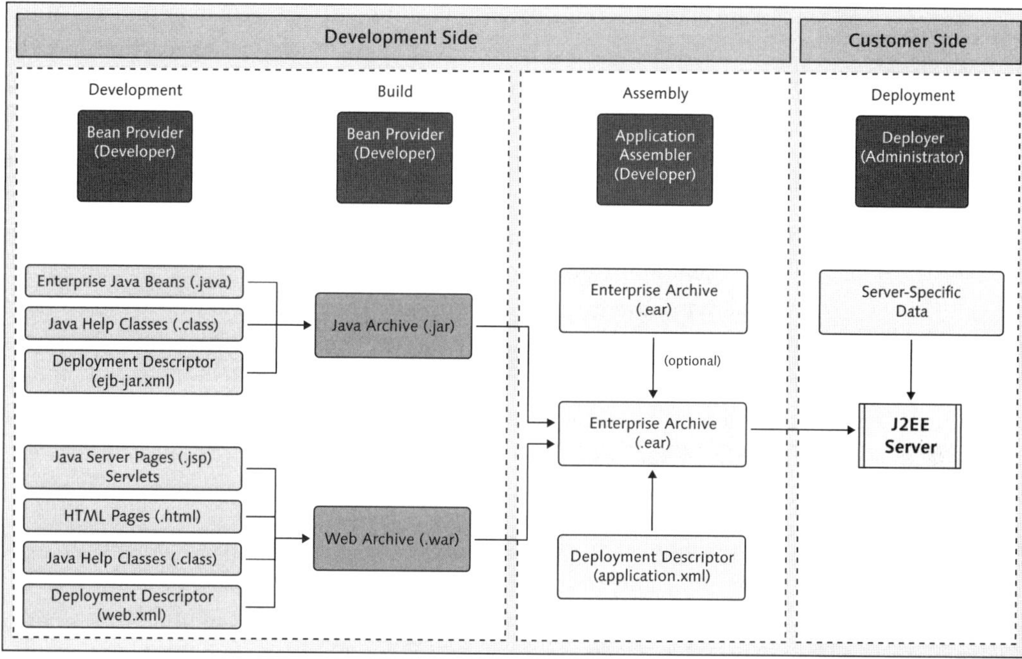

Figure 15.3 The Standard Java Development Process

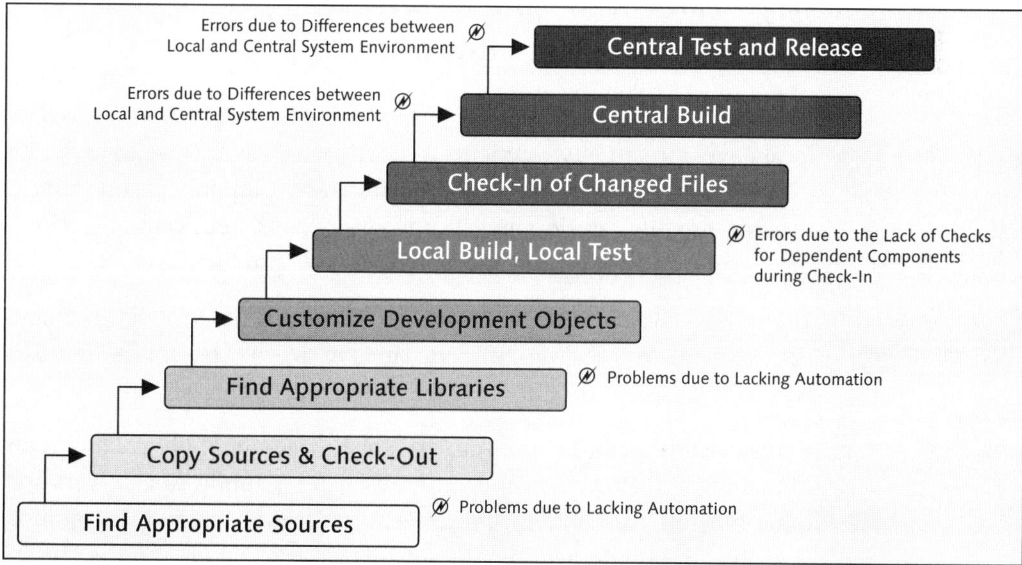

Figure 15.4 Possible Mistakes in the Java Development Process

Like ABAP applications, Java applications can exist in different versions. Therefore, before a developer creates a new or changes an existing application, he must be sure to use the correct versions of source code and libraries that were used. Often, to use the different versions within different development steps, the IDE configuration must be changed. When the correct versions of all necessary sources have been found and checked out of the central file directory, local development can begin. The developer then creates his own builds from time to time—based on the respective operating system environment—to test his application locally. After the development is completed, the changed sources are copied back to the central directory. Errors might occur during this process if, for example, referenced objects have been changed by other developers and copied back into the central directory. When testing on the central system, this can lead to different runtime environments compared to the developer's computer.

These problems do not occur when developing in ABAP because the development and runtime environments are provided centrally on one system. The goal of the NWDI is therefore to avoid the problems of standard Java development and to use the ABAP concepts instead.

15.3 Parts of the SAP NetWeaver Development Infrastructure

The SAP NetWeaver Development Infrastructure (NWDI) consists of local development environments, the SAP NetWeaver Developer Studio (NWDS), and additional server-based software components and services that can provide development teams with a consistent central environment and thus support the entire lifecycle of a product.

SAP NetWeaver Developer Studio

The SAP NetWeaver Developer Studio (NWDS) is the SAP development environment for creating different kinds of SAP J2EE applications. The NWDS is based on the Eclipse open source development platform.

Using existing tools, Eclipse supports the development of Java programs in many ways. However, integration with J2EE application servers and other functions required for the SAP environment is missing. Integration is enabled by implementing plug-ins, which are included in the NWDS installation package – see also figure 15.5.

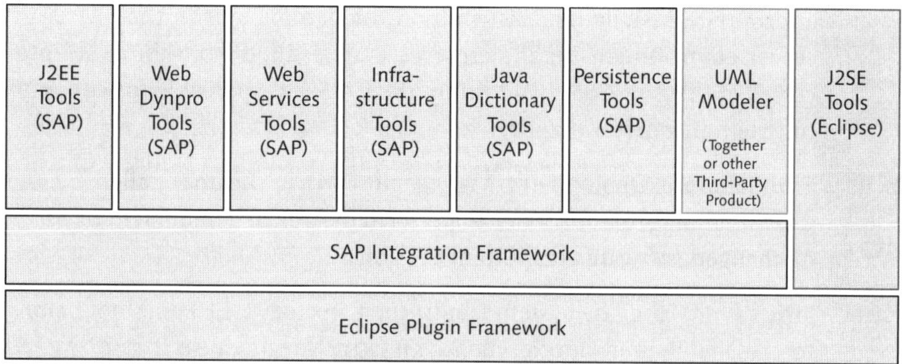

Figure 15.5 Eclipse and the SAP NetWeaver Developer Studio

Local and team-oriented development, testing, and deployment of business applications are supported through versioning. In addition, tools for different kinds of application development are included, such as Web-Screen tools for creating web interfaces or J2EE tools for developing J2EE applications such Enterprise Java Beans. By using these tools, and by integrating them with the other components of the SAP NetWeaver development environment discussed in the following sections, it is possible to fully support the Java development process. For a graphical overview see also figure 15.6.

Design Time Repository

The central storage and versioning of the Java sources and other resources required for development is taken over by the Design Time Repository (DTR). To enable development in a team, an automated conflict detection, and the corresponding conflict resolution for different versions, is also provided. Together with the SAP NetWeaver Developer Studio, the DTR allows for the support of all projects, such as Web Dynpros or Enterprise Java Beans.

Component Build Service

The Component Build Service (CBS) is responsible for creating runtime objects such as Java archives, which can later be deployed in the J2EE Engine. The CBS allows for incremental builds, as well as for an automated rebuild of dependent software components, by reading the necessary resources from the DTR. The component builds are based on the SAP component model.

Change Management Service

The Change Management Service (CMS) controls the transports and deployments in the development environment by carrying out the appropriate installation, distribution, or deployment in the SAP J2EE server environment for the archives that resulted from the build processes of the SAP CBS. In addition, the CMS is responsible for configuring the transport landscape.

Software Deployment Manager

The Software Deployment Manager (SDM) is the tool called by the Change Management Service to perform the actual deployment of a new or changed software component version.

System Landscape Directory

Strictly speaking, the System Landscape Directory (SLD) does not belong to the NetWeaver Development Infrastructure because it can be used for many other purposes without even using the development environment. However, the NWDI builds on the SLD as a central server application to access information about the existing system landscape, the software components contained in it, and the name range reservation (name server).

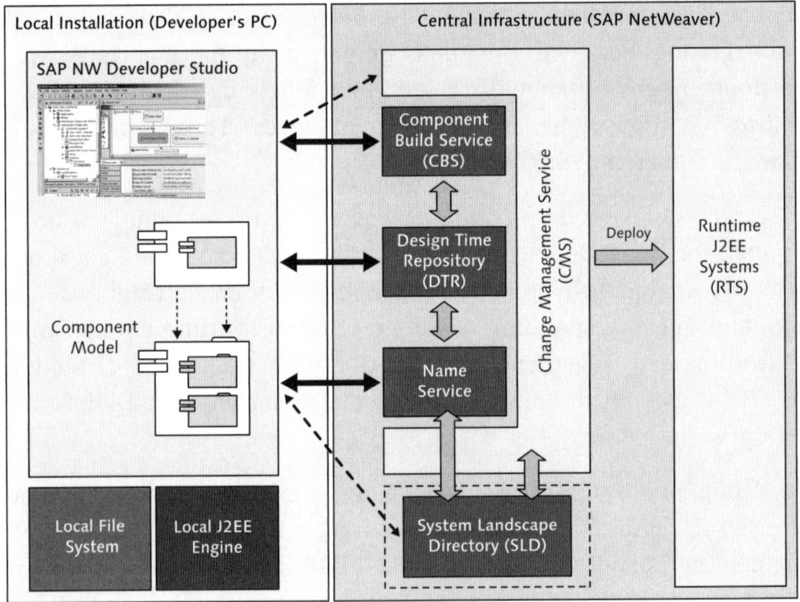

Figure 15.6 Parts of the SAP NetWeaver Development Infrastructure

Software component model

The development of Java applications in the NWDI is based on the SAP software component model. Using this model, software projects can be systematically structured because programming units—which can be maintained and reused in a more optimal way—can be used from the beginning. The components can use other components in a defined and controlled way by making only specific functions available via a set of public interfaces—the public parts. In addition to the componentization of the development process, using a name server within the SLD helps avoid naming conflicts for software objects, even with distributed development. These conflicts will not be apparent during local development or in a local test. However, when the different software objects are brought together in a common runtime environment, any error—up to and including the deactivation of the applications—can occur.

To protect production systems from premature additional developments in the local or central development systems, the production and development environments must be strictly separated. Aside from that, ideally a stable runtime environment should exist, reflecting the software status of the production system to test new developments. To accomplish these goals, SAP recommends a four-system landscape (see Figure 15.7). The four systems represent the different process states, where DEV and CONS stand for the two possible development states of the software components.

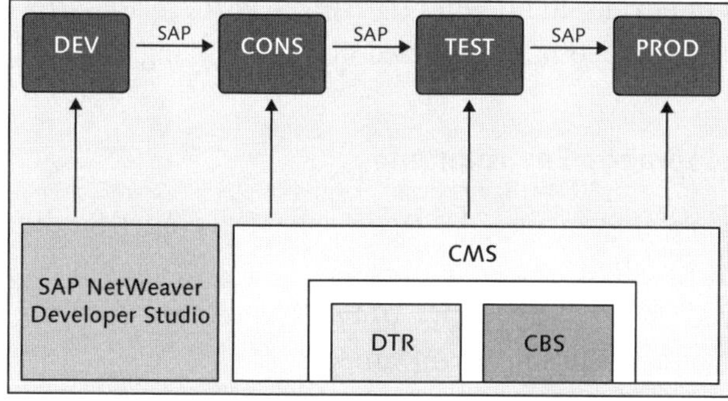

Figure 15.7 Four-System Landscape in the NWDI

The central development system DEV is used by individual developers to test their local developments in a larger context. This means that the interaction with developments of other programmers can be tested. In the consolidation system CONS and the test system TEST, either certain fixed states of software components are consolidated or a complete test, for example, an integration test, is carried out. Only after successful testing can the new development be imported into the production system

PROD. The transports between the different systems are then started and monitored by the CMS.

[+] As mentioned previously, the SAP NetWeaver Development Infrastructure has defined four systems per default. However, you do not necessarily keep four runtime systems ready, even though this would make sense in light of the different tests within the Java environment. If, for example, a transport landscape with only three systems exists for parallel ABAP-based systems, you could also adapt the runtime systems to the Java transport landscape. In this case, you would build up runtime systems for only DEV, TEST, and PROD. Irrespective of this scenario, there would still be a workspace in the DTR and a build space for the CONS system in the CBS, on the basis of which the deployments would be built.

15.4 Configuration of the SAP NetWeaver Development Infrastructure

Before the SAP NetWeaver Development Infrastructure can be used, it must be installed and configured. Depending on how the NWDI will be used or which types of development will be performed, there are different scenarios that are described in more detail in the following sections.

15.4.1 Local Development Environment

Java applications are created in the SAP NetWeaver Developer Studio. Because the NWDS is installed on a developer's PC, the applications created must be deployed on the J2EE Engine of SAP NetWeaver AS. Thus, the J2EE Engine serves as a runtime environment.

[+] In ABAP-based systems, developments are carried out via the ABAP Workbench. Because the ABAP Workbench is part of SAP NetWeaver AS ABAP, it can be used both as a development and as a runtime environment.

This illustrates that the development of Java applications generally consists of a combination of local development and testing, on the one hand, and central testing, deployment, and execution on the other hand.

[+] If, aside from the development of Java applications, an ABAP development and runtime environment is required, SAP NetWeaver AS ABAP

+ Java needs to be installed instead of SAP NetWeaver AS Java. This is the case, for example, if the interfaces must be created in Java, but data access takes place via an ABAP-based system.

In this case, the order of the installation steps is as follows:

1. Installation of SAP NetWeaver AS (Java or ABAP + Java)
2. Local installation of the SAP NetWeaver Developer Workplace, which consists of the SAP NWDS and local SAP NetWeaver AS Java
3. Optionally, the installation of additional SAP NetWeaver Developer Workplaces

The recommended hardware requirements for installing the SAP NWDI can be found in SAP Note 737368, based on the applicable development scenario. The following are the requirements for a PC with SAP NWDS: on the hardware side, 2GB RAM, a CPU with a clock rate of 2GHz and approximately 3GB available disk space; on the software side, Windows 2000 SP3 or Windows XP, with Internet Explorer Version 5.5 or higher. [+]

15.4.2 Overview of the Different Development Scenarios

The SAP NetWeaver Development Infrastructure supports several development scenarios, which are based on each other, as follows:

- **Scenario 1—team-oriented development**
  Although it is possible to wholly support pure Java and J2EE projects with this scenario, you cannot carry out any Web Dynpro development. If you decide to work in software components later on, there is no tool support to migrate existing developments to the component model. Because this involves manual effort, you must determine early on which scenario should be used.
- **Scenario 2—development of software components**
  Unlike Scenario 1, this scenario allows you to develop software components. However, it still uses only the DTR and you must therefore carry out the build process or deployment manually.

  As with Scenario 1, SAP also does not provide any automatic migration tools to higher scenarios for this scenario. Therefore, this is considered a demo scenario for developing in software components.

- **Scenario 2+ — development of software components with a track**
  This scenario allows you to develop software components, provides you with the complete range of administrative functions, and allows you to use the build environment.
- **Scenario 3 — development with multiple layers**
  This scenario is necessary if different software components that depend on one another need to be developed in parallel. Because this scenario enables you to combine different tracks and therefore develop interdependent applications, it is considered an extension of the second scenario.

Scenario 1: Team-Oriented Development

Small development teams

In general, this scenario is recommended for only smaller development teams that do not require any central administration. Development should be restricted to pure Java and J2EE applications. The components of the SAP NWDI used in this case are the DTR for the storing and versioning of program sources, as well as the SAP NWDS for the actual development process. Because no components are used, neither the CBS nor the CMS is required.

Installation and configuration

The order of installation and configuration steps is as follows:

1. Installation of SAP NetWeaver AS Java.
2. Deployment of NWDI components on this server.
3. Installation of the SAP NetWeaver Developer Workplaces (with the NWDS and, optionally, local SAP NetWeaver AS Java).
4. Configuration of the DTR servers, specifically the creation of the workspaces, the user management system, and the users and their authorizations upon which they are based.
5. Configuration of DTR client definitions for all NWDS in use.
6. Selection of files for automatic storing in the DTR.
7. Setup of runtime systems in the DTR.
8. Setup of manual or automated processes for Software Change Management (optional).

In this scenario (see Figure 15.8), developers each have their own local development environment consisting of the SAP NetWeaver Developer Studio and, optionally, local SAP NetWeaver AS Java for running tests. The development takes place in the NWDS. The Design Time Repository (DTR) is used to centrally provide program sources to all team members. In the DTR, the sources and their versions are stored in files and directories, and a concurrent development on their basis is appropriately controlled.

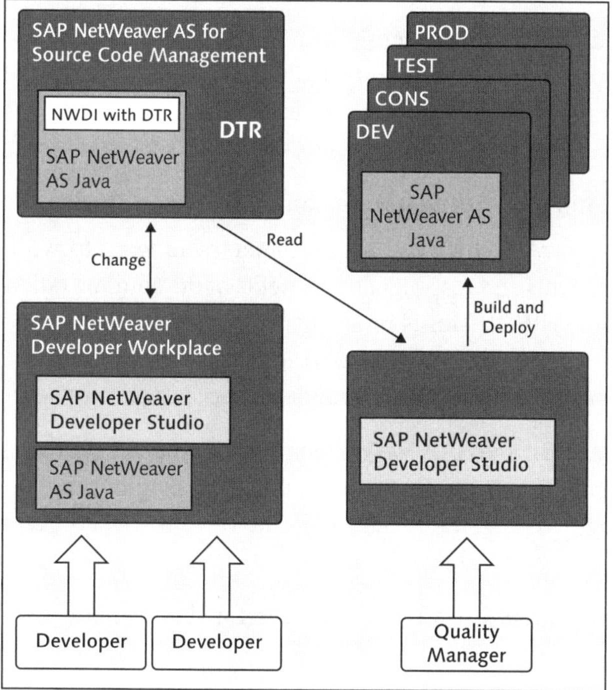

Figure 15.8 Example of a System Landscape for Scenario 1

The developed applications are then compiled and assembled with the integrated tools of the NWDS. The deployment of the applications is performed manually from the NWDS by starting the SAP Deployment Manager.

In this scenario, it is the quality manager's responsibility to maintain different states of the program sources in the DTR. To meet this requirement, different DTR workspaces should be created for development and consolidation.

Scenario 2: Development with Software Components

Small teams

This scenario is appropriate for smaller development teams if you do not want to restrict development to pure Java and J2EE applications, or, if you want to test how to use software components in development and how to modularize programming by defining their dependencies. As with the previous scenario, the only components of the SAP NetWeaver Development Infrastructure used here are the DTR for the storing and versioning of program sources and the SAP NWDS for the actual development process.

Installation and configuration steps

The installation and configuration steps—and the parts and tasks of the NWDI—in this scenario are the same as those in Scenario 1, with one exception: you can use the SAP component model.

Scenario 2+: Development with Software Components in a Track

All advantages in administration and automation

This scenario (see Figure 15.9) is ideal for customers who want to work with software components and reap all of the benefits of the administration and automation of the NWDI. This is the scenario that can be used, aside from Scenario 3, to customize Web Dynpros for Employee Self Service (ESS) and Management Self Service (MSS) to meet special requirements.

It uses all components of the SAP NetWeaver Development Infrastructure: the Design Time Repository for storing and versioning of program sources, the Change Management Service, and the SAP NetWeaver Developer Studio for the actual development.

Installation and configuration steps

The order of installation and configuration steps for this scenario is as follows:

1. Installation of SAP NetWeaver AS Java.
2. Setup and activation of the SLD.
3. Installation of one or several AS Java instances for the NWDI components.
4. [+] Although the different components of the NWDI such as DTR, CBS, and CMS, as well as the System Landscape Directory (SLD), can be installed on a server, for performance reasons, SAP recommends that you install at least the DTR and the CBS on separate hosts. For basic information about hardware requirements, see SAP Note 737368.

5. Deployment of the NWDI components.
6. Installation of the SAP NetWeaver Developer Workplaces (with the NWDS and, optionally, local SAP NetWeaver AS Java).
7. Installation of SAP NetWeaver AS Java as a central test system.
8. Creation and setup of the user management system, and the users and authorizations on which it is based.
9. Creation of a domain and a track in the CMS.
10. Check-in and import of the required program sources.
11. Customization of the authorization for the DTR workspaces.
12. Import of the development configuration.

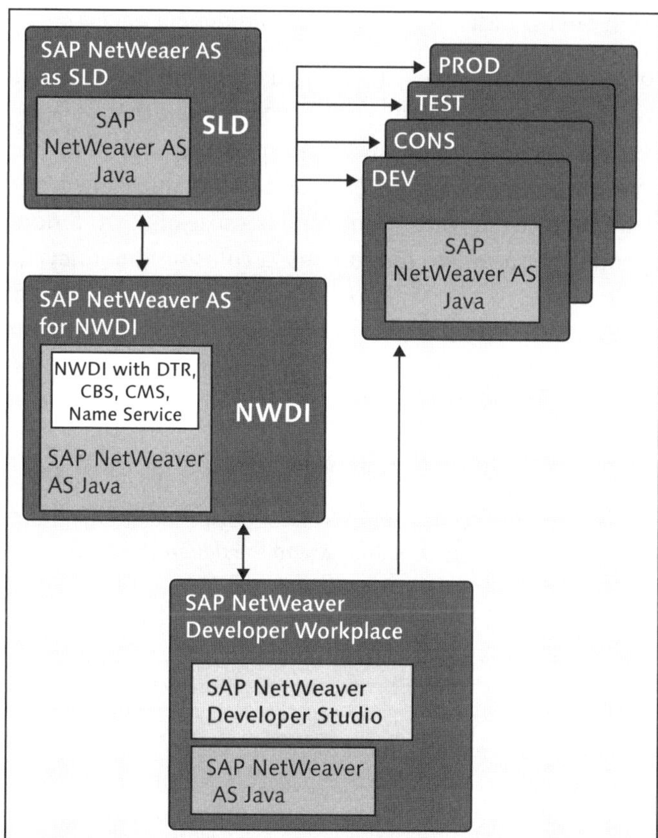

Figure 15.9 Example of a System Landscape for Scenario 2+

As with the previous scenarios, every developer has his own locally installed SAP NetWeaver Developer Studio and SAP NetWeaver AS Java. The DTR is also used as a central storage location of the sources. However, by using the software components, the developers can distribute their programs among team members to create smaller, reusable, more modular units that are easier to use and maintain.

This is achieved via the type of encapsulation or by sharing only certain interfaces, that is, the public parts. In addition, by completely using the NWDI, some processes are automated; for example, in SAP NetWeaver Developer Studio, DTR access is set up automatically by importing the configuration of the development environment (development configuration). A special component build can now also be created in the SAP NWDS, which creates components based on their types and dependencies.

SAP component model

The advantage of the SAP component model as an extension of the classes and interfaces visibility concept already contained in Java is that—via the extension by the development and software components—each of these components is visible in one direction only and is exactly defined, via public parts, as an interface. For this reason, and because of the additionally defined dependency on other components, a collision due to cyclic interdependencies of the components is not possible. The builds are therefore always provided with the current libraries, and the creation of the previously mentioned "incremental builds" is possible only by using these extensions.

Example

Figure 15.10, which shows the Web Dynpro Explorer perspective of the SAP NetWeaver Developer Studio, helps you understand the dependencies of the individual development components and the builds.

The dependencies of com.sap.budget.mss are visible via USED DCs (such as com.sap.aii.proxy.framework or com.sap.aii.util.misc). If, for example, an object of the development component com.sap.aii.proxy.framework is changed, a build request is automatically created in the CBS. The same applies to dependent development components—in this case com.sap.budget.mss—which are then rebuilt via another build request. For example, if other development components use the interfaces shown under PUBLIC PARTS (in this case only BudgetInfo), these components would be rebuilt automatically when there are changes to com.sap.budget.mss because the other development components entered com.sap.budget.mss as Used DCs.

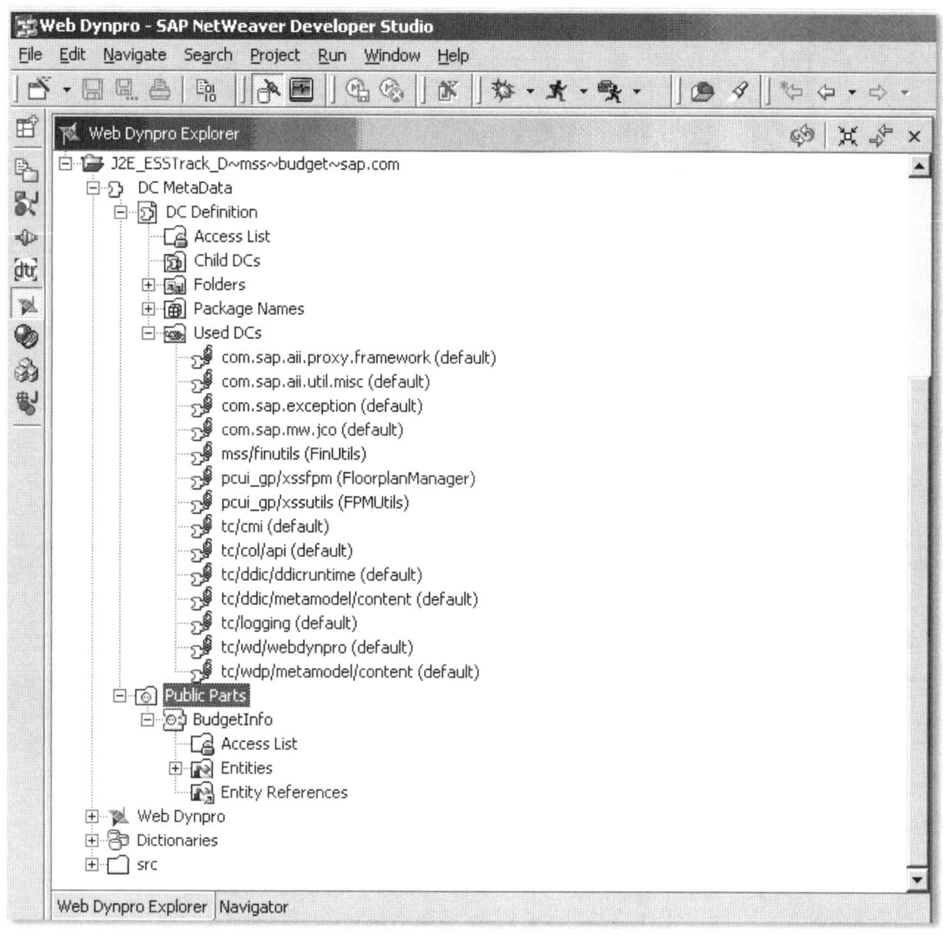

Figure 15.10 Example of the Dependencies of Development Components

By using the Component Build Service (CBS), you no longer need to use command line tools and individual build scripts to create a central component build. The CBS creates builds from components and their dependent objects on demand, and also provides ready-to-use libraries and deployment tools for developers and runtime systems. The process of software distribution is now automated as well, by implementing the SAP Change Management Service (CMS). The CMS is responsible for transporting the software—that is, program sources and libraries—within the landscape, and supports the automatic deployment of executable programs on the relevant servers.

Scenario 3: Layered Development

Parallel development

This scenario is an extension of Scenario 2+ in that several software components that are based on each other are developed in parallel. The development can be coordinated hierarchically. The requirements regarding the system landscape and the individual tasks therefore correspond to those of Scenario 2+, except that more J2EE Engines might be necessary for testing the applications. This is the scenario SAP uses for software development. Figure 15.11 shows an example of the various software layers.

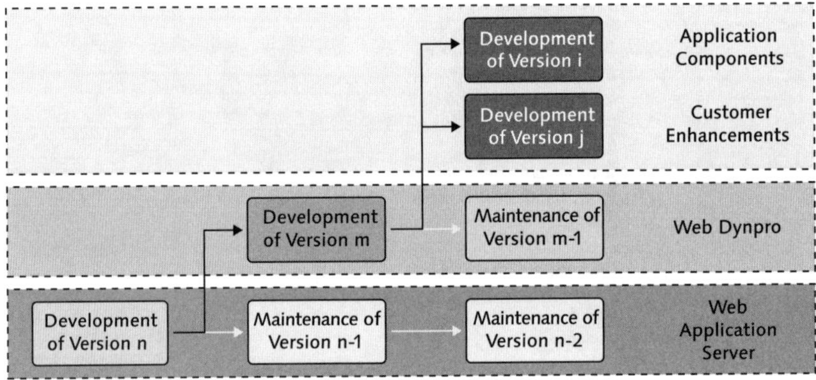

Figure 15.11 Different Layers in the Java Development Process

15.5 Configuration of the SAP NetWeaver Development Infrastructure

After the basic demands on specific services and components for using the NWDI have been introduced in the previous chapters, we will now describe the configuration of the individual parts so you can use manual or automated processes in the SAP Software Change Management. Because the individual scenarios are built on each other, we will discuss the configuration of Scenario 2+ in particular because it requires all parts of the NWDI and therefore also reflects the DTR configuration for Scenarios 1 and 2.

Figure 15.12 gives you an overview of all of the steps to be carried out during Java development; the details will be described throughout the rest of this chapter. Before you can begin the actual development, you must determine the parts that make up the software, and in which environment the development should take place. After the development has been completed, it is distributed using other parts of the NWDI.

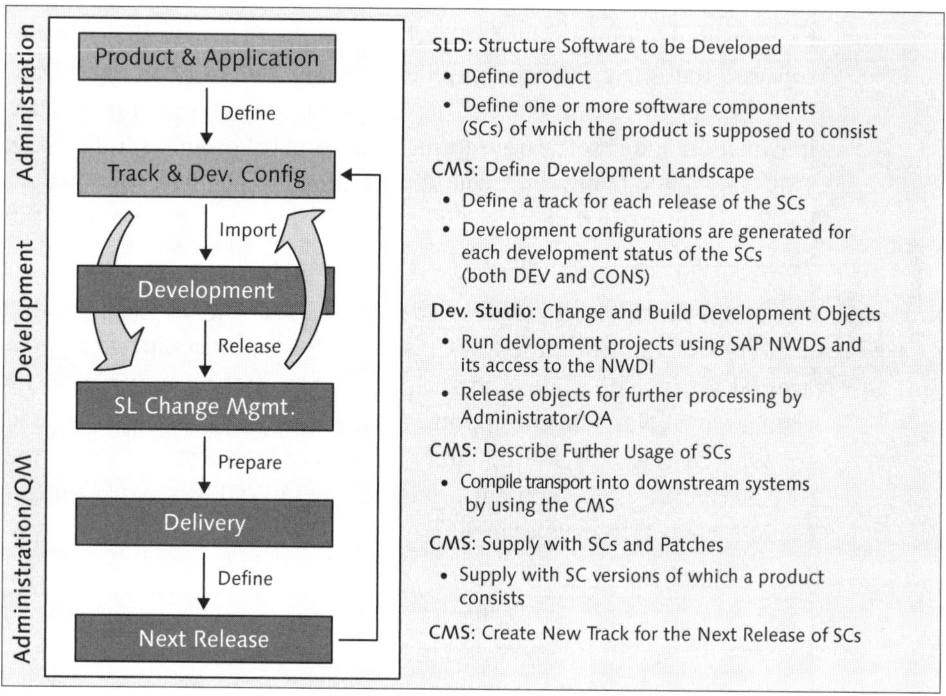

Figure 15.12 The Lifecycle in Java Development

15.5.1 Configuration of the System Landscape Directory

To map the complex business processes of today, a multitude of different software components are required on different hardware platforms. Dependencies exist between the components regarding installation requirements, software updates, and the interfaces that connect them. Therefore, the administration of such a system landscape can become complex and difficult to handle. In general, the System Landscape Directory (SLD) facilitates the administration of an SAP system landscape by serving as a central storage for this information. All installable and installed components of a system landscape are stored based on the standard Common Information Model (CIM), which provides a general, flexibly extensible schema for the description of such components, and has been enhanced by SAP with proprietary SAP-specific classes.

Automatic registration

Information about the installable SAP software components is provided by SAP on a regular basis as data packages that can be imported into the System Landscape Directory (SLD). The SAP software components can be registered automatically and cyclically in the SLD with their current software status (e.g., version numbers, current patch levels, and dependencies on other components). Furthermore, you can manually enter information about software statuses of third-party products in the SLD. This way, the SLD provides you with a complete picture of the system landscape in its current state. Figure 15.13 gives you an idea how the SLD is embedded in a system landscape.

Universal data source

The SLD is therefore also ideal as a data source for other applications that are very different from the NWDI, such as the Software Lifecycle Manager (SLM), which can be used as a planning tool for executing software changes as of NetWeaver Support Package Stack 12. It can also be used for Web Dynpros for storing target systems of web services, or for the SAP NetWeaver Development Infrastructure (NWDI), to manage information relevant to development.

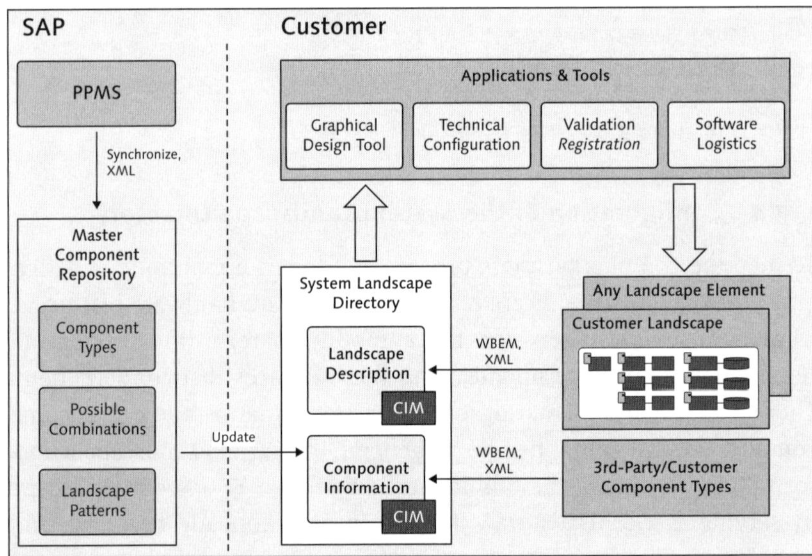

Figure 15.13 Data Flow between SLD and other Components

The SLD is a server application that communicates with clients only via Hypertext Transfer Protocol (HTTP or HTTPs). The SLD is installed automatically during the installation of SAP NetWeaver AS Java, but must be appropriately configured and activated before it can be used. The following is an overview of the individual steps required for this purpose:

- Change the virtual memory size (depending on the creator of the JRE/JDK) to at least 512 or 1024 MB using the J2EE config tool.
- Create users and roles depending on the system used as the User Management Engine (UME).
- Log on to the SLD with a user belonging to either the J2EE administrators group or to the SAP_SLD_ADMINISTRATOR group; this access is performed via a browser using the address *http://SLD-Host:Port/sld*.
- Specify basic SLD settings such as persistence and Object Server via ADMINISTRATION • SERVER SETTINGS.

  In the OBJECT SERVER area, you can enter the name range known from the ABAP environment without "/". This name range can be requested in the SAP Service Marketplace at *http://service.sap.com/NAMERANGES*. If this is not what you want, you should enter the host name of the SLD. In this case, however, the SLD can no longer be used for name range reservations in the NWDI.
- From the administration window, start the SLD server.
- From the administration window, also start the SLD bridge; this is necessary only if the systems of the system landscape should automatically report their current status to the SLD. The SLD bridge is required for converting the formats of the various system data to the Common Information Model (CIM) format used by the SLD.

  It is also possible to operate several SLDs in a system landscape. This can be the case, for example, in very large system landscapes or where there are special demands on network topologies or security restrictions. The SLD bridge can then exchange the data of an SLD system with that of another SLD system. More detailed information can be found in the document *Planning Guide* in the SAP Service Marketplace at *http://service.sap.com/SLD • Media Library*.

- Initial data import of the SAP product and software component description via ADMINISTRATION • IMPORT.

  The file required for this can be found in the SAP Service Marketplace at *http://service.sap.com/SWDC • Entry by Application Group • Additional Components • SAP Master Data for SLD* and in the corresponding subdirectories. What you need is the appropriate `CRContent` file. If an initial import has already occurred, only the `CRDelta` file is necessary. If an extension of the SLD CIM model is required, this is determined at the beginning of the data import. You would then have to first import the appropriate `CIMSAP` file. Additional explanations can be found in SAP Note 669669.

- Configuration of data providers.

  This procedure varies depending on whether an ABAP- or a Java-based system should register with the SLD. ABAP-based systems only register via RFC; Java-based systems can also transfer their data directly to the SLD bridge via HTTP. Details can be found in the *Post-Installation Guide*, which is available in the SAP Service Marketplace at *http://service.sap.com/SLD • Media Library*.

  Please note that only ABAP-based systems from SAP ERP 4.0B and higher, as well as Java-based systems from SAP NetWeaver AS J2EE 6.30 and higher, can automatically register with the SLD. For ABAP-based systems, a minimum Support Package status is required, which is listed in SAP Note 584654.

- Register the SLD.

  This step is required for only the SLD. Using the path HOME • TECHNICAL LANDSCAPE • NEW TECHNICAL SYSTEM, you first create a system for SAP NetWeaver AS Java in which the SLD has been activated, or the system is created automatically for this SAP NetWeaver AS Java by activating the SLD registration services from the Visual Administrator. Then, using the path HOME • TECHNICAL LANDSCAPE • NEW TECHNICAL SYSTEM, a system landscape directory entry is set up based on this system.

- If the name range reservation is used in the NWDI, the SLD that fulfills the name server function must be appropriately registered in the DTR after the DTR has been set up.

15.5.2 Setting Up Users and Authorizations

The correct setup of users, and their roles and authorizations significantly contributes to whether the developments can be carried out in a coordinated way and, for example, whether a dual control for acceptance and tests, or a division of tasks between the actual development activity and the transportation, is possible. In this context, a distinction is made between the following users in the NWDI area:

NWDI users

- Developers who work in both their SAP NetWeaver Developer Studio and in the SAP NetWeaver Development Infrastructure (NWDI). They must have access to the SLD and the other NWDI components.
- An NWDI administrator who needs access to all components of the NWDI. However, for the configuration in the CMS, it is not really necessary to access the SLD; this can be done by an SLD's own administrator.
- Change Management Service (CMS) users who carry out a variety of activities in the SLD, CMS, DTR, and CBS that are necessary for setting up the NWDI and operating the CMS.

Ideally, the development in the NWDI is hierarchically structured and its procedure corresponds to that illustrated in Figure 15.14.

Table 15.1 shows how these users can be assigned to various roles and user groups.

NWDI Role	User	UME Role	UME Group
Member of Development Team	Developer_1 Developer_2 Developer_n	NWDI.Developer	NWDI.Developers
NWDI Administrator	NWDIadmin	NWDI.Administrator	NWDI.Administrators
(internal user)	CMSuser	NWDI.Administrator	NWDI.Administrators
Transport Manager Quality Manager	NWDImanager	NWDI.Manager	NWDI.Managers
Software Architect Landscape Administrator	Administrator	NWDI.Administrator	Administrators NWDI.Administrators

Table 15.1 Assignment of Users to Roles and User Groups

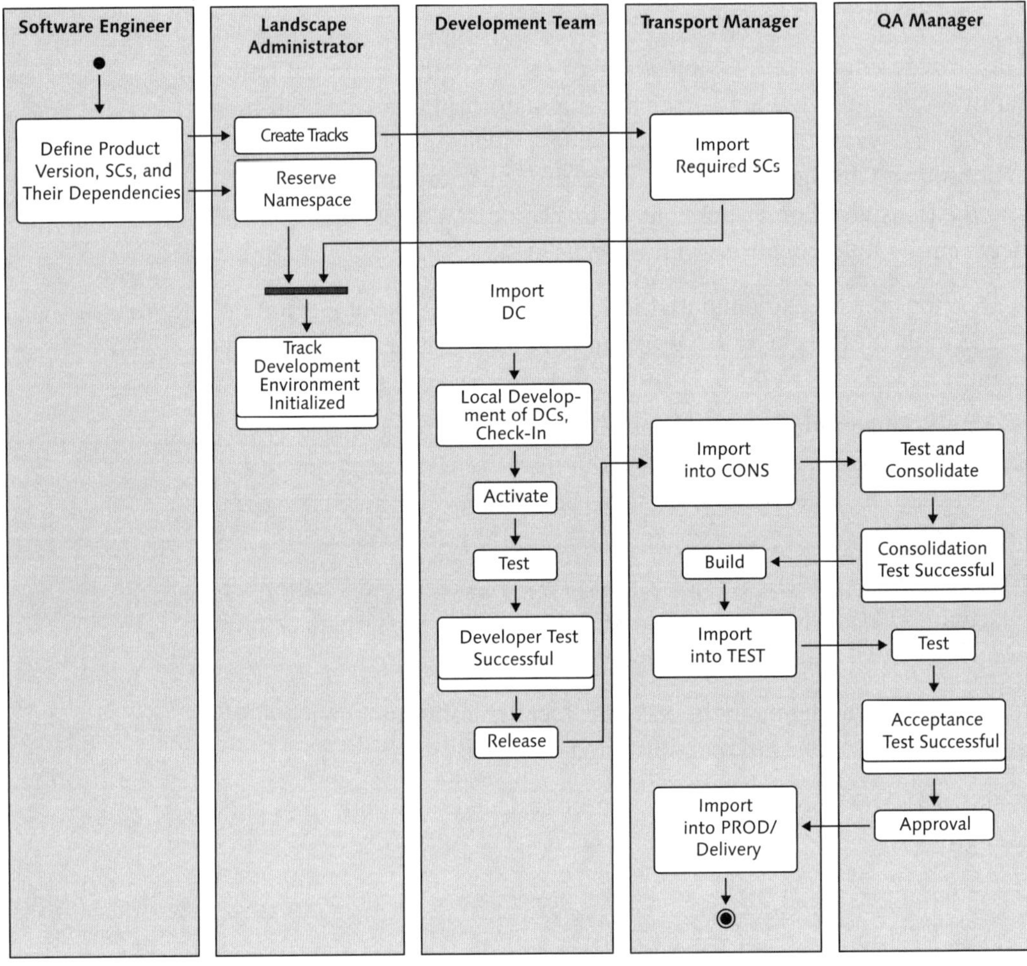

Figure 15.14 Hierarchical Structure of Java Development

CMSuser Although the CMSuser needs to be created, it should not be assigned to a person—it is used only internally by the CMS. This user is made known to the NWDI in the domain definition.

NWDI Administrator The NWDI Administrator, aside from having the authorizations of the NWDI Manager, also has administrator authorizations so that he can carry out special restore options, for example, in the event of an error that would require extended authorizations. Possible assignments of users to UME activities or security roles of the SLD are listed in Table 15.2.

User/Role	UME Activity	Java Security Role
NWDI.Developer	CBS.Developer CMS.Display CMS.Export	LcrInstanceWriterNR
NWDI.Adminstrator	CBS.Administrator CMS.Administrate	LcrInstanceWriterAll
CMSuser	CBS.Administrator CMS.Administrate	LcrInstanceWriterAll LcrInstanceWriterLD
NWDI.Manager	CBS.Developer CBS.QM CMS.Administrate	LcrInstanceWriterNR LcrInstanceWriterCR LcrInstanceWriterLD
Administrator	CBS.Administrator CMS.Administrate	LcrInstanceWriterAll LcrAdministrator

Table 15.2 User Assignments to UME Activities and SLD Roles

[+] If no central ABAP system or LDAP is used for user management, but users are created in the local UME and the SLD is installed on a separate J2EE Engine, users (in this example Developer_1 or CMSuser) must be created in all UMEs with the same authorizations and passwords. With respect to the SLD, the assignment needs to be done via VISUAL ADMIN • SERVER • SERVICES • SECURITY PROVIDER • SAP.COM\COM.SAP.LCR*SLD • SECURITY ROLES.

In addition, the authorizations for the DTR must be assigned. The corresponding detailed description can be found in the online help at *http://help.sap.com* • DOCUMENTATION • SAP NETWEAVER • ENGLISH • APPLICATION PLATFORM • JAVA TECHNOLOGY IN SAP NETWEAVER AS • ADMINISTRATION MANUAL • ADMINISTRATION OF SAP NWDI • CONFIGURING USER MANAGEMENT IN SAP NWDI • USER AUTHENTICATION AND USER AUTHORIZATION • CONFIGURING DTR CLIENTS.

15.5.3 Setting Up SAP NetWeaver Developer Studio

Finally, every SAP NetWeaver Developer Studio must be set up and configured appropriately, which is usually done by the responsible developer.

Storage location for different data types

Depending on the scenario chosen, the storage location for different data types is specified first. Unlike Scenarios 1 and 2, Scenarios 2+ or 3 do not store the .project and .classpath types. This is checked in the NWDS via the menu path WINDOW • PREFERENCES • TEAM • IGNORED RESOURCES. For Scenarios 2+ and 3, the checkboxes for the .project and .classpath types must be enabled.

If SAP NetWeaver AS Java was installed locally along with the NWDS, it must be set as a runtime environment. This is done via the menu path WINDOW • PREFERENCES • SAP J2EE ENGINE. If no local J2EE Engine is used, another SAP NetWeaver AS Java must be entered as a remote host, which will then serve as a runtime environment for the NWDS.

Development configuration pool

To enable access to the configuration (development configuration) in the SLD, the development configuration pool must be maintained in the NWDS settings. There, the URL of the SLD is entered via the menu path WINDOW • PREFERENCES • JAVA DEVELOPMENT INFRASTRUCTURE • DEVELOPMENT CONFIGURATION POOL.

15.5.4 Creating Products and Software Components

As mentioned previously, using software components allows a reasonable structuring of large projects into reusable units that are easier to handle. Figure 15.15 gives you a better idea of how the elements of the SAP component model are related to one another.

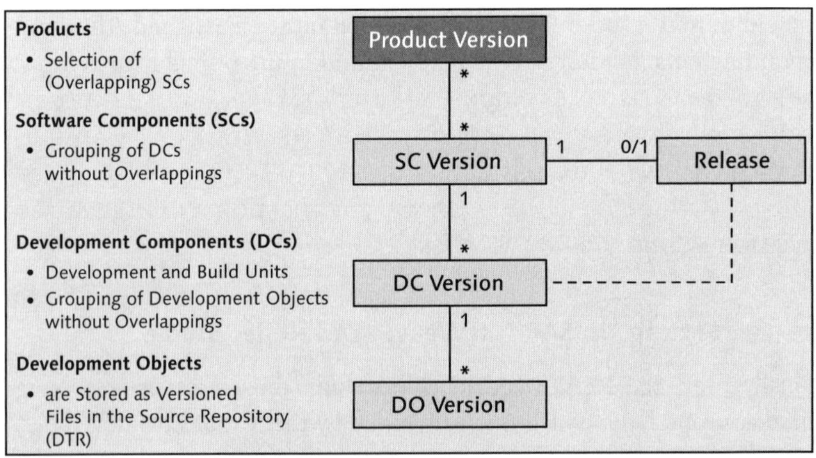

Figure 15.15 Elements of the SAP Component Model

Development component

A development component (called DC in the text that follows) is a kind of container for development objects in Java and thus forms the smallest build unit. A DC has defined, external interfaces and is otherwise known as a *black box*. DCs can use other DCs via their interfaces (public parts) and are therefore the elementary, reusable units of the component model.

Development object

A development object (called DO in the text that follows) is a part of a DC that provides portions of the DC functionality. This can be a Java class, a table definition, a JSP, or other objects.

Software component

Software components (called SC in the text that follows) connect DCs for the delivery and deployment to larger units. Ideally, the corresponding business processes can therefore be connected.

Release

A release identifies a bigger step in the development process that usually involves the provision of new or updated functionality.

Product

A product consists of one or more software components.

Products and software components are created in the SLD via the menu path HOME • SOFTWARE CATALOG (see Figure 15.16).

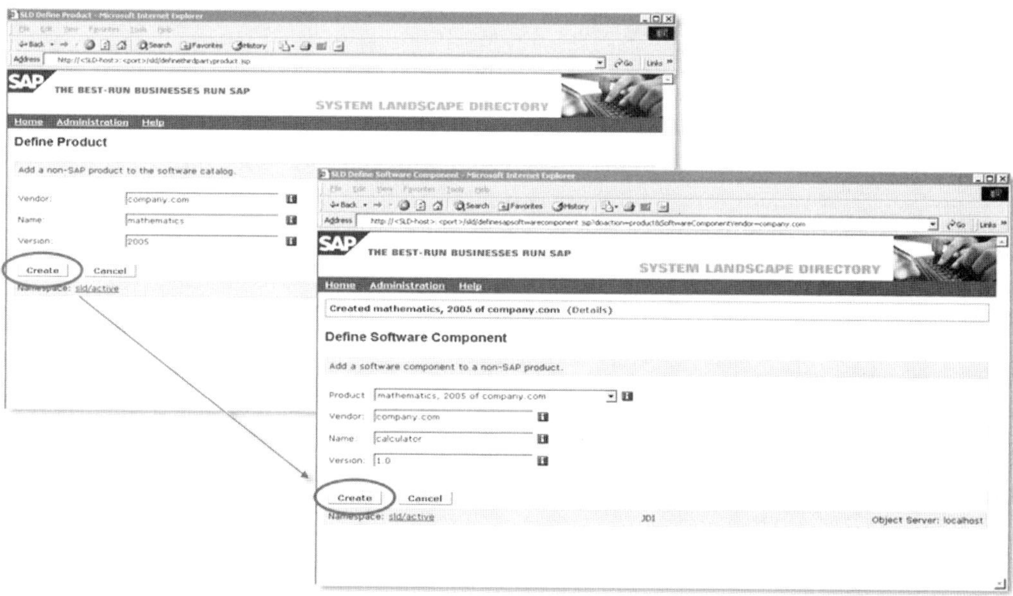

Figure 15.16 Products and Software Components in the SLD

Both products and software components must be created before starting the development process if this is necessary for your own development components. In the SLD, the dependencies of this software component are specified, and this, in turn, determines the dependencies for the central build. These conditions are maintained via the path SLD HOME • SOFTWARE CATALOG • PRODUCT VERSION • SOFTWARE COMPONENT • USAGE DEPENDENCY. For Java software component development, the dependency must be selected in the BUILD TIME context.

15.5.5 Creating a Domain and Track in the Change Management Service

To be able to structure the transport landscape, a Change Management Service (CMS) domain must be created. A CMS domain describes the part of the development landscape that is administered using the Change Management Service. The CMS domain stores the following information:

- The transport directory in which the transport information is stored
- The CMS administrative user (referred to previously as CMSuser) who executes the various tools
- The SAP NetWeaver AS Java running the CMS

The individual tracks in which the software components are developed are later created within this CMS domain and connected to the transport landscape. A domain is created with the CMS user interface, which is called from a browser using the address *http://<HOST>:<Port>/devinf* • *Change Management Service*. For this purpose, you need to log on to the screen with a user who belongs to the NWDI.Administrators group. You can then specify the settings according to those shown in Figure 15.17.

[+] Note that the data for DOMAIN NAME and CMS NAME is stored in the SLD and can therefore be assigned only once. The domain name can consist of a maximum of three letters or digits.

Development track

After a domain for structuring the transport landscape has been created, a development track is created in the next step. Additional parts that represent a track are shown in Figure 15.18.

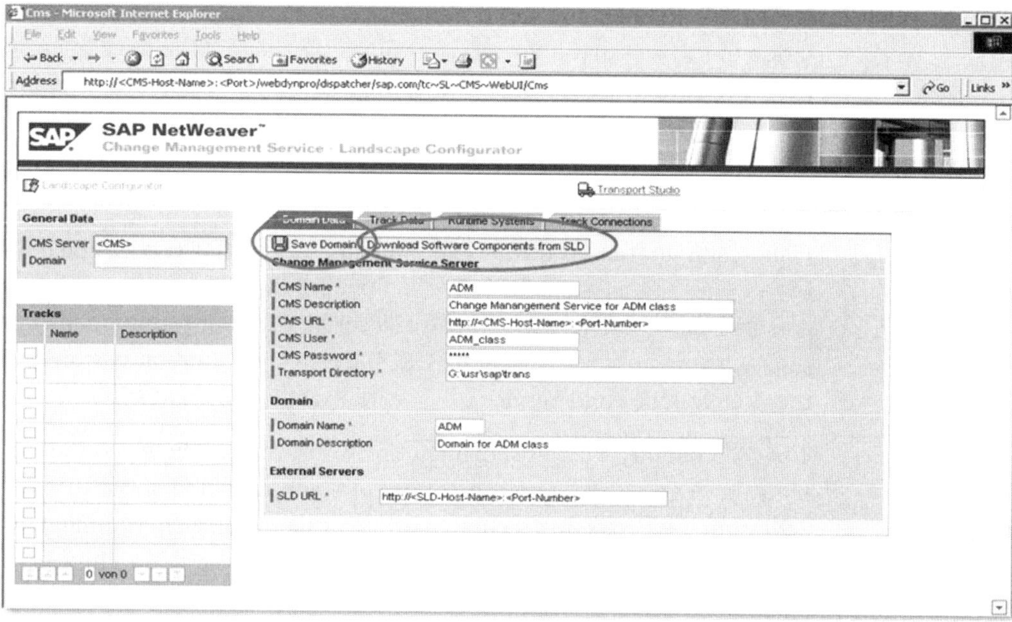

Figure 15.17 Creating a Domain

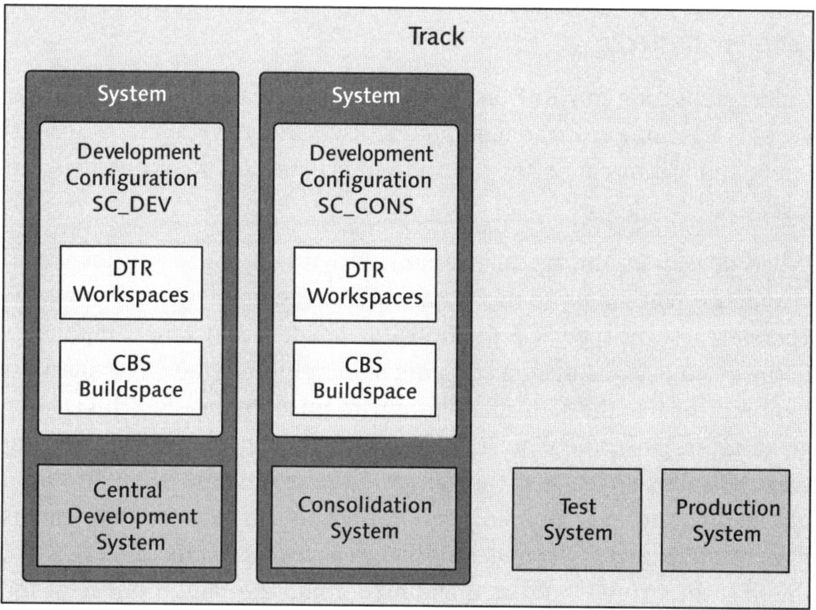

Figure 15.18 Parts of a Track

The development structure (development configuration, called configuration in the text that follows) determines the view of the developer on the development landscape. The configuration describes the software components to be developed and thus organizes access to the NWDI. Therefore, all developers working with the same configuration work with the same objects. This ensures consistency.

Every configuration in the Design Time Repository (DTR) is assigned up to two workspaces—one for active and one for inactive program sources. A workspace contains the sources of a certain software component status. Workspaces are accessed via URLs. Every configuration is stored in the Component Build Service (CBS) with exactly one build space.

The CMS handles the transporting of software changes between the systems. In general, a system can consist of a configuration and a runtime environment; that is, just a configuration, just a runtime environment, or both, depending on whether program sources or deployable archives will be transported. A system is connected to a development status (development, consolidation, test, or production).

The track contains all configurations and all runtime environments that are necessary to develop, test, and use one or several software components productively.

[+] Unlike transports in ABAP, a separate track is created in the NWDI for every release of a software component. In ABAP, developments for different applications are often transported via one and the same transport layer.

When developing in tracks, you must provide the CBS with the corresponding environment so that it can build the components appropriately. Therefore, if you specified additional, dependent software components in the product and software component definition in the SLD, you must transport them to the corresponding environment of the CBS. This is done via check-in. First, the required software components must be copied to the CMS/Inbox directory of the transport directory. In the transport studio of the CMS, the corresponding track for which the software components have been defined as dependent is then selected. Using the CHECK-IN tab, the relevant archive is selected and placed into the import queue of the development system using CHECK-IN. Finally, the software components must be imported, which is done in the CMS transport studio via DEVELOPMENT, by releasing the queued software components for import. This must be done for all systems for which the track has been created.

15.5.6 Creating a Development Component

Configurations (development configurations) are created and stored in the CMS. The SLD contains the information about the CMS in which the relevant configuration is stored. The configuration is then imported from the CMS into the NWDS. This way, the development environment is available for a specific software component in the current development state. Therefore, every development process starts with selecting a configuration.

Configuration import

The configuration import is done from the DEVELOPMENT CONFIGURATION perspective of the NWDS. However, the URL to the SLD must have been maintained beforehand. After the import process has completed, a tree structure for the configuration and the software component is displayed in the INACTIVE DC VIEW window of the NWDS. A new development component can now be created from the DEVELOPMENT CONFIGURATION perspective by right-clicking on the new software component and selecting CREATE NEW DC. You can then enter the necessary data in the windows that display. Afterwards, you should immediately create an activity.

Activity

An activity contains a set of changes that are carried out by a user and are then assigned to a workspace. In Java development, this is known as a change list.

15.6 Developing in the SAP NetWeaver Development Infrastructure

After the NWDI, tracks, and development configurations have been set up according to the previously discussed steps, actual development can commence. Figure 15.19 illustrates the individual steps of the development process and how the different NWDI parts are used in this process.

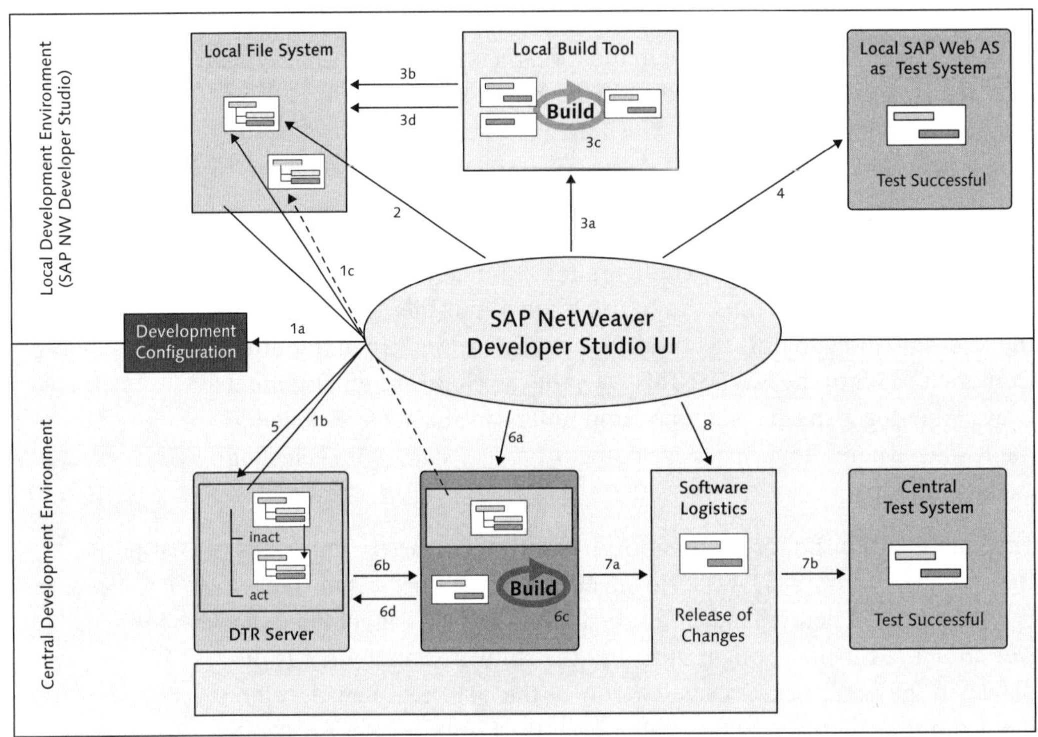

Figure 15.19 Development Process using the NWDI

Selecting the development configuration

The development configuration is the development environment for the various software components in their current state. Therefore, every development activity starts with selecting the development configuration. Because the configuration is created and stored in the CMS, it is imported into the NWDS in Step 1a. Thus, local files are synchronized with the sources of the DTR (Step 1b) and the archives of the CBS (Step 1c). In the next step, sources are recreated or existing sources are corrected (Step 2). They can then be used to create a local build whenever a local test is needed. This can be started from the NWDS (Step 3a). First, the sources and necessary archives are loaded (Step 3b). The build process is then started automatically (Step 3c). Next, the archives created during this process are written back to the local file system (Step 3d).

The results of this local build are then used to be tested on the local test system (Step 4).

After a successful test, the sources in the DTR are updated to the current state (Step 5). After this has been completed, the central build can be started from the NWDS (Step 6a). For this purpose, the sources and additional, necessary archives are loaded into the CBS (Step 6b), after which the automatic build is started (Step 6c). After the build has been successfully completed, the sources in the DTR are automatically activated (Step 6d).

Deployment

Next, automatic deployment of the generated archives in the central test system is started using the CMS (Steps 7a and 7b). A common test can then be carried out in the central test system together with other software components. If this test completes successfully, the activities are released and the changes are exported and placed into the import queue of the consolidation system.

15.6.1 Creating a J2EE Application

J2EE applications are created in the J2EE DEVELOPMENT perspective of the NWDS. This perspective enables consistent access to all development objects of a J2EE application.

[+]

The J2EE DEVELOPMENT perspective is by default shown automatically when a J2EE project is started. If, for example, a web service or a Web Dynpro needs to be developed, the corresponding perspective should be selected using the menu path WINDOW • OPEN PERSPECTIVE • OTHER.

J2EE Explorer

A central part of this perspective is the J2EE Explorer. It offers a logical, structured composition for the local project structure, as well as a reasonable starting point for activities that make sense here such as creating or changing development objects. When an object is selected from the J2EE Explorer by double-clicking, the appropriate editor is started by default (for example for XML, JSP, or HTML). If new objects need to be created, wizards provide corresponding support.

Java Server Pages

Usually, Java Server Pages (JSPs) are used as part of the presentation logic, which is created in the NWDS in the context of web module projects. This context can easily be created from the context menu of the NWDS via an entry of the relevant development component in the J2EE DC Explorer. After a JSP has been created, the JSP Editor starts automatically. This editor consists of two views—a preview of what the HTML program will look like in a browser, and a source code view in which the program can be displayed and edited in parallel.

Enterprise Java Beans

Similar to JSPs, Enterprise Java Beans (EJBs) are built from the J2EE DC Explorer. First, however, you need to create an appropriate development component.

Enterprise applications

A J2EE application is created and deployed from an enterprise application project in the form of an Enterprise archive (.ear file). Additional JSP or EJB modules can then be added to this file.

[+]

How the various archives are composed and assembled is shown in Figure 15.3.

15.6.2 Creating a Local Build and Carrying Out the Local Tests

When a local build is started from the NWDS, a .ear archive is created from the enterprise application project. When this local build has been carried out, the sources that have been created are compiled in the local context of the versions of the referenced objects. If necessary, .jar or .war archives are generated simultaneously for the referenced projects (web module project or EJB module project, respectively). Aside from the .jar and .war archives, the .ear archive also contains the deployment descriptors. Optionally, other libraries can be added to the .ear archive. When the local build has been carried out successfully, the application that has been created can be deployed and tested on the developer's local SAP NetWeaver AS Java.

15.6.3 Check-in of Changes

In the SAP NWDI, the Design Time Repository (DTR) has the task of managing the versions of program sources to enable larger teams to work on the software development. Therefore, the DTR must be informed about the planned changes at the beginning of a development activity by creating an activity in which the change information is stored. Afterwards, the program sources are checked out and changed in the local NWDS. When the program changes have been completed, the sources are checked into the DTR again. Using the DTR check-in mechanism, the changes become active when the activities are released and are visible to all developers.

By activating the changes in the second step, they are rebuilt so that the sources (libraries) become visible for all other developers and any additional development components that use them.

DTR clients and DTR server

The DTR consists of two parts—the DTR clients and the DTR server. The primary activities of the individual developers—such as check-in and check-out and the correction of sources—take place in the NWDS. The DTR server handles file versioning. The various resources are accessed in the context of a workspace, and versions are administered in the context of the activities. Therefore, a workspace references a set of resources each in exactly one version. As an alternative, one resource can be referenced in several workspaces. For the Employee Self Service (ESS) example, this means that ESS_DEV can be referenced with MSS_CONS. Because the files in a workspace form a software component, every workspace corresponds to the status of the sources for this software component.

When a versioned resource is changed or deleted, a new version is created for this resource. Every resource version created in a workspace receives a unique number. This consecutive number reflects the order in which the versions were created in the workspace. The DTR shows the relationship between the individual versions of a versioned resource as a version graphic. Changed sources are always checked into the inactive workspace of the DTR. Both the inactive and the active workspace show a version of the files that are stored in the DTR.

The DTR client functions are only necessary for administrative activities such as sync-to-date, defining the ACLs, and deleting software components from the NWDS.

Example

Figure 15.20 shows that File 2 has been modified several times already. After the last change, Version 3 was generated during the check-in. However, the changes were last activated with Version 1 so that the active workspace shows this version.

After check-in, the changes that were made are also available to other developers. When required, development components are checked out; the active versions of the development components are always transferred to the local PC when the inactive versions of a developer's own development components are checked out.

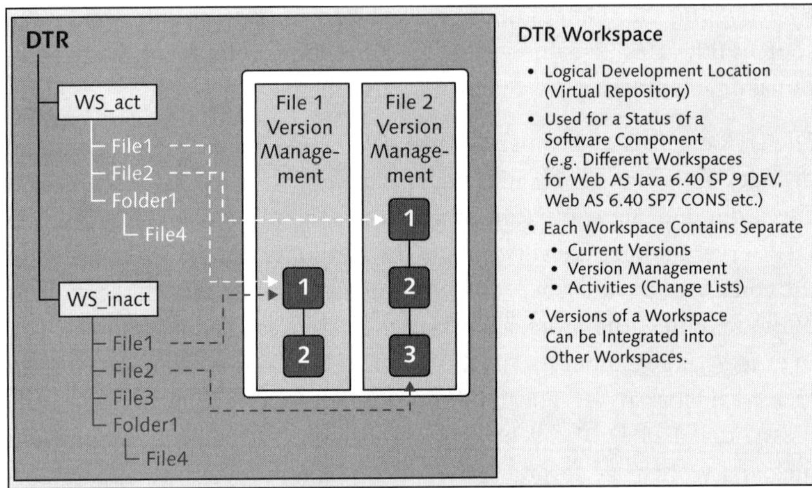

Figure 15.20 Structure of the Design Time Repository (DTR)

15.6.4 Activation in the CBS, Central Deployment, and Central Test

In the next step, after the resources have been checked into the inactive workspace, the application is activated. After a build has been once carried out completely for the first time—because the SAP NetWeaver Development Infrastructure is based on the component model—only the changes to the sources and to the dependent development components need to be carried out in the future (incremental build), which will be processed much faster. During the activation—started from the NWDS—the request for a build is first sent to the CBS. The CBS then tries to create a central build using the selected sources.

Result of the activation

The result of this activation is that runtime objects are now available. If the activation was successful, the build space of the changed software component is filled with the generated archives, and the active workspace in the DTR also shows the current file version. This process ensures that the active workspace in the DTR contains only sources of successful builds and that the active workspace is always synchronized with the build space. In Figure 15.21 this principle is illustrated. Build spaces always contain the appropriate version of the software components of a development configuration so that a consistent development environment is always available for developments in larger groups. After successful activation, if the system is set up accordingly, the application can be deployed automatically in the central development system of the track used. There, its interaction with successfully activated applications from other development teams can be tested.

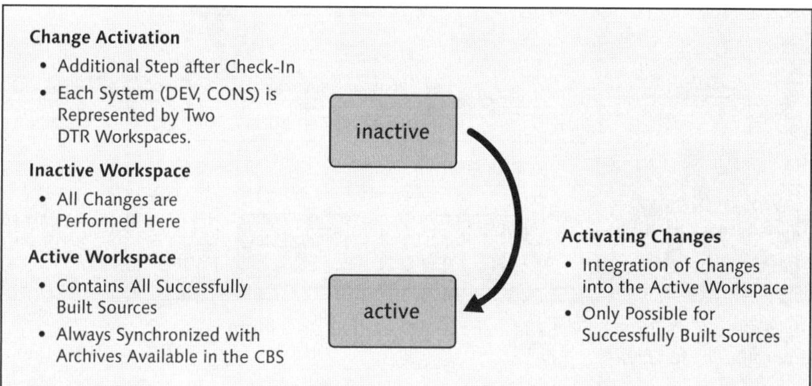

Figure 15.21 Interaction between the Component Build Service (CBS) and the Design Time Repository (DTR)

15.6.5 Release of Changes to the Consolidation System

When the development has been completed, and the developers involved have checked in their sources and tested them in the central development system, the changes can be released for transport to the consolidation system. This is comparable to the release of change requests in the development system of an ABAP system. Unlike with ABAP, however, in this situation transport requests are not written to an import buffer on the file system but are stored sequentially in the NWDI database.

15.7 Transporting Java Projects

After the developments have been successfully tested and released in the central development system, they are transported to the subsequent systems. This process is controlled by the CMS. A track contains the development configuration, as well as the corresponding runtime systems for the various development statuses of the software components, and, by default, consists of a four-system landscape (see Figure 15.22).

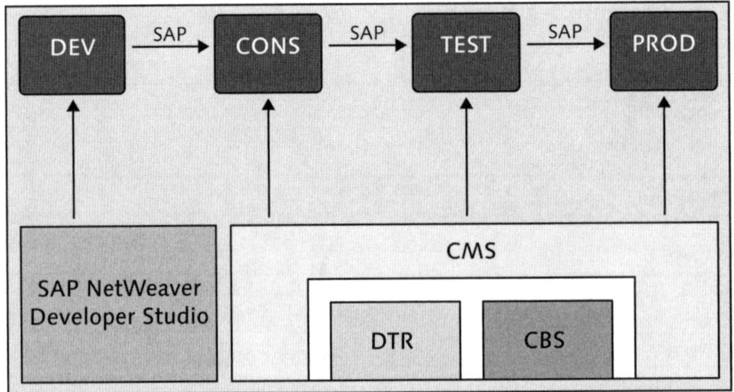

Figure 15.22 Four-System Landscape as a Standard Development Environment for Java

Test

In the central development system DEV, the sources that have been created are tested for their interaction with other developments. The CONS consolidation system is used for consolidating a specific status of a software component and for additional tests of this component. During this process, an additional version of this software component is created based on the status in CONS. This new version is then used to carry out the integration test in TEST before the import into the production system PROD finally happens.

These four system roles can be assigned to specific runtime systems in which the deployment is automatically effected during the import, and which enable testing the software component versions in their corresponding development status. Figure 15.23 illustrates this path of transport steps in a track.

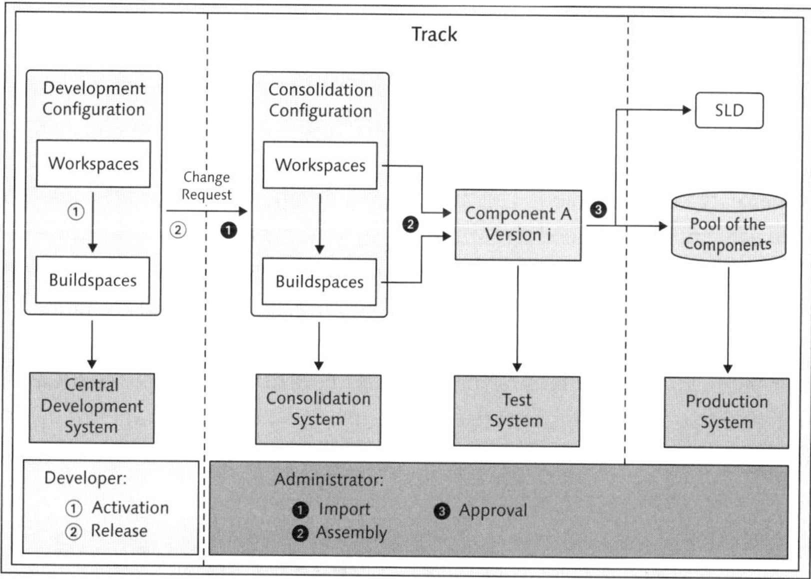

Figure 15.23 Overview of Transports Within a Track

Example

After the newly created or changed sources have been checked in, the developer can transfer the changes to the Component Build Service (Developer, Step 1). The CBS tries to reinterpret all components that are directly or indirectly affected by these changes. If this can be done without problems, the changes are accepted and the results of all developers of the same development configuration are made available in the form of archives or libraries. If the activation and the developer test were successful, the developers release their activities in the NWDS and transfer the changes to the CMS (Developer, Step 2). All activities selected by the developer are then summarized in a change request and placed into the import queue of the consolidation system.

With the import into the consolidation system (Administrator, Step 1), the system administrator integrates the released changes into the DTR workspace of the consolidation system and the CBS automatically compiles the changed software components. After testing the application functions, the CMS creates a new version of the application based on the status in the consolidation system (assembly) and prepares it for further transport to the test system (Administrator, Step 2). After the subsequent import into the test system and the integration test have taken place in this system, the quality manager can approve the transport of the software components to the production system (Administrator, Step 3).

15.8 Summary

Using the SAP NetWeaver Development Infrastructure reduces the risks of the Java development process, which were presented at the beginning of this chapter and occur most often during development where large teams are involved. This is because the operations that can lead to inconsistencies in the development process, such as obsolete libraries or archives, are improved by controlling the processes centrally. With a centrally available build service, a new build can be created on demand from the NWDS. This can reduce the time required for resolving errors compared to builds that are initiated and controlled only centrally. Figure 15.24 shows, as a comparison to Figure 15.4, the advantages of using the NWDI.

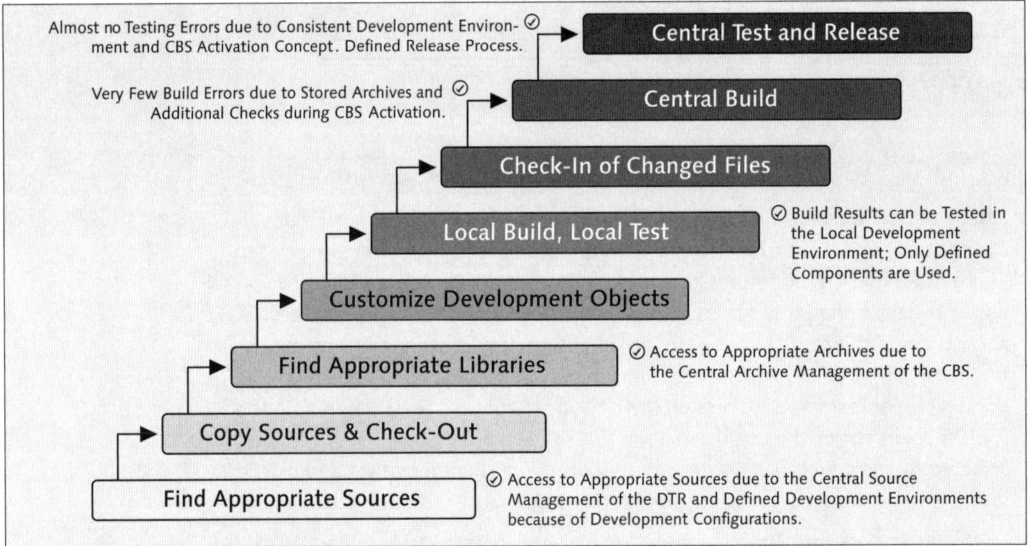

Figure 15.24 Benefits of Using the SAP NetWeaver Development Infrastructure

15.9 Questions

1. **Which of the following statements about the NetWeaver Development Infrastructure (NWDI) are correct?**
   A. It consists of several coordinated tools for designing, developing, and testing Java programs.
   B. It can be used as both a local and central development environment.
   C. It is not suitable for teams with several developers.
   D. It is not suitable for transporting ABAP and Java components.
2. **Which functions are fulfilled by the SAP Design Time Repository (DTR)?**
   A. The DTR takes care of the central storage, versioning, and management of Java sources.
   B. The DTR provides automated conflict verifications.
   C. The DTR can also store Word files.
   D. The DTR manages archives that are required for software development.
3. **Which functions are fulfilled by the SAP System Landscape Directory (SLD)?**
   A. It is a tool for central user management.
   B. It stores information about the system landscape.
   C. It works like a central data cache.
   D. It stores version information about the installed software components.
4. **Which of the following services are required for Java transports?**
   A. Java Activation Framework (JAF)
   B. Design Time Repository (DTR)
   C. Component Build Service (CBS)
   D. Change Management Service (CMS)
   E. Enterprise Information System (EIS)

5. **Which of the following statements are correct with regard to tracks, systems, and development configurations?**
   A. A track always contains exactly one development configuration.
   B. A track contains multiple systems.
   C. A system consists of a development configuration and a runtime environment.
   D. A track serves to develop various software components in different releases.
   E. A track serves to develop only one release of a specific software component.
6. **Which of the following statements are correct with regard to Design Time Repository (DTR) and Central Build Service (CBS)?**
   A. The DTR consists of one active and one inactive workspace.
   B. The development components can be used by other developers by checking in at the DTR.
   C. The development components can be used by other developers through activation in the CBS.
   D. If the central build fails, the elements of the active workspace enter the inactive workspace.
7. **Which of the following statements are correct with regard to the transport of Java objects?**
   A. The objects are automatically activated when requests are imported into the consolidation system.
   B. Like in the ABAP environment, only individual development objects and (generally) not entire software components are imported into the production system.
   C. During the assembly step, only references to required software components are created.
   D. During the assembly step, all required software components are included in the archive to be created.

Along with ABAP objects, the enhanced Change and Transport System (CTS+) enables you to transport Java objects and SAP-related non-ABAP applications in the system landscape. It also allows for managing non-ABAP systems in the transport domain of an ABAP system.

16 Enhanced Change and Transport System

The enhanced Change and Transport System (CTS+) enables you to transport ABAP and non-ABAP objects together in a single transport request. During the import into the Transport Management System (TMS), the system performs the appropriate deployment step for the non-ABAP objects automatically.

Transportable objects

You can transport the following objects using the enhanced CTS:

- Java- and J2EE-based objects (see Chapter 15)
- Software Component Archives (SCAs)
- Enterprise Application Archives (EARs)
- Software Deployment Archives (SDAs)
- SAP NetWeaver Portal objects:
  - Portal Archives (PARs)
  - Enterprise Portal Applications (EPAs)
- Knowledge Management objects (KM content and configurations)
- SAP NetWeaver Process Integration objects: Integration Builder and Integration Directory objects (TPZ)
- System Landscape Directory Content objects: products, software components, technical systems, and business systems

Figure 16.1 illustrates the CTS+ concept. Various development environments link to the ABAP transport system and transfer software changes in the form of archive files and transport requests. After the transport requests have been imported, the system transfers the archive files to the target non-ABAP system and imports and activates them automatically. The software is centrally distributed via the ABAP Change and Transport System.

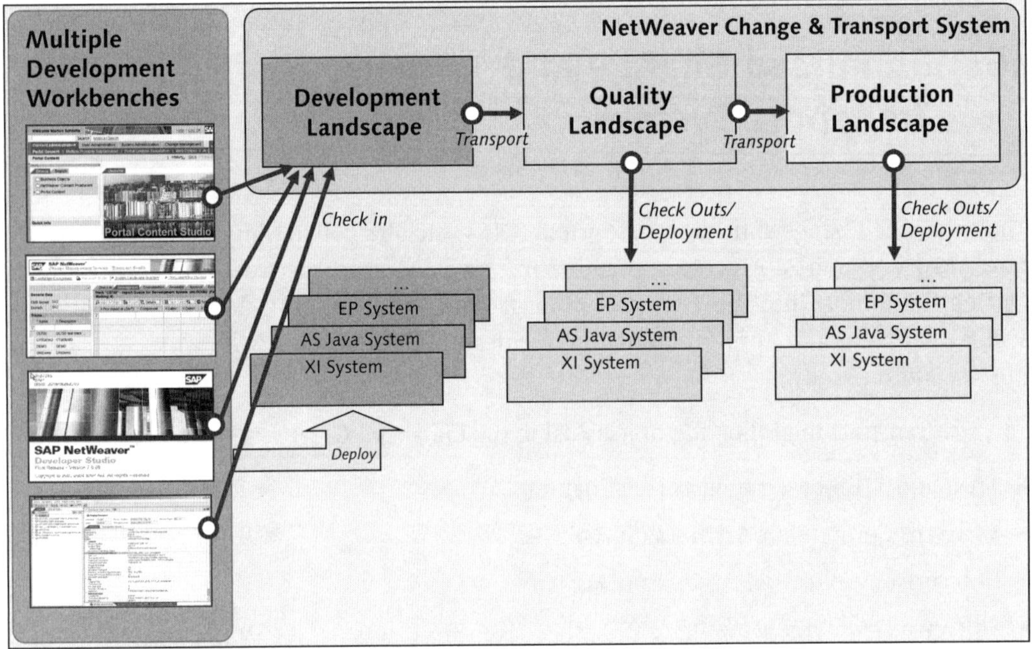

Figure 16.1 The Concept of the Enhanced Change and Transport System

Advantages of the enhanced Change and Transport System

Both the ABAP Change and Transport System and the SAP NetWeaver Development Infrastructure (NWDI) already provide comprehensive functions to distribute changes. However, the following aspects haven't been covered sufficiently:

- Synchronized transports into dual-stack systems
- Distribution of changes in a portal landscape

- Standardized user interface to distribute and track changes in the entire solution landscape
- The option to also configure flexible transport routes for non-ABAP systems
- The integration of non-ABAP systems with the Change Request Management or other change management tools

These issues were addressed by introducing the enhanced Change and Transport System.

16.1 Overview and Architecture

To use the enhanced Change and Transport System, you need at least one SAP NetWeaver 7.0 ABAP and one SAP NetWeaver 7.0 Java stack. Ideally, the necessary components for the CTS+ should be located on an SAP NetWeaver 7.0 dual-stack system. SAP Solution Manager is often used as the central transport management system (see Chapter 19). However, instead of SAP Solution Manager functions, the enhanced Change and Transport System only requires SAP NetWeaver technology.

Figure 16.2 illustrates the components required for the enhanced Change and Transport System.

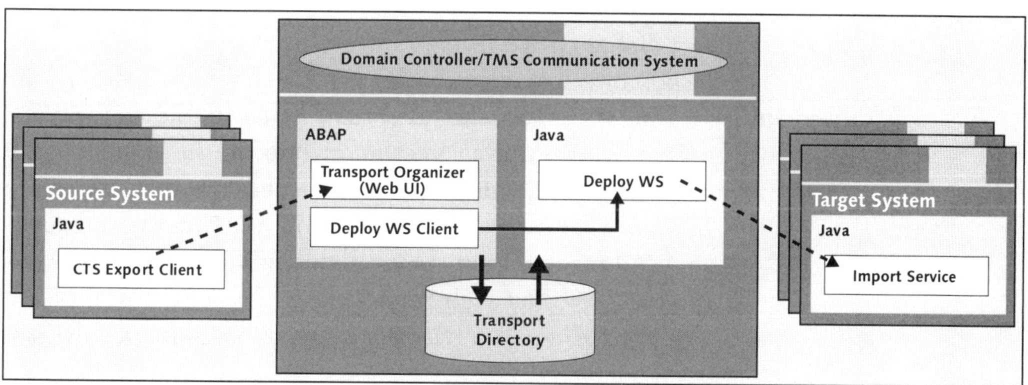

Figure 16.2 The Components of the Enhanced Change and Transport System

Components

The necessary components are:

- **Domain Controller (ABAP)**
  The Domain Controller is the system in which the TMS transport routes are set up.
- **TMS communication system (ABAP)**
  The TMS communication system is the ABAP system in which the transport program `tp` is triggered to perform the import steps. Usually, the Domain Controller is the same system as the communication system.
- **Deploy Web Service (Java)**
  The Deploy Web Service is a Java web service that communicates with the deployment tools of non-ABAP systems. The transport program `tp` communicates with the CTS Deploy Web Service to deploy non-ABAP objects.
- **Deploy Web Service Client**
  To enable the transport control program `tp` on SAP NetWeaver AS ABAP to communicate with the Deploy Web Service on SAP NetWeaver AS Java, a Deploy Web Service Client (Deploy Proxy) is required for ABAP.
- **Transport Organizer Web UI (ABAP)**
  The Transport Organizer Web UI is an ABAP Web Dynpro application used to create and modify transport requests for non-ABAP systems.
- **Transport directory (ABAP)**
  The transport directory is the directory in which the transport files are stored. During the export, the ABAP stack writes the files to the directory and reads them during the import into the successor system. In contrast to an ABAP-only transport, a subdirectory is created in the `<DIR_TRANS>/data` directory for each non-ABAP transport request. The non-ABAP files are then stored in this subdirectory. During the import, the CTS Deploy Web Service reads the non-ABAP files and passes them to the import service (for example, Software Deployment Manager of the target system).
- **CTS Export Client**
  The CTS Export Client is the non-ABAP development system in which the changes are carried out and exported. As of a particular Support

Package status in the non-ABAP system, the system can establish a direct RFC connection from the development system to the Transport Domain Controller. It is thus possible to transfer non-ABAP objects directly from the development environment to a change request. This scenario is also known as *close coupling*.

- **Import service**

  The import service is the import method of non-ABAP applications. Currently, CTS+ supports the following import methods:

  - Software Deployment Manager
  - XI import method
  - SLD import method
  - KM import method

  When importing non-ABAP objects, the transport control program `tp` calls the CTS Deploy Web Service on the Java stack. The CTS Deploy Web Service, in turn, triggers the import service of the non-ABAP application (for example, Software Deployment Manager), which imports and activates the objects in the target system.

16.2 Performing Transports for Non-ABAP Objects

Loose coupling

When transporting non-ABAP objects, you distinguish between loose coupling and close coupling scenarios. For loose couplings, the developer exports the non-ABAP objects from the development system into an export file in the file system, as before. However, the export file is not directly imported into the target system but is instead uploaded to a transport request as a transport object of type FILE.

Close coupling

For close couplings, no direct RFC connections exist between the non-ABAP development system and the Transport Domain Controller. It is thus possible to transfer non-ABAP objects directly from the development environment to a change request, which is similar to a transfer from the ABAP Editor. Close couplings are possible in the following SAP NetWeaver applications: Portal, XI, NWDI, and SLD as of NetWeaver 7.0, Support Package stack 14. The following section describes the export process from a Portal development environment (Portal Content Studio).

16.2.1 Export of a Portal Development from the Portal Content Studio

Figure 16.3 shows an example of a Portal development in the Portal Content Studio.

In this example, a developer developed a Portal application in the Portal Content Studio. With the transport package editor, he bundled all required objects into a transport package. Now he can transfer the transport package directly to a transport request. To do so, he selects the CTS export method in the transport package editor. The system prompts to add the transport package to the corresponding transport request. The developer uses the START EXPORT button to attach the transport package to the transport request.

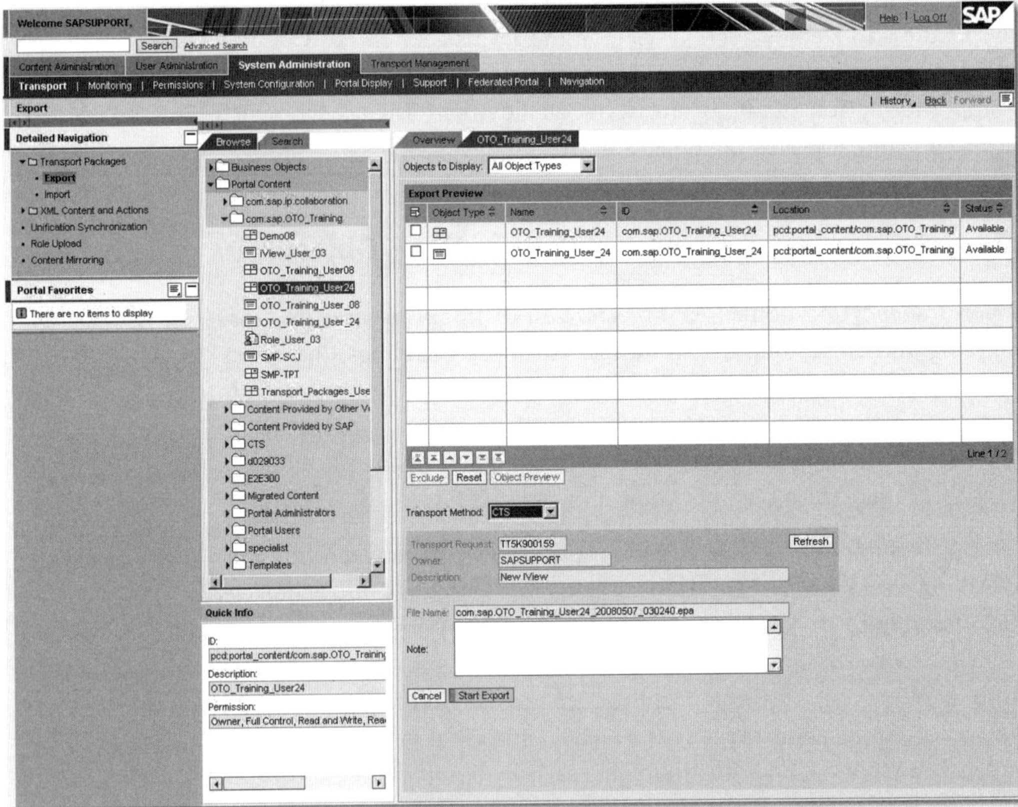

Figure 16.3 Coupling of the Portal Content Studio with the Transport Organizer

16.2.2 Transport Organizer Web UI

Transport Organizer Web UI

The Transport Organizer Web UI provides all of the functions you need to process and manage your transport processes for non-ABAP objects. It is an enhancement of the common Transport Organizer (Transaction SE09). The user interface and the option to create transport requests for non-ABAP development systems are the most important improvements. Furthermore, it also enables you to define a transport request as the standard transport request.

Standard transport request

For non-ABAP development systems, one standard request must be defined for each user. The standard request is then used to store changes for this user. The objects are directly attached to the transport request and not in a task. Each developer has its own transport request.

Transport request for a non-ABAP development system

Figure 16.4 shows a transport request that was created using the Transport Organizer Web UI in the OTO system for the non-ABAP development system EPD. The name of this transport request begins with EPD. The administrative information on this transport request is stored in the OTO system.

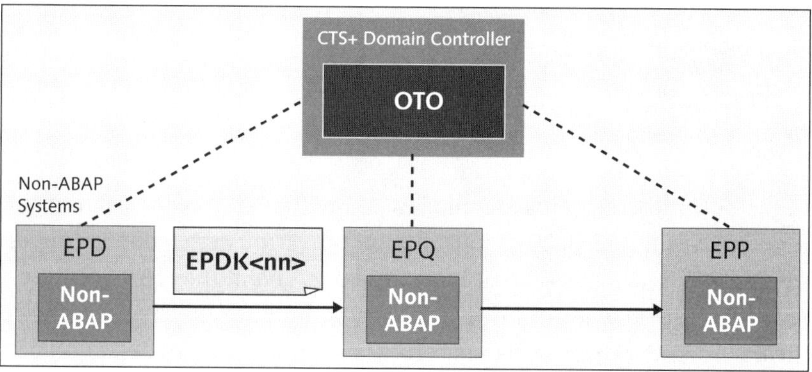

Figure 16.4 Transport Request for a Non-ABAP Development System

The Transport Organizer Web UI consists of a top and a bottom screen area, as shown in Figure 16.5.

In the top screen area (general settings and activities), you can process and manage your transport requests or the transport requests of another user by means of various buttons. The transport requests are displayed in a request list, which is output as a table. This table lists the transport request number, the DESCRIPTION of the transport request, and the OWNER.

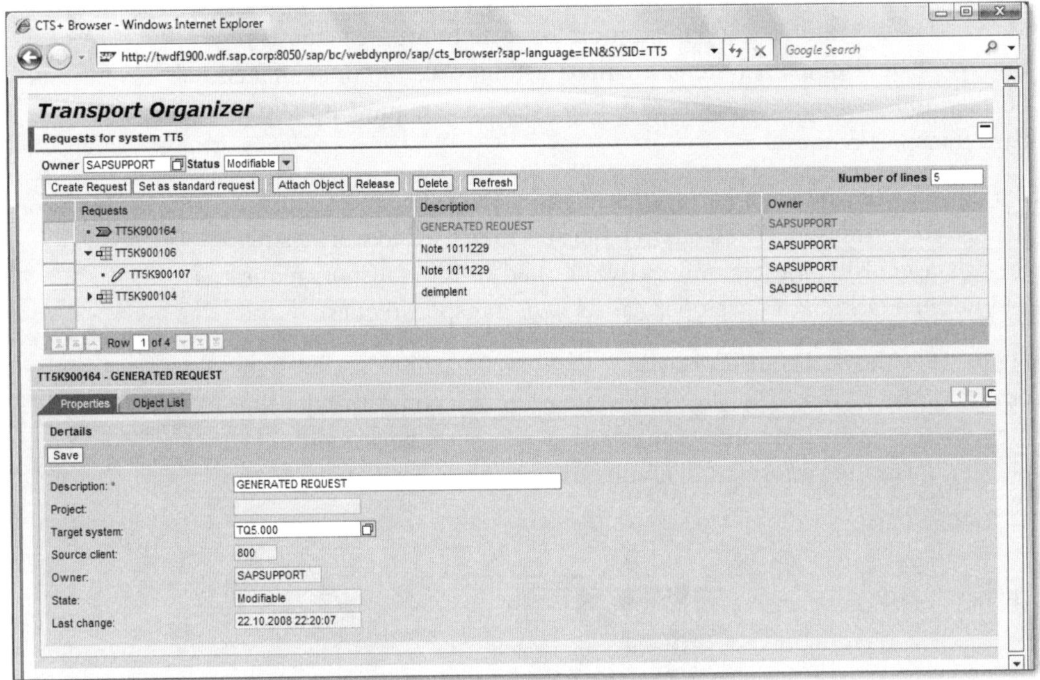

Figure 16.5 Transport Organizer Web UI

Detail view

In the bottom screen area (detail view of the transport requests), the system displays the respective information on various tabs, depending on the settings and activities that were implemented in the top screen area. Aside from displaying transport requests, the bottom screen area also includes auxiliary functions you can use to, for example, delete objects attached to transport requests.

General Settings

You must configure the following settings in the top screen area before you can start to process transport requests:

- **Owner**
  When you call the Transport Organizer Web UI, the OWNER field displays your user name. Thus, you can display all transport requests you have created with your user name. The respective authorization also enables you to display and edit the transport requests of other authorized users.
- **Status**
  The (request) status displays whether a transport request is still being processed (MODIFIABLE) or has already been released.
- **Time of release**
  When you select a time (for example, since yesterday) in the dropdown menu, you can view all released transport requests from this point in time.

Activities

In the top screen area, you can perform the following activities:

- Create transport requests
- Define transport requests as standard transport requests. For non-ABAP development systems, one standard request must be defined for each user. The standard request is then used to store changes for this user.
- Attach objects (files) to a transport request. To do this, you have the following two options (depending on the application used):
  - Attach objects via the file system (loose coupling)
  - Attach objects directly in the application (close coupling)
- Release transport requests
- Delete transport requests in the Transport Organizer Web UI

Finally, you can import the transport requests with non-ABAP objects in Transaction STMS.

Detail View of the Transport Requests

The bottom screen area provides the following display and change functions, which you can select via the corresponding tabs:

- Properties of a transport request
- Object lists in the Transport Organizer Web UI
- Log display in the Transport Organizer Web UI

Properties of a Transport Request

The properties of a transport request function displays the detailed properties of a transport request after you select it in the top screen area. It lists the owner, the transport state, the corresponding project, the source client, and the date of the last change (LAST CHANGE). If necessary, you can change the following properties manually:

- Description
- Project
- Owner (using the CHANGE OWNER BUTTON)
- Target system
- Attributes

Object Lists in the Transport Organizer Web UI

The OBJECT LIST tab displays a list of the files that are attached to a transport request. This helps you avoid attaching the same file several times, for example. It also enables you to delete objects from the object list.

Log Display in the Transport Organizer Web UI

After having released a transport request, you can view the respective transport request logs in the Transport Organizer Web UI and track the status of the transport request.

The STATUS column may indicate the following:

- Transport request is in the import queue
- Export/deployment finished successfully
- Not yet flagged for import
- Import canceled

The table lists the source system of the transport request as well as all target systems to which a transport route was configured. It also displays the target systems into which the transport request was imported by manually forwarding it.

16.2.3 Import Transport Requests with Non-ABAP Objects

To make transported objects available in the target system, you must import them into this system. As is the case with ABAP systems, these objects are imported using Transaction STMS (see Chapter 13).

You can integrate Transaction STMS into the Portal via a transactional iView (see Figure 16.6) so that the Java developer doesn't have to log on to the SAP ERP system to import the objects.

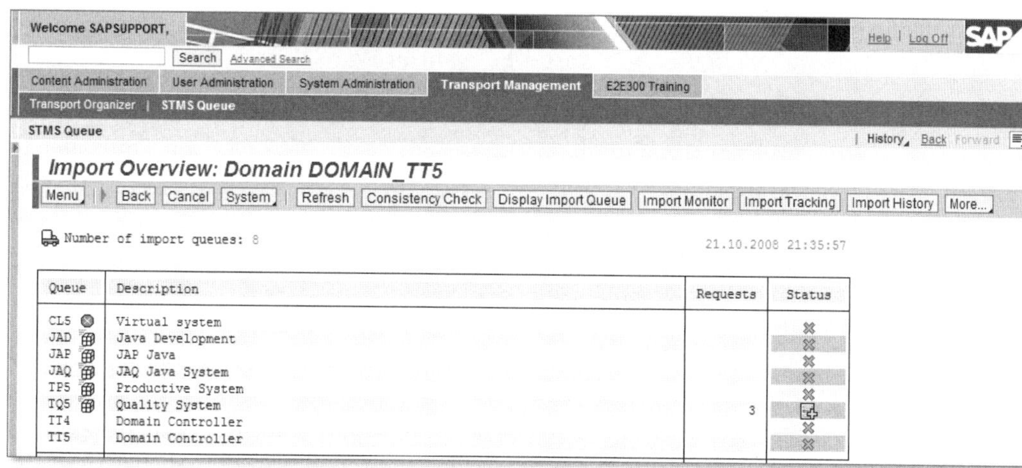

Figure 16.6 iView for Transaction STMS in the Portal

16.3 Configuration of the Enhanced Change and Transport System

Non-ABAP systems

Non-ABAP systems are based on SAP NetWeaver Application Server Java or on non-SAP systems. Non-ABAP systems are treated as virtual systems in the CTS; that is, they require an ABAP communication system on which the transport control program `tp` runs. For source systems, the Transport Organizer is used on this communication system as well.

Dual-stack systems

Dual-stack systems consist of one SAP NetWeaver Application Server ABAP and one SAP NetWeaver Application Server Java. Before you can configure the AS Java of a dual-stack system, you need to integrate the dual-stack system into the transport domain and configure it.

Configuration options for non-ABAP and dual-stack systems

In transports, non-ABAP and dual-stack systems can serve as source and target systems. When you create non-ABAP or dual-stack systems as source or target systems in your transport landscape, they are automatically configured with the default settings. If you want to change these settings, you can adapt them to the processes in your system landscape using parameters.

16.3.1 Setting up the ABAP Stack

You must implement most of the settings for ABAP stacks in Transaction STMS. In addition, you need to establish a connection to the Java stack and configure the Transport Organizer Web UI, as follows:

- **TMS Domain Controller**
  You must define the ABAP system as the TMS Domain Controller in Transaction STMS.
- **TMS communication system**
  A non-ABAP system requires an ABAP system as the TMS communication system, which is defined via the COMMUNICATION_SYSTEM transport parameter.
- **Transport Organizer Web UI**
  You need to activate the ABAP Web Dynpro application, CTS_BROWSER, for a particular client (e.g., client 001) in Transaction SICF. The NON_ABAP_WBO_CLIENT transport parameter defines the client in which the transport requests are created for non-ABAP applications.
- **Deploy Web Service Client**
  - HTTP connection: The HTTP connection (recommended name: CTSDEPLOY) for the connection to the Java stack must be created in Transaction SM59.
  - Logical port: The logical port (recommended name: CTSDEPLOY) for the Java Web Service Deploy Proxy must be created in Transaction LPCONFIG in client 000.

16.3.2 Setting up the Java Stack

Only the Web Service Deploy Proxy must be located on the Java stack. You can check this in the Web Service Navigator (see Figure 16.7). If the service is not on the Java stack, proceed as described in SAP Note 1076189.

Figure 16.7 Web Service Navigator

16.3.3 Setting up the TMS System Landscape

Chapter 8 already explained the setup and configuration of the TMS system landscape. Consequently, this chapter only discusses the special characteristics for non-ABAP systems.

Creating non-ABAP systems

The enhanced Change and Transport System also introduced a new TMS system category: the non-ABAP system. Figure 16.8 illustrates how you can set up such a system using Transaction STMS, OVERVIEW • SYSTEMS and thenCREATE·• NON-ABAP SYSTEM. All pure Java systems require this system category, for example for SAP NetWeaver Portal or the System Landscape Directory.

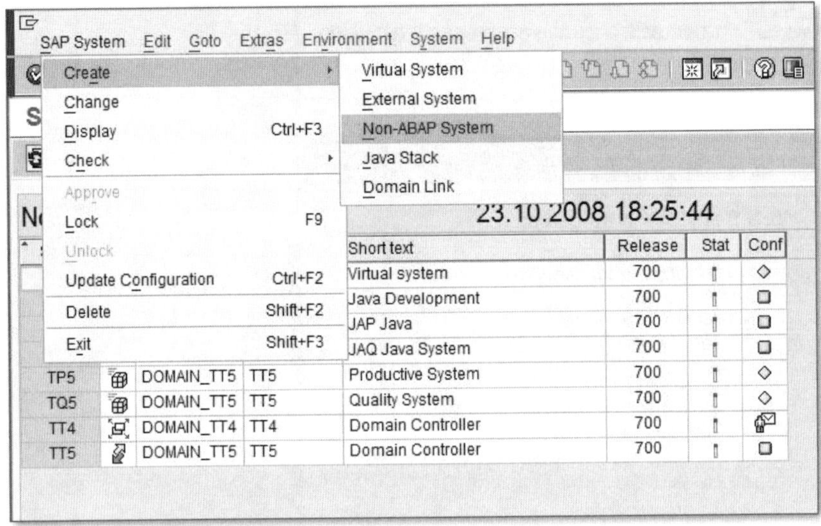

Figure 16.8 Creating Non-ABAP Systems

SAP also introduced additional transport parameters for non-ABAP systems. These parameters are predefined automatically when you use the menu described previously. You can check and change them in Transaction STMS: Transaction STMS, SYSTEM OVERVIEW • CREATE·• SID • TRANSPORT TOOL tab.

You can enhance already existing dual-stack systems (for example, SAP NetWeaver PI) with the new transport parameters for the Java stack to also transport non-ABAP objects. To add the required transport parameters, use the CREATE • JAVA STACK function from the previously discussed menu.

The TMS: CONFIGURE NON-ABAP SYSTEM dialog box opens (see Figure 16.9).

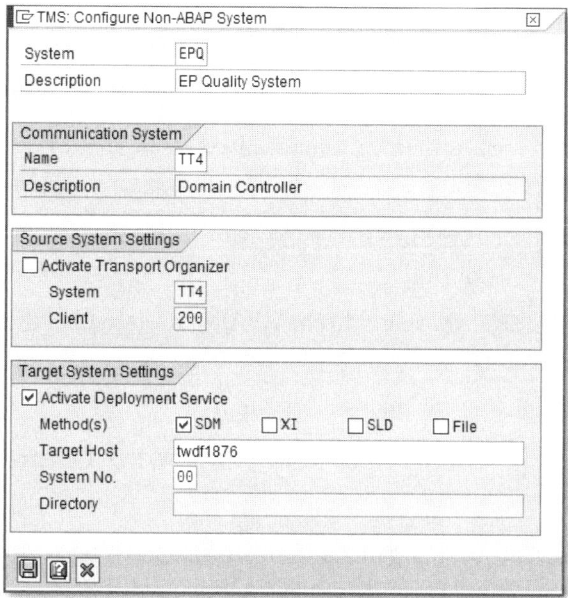

Figure 16.9 The Configure Non-ABAP Systems Dialog Box

1. Create the non-ABAP system, including its system ID and description.
2. Define the CTS system as the communication system.
3. If you want to configure your system as the source system, set the ACTIVATE TRANSPORT ORGANIZER flag in SOURCE SYSTEM SETTINGS, and specify the client in which you want to use the Transport Organizer.
4. If you want to configure your system as the target system, set the ACTIVATE DEPLOYMENT SERVICE FLAG in TARGET SYSTEM SETTINGS. Select the respective deployment methods, and fill in the remaining fields appropriately. Enter the corresponding system user and password for the selected deployment methods.
5. Save your settings, and confirm the distribution of the TMS configuration.

The system now automatically generates all required parameters and their corresponding values as default settings. When you select your system in the system overview, you can display these parameters on the TRANSPORT TOOL tab.

16.3.4 Configuration Parameters for Non-ABAP Source Systems

You must configure the following parameters in the non-ABAP development system. The system creates them automatically when it creates the menu path described previously.

- COMMUNICATION_SYSTEM: the SID of the ABAP communication system (e.g., the Domain Controller)
- NON_ABAP_WBO_CLIENT: the client in the ABAP stack in which the Transport Organizer Web UI was activated.
- NON_ABAP_SYSTEM: 1 (not for dual-stack systems)

Dual-stack systems require only the NON_ABAP_WBO_CLIENT parameter.

[+] All clients in which the Transport Organizer Web UI runs must be set to Automatic recording of changes (Transaction SCC4).

The close coupling scenario additionally includes the WBO_GET_REQ_STRATEGY and WBO_REL_REQ_STRATEGY strategy parameters. They are explained in the following section.

16.3.5 Configuration Parameters for Non-ABAP Target Systems

Test and production systems receive transport requests with non-ABAP objects. The communication system of a target system must communicate with the transport control program `tp` and the Deploy Web Service Client to trigger the import of the non-ABAP objects into the Java systems. The enhanced Change and Transport system supports the applications outlined in Table 16.1:

Applications	Transport Parameters
Import via Software Deployment Manager (for the EP, KM, NWDI applications)	DEPLOY_URL
Import of PI/XI objects	DEPLOY_XI_URL
Import of SLD objects	DEPLOY_SLD_URL
File transfer	DEPLOY_OUTBOX

Table 16.1 Applications Supported by CTS+

You must set the following parameters for non-ABAP target systems:

- COMMUNICATION_SYSTEM: the SID of the ABAP communication system (e.g., the Domain Controller)
- DEPLOY_DATA_SHARE: the Transport directory (e.g., `<DIR_TRANS>\data`)
- DEPLOY_URL or DEPLOY_SLD_URL or DEPLOY_XI_URL or DEPLOY_OUTBOX
- DEPLOY_WEB_SERVICE: CTSDEPLOY (name of the logical port that is created) for the connection to the Java Web Service Deploy Proxy
- NON_ABAP_SYSTEM: 1 (not for dual-stack systems)

16.3.6 Connection of the Development Environment to the Transport System (Close Coupling)

Close coupling

If you want to transport objects from an SAP NetWeaver PI or SAP NetWeaver Portal application, you must establish a connection between the application and the transport system, called a close coupling. This variant provides the highest level of automation. Similar to ABAP systems, you can store developments in non-ABAP systems directly in a transport request. However, this scenario requires a particular minimum Support Package status in the non-ABAP development system.

Loose coupling

If a close coupling is not possible, you must use the *loose coupling* scenario. In this case, the non-ABAP development system is not connected to the Transport Organizer Web UI. The developer works in the development environment as usual. At the end, he exports the changes into an export file. In a second step, a transport request is created in the Transport Organizer Web UI and the exported file is attached to the transport request. Finally, the transport request can be released.

- Close coupling enables you to call the transport request directly from the non-ABAP development system. The interim step—that is, exporting the changes into the file system and then uploading them into the transport request—is not required. The transport process involves creating a transport request for the respective development system, attaching the non-ABAP object, and releasing the transport request.

Creating a Transport Request

The WBO_GET_REQ_STRATEGY transport parameter controls how the transport request is created. The following values are possible:

- **TAGGED**
  You must create the transport request in the Transport Organizer Web UI and manually define it as the standard request for the respective user.
- **SMART**
  The system checks whether a standard request exists for the user. If not, it automatically creates a new transport request and defines it as the standard request.

Attaching the Non-ABAP Objects

Standard request

For SAP applications (SAP NetWeaver Portal, PI, NWDI or SLD systems) that are closely coupled to the CTS system (close coupling), you can by default attach objects directly from the application. The data is transferred to the CTS server via the SAP Java Connector (JCo) connection. In this case, the WBO_FILE_TRANSFER parameter is by default set to STREAM.

If you want to transfer the data via a file system (share) or a Network File System (NFS) for performance reasons, you must set the WBO_FILE_TRANSFER parameter to SHARE.

Releasing a Transport Request

The WBO_REL_REQ_STRATEGY transport parameter controls how the transport request is released. The following values are possible:

- **MANUAL**
  You must manually release the transport request in the Transport Organizer Web UI. This is the same procedure as for ABAP systems.
- **AUTO**
  The system releases the transport request automatically when an object is attached. In this case, a transport request can only transport one non-ABAP archive. The developer is responsible for releasing the transport requests.

RFC connection

To connect the non-ABAP development system to the enhanced Change and Transport System, you must establish an RFC connection from the development system to the Domain Controller. The necessary RFC connection is *sap.com/com.sap.tc.di.CTSserver*. You must enter it in the DESTINATION SERVICE area of the respective development system's Visual Administrator (see Figure 16.10). The SAP online help contains detailed instructions for this.

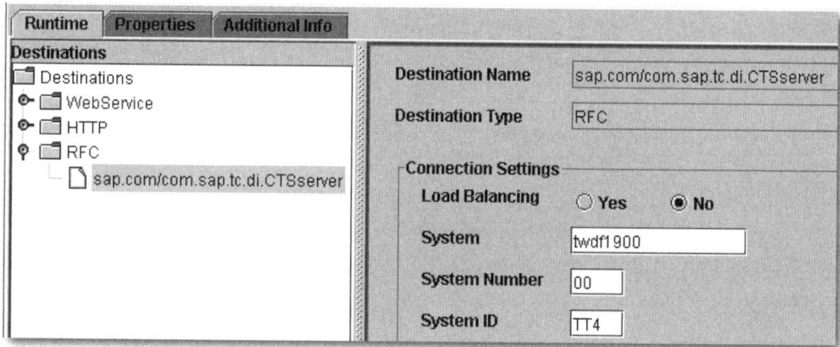

Figure 16.10 Connecting the Development System to the Domain Controller in the Visual Administrator

16.4 CTS+ Transport Landscapes

This section contains configuration examples for typical transport landscapes that are often used in day-to-day work situations. It describes scenarios for a non-ABAP system and a dual-stack system. In addition, it also introduces a Portal development landscape in which Java developments are implemented using the SAP NetWeaver Development Infrastructure.

16.4.1 Non-ABAP System

This section describes the CTS+ configuration for a plain non-ABAP system, for example SAP NetWeaver Portal. A plain non-ABAP system has only one Java stack and no ABAP stack. Thus, it requires an external Domain Controller to configure the TMS settings.

The non-ABAP transport landscape consists of three systems (see Figure 16.11): the EPD development system (configured as the source system), the EPQ test system, and the EPP production system.

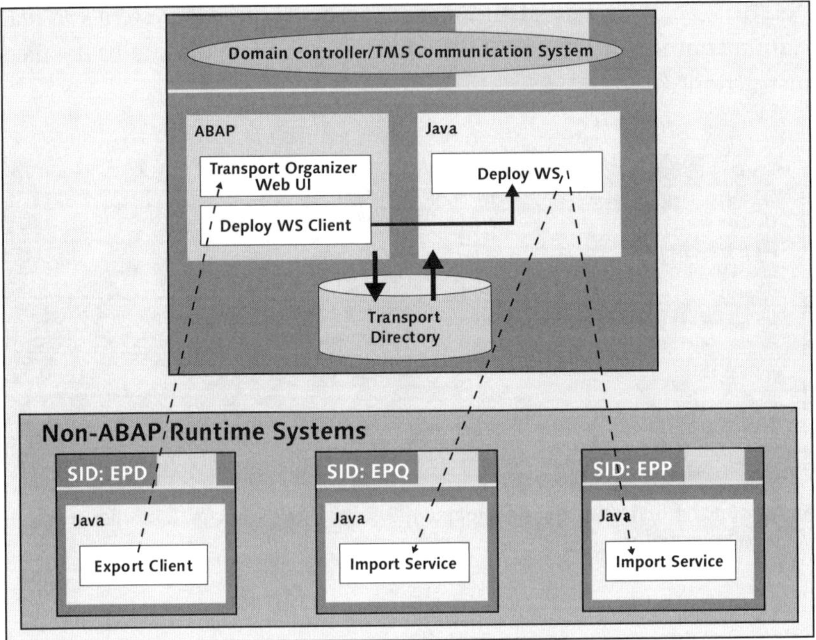

Figure 16.11 Example of a Non-ABAP Transport Landscape

The two latter systems were configured as target systems. The transport parameters are set in the Domain Controller. For the example shown in Figure 16.11, they could look as follows:

- For the EPD system:
  - COMMUNICATION_SYSTEM = (e.g., DCS)
  - NON_ABAP_SYSTEM = 1
  - NON_ABAP_WBO_CLIENT = (e.g., 001)
  - WBO_GET_REQ_STRATEGY = SMART (close coupling)
  - WBO_REL_REQ_STRATEGY = MANUAL (close coupling)
- For the EPQ and EPP systems:
  - COMMUNICATION_SYSTEM = (e.g., DCS)

- DEPLOY_DATA_SHARE = <DIR_TRANS>\data
- DEPLOY_URL = http://< hostname>:< SDMport>
- DEPLOY_WEB_SERVICE = CTSDEPLOY
- NON_ABAP_SYSTEM = 1

16.4.2 Dual-Stack System

This section describes the CTS+ configuration for a dual-stack system, for example, SAP NetWeaver PI. In this case, you can use the already existing TMS configuration for the ABAP stack. In addition, you must configure the CTS+ components.

tp and Deploy Web Service

Each target system triggers the import process with the transport control program `tp`, which runs on the local system (same behavior as in ABAP). The Deploy Web Service also runs on the Java stack of each target system. The Deploy Web Service Client—which consists of the HTTP connection and the logical port—must be configured on the ABAP stack of each target system.

The example in Figure 16.12 shows the configuration for an SAP NetWeaver PI landscape that consists of a PID development, a PIQ test system, and a PIP production system. The target systems must use the DEPLOY_XI_URL parameter. The PID system requires the parameters for the source systems. PIQ and PIP are the target systems and require the Java stack parameters for the target systems. The PIP production system serves as the Domain Controller. The transport parameters are as follows:

- PID system
  - NON_ABAP_WBO_CLIENT = (e.g., 001)
  - WBO_GET_REQ_STRATEGY = SMART (close coupling)
  - WBO_REL_REQ_STRATEGY = MANUAL (close coupling)
- PIQ and PIP systems
  - DEPLOY_DATA_SHARE = <DIR_TRANS>\data
  - DEPLOY_XI_URL = http://<hostname>:<Javaport>
  - DEPLOY_WEB_SERVICE = CTSDEPLOY

[+] If you also want to use the test system for emergency corrections, you need to configure the Transport Organizer Web UI for this system as well. In this case, the PIQ system serves as the source and target system.

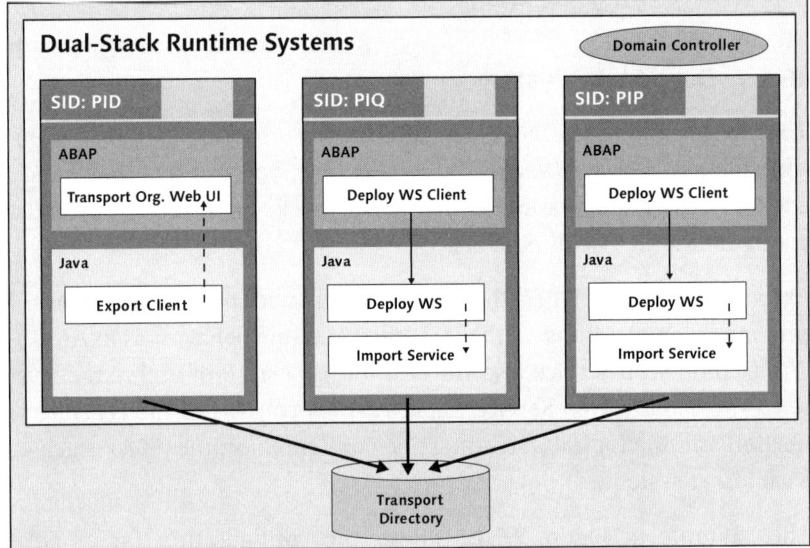

Figure 16.12 Example of a Dual-Stack Transport Landscape

16.4.3 Combined CTS+ Applications

NWDI and SAP NetWeaver Portal

Frequently, multiple SAP applications run on the same system. In this case, you must also combine the CTS+ settings for these multiple applications.

Figure 16.13 shows a Portal development landscape in which Java developments are implemented using the SAP NetWeaver Development Infrastructure. This scenario is common because the Portal development environment, called *Portal Content Studio*, only enables developments of Portal content, such as HTML pages, iViews, or navigation bars. You cannot develop complex program processes and applications in the Portal Content Studio. For this, you need the Developer Studio and the SAP NetWeaver Development Infrastructure.

The Portal content is developed in the Portal development system. The archives are transferred to a CTS+ transport request.

The Java source code is in the NWDI. It is developed using the Developer Studio and imported from the NWDI into the Portal development system (see Chapter 15). Next, the Java archive files are generated. They are also transferred to a CTS+ transport request. This request can contain Portal content and Java applications at the same time, which means that you can transport dependent objects simultaneously.

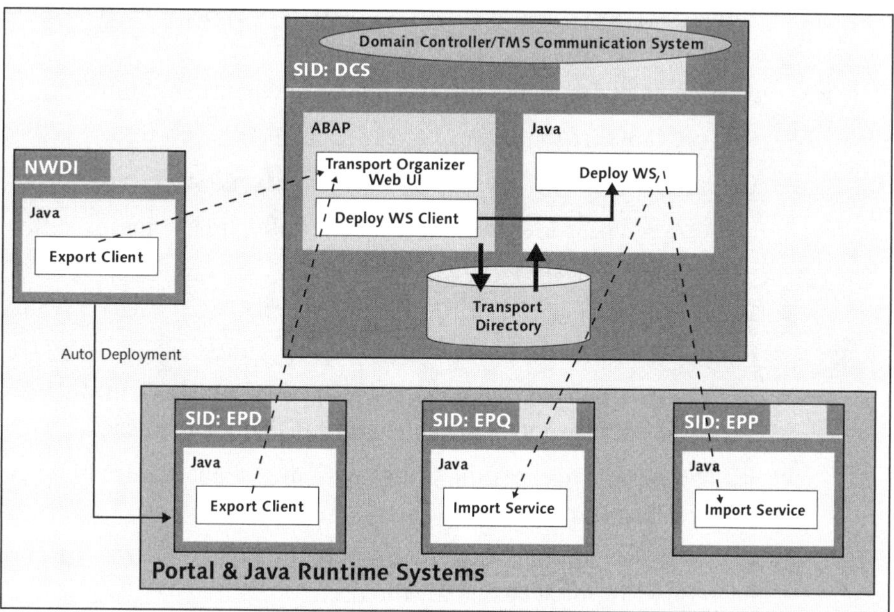

Figure 16.13 Example of an SAP NetWeaver Portal Landscape with NWDI

The CTS+ controls the import into the test and production systems. You can use the Software Deployment Manager to import the NWDI and Portal Content Studio archives. To do so, you only have to configure the *DEPLOY_URL = http://<SDM-hostname>:<SDMport> deploy parameter for the target systems.*

16.5 Questions

1. **Which objects can be imported with the Software Deployment Manager?**
   A. Software Deployment archives
   B. Software Component archives
   C. Java patches
   D. ABAP Support Packages
2. **Which are advantages of the enhanced Change and Transport System?**
   A. Tracking parameter changes in heterogeneous environments
   B. Software distribution of non-ABAP objects
   C. Simultaneous distribution of changes in dual-stack systems
   D. A shared user interface to distribute software changes in different development environments
3. **What effects does the WBO_REL_REQ_STRATEGY = AUTO transport parameter setting have?**
   A. A new transport request is created in the Domain Controller if a standard transport request is not available for the user.
   B. The system releases the transport requests automatically when an object is attached.
   C. The application displays an error message if a standard transport request is not available for the user.
4. **Where is the enhanced Change and Transport System configured?**
   A. In the configuration of the Transport Management System (TMS)
   B. In the Instance profile of the Java stack
   C. In the Instance profile of the ABAP stack

5. **How can you simultaneously distribute changes in business processes that run in ABAP and Java systems, for example, in the ESS/MSS scenario?**

   A. The enhanced Change and Transport System enables you to create transport requests that contain ABAP and Java objects.

   B. The enhanced Change and Transport System enables you to define dependencies between transport requests in the ABAP and Java stack.

   C. The SAP NetWeaver Development Infrastructure (NWDI) enables you to define dependencies between transport requests in the ABAP and Java stack.

SAP provides several methods to correct errors that have occurred in your SAP system. This chapter describes these methods, the contents of the changes involved, and recommendations for project implementation.

17 Maintaining SAP Software

In this chapter, you will learn about the software maintenance strategies and tools provided by SAP and, in particular, about Support Packages and SAP Notes. Support Packages correct all errors that have been identified within a specific time period in a system, whereas SAP Notes correct individual errors as they occur. This chapter also explains the modification adjustment steps you need to take when importing Support Packages.

The tools discussed in this chapter are as follows.

- The Note Assistant (Transaction SNOTE), used to import Notes with code corrections. Tools
- The SAP Patch Manager (Transaction SNOTE), used to import Support Packages.
- The SAP Add-on Installation Manager (Transaction SAINT), used to import add-ons and delta upgrades.
- The SAP Java Support Package Installation Manager, used to import Java Packages.

This chapter is intended primarily for system administrators and technical consultants who are responsible for maintaining and updating an SAP ERP system landscape. Nonetheless, project leads and strategic consultants will also benefit from this information because it is helpful for planning package upgrades and for estimating the time and staff costs involved. Experience shows that the main factors causing difficulties in

Support Package implementation projects are the required downtime, the time and effort necessary for testing, and the indispensable code freeze. Section 17.3 addresses these aspects, and also describes the benefits gained from importing Support Packages.

Section 17.4 focuses on the maintenance of Java-based systems in particular, which in many respects is different from the maintenance of ABAP systems.

17.1 Making Manual Corrections on the Basis of SAP Notes

If a specific problem occurs with the SAP ERP software and this problem is corrected, details of the correction are published in an SAP Note. The correction is also included in the next Support Package.

If the problem is particularly urgent, you may not be able to wait for the Support Package and will have to manually make the correction with the help of an SAP Note.

SAP provides the SAP Note Assistant to enable customers to import SAP Notes. This tool considerably reduces the amount of manual work required to implement the Note and make modification adjustments later on.

Particularly important Notes—such as those about faults with serious consequences including system downtime and data inconsistencies—are classified as HotNews and are published on the SAP Service Marketplace.

17.1.1 SAP HotNews

SAP HotNews items are SAP customer Notes with Priority 1 (very high). These Notes contain the solutions to problems that could cause a system breakdown or data loss in the SAP system. Therefore, if one of these Notes applies to your system, it is very important that you take it seriously.

Process

The new SAP HotNews process enables you to display only HotNews items that are relevant to your areas. The shared personalization interface for SAP HotNews and SAP TopNotes (see the text that follows) allows you to create multiple filters for the applications you use (such as SAP ERP or SAP CRM). Using the filter maintenance functions, you can select your products (such as SAP ERP), product versions (such as SAP R/3 4.6C), software components (such as SAP Basis 4.6C), and Support Packages, and the system returns only the HotNews items that are relevant to your criteria.

SAP HotNews items are located in the SAP Service Marketplace under the */notes* Quick Link: *http://service.sap.com/notes*. (You need a Service Marketplace user to be able to view this content.)

Newsletter

You can also have the SAP HotNews that are of interested to you emailed to you in the SAP Service Marketplace newsletter. To subscribe to the relevant topic area—NEWS FOR ADMINISTRATORS (INCL. SAP HOTNEWS)—of the SAP Service Marketplace newsletter, you need to configure the required settings in the SAP Service Marketplace under MY PROFILE. You will then be informed automatically as soon as there is a new SAP HotNews item that is relevant to your settings.

If you receive an SAP HotNews item with information that is extremely important for the operation of your SAP system, you should confirm receipt of this item in the SAP Service Marketplace. When you do so, this HotNews item is no longer displayed to you. SAP is also notified that you have read the HotNews item and that you have taken the recommended measures.

As an SAP system administrator, you should regularly review all SAP HotNews items, or ensure that this is done and, if necessary, proactively implement applicable items in your system. Figure 17.1 shows the SAP HotNews Browser in the SAP Service Marketplace.

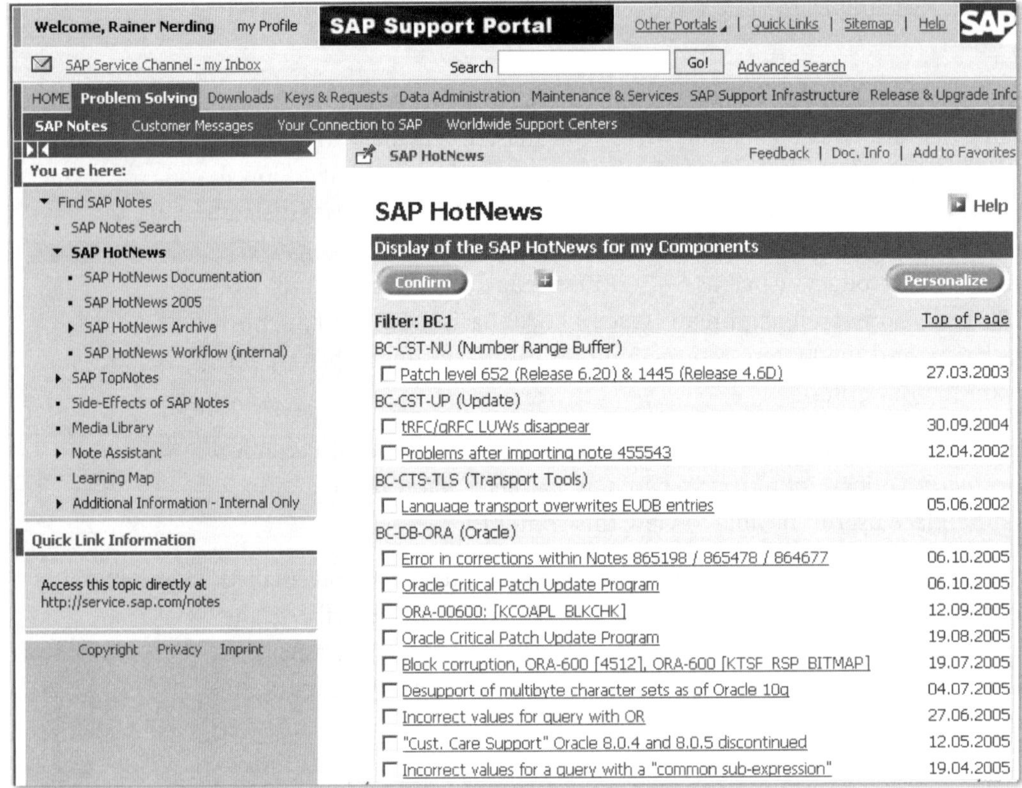

Figure 17.1 SAP HotNews Browser in the SAP Service Marketplace

17.1.2 SAP TopNotes

SAP TopNotes are the most important SAP Notes in a component or subcomponent (such as FI-AR). These are the Notes that are most frequently attached to customer problem messages. Every month, the system identifies the ten most common messages for the component in question. Then, the TopNotes are checked manually, and other important SAP Notes can be added to them or replace them. This concept is described in detail in Note 557703.

SAP TopNotes are also located in the SAP Service Marketplace under the */notes* Quick Link (*http://service.sap.com/notes*). As with SAP HotNews, you can also be notified of new SAP TopNotes by email.

17.2 Implementing Notes with the SAP Note Assistant

Transaction SNOTE

The SAP Note Assistant (Transaction SNOTE, see Figure 17.2) can automatically implement Notes that contain corrections to source code. Other changes, such as Customizing changes or changes to a table cannot be automatically implemented. Always make sure to read the Note carefully before implementing it using the Note Assistant. It may contain information about prerequisites, interdependencies, and references to clean-up steps you'll need to consider in the implementation process.

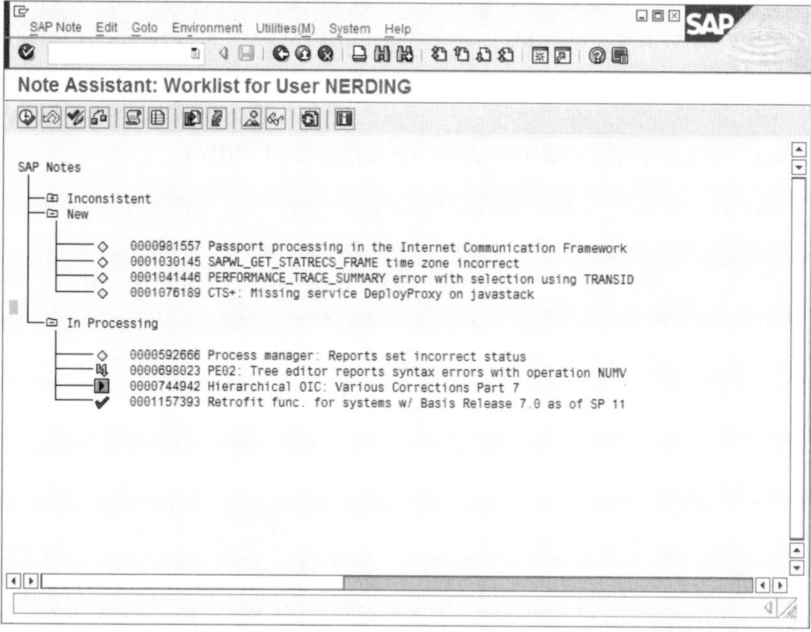

Figure 17.2 The SAP Note Assistant

The Note Assistant provides the following functions:

- **Reporting**
  Provides an overview of the existing Notes and their processing status, and of all the source-code corrections that have been implemented to date.

- **Project administration**
  Allows you to assign Notes to processors, which can then set the processing status. The system notifies you if a Note has an inconsistent status.
- **Retraceability**
  Means that the system automatically logs the processing steps.
- **Error correction**
  Enables you to automatically implement source-code corrections (correction instructions) that are described in Notes.
- **Integration**
  When Support Packages or upgrades are imported, the system automatically identifies the Notes that the Support Package or upgrade resolves and which correction instructions have to be reimplemented.

17.2.1 Registering Manually-Implemented Notes

If you implemented corrections from Notes in your SAP system before installing the Note Assistant, you can retroactively "notify" the Note Assistant of this fact. Because the Note Assistant cannot automatically determine whether a Note correction was implemented in your system manually (that is, without the use of the Note Assistant), this is important to do. Proceed as follows:

1. In the ABAP Editor (Transaction SE38), call the program `SCWN_REGISTER_NOTES`.
2. In the program's input screen, enter the numbers of the Notes you want to register and that have been fully implemented.
3. This can cause the following situations to occur:
   - If you created a Remote Function Call (RFC) connection to the SAPNet-R/3 frontend, the program automatically loads the Notes to be registered into your system's database.
   - If you did not create an RFC connection, first load the Notes to be registered from the SAP Service Marketplace. Then, upload the Notes in the Note Assistant.

4. The program checks whether the Notes are valid for your release and Support Package level. It also verifies whether the Notes are already registered as having been implemented in the Note Assistant. The system then outputs the results of these checks to a list.
5. To register the Note, select PROGRAM • EXECUTE.

[+] To be able to register the Note as implemented, the system has to enter the details of the Note and the objects it corrected in a change request. When you transport this request, you are registering the Note as implemented, even in your downstream systems. If it is not possible to include the Note and its objects in one request—because, for example, some objects have already been locked in other requests—the system will reject the registration.

17.2.2 Processing Notes

To correct an error in a program using the Note Assistant, proceed as follows:

1. Load the Note into your system. During the loading process, the Note Assistant checks whether the characteristics of the Note (software component, release level, and Support Package level) match those of your system. It then states whether the corrections can be implemented.

   Only Notes with source-code corrections (correction instructions) can be automatically implemented.
2. Read the Note description carefully.

   The Note description may contain information about prerequisites and interdependencies, and references to post-processing steps (for example, changes that need to be made to a table), which the Note Assistant does *not* automatically recognize. If you do not read and, if required, act upon this information, serious problems can result. It is therefore absolutely imperative that you read the Note before you start the implementation.
3. Determine whether the Note is relevant to you. Classify the Note in accordance with the processing status.

4. Implement the correction.
5. Carry out any post-processing steps that may be specified in the Note.
6. Test whether the error has been successfully corrected.
7. Set the processing status to COMPLETED.
8. Release the transport request and import the corrections into the downstream systems in your system landscape.

Search Note

Note Browser

The Note Browser enables you to search through all SAP Notes in your system. It also displays Notes that are assigned to another processor and Notes that have already been implemented. Proceed as follows:

1. Select a search criterion for the Note:
   - Note number
   - Application component
   - Processing status
   - Implementation status
   - Processor
2. Select which option you require:
   - Restrict the selection process to certain software components and their releases.
   - Sort the Notes according to their number or the application component to which they belong.
3. Confirm your selection.

The Note Browser then displays a list of the Notes that match your criteria, including their Note number, short text, component, processing status, implementation status, and user (see Figure 17.3). You can also implement Notes directly from the Note Browser.

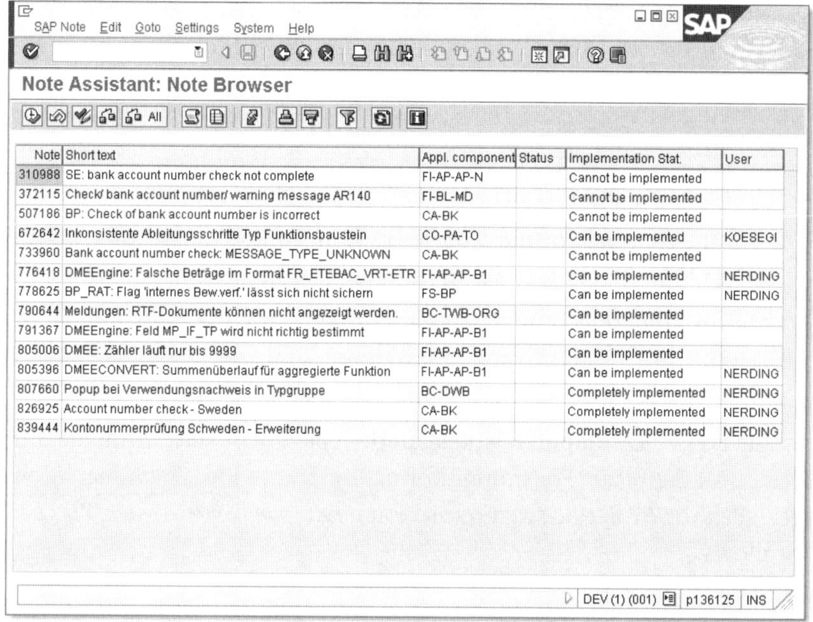

Note	Short text	Appl. component	Status	Implementation Stat.	User
310988	SE: bank account number check not complete	FI-AP-AP-N		Cannot be implemented	
372115	Check/ bank account number/ warning message AR140	FI-BL-MD		Cannot be implemented	
507186	BP: Check of bank account number is incorrect	CA-BK		Cannot be implemented	
672642	Inkonsistente Ableitungsschritte Typ Funktionsbaustein	CO-PA-TO		Can be implemented	KOESEGI
733960	Bank account number check: MESSAGE_TYPE_UNKNOWN	CA-BK		Cannot be implemented	
776418	DMEEngine: Falsche Beträge im Format FR_ETEBAC_VRT-ETR	FI-AP-AP-B1		Can be implemented	NERDING
778625	BP_RAT: Flag 'internes Bew.verf.' lässt sich nicht sichern	FS-BP		Can be implemented	NERDING
790644	Meldungen: RTF-Dokumente können nicht angezeigt werden.	BC-TWB-ORG		Can be implemented	
791367	DMEEngine: Feld MP_IF_TP wird nicht richtig bestimmt	FI-AP-AP-B1		Can be implemented	
805006	DMEE: Zähler läuft nur bis 9999	FI-AP-AP-B1		Can be implemented	
805396	DMEECONVERT: Summenüberlauf für aggregierte Funktion	FI-AP-AP-B1		Can be implemented	NERDING
807660	Popup bei Verwendungsnachweis in Typgruppe	BC-DWB		Completely implemented	NERDING
826925	Account number check - Sweden	CA-BK		Completely implemented	NERDING
839444	Kontonummerprüfung Schweden - Erweiterung	CA-BK		Completely implemented	NERDING

Figure 17.3 The Note Browser Displays All Notes That Have Been Implemented Using the SAP Note Assistant

Load Note

You can load SAP Notes into your system from the SAP Service Marketplace or the SAPNet-R/3 frontend, using either a direct RFC connection (Note download) or by file transfer (Note upload). Note download has the following benefits:

- You can transfer the Note in the Note Assistant from the SAPNet-R/3 frontend directly to your system.
- If the Note in question specifies other Notes as prerequisites, the Note Assistant automatically downloads these in the implementation process.
- You can download updated versions of the Notes with the touch of a button.

To download a Note, you must create an RFC connection to the SAPNet-R/3 frontend. To upload a Note, a permanent RFC connection to the

SAPNet-R/3 frontend is not necessary. Instead, first load the required Note from the SAP Service Marketplace and save it locally on your PC. Then, upload the Note from inside the Note Assistant.

To download a Note, proceed as follows:

Procedure for Note download

1. Select GoTo • Download SAP Note in the Note Assistant.
2. Enter the numbers of the Notes you want to download. You can use the selection function to select individual Notes or a list of Notes.
3. Confirm your selection. The system then loads the matching Notes from the SAPNet-R/3 frontend into your database.

Procedure for Note upload

For Note Upload to be available, the SAP Download Manager must be installed on your computer. Notes can then be downloaded from the SAP Service Marketplace. For more information on the SAP Download Manager, see the SAP Service Marketplace at *service.sap.com/swcenter*. Proceed as follows:

1. Select the Note in question from the SAP Service Marketplace under *service.sap.com/notes*.
2. Select Download. The Note is added to your Download Basket. Repeat this process as many times as necessary.
3. To save the selected Notes to your local PC, start the SAP Download Manager. Select Download. The Notes are saved as files to the local directory you specified.
4. In the Note Assistant, load the Note files into your system using the Note Upload function (GoTo • Upload SAP Note).

After you have successfully downloaded or uploaded a Note that was not previously in your system, it is listed with processing status New.

Classify Note

Classifying a Note allows you to specify the relevance or processing status of a Note. Read the Note carefully and decide whether its content is relevant to the situation in your system. Then proceed as follows:

1. If the Note is relevant, set its status to In Processing (see Figure 17.4). This informs other users that you are already processing this Note.

2. Closely follow the recommendations given in the Note. If the Note contains a correction instruction, implement it in your system.
3. If you want to assign the Note to another processor, enter the user name of the processor.

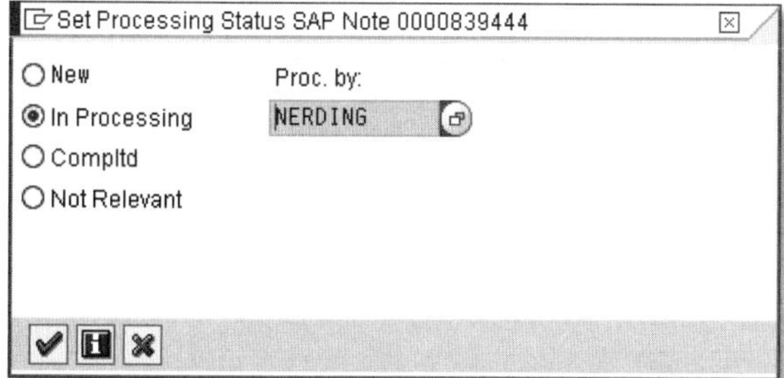

Figure 17.4 Processing Statuses for Implementing Notes

All of your actions are recorded in the log file for the Note. You can also enter additional comments in the log file, for instance, information you may want to pass on to another user.

If the Note is not relevant to you, set the processing status to NOT RELEVANT. This signals to you and all other users that this Note can be disregarded.

Implement Correction Instruction

A function exists that implements the correction instruction contained in a Note. If you have previously modified the object that is the subject of a correction instruction, you can also adapt the correction to your modifications.

To implement the correction instruction of a Note in your system, proceed as follows: **Preparations**

1. Place the cursor on the title of the Note in the initial screen of the Note Assistant and select SAP NOTE • IMPLEMENT SAP NOTE. First, the system checks which correction instruction from the Note is appropriate for your release and Support Package level. It then checks whether any corrections from other Notes are a prerequisite to the implemen-

tation of this correction. If there are prerequisite Notes, the system displays these in a dialog box.

- If you have an RFC connection to the SAPNet-R/3 frontend, you can automatically download these Notes by confirming the dialog box.
- Otherwise, load them from the SAP Service Marketplace and then upload them using the Note Assistant.

If the prerequisite Notes are relevant to your system, they are then displayed in the order in which they need to be implemented (see Figure 17.5). If possible, the system implements all prerequisite Notes in one step.

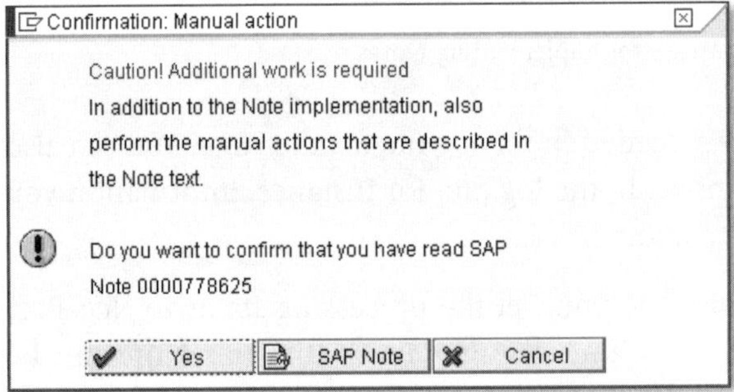

Figure 17.5 Prerequisite Notes

[+] Read the prerequisite Notes as carefully as you would any other Notes.

If any prerequisite Notes are not relevant (for example, because they have already been imported in a Support Package), the Note Assistant automatically assigns the correct status to them and does not display them in the list. To view these Notes, call the Notes Browser and select the NOT RELEVANT processing status.

2. Before the system corrects the objects, it opens a dialog box in which you can select the change request.

Select request

Either select a suitable change request, or create a new one.

The Note (R3TR NOTE), including all correction instructions (R3TR CINS) and all changed objects, is entered into the request. The transport request then transports all corrections to the downstream systems.

[+] Note that all objects to be corrected, plus details of the Note, must be entered in a request. This is the only way to ensure that the corrections are transported in their entirety to the downstream systems.

No SSCR key is required for automatically implementing Note corrections.

Change objects

3. A dialog box opens that lists all of the objects to be changed. A traffic light icon shows whether the system can automatically implement the correction.

   Click on the object name to open an editor. The editor shows you the changes in detail.

   If you previously modified the objects to be corrected, the Note will have a yellow traffic light. You can then adapt the corrections to suit your modifications (also see the section "Split-Screen Editor").

   If you make manual changes when implementing Notes, the system cannot judge whether the corrections have been implemented properly. Therefore, you must confirm in a separate dialog box that the corrections can be classified in the system as fully implemented (see figure 17.6).

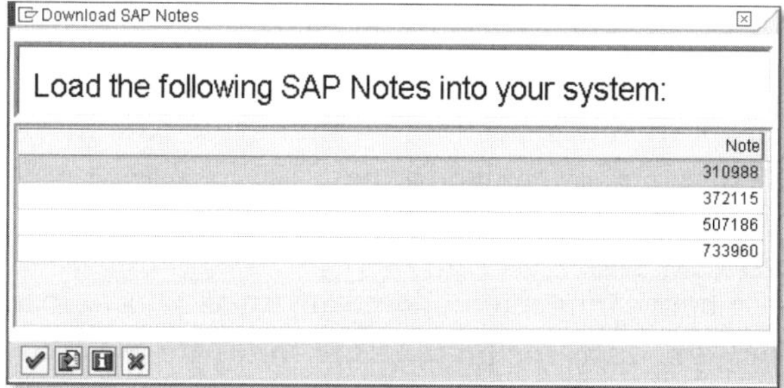

Figure 17.6 Additional Manual Action Required in Note Implementation

[+] If the system cannot automatically implement a correction, even though the objects in question were *not* previously modified, you should first attempt to import the Note using the split-screen editor. In many cases, minor differences in the source code cause the automatic implementation to fail. If the implementation still doesn't work, it is probably because the Note contains an error of some sort. If this happens, contact SAP Support by creating a problem message under the Note's component (for example, FI-AR-CR).

Syntax checking

4. Check that the corrected objects do not contain any syntax errors. This is particularly important if they also contain customer-specific modifications. Note that currently the system can automatically implement only source-text changes. If any other changes are required (changes to Dictionary objects, for example), they are described in the Note text and must be manually implemented in your system.

Testing

5. After implementing the corrections, test the function in question to ensure that it has been fully corrected by the Note.

   You can display all objects that were corrected by the Note; simply select GoTo • Corrected objects to call the modification browser.

Completed

6. Set the processing status to Completed.

[+]

In exceptional cases, you can remove correction instructions that you have implemented. This undoes all implemented changes. The Note in question remains in your system and is reset to the status it had prior to it being implemented. To remove certain correction instructions, select SAP Note • Reset SAP Note Implementation.

Release

7. After you have solved your problem via the Note, release the change request that was created when you implemented the correction instruction. This transports the corrections and the Note data to the downstream systems in your system landscape.

Note queue

If a particular Note has prerequisite Notes, the Note Assistant identifies these when the Note is being implemented and instructs you to load them into your system. As soon as the prerequisite Notes are available, the Note Assistant displays the Note you selected along with all additional Notes in a dialog box called the Note queue (see Figure 17.7). The Notes have to be implemented in the order shown in the Note queue. Before you start the implementation process, read the prerequisite Notes as carefully as you would any other Notes.

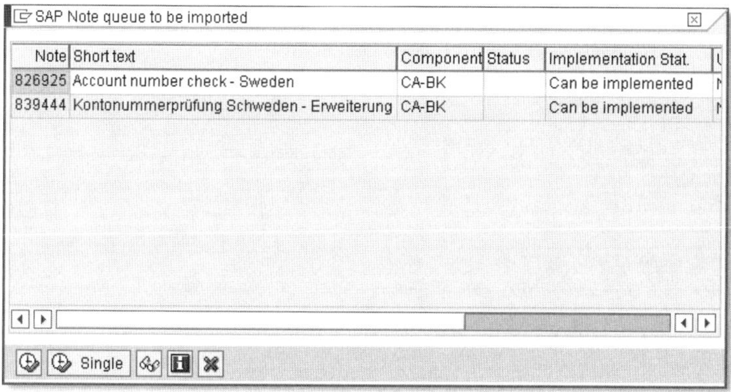

Figure 17.7 Implementing a Note Queue

You have the following options:

- **Implement multiple Notes in one step**
  The system implements as many of the specified Notes as possible, in one step, in sequence. The Notes that can be implemented at the same time are highlighted in color.

  The system can implement multiple Notes in one step only if all corrections can be transferred in unmodified form from the Notes. If you have made your own modifications to the includes in question, the system may be unable to insert individual changes. The system always implements such Notes individually so that you can adapt your modifications.

- **Implement all Notes individually**
  The system implements the specified Notes individually. This option allows you to review in detail what source code changes belong to which of the specified Notes, and to modify the changed source code, if necessary.

- **Cancel SAP Note implementation**
  The system does not make any changes to the source code.

Confirm changes

The CONFIRM CHANGES dialog box shown in Figure 17.8 displays which objects will be changed by the Note implementation, and whether the Note Assistant can copy in the changes. If you confirm this dialog box, the system implements the corrections into the specified objects. If you select Cancel, the system does not make any corrections.

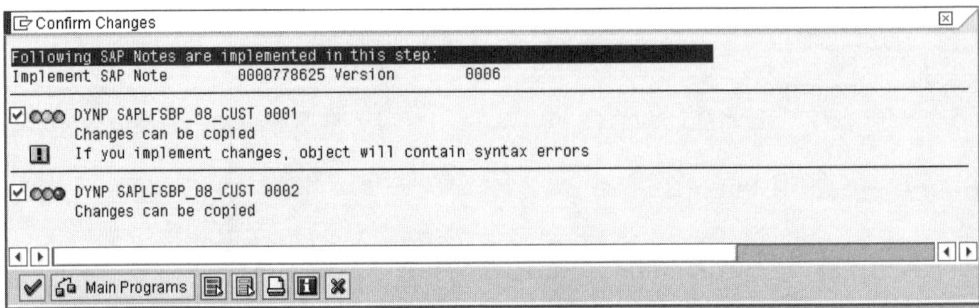

Figure 17.8 Display of Objects to Be Changed

The 'traffic light' icons show you whether the corrections in a Note can be implemented. The different colors have the following meanings:

- **Green light**
  The corrections can be implemented without any changes.
- **Yellow light**
  Some of the corrections can be implemented.

  Before you confirm the implementation, you should adapt the corrections so that the object changes can be imported correctly. To do this, click on the object name or on the traffic light icon. The split-screen editor opens, where you can edit the source code.
- **Red light**
  The object changes cannot be implemented.

  This can occur for a variety of reasons; for example, the object has to be created from scratch, or is locked by another change request.

  A corresponding message text exists for every object (for example, Corrections that have not been included completely). If you click on the text, the system displays the appropriate long text with detailed information.

To implement the corrections, select all of the objects for which you want to implement corrections and select CONTINUE.

[+] Note that only the objects you selected will be changed.

Split-screen editor

The split-screen editor shown in Figure 17.9 provides a detailed display of all corrections in an object. You can use this editor to adapt the corrections to your own modifications, if necessary.

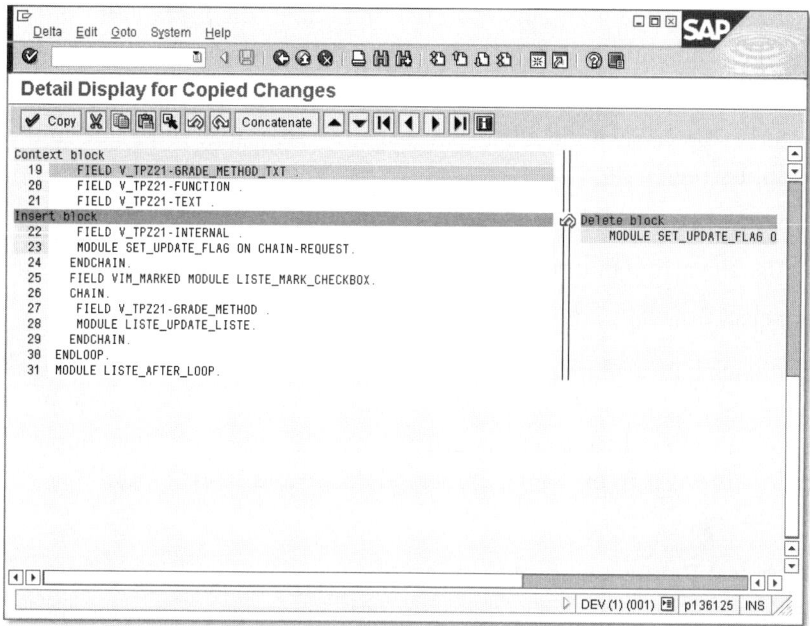

Figure 17.9 Split-Screen Editor

The split-screen editor is divided into two areas:

- On the left-hand side of the screen, you see the source code as it looks after the changes have been implemented. The changes are highlighted in color. You can edit the source code in this portion of the screen.
- On the right-hand side of the screen, you see the parts of the program that have been deleted, and the corrections the Note Assistant cannot implement automatically. These deletions and corrections are displayed in the form of context blocks, delete blocks, and insert blocks.

You can do the following on the left-hand side of the screen:

- Manually edit the program
- Select, cut, copy, and paste blocks

  To select a block that is highlighted in color, place your cursor on the header line and choose SELECT. You can also select multiple lines. [+]

To do so, place your cursor on the first line of the block you want to select and choose SELECT. Then place your cursor on the last line and choose SELECT again.

- Select UNDO to undo all changes, step by step, that you made in the split-screen editor.
- Select REDO to restore all changes you undid.
- Use the arrow buttons to go to the next or last change.
- Select CONCATENATE to attach two lines to each other.

If a block has been inserted or deleted, the UNDO/REDO button appears between the left- and the right-hand side of the editor. You can use it to undo or redo individual changes. The technical function of the undo and redo buttons is to exchange individual delete and insert blocks.

Technical Details on Correction Instructions

Technical details on correction instructions contains information on the following topics:

- The format of correction instructions
- The validity of correction instructions
- Prerequisites for correction instructions

Format

Correction instructions describe how the source code of ABAP programs has to be changed to resolve an error. These instructions are located at the end of each SAP Note. You use correction instructions to automatically correct the source code of ABAP programs, ABAP includes, function modules, method implementations, dynpro flow logic, and type groups.

Every change contains information about the object (for example, the include or the function module) and the modularization unit (such as the FORM routine) in which it will be made. The location of the change is identified by the unique number of the unchanged lines that directly precede the lines to be changed (context block). The lines to be deleted are then listed (delete block), followed by the lines to be inserted (insert block). A correction instruction can consist of multiple context blocks, delete blocks, and insert blocks.

When automatically implementing a correction instruction, the system finds the context blocks in the include or function module to be corrected, checks whether the context blocks follow the lines to be deleted, and replaces these lines with the lines to be inserted.

If the include or function module to be corrected contains customer modifications, sometimes the system cannot find the context blocks specified in the correction instruction, or in the lines to be deleted. In other words, the system cannot fully implement the correction. In this case, you can use the split-screen editor to adapt the corrections in the Note to your modifications.

Since 1998, correction instructions have been formalized to such a degree that they can be implemented automatically. However, older Notes may still be in non-standardized format, and the Note Assistant will be unable to automatically completely implement these Notes. However, as mentioned before, you can manually edit the source code, using the split-screen editor. It is recommended that you do this to ensure that the Note Assistant can register the Note in your system.

Validity of Notes

Every correction instruction specifies the release and Support Package levels in which you can implement the correction instruction. These levels are known as the *validity range* of the correction instruction .

For example: if an error is detected in Release SAP_BASIS 7.00, and Support Package 5 corrects this error, the validity period of the correction instruction in question will be specified as "SAP_BASIS 7.00, Support Packages 1–4."

A Note can also specify that a correction instruction may not be implemented if the system contains a specific software component (such as an add-on). This may be the case if, for example, a correction makes changes to a part of a program that is required in its unmodified form by another software component.

If such a condition exists, this information displays in the header area of the correction instruction under *Invalid for <software component, release, Support Package level>*.

The Note Assistant automatically checks the validity and implements a correction instruction only if the status of the system is included in the specified validity area.

Prerequisites In certain cases, correction instructions can be implemented only if other correction instructions have already been implemented. This is due to interdependent changes made to the same points in the source code, or to semantic dependencies.

These dependencies are described in the header area of the correction instructions. If there are dependencies, you will have to implement not just one Note, but a series of Notes.

Log File

A log file is created when you download a Note (see Figure 17.10). A log file contains information about all of the main processing steps, including the date, time, system, and user in question, allowing you to trace the steps that have already been taken.

You can also save your own notes or remarks in the log file, provided that you are entered as a processor for this Note.

The information in the log file cannot be deleted.

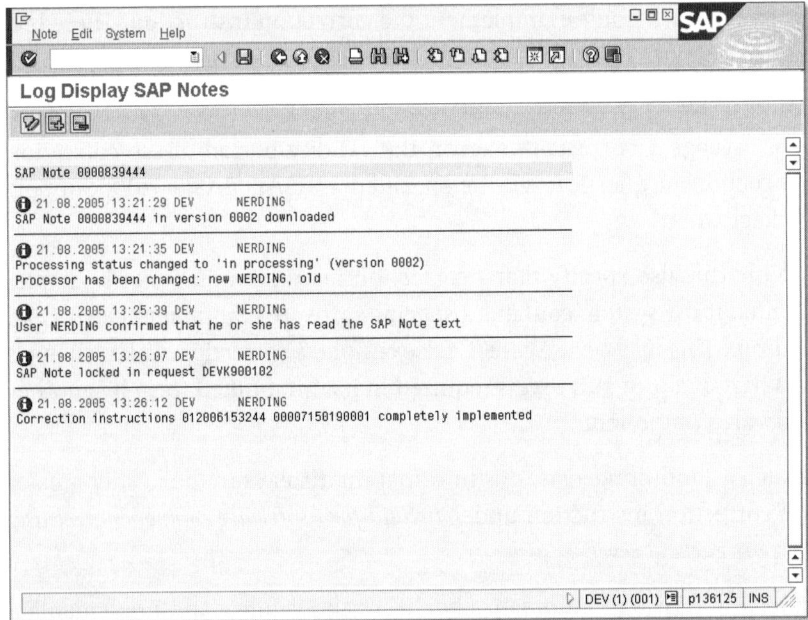

Figure 17.10 Log File

Update Note

Updating a Note allows you to adjust the version of a Note in your system to the current version in the SAPNet-R/3 frontend. You can thus check at any time whether the Notes in your system are up to date. If necessary, the system downloads the latest version.

You have the following options:

- Adjust an individual Note from within the Notes display
- Adjust all Notes listed in your worklist
- Adjust all Notes listed in the Notes browser

[+] Notes can be automatically updated only if you have set up an RFC connection to the SAPNet-R/3 frontend.

To update a Note, proceed as follows:

1. Choose DOWNLOAD LATEST VERSION OF SAP NOTES.

   The system checks whether your system contains the latest versions of the Notes listed on the screen.

   It also displays—in a dialog box—any Notes that SAP has changed since the last time you downloaded them.

2. To download the latest versions of these Notes, click OK in the dialog box.

If the current Note was changed, and therefore has to be reimplemented, the Note Assistant displays this Note in your worklist under the INCONSISTENT heading. In this case, all you have to do is reimplement the Note.

Post-Processing Support Packages

A Support Package contains a collection of error corrections. Support Packages can be imported only in their entirety and only in the specified order. Every correction in a Support Package is documented in a Note.

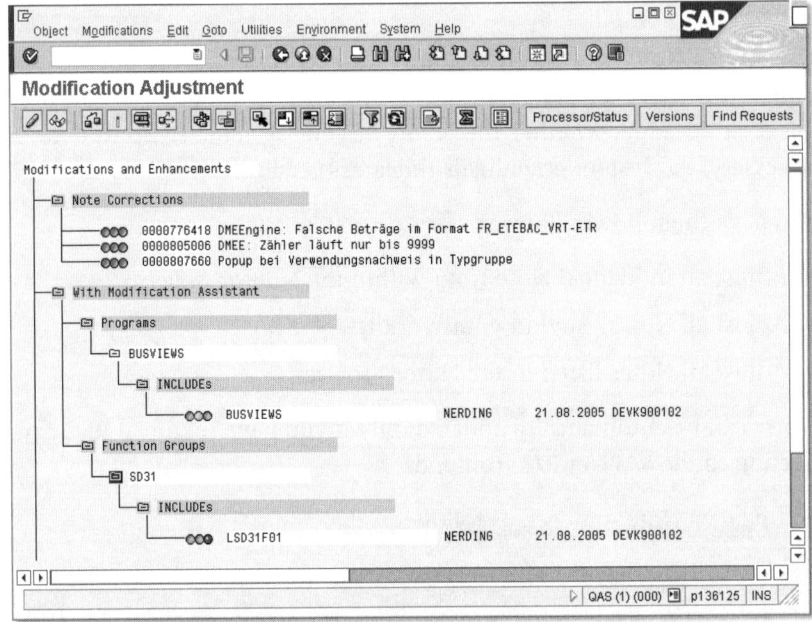

Figure 17.11 Post-Processing Support Packages in Transaction SPAU

After you import a Support Package, you must execute the modification adjustment using Transaction SPAU as shown in Figures 17.11 and 17.12. The scenarios that can arise are as follows.

Correction implemented via a Note and contained in the Support Package (traffic light icon with no colors)

1. When a Support Package is imported, the system automatically checks whether you have previously implemented individual corrections from this Support Package in the form of Notes. In the modification adjustment function (Transaction SPAU), these Notes are displayed with a traffic light icon with no colors and are therefore marked as obsolete.

   You must reset the objects they contain to their original SAP status. You can do this in one of the following ways:

   - Click on the traffic light icon.
   - Position the cursor on the Note number. Choose Reset to Original.

   A dialog box opens. In this box, confirm that you want to reset the Note correction to the original status.

   If you have selected multiple Notes corrections, you can choose Reset All, and the dialog box does not open.

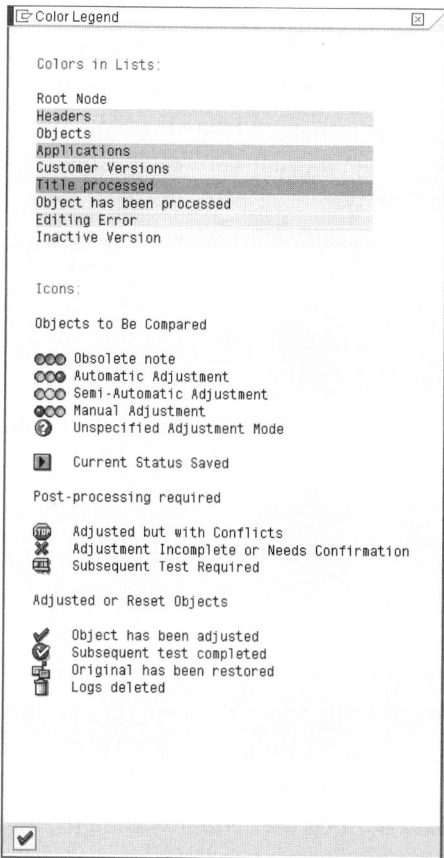

Figure 17.12 Color Legend in Transaction SPAU

Note implemented, but not contained in Support Package (yellow traffic light icon)

2. The system checks whether corrections that you have previously implemented via a Note have been overwritten by a Support Package that did not contain these corrections. If this is the case, you will have to reimplement these Note corrections. The system displays these Notes in the modification adjustment (Transaction SPAU) with a yellow traffic light.

   Click on the traffic light to start the reimplement process for the Note.

   These Notes are also displayed in your worklist with the status INCONSISTENT, which mean they have to be reimplemented. To start the reimport, choose IMPLEMENT SAP NOTE.

Correction implemented via a Note and contained in the Support Package, but Note version is different (yellow traffic light icon)

3. The system checks whether you have previously implemented individual corrections from the Support Package into your system via Notes. If the Note version in the Support Package is more current than the Note that was implemented in your system using the Note Assistant, the modification adjustment function cannot reset the objects in the Note to their original status. The system displays this Note with a yellow traffic light.

   In this case, proceed as follows:

   - Call the Note Assistant.
   - Download the latest version of all Notes.
   - Recalculate the adjustment modes in the modification adjustment. Then choose GoTo • Determine Adjustment Mode.

   If SAP has not changed the Note, its traffic light icon has no colors. You can reset it to its original status as described in step 1.

   If SAP has changed the Note, its traffic light icon is yellow. In this case, proceed as described in step 2.

Note has been implemented, although parts of it are contained in the Support Package (green traffic light icon)

4. An example of this scenario would be a Note that contains several correction instructions, each of which has a different validity period. This can have the following effect: When a Support Package is imported, one correction instruction may become obsolete, whereas another may still be valid. In such cases—which are, admittedly, rare—the Note has a green traffic light icon.

   If you click on the icon, correction instructions that are no longer relevant are reset to their original status.

Adjustment mode for Note implementation unspecified (green question mark)

5. The adjustment modes for Notes corrections are calculated in a background process after a Support Package is imported. However, if for some reason this process is not started, or if errors occur, a green question mark is displayed in front of the object in the hierarchy display. Click on the question mark to restart the process. This process can take a few minutes to complete.

[+] If an object contains your own modifications and Note corrections, you must first process the Note corrections in the modification adjustment function (SPAU), and then adjust your own modifications.

The system does not support modification adjustments in the WITH MODIFICATION ASSISTANT subtree if the object is contained in Note corrections that have not yet been adjusted, or reset to their original status.

In all cases, in a modification adjustment—or when correction instructions are reset to their original status—the objects contained in the Note are placed into transport requests. This ensures that they are transported to the downstream systems.

17.2.3 Implementation Status and Processing Status of Notes

The Note display in the Note Assistant contains two statuses: IMPLEMENTATION STATUS and PROCESSING STATUS. The implementation status of a Note is determined by the system, based on existing information. The processing status is specified by the user.

You should note that the system checks whether the processing status you specify is consistent with the implementation status of the correction instructions.

For example, you may set the processing status to COMPLETED only if all relevant corrections have been implemented (implementation status COMPLETELY IMPLEMENTED or CANNOT BE IMPLEMENTED).

If the implementation status changes afterwards and if it is no longer consistent with the processing status (for example, after a Support Package is imported), the system marks this Note as INCONSISTENT in the Note overview.

Implementation Status

If a Note contains correction instructions, the implementation status indicates whether all relevant correction instructions of the Note have been implemented in the system.

The system automatically sets the implementation status. The possible values are as follows (see Figure 17.13):

- **Incompletely implemented**
  Not all relevant correction instructions have been implemented, or a particular correction instruction has not been implemented completely.

The objects in question are therefore considered to be in an inconsistent state, and you should reimplement the relevant Note.

- **Obsolete version implemented**
  SAP has corrected a Note that contained errors. Reimplement the Note in your system.
- **Can be implemented**
  The Note contains correction instructions you can implement in your system, if necessary.
- **Completely implemented**
  The corrections in the Note have been fully implemented in your system. In this case, you don't have to take any action.
- **Cannot be implemented**
  The Note does not contain any correction instructions you can implement in your system. In this case, you do not have to take action.
- **Obsolete**
  After you implemented the corrections in the Note, you imported a Support Package that also contains these corrections. The error has therefore been resolved completely.

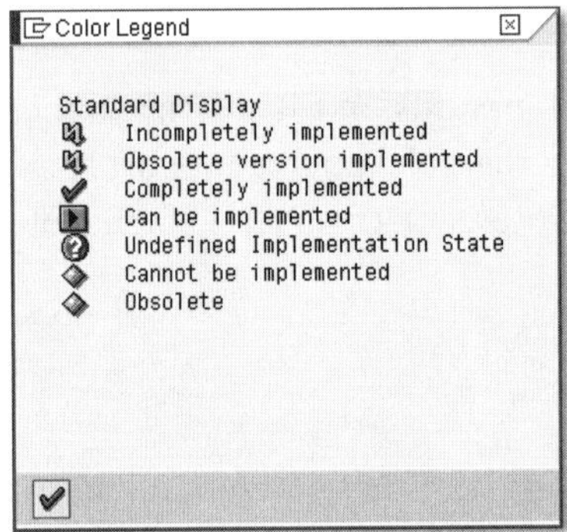

Figure 17.13 Possible Implementation Statuses of a Note

Processing Status

The processor of a Note sets its processing status. This status tells other users and the system whether this Note has already been processed and if so, to what extent. This status is set in the Note Assistant and can be one of the following:

- **New**
  The Note has been loaded into your system but has not yet been processed.
- **In processing**
  The Note is being processed.
- **Completed**
  The instructions in the Note have been executed and any corrections have been implemented in the system. Therefore, processing is completed.
- **Not relevant**
  The Note has been read and classified as not relevant. A possible reason for this is that it pertains to a function that you do not use.

17.3 ABAP Support Packages

SAP regularly publishes Support Packages for different types of program correction and updates, both for ABAP and Java.

Support Packages can be downloaded from the SAP Service Marketplace under the Quick Link */swdc*. SAP also provides collections of Support Packages on CD-ROM. You can order these Support Packages from the SAP Software Shop at *http://service.sap.com/softwarecat.*

SAP provides a range of tools that make it easy and convenient for you to obtain Support Packages and import them automatically.

Side effects of SAP Notes

The new reporting tool for *side effects of SAP Notes* helps you avoid any undesirable side effects of Support Packages after you import them. This tool discovers whether the SAP Notes in a Support Package could have side effects on other areas of your SAP system, and outputs a list of additional SAP Notes you should implement to prevent these side effects from happening.

Benefits of Support Packages

Support Packages provide the following benefits:

1. **Proactive solution of known problems**
   Support Packages solve known problems that have occurred in other SAP customers' systems, and thus proactively remove potential problems. This, in turn, leads to better system stability.

2. **Prerequisite to problem-solving**
   In rare cases, a problem can be solved only if a certain Support Package has been imported. In such cases, it is not possible to solve the problem with a series of Notes. If the problem in question occurs, the required Support Package will have to be imported at short notice. The older the Support Package status, the higher the risk becomes.
3. **Improved repair and maintenance**
   If a problem occurs, it is easier to find a solution if the latest Support Package has been imported. This is because you can exclude from the possible solutions all Notes that are contained in the Support Packages that have already been imported.
4. **Reduced repair and maintenance**
   If you import the Support Packages for your system, there is no need to import all of the individual Notes. If the kind of error occurs that necessitates the implementation of a Note, this Note may have several prerequisite Notes that also have to be implemented. If you don't have the latest Support Packages, the list of prerequisite Notes may be very long, thus increasing the amount of time and effort required for error correction.
5. **Prerequisite for implementation projects**
   An up to date Support Package is often a prerequisite for the implementation of new functionality in a system. In such cases, if the Support Package level is not current, the implementation process will have to be put on hold until the appropriate Support Package is imported.
6. **Prerequisite for interfaces to other SAP systems**
   In some cases, it is necessary to import the latest Support Packages so that other SAP systems with newer Support Packages can use interfaces to your system.
7. **Statutory changes**
   Support Packages comply with the latest statutory requirements. This is especially relevant to the HR area, but also to statutory changes in the FI/CO area.
8. **Prerequisite for importing Enhancement Packages**
   SAP ERP 6.0 as well as most applications based on SAP NetWeaver 7.0 provide new functions in Enhancement Packages. These enable the customer to import software innovations more frequently and with little additional effort. Enhancement Packages each require a current Support Package stack.

Support Packages contain quality improvements to the SAP system and make any adjustments that may be necessary (due to statutory changes, for example). They do this by replacing the affected objects in your system.

Every Support Package is valid for one specific release level (but for all databases and operating systems) and has a prerequisite number of predecessors. An upgrade of the next release level or correction level contains all Support Packages for the preceding levels that were available when the upgrade was delivered.

Support Package Manager

The Support Package Manager ensures that Support Packages are imported only in the predefined order.

To prevent problems from occurring, import Support Packages at regular intervals. This is the best way to keep your system landscape up to date.

Java Support Packages

Java Support Packages contain corrections and updates to Java components. They are delivered in the form of software component archives (SCAs). Unlike ABAP Support Packages, Java Support Packages always contain the full version of the development component in question. It is therefore sufficient to import only the latest one. If dependencies exist between the current Java Support Package and other Java Support Packages, they are described in an SAP Note.

Java Support Packages have been delivered since SAP Web Application Server (SAP Web AS) 6.20 and are imported using the Software Deployment Manager (SDM). The SDM is delivered with the SAP Web AS from Version 6.20 on. SAP Note 544244 contains more detailed information on this topic. As of SAP NetWeaver 7.00 you are also provided with the Java Support Package Manager (JSPM). This is a Java-based tool for implementing Java Support Packages, patches, and Support Package stacks. The use of JSPM is similar to the use of SPAM. Java Support Packages and patches are discussed in detail later in this chapter.

17.3.1 Applying ABAP Support Packages

Support Package Manager

The Support Package Manager (SPAM) enables you to import SAP Support Packages into your system easily and efficiently.

You can open the SPAM in one of the following ways:

- ▶ Choose SAP MENU • TOOLS • ABAP WORKBENCH • UTILITIES• MAINTENANCE • SUPPORT PACKAGE MANAGER.
- ▶ Enter Transaction code SPAM.

[+] The SAP Add-on Installation Tool (SAINT) provides functionality that is similar to Transaction SPAM. However, SAINT also lets you implement add-ons and delta upgrades of individual ABAP software components. If you need to upgrade software components with the Support Package stack, Transaction SAINT is frequently used instead of Transaction SPAM. However, using SAINT is similar to using SPAM; therefore, only Transaction SPAM (see Figure 17.14) is described in detail here.

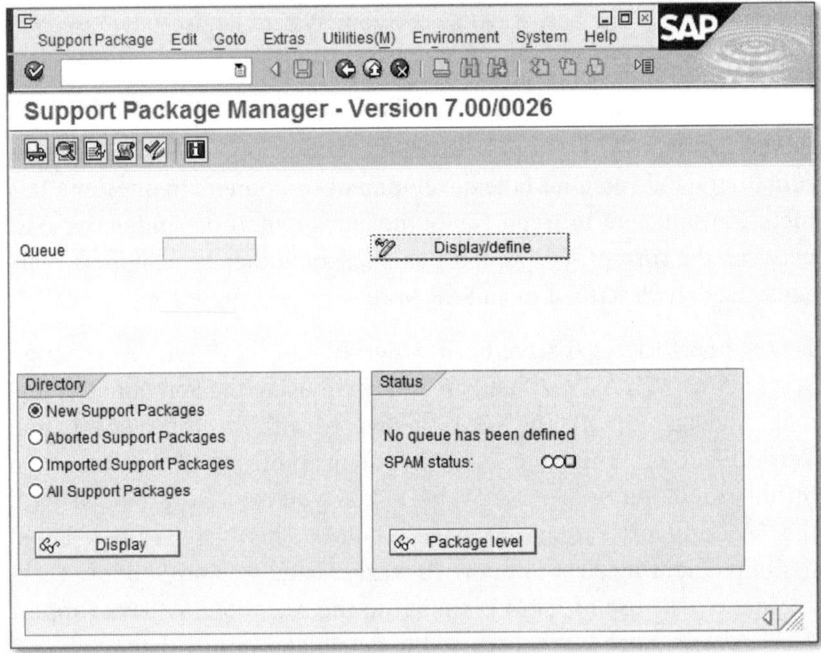

Figure 17.14 The Initial Screen of Transaction SPAM

Features

The Support Package Manager has the following features:

- ▶ **Support Package loading**
  You can load Support Packages into your system from the SAP Service Marketplace, the SAPNet-R/3 frontend, or from collection CDs.

- **Restartability**
  When the Support Package Manager imports a Support Package into your system, it adheres to a fixed order of steps.

  If the import process has to be canceled for any reason, you can resume processing at a later stage from the point that had been reached.
- **Display import status**
  You can use the Support Package Manager to identify the current import status of your system.
- **Special import procedure**
  A special import procedure minimizes downtime.
- **Start time control**
  The individual phases of the Support Package Manager are grouped into modules. This allows you to set the start time of the modules to any time you like.
- **Background processing**
  You can also schedule the modules to run in background processing, with predefined start times.

You need the following authorizations to be able to use all of the Support Package Manager functions:

- S_TRANSPRT
- S_CTS_ADMIN

Authorizations

Both authorizations are contained in the S_A.SYSTEM authorization profile.

If you log on to client 000 and your user master contains the relevant authorization profile, you can use all of the Support Package Manager functions. If you log on to another client, or if you don't have the required user profile, you can use only the display functions.

You can only assign this authorization profile to the system administrator. Also, only the system administrator should have authorization for the following actions:

- Download Support Packages
- Import Support Packages
- Confirm successfully imported Support Packages
- Reset the status of a Support Package

Settings

Choose EXTRAS • SETTINGS to open a dialog box in which you can configure general settings for the Support Package Manager. These settings affect the behavior of the system when loading and importing all types of Support Packages. One exception is SPAM/SAINT updates, which have special predefined settings.

You only have to configure the settings once because they are saved and used every time the Support Package Manager is called. Note that these settings also apply to the SAP Add-On Installation Tool.

An exception to this is the settings for the *Downtime-minimized* import mode: This does not automatically apply to the Add-On Installation Tool.

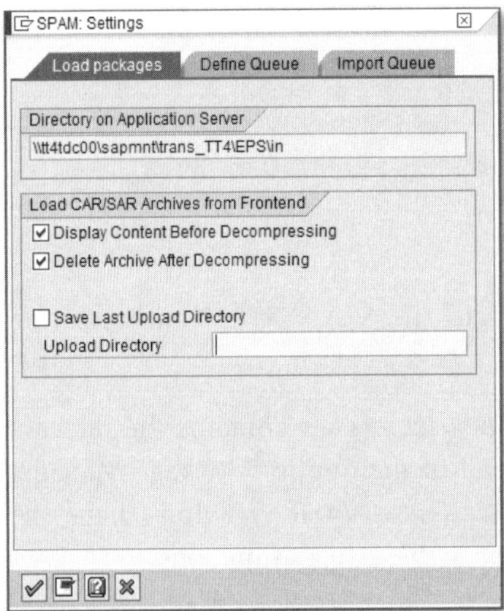

Figure 17.15 Load Packages Tab

On the LOAD PACKAGES tab, you can change or check the following properties (see Figure 17.15):

- **Directory on Application Server**
  Shows the application server directory in which the Support Packages are stored.

Load Packages tab

- **Load CAR/SAR Archives from Frontend**
  - **Display Content Before Decompressing**
    Allows you to specify whether you want to view a dialog box containing the archive content before the CAR/SAR archive is decompressed. This is selected by default.
  - **Delete Archive After Decompressing**
    Allows you to specify whether the CAR/SAR archive that was transferred to the application server should be deleted after it is successfully decompressed. This is selected by default.
  - **Save Last Upload Directory**
    Allows you to specify whether the most recently used upload directory on your frontend computer should be saved. If you select this option, this directory is automatically displayed as the start directory in the archive selection dialog box the next time you use this transaction. You can also enter an upload directory of your choice in the UPLOAD DIRECTORY field. This directory is then displayed as the start directory in the archive selection dialog box.

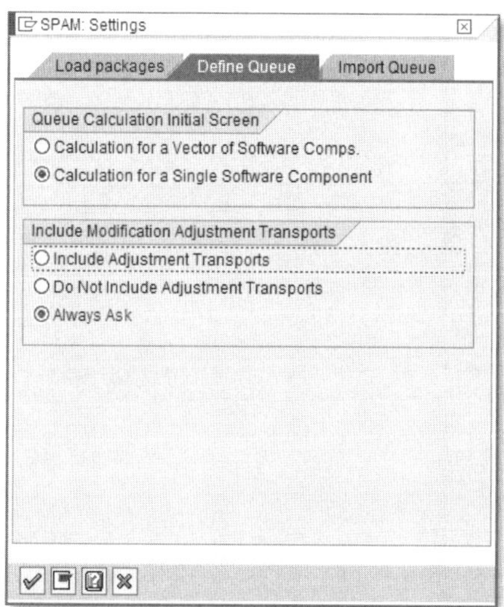

Figure 17.16 Define Queue Tab

On the Define Queue tab, you can change or check the following properties (see Figure 17.16):

Define Queue tab

- **Queue Calculation Initial Screen**
  You can specify the queue calculation method you want to be provided with by default when entering the queue definition screen:
  - **Queue calculation for a Vector of Software Comps (components)**
    The Support Package queue calculation takes place for multiple software components based on the target Support Package level that has been defined for each software component (see section "Define Queue," marginal text: "Define queue on the basis of multiple software components").
  - **Queue Calculation for a Single Software Component**
    The Support Package queue calculation is done by selecting one software component and the highest Support Package for this software component (see section "Define Queue," marginal text: "Define queue on the basis of target Support Package").
- **Include Modification Adjustment Transports**
  You can specify whether you want to include SPDD and SPAU adjustment transports.

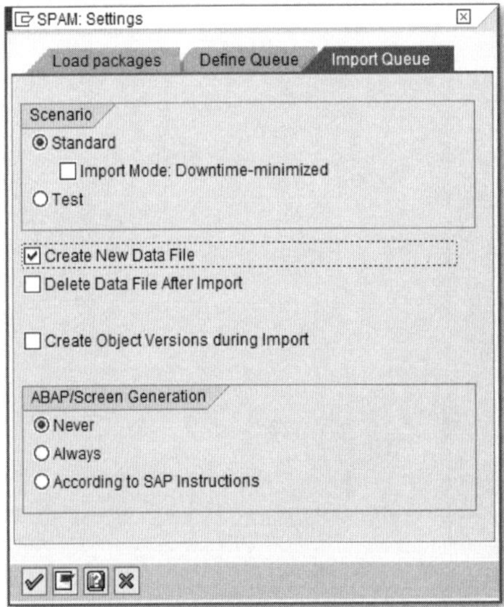

Figure 17.17 Import Queue Tab

On the IMPORT QUEUE tab, you can change or check the following properties (see Figure 17.17):

Import Queue tab

- **Scenario**
  By selecting the scenario, you determine which actions will be carried out during the import of the Support Package:
  - **Standard**
    Select the standard scenario if you want to import Support Packages completely and execute all of the steps involved.
  - **Import Mode: Downtime-minimized**
    If you select the standard scenario, you can also select the downtime-minimized import mode to reduce the downtime. This is not selected by default. If you do not select this option, Support Packages are imported using the conventional method. For more information on this import mode, see the relevant section that follows.
  - **Test**
    The test scenario lets you determine whether you need to carry out a modification adjustment, or whether conflicts exist that need to be resolved before the import—that is, before the Support Package is imported. No data or objects are imported into your system in the test scenario.
    There is no test scenario for SPAM/SAINT updates. Therefore, if you select this option when importing a SPAM/SAINT update, it is ignored.
- **Create New Data File**
  This option allows you to specify whether the data files in the EPS packages should be decompressed with every attempted import. It is selected by default.

  If you have a multisystem landscape with a shared transport directory, it is best to select this option in only the first system into which you import Support Packages, and to deselect it in the downstream systems. This saves time in the import process because the data files do not need to be created again in the downstream systems.

- **Delete Data File After Import**
  This option allows you to specify whether the data files should be deleted after a Support Package is imported. This helps to save disk space and is selected by default.

  If you have a multisystem landscape with a shared transport directory, it is best to deselect this option because the data files do not need to be created again in the other systems (see the list item "Create New Data File").

- **Create Object Versions during Import**
  This option does not apply to SPAM/SAINT updates.

  It allows you to specify whether versions should be created of the Support Packages' objects during the import process. This option is deselected by default. This is because versioning makes sense only if it is activated for all imports, and also because it can take a long time and takes up a lot of space in the database.

  [+] Note that if version creation is activated in the transport tools' configuration in the Transport Management System (Transaction STMS), you must set the `VERS_AT_IMP` parameter to `ALWAYS`.

- **ABAP/Screen Generation**
  These options allow you to specify whether the programs and screens that come with the Support Package should be generated during the import.

  They have no effect with SPAM/SAINT updates.

  - **Never**
    If you select this option, the programs and screens are generated only when they are called for the first time.

  - **Always**
    If you select this option, the programs and screens are always generated. Note that the generation process can take a very long time to complete, and may cause errors.

  - **According to SAP Instructions**
    If you select this option, the programs and screens are always generated if the generation option is activated during the import process for these Support Packages.

Import Phases and Modules

All actions the import tools perform run in *phases*. These phases, in turn, are grouped into modules. The modules have the following properties:

- You can run them individually.
- You can start them in a background process.
- You can set the start time of the modules to any time you like.

Description of import process

The import process is subdivided into the following modules:

- **Preparation module**
  This module carries out all of the preparation and testing steps (such as a test import and add-on conflict checking). It can run during live operation.

  After you have run the Preparation module, you can reset the queue. If you proceed to the Import 1 module and do not reset the queue, the data is changed in the database and you will not be able to reset or delete the queue from this point on.
- **Import 1 module**
  This module imports and activates Dictionary objects (and carries out a modification adjustment of Dictionary objects, if necessary). Any changes that are made in the process of importing and activating the Dictionary are still in an inactive state in the system. This means that the runtime system cannot "see" these changes yet. If you are sure that manual changes do not need to be made and that no transports will be imported into the system, this module can also run during live operation. This is usually the standard in production systems.
- **Import 2 module**
  This module carries out the remaining import steps, including the activation of inactive Dictionary nametabs. To avoid inconsistencies, this module cannot run simultaneously with live operations, because it imports changes to various transport objects.
- **Clean-Up module**
  This module handles all post-import ("clean-up") steps, especially modification adjustment for Repository objects. Live operations can resume after all modifications have been adjusted.

[+] Because the package import process can be stopped after every module, it is possible to run the Preparation and Import 1 modules during live operations. After the system has been transferred to non-live operations, the Import 2 module and, if necessary, the modification adjustment can be carried out, after which live operations can resume.

[+] Make sure that no company-specific transports, aside from modification adjustment transports, occur when the Import 1 module has been started, and that no manual changes are made to Repository objects (ABAP programs and Dictionary objects). Moreover, the search helps may be inconsistent during the time period between running modules Import 1 and Import 2. This time period should be kept as short as possible.

Import phases The Support Package Manager uses the status bar to indicate which phase is currently being executed. If you want to know which phases are executed for which scenario (test or standard scenario), run program `RSSPAM10`.

SAP Add-on Installation Tool

The SAP Add-on Installation Tool (SAINT) provides functionality that is similar to Transaction SPAM. However, SAINT also lets you implement add-ons and delta upgrades of individual ABAP software components. If you need to upgrade software components with the Support Package stack, you need to use Transaction SAINT instead of Transaction SPAM. Moreover, Transaction SAINT enables you to use multiple parallel processes for the R3trans import and for background processing. However, this is only possible for specific packages that consist of multiple object bills of material, for instance, ERP Enhancement Packages.

Import SPAM/SAINT Update

SPAM/SAINT updates (known as SPAM updates for short) provide you with updates and improvements to the Support Package Manager and the SAP Add-On Installation Tool. Every release comes with a SPAM update, which is then updated as necessary over time. It is stored in the following locations in the system:

- In the short description; for example, SPAM/SAINT update version <REL>/0001
- In the package name; for example, *SAPKD<REL>01*

[+] We recommend that you always import the latest version of a SPAM update before importing Support Packages or Installation Packages.

Canceled packages

A SPAM update can be successfully imported only if the system does not contain any canceled packages. If the system does contain such packages, a dialog box informs you of this fact and you can do one of two things:

- Fully import the queue and then import the SPAM update.
- Delete the queue, import the SPAM update, and then import the queue.

Note that you can delete the queue only if the Import 1 module has not yet been started (up to phase SCHEDULE_RDDIMPDP).

To import a SPAM update, proceed as follows:

1. Open the Support Package Manager (Transaction SPAM).
2. Check that the SPAM update in question is more up to date than the version that is currently on your system. (The latest version is displayed in the title bar of the Support Package Manager.)
3. To import the latest version, choose Support Package • Import SPAM update. SPAM updates are automatically confirmed after they have been successfully imported.

Loading Support Packages

Before you can import a Support Package, you must load it from the SAP Service Marketplace (see Figure 17.18).

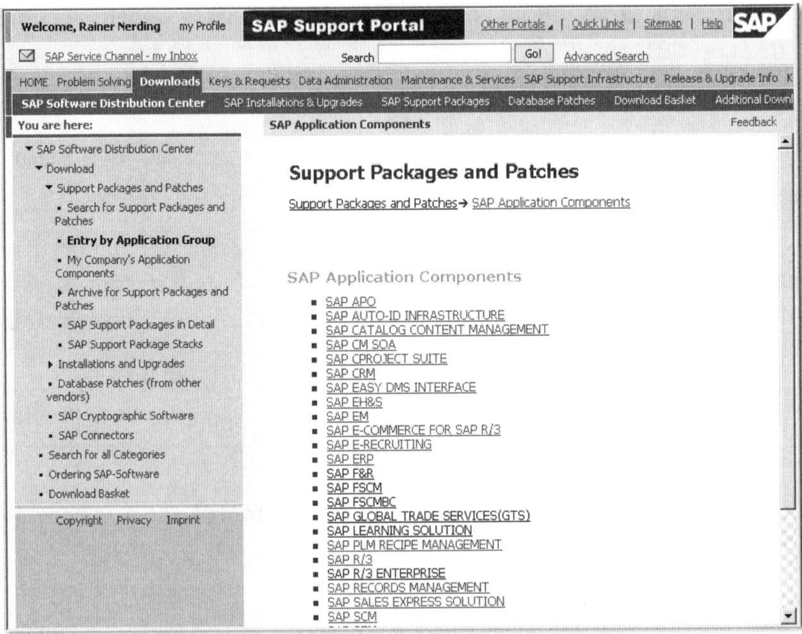

Figure 17.18 Loading Support Packages from the SAP Service Marketplace

Load Support Packages from the SAP Service Marketplace or CD

Support Packages in the SAP Service Marketplace are in compressed format. You therefore have to *decompress* them before using them.

If the archives are located on your frontend computer, you can transfer them directly to the application server from within the Support Package Manager and decompress them there. However, if the archives are larger than 10MB, proceed as follows:

1. Load the Support Packages from the SAP Service Marketplace or mount the relevant CD.
2. Log on with the following operating system-dependent user:

Operating System	User
Unix	<sid>adm
IBM eServer iSeries	<SID>OFR
Windows	<SID>adm

3. Switch to the following operating system-dependent subdirectory in your system:

Operating System	Subdirectory
Unix and IBM eServer iSeries	trans
Windows	TRANS

4. Use the following operating system-dependent command to decompress the archive that contains the Support Packages:

Operating System	Command
Unix	SAPCAR -xvf /<CD_DIR>/<PATH>/<ARCHIVE>.CAR
IBM eServer iSeries	SAPCAR '-xvf /QOPT/<VOLID>/<PATH>/<ARCHIVE>.CAR'
Windows	SAPCAR -xvf <CD_DRIVE>:\<PATH>\<ARCHIVE>.CAR

   The decompressed Support Packages are then automatically placed in the EPS inbox of your transport directory (Unix and IBM eServer iSeries: /usr/sap/trans/EPS/in; Windows: <DRIVE>:\usr\sap\trans\EPS\in).

5. Load the Support Packages into your system using SUPPORT PACKAGE • LOAD PACKAGE • FROM APPLICATION SERVER.

   A list of the Support Packages you just uploaded displays. They are now known to the SAP system with all of their attributes and can be handled correctly by the Support Package Manager.

6. Choose BACK to return to the Support Package Manager's initial screen.

7. Define the queue.

Load from frontend

If you want to load the archives (*.CAR/*.SAR) from the frontend to the application server, and if the archives are smaller than 10MB, proceed as described in the list of steps that follows. If the archives are greater than 10MB, the procedure described here will not be efficient. In this case, first transfer the Support Packages to the application server—via FTP, for example—and then load them from there.

1. Open the Support Package Manager (Transaction SPAM).
2. Choose Support Package • Load Packages • From Frontend. The dialog box for archive selection opens.
3. Select the relevant archive. This archive is transferred to the application server. The archive's table of contents is read and then displayed in a dialog box.
4. Select Decompress to transfer the archive to the application server and decompress it. If you select the New Support Packages option and choose Display under Directory in the initial screen, the corresponding package is displayed in the Support Package Manager after the archive has been decompressed.

Define Queue

The queue determines which Support Packages are imported into your system by the Support Package Manager, and in what order. If the queue has not yet been fully defined, you now have to define the queue, making your selection from the available Support Packages. If the queue has been fully defined, it is simply displayed, and you cannot change it. However, you can delete the queue entirely, if required, by choosing Delete Queue.

[+] Note that you can delete the queue only if the Import 1 module has not yet been started (up to phase SCHEDULE_RDDIMPDP).

The Support Package Manager ensures that only Support Packages that are suitable for your system are displayed in the queue. Support Packages that are intended for another release, or for an add-on that you have not installed, don't appear in the queue, even if you loaded them into your SAP system.

You can define the queue on the basis of either the software components in your system or a target Support Package as shown in figure 17.19.

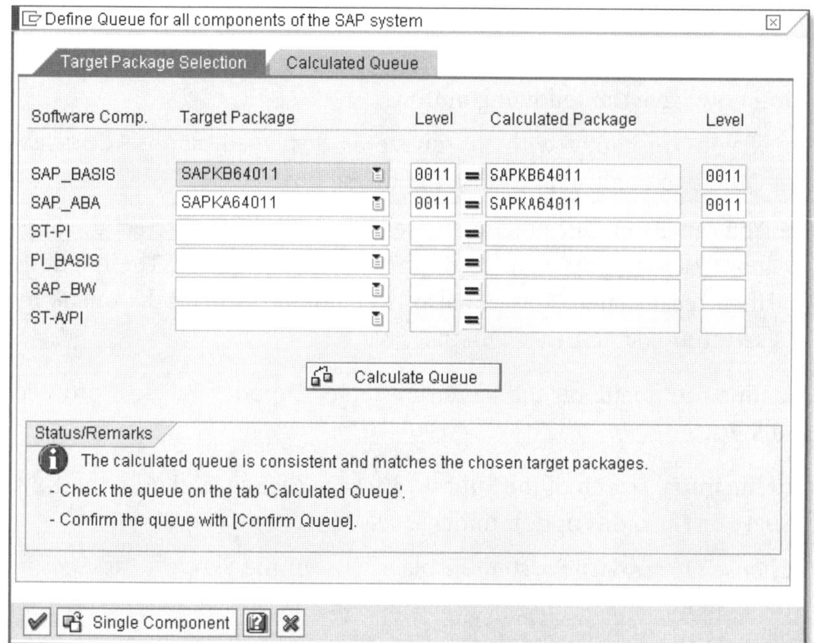

Figure 17.19 Defining the Import Queue

To define a queue on the basis of software components, proceed as follows:

Define queue on the basis of software components

1. Click DISPLAY/DEFINE in the initial screen of the Support Package Manager.
   The COMPONENT SELECTION dialog box appears, and the list of installed software components is displayed (such as SAP_BASIS, SAP_HR, SAP_BW).
2. Select the component you want.
   Alternatively, you can calculate a common queue for all software components in the system by selecting ALL COMPONENTS.
3. The queue is then displayed. The queue contains the Support Packages available for the selected component(s) in your system, and possibly also any Support Packages required for other components, Conflict Resolution Transports (CRTs), and any associated add-on Support Packages.

If you want to define the queue for another software component, select NEW COMPONENT.

4. You now have the following options:
   - If you are happy with the queue as displayed, choose CONFIRM QUEUE to confirm and close the dialog box.
   - You can also reduce the queue selection. To do this, select the Support Package you want to be the last in the queue. The queue is then recalculated. You can also explicitly recalculate the queue by selecting RECALCULATE QUEUE.

Define queue on the basis of target Support Package

To define the queue on the basis of a target Support Package, proceed as follows:

1. In the initial screen of the Support Package Manager, choose the NEW SUPPORT PACKAGES option under DIRECTORY.
2. Choose DISPLAY. The system displays a list of the Support Packages in the system.
3. Place your cursor on the Support Package you need and click CALCULATE QUEUE. The queue is displayed. It contains the Support Packages available in your system for the target Support Package, and possibly also any Support Packages required for other components, Conflict Resolution Transport (CRT), and any associated add-on Support Packages.
4. Proceed as described under Step 4 in the section "Define Queue," marginal text: "Define queue on the basis of software components."

Queue rules

The following rules apply when you create a queue:

- Support Packages for a selected component are placed in the queue in sequence.
- If Support Packages in the queue are linked to Support Packages of another component (such as another predecessor relationship or a required CRT), other Support Packages are added to the queue until all predecessor relationships are accounted for.

[+] Note that the Support Package Manager takes into account the configuration of your SAP system and places only the Support Packages your system can accept into the queue.

Import Queue

The Support Package Manager provides the following two scenarios for importing Support Packages or the queue:

Test scenario

The test scenario is used to identify any conflicts or problems (for example, repairs that have not been released) before the actual import process. The test import creates the list of objects to be adjusted in Transactions SPDD and SPAU, and should therefore be run during the project preparation phase.

This scenario allows you to estimate—and, possibly, minimize—the time and effort required to import Support Packages. No data is imported into the system in this scenario, and if errors occur, you can continue the import without having to correct them. You must explicitly select the test scenario.

[+]

Note that after the test scenario has run, the queue is empty again and you will have to redefine it. You will then also have to explicitly select the standard scenario.

Standard scenario

In the standard scenario, the Support Packages contained in the queue are fully imported. If errors occur, you can continue and complete the import only after you have removed or resolved them.

After you have selected the standard scenario, you can choose between the conventional import mode and the *downtime-minimized* import mode. The latter reduces the downtime.

Proceed as follows to import the queue in the standard scenario:

1. To set the standard scenario, select EXTRAS • SETTINGS.
2. On the IMPORT QUEUE tab, select STANDARD and configure the other import settings.
3. Select the import mode you need to use.
4. Select SUPPORT PACKAGE • IMPORT QUEUE. You can also use this function to resume an import procedure that was previously canceled.
5. The dialog box for selecting the start options opens. Specify the required start options and confirm the dialog box.

The Support Package Manager then completes the import, in accordance with the import mode and start options you selected.

Conventional import mode

If you accept the standard start options without changing them, the Support Package Manager handles the entire import process in the dialog box. The status bar provides you with information about the progress of the import and the current phase of the Support Package Manager. Note that your system should no longer be live at this point.

If you selected a start time or CONTINUE MANUALLY for the Import 2 module, you can keep the system in productive mode until the Import 2 module starts.

Downtime-minimized import mode

If you accepted the standard start options without changing them, you can keep the system in live mode for the time being, because the Support Package Manager will explicitly ask you to stop live operations when the time comes.

As usual, the Support Package Manager carries out all of the preparatory and checking steps (Preparation module). It then imports the inactive objects (Import 1 module), during which process the system can stay live.

The development environment is locked when the Import 1 module starts, so that objects are not unintentionally modified. Therefore, the consistency of the system is not jeopardized when objects are accessed by this module.

The Support Package Manager then notifies you in a dialog box that you have to stop productive operations for the next import module (Import 2).

- Click on CANCEL to do this in an orderly manner.

  Close any background jobs that are running. Request all users to close any transactions they are running and to log themselves off from the SAP system.

- Click on CONTINUE to continue the import.

  The Import 2 module activates the objects that were previously imported in an inactive state and imports the remaining objects from the Support Packages in the queue.

After this module has finished, the Support Package Manager informs you that you can resume live operations in the system, provided that no changes, or at most only small changes, were made to SAP objects.

- If you made changes to SAP objects, the Support Package Manager instructs you to finish the modification adjustment process.

  If you have to adjust Dictionary objects (Transaction SPDD), you must do this immediately, whereas with Repository objects (Transaction SPAU), you can adjust the objects immediately, at a later point, or in parallel with the clean-up steps after importing a Support Package. To do this, proceed as described in Chapter 18, Section 18.3.

- To complete the import process, select IMPORT QUEUE again.

  The clean-up steps are carried out on the next import module (Clean Up), and the import process is completed and closed.

Defines start options

You can define the start options for the individual modules according to your system requirements. If you confirm the dialog box without configuring any specific settings of your own, the import tool uses the standard settings of the selected import mode. You can store any settings you configure as a template for future import procedures.

The tabs in the START OPTIONS FOR THE QUEUE dialog box (see Figure 17.20) allow you to select the options you need for every module:

- **Start in dialog immediately**
  Select this option if you want this module to start running immediately in the dialog box. If you select this option for multiple modules, they are executed immediately, one after the other. The mode remains blocked for the duration of the import.
- **Start in background immediately**
  Select this option if you want this module to start running immediately in the background. If you select this option for multiple modules, they are executed immediately, one after the other.
- **Start in background later**
  Select this option if you want this module to start running in the background at a later time. Specify the start date and start time in the input fields. The NO START AFTER option lets you specify that this

module should run only during the period between PLANNED START and NO START AFTER. If no background process is available in this time period, this module is not started.

- **Manual Start/Continue Manually**
  Select this option if you want to manually start processing of this module. The import tool stops the processing process after the previous module has finished.

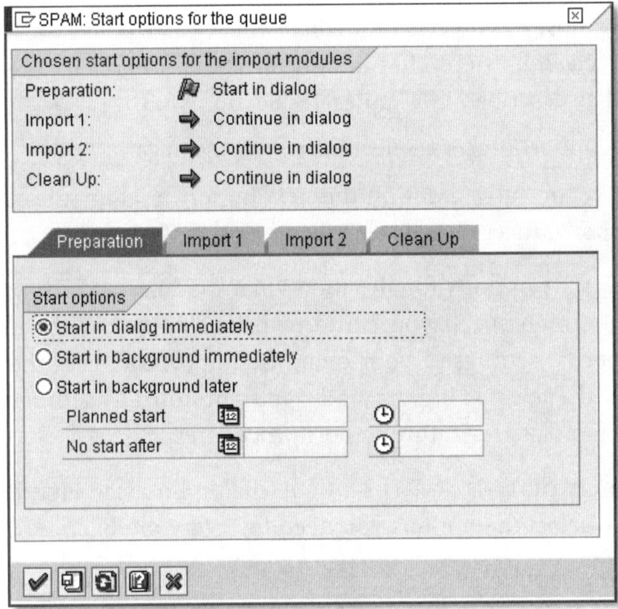

Figure 17.20 Defining the Start Options

Standard settings if conventional import mode is used in unchanged form

If you selected the conventional import procedure (DOWNTIME-MINIMIZED is not activated), the following standard settings apply:

Module	Option
Preparation	Start in dialog immediately
Import 1	Continue in dialog immediately
Import 2	Continue in dialog immediately
Clean Up	Continue in dialog immediately

If you have selected the downtime-minimized import mode, the following standard settings apply:

Standard settings if Downtime-minimized import mode is used in unchanged form

Module	Option
Preparation	Start in dialog immediately
Import 1	Continue in dialog immediately
Import 2	Continue manually
Clean Up	Continue manually

Downtime-minimized Import Mode

As a rule, the process of importing the latest OCS packages (Support Packages, Add-on Installation Packages, and add-on upgrades) requires a relatively long system downtime due to the size and scope of these packages. Although the system is not restarted in the import process, it should still not be used for live operations during this process. This restriction is a distinct disadvantage in many live systems.

Therefore, the downtime-minimized import mode was developed to reduce the downtime required for package imports. This mode enables you to import the majority of import objects while keeping the system live. The objects in question are program code and program texts. Therefore, downtime can be reduced greatly if a package contains a high proportion of program code and texts. (This figure is approximately 70-80% for SAP Basis and SAP R/3 Support Packages.)

Inactive objects

In downtime-minimized import mode, the objects are imported into the database in an inactive state and are mostly "invisible" to the system. The system can continue to stay live.

This procedure contains new actions (activation of inactive objects) and more organizational steps than the previous mode, which means that the import process takes longer. The efficiency and time-savings in the non-live phase of this mode, as compared to conventional mode, depend on two things: the proportion of inactively imported objects of the overall volume of imported data, and the amount of time consumed by additional actions that have to be carried out during the downtime (such as the handling of after-import methods and XPRAs).

[+] Import the packages in queues that are as large as possible. Ideally, put all packages in one queue.

Note, however, that in some cases Support Packages cannot be imported in one queue using the Support Package Manager. Consult the relevant SAP Note in your release for more information.

Because the inactively imported objects are stored in the database at the same time as the active versions, more space is temporarily required in the database.

Activating the objects

The objects are activated later by a predefined process that is provided by the import tool (Support Package Manager/SAP Add-On Installation Tool). Nevertheless, inactive objects are not fully isolated from the system, which means that parallel changes can cause unwanted activations and therefore system inconsistencies.

During the import, you should ensure the following:

- That there is enough free storage space in the database
- That there are no simultaneous imports of transport requests
- That the development environment is not in live use

Use downtime-minimized import mode in the following situations:

- In live systems
- In test systems, if you want to test the expected downtime in the live system

During the import process, you should treat the systems like live systems (no manual changes to program objects, and no parallel imports of other transport requests).

Do not use downtime-minimized import mode in the following situations:

- In development systems or in systems into which a lot of regular imports are made (such as QA or test systems)

  System consistency cannot be guaranteed during the import if manual changes are made to program objects, or if other transport requests are imported at the same time.

- To import Support Packages to BBP/CRM systems

  The additional preparation and clean-up steps required by the special Support Package Manager for BBP/CRM mean, in effect, that the entire import process takes place during downtime.

- To import preconfigured systems (SAP Best Practices) using the Add-On Installation Tool

Importing Support Packages into a System Landscape

Support Packages can be imported in groups or individually. If you have multiple SAP ERP systems, you must import Support Packages into each of these systems.

Three-system landscape

You can use the previously discussed procedure to import Support Packages into your landscape's development system, but the procedure is different for the other SAP ERP systems in your landscape, especially if you have to carry out a modification adjustment. Figure 17.21 shows an example of how Support Packages can be distributed in a three-system landscape.

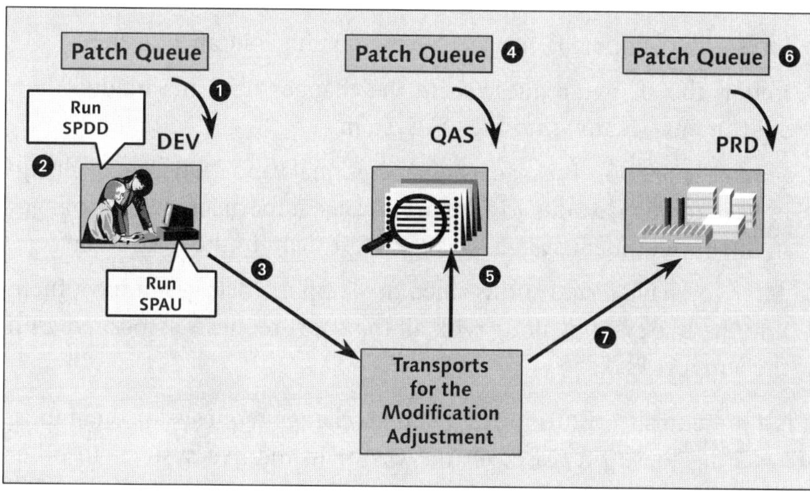

Figure 17.21 Distribution of Support Packages in a Three-System Landscape

Ideally, all SAP ERP systems have the same release level, as is the case after they are installed, after an SAP ERP release upgrade, or after the rollout in the implementation phase. If this is the case, you can import one or more Support Packages the same way you import change requests:

1. Import the Support Packages into the development system. The system adjusts all objects that were imported with the Support Package and that have been modified by the customer:
    - You may need to carry out a modification adjustment for the Dictionary objects using Transaction SPDD in the development system. The changes that result from the adjustment can then be included in a change request. This change request can be used to transport the modification adjustment of the ABAP Dictionary objects to other systems.
    - You may need to carry out a modification adjustment for the ERP Repository objects using Transaction SPAU. The changes that result from the adjustment can then be included in a change request. This request can be used to transport the modification adjustment of the Repository objects to other systems. If enhancements were used to make changes to the SAP ERP system (see Chapter 2), there is no need for an adjustment because enhancements don't result in modifications.
2. Import the Support Packages into the quality assurance system.
3. Import the change requests with the changes from the modification adjustments (if any) into the QA system.
4. Verify the Support Package using operational validation tests. If changes have to be made due to Support Package imports, make the changes in the development system and then test them in the QA system.
5. After you have tested and verified the Support Packages, import them into the live system, along with all transport requests associated with the Support Packages.

It is a prerequisite of this process that no change requests for the import are waiting to be processed in the QA or in the live system. In other words, the SAP systems—especially the QA and live systems—must all have the same release level. The validation process in the QA system ensures that the Support Package and all of the change requests that result from the modification adjustment can be imported into the live system.

Support Packages and Development Projects

It is more difficult to schedule Support Package imports if large development projects are ongoing in your system landscape. This is because you are not supposed to make transports between systems with different Support Package levels. Therefore, development projects cannot be imported into the live system until the Support Packages have been imported into all systems in the landscape.

Despite efforts to keep this "code freeze" period as short as possible, experience shows that one to two weeks have to be allotted for the SPAU adjustment in the development system, and approximately two to four weeks must be scheduled for the integration test in the QA system that follows. Of course, these time periods are average values and will vary from system to system.

SAP Code Inspector

The time and effort required for the SPAU adjustment increases as the number of modified and customer-specific objects increases. In addition to the objects listed in SPAU, any customer-specific objects that access standard SAP code also have to be checked. The SAP Code Inspector (Transaction SCI) is an automated tool for performing this task, and lets you carry out an extended syntax check for all customer-specific objects.

The time and effort required for this check depends on the number of business processes in use. The SAP system administrator has to decide whether to test only the most important business processes, or whether more minor processes should also be included in the test. Therefore, it is necessary to categorize the business processes according to their importance (ABC analysis) in advance. A well-organized test management process and the ready availability of automated test cases (eCATT) reduce the time and effort required for the test, and thus shorten the duration of the code freeze period.

Before Support Packages are imported into the development system, any open change requests should be released and imported to the downstream systems. After the Support Packages have been imported into the development system and the SPAU adjustment is complete, you may be able to resume development work in the development system. However, it's still possible that errors detected in the Support Package tests may be difficult to solve in the development system because the development system may have a more up to date software release. The safer option is therefore to resume work in the development system only if the Support Packages have been tested and found to be error-free. In all cases, all transports in the QA system must be suspended for the duration of the integration test.

Because of these effects on development projects, the timing of Support Package imports must be carefully planned and coordinated with the development project teams.

Some SAP customers first test Support Package imports and the SPAU adjustment in a sandbox environment, to minimize the code freeze period. Initial unit tests can also be carried out in the sandbox system.

You can also use the latest Support Package level for the relevant development projects, and then transport the changes along with the Support Packages through the maintenance landscape. This has the advantage that only one test is required for Support Packages and development projects. Note that this approach requires a phase-based system landscape, as described in Section 3.6.2.

17.3.2 Modification Adjustment

If Support Packages include objects that have been modified in the customer system, you need to implement a modification adjustment. Here, you have the following options: keep the modified version, accept the new standard SAP version, or adjust the two versions manually. The new standard SAP version remains active unless an adjustment has been carried out. Ideally, the modification adjustment needs to be implemented only in the development system. The resulting SPDD and SPAU transports can be integrated in the Support Package queue for the downstream systems.

Chapter 18, Section 18.3 deals with the topic of modification adjustment in greater detail. Thus, we will not discuss it further at this point.

17.4 Java Corrections

ABAP corrections are delivered via SAP Notes or Support Packages. SAP Notes contain correction instructions that can be used to insert selected code lines into existing code. This lets you correct errors individually and in an isolated manner. In Java systems, these isolated changes are not possible, and you need to at least update the entire development component.

SAP component model

Figure 17.22 shows the SAP component model. Products consists of multiple software components, which comprise multiple packages (ABAP) or development components (Java). These, in turn, are containers for individual development objects that belong together logically and are interdependent.

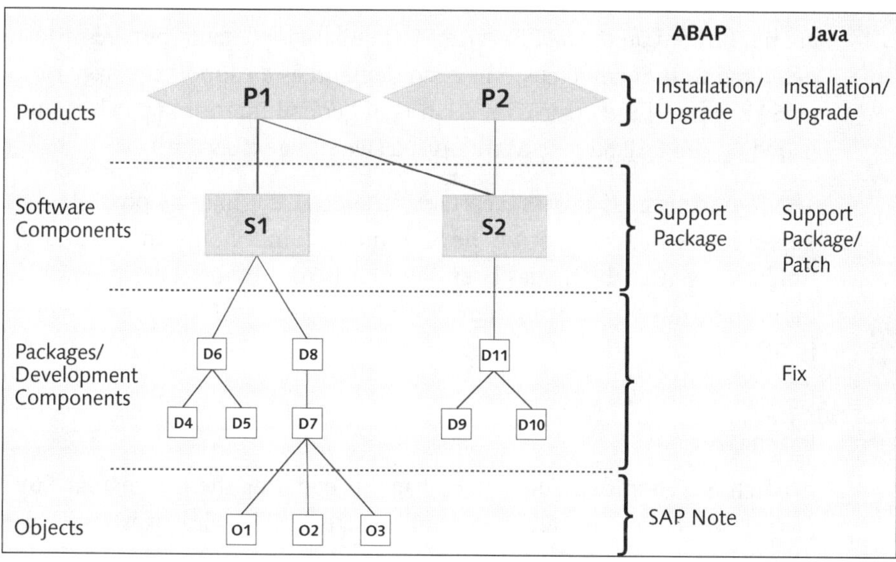

Figure 17.22 SAP Component Model

17.4.1 Java Correction Types

Software maintenance is available for products, software components, and development components. Products are installed or upgrades to a higher release level are implemented. A release consists of multiple software components that contain new functions and improvements.

Support Packages

JSPM In contrast to ABAP, a Support Package does not just contain the changed objects, but all objects of a software component. Therefore, in Java, you only have to import the last Support Package; in ABAP, you have to import all predecessors in the correct sequence. This means that Java Support Packages are cumulative. The common file format is SCA, which is implemented using the Java Support Package Manager (JSPM).

Fixes

Fixes are full deliveries of a development component. In other words, they contain all objects of this particular development component. A fix is the smallest delivery unit of corrections and usually solves one specific problem. Fixes are provided only in emergency cases if an urgent preliminary correction is required before the next Support Package is available. They are not offered on the SAP Service Marketplace by default, but are instead delivered to individual customers on demand as a support message or in an SAP Note. If the error correction is of general interest, a patch is published on the SAP Service Marketplace (see the next section).

The import of fixes carries a certain risk because it may be possible that dependencies exist to other development components that will stop functioning after the fix has been imported. You should therefore implement fixes only in coordination with SAP Support. Fixes are delivered in SDA file format.

Patches

A patch is a modified Support Package. It contains the last regular Support Package and also all important and generally valid fixes that have been compiled since the release of the last Support Package. Just like a Support Package, a patch is a full delivery of a complete software component. The common file format is SCA. Patches are created by SAP on request and are published in the SAP Service Marketplace, for instance, if serious problems have emerged. Usually, patches are created only for the latest Support Packages.

You can download both Support Packages and patches from the SAP Service Marketplace under the Quick Link *http://service.sap.com/swdc* (see

Figure 17.24). You must decide whether you want to import the last Support Package or also integrate the latest patch. Under the INFO link of a patch you can find a list of Notes available for the patch. If these Notes are relevant for your system, you should integrate the patch. If you click on the INFO link of a Support Package, you are provided with a summary that describes all corrections in a Support Package.

Figure 17.23 shows the three different Java correction types: Support Packages, Fixes and Patches.

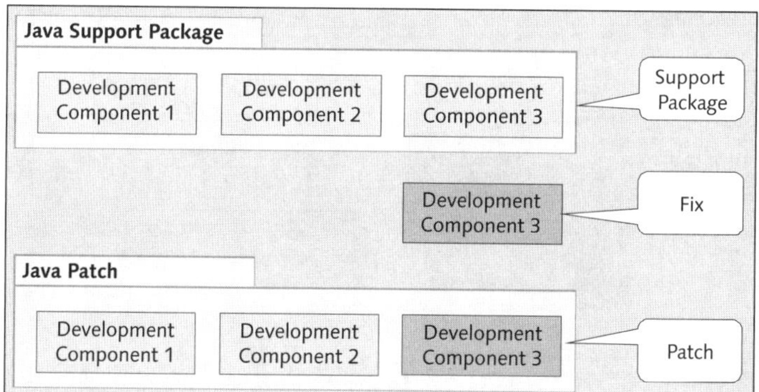

Figure 17.23 Java Support Packages, Fixes, and Patches

Figure 17.24 Java Support Packages and Patches in the SAP Service Marketplace

17.4.2 Version Information of a Java System

You can view the version information of a Java-based system on the component information page. The URL is *http://<hostname>:<port>/sap/monitoring/ComponentInfo* (see Figure 17.25).

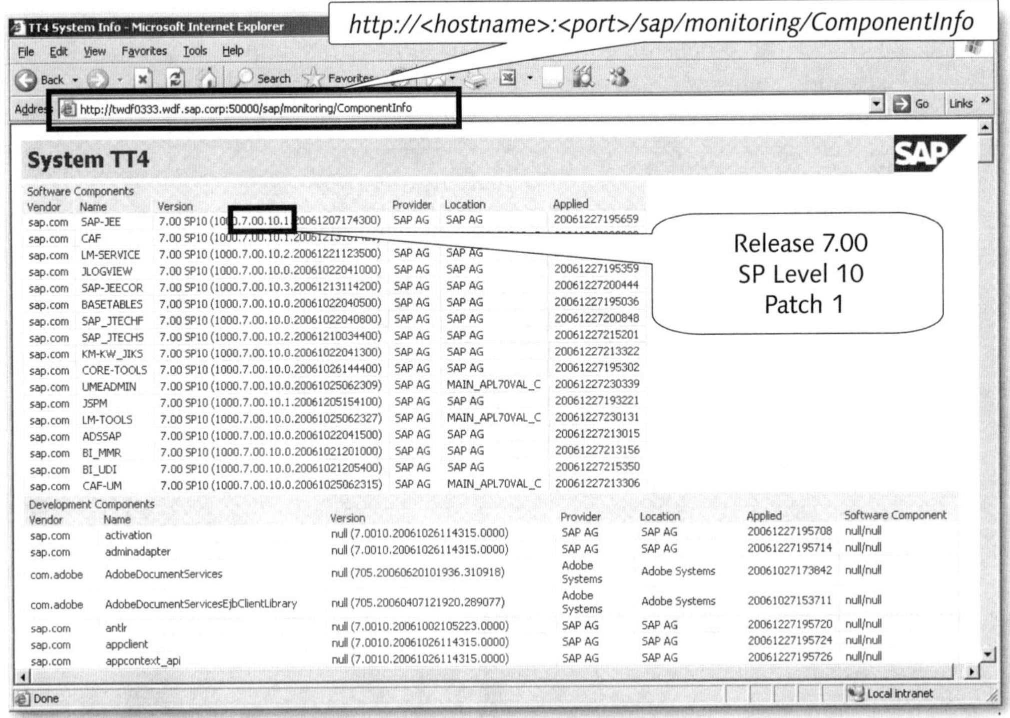

Figure 17.25 Version Information of a Java System

For each software component, the version information indicates the release level, the Support Package level, and the patch level.

SCA Java Support Packages are delivered in *Software Component Archive* (SCA) format. A software component archive comprises the following attributes:

- Vendor
  The manufacturer of the software, for example, sap.com.
- Name
  The name of the software component, for example, SAP-JEE. Vendor and name form a unique key for the software component. Components with identical names and different manufacturers are considered to be different.
- Release
- Support Package level
- Patch level
- Counter
  The counter includes the release, Support Package level, patch level, and time stamp, for example, 1000.7.00.2.0.20050524093600. In this example, 7.00 is the release, 2 the Support Package level, 0 the patch level, and 20050524093600 the time stamp.
- Provider
  The provider who created the software component, for example, SAP AG.

17.4.3 Java Support Package Manager (JSPM)

The Java Support Package Manager (see Figure 17.26) was implemented in SAP NetWeaver 7.0 to facilitate the import of Java Support Packages. In previous releases, Java Support Packages had to be imported using the Software Deployment Manager (SDM). The JSPM can also be used to import new software components or business packages. In addition, the JSPM identifies software components that have been modified and provides a modification adjustment in connection with the SAP NetWeaver Development Infrastructure (NWDI).

The JSPM is a Java-based program whose user interface is called at the operating system level. The script is go.bat and it is stored in the directory, *\usr\sap\<SID>\<Instance>\j2ee\JSPM*. The structure of the JSPM is similar to Transaction SPAM in ABAP systems and provides similar functions.

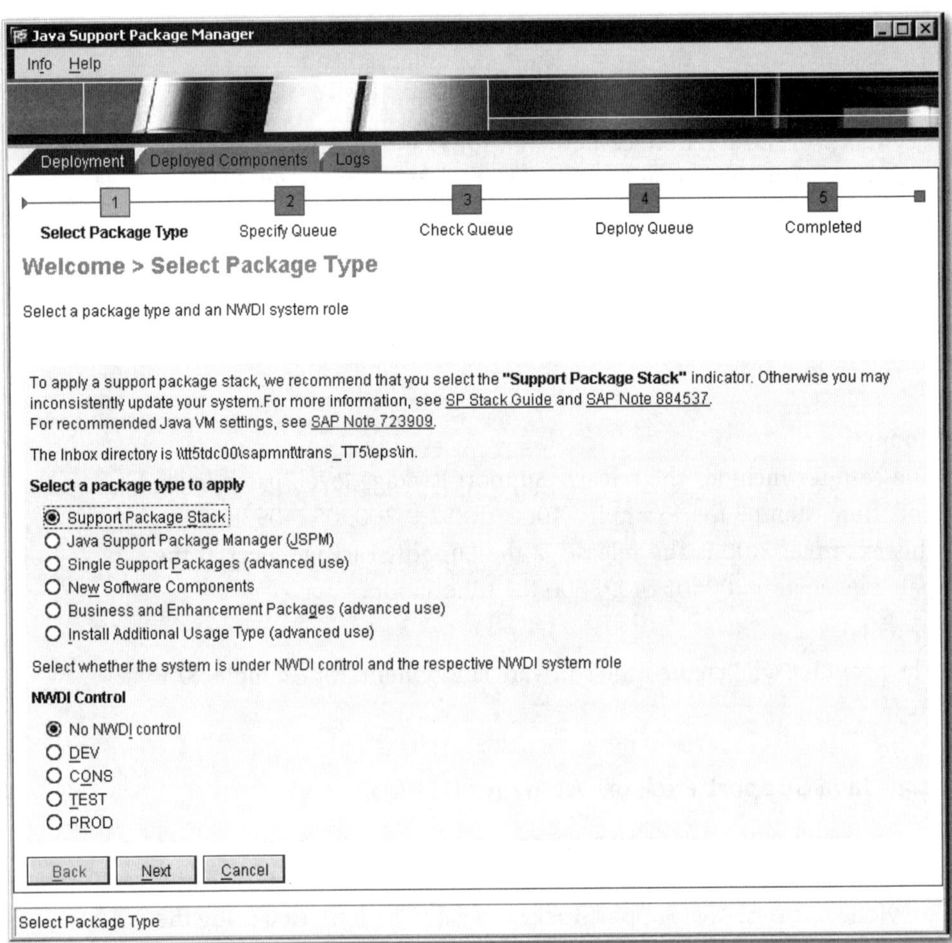

Figure 17.26 Java Support Package Manager

The JSPM establishes a connection with the Software Deployment Manager (SDM) to import Support Packages and new software components. The SDM implements additional validation steps for the packages and imports them into the Java application after the check has completed successfully.

Advantages of JSPM

SAP continuously provides new technologies and applications based on SAP NetWeaver Applications Server Java (AS Java). It is therefore important that these innovations can be imported safely and easily. JSPM was developed to address this issue and has the following advantages:

- **Improved user interface**
  The JSPM has a graphical user interface whose structure is similar to the installation and upgrade tools SAPinst and SAPJup. Its functions and operating elements are extensively adapted to the proven ABAP Support Package Manager (Transaction SPAM), and the status of the import can be monitored. The import process is logged comprehensively and can be restarted if an error occurs. The JSPM also informs you if a restart of the J2EE Engine is necessary during the import process.
- **Check for Support Package prerequisites**
  Prior to the import, the JSPM checks whether all prerequisites are met for importing the Support Packages—in particular, whether dependencies to other software components and their Support Packages exist.
- **Update of the SAP kernel and additional operating system files**
  The JSPM can update both the software component within the Java Application Server and the associated operating system files, for instance, the SAP kernel or the Internet Graphics Server (IGS). These files can also be distributed in a high-availability cluster environment.

  Prior to importing the actual update, the JSPM can update itself and the Software Deployment Manager (SDM).

  As a result, the JSPM automates the import of updates extensively and carries out many steps that previously had to be implemented as additional manual steps.
- **Import of a complete Support Package stack**
  The JSPM can import a complete Support Package stack, including the appropriate SAP kernel, into the system. During this process, the stack configuration file, which was created when the stack was downloaded from the SAP Service Marketplace, is evaluated. You can set restrictions to a specific system usage type. You can also integrate patches that are more up to date than the stack to be imported if these patches have previously been downloaded to the Support Package inbox.
- **Modification adaptation in connection with the NWDI**
  In some scenarios, SAP provides the Java source code which can then be modified by the customer—for example, in the SAP ERP scenarios

ESS/MSS or Biller Direct. During the import of Support Packages, the modifications are supposed to remain unchanged and not be overwritten by the SAP standard. This is provided by the JSPM in connection with the SAP NetWeaver Development Infrastructure (NWDI). First, the new Support Package is imported in NWDI where the modification adjustment takes place. Then, the modified archive is imported into the runtime system.

Software shipment units

The following shipment units can be imported using the JSPM:

- **Support Package stacks**
  Support Package stacks are coordinated combinations of Support Packages for all components of an application. They were introduced to reduce the wide range of possible software versions in customer systems. Moreover, the Support Package stacks are already tested intensively at SAP. For more information about Support Package stacks refer to Section 17.5. A Support Package stack may contain the following packages:
  - Archives for different software components (SCA). These archives can be both Support Packages and patches, which means that you can integrate the latest patches with the Support Package stack. After the corresponding software components have been modified, you can implement an adjustment using the NWDI.
  - Update for the Software Deployment Manager (SDMkit.jar)
  - SAP kernel (SAPEXE.SAR and SAPEXEDB.SAR)
  - Archives for the Internet Graphics Server (IGS)
  - Configuration file of type XML that contains a description of the stack's software components as well as the corresponding support package and patch level
- **Individual Support Packages and patches**
  SAP provides Support Packages for every software component. If dependencies exist between the current Support Package of different software components, they are described in an SAP Note.

  In addition, you can import "patched" Support Packages or patches. For example, patch 2 of Support Package 3 contains fixes that were created after the Support Package had already been released.

The file format of Support Packages is SCA, JAR, or SAR. Using the NWDI, you can only modify Support Packages of type SCA.

Java Support Packages always contain all objects of a software component. Therefore, you only have to import the latest Support Package and not all predecessors in the correct sequence, as is the case in ABAP. This is the major difference in the software logistics of ABAP and Java systems.

- **New software components**
  New software components of SAP and SAP partners.
- **Business packages for SAP Business Suite applications**
  Business packages for applications of SAP Business Suite are new Java-based applications that are integrated with the SAP Business Suite applications. For example, business packages exist for the ESS/MSS scenario. These contain applications and user interfaces in the Portal that are integrated with the new business processes in the SAP ERP backend. Usually, the version of the business packages must be coordinated with the version of the backend application.

17.4.4 Importing Java Support Packages

This section provides guidelines and tips on how you should import Support Packages into the Java stack. The links provided are valid for Release SAP NetWeaver 7.0. Similar links exist for other releases.

Step 1 — Planning

From the SAP Service Marketplace, download the latest Support Package Stack Guide for your Support Package level, which can be found under *http://service.sap.com/maintenanceNW70*. The latest information is provided in the Notes, which can be found under *http://service.sap.com/sapnotesNW70*. The most important SAP Notes are as follows:

- 724452: Central Note for SAP NetWeaver Java Server 04/2004s
- 852008: Release Restrictions for SAP NetWeaver 7.0
- 879289: Support Package Stack Guide — SAP NetWeaver 7.0
- 891983: JSPM: Central SAP Note SAP NetWeaver 2004s AS Java

Consult the SAP online help to get additional information about enhancements and changes that are imported with the new stack. The online help can be found under *http://help.sap.com/NW70*. Click on the RELEASE NOTES link and select your Support Package stack.

Cluster environments In certain cases, the JSPM stops the system or individual instances and restarts them again after a specific period of time. This is necessary for replacing the SAP kernel, for example. If you use a high-availability cluster solution, you must switch it off during the import process so that the JSPM can exclusively stop and start the instances.

JDK update In some cases, it is necessary to renew the Java Development Kit (JDK) before you can import Support Packages. This is described in SAP Note 718901. Note that the JVM path may change. In this case, you must adapt the new path on all dialog instances.

Integrate patches Check whether the SAP Service Marketplace provides you with patches for the Support Package stack to be imported. These can be found under *http://service.sap.com/swdc • Download • Support Packages and Patches*. Click the INFO button of the respective patch to view the corrections contained in it. In general, SAP does not recommend integrating the latest patches because they may not be tested in the context of the Support Package stack and may cause new problems. However, if the corrections are relevant for your system, you should integrate the patches. SAP Note 1080821 describes how patches are imported with a single step using the Support Package stack option. This is possible as of JSPM 7.0 Support Package 14.

Step 2 — Preparation

First, create a backup of the Java system and the database.

Download the required Support Packages from the SAP Service Marketplace. The files can be found under *http://service.sap.com/sp-stacks*. For all systems based on NetWeaver 7.0, you must download the files using the Maintenance Optimizer of the SAP Solution Manager. During the download, a stack definition file of type XML is created. Copy the Support Pack stack files and stack definition file to your JSPM inbox directory.

Ensure that the JSPM inbox is configured correctly. Usually, the path is: `/usr/sap/trans/EPS/in`. This path must be set in the instance profile (Parameter DIR_EPS_ROOT) and in the JSPM configuration file (`usr\sap\<SID>\SYS\j2ee\JSPM\param\jspm_config.txt`). There, the parameter `/jspm/inbox` must indicate this path. The operating system user, <sid>adm, requires read access to the JSPM inbox.

Refer to the SAP online help and the respective Support Package Stack Guide for more detailed instructions. These can be found under *http://service.sap.com/maintenance NW70*.

Step 3 — Perform Update

Log on to the central instance as <sid>adm. The J2EE Engine and the SDM server must be running. No application may be connected to the SDM server because only one connection may be established to this server. If, for example, a user is connected to the SDM server via the SDM GUI, the JSPM cannot establish a connection with the server at the same time. Start the JSPM and enter your SDM password. Proceed as described in the Support Package Stack Guide. After the import has been completed successfully, you can fill in the feedback form.

17.5 Support Package Stacks

In 2003, SAP added *Support Package stacks* (SP stacks) to its Support Package strategy for some product versions. This new strategy supports the import procedure for most customers and Support Packages, improves quality and service, and thus reduces ongoing operating costs.

The increasing range and complexity of components within individual product versions makes it necessary to improve the transparency of Support Packages and patches, and to clearly specify the recommended or permitted combinations. Therefore, a new SP stack is compiled for every product version that is updated via the new strategy, usually on a quarterly basis. This stack contains the optimal combination of Support Package and patch levels for the individual components at the time of the stack release.

Therefore, SP stacks are combinations defined by SAP for each product version. SAP recommends that you import these stacks on a regular basis. Although the underlying technology of the individual Support Packages and patches does not change with this stack approach, an SP stack should be regarded as a whole. In other words, although you should take into account any minimum requirements of or dependencies between the individual components, the Support Packages and patches contained in the stack must be imported together.

Benefits

By reducing the range of theoretically possible combinations to practical, real-world combinations, several benefits result for the customer:

- The quality of the individual Support Packages is improved because other associated components are maintained to a known minimum level. As a result, corrections are less complex and of a higher quality.
- Quality and compatibility within the set combinations are improved because SAP's own tests can focus more on these combinations.
- Download pages that are tailored to SP stacks make it easier to download required Support Packages and patches.
- Import instructions can also be tailored to the combination to be imported, reducing the time and effort required for the import process.
- The general level of knowledge about any restrictions, and transparency about side effects and their solutions, are better overall for SP stacks than for individual combinations. Potential problems can be prevented and, when they occur, solved more effectively. This, in turn, reduces operating costs.

Reducing TCO

SP stacks support the requirements of customers with live applications for regular Support Package and patch recommendations, and their need for minimum total cost of ownership (TCO). For customers with upgrade or implementation projects, the minimum requirements may involve other (higher) recommendations than the most recent SP stacks.

Implementing SP stacks leads to a reduction in complexity, increased quality, improved transparency, and simplified repair and maintenance. SP stacks further reduce the risks to live operations and help expedite the resolution of problems. They are another step toward reducing total cost of ownership (TCO).

After an SP stack is released, details of the relevant information and download site are available from the SAP Service Marketplace via the Quick Link */sp-stacks*, as shown in Figure 17.27.

Download

Additional information on specific SP stacks is available from the relevant Release and Information Note (RIN), which is available via a link on the previously mentioned page.

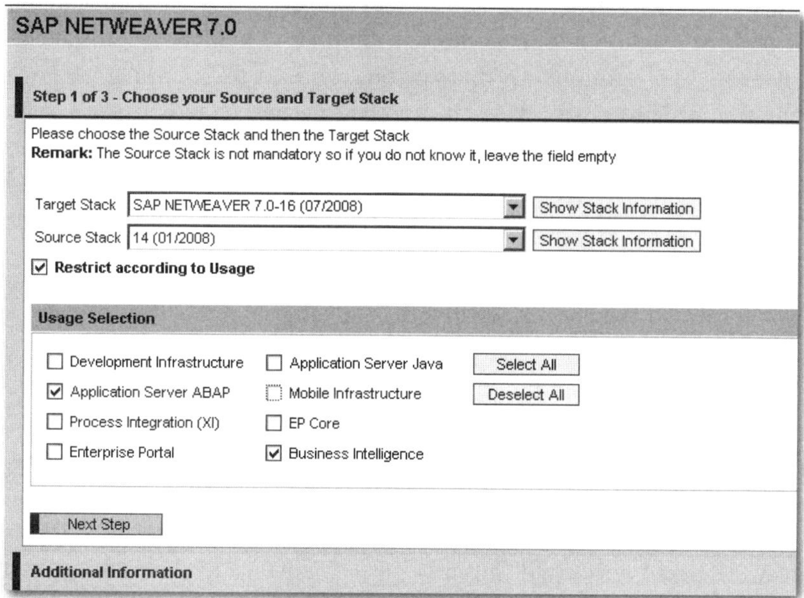

Figure 17.27 Downloading Support Package Stacks from the SAP Service Marketplace

17.5.1 SP Stack Strategy with the Usual Import Procedure

It has been established that most customers carry out planned maintenance for each live application between one and four times a year, and that this maintenance process usually covers all of the components of each application.

In practice, the frequency of planned maintenance operations depends on many factors. These include the following:

- The customer's specific situation (projects, live status, etc.)
- The product in question (technical factors, statutory changes, etc.)
- The benefits of having the latest release when support is required
- The customer's assessment of the risk of encountering known errors (and therefore, of incurring unnecessary costs and having to react at short notice)
- The expected costs of a planned maintenance operation

As a result, a standard rule for calculating the optimal time and frequency of planned maintenance operations does not exist. Customers decide on the optimal conditions, taking into account their individual circumstances. However, SAP recommends that customers run a planned maintenance operation at least once a year, and preferably two to four times a year, regardless of whether problems have arisen. This keeps the risks previously outlined manageable. SAP assumes that the latest SP stack will be imported as part of a planned maintenance operation, and that the SP stacks in use in a system landscape are not retained beyond one year. As mentioned before, if problems occur, SAP can instruct customers to import the latest Support Packages or patches, independently of the SP stack cycle.

Unexpected problems

Unexpected problems can occur at any time, regardless of planned maintenance operations. They have to be fixed as quickly and straightforward as possible. A range of different mechanisms is available for this purpose, and the decision which device to use depends on the affected component and the actual problem. These mechanisms include correction instructions for ABAP-based tracks (which can solve problems relatively localized, and in a targeted way) and Java Support Packages (which, for technical reasons, usually contain other problem solutions and whose effects are therefore not as restricted to the local environment as ABAP-based tracks are).

The SP Stacks strategy goes hand in hand with the general combination of planned maintenance and specific corrections that are provided in the meantime:

- The frequency with which SAP provides Support Package stacks depends on the age and maturity of the product. For new releases, new Support Package stacks are delivered every two months. For older releases, SP stacks are provided only twice per year.

- The frequency of SP stack deliveries is intended to complement the frequency of planned maintenance operations. This does not mean, however, that planned maintenance must be carried out at the SP stack interval. Based on your assessment of the previously discussed factors, you can temporarily postpone the import of an SP stack, provided that your system does not contain any errors that necessitate the import of up to date Support Packages or patches. You can catch up with any Support Packages you postpone when you import the next SP stack.
- SP stacks contain Support Package combinations that you should change only in exceptional cases; for example, if a problem has occurred that can be solved only by a change. In such cases, you should keep the modification as small and as local as possible. Of course, you can also import new Support Packages or patches as a preventative measure if circumstances in the system indicate that the error in question is likely to occur. However, in many cases, you will be able to make a local correction via the correction instruction in a Note, for example.
- Components of an SP stack that are not in use, or not in live use, in a system landscape do not have to be patched when an SP stack is imported, provided they have no technical or logical dependencies with any components that are in active use. You should note, however, that the Support Package or patch levels of components that are in use cannot be lower than the levels of the combination set in the SP stack.

If unexpected problems are identified in an SP stack, they will usually affect only a few customers. Therefore, it is not necessary to change the general recommendation for the planned maintenance processes.

Release and Information Note

Instead, a Release and Information Note (RIN) is used to inform all customers of the general release of an SP stack, possibly including information about potential problems. As discussed previously, notification of critical errors is communicated via HotNews Notes. A special reporting tool in the SAP Service Marketplace can be used to find out about known side effects of all types of Support Packages (Quick Link *http://service.sap.com/side-effects*).

Any differences between Support Package levels or patch levels and the relevant SP stack should be documented in Notes. This approach is used only for problems or other special cases (such as statutory changes or for customers' project or implementation phases). This also applies to Support Packages or patches that have been created since the last SP stack, and that will be part of subsequent SP stacks.

It is also possible that Support Packages or patches may exist that are more up to date than those contained in the last SP stack. Nevertheless, as long as your system is not experiencing any problems, the general recommendation is that you use the combination contained in the latest SP stack. Any Support Packages or patches that are created in the interim are reserved for the special cases mentioned previously.

Full-stack approach

The full-stack approach applies to Java-based systems in particular. This means that you always have to import the complete stack. Deviating combinations have not been tested and frequently cause problems. Individual Support Packages should only be imported in coordination with the SAP support team.

17.5.2 Cross-System Support Package Stacks

In some cases, it may be necessary to import the same Support Package stack across the system, for instance, if the ESS/MSS scenario runs on an ERP backend system and in an external Portal. In this case, the Support Package levels of the Web Dynpro sources that are imported into the portal must match with the Support Package levels in the SAP ERP backend. At the same time, they are also part of the Portal stack so that the entire Support Package stack in SAP NetWeaver Portal must correspond to the Support Package stack in the SAP ERP backend. A similar situation applies to Web Reporting in SAP NetWeaver BI 7.0.

17.5.3 Details of the Components in SAP Support Package Stacks

Based on one "leading" application component, SP stacks represent a combination of preset or recommended Support Package levels and patch levels of product version's other components. Dependencies are defined step-by-step in a "top-down" fashion (see the example that follows).

For some components such as the SAP GUI, stacks specify one level for each possible release. Other components may be optional; that is, the relevant Support Package or patch level must be fulfilled only if the component in question will be in use in a production system (for example, an SAP ERP Enterprise Extension).

The basic rule is that the other components must have at least the specified level for you to be able to import a Support Package for the leading component. Also, a higher level is recommended for most components only for problems where a local correction (such as a correction instruction) or a workaround does not exist.

Components

An SP stack can consist of the following:

- A Support Package level of a leading application component (such as SAP_APPL 4.6C), which serves as the name of the SP stack.
- A Support Package level of the application basis (such as SAP ABA 4.6C) that is a prerequisite for the previously mentioned application Support Package and that would not usually be overwritten until the next SP stack.
- A Support Package level of the basis layer (such as SAP Basis 4.6C) that is a prerequisite for the previously mentioned ABAP Support Package and that would not usually be overwritten until the next SP stack.
- A recommended kernel patch level (such as SAP KERNEL 4.6D) that would not usually be overwritten until the next SP stack, provided that there are no problems. This kernel patch level is intended for use on the operational level and can be higher than the upgrade level for the release in question (in this case, follow the instructions in the upgrade documentation or the relevant Notes).
- A minimum patch level for every possible SAP GUI release (such as 4.6D/6.20 for Windows, and 6.20/6.30 for Java). Note that the releases in this case should initially be regarded as alternatives and that each patch level is a minimum requirement that can be overwritten at any time. This minimum requirement within an SP stack will be increased only in exceptional cases. However, because the SAP GUI is a component of almost all SAP products, the requirements of the SP stacks of different products that are used in parallel must be coordinated with each other. In this case, it is the maximum required SAP

GUI release with the maximum required patch level that is relevant. Other conditions may also arise in the context of product-specific GUI add-ons.

- A minimum patch level for every possible SAP ITS release (such as 4.6D, 6.10, and 6.20) is recommended. The different releases should be regarded as alternatives, similarly to the SAP GUI.
- Optional components might require the specified level only when the component in question is in production use.

17.5.4 SP Stack Calendar

Either the product versions listed in the SP stack calendar (see Figure 17.28) are already supported by SP stacks, or SP stacks will be introduced for them in the near future. Every SP stack is "led" by a particular component or Support Package track, and the relevant Support Package is a central component of this. After the first SP stack is released, this signals the start of the new strategy for that product version.

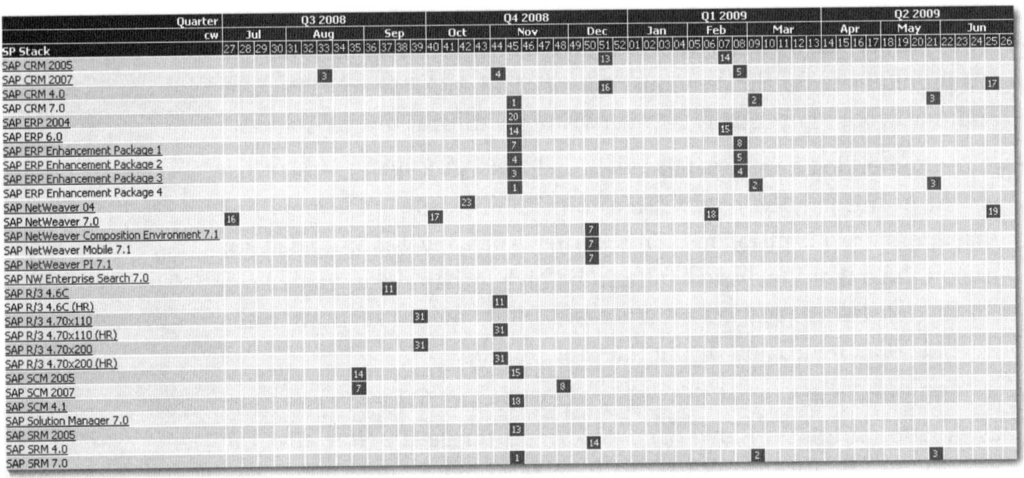

Figure 17.28 Support Package Stack Calendar

17.6 Side Effects

The SAP Service Marketplace has a reporting tool that helps you avoid unwanted side effects. Side effects can occur in rare cases after a Support Package or an SAP Note has been imported. The tool enables SAP customers to reduce their internal support costs and increase the stability of their SAP solution.

SAP Support Packages consist of several SAP Notes, each of which contains software corrections. Importing Support Packages and Notes increases system stability and protects the system from known problems. Nonetheless, it can still happen that a Note that is intended to solve one problem can actually cause another problem. To solve this new problem, a new Note is created that is linked to the first Note.

This tool is intended to make these dependencies easier to handle. If you're importing a Support Package or an SAP Note, you can search for any known side effects and correct these, if necessary. The tool enables you to proactively prevent problems that could occur after an import.

Information about side effects is defined in the Note attributes. The reporting tool identifies all side effects that will be caused by the Notes contained in the Support Package. Therefore, to protect your system from unwanted side effects, import these Notes after you import the Support Package.

Side effects of an individual Note

The Quick Link *http://service.sap.com/notes in the* SAP Service Marketplace provides information about known side effects of individual SAP Notes (see Figure 17.29).

Side effects of Support Package queues

To obtain a list of all of the side effects of a Support Package or an SP stack, use the reporting tool in the SAP Service Marketplace (Quick Link: *http://service.sap.com/side-effects.)*

Use this tool just before you import a Support Package to see the most up to date list of side effects.

Side effects that have already been eliminated by other Support Packages in the same queue are automatically removed from the results list. This list is tailored to your Support Package queue. It is sorted by application component, so that you can easily skip Notes that belong to applications you do not use.

Figure 17.29 Side Effects of an Individual Note

Note that it can take several hours to create the results list. The system sends you an email when the list is complete. Figure 17.30 shows the beginning of a side-effect report.

SAP began side-effect reporting in July 2003. Complete information on the side effects of earlier Notes is not available.

Report on Side-Effects of SAP Notes

Help

This report provides an overview of currently known side-effects of Notes contained in a Support Package. The list also includes pointers to other notes, which are able to resolve undesired side-effects.

You have requested the side-effects notes for the following:

Product:	SAP R/3 ENTERPRISE		
Product version:	SAP R/3 ENTERPRISE 47X110		
Component:	EA-APPL 110	Support packages:	SAPKGPAA17 to SAPKGPAA19
Component:	EA-IPPE 110	Support packages:	SAPKGPIA16 to SAPKGPIA18
Component:	PI 2003_1_470	Support packages:	SAPKIPZH58 to SAPKIPZH59
Component:	PI_BASIS 2003_1_620	Support packages:	SAPKIPYH57 to SAPKIPYH57
Component:	SAP ABA 6.20	Support packages:	SAPKA62036 to SAPKA62041
Component:	SAP APPL 4.70	Support packages:	SAPKH47019 to SAPKH47022
Component:	SAP BASIS 6.20	Support packages:	SAPKB62036 to SAPKB62041

Results:

Appl. Area	Note Number	Note Version (s)	In Support Package	Note Version	Appl. Area	Solving Note Number	Note Version
AC-INT	0000561175	0001 to 9999	SAPKH47022	0020	AC-INT	0000794974	0001
AP-MD-BP-UI	0000736239	0001 to 9999	SAPKA62041	0002	AP-MD-BP-UI	0000856200	0002

Figure 17.30 Side Effects of Support Package Queues

17.7 Questions

1. **What are the benefits of importing SAP Support Packages?**
   A. Proactive solution of known problems
   B. Functional extensions to SAP software
   C. Improved ease of maintenance and reduced time and effort for repairs and maintenance
2. **Which of the following statements are true with regard to the SAP Note Assistant?**
   A. It simplifies the maintenance of programs in the customer namespace.
   B. It enables you to import Notes that contain code corrections.
   C. It simplifies the process of making changes to Data Dictionary objects.
   D. It identifies dependencies between SAP Notes.
   E. It can replace the process of importing Support Packages.
3. **Which of the following statements are true with regard to Support Packages?**
   A. They change the SAP standard of your SAP system before the next release upgrade.
   B. You can import all types of Support Packages into all SAP systems, regardless of the components installed in the target system.
   C. Support Packages are available only to customers who are taking part in the ramp-up.
   D. Different types of Support Packages may be required for SAP systems with different components.
4. **Which of the following statements are true with regard to the SAP Patch Manager?**
   A. The Patch Manager ensures that Support Packages are imported in the correct order.
   B. The SAP Patch Manager does not check whether the type of Support Package you want to import is suitable for your SAP ERP installation. You have to determine whether you need a particular Conflict Resolution Transport, for example.

C. The SAP Patch Manager does not allow you to protect SAP objects you have modified. These objects are automatically overwritten.

D. The SAP Patch Manager automatically opens Transactions SPDD and SPAU for the modification adjustment process, if required.

5. **Which of the following statements are true with regard to Support Package stacks?**

   A. Support Package stacks are combinations of Support Packages that are recommended by SAP.

   B. Support Package stacks should be imported only if an urgent problem is preventing an import from being carried out.

   C. Support Package stacks are Support Package combinations that have been particularly well tested by SAP.

   D. The SAPGUI version also must be upgraded to the latest level with every Support Package stack upgrade.

6. **Which of the following statements are true with regard to ABAP and Java corrections?**

   A. An ABAP Support Package always overwrites all objects of a software component.

   B. A Java Support Package always overwrites all objects of a software component.

   C. An individual ABAP program can be changed using an SAP Note that contains a correction instruction.

   D. An individual Java program can be changed using the Software Deployment Archive (SDA).

7. **Where can you find version information about a Java system?**

   A. Under *http://<hostname>:<port>/sap/monitoring/ComponentInfo*

   B. In the SAP System Landscape Directory (SLD)

   C. In the system status information of the ABAP stack (only for dual-stack systems)

   C. In Transaction SPAM of the ABAP stack (only for dual-stack systems)

To adapt an SAP system to the requirements of changed business processes and legal regulations, you can implement the required functions by upgrading to a higher SAP product version. In highly integrated system landscapes in particular, this creates various challenges for a successful project implementation. This chapter describes these challenges as well as related areas, such as using SAP Enhancement Packages and converting to Unicode.

18 SAP Software Release Upgrade

This chapter describes general guidelines you should follow when upgrading to a different release of SAP software. These guidelines should be regarded as a supplement to the corresponding upgrade guidelines, which contain the individual steps and necessary actions. Although this chapter does not provide a detailed explanation of these administrative actions, it should prove useful to system administrators and technical consultants who implement the upgrade, as well as project leads who support the planning of the upgrade project. In particular, this chapter addresses the general recommendations and services in more detail, in addition to describing the technical upgrade procedure. SAP Solution Manger, which is described in more detail in Chapter 19, is an additional information source and tool for implementing the upgrade project.

18.1 Lifecycle of an SAP Production System

Over time, your SAP production system undergoes a development process that enables you to better respond to changing business requirements. Aside from the corrections mentioned in the previous chapters using SAP Notes or Support Packages, you will, for example, have carried out Customizing changes for currency adjustments, created new clients or company codes for additional company sites or subsidiaries, or implemented additional components. Furthermore, you will frequently want to implement a new function in the system. SAP delivers new functions to customers primarily in new releases.

18.1.1 SAP Release and Maintenance Strategy

For efficient planning and support of your production environment's lifecycle, you should know SAP's release and maintenance strategy.

Within the scope of maintenance, aside from the corrections in Notes that have been mentioned already in several places in this book, SAP develops new functions and adaptations to meet current technology requirements. It is therefore possible to use improved hardware or newer versions of databases or operating systems, for example. Often, this is possible without changing the release by importing a newer version of the SAP kernel.

Standard maintenance

For planning, it is important to know the timeframe for SAP software maintenance. Standard maintenance lasts five years for SAP products that use SAP NetWeaver '04 or later as a technology platform. This means that within this time frame, all Note or Support Package corrections as well as legal adjustments—for example, tax rates in payroll accounting—are covered in the maintenance fees. For an increased maintenance fee corrections can be delivered for one or two more years. After this period, that is, eight years after implementing a release, corrections are only created individually within the scope of customer-specific maintenance and are fees are charged by the effort required.

5-1-2 maintenance strategy

For most SAP customers, this timeframe is more than adequate because this strategy—also called 5-1-2 maintenance strategy—provides eight years of planning reliability (see Figure 18.1). However, the need to use a new functionality often arises earlier. Extensions or completely new application functions are usually implemented in a new release, which is why the question of whether to change to customer-specific maintenance usually does not come up. Because SAP ensures that the release change is supported by the corresponding tools and methods, the applications already implemented can still be used with only very small adjustments. Because the required effort is thus much smaller than with a new installation, the decision whether to upgrade is less difficult to make.

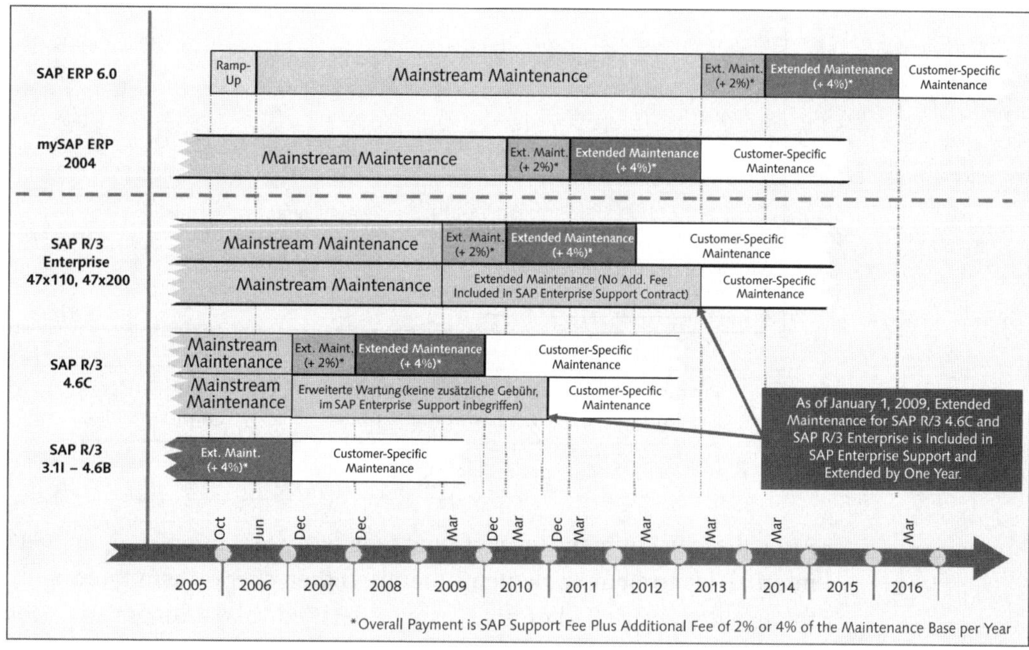

Figure 18.1 Phases of the 5-1-2 Maintenance Strategy using SAP ERP as an Example

With the previously used release strategy, the latest extended business processes and functions were first delivered in a "functional release" to a limited number of customers. In addition, SAP recommended not to use these functional releases in production because there was only limited support for corrections via Support Packages. These were created primarily for the "correction release," which contained adaptations and necessary improvements based on the functional release. The correction release was then made available to all customers. The maintenance timeframes between the functional release and the correction release varied, which is why users of a functional release had to either import a Final Delta Patch or perform an upgrade for the correction release.

Ramp-up procedure

In contrast to these previously used installation procedures or release types, SAP now introduces new releases using what is called a ramp-up procedure (see Figure 18.2).

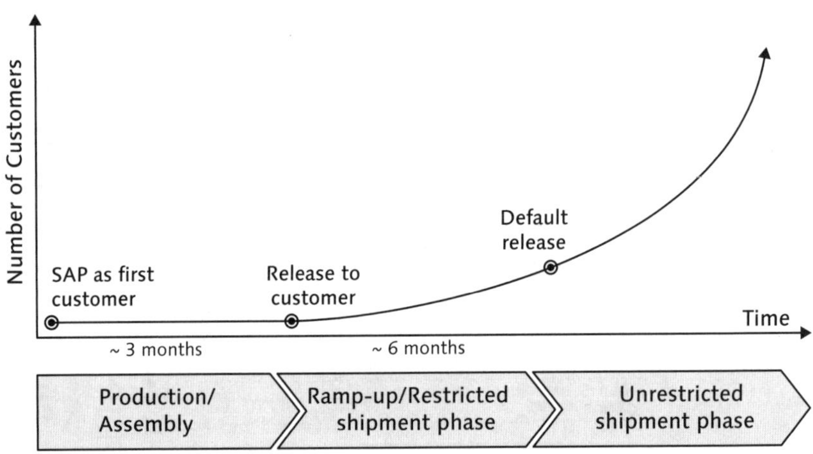

Figure 18.2 Time Schedule of the Ramp-up Procedure

After the development of new functions has been completed, an SAP-internal department implements them and then checks them thoroughly for an extended period of time, using a detailed validation process. This process covers everything from documentation to installation or upgrade procedures to Customizing and the use of specific functions. This ensures that the small number of ramp-up customers receives software that can be used in production immediately. A good selection of ramp-up customers from highly diverse usage areas guarantees hat an extensive portion of the application will be verified further. SAP provides enhanced support for this purpose to solve problems as quickly as possible. When the stability criteria for the ramp-up have been met, the ramp-up is completed and the new release is made available to all clients.

18.1.2 Upgrade Motivation

What motivates SAP customers to change their software release? To answer this question, a large-scale survey was conducted in 2004. More than 700 SAP customers were interviewed about upgrades and, among other things, asked about the motives for a release change.

As you can see from the survey results shown in Figure 18.3, the main reason for a release change is the demand for new application functions or the use of current technology standards, followed by the intention to remain within the standard maintenance. Furthermore, aspects of cost reduction and improved operation optimization are becoming increasingly important, especially with regard to the current release, SAP ERP 6.0. Additional results of this survey, as well as recommendations based on it, are discussed in Section 18.8.

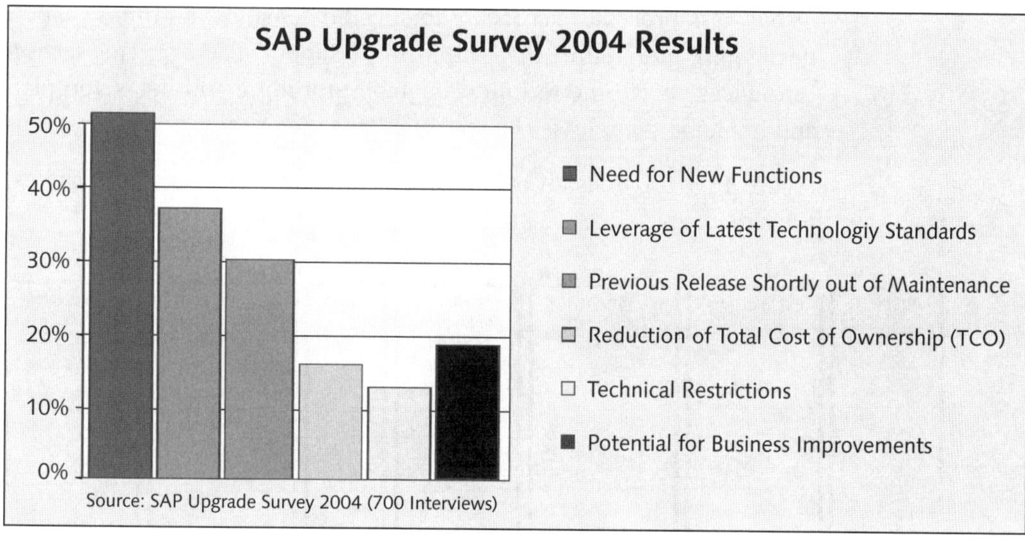

Figure 18.3 Motivation for a Release Change

Planning

Therefore, good planning of an upgrade project requires synchronizing your IT strategy with the SAP maintenance strategy. With the 5-1-2 maintenance strategy, you can do so with more flexibility. As a result, you should determine before the end of the standard maintenance time of five years whether it makes sense to perform a release change in parallel with potential other running projects, for example, or if it would be better to use a maintenance extension. In the context of rapid changes in information technology and your business processes, an upgrade should be considered a day-to-day process. SAP Enhancement Packages facilitate this considerably because what they provide lies somewhere in between Support Packages and upgrades with regard to changes to objects and options for the implementation of new functions. SAP Enhancement Packages are described in detail in Section 18.5.

18.2 Release Change Process

In contrast to Support Packages, which contain only a small number of new Repository objects, a release change includes a large number of elementary changes and new objects as a result of new functionality. New applications require corresponding Customizing to enable mapping of business processes according to specific demands, and these activities require more effort than importing a Support Package. This section introduces you to the technical upgrade procedure and helps you plan and implement a release change.

Figure 18.4 provides an overview of the main phases of the technical upgrade procedure.

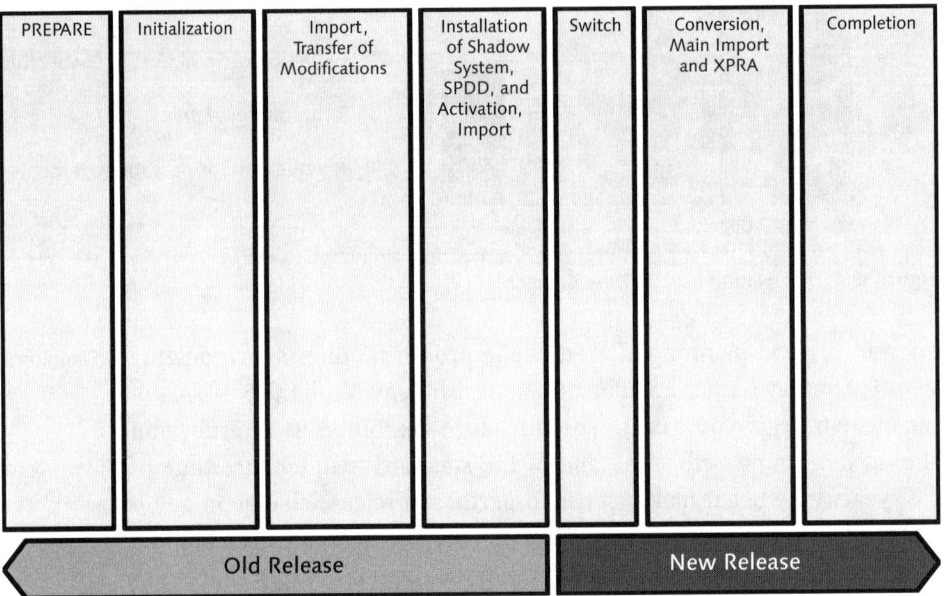

Figure 18.4 Overview of the Technical Upgrade Procedure

PREPARE During the initial phase of an SAP software release change, the PREPARE script is run at the operating-system level. This script performs preliminary checks that save time for the actual upgrade procedure. It checks, for example, the available disk space or the existence of corrections in change requests that have not yet been released. If necessary, you can adapt your SAP system according to the results of this check. For example, you might need to increase the size of the tablespaces and make additional disk space available.

ASU Toolbox

A portion of the upgrade preparations that is of particular importance for the application—and that is also known as ASU (*Application Specific Upgrade*)—has been integrated with PREPARE for SAP ERP 6.0 and SAP NetWeaver BI 7.0 upgrades, on the basis of Service Release 3 and subsequent releases. Before this improvement, you had to import the programs of the ASU Toolbox into the system using a transport. As described in SAP Note 623723, some of the errors in the application components and problems due to missing display or background variants were then eliminated. The newly designed ASU Toolbox now provides a framework that generates a client-independent task list using an XML file. The task list is then processed during the upgrade. You can display the task list via Transaction /ASU/UPGRADE.

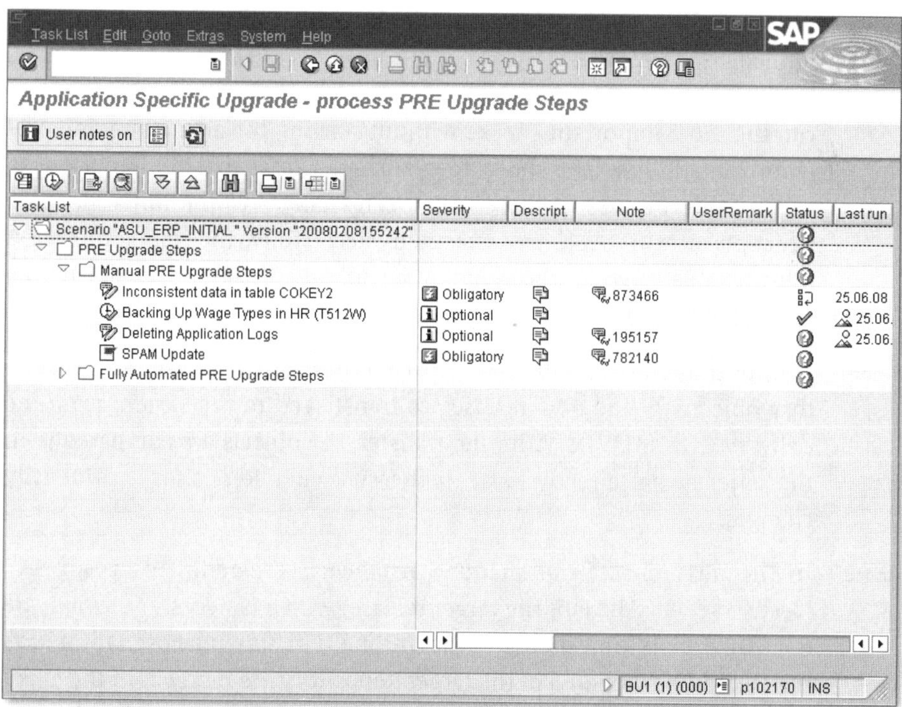

Figure 18.5 ASU Status During Upgrade Preparations

The basic conditions for using the new ASU Toolbox, such as the required ST-PI add-on version, are listed in SAP Note 1000009. This Note also describes how you should process the individual tasks and how you can generate your own steps for this. Figure 18.5 gives you an impression of what thc ASU toolbox looks like.

[+] To solve the report variant-related problems mentioned earlier, you should execute the *pre-processing* module in PREPARE because the first step of the "variant savior," JOB_RASUVAR1, is performed in this module. Additional information can be found in SAP Note 712297.

The following phases of the ASU toolbox, which are no longer part of the preparations, are then executed by the R3up program or, as of SAP software releases based on SAP NetWeaver 2AS ABAP 7.0, by SAPup.

Initialization

During the initialization phase, some of the PREPARE checks are repeated. After you have resolved all problems that were reported during the execution of PREPARE, the initialization phase should run smoothly. Some of the checks are repeated because it is advisable to run PREPARE not only immediately before the upgrade, but as early as several weeks beforehand; PREPARE can be repeated several times. This ensures that you can run the most important checks without starting the actual upgrade program, but still have the ability to evaluate all areas that are important to the upgrade process. If there have been changes to the initial upgrade situation after PREPARE was executed successfully, the upgrade process must be able to verify the situation again, which takes place during the initialization phase.

Import

During the "import and transfer of modifications" phase, the Repository objects for the new release are transferred to the system from the delivery CDs or DVDs. After the transfer, the objects are compared with the objects that already exist in the customer Repository to identify changes.

Shadow instance

In the next phase, the shadow instance is created. This is an SAP NetWeaver AS ABAP of the target release, which is necessary to activate data Dictionary objects before downtime. For this purpose, all objects that should be included in the target Repository are merged. In the event of data Dictionary object conflicts, you must first synchronize the two versions using Transaction SPDD. This synchronization must be carried out with great care because there is a risk of data loss if it is not done correctly. When the synchronization has completed, the activation is started. Contrary to what you might expect from, for example, Transaction SE11, this activation does not create a corresponding version of these objects in the database. Instead, it creates a new version of the *runtime object* that is needed for the structure changes calculated in a subsequent step.

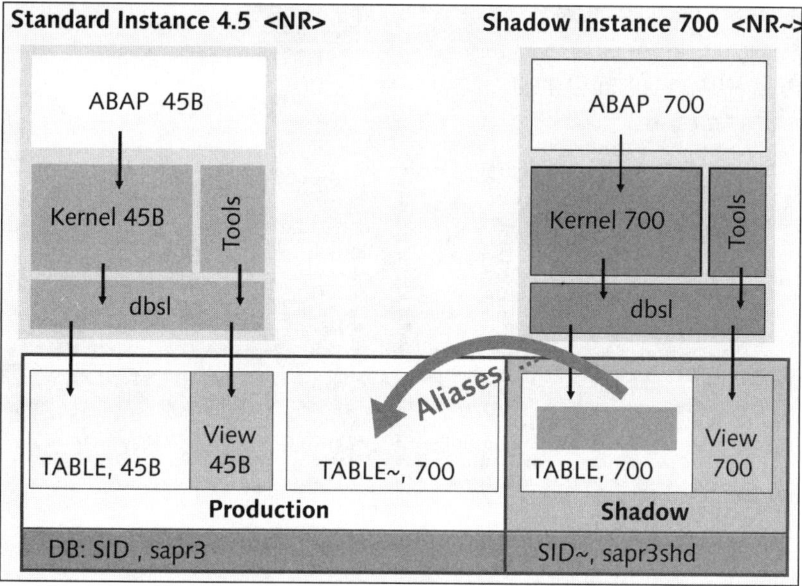

Figure 18.6 Interaction of the Shadow Instance and the Standard Instance

The downtime required for the upgrade process starts, at the latest, with the switch between the object versions. At this stage, the change to the new kernel and Repository versions takes place.

Conversion, main import, and XPRA

Finally, during the "conversion, main import, and XPRA" phase, the changes caused by the new Repository are written to the database. During these steps, the system is not available—this is called the system "downtime." Depending on various factors, downtime can last for several hours. After certain table imports and logical adaptations have been performed, the system is available with the new functions.

Completion During the "completion" phase, additional actions are taken with regard to the last adaptations of objects, and the call for synchronizing the remaining Repository objects in Transaction SPAU is started. The post-processing steps for the ASU Toolbox are also performed during this phase. Figure 18.7 gives you an idea of what can be included in such activities.

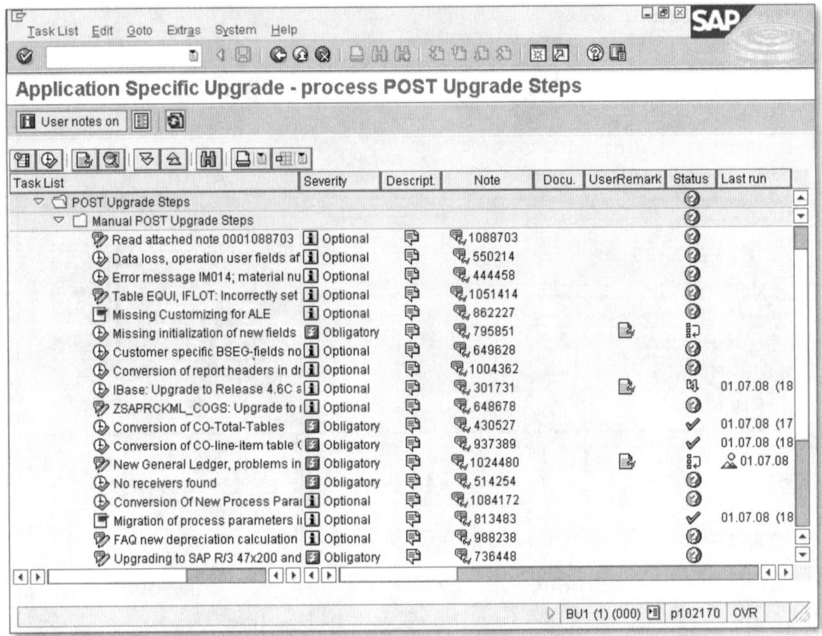

Figure 18.7 ASU Status at the End of the Upgrade

18.2.1 SAP System Switch Upgrade Procedure

The SAP System Switch Upgrade procedure was introduced with the upgrades to systems with SAP Web AS ABAP 6.10 and higher. It replaces the previously used Repository switch procedure.

Previous SAP system upgrade procedures were performed by importing the new Repository objects into the system, using a well-defined sequence of transports. However, with increasing numbers of objects and therefore more and larger transports, the system was in a state between the start and target release for longer amount of time, during which it could not be used. As a result, following the generally held belief that the number of SAP Repository objects usually by far exceeds the number of customer Repository objects, and that the size of the application tables is a multiple of the size of the Repository tables, the Repository switch upgrade was developed. This means that the new Repository is positioned adjacent to the Repository still in use, to exchange it with the old Repository in one operation. After this process, to complete the upgrade, all you have to ensure is that the application data matches the new Repository objects. An analysis of many upgrade runtime evaluations results, from the downtime statistics for Repository switch upgrades, is shown in Figure 18.8.

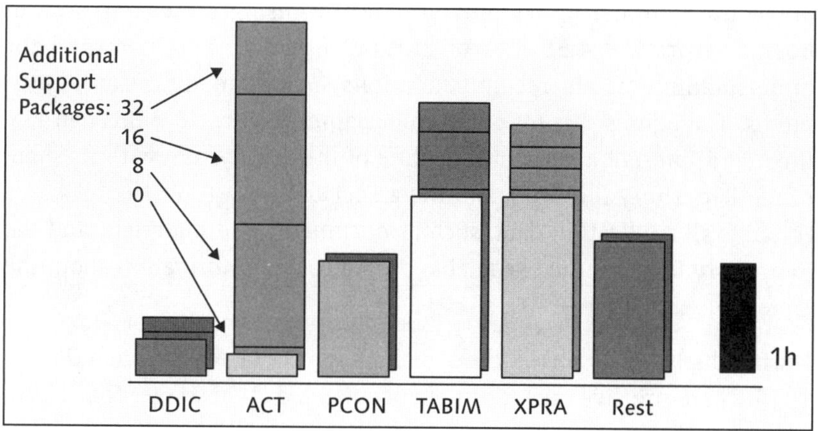

Figure 18.8 Changes of Downtime Depending on the Number of Included Support Packages for the Repository Switch Upgrade

Activation

As you can see, the activation time (ACT phase) increases with the number of Support Packages included in the upgrade. Thus, every customer had to make the decision whether to import as many Support Packages as possible during an upgrade project to reach a current software state, or to stay at a comparatively old correction level without Support Packages, to have less downtime.

The reason for this result is that a runtime version of the SAP data Dictionary must exist for all data Dictionary objects to be able to adapt the objects in the database. To save time, SAP delivers this version along with the CDs or DVDs for the new release. Objects that are carried over into the new Repository from the set of Support Packages, however, do not have this information and must therefore be activated. This step must also be performed for the objects that are carried over into the new release due to customer developments. Because activation alone can take several hours, especially for upgrades to releases with a lot of Support Packages, it was necessary to find a way to save this time in favor of reduced downtime. The result of this optimization is the SAP System Switch Upgrade.

18.2.2 SAP System Switch Upgrade in Detail

This section details the phases of the currently used technical upgrade procedure outlined in the previous section, using the example of an upgrade from R/3 4.5B to SAP ERP 6.0 ECC 6.0. This is critical for understanding certain recommendations such as modification adjustments. The figures that follow in this chapter (Figure 18.9 through Figure 18.16) present a schematic outline of the SAP system with its share of the Repository (bottom), and the associated data (top). The data area contains all application data, such as documents and materials, and the Repository includes the executable programs and information about the table structure.

PREPARE phase

During the PREPARE phase, the actual system is not yet modified (Figure 18.9). Therefore, live operations are not affected at this stage. To perform activation that is later required in advance, a small instance with basic functionality of the target release is installed in parallel to the existing instance, after several checks have been completed.

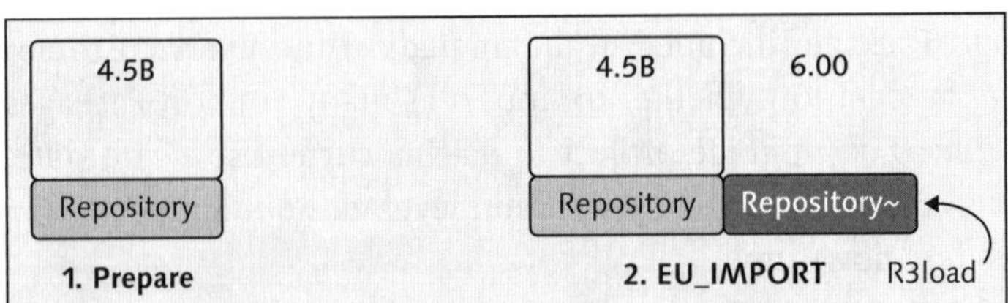

Figure 18.9 PREPARE Phase and EU_IMPORT Phase

Initialization phase

As mentioned previously, the initialization phase runs some of the PREPARE phase checks again. During the individual data transfer steps, the program R3load loads the data from the upgrade CDs to the database. A trick is used here that is important for a fast switch: The data is stored in a second Repository, parallel to the existing Repository. Because this area of the database is created with a changed name (all relevant names are extended by "~xx", where "xx" represents a specific release), normal operation is not affected. These areas are not visible to standard SAP programs such as, for example, the kernel. After the Repository information has been created, the tables that are delivered with the new release—and which do not yet exist in the database—are created.

To ensure that customer developments are not lost during the upgrade, the last part of the data transfer ensures that these objects are saved. They are either moved directly into the new Repository following certain rules, or a copy of the current version is stored in the version database (see Figure 18.10).

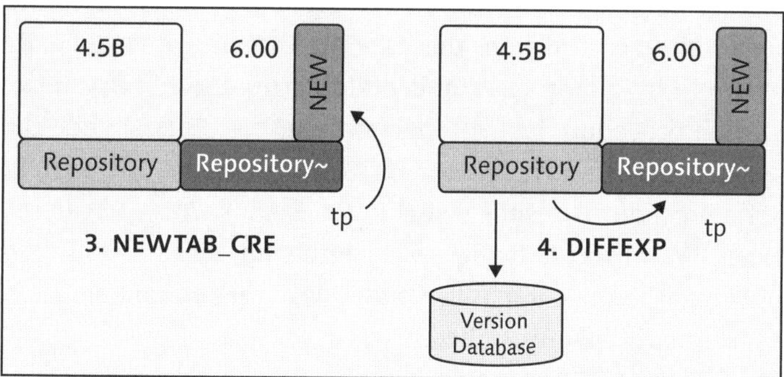

Figure 18.10 Creation of New Tables and Salvaging of Modifications and Customer Developments

SPDD adjustment

Now that all objects exist in the new Repository, the shadow system will be built next (see Figure 18.11). For SAP ERP 6.0 ECC 6.0, this is SAP NetWeaver AS ABAP with Release 7.0 (see also Figure 18.6). Initially, the modification adjustment for data Dictionary objects such as tables or data element definitions must be performed if these objects have been changed. This is done using Transaction SPDD. More details about the modification adjustment can be found in the section "Modification Adjustment."

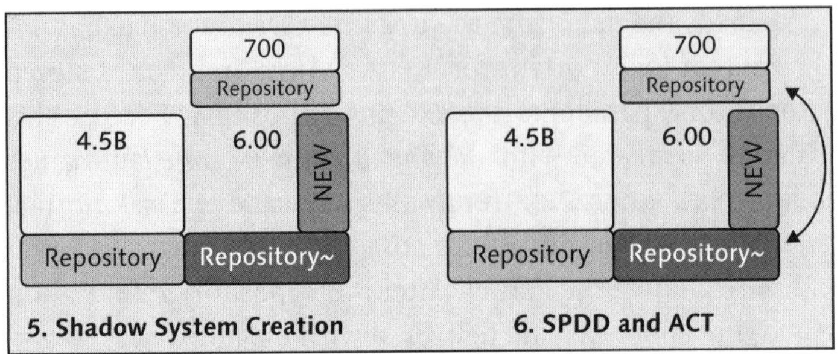

Figure 18.11 Creation of the Shadow Instance, Execution of SPDD, and Activation

Due to the chronology of the process, it is apparent that you need to determine the future structure of a table before the runtime information is being created in the "activation" step. The second instance is required because the old release does not usually know the rules with which runtime objects are created in the new release. Therefore, in the old Repository switch upgrade procedure, both the SPDD adjustment and the activation are time-critical steps that take place during downtime. By reorganizing the individual phases and building up another "system," the system switch procedure lets you perform these activities while the system can still be used in production. However, even the SAP System Switch Upgrade procedure uses the switching mechanism, as you can see in the next step. When the activation has completed, and the collected data has been copied to the database area that will still be available later, the shadow system will be uninstalled.

ICNV phase

Finally, in the ICNV phase, any potentially pending table conversions can be started concurrently with live operations, to save some downtime (see Figure 18.12). Downtime is also reduced by copying specific data in advance during the "shadow_import." Database mechanisms ensure that data that was changed during live operations after the copy action is copied again. This will be done during downtime, because it is vital to ensure data consistency.

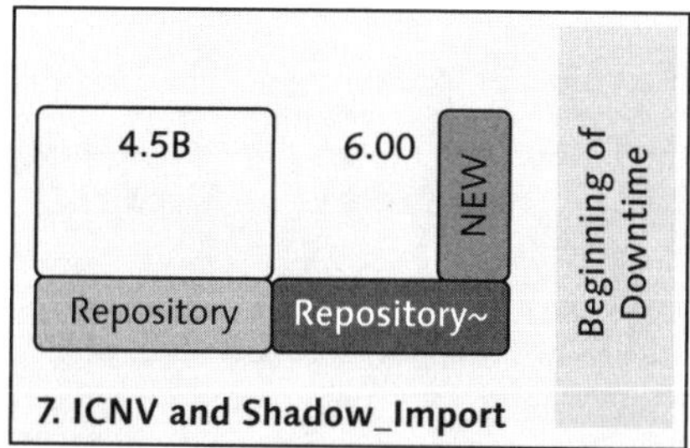

Figure 18.12 Final Activities Before Downtime

The upgrade then stops just before the step that starts the system downtime. Therefore, the production system can be stopped at a specific time; for example, on a Friday evening after completing your workday activities. When downtime starts, the old Repository is deleted. Because it was created according to a specific naming convention, this action can complete in a matter of minutes. Next, the switch is performed. The names of the Repository that was previously created in parallel are changed to new names by using a quick database operation. At this stage, the new programs and transactions are, in theory, already available.

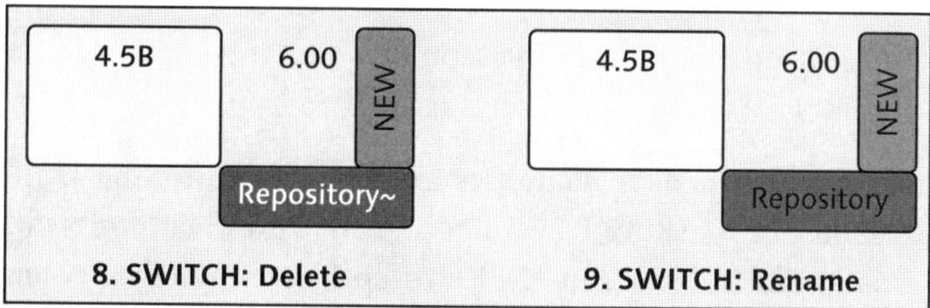

Figure 18.13 Actions During Switching

As you can see in Figure 18.13, however, the area with the application data is not located above the new Repository. This shows that tables were extended or changed in some way during the upgrade process. The adaptation of the data to these new structures is carried out in the next phase, the conversion (see Figure 18.14). Using the data determined during the activation, these changes are calculated and, depending on the result of these calculations, the table is adapted to the application data in the database. This can be reflected in the creation of new indexes and the extension or deletion of several fields in the table structure.

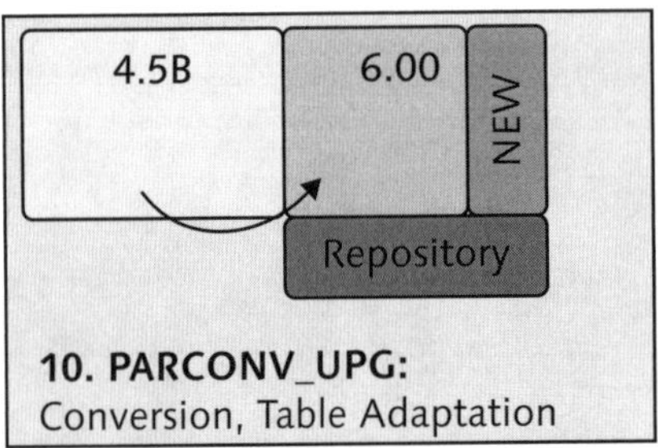

Figure 18.14 Adaptation of the Table Structures Between Database and Repository

[+] Because operations are carried out in the database, the runtime depends primarily on the size of the objects to be edited. In addition, in this phase, the result of the SPDD adjustment needs to be considered. If, during the adjustment, it is determined that a field needs to be deleted from a table, not only the field is deleted from the data Dictionary but also the associated data in the database. Because such a change—a field deletion—cannot be carried out directly from the database, a table conversion takes place, which is performed via ABAP programs. For this, the remaining fields of this table are copied row by row—a process that for large tables can take a long time to complete.

The following section about modification adjustments provides an example.

TABIM_UPG

Now that the tables for the data Dictionary are consistent after the adaptations were made, the "TABIM_UPG" step includes the final import of Customizing data. The subsequent "XPRA" step (*Execution of Programs After put*) logically adapts specific tables (see Figure 18.15). For example, if it makes sense to copy data from existing tables to the new tables or to adjust the data in some way to use new functions, this adaptation takes place during this step.

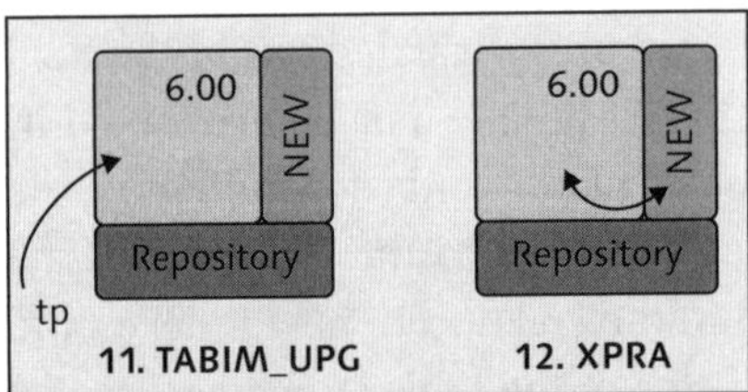

Figure 18.15 Final Table Import and XPRA

During the "completion" step, after all technical and application-relevant adaptations have been carried out, objects that were inactive before downtime are now also copied as inactive versions. If necessary, an adjustment of Repository objects that do not belong to the data Dictionary is provided via Transaction SPAU (see Figure 18.16).

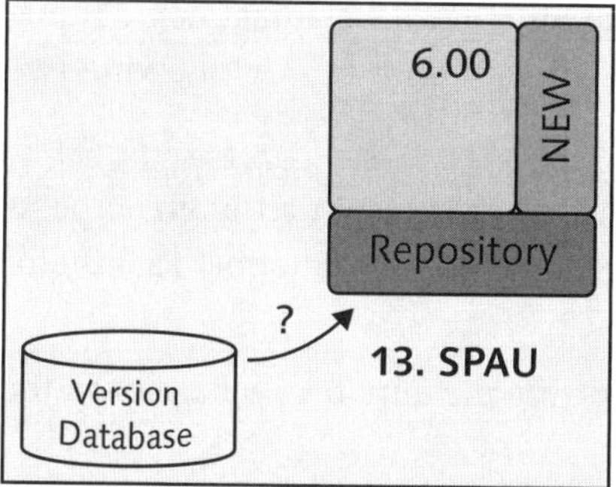

Figure 18.16 Adjustment of Repository Objects via SPAU

18.3 Modification Adjustment

The standard version of the SAP system can be adapted to an operational work environment at different levels, as follows:

- Customizing
- Personalization
- Provided extensions (Business Add-Ins)
- Enhancements
- Customer developments
- Modifications of the standard version

In most cases, the software can be adapted to processes without modifications. If modifications are required, however, when applying SAP Notes, importing SAP Support Packages, and changing releases, you will have to repeatedly check your changes and adapt them, if necessary, to ensure that they still work after upgrading the SAP software version.

Importing new standard objects

When new standard SAP objects are imported either by importing Support Packages or through an SAP release change, the SAP system detects the modifications that were made to the SAP Repository objects. In other words, if you change a Repository object delivered by SAP, you modify the default version of this object. This customer modification of the standard SAP version must be compared with the new version of the object delivered by SAP. This process is called modification adjustment. Therefore, a modification adjustment is necessary only in the following two situations:

- SAP delivers an object in a Support Package or in an upgrade package that is different from the version of the last Support Package or release.
- You changed the object since importing the Support Package or in the old release.

If SAP modifies an object that has not been modified by you, its new version is used. A modification adjustment is also not required if you change an SAP object of which a new version is not delivered by SAP. Customer-developed objects are also unaffected by the modification adjustment.

For the modification adjustment you must determine the differences between the objects and then decide which properties the objects should have in the updated SAP system. You should adjust all objects you changed and that are included in the new SAP delivery.

Transaction SPDD or Transaction SPAU

Depending on the category of the relevant object, you must use either Transaction SPDD or Transaction SPAU for the modification adjustment (see Table 18.1). Transaction SPDD is used for most ABAP Dictionary objects and must be executed before activating the new ABAP Dictionary objects. Transaction SPAU is used for most Repository objects and is run after activating the new Repository objects.

Transaction	Object Category
SPDD	Domains, data elements, tables
SPAU	Reports, menus, screens, views, lock objects, matchcodes

Table 18.1 Transactions for the Modification Adjustment of Different Object Categories

The Support Package Manager SPAM or the release change program SAPup automatically asks you at the appropriate stage to perform a modification adjustment. A modification adjustment leads to one of the following results:

- The modification adjustment is refused, that is, the old object is replaced with the new standard SAP version. This is called "reverting to the standard SAP version."
- You do not revert to the standard SAP version. If you choose this option, the corresponding transaction for the modification adjustment is displayed (Transaction SPAU or Transaction SPDD). You can then keep the modification as is or create a new modification by merging the new SAP version with the existing changes.

[+]

You should never ignore a request for modification adjustment. If you do, the modified objects are automatically overwritten with the new SAP Repository. Even if you decide in favor of the new standard SAP object, you should use the explicit reversion procedure in Transaction SPDD and Transaction SPAU. This way, you will not be asked to perform another modification adjustment for the same modifications in subsequent release changes. Thus, using the reversion procedure saves time in future release changes.

Modification adjustment for data Dictionary objects

During the modification adjustment for data Dictionary objects, you need to be particularly careful if you want to revert to the standard SAP version. Often, tables are modified by being extended by customized fields such the field E in the example shown in Figure 16.13. If SAP delivers a new version of this table (extended by the field D), you are prompted to perform a modification adjustment.

If you then revert to the standard SAP version during the adjustment, you not only delete the field E from the table description, but you also delete the values of this field from the database via a conversion. However, if you keep your modification, errors can occur in SAP programs during the upgrade or during subsequent operation because the expected field D cannot be accessed. Therefore, one reason for the adjustment could be to create a new modification of both your own modification and the SAP extension.

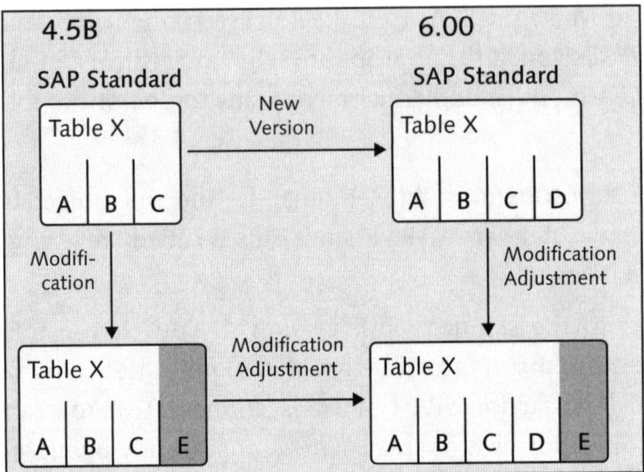

Figure 18.17 Options During the Modification Adjustment for Tables

Aside from the modification adjustments for tables, adjustments also exist for other Repository objects such as menus, text elements, dynpros, and reports.

Example: Modification Adjustment for Programs

Figure 18.18 shows the source text of the standard SAP object, M07DRAUS. The customer added new functions to this program in the source text lines 12–14. The program is now delivered in a Support Package with the additional source text lines 10 and 13 to correct a reported error.

Because the SAP standard was modified and a new version was delivered, the adjustment is offered in Transaction SPAU. The customer has the following options:

He can accept the new SAP standard and lose the functions he implemented in lines 12–14 of his modified version.

He can decline the new standard SAP version and forego the correction delivered in lines 10 and 13.

He can accept the new SAP standard and manually add lines 12–14 so that the additional check required by the customer still takes place.

If the modification adjustment using Transaction SPAU is not carried out, the new SAP version is implemented automatically and the state of these objects remains set to modified. However, the adjustment can still be performed later using the information from the version database.

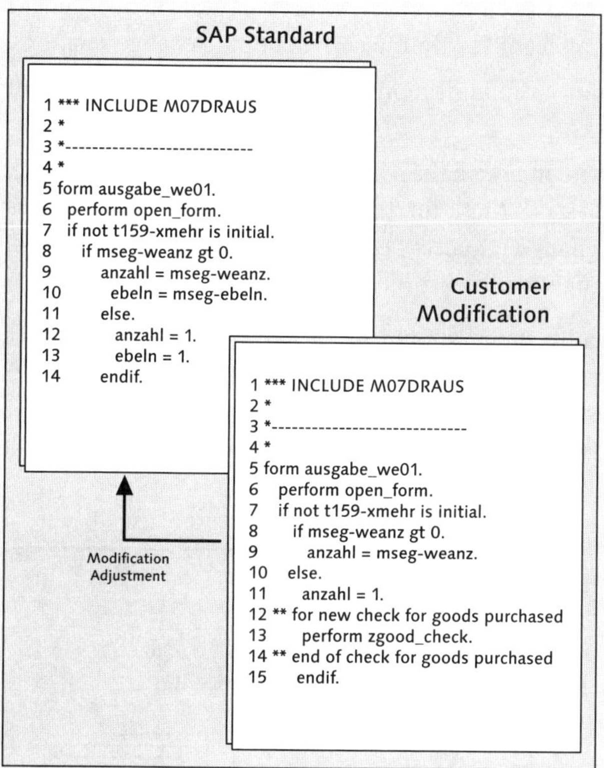

Figure 18.18 Source Texts of the New SAP Standard and the Customer Modification

18.3.1 Modification Adjustment During Release Changes

During the change to a new SAP release, use the following standard procedure for the modification adjustment (see Figure 18.19):

Standard procedure

1. Create two change requests in the Workbench Organizer (Transaction SE09): one for the modification adjustment using Transaction SPDD and one for the modification adjustment using Transaction SPAU.
2. Create one task for every developer who is involved in the modification adjustment.
3. Using Transaction SPDD or SPAU respectively, the developers must determine whether the modifications should be kept or discarded. While processing the object list, the developers should mark an object

as Done when it has been completely processed. All changes must be recorded in the relevant task in the corresponding change request.

4. After completing the modification adjustment, the developers must release their tasks.
5. When all modified objects in the list are marked as Done, you must flag the change requests as Mark for Transport. However, you should not yet release the change requests because `SAPup` automatically releases and exports change requests at the end of the release change.

The modification adjustment should be carried out by developers and not by SAP system administrators. The employees responsible for the modifications must be involved in the release change process and be present at the time. They should also review the entire documentation of every modified object.

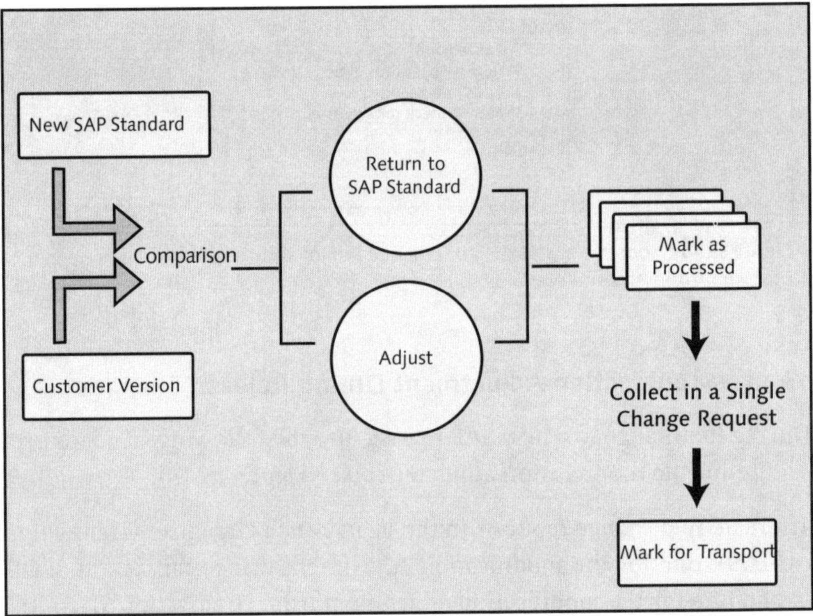

Figure 18.19 Modification Adjustment Process

[+] The more modifications exist and the more complex they are, the longer the release change process takes in a development system.

In subsequent release changes in the other systems of the system landscape, SAPup detects the existence of change requests resulting from Transactions SPDD and SPAU and prompts you to import them. When you import the change requests into these systems, you do not need to make the same modification adjustment in every system.

If you agree to import the change requests, the modifications in the change requests are automatically compared with the corresponding objects in the target system, and the results of this comparison are displayed.

During the release change, all you need to do is confirm that the changes from these change requests should be applied.

Ideally, the result of the comparison is that all systems in the system landscape received identical modifications before the release change. This is the case, for example, if you used the recommended procedure, that is, if you created all modifications in the development system and then distributed them to the downstream systems prior to the release change. If the comparison shows that a change request contains all modifications existing in the current system, SAPup skips the request for modification adjustment and directly continues with activating the ABAP Dictionary. Even if not all objects can be supplied with the automatic adjustment transport, it is often useful to use it anyway to not to have to process this part again later.

One prerequisite for a release change in the remaining systems of the system landscape is that the global change option is set to Modifiable (for the time of the release change).

Adjustment transport

Two procedures exist for importing the adjustment transport:

- The automatic procedure mentioned previously, where SAPup detects the adjustment transports from the other systems of the system landscape and imports them during the upgrade
- A manual transport; for this, you create a typical transport for which the release is not controlled by SAPup and which is marked for further upgrades. Specifically, this method is used if only a short code freeze period (during which no further developments can take place) is scheduled. After the upgrade, the manual transport can be imported as easily as any standard transport.

SAPup treats the adjustment transport that is integrated in the upgrade as if it were another set of objects belonging to the upgrade and merges it in the correct order into the upgrade procedure. Thus, the objects of the transport are transferred to the new Repository even before the system downtime. If the SPAU adjustment transport is imported manually after the actual upgrade, system downtime will be extended by the duration of this import.

[+] Therefore, if downtime is an important factor for you and the SPAU adjustment transport requires several hours for the import, you should try to avoid the subsequent transport. Instead, you should integrate the SPAU transport into the upgrade. When asked for an adjustment transport, you can also proceed by providing SAPup with an adjustment transport different from the one originally exported. SAP Note 68678 describes the corresponding procedure in detail.

[+] In any case, you should test—in a test upgrade—the procedure and its result for both the automatic adjustment transport and, in particular, for the subsequent change of the automatic adjustment, to avoid potential errors or data inconsistencies in the production system!

18.3.2 Modification Adjustment During the Import of Support Packages

When importing Support Packages, the option to integrate SPDD or SPAU requests in the Support Package queue exists only since SPAM version 0020 in the SAP Web AS 6.x releases. If you need to adjust a large number of modifications, this procedure ensures benefits with respect to time and security when compared with a manual adjustment. Proceed as follows:

Procedure

1. Start importing the selected Support Package queue via the Support Package Manager in Transaction SPAM in the development system.
2. If you modified SAP Dictionary objects and if these objects are imported together with the Support Package, the Support Package Manager stops automatically. You must then adjust these objects using Transaction SPDD.

3. Create a change request in the Workbench Organizer (Transaction SE09) for the modification adjustment using Transaction SPDD. Also create one task for every developer who is involved in the modification adjustment.
4. After the adjustment is completed, the developers must release the tasks and inform you about this so that you can release the request in Transaction SPDD via Utilities • Mark for transport and mark the request for import into subsequent systems.
5. Continue importing the Support Package queue.
6. If you modified SAP Repository objects and if these objects are imported together with the Support Package, the Support Package Manager stops automatically. You must then adjust the Repository objects using Transaction SPAU.
7. Create a change request in the Workbench Organizer (Transaction SE09) for the modification adjustment using Transaction SPAU. Also create one task for every developer who is involved in the modification adjustment.
8. After the adjustment is completed, the developers must release the tasks and inform you so that you can release the request in Transaction SPAU via Utilities • Mark for transport and mark the request for the import into subsequent systems.
9. Finish the import of the Support Package queue by continuing the import in the Support Package Manager.

Importing adjustment changes

The SPDD or SPAU request can subsequently be used to import the adjustment changes into the other systems in the landscape systems. Proceed as follows:

1. Start the Support Package Manager using Transaction SPAM and select the same Support Package queue as the one you imported into the development system.
2. After selecting the Support Package queue, you're asked in Transaction SPAM whether you want to integrate modification adjustment transports (this query can be suppressed using the Support Package Manager settings). When you confirm the request, the existing adjustment transports are displayed in a dialog box. To add the adjustment transports to the Support Package queue, select Accept selected adjust-

ment transports. For every adjustment transport listed, the status field displays if it matches the current Support Package queue and can therefore be integrated—matching adjustment transports are already selected in the table. An adjustment transport "matches" the queue if the target Support Package status of the current queue corresponds to that of the export system at the time of exporting the modification adjustment transport.

3. The selected adjustment transports are then integrated into the Support Package queue. If a modification adjustment transport is imported as part of a Support Package queue, it is removed from the normal transport flow for Workbench requests. Automatic forwarding to the follow-up system does not take place. For example, if you use the typical three-system landscape of development system (DEV), quality assurance system (QAS), and production system (PRD), the modification adjustment transport is placed into the import queue of the QAS system after being exported from the DEV system. The integration of the adjustment transport into a Support Package queue in the QAS system now leads to the removal of this transport from the QAS import queue. Because transport forwarding does not take place during the import of a Support Package queue, the adjustment transport is not forwarded to the import queue of the PRD system. That is, the modification adjustment is not imported with the Transport Management System into your PRD system. As in the QAS system, you should then import the adjustment transport as part of a Support Package queue into the PRD system.
4. Start importing the Support Package queue from Transaction SPAM.

[+] Ensure that, respectively, only Dictionary objects exist in the SPDD request and only Repository objects exist in the SPAU request. Otherwise, severe problems might occur because transport steps for the adjustment request would also trigger actions for the Support Package import.

Manual SPDD adjustment

If you do not use Version 0020 of the Support Package Manager in SAP Web AS Release 6.x or use a lower SAP Basis release, the SPDD adjustment must be carried out manually. To do so, customize the objects displayed in Transaction SPDD according to your needs using Transaction SE11 and save them without activating them. However, for the SPAU adjustment, you can create a transport request in the development system in which you integrate the adjusted Repository objects. These objects can be imported via the TMS import function after the Support Package queue has been completely imported into the follow-up system; in this case, you can ignore the request for adjustment made by Transaction SPAU. However, as a precaution, after importing your adjustment transport, you should review the modification browser, the version information of the adjusted objects, and the corresponding code to ensure that this action was carried out correctly.

[+] You should never directly import the transport request you created for the SPDD adjustment with transport tools, such as the TMS, especially when using the specific downtime-optimized procedures in SPAM or SAINT. Otherwise, inconsistencies may occur in the system.

18.3.3 Modification Assistant

To simplify the modification adjustment during an upgrade or Support Package implementation, the modification assistant was introduced with SAP Release R/3 4.5. To ensure that it is used, go to a specific modification mode when calling the ABAP Workbench editors to modify standard version objects. In this mode, the original object is protected and can be changed only by using the buttons provided specifically for this purpose (see Figure 18.20). Changes are logged via the modification assistant to enable a quick and detailed overview of modifications and to reduce the upgrade effort.

Figure 18.20 Modification Assistant Change Options

The modification assistant provides support in the following functions of the ABAP Workbench:

- ABAP Editor
- Class Builder
- Screen Painter
- Menu Painter
- Maintenance of text elements

- Function Builder
- ABAP Dictionary
- Documentation

Modifications to ABAP Workbench objects that are not supported by the modification assistant are logged and displayed in the overview. During the upgrade, modifications to these objects are adjusted using traditional methods.

Leave modification assistant on (active)

In general, SAP recommends leaving the modification assistant on (active), even if the modification of the object is a bit more complex, because it simplifies the modification adjustment. You can get an overview of the modifications you made and can easily reset the object to its original state. The modification assistant can be turned off; however, you will then no longer receive any detailed information about your modifications and must implement the adjustment manually via version management. Because the modification logs are based on the original version that was imported with the last upgrade or Support Package and record only the differences between the original and modified versions of the object, this information is lost if you turn off the assistant. Therefore, the modification assistant cannot simply be turned on again later.

```
MODULE USER_COMMAND_0100 INPUT.
  CASE OK_CODE.
    WHEN 'SHOW'.
      CLEAR OK_CODE.
      SELECT SINGLE * FROM SPFLI WHERE CARRID = SPFLI-CARRID
*{   REPLACE        MODK920030                                   1
*\                                AND  CONNID = SPFLI-CONNID.
                                  AND  CONNID   = SPFLI-CONNID
                                  AND  CITYFROM = SPFLI-CITYFROM
                                  AND  CITYTO   = SPFLI-CITYTO.
*}   REPLACE
*{   INSERT         MODK920030                                   2
    WHEN 'CHNG'.
      PERFORM CHANGE_SPFLI.
*}   INSERT
    WHEN SPACE.
    WHEN OTHERS.
      CLEAR OK_CODE.
      SET SCREEN 0. LEAVE SCREEN.
  ENDCASE.
ENDMODULE.                 " USER_COMMAND_0100  INPUT
```

Figure 18.21 Changes Using the Modification Assistant

[+] As you can see in Figure 18.21, line 16 was replaced with lines 17 to 19; in addition, lines 22 and 23 were inserted. The figure also shows the MODK920030 transport request in which these changes were recorded. It is therefore easy to understand that changes carried out using the modification assistant can be easily adjusted with newer versions.

As mentioned previously, the modification assistant was introduced with Release R/3 4.5. If you implement an upgrade from a release prior to 4.5A to a release higher than 4.5A, all objects modified by you and redelivered by SAP are displayed in Transaction SPAU in the Without Modification Assistant category. Objects that cannot be versioned and that have not been managed by Transaction SPAU are also displayed here. The adjustment of these objects must then be carried out manually and supported by version management.

SAP online help provides additional information about the modification assistant and the adjustment.

18.4 Upgrade Strategies for a Transport Landscape

Follow the transport route

In a transport landscape, release changes should be performed in exactly the order defined by the transport route. The modification adjustment for a release change is carried out in the development system and is then transported along the transport route to downstream systems.

When planning a system landscape for an upgrade, not only the modification adjustment plays an important role. You might also need to check—in a preliminary study—whether the target release even fulfills your needs for new functionality. Furthermore, you don't want to paralyze the existing development system with the upgrade. To address this, in addition to the existing landscape, you could create a sandbox system—for example, a copy of the existing system. There could also be demands from various projects requesting a short code freeze period. This can rarely be accomplished within a three-system landscape. Furthermore, development and Customizing tasks for different release statuses must be performed in separate SAP environments as described in Chapters 4 and 6. The following sections introduce different system landscapes that can be used for upgrades.

18.4.1 Release Change in a Three-System Landscape

Upgrade sequence

In a release change in a three-system landscape, the upgrade tasks need to be performed in the following order (see Figure 18.22):

1. Implement the release change and the modification adjustment in the DEV development system.
2. Implement the release change in the QAS quality assurance system or in a copy of the PRD production system. The latter option is preferable. Then, import the change requests with the results of the modification adjustment into the QAS system, and test and validate the functionality of the system.
3. Implement the release change in the PRD production system. Import the change requests with the results of the modification adjustment into the PRD.

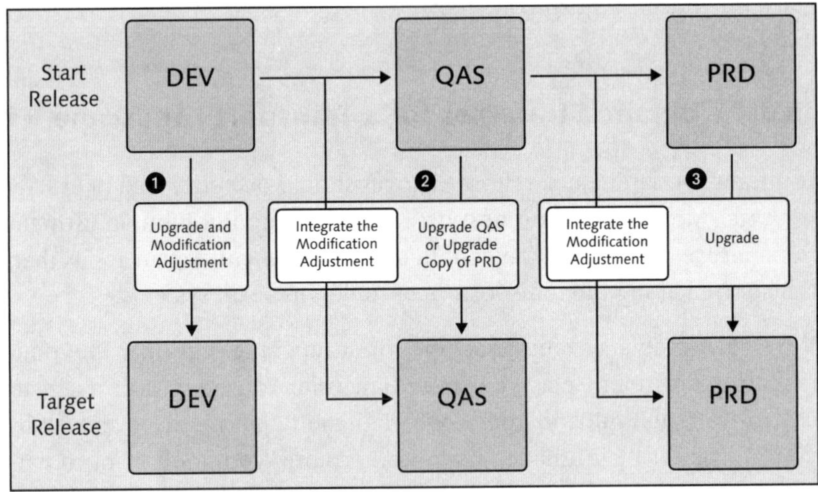

Figure 18.22 Order of the Release Changes in a Three-System Landscape

The three-system landscape is the standard landscape recommended by SAP for live operations. As you can tell from the modification adjustment sequence above, the processing during an upgrade follows the normal transport route as well. However, this also shows that this landscape cannot meet all requirements. The most important aspect in this regard is the missing maintainability of the production system during the upgrade of DEV and QAS. When the development system is in the upgrade phase, there is no system available to implement potentially necessary corrections for problems in the production system, unless you make these corrections in the test or production system. This, however, carries certain risks (regardless of the system in which you make the changes): making the changes poses a risk in and of itself, and the results achieved with the upgrade of the development system can no longer be completely transferred to downstream systems. The time period for which these risks exist is the duration of the test system upgrade, including the time reserved for testing.

18.4.2 Release Change with an Additional Development System

If you have a fourth system available, you can avoid some of the problems you would encounter using the standard three-system landscape. In this case, you would, for example, proceed as shown in Figure 18.23.

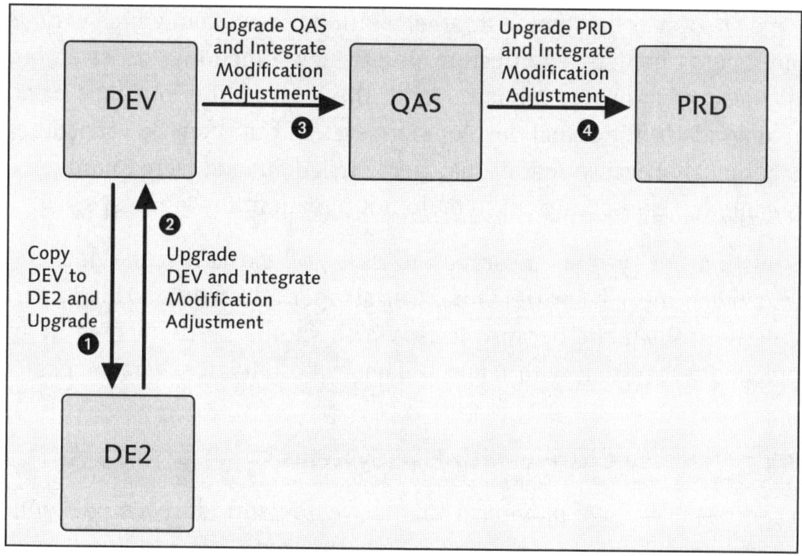

Figure 18.23 Upgrade in the Three-System Landscape with an Additional Development System

System copy of the development system

With this setup, a system copy (DE2) of the development system (DEV)—on which the upgrade is carried out—is first created. When carrying out the upgrade, adjusting the modifications, or validating new functions in the DE2 system, you can still maintain the existing release in the original system landscape. When the work on the DE2 system is completed, the upgrade of the actual development system and then the upgrade of both the test and the production system are carried out as described previously.

Drawbacks

This procedure has certain benefits, but also drawbacks. Aside from the additional hardware you will need for the second development system, you will also need to manually recreate all developments and corrections on the new DE2 development system that were carried out on the DEV development system after the system was copied from DEV to DE2. However, new developments to the new release after the DEV upgrade can be carried out easily via normal transports. Therefore, in an environment in which extensive project work is still being done in the old release, the maintenance effort is proportionally high.

However, you can also see this system landscape from a slightly different perspective in that the development system does not directly produce a new development system, but rather a sandbox system in which various components such as new Customizing or new functions are tested but not saved as transport requests. With the information you thus have, the upgrade in the actual development system can often be carried out more quickly because actions that were carried out and were found to be unwanted in the sandbox system do not remain in the landscape.

In this kind of system landscape the issue still exists that the development work must be frozen for a certain period of time. This is particularly problematic because tests, which should be performed in an upgraded test system with relevant data, can often last several weeks.

18.4.3 Release Change with Five Systems

Phase-based development environment

In contrast to the two previous variants, we now introduce a model with five systems. If you are planning a release change to gain additional functionality, such as implementing a new SAP component—for example, PP, MM, or HR—you must configure a "phase-based development environment." This is an environment in which you can map different phases of the development process—different release statuses in this case—to help you avoid long development freezes. While the new release is being configured, you can still implement supporting Customizing and development work for the current release in production operation, and you can also take more time for the tests in the new release when using such a system landscape. The following example describes in detail which actions and customizations should be expected.

Example: Phase-Based Release Change in a System Landscape

An enterprise is in live mode with the ERP application components Financial Accounting, Logistics, and Human Resources. The current ERP implementation consists of a standard three-system landscape with one development system (DEV), one quality assurance system (QAS), and one production system (PRD).

The enterprise plans to change from R/3 Release 4.5B to SAP ERP 6.0 ECC 6.0. To support this release change, two additional SAP ERP systems are installed, for two reasons: testing and verifying the new ERP release is considered time-consuming, and required maintenance changes must be imported into the production operation every two months.

To support the production operation with changes every other month (production support), the PPS system is created using a system copy of the development system. A system copy of the existing QAS system is used for creating another quality assurance system, PQA. The PPS and PQA systems now provide production support for the PRD production system. All employees who are involved in Customizing and development and need to make changes together with the production support will do so in the PPS system. Tests and validation take place in PQA. After acceptance, the corrections are imported into the PRD production system. All changes are documented so that they can also be implemented in the DEV system after the release change. The synchronization is necessary to ensure consistency among all ERP systems.

The PPS system enables the technical team to implement the release change to SAP ERP 6.0 ECC 6.0 in the DEV and QAS systems. When the release change has been completed and all available Support Packages have been imported, the Customizing and development team of the new implementation phase begins with the release Customizing in DEV. All Customizing and development changes made in PPS are also implemented in DEV. After the unit tests have been completed, the changes are released and exported to QAS for verification.

The three-system landscape is now a five-system landscape (see Figure 18.24).

Figure 18.24 Five-System Landscape Consisting of Different Releases

The initial proposal of configuring the Transport Management System (TMS) to enable the implementation of the release change and provide production support at the same time is illustrated in Figure 18.25.

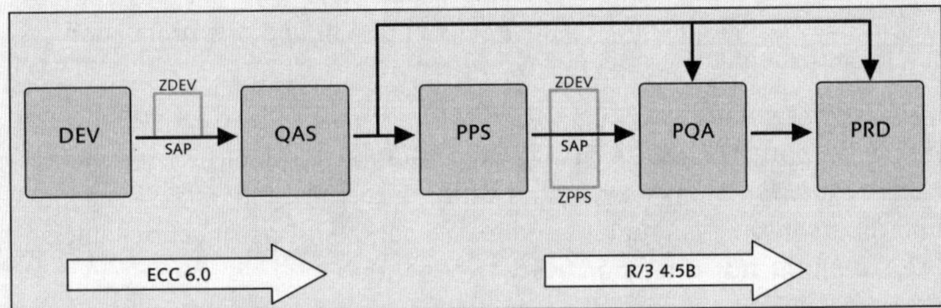

Figure 18.25 Five SAP Systems Connected Through Transport Routes

From a technical perspective, this initial proposal is feasible; however, the system administrators are worried because the import queues of PQA and PRD receive changes from both development systems DEV and PPS.

The import of change requests from DEV into PPS, PQA, and PRD before the release change could be prevented using the `sourcesystems` transport profile parameter. This solution is not completely satisfying, however, because the existence of change requests from R/3 Release 4.5B and from SAP ERP 6.0 ECC 6.0 in the import queues of PPS, PQA, and PRD could lead to confusion.

Another proposal is to create a second transport directory for DEV and QAS. The existing transport directory would be used for maintaining the import queues of PPS, PQA, and PRD and would receive only change requests for production support. Although this solution is also feasible, it requires that no one uses the TMS to copy change requests between different transport directories because this would automatically add change requests from SAP ERP 6.0 ECC 6.0 to the import queues of PPS, PQA, and PRD. Using authorizations, you can restrict the TMS access and thereby lessen this risk but this does not completely eliminate it.

Therefore, the TMS configuration proposal illustrated in Figure 18.26 is eventually accepted. This involves the creation of the virtual R50 system whose import queue receives a list of sequential change requests from SAP ERP 6.0 ECC 6.0 that need to be imported into the PPS, PQA, and PRD systems after the release of these systems has been changed to SAP ERP 6.0 ECC 6.0.

While the release change is prepared in PRD, change requests are imported from DEV to QAS for verification and then delivered to R50. In the next step, the import buffer is copied from R50 to create an import buffer for PQA; the release change is carried out in PQA.

Change requests are imported to ensure that the change from R/3 Release 4.5B to SAP ERP 6.0 ECC 6.0 can be completed without problems. If the tests run successfully, the release change is carried out in the PRD system. Then the import buffer is copied from R50 to create an import buffer for PRD, and the change requests are imported from SAP ERP 6.0 ECC 6.0 into the PRD production system. Eventually, release change, import buffer copy, and change request import are effected in PPS.

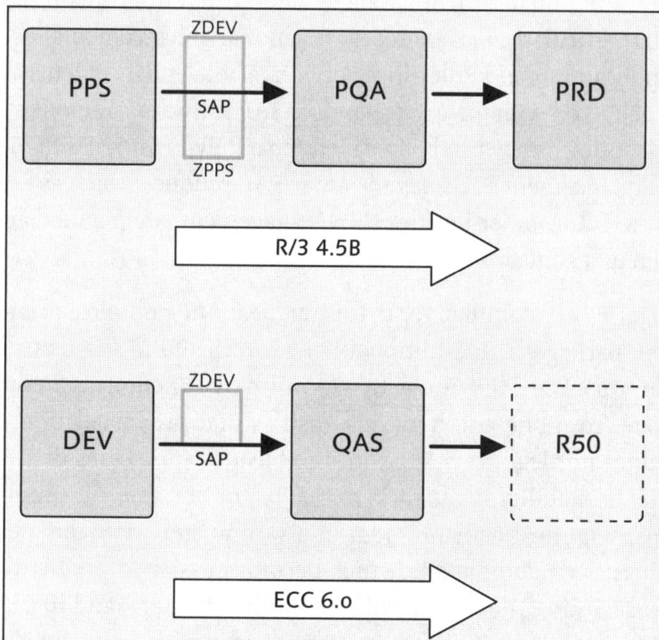

Figure 18.26 TMS Configuration with Virtual System

18.5 SAP Enhancement Packages

As described in the previous chapters, release changes provided by SAP allow you to add new functions to an existing system. However, as you have also read, because a new release is always delivered as a complete package, it also requires a certain amount of effort, for example, to test all business processes or adapt particular custom developments to the new release.

In addition, SAP Support Packages also contain changes to supply an existing system with corrections and new legal adaptations. This approach ensures the stability of the business processes to a great extent, but you cannot use it to implement all of the new functions.

Concept

SAP Enhancement Packages enable you to meet all requirements regarding flexibility and innovation and still retain the stability required of business processes. SAP Enhancement Packages (short SAP EhP) contain new developments, particularly in the area of functional enhancements, user interface simplifications, and Enterprise Services. These enhancements are bundled and delivered with the corresponding SAP software components. With a few exceptions, they can be installed separately in an SAP ERP 6.0 system. SAP Enhancement Packages for other SAP products, such as SAP NetWeaver or SAP Customer Relationship Management, are planned and should be used in a similar way to that described for SAP ERP.

Delivery

SAP EhP deliveries are cumulative, that is, an SAP EhP contains all previous SAP EhP packages. An additional benefit of SAP EhPs is that the installation of a package and the activation of new functions are completely separate from one another. This ensures that the installation of an SAP EhP does not lead to changes to the business processes or user interfaces, that is, stability is retained to the extent possible. To use the new functions, you must activate them in a second step after the technical import has been completed. It thus becomes easier to predict the resulting changes—described in detail later in the chapter—and to plan the work that will be required for adaptations to processes or for end user training. The SAP Switch and Enhancement Framework, which is described in Chapter 10, Section 10.4, is the technology that enables the separation between the import and the activation.

Another advantage of SAP EhPs is that the planned delivery intervals—one package per year—make new functions available more quickly than is the case with new main releases containing major changes.

In addition to the delivery of SAP EhPs, SAP will continue to distribute corrections and legal adaptations via SAP Support Packages. The maintenance duration for SAP EhPs will be as long as the maintenance duration for the underlying SAP product. For example, the standard maintenance for SAP ERP 6.0 is in effect through the first quarter of 2013, followed by two years of extended maintenance or another year of customer-specific maintenance.

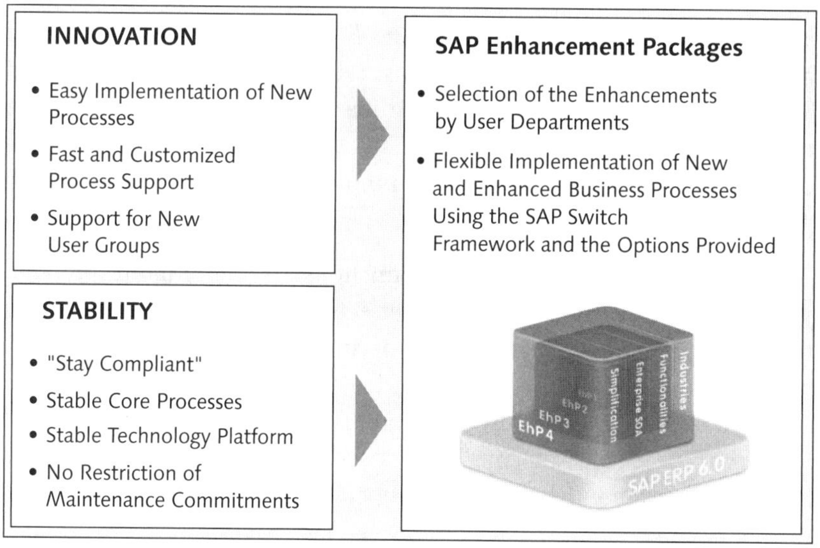
INNOVATION
• Easy Implementation of New Processes
• Fast and Customized Process Support
• Support for New User Groups
STABILITY
• "Stay Compliant"
• Stable Core Processes
• Stable Technology Platform
• No Restriction of Maintenance Commitments
SAP Enhancement Packages
• Selection of the Enhancements by User Departments
• Flexible Implementation of New and Enhanced Business Processes Using the SAP Switch Framework and the Options Provided
EhP 2
EhP 3
EhP 4
Simplification
Enterprise SOA
Functionalities
Industries
SAP ERP 6.0

Figure 18.27 Innovation and Stability through SAP Enhancement Packages

Figure 18.27 provides you with an overview of the advantages of using SAP Enhancement Packages. You can find more information on the business processes that are installed together with the corresponding SAP Enhancement Package in the Masterguide, which can be downloaded for the various SAP EhP versions from the SAP Service Marketplace at *http://service.sap.com/instguides*.

18.5.1 Implementation Activities for SAP Enhancement Packages

Discover

The first step for using a new function that is delivered with an SAP Enhancement Package is the appropriate planning (*discover phase*). The following sections describe examples for the currently available SAP Enhancement Package for SAP ERP; for SAP EhPs for other products, the web addresses for the SAP Service Marketplace or SAP Notes may differ.

The SAP Service Marketplace at *http://service.sap.com/erp-ehp* provides detailed information to support your planning process. You can run comprehensive checks for the required new functions (called *business functions*) using the content found here, which is categorized into general documentation, presentations, release notes, test catalogs, and learning maps. The SAP Solution Browser also contains information on SAP Enhancement Packages. It enables you to answer business process owners' questions about which innovations can be used for which processes.

Evaluate

After you have discovered business functions that are of interest to you, you should check and evaluate the effects of using these functions on the existing system (*evaluate phase*). This information is stored in the corresponding documentation (see Figure 18.28) as well as in the release notes. In particular, the information on resulting changes and additional SAP products or software components necessary for using the functions help you determine the corresponding effort.

Install

To install an SAP EhP, a minimum Support Package status is required for the respective SAP product (currently only SAP ERP 6.0). This status does not depend on the desired SAP EhP version and is defined in SAP Notes, for example, for SAP EhP3 in SAP Note 1095233. You must also check, using SAP Note 1117309 for example, whether the already installed add-ons are compatible or have additional prerequisites.

[+] To reduce the installation effort for SAP Support Packages and SAP Enhancement Packages—for modification adjustments or tests, for example—you should import all changes in a single step.

HCM, ESS for Personal Information

Technical Data	
Technical Name of Business Function	HCM_ESS_CI_1
Type of Business Function	Enterprise Business Function
Available as of	SAP enhancement package 3 for SAP ERP 6.0
ECC Software Component	EA-HR 603
ECC Application Component	Employee Self-Service (PA-ESS-XSS)
Business Intelligence Content	Not relevant
SAP Enterprise Services	Not relevant
JAVA Software Component	SAP-ESS 603
Portal Content	*Business Package for Employee Self-Service (SAP ERP) 1.31*
Additional components in other SAP applications	Not relevant
Other business functions you need to activate	Human Capital Management (EA-HR)

You can use this business function to provide better support for the administration of employees from many different countries. The enhancements for the Employee Self-Service (ESS) *Personal Information* area ensure that your employees can maintain foreign addresses in ESS using either the correct country-specific format, if available, or an international address format.

EXAMPLE
If an employee wants to enter a permanent home address in France, he or she can do so using the correct country address format, as the appropriate fields for French addresses are provided.

This business function allows you to customize *Personal Information* screens, for example, by adding or removing fields, adapting the screens according to your specific requirements. It is also possible to customize the Overview screens of applications in this area, allowing you to adapt the screens to suit your needs.

Prerequisites

- You have activated the Enterprise Extension *Human Capital Management* (EA-HR) in your back-end system.
- You have activated the business function *HCM, ESS for Personal Information* in your back-end system.

Figure 18.28 Sample Documentation for a Business Function

After having checked the basic prerequisites, you assign the business functions selected in the steps described previously to the installable technical usages, such as ABAP or Java components and Portal or XI content. For SAP EhP3, for example, this assignment is defined in SAP Note 1083576 (see Figures 18.29 and 18.30). The assignment indicates whether the function can be implemented via an update of the relevant software components on the SAP ECC server or whether you must also make the respective changes in the integrated SAP NetWeaver Portal.

Business Function	Business Function (Technical Name)	TechUsage (PPMS)	ABAP Product Instance	Java Product Instance	Portal Content	XI Content	BI Content
Travel Management	FIN_TRAVEL_1	**HCM - Travel Management**	Human Capital Management	---	All BP	All XI Content	---
TRM: Hedge Management, New Instruments, New Key Figures	FIN_TRM_LR_FI_AN	**Financial Services**	Financial Services	---	---	---	BI 7.0.3 SP8
HCM, Administrative Services 01	HCM_ASR_CI_1	**HCM - Administrative Services**	Human Capital Management	---	All BP	---	---
HCM, Empl. Interaction Center 01	HCM_EIC_CI_1	**Human Capital Management**	Human Capital Management	---	---	---	---
HCM, SAP E-Recruiting 1	HCM_ERC_CI_1	**ERecruiting on ECC Srv w/ XI**	E-Recruiting	---	---	All XI Content	---
HCM, SAP E-Recruiting 1	HCM_ERC_CI_1	**ERecruiting Stand-alone w/ XI**	SAP E-Recruiting	---	---	All XI Content	---
HCM, SAP E-Recruiting - Search 1	HCM_ERC_SES_1	**ERecruiting on ECC Server**	E-Recruiting	---	---	---	---
HCM, SAP E-Recruiting - Search 1	HCM_ERC_SES_1	**ERecruiting Stand-alone**	SAP E-Recruiting	---	---	---	---
HCM, ESS for Concurrent Employment and Global Employee	HCM_ESS_CE	**HCM Self Services**	Human Capital Management	SAP XSS (Self Services)	All BP	---	---
HCM, ESS for Personal Information	HCM_ESS_CI_1	**HCM Self Services**	Human Capital Management	SAP XSS (Self Services)	All BP	---	---
HCM Localization Topics	HCM_LOC_CI_1	**HCM Self Services**	Human Capital Management	SAP XSS (Self Services)	All BP	---	---
HCM, Learning Solution 01	HCM_LSO_CI_1	**HCM - Learning Solution**	Learning Solution	SAP Learning Sol-Client (Auth) SAP Learning Sol-Frontend CP SAP Learning Sol-Client (Learn)	All BP	---	---
HCM, Enterprise Learning	HCM_LSO_VLR	**HCM - Learning Solution**	Learning Solution	---	All BP	---	---

Figure 18.29 Part of SAP Note 1083576 with Dependencies of the Business Functions

Nr	603 ABAP Product Instance	Software Component 1	Software Component 2	Software Component 3	Software Component 4	Software Component 5
1	**Discrete Ind. & Mill Products**	SAP_APPL 6.03	EA-APPL 603	ECC-DIMP 603		
2	**Oil&Gas**	SAP_APPL 6.03	IS-OIL 603			
3	**Catch Weight Management**	SAP_APPL 6.03	IS-CWM 603	FINBASIS 603	SEM-BW 603	
4	**Hospital**	SAP_APPL 6.03	IS-H 603			
5	**Public Sector Accounting**	SAP_APPL 6.03	FI-CA 603	IS-PS-CA 603	EA-PS 603	
6	**Insurance**	SAP_APPL 6.03	FI-CA 603	INSURANCE 603		
7	**Media**	SAP_APPL 6.03	EA-APPL 603	FI-CA 603	IS-M 603	
8	**Utilities/Waste&Recycl./Telco**	SAP_APPL 6.03	EA-APPL 603	FI-CA 603	IS-UT 603	
9	**Leasing/Contract A/R & A/P**	SAP_APPL 6.03	EA-APPL 603	FI-CA 603	FI-CAX 603	
10	**Oil&Gas with Utilities**	SAP_APPL 6.03	EA-APPL 603	IS-OIL 603	FI-CA 603	IS-UT 603
11	**Retail**	SAP_APPL 6.03	EA-RETAIL 603			
12	**Global Trade**	SAP_APPL 6.03	EA-GLTRADE 603			
13	**Financial Supply Chain Mgmt**	SAP_APPL 6.03	FINBASIS 603	SEM_BW_603		
14	**Central Applications**	SAP_APPL 6.03	EA-APPL 603			
18	**Defense**	SAP_APPL 6.03	EA-APPL 603	EA-DFPS 603	ECC-DIMP 603	
19	**Defense for Public Admin**	SAP_APPL 6.03	EA-APPL 603	EA-DFPS 603		
20	**Financial Services**	SAP_APPL 6.03	EA-FINSERV 603			
15	**Strategic Enterprise Mgmt**	FINBASIS 603	SEM-BW 603			
16	**Human Capital Management**	EA-HR 603				
17	**Learning Solution**	EA-HR 603	LSOFE 603			
21	**E-Recruiting**	ERECRUIT 603				

Nr	Java Product Instance	Software Component 1	Software Component 2	Software Component 3
1	**SAP FSCM - Biller Direct**	FSCM-BILLER DIRECT 6.02		
2	**SAP Integration for SWIFT**	SWIFT 602		
3	**SAP Learning Sol-Client (Auth)**	LSOAE 602 (AUTHORS ENVIROMENT)		
4	**SAP Learning Sol-Client (Lern)**	LSOOP 602 (OFFLINE PLAYER)		
5	**SAP Learning Sol-Frontend ABAP**	LSOFE 602 (FRONT END)		
6	**SAP Learning Sol-Frontend CP**	LSOCP 602 (CONTENT PLAYER)		
7	**SAP Retail Store Applications**	IS-R-SRS 602		
8	**SAP Utility Customer E-Service**	SAP UCES 6.02	SAP JAVA DATA DICTIONARY 5.0	
9	**SAP XSS (Self Services)**	IS FS ICM APP 603	SAP ESS 603	SAP PCUI_GP 603

Figure 18.30 Part of SAP Note 1083576 with Description of the Technical Usages

When you have identified the relevant components, you must download the necessary software packages from the SAP Service Marketplace. For this purpose, you need to consider the dependencies and requirements of the necessary SAP Support Packages, the desired SAP Enhancement Packages, and any additional SAP Support Packages for corrections. As an integral component of SAP Solution Manager, the SAP Maintenance Optimizer— described in detail in Chapter 19—can be very helpful for these activities because it already determines the dependencies when specifying the technical components, and then downloads the corresponding files from the SAP Service Marketplace. During this process, it creates the appropriate XML file, which is transferred to the import tools, and thus ensures a consistent status for the software to be imported.

Support Packages

As mentioned previously, specific Support Packages also exist for SAP Enhancement Packages. The initial version of, for example, Package EA-APPL 603—this is the short description for EhP 3 in SAP ERP 6.0 ECC 6.0—corresponds to the SP01 maintenance status for EA-APPL 602 or the SP11 maintenance status for EA-APPL 600. If the Maintenance Optimizer or import tools are installed, these software statuses are identified, and the system automatically determines a minimum Support Package version for the higher Enhancement Package status and requests it for integration.

[+]

Please note that SAP Enhancement Packages cannot be uninstalled from a system (similar to add-ons). If you first want to check the functions of one or more business functions for their usage options with regard to your business processes, you should do so in a sandbox system instead of in your development system.

When installing the queue that consists of SAP Support Packages and SAP Enhancement Packages, you should perform the same steps you would perform when importing only SAP Support Packages, that is, adapt the developments and test your business processes. The scope of the tests of the new SAP EhP functions depends on whether you want to activate their functions immediately after the installation or at a later point in time.

Activate

As already mentioned, the import of SAP EhPs alone doesn't make the new function available. You must also activate the corresponding business function to use the new program parts (activate phase). To do so, call Transaction SFW5. This is the central transaction for controlling the various activities for the business functions. Using the overview in this transaction, you can, for example, display current or planned statuses, or view additional information such as release notes, test case descriptions, and possible dependencies (see Figure 18.31). SAP Note 1066110 provides more information on the installation of the respective documentation.

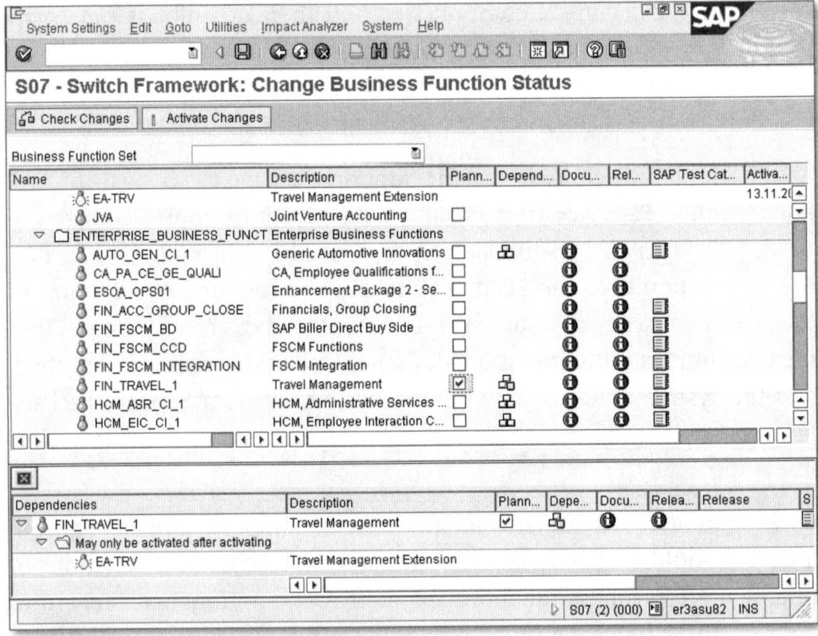

Figure 18.31 Activation of a Business Function Displaying the Dependencies

Activating business functions

To activate a business function, proceed as follows:

1. Prepare the system for the activation, for example, by unscheduling batch jobs and locking the system for other users.
2. Enter Transaction code SFW5.
3. Select the desired Business Function Set from the list (you can only select one at a time) and then the required business functions.
4. Set the planned status to Active, and select Check Changes.
5. If no error is found, select Activate Changes.
6. When the activation is completed, you can re-schedule batch jobs, and users can use the system again.

With the activation, the system starts a job that generates the corresponding parts—for example, of the programs or function modules—via the switch framework or it activates BC Sets in the background. Because changes in the system are minor, downtime is reduced when compared with a complete release change—you should expect an average runtime of 30 to 120 minutes.

Test and go live

You can test the new functions immediately after their activation. To do so, you can use the standard templates for test cases. Figure 18.32 shows a representative example. Because the switch framework enables you to activate only selected new functions, it is easier to test them or train end users for exactly these enhancements. As described for the activate phase, you can call the test cases in Transaction SFW5 when the installation of an SAP EhP is completed. From there, you can navigate to the SAP Test Workbench to document the test results. If you manage your tests and test cases centrally in SAP Solution Manager, you can also transport the test cases to SAP Solution Manager using a transport request. If you need detailed information on the test cases before you perform the installation, you can access the corresponding texts in the SAP Service Marketplace at *http://service.sap.com/erp-ehp*.

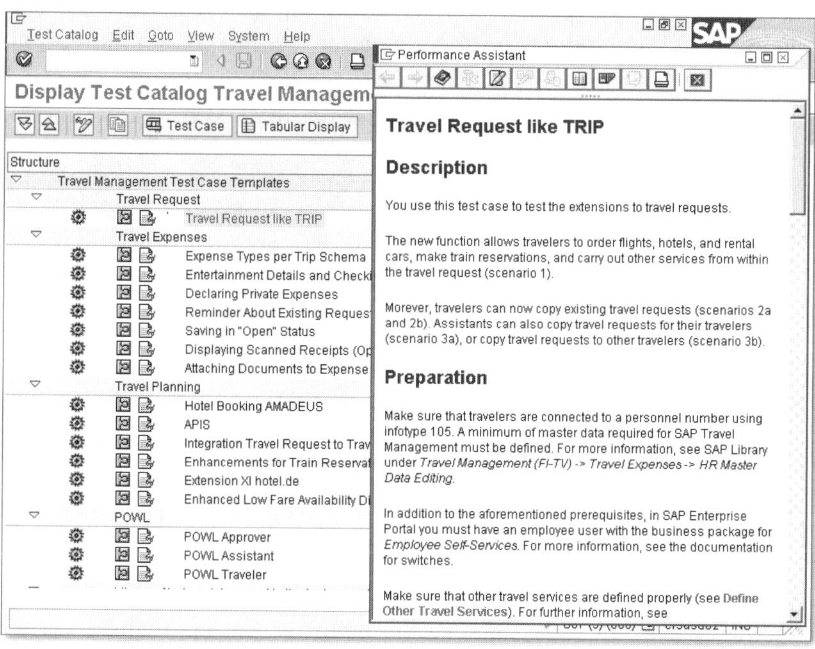

Figure 18.32 Sample Test Case Description of a Business Function

18.5.2 Technical Implementation

Various tools are used to install SAP EhPs. One of these tools is the SAP Solution Manager Maintenance Optimizer, which guides you through the individual installation steps and simplifies the process by determining the required software packages and also downloading them. In addition, you use import tools, which are briefly introduced here for the different SAP products:

XI/PI content

If SAP NetWeaver PI requires changes, these are implemented by installing the *XI/PI content*, which corresponds to the PI version used. You can find the XI/PI content for an SAP application in the SAP Service Marketplace at *http://service.sap.com/swdc* • DOWNLOAD • SUPPORT PACKAGES AND PATCHES • ENTRY BY APPLICATION GROUP • SAP CONTENT • ESR CONTENT (XI CONTENT) • <XI CONTENT SOFTWARE COMPONENT> • <XI CONTENT SOFTWARE COMPONENT VERSION> (the name and version of the software component are defined in the application's Masterguide). You import the XI content into the Integration Repository by first copying the provided export files into an import directory of the Integration Builder's host and then performing the import using a menu in the Integration Builder. In the following steps, <systemDir> refers to the path for the host's system directory (usually, <systemDir> = "\usr\sap\<SAPSID>\SYS\global"). Proceed as follows:

1. Get the export files for the XI content of the cross-system application. The naming convention allows for an assignment to their Support Package level. For example, SCM4003_00.ZIP and SCMBASIS4003_00.ZIP indicate SP level 03 with patch level 0 of the XI content.

[+] You do not overwrite the content that has already been imported to the Integration Repository when importing XI content with an older version. Support Packages for XI content always contain the previous objects as well as the changes and enhancements that should be delivered with this Support Package.

2. Copy the export files into the import directory for the Integration Repository (<SYSTEMDIR>\XI\REPOSITORY_SERVER\IMPORT). If the files are zipped, you have to unzip them before importing them. The system generates the import directory when the Integration Builder is called for the first time.

[+] The actual export files have the extension .tpz. You must not unzip these files and should store the ZIP files for error analysis.

3. Log on to the SAP system on which the Integration Builder is installed. To call the initial screen of the Integration Builder, start Transaction SXMB_IFR, and click on INTEGRATION REPOSITORY.
4. After starting the Integration Builder, select the files from the import directory and import the XI content by choosing TOOLS • IMPORT DESIGN OBJECTS. The sequence in which the export files are imported is not critical.
5. After a successful import the Integration Builder moves the imported TPZ files into the <SYSTEMDIR>/XI/ REPOSITORY_SERVER/IMPORTEDFILES directory. The Support Package level of imported software component versions is specified on the Integration Builder's DETAILS tab of the respective software component version.

Java software components and Portal content

The actual installation of the Java software components and the Portal content is carried out using the JSPM. The necessary data for the SAP NetWeaver Portal content is stored in the */portal_content* subfolder where each business package has its own subfolder with the required file. The Java instances SAP ERP 2005 – SAP NW – EPCore or SAP ERP 2005 – SAP NW – Enterprise Portal are the basis for the installation. In addition to the business packages that should be installed, you must install the business packages BP ERP05 Common parts 1.31 and BP TECHNICAL INFORMATION 1.30.

To use the SAP XSS component (Self-Services), you also need the Java instances SAP ERP 2005 – SAP NW – EPCore or SAP ERP 2005 – SAP NW – Enterprise Portal. The other files for the installation are stored in the /JAVA_SERVER_COMPONENTS/SAP_XSS_SELFSERVICE subfolder. In this context, you must consider several dependencies, for example, the dependency on the SAP PCUI GP or IS FS ICM APP 603 packages. You can find additional information in SAP Note 1100230 or—more conveniently—via the automatic determination in the SAP Solution Manager Maintenance Optimizer. Proceed as follows:

1. Log on to the J2EE Engine on which the components should be installed as <SID>adm.
2. Copy the required files into the standard directory for SAP Support Packages /USR/SAP/TRANS/EPS/IN.

3. Call JSPM using the GO script, which is located in the file system in the /USR/SAP/<SID>/<CENTRAL_INSTANCE>/J2EE/JSPM directory. Depending on the installation category, the name for the central instance is either JC<xx> or DVEBMGS<xx>, where <xx> stands for thc number of the central instance.
4. Enter the SDM password to log on to the SDM.
5. If you are using the JSPM for the first time, you must first upgrade it to the latest release before you can deploy additional packages. To do so, select the JAVA SUPPORT PACKAGE MANAGER option on the DEPLOYMENT tab, and update the SAP.COM/JSPM software component to the target status of the Support Packages. When the upgrade is completed, you must restart the JSPM and log on again with the SDM password.
6. On the DEPLOYMENT tab, select the BUSINESS AND ENHANCEMENT PACKAGES option. You should use the SUPPORT STACKAGE STACK option determined by the SAP Maintenance Optimizer. Otherwise, select the relevant files from the files you copied into the inbox and, if necessary, deselect the files that you do not need.
7. The JSPM now checks the installation queue for consistency. Therefore, you must check the status of the log files—when the statuses OK and WARNING are displayed, you can continue the import; when REVISE is displayed, the deployment cannot be carried out. In this case, the information under SHOW DETAILS may be helpful.
8. Start the installation with the START button. If dialog instances are active, JSPM prompts you to stop them. JSPM also informs you that the system will be stopped before actually stopping it.
9. When the import is completed with DEPLOYED or DEPLOYED WITH WARNING, the import process has been successful. Nevertheless, you should check the log files and status via the DEPLOYED COMPONENTS tab. The ERROR or NOT DEPLOYED status indicates a problem, which you should analyze using SHOW DETAILS.

   After troubleshooting, you can start a new deployment by resuming it.
10. In a Unix environment, to complete the process, you must also adapt the authorizations of the kernel binaries.

ABAP software components

To install the ABAP software components, until a special tool—the SAP Enhancement Package Installer—is available, only Transaction SAINT can be used. Because Transaction SAINT is based on the technology of Transaction SPAM and has been used for the installation of ABAP add-ons for quite a while, it is a technically sophisticated and sufficiently known tool. However, for the installation of SAP EhPs, you need the most up-to-date version of Transaction SAINT (this is installed using the SPAM update), which must be at least version 25. Proceed as follows:

1. Load or copy the required Support Packages and Enhancement Packages into the Support Package inbox (usually into *DIR_TRANS/eps/in*).
2. Log on to client 000, and call Transaction SAINT from it.
3. Refresh the software package information by selecting START and then selecting LOAD – FROM APPLICATION SERVER.
4. Load the XML file with the Enhancement Package stack information you created using the SAP Solution Manager Maintenance Optimizer by selecting Stack Configuration, or select the required Enhancement Packages, add-ons, or Support Packages directly in Transaction SAINT.
5. Select Continue to start the queue calculation of the software packages that should be installed.
6. Check the queue calculation logs for errors—for example, for an insufficient Support Package status or missing packages—and, if necessary, repeat the calculation after having completed the corrections.
7. Select Continue to initiate the installation of the software packages. The system prompts you to enter a valid password for add-ons and Enhancement Packages respectively—for EhP3, the password can be found in SAP Note 1083533.
8. Decide whether you want to include modification adjustment transports in the installation queue.
9. Select the import mode for the installation queue—you can choose between the normal mode and the DOWNTIME_MINIMIZED MODE.
10. If necessary, carry out the modification adjustment. This must be done if you didn't integrate an adjustment transport or if the trans-

port does not include all objects that should be adjusted. If required, Transaction SAINT will provide the respective jump via the selection of the relevant modifications.

11. Confirm the successful import of the software packages.

[+] Both the calculation of the stack combination and the check in the import tools ensure that you do not mix different EhP version packages. For example, you cannot install B. SAP_APPL 603 together with EA_HR 602. In this case, the EA_HR package would also be changed to Version 603. The system also checks the dependencies within an ABAP instance when activating the business functions. However, this is not possible across different instances. For example, with regard to content, it is not possible between the ERP instance and the SAP NetWeaver BI system.

[+] Only by using upgrade tools, which are delivered with the SAP ERP 6.0 Service Release SR3 upgrade, can you integrate SAP Enhancement Packages directly into the upgrade procedure. This is similar to integrating SAP Support Packages. The preparations correspond to the actions described previously for determining and creating the XML file using the SAP Solution Manager Maintenance Optimizer. If you consider using the SAP EhP3 functions, you should integrate the relevant packages with the upgrade. With the upgrade activities, you already perform the corresponding application tests, and the runtime for the import at a later stage is omitted almost entirely.

SAP EhPI

In particular, when many and large software packages are involved, the import of the SAP Enhancement Packages using the SAINT tool may take several hours because of the technology used. Even if you use parallel R3trans processes, which you can activate in the SAINT options, the process only improves when the packages provided contain appropriately prepared transports. Using the DOWNTIME_MINIMIZED option also only insignificantly reduces the amount of time during which you cannot use the system for production. Therefore, SAP developed a new tool, the *SAP Enhancement Package Installer* (EhPI), which piloted with SAP Enhancement Package 3 and will be generally available for later Enhancement Package versions.

The SAP Enhancement Package Installer uses technology that is similar to the SAP System Switch Upgrade. Here, the packages are also first copied and then switched to the new version at a later stage. This means that preparations for the import can be made in parallel to live system operation to be able to resume operation after a relatively short downtime.

To keep the import process as simple as possible, SAP EhPI uses a roadmap that illustrates the installation steps as grouped into phases (see Figure 18.33).

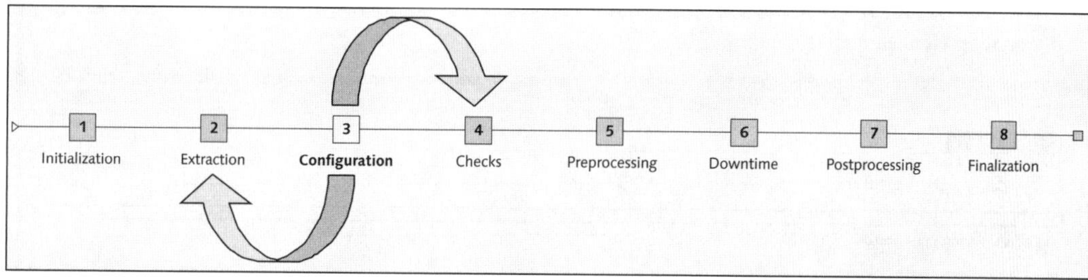

Figure 18.33 Phases of the EhPI Roadmap

Phases

As shown in the figure, SAP EhPI enables you to go back to the previous step (BACK) or continue the installation with the next step (NEXT). The meaning of the different steps—see Figure 18.34 for a detailed example—is briefly described as follows:

1. INITIALIZATION analyzes the SAP system and creates the information for the installation GUI.
2. EXTRACTION unpacks the software packages that are required for the installation.
3. DURING CONFIGURATION, YOU specify system-specific information, such as user passwords or additional Support Packages.
4. CHECKS checks whether the requirements for the installation of the SAP Enhancement Packages are met.
5. PREPROCESSING creates the parallel instance and executes further preparatory steps.
6. DURING DOWNTIME, the software packages of the SAP EhPs are switched to the new versions.
7. POSTPROCESSING saves the log files and initiates the necessary postprocessing steps.

8. Finalization deletes no longer required files and directories and completes the installation.

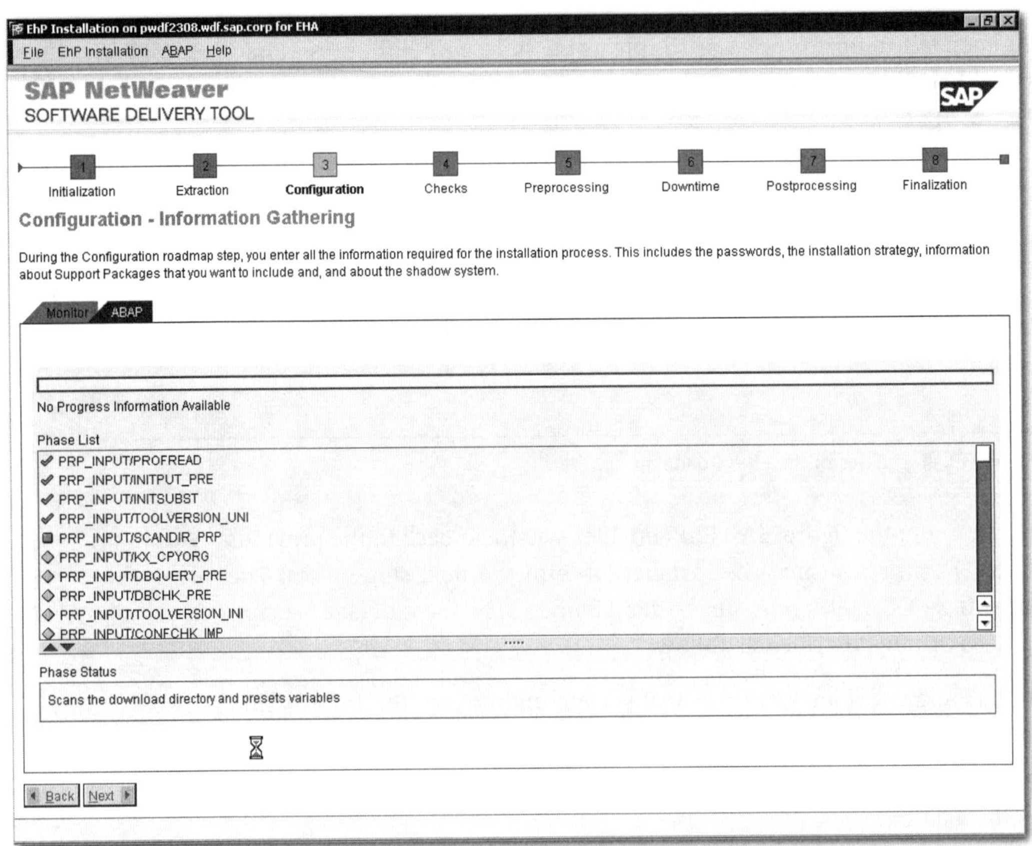

Figure 18.34 Progress Display in the SAP Enhancement Package Installer

18.6 Upgrades and Unicode

Unicode is an international standard that assigns the characters of almost every existing language and script to a consistent and unique Unicode value. This value uses a hexadecimal notation and is usually supplemented by a meaningful description (see Table 18.2).

Character	Unicode Value	Unicode Description
A	U+0041	LATIN CAPITAL LETTER A
Ä	U+00C4	LATIN CAPITAL LETTER A WITH DIAERESIS
α	U+03B1	GREEK SMALL LETTER ALPHA
ظ	U+0638	ARABIC LETTER ZAH
א	U+05D0	HEBREW LETTER ALEF

Table 18.2 Sample Unicode Notation

This uniqueness of the characters is an advantage of Unicode as compared to other, often incompatible, single code pages—such as the example of ISO 8859-1 (Latin-1) shown in Figure 18.35.

<table>
<tr><th></th><th>0</th><th>1</th><th>2</th><th>3</th><th>4</th><th>5</th><th>6</th><th>7</th><th>8</th><th>9</th><th>A</th><th>B</th><th>C</th><th>D</th><th>E</th><th>F</th></tr>
<tr><td>0</td><td></td><td></td><td></td><td></td><td></td><td></td><td></td><td></td><td></td><td></td><td></td><td></td><td></td><td></td><td></td><td></td></tr>
<tr><td>1</td><td></td><td></td><td></td><td></td><td></td><td></td><td></td><td></td><td></td><td></td><td></td><td></td><td></td><td></td><td></td><td></td></tr>
<tr><td>2</td><td>SP</td><td>!</td><td>"</td><td>#</td><td>$</td><td>%</td><td>&</td><td>'</td><td>(</td><td>)</td><td>*</td><td>+</td><td>,</td><td>-</td><td>.</td><td>/</td></tr>
<tr><td>3</td><td>0</td><td>1</td><td>2</td><td>3</td><td>4</td><td>5</td><td>6</td><td>7</td><td>8</td><td>9</td><td>:</td><td>;</td><td><</td><td>=</td><td>></td><td>?</td></tr>
<tr><td>4</td><td>@</td><td>A</td><td>B</td><td>C</td><td>D</td><td>E</td><td>F</td><td>G</td><td>H</td><td>I</td><td>J</td><td>K</td><td>L</td><td>M</td><td>N</td><td>O</td></tr>
<tr><td>5</td><td>P</td><td>Q</td><td>R</td><td>S</td><td>T</td><td>U</td><td>V</td><td>W</td><td>X</td><td>Y</td><td>Z</td><td>[</td><td>\</td><td>]</td><td>^</td><td>_</td></tr>
<tr><td>6</td><td>`</td><td>a</td><td>b</td><td>c</td><td>d</td><td>e</td><td>f</td><td>g</td><td>h</td><td>i</td><td>j</td><td>k</td><td>l</td><td>m</td><td>n</td><td>o</td></tr>
<tr><td>7</td><td>p</td><td>q</td><td>r</td><td>s</td><td>t</td><td>u</td><td>v</td><td>w</td><td>x</td><td>y</td><td>z</td><td>{</td><td>|</td><td>}</td><td>~</td><td></td></tr>
<tr><td>8</td><td></td><td></td><td></td><td></td><td></td><td></td><td></td><td></td><td></td><td></td><td></td><td></td><td></td><td></td><td></td><td></td></tr>
<tr><td>9</td><td></td><td></td><td></td><td></td><td></td><td></td><td></td><td></td><td></td><td></td><td></td><td></td><td></td><td></td><td></td><td></td></tr>
<tr><td>A</td><td>NBSP</td><td>¡</td><td>¢</td><td>£</td><td>¤</td><td>¥</td><td>¦</td><td>§</td><td>¨</td><td>©</td><td>ª</td><td>«</td><td>¬</td><td></td><td>®</td><td>¯</td></tr>
<tr><td>B</td><td>°</td><td>±</td><td>²</td><td>³</td><td>´</td><td>µ</td><td>¶</td><td>·</td><td>¸</td><td>¹</td><td>º</td><td>»</td><td>¼</td><td>½</td><td>¾</td><td>¿</td></tr>
<tr><td>C</td><td>À</td><td>Á</td><td>Â</td><td>Ã</td><td>Ä</td><td>Å</td><td>Æ</td><td>Ç</td><td>È</td><td>É</td><td>Ê</td><td>Ë</td><td>Ì</td><td>Í</td><td>Î</td><td>Ï</td></tr>
<tr><td>D</td><td>Ð</td><td>Ñ</td><td>Ò</td><td>Ó</td><td>Ô</td><td>Õ</td><td>Ö</td><td>×</td><td>Ø</td><td>Ù</td><td>Ú</td><td>Û</td><td>Ü</td><td>Ý</td><td>Þ</td><td>ß</td></tr>
<tr><td>E</td><td>à</td><td>á</td><td>â</td><td>ã</td><td>ä</td><td>å</td><td>æ</td><td>ç</td><td>è</td><td>é</td><td>ê</td><td>ë</td><td>ì</td><td>í</td><td>î</td><td>ï</td></tr>
<tr><td>F</td><td>ð</td><td>ñ</td><td>ò</td><td>ó</td><td>ô</td><td>õ</td><td>ö</td><td>÷</td><td>ø</td><td>ù</td><td>ú</td><td>û</td><td>ü</td><td>ý</td><td>þ</td><td>ÿ</td></tr>
</table>

Figure 18.35 Characters of the ISO 8859-1 Code Page (Latin-1)

The top area of Figure 18.35 shows the characters of the US7ASCII code page, which is also part of all other code pages. Technically, a single code page can thus only properly map the languages of one language group. All other characters that are not included, such as α (expressed as xE1 in ISO 8859-7), require a separate, additional code page to be displayed.

Several code pages installed in parallel starting with SAP ERP 3.1I were the method chosen to meet the requirements for a global system, under the MDMP (*Multi-Display Multi-Processing*) concept. Every user and sys- MDMP tem process is assigned an ISO code page as an attribute that is either transferred or inherited, for example, when logging in. For additional support, the necessary language-dependent texts are then identified using the SPRAS table field. The technology used in this process, however, can be regarded as a proprietary SAP solution—particularly between ABAP applications and the SAP GUI. This is because the SAP GUI passes a logon language to the ABAP server and can transfer characters that were returned to the GUI, such as texts of a wrong code page, without manipulation. Because this is not possible with applications that run using a web browser, there is risk of data corruption.

Internet communication

Because of its advantages regarding the use of XML, Java, and HTML, Unicode has become the code page for Internet communication. This, in turn, also intensifies the use of Unicode in SAP systems for smooth data exchanges. Currently, new installations that are based on SAP NetWeaver 7.0 and higher are thus delivered only in Unicode. When you upgrade systems with only one code page to products based on SAP NetWeaver 7.0, using Unicode is not mandatory, but it is recommended. However, this does not apply to upgrades for MDMP systems. These have to be converted to Unicode after the upgrade and before live operations are started, unless you sign a disclaimer waiving your right to any claims against SAP in case of data inconsistencies that may occur as a result of its use.

If a system is not directly installed as a Unicode system, SAP enables Unicode conversion based on the system copy that was originally used for OS and/or DB migrations. First, existing database content is exported to a database-independent format and simultaneously converted to Unicode. This data is then imported to a newly installed Unicode database instance. In contrast to an OS/DB migration, for the Unicode conversion a vocabulary must also be created. The export tools can then convert the characters properly on the basis of this vocabulary. Furthermore, all ABAP programs must comply with the strict rules of the Unicode syntax check. The book *Unicode in SAP-Systemen* by N. Bürckel, A. Davidenkoff, and D. Werner (SAP PRESS, 2007) provides more information on these steps and the necessary adaptations with regard to the different interface categories.

[+] Because the same tools are used for Unicode conversion and OS/DB migrations, the conversion to Unicode provides an excellent opportunity to combine a platform or database change with the Unicode project.

The Unicode capability of SAP systems is provided as part of SAP Web AS 6.10 (with the exception of z/OS; there, Unicode is available only as of SAP NetWeaver AS 6.40). SAP Note 79991 lists the availability for the various SAP products that are based on these systems. This holds true, for example, for ERP SAP R/3 Enterprise 4.7 2.00 or for SAP BW 3.5; SAP NetWeaver XI 3.0 or SAP EP 6.0 are only available as Unicode versions. If a release is released for Unicode, all subsequent releases are also automatically released for Unicode.

As a result, with R/3 4.6C, for example, you must upgrade to a Unicode-enabled release prior to the Unicode conversion. Because of the restrictions described previously for MDMP systems, a direct upgrade to SAP ERP 6.0 is generally not recommended. Instead, you should first upgrade to SAP R/3 Enterprise 4.7 2.00 and then perform the Unicode conversion before upgrading to SAP ERP 6.0.

Unicode conversion steps

What actions are necessary for the entire Unicode conversion? The export and import of the database described previously are the last steps in a chain of various work packages for the conversion project. Figure 18.36 provides an overview of the activities that are part of a Unicode conversion project.

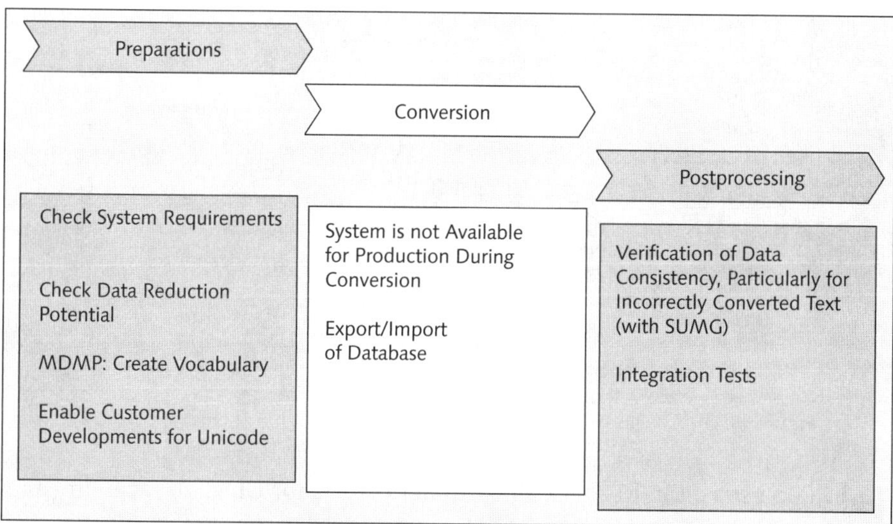

Figure 18.36 Overview of the Activities of a Unicode Conversion Project

Unicode preparations

When, within the scope of the preparations, the basic conditions such as released operating system and database combinations are checked, you should also check whether you can reduce the amount of data, for example, via archiving. Especially with very large databases, this lets you reduce the runtime—and thus the system downtime—to a great extent.

You also must adapt all customer programs so that they comply with the strict rules of the Unicode syntax check. Depending on the number of customer developments, this may involve several weeks of adaptation work. To support you in adapting the programs, SAP developed Transaction UCCHECK (see Figure 18.37). In this transaction, the respective correction notes are added to the faulty objects, and you can navigate from this transaction to the ABAP Workbench to implement the corrections.

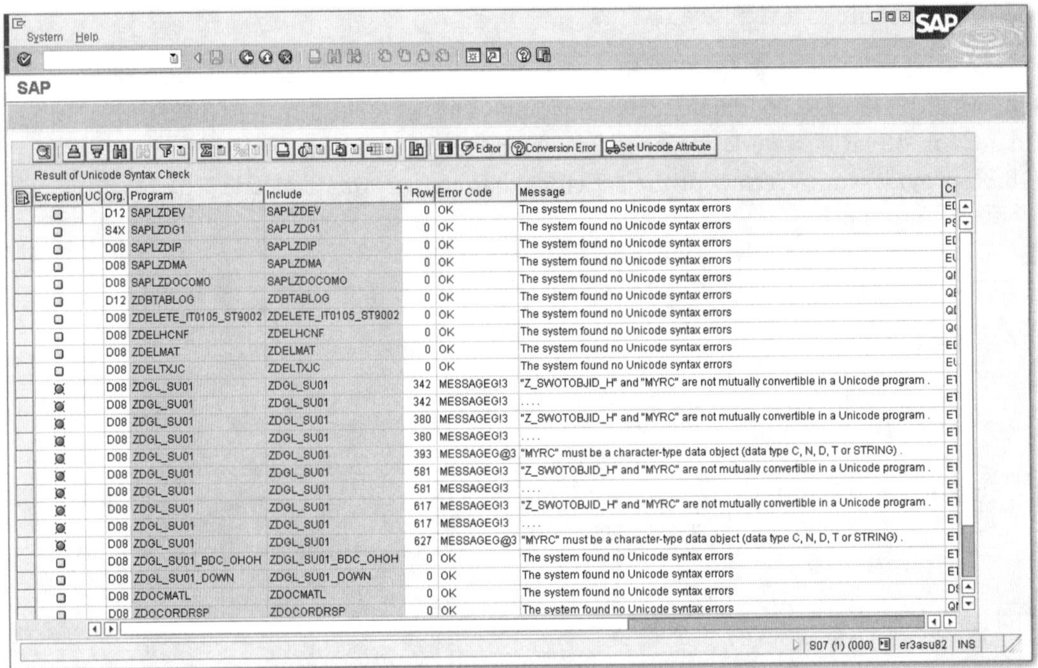

Figure 18.37 Checks with Transaction UCCHECK

[+] Because you must check all customer objects for Unicode capability and adapt them, in this context, it is useful to delete unnecessary or unused objects.

Even if you implement an upgrade project without Unicode conversion, you can and should make the adaptations within SPDD or SPAU with regard to their Unicode capability. You will then not have to adapt these objects in a subsequent Unicode project. [+]

Figure 18.38 is a graphical representation of the steps of a Unicode Conversion project that will now be explained in more detail. To prepare an MDMP system, you must also execute Transaction SPUMG or SPUM4. These transactions perform consistency checks and categorize the tables. They also check all areas of the database that are not uniquely identified by a language key. These checks then create a system vocabulary that is required for correctly assigning texts during the database export. However, before the vocabulary can be used, you must first assign the correct language key to the vocabulary, either automatically or manually.

R3load

During the initial step of the Unicode conversion, the `R3load` tool uses the previously created vocabulary to write the entire content of the database to the file system. In the next step, `R3load` imports the data to a database converted to Unicode. Because these export and import activities may take several hours, particularly for large databases, you should check and optimize the options for acceleration in test systems before implementing them in the production system. These options are provided in the context of a parallelization of `R3load` or when using multiple tools, such as Table Split.

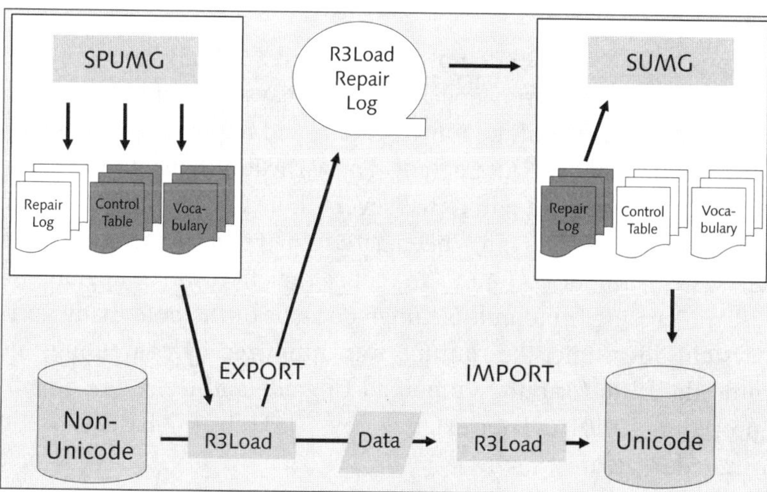

Figure 18.38 Concept of an SAP Unicode Conversion

After the import, you must perform certain post-processing steps before you can release the system to end users. Specifically, this includes processing pool tables, adapting system parameters, and post-processing incorrectly converted texts using Transaction SUMG. In this context, you must first perform the automatic repairs of the SPUMG reprocess logs before you can manually process the corrections.

Combining the processes that were described previously as relevant for a Unicode conversion together with an upgrade may result in very long system downtimes due to the possibly long runtimes for the preparatory steps and the actual conversion.

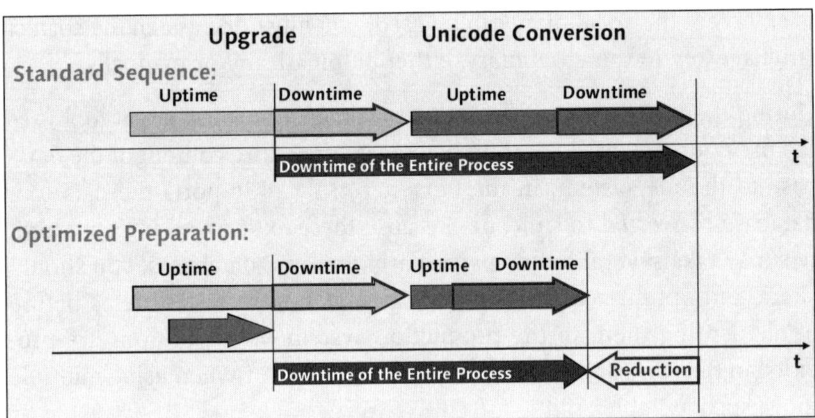

Figure 18.39 Activity Sequence of an Upgrade and a Unicode Conversion

The arrows in Figure 18.39 do not necessarily realistically represent the actual runtimes of the various phases. For SAP systems with a database size of 1 terabyte, the runtime for the export and import is often longer than the runtime for the SAP upgrade. For MDMP systems, the vocabulary creation may take an additional several hours or even days. Based on customer data analyses it has been determined that a large number of MDMP systems run on R/3 4.6C. To reduce the effort for an upgrade to SAP ERP 6.0 arising from multiple upgrade steps or the potentially very long system downtime, the runtime was optimized by combining the two procedures (to form the Combined Upgrade and Unicode Conversion procedure [CU&UC, later extended by TU&UC]). The basic concept is illustrated in Figure 18.39.

The book *SAP NetWeaver Application Server Upgrade Guide* by B. Vanstechelman, M. Mergaerts, and D. Matthys (SAP PRESS, 2007) contains a detailed description of all of the activities required for these procedures.

18.6.1 CU&UC

The CU&UC procedure (see Figure 18.40) was developed for the SAP R/3 4.6C upgrade. In this context, porting Transaction SPUMG into Release R/3 4.6C—which is executed as SPUM4—was the adaptation that had to be made. The system vocabulary can now be generated directly in the production system.

Because Transaction SPUM4 is imported to the system using the tool import of PREPARE and the vocabulary checks may take several days, you must execute PREPARE as early as possible. This is particularly relevant because database checks in the production system with SPUM4 may involve additional load. [+]

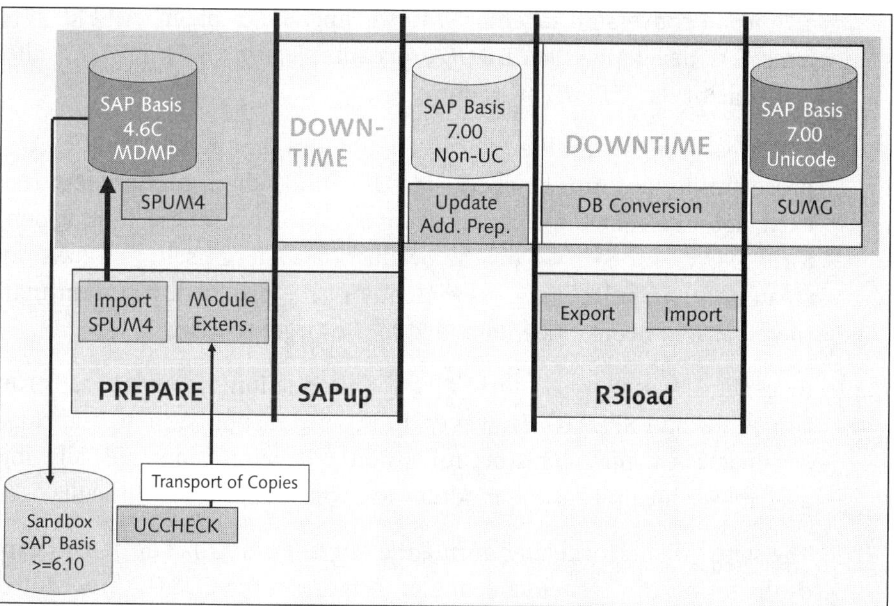

Figure 18.40 Overview of the Technology for the CU&UC Procedure

UCCHECK

Transaction UCCHECK is a critical transaction of the Unicode conversion that cannot be ported. As a result, you must make the changes to customer developments in a system that runs at least SAP Web AS 6.10. This system is usually created from a system copy of the development system that is then upgraded to the target release. The corrections implemented in this system are later provided as a transport of copies to the system that should be upgraded.

SAPup, which was also adapted, can then integrate these transports into the upgrade. It also creates the required Unicode runtime objects before downtime and ensures that the upgrade and Unicode steps are synchronized.

18.6.2 TU&UC

As already mentioned, Transaction SPUMG is responsible for creating the system vocabulary. However, it cannot be ported to systems lower than SAP R/3 4.6C, because the required object-oriented ABAP programming elements are only available as of this release. To be able to perform a Unicode conversion together with the upgrade of older SAP ERP systems, SAP developed the CU&UC procedure. Figure 18.41 illustrates the principle of the TU&UC procedure.

Because a system with the target release is also required for the CU&UC procedure to perform the checks via UCCHECK, the procedure lets you exchange different information using SAPup. Because you cannot perform SPUMG or SPUM4 on the production system itself, you have to create the vocabulary in a system copy of the production system that therefore first needs to be upgraded to the target release.

[+] In general, you can also just copy the production system to perform UCCHECK and SPUMG. However, in the production system, and thus also in its copy, version history for customer developments is usually not available, which makes the modification adjustment more difficult.

The steps you perform later during the upgrade and Unicode conversion of the production system are similar to those of the CU&UC procedure. In the PREPARE and upgrade processes, the objects that were enabled for Unicode syntax and the events of the vocabulary check are integrated before Unicode conversion takes place.

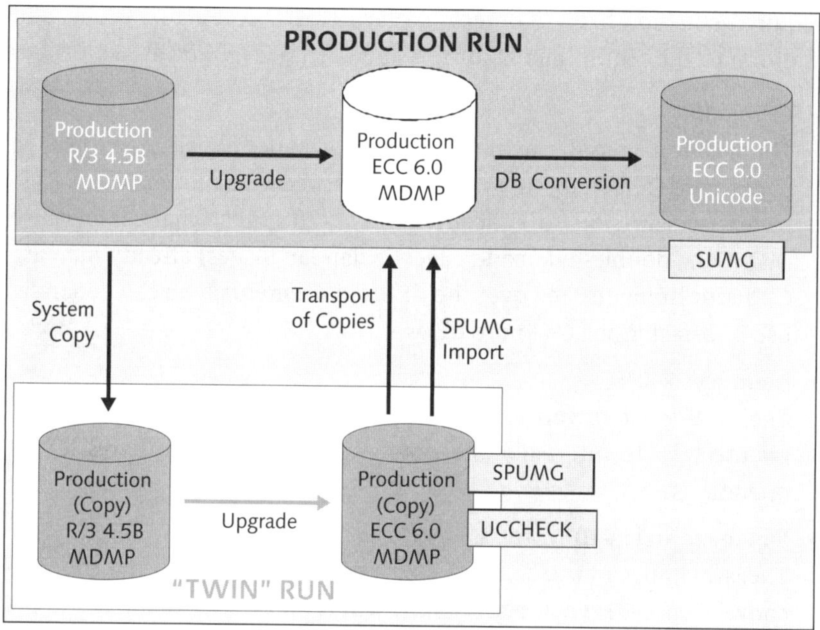

Figure 18.41 Overview of the TU&UC Technology

The disadvantage of the TU&UC procedure that arises from creating a system copy of the production system is also an advantage, compared with the CU&UC procedure. In contrast to the ported SPUM4, SPUMG has more comprehensive options for setting the language key. Furthermore, the creation of the vocabulary in a system copy involves no additional system load in the production system. [+]

When creating the system vocabulary during the TU&UC procedure, you must keep in mind that the twin system is older than the production system at the time of the upgrade. This leads to some differences in the dataset that may also lead to more manual processing efforts after the Unicode conversion with Transaction SUMG.

18.6.3 Unicode Hardware Requirements

Aside from the additional activities you have to perform for the Unicode conversion, you also have to ensure that sufficient hardware resources are provided. For the different areas, the average additional hardware requirements you have to determine for CU&UC or TU&UC projects in addition to the requirements for the upgrade are as follows:

Additional hardware requirements

- **CPU: +30%**
  The additional requirement for CPU performance depends on the code pages used before the upgrade. For systems with one installed code page, a conversion to Unicode involves the most changes because MDMP or double-byte code pages (Asian languages) already increase CPU requirements. To cover the CPU requirements, you can generally use 30% faster or 30% more CPUs.
- **Memory: +50%**
  The additional memory is required because SAP application servers use UTF-16 internally and now require at least two bytes for all operations.
- **Database size: +10 ... +60%**
  The large range of the database size increase as a result of the Unicode conversion has several reasons. Growth is greater for smaller systems (< 250 GB) and, independent of the database size, there is the factor of the Unicode encoding of the database itself. Databases that use UTF-8, such as IBM DB2/UDB or Oracle, increase in size only slightly; IBM DB2/iSeries or DB2/zOS with UTF-16, however, have a rather high database growth. Another factor is whether you used a 1-byte or 2-byte code page and how the characters are distributed between the ASCII area and the code page-specific characters. However, after the Unicode conversion is completed, the database size often decreases, independent of the conversion. This is due to the export/import procedure used and the resulting reorganization of the data.
- **Network (SAP GUI): no changes**
  No changes arise from the compression that is used for the communication between the application server and the frontend via the SAP GUI protocol.
- **Network (backend side): +30%**
  In contrast to the SAP GUI communications, data transfer between the application servers takes place based on UTF-16. This results in additional requirements similar to the additional memory require-

ments. For the communication between the application server and the database, the requirement for network bandwidth (as mentioned for the change of database size) depend on the Unicode encoding used for the database system.

18.6.4 Unicode Transports

During a conversion project—with or without upgrades—it is often necessary to perform transports between Unicode and non-Unicode systems. Although these transports are generally possible, you must keep in mind certain restrictions:

- **Transports from Unicode to non-Unicode**
  This may be the case, for example, when, because of urgent maintenance tasks, changes must be transported from a development system that has already been converted to Unicode into a test or production system that has not yet been converted. Problems may arise when the Unicode characters in the target code page are not supported, for example, if a Russian character is transported into a system on which only the Latin-1 code page is installed. These characters are usually converted into the hash sign (#).
- **Transports from MDMP to Unicode and vice versa**
  As is also the case with data transfer via other interfaces, conversion-related problems may arise with language-independent data in this scenario. Language-independent data is data that is contained in tables without the SPRAS language key. Using the Charset parameter, as described in SAP Note 80727, you can define which basis should be used for transports to convert the data. However, for this you may need to update the `R3trans` program. In this scenario, unknown characters are also converted into hash signs.
- **Transports from Unicode** to **a system lower than SAP Web AS 6.10**
  Transports from Unicode systems to systems <= 4.6D are currently not technically possible.
- **Transports from a system lower than SAP Web AS 6.10 to Unicode**
  Transports from, for example, an SAP R/3 4.6C system to a Unicode system such as SAP ERP 6.0, are generally possible. For the import,

the system sets the Unicode flag automatically so that the Unicode syntax check is automatically carried out for these objects. However, this may also lead to problems because these objects are not necessarily Unicode-enabled and thus might not run in the Unicode system.

[+] When upgrades and Unicode are combined, in addition to the issues already mentioned, problems arising from transports between different SAP releases may occur. As a result, as already described, you should not perform transports between different release and code page statuses.

SAP Notes 80727, 330267, 638357, and 775114 provide information and updates for the problems discussed.

18.7 Java Upgrade

SAP NetWeaver 7.0 is the first development that enables an SAP upgrade of a Java instance. For this purpose, however, the starting release must be SAP NetWeaver '04 Support Package Stack 9 or any SAP product that is based on this Java instance. The deployed upgrade tool, `SAPJup`, uses—to the extent possible—the technologies you already know from the upgrade tool for ABAP instances, `SAPup`.

SAPJup

`SAPJup` is characterized by options to protect customer data or other application data configured in the J2EE Engine or to adapt it to the new release (see Figure 18.42). You can also integrate with the upgrade SAP Support Packages and modified Java archives—for example, from third-party suppliers—for the target release to avoid retroactive installation work. For SAP Support Packages, equivalence information among the different releases is checked to avoid older software statuses in the system that were implemented with the upgrade. In addition to this, `SAPJup` automatically identifies the installable technical usages to determine the correct software packages for the target release. These usages cannot be compared with those of SAP NetWeaver '04: For example, Technical Usage EP contains the KMC, UWLJWF, and CAF GP packages in addition to EP.

Similar to the ABAP upgrade, the Java upgrade only upgrades the central instance to the new release. You have to manually stop the application servers involved in the upgrade and update them to the new version with SAPinst after the upgrade has been carried out.

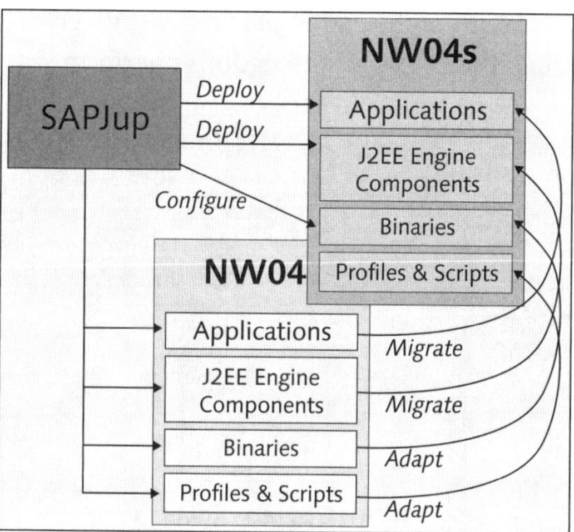

Figure 18.42 SAPJup Activities

To control SAPJup, a user interface called Java SDT GUI is available. It is similar to the SAPup upgrade wizard but does not distinguish between roles, such as observer and administrator. Furthermore, it only allows for one GUI connection.

Overall, a Java upgrade is much easier to implement than an ABAP upgrade and usually also requires less time. After preparations are completed, the main task of SAPJup is to deploy the new software components. Because modification adjustments and activation of data Dictionary elements are not necessary for this upgrade, the process does not require a shadow instance.

Synchronized upgrade

For dual-stack systems (that is, systems with a combination of ABAP and Java instances), upgrade procedures are synchronized. See Figure 18.43 for an overview of the tools that are involved. In this case, you must perform both the PREPARE and the upgrade activity. To ensure synchronization, you must start the ABAP upgrade first. The steps then usually run in the corresponding instance independent of each other; only three steps have to be performed in parallel. However, this is ensured by the automatic adjustment. This applies to the start of downtime, for example. If SAPJup reaches downtime, it does not continue its work until SAPup reaches downtime as well. Another critical point is the kernel switch executed by SAPup. Here, both upgrade tools must reach the respective phase before the kernel is switched. Finally, at the end of the upgrade, when the profile parameters are modified, the last synchronization is performed.

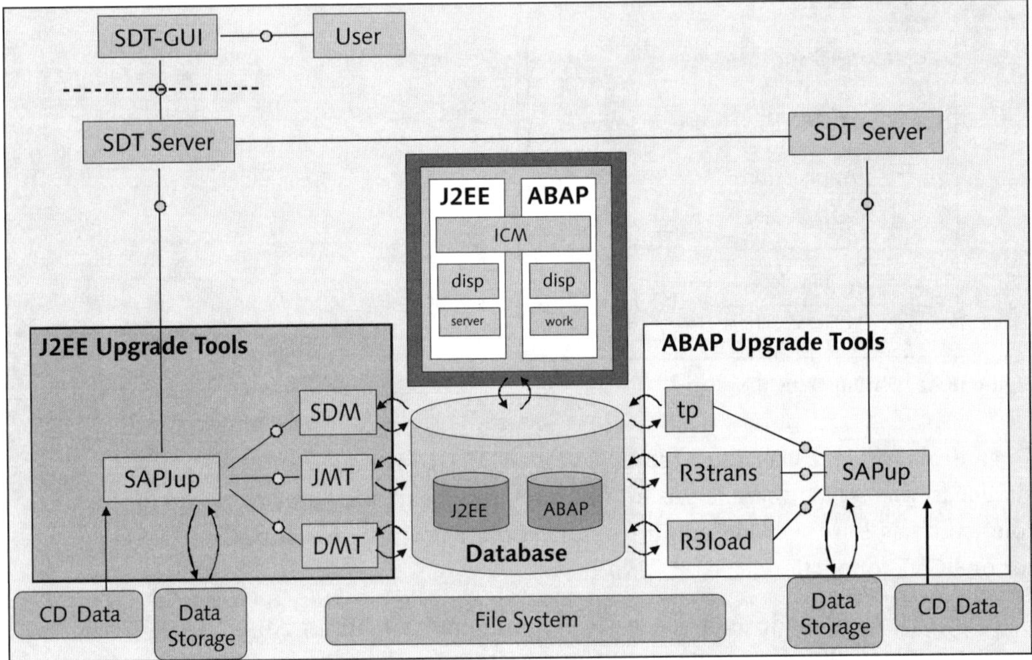

Figure 18.43 Interaction of the Upgrade Tools for ABAP and Java

You can find general information about the Java upgrade in the upgrade guide in the SAP Service Marketplace at *http://service.sap.com/upgradenw2004s*. This guide provides preparatory steps for the implementation of the Java upgrade, for example, checking the Java Development Kit version used, as well as the memory and virtual machine settings.

To prepare for the Java upgrade, proceed as follows (this example uses a Unix system):

1. Log on to the system as user <sid>adm.
2. Copy the Java Upgrade Master CD to a subdirectory such as /sapcd/UPGMSTR_JAVA.
3. Create the /USR/SAP/JUPGRADE Java upgrade directory and navigate to this directory using the cd /USR/SAP/JUPGRADE command.

4. Decompress the fixbuffer for the Java upgrade using the `SAPCAR -xvf <fixbuffer>.SAR` command; this creates a UPG and an INFO file required by `JPREPARE`.
5. Start Java `PREPARE` using the `/sapcd/UPGMSTR_JAVA/JPREPARE` command. `JPREPARE` creates the fixbuffer and additional files in the /USR/SAP/JUPGRADE directory and outputs a message that the SDT server can now log on to <host>/<address>.
6. Start the respective user interface via *http://Host:6239* (port 6239 is the default location, which can be customized with <http-PORT> in the /USR/SAP/JUPGRADE/SERVER/SDTSERVER.XML file) and by clicking the START J2EE UPGRADE FRONTEND link. The system opens a Java Web Start popup window that displays the actual SDT GUI. See Figure 18.44 for an overview of the tools and standard ports being used.

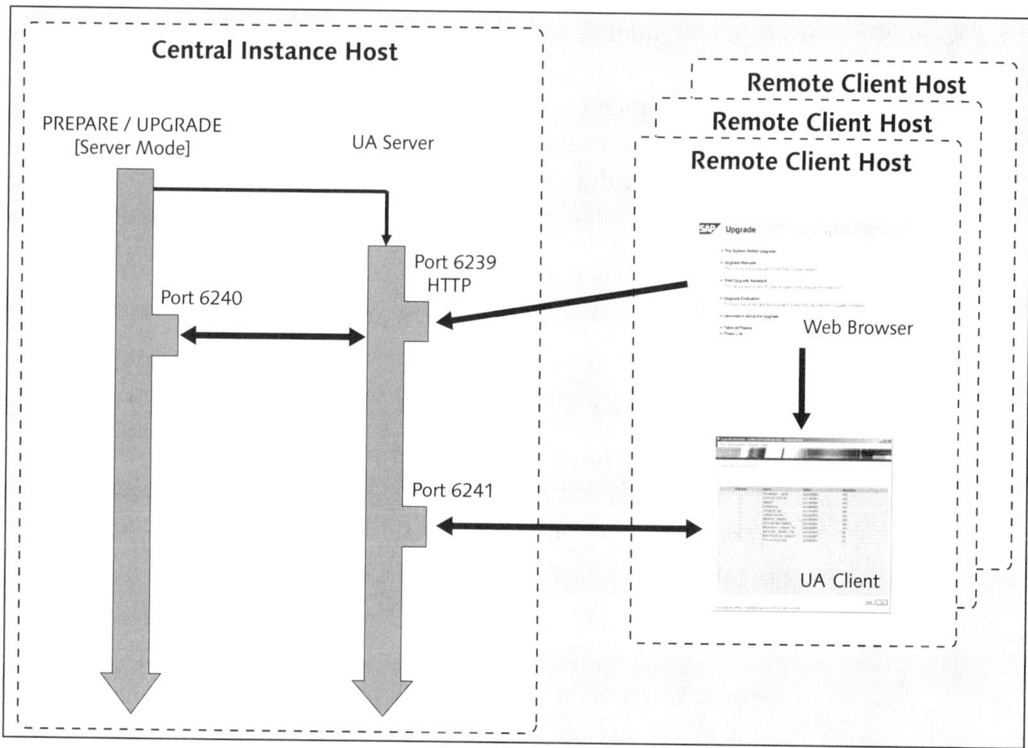

Figure 18.44 User Interface for SAPJup, Including the Technical Components

Java PREPARE

Similar to ABAP PREPARE, Java PREPARE consists of several modules that check the source release, collect the required software—such as upgrade CDs and SAP Support Packages for the upgrade—and evaluate the target configuration. They are as follows:

- INITIALIZATION and EXTRACTION are used to enter system data, for example, SID, system SID, the password for the SAP superuser, the CD mount points, the upgrade password, and the SAP Solution Manager key.
- IN CONFIGURATION, the target system is adapted by selecting the corresponding SAP Support Packages. These SCAs are searched in the DIR_TRANS/EPS/in directory and provided for selection in the SDT GUI.
- GENERAL CHECKS and FINALIZATION check certain system requirements, such as the JDK version that should be used by the target release.

Steps for the SAP Java upgrade

As already mentioned, the steps for the Java upgrade are much easier. You should not start with the downtime steps until all user activities have come to an end and the database and the upgrade directory have been backed up. For dual-stack upgrades, the ABAP upgrade must have reached the downtime phase and the central instance needs to be isolated. Proceed as follows:

1. Stop all J2EE dialog instances.
2. Log on to the system as user <sid>adm.
3. Navigate to the /USR/SAP/JUPGRADE/EXE UPGRADE DIRECTORY.
4. Call the upgrade program via ./UPGRADE.
5. When the program starts, the system prompts you to start the SDT GUI. Do so via *http://Hostname:6239* and by clicking the START J2EE UPGRADE FRONTEND link (through which the actual SDT GUI is started).
6. Start the Java upgrade by selecting CONTINUE.
7. SAPJup now exchanges the central elements, for example, the SAP kernel and SDM, before continuing with the different deployment steps. In this process, first the J2EE Engine core module, followed by the database and file system modules, are replaced before the offline deployment, online deployment, and additional components added by JPREPARE are executed using the SDM. For this purpose, SAPJup starts and stops the J2EE Engine as necessary.

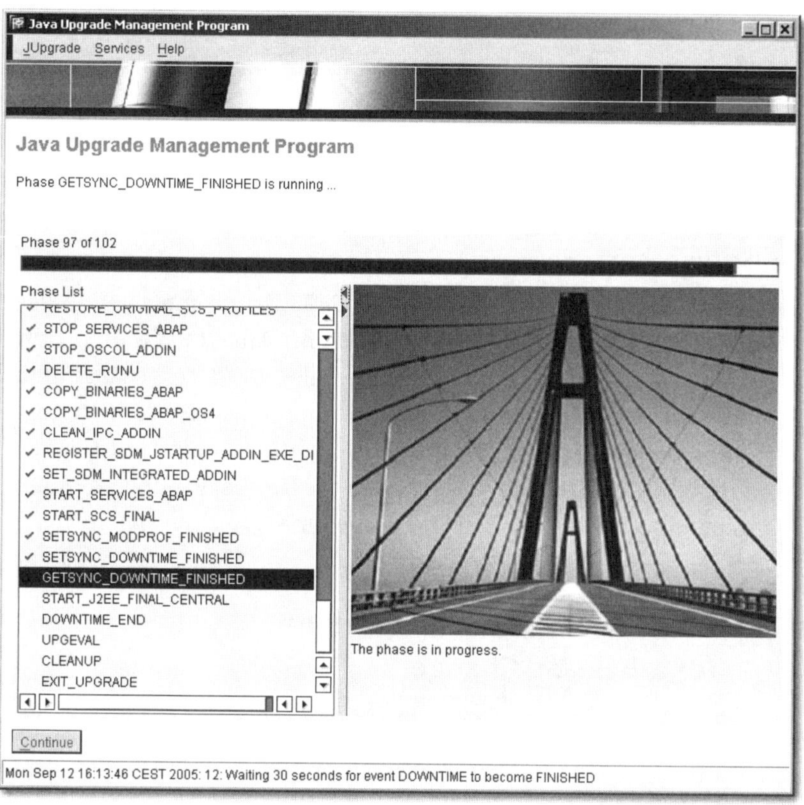

Figure 18.45 Processing the Upgrade Phases of SAPJup

The following steps are performed (see Figure 18.45 for a screenshot of an example process step):

- Stopping the system
- Deactivating the UME user data to ensure that the SAP* user is the only user that can access the system
- Updating the kernel, SAP MMC (Windows only), IGS, and SDM
- Undeploying and deploying SLOT1 (file system deployment)
- Undeploying and deploying SLOT2 (database deployment)
- Adapting the profiles and the J2EE Engine start sequence
- Undeploying and deploying SLOT3 (offline deployment)
- Migrating the J2EE Engine core data (Java migration toolkit)

- Starting the system in safe mode
- Undeploying and deploying SLOT4 (online deployment)
- Starting the application migration (application migration container)
- Stopping the system
- Reactivating the original UME user data
- Starting the system
- At the end of the Java upgrade, the SDT GUI prompts you to back up the database and file system content. After this, the post-processing steps, such as installing the dialog instances, changing the password of the J2EE administrator due to stricter security regulations, updating SLD content, and additional steps must be performed. These steps are described in the NetWeaver upgrade guide, depending on the product and usage type.

18.8 Additional Recommendations for a Release Change

After the rather technical descriptions of the previous sections, this section introduces general recommendations for carrying out a release change and provides an overview of useful tools and services.

18.8.1 Upgrade Tools and SAP Upgrade Service Offers

Upgrade project phase DISCOVERY and EVALUATION

As already mentioned in the introductory section about upgrades, not only technical aspects need to be considered during an upgrade project. The course for the project is set long before the upgrade program is started for the first time. Here, the general rule applies as well: An SAP upgrade project is a "real" project and should be planned carefully.

In the customer survey mentioned previously (see Section 18.1.2), customers were also asked about the challenges during the planning phase of an upgrade. It turned out that customers have problems especially when it comes to finding the right time for an upgrade. They also frequently have difficulties estimating both the effort and costs involved (see Figure 18.46). Naturally, challenges vary depending on the level of knowledge and experience. After you have carried out an upgrade project for the first time and ensured that it was well documented, you can produce a good estimate for another upgrade project based on this data, even though the volume or the system landscape that will be changed will not always be directly comparable.

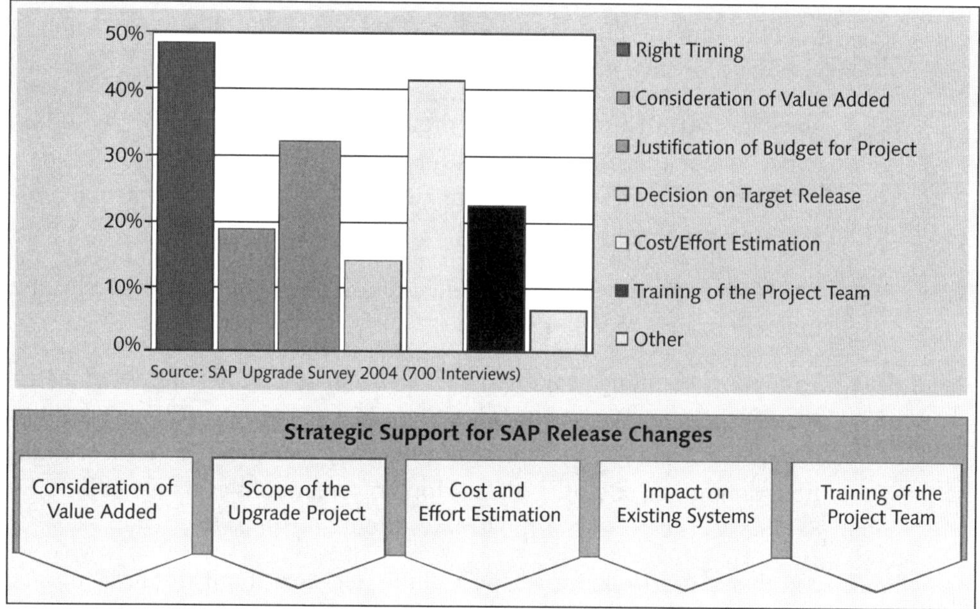

Figure 18.46 Challenges Before the Start of an Upgrade Project

Among SAP customers, the following procedure has proven to be a best practice for the discovery process:

- Collecting preparatory documents from the IT department, for example, by participating in SAP events or searching for information in the SAP Service Marketplace
- Together, the IT department and the representatives of the various business areas evaluate the options the new release provides. For this purpose, SAP delivers the SAP Solution Browser, a tool that provides support for the evaluation of new functions, particularly in SAP

ERP Solution Browser

ERP 6.0. The SAP Service Marketplace provides more information on this topic at *www.service.sap.com/upgrade* • UPGRADE TOOLS • SAP ERP SOLUTION BROWSER.

- The new functions are analyzed using additional details with regard to their value for the business processes. If required, you can also obtain specific information in delta workshops.
- A demo system, which you can set up, for example, in a sandbox environment, allows you to test the functions in detail without side effects for the existing system.

[+] You can obtain comprehensive information (for example, on the effort expected for the modification adjustment and the application adaptation) when you create a sandbox system before you start the actual project. This improves planning of the real upgrade project.

The IT and user departments define the costs, risks, and procedure of the upgrade project together.

SAP Upgrade Experience Database

To support planning, it is often useful to obtain reference values or statistics of other customers' upgrades. The SAP Upgrade Experience Database provides information on planning-relevant data, such as project duration, downtime, and other data. More information is available in the SAP Service Marketplace at *http://service.sap.com/upgradedb*.

Another critical planning aspect is the decision about the best time to implement the project. In this context, as already mentioned, uninterrupted, standard support as part of the 5-1-2 maintenance needs to be considered. However, the maintenance dates for the operating system and database or pending hardware maintenance should also be examined. The analysis of the system that should be upgraded is not the only relevant aspect; the planning of larger projects in your enterprise, such as roll outs or system consolidations, should also be taken into account.

Upgrade project phase for executing the upgrade

After all decisions have been made during the upgrade project preparation phase, the upgrade is performed. The survey mentioned previously also covered questions about problematic areas during the execution of the upgrade, which led to the results shown in Figure 18.47.

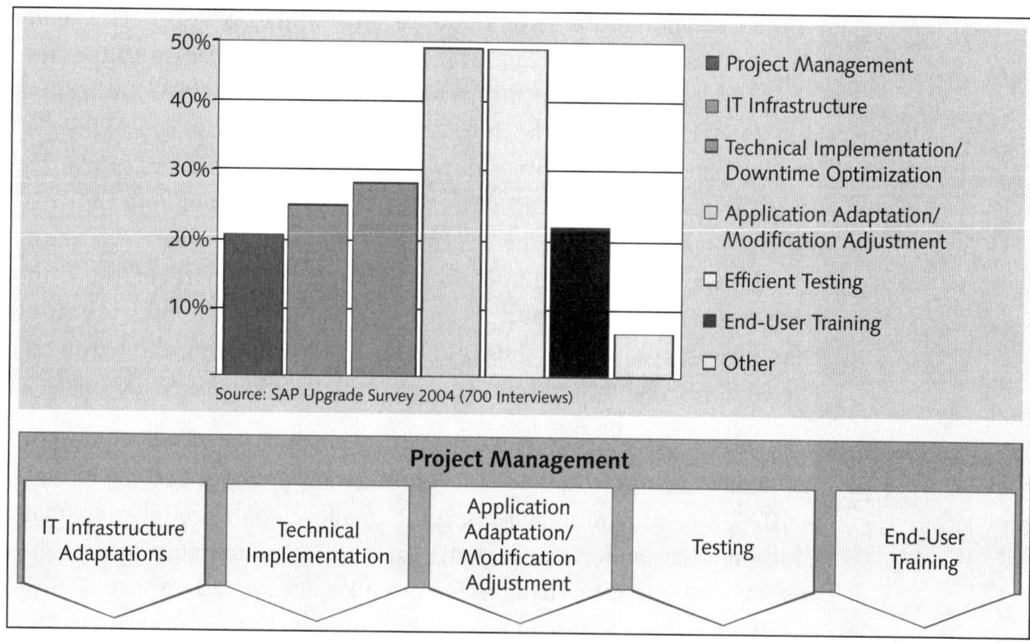

Figure 18.47 Challenges During the Execution of a Release change

You can see that the areas of testing and modification adjustment or customizing the application required the greatest effort and therefore usually incurred the highest costs, even exceeding the areas of end-user training and additional hardware purchases. As a result of this survey, SAP also combined appropriate tools and services to support you individually in the most important areas. We will now explain these areas in detail.

IT infrastructure

Especially if several interim releases were skipped, it is often necessary during a release change to upgrade the hardware as well. Adapting the hardware can also influence the decision on the upgrade timing if, for example, specific leasing contracts exist. With regard to the IT infrastructure, the database and application server hardware is considered first. Additional hardware requirements are often derived from increasing the functionality used in a new release. This implies an adaptation not only for the SAP software, but also for the operating system and database software. You can obtain initial information by carrying out a Quick Sizing project. Note that this can only be considered an approximation because the Quick Sizer calculates its workload in SAPS based on the document volume or the expected number of users. The actual usage of the system and the projection of the current data to the new release are only possible using an Analysis Session of the SAP Going Live Functional Upgrade Check (short: SAP GLFU). For this purpose, the system load is calculated from a download of your system and converted using the appropriate factors. This allows an evaluation of both the existing and planned servers for coverage of the expected load. Therefore, the SAP GLFU should be booked well in advance—particularly, if the system already shows poor performance in its starting release—to be able to react accordingly during the project by adapting the hardware. The GLFU can be ordered directly from the SAP Service Marketplace at *http://service.sap.com/servicecat*.

[+] SAP Notes such as Note 778774, *Hardware Requirements ECC 5.0* or Note 901070, *Hardware Requirements ECC 6.0*, allow you to roughly estimate additional hardware requirements for a technical upgrade project that arise during a release change. For example, an upgrade from R/3 4.6C to ERP ECC 6.0 leads to additional requirements of approximately 55% more memory and approximately 22% more CPU capacity.

Frontend

In addition to server changes, it is often necessary to replace the frontend PCs. This is, in part, a result of the demands on CPU speed or main memory to enable the display of enhanced User Interfaces. In addition, it results from the necessity to install a new operating system version with increased hardware requirements on the PCs. Another aspect to consider is the network infrastructure between the application server and frontend PCs. Especially as of the changes introduced with Release R/3 4.6C, and thereby enhancing usability—keyword "Enjoy SAP"—there is an increase in the network load. Unlike before, when parts of lists were transferred to the PC and every scroll operation in these lists required new processing on the application server, the entire list is now on the PC and scrolling takes place there as well. In addition, many transactions that used to be executed using several dialog box steps have been converted to control-based transactions in which much of the required additional information is available right from the start. Thus, the network load of a transaction can increase, on average, from 3 to 4 KB to 6 to 9 KB. If instead of the SAP GUI for Windows, the SAP GUI for HTML is used, via the Internet Transaction Server (ITS), for example, this value can even be higher. If current network usage is unknown, you can get an estimate using a whitepaper that is provided in the SAP Service Marketplace at *http://service.sap.com/erp-inst*.

Application adaptation

To keep the application adaptation activities to a minimum, this adaptation is carried out to a large degree by the upgrade, for example, in the form of XPRA reports. Additionally, SAP combined the other adaptations in upgrade and delta Customizing. Upgrade Customizing refers to the extensions of Customizing that are necessary due to the improved capabilities of an already existing process step for the new release. Delta Customizing is designed for processes that were newly imported into the system during the release change. Both Customizing activities can easily be filtered in the Customizing IMG. This reduces the adaptation tasks to a minimum. Nevertheless, you should take your time and perform this adaptation in the development system after the upgrade and integrate it in the transport requests. As a result, these supplementations can be easily transferred to the other systems in your system landscape.

Testing

Testing should be considered one of the main efforts in an upgrade project. The more different modules, custom developments, and interfaces are used, the more testing is required. Fortunately, there are several tools and services to assist you.

In SAP NetWeaver 7.0 underlying SAP ERP 6.0, for example, there is a comprehensive Test Workbench, which, when compared to the SAP 4.x Basis releases has been particularly improved in its support of automatic tests. eCATT, an enhancement of the proven CATT, allows you to create automatic test cases for all SAP GUI-based transactions, even if these use control technologies. In addition, the execution of test cases beyond system boundaries has been improved. Therefore, you can now create automatic tests that can verify cross-system business processes. At the same time, this tool can be integrated with the SAP Test Workbench. The Test Workbench now enables the central creation of test plans for different application cases. These test plans can be divided according to various criteria, and smaller work packages can be assigned to different users. After logging on to the workbench, users will find their individual worklist covering both automatic and manual tests. From there, they can start the tests, read corresponding documents such as test case descriptions, and store test results as statuses such as "test successful," "subsequent test required," and so on. Because the statuses can be stored centrally, current evaluations regarding the test process can be created very easily.

Because tests can be stored and validated centrally and the automatic eCATT test cases can be run across system boundaries, you should use the Test Workbench within SAP Solution Manager. The corresponding transport- and upgrade-relevant scenarios you can implement in SAP Solution Manager are described in Chapter 19.

[+] In addition to the already mentioned creation of a sandbox system to support project planning, it has proven to be helpful to create a project test system from a copy of the production system during the upgrade activities. Here, you can test the development adaptations or new functions in end user and regression tests. You should use the dataset that is later available in the production environment for these tests. This type of system also enables you to realistically estimate the expected upgrade downtime.

End user training

The more releases that are skipped in an upgrade and the more new functions that are used or modifications that are replaced with the standard SAP version, the greater the need to train end users in handling the system. This holds especially true if users work in many different locations. Because training in a traditional classroom implies extensive traveling and therefore high costs, it is advisable to train users via the existing network infrastructure using eLearning. SAP provides the SAP Tutor program for this purpose.

SAP Tutor

SAP Tutor lets you create training materials by capturing any Windows-based screen output such as the SAP GUI or web browsers. In addition, texts and interaction fields can be stored along with the recorded screen sequences. Through the texts, task descriptions or explanations, for example, can be added, which can be read aloud by the system using an integrated speech engine. Using the interaction fields, you can edit the images displayed so that you can simulate transactions, data entries, and much more without actually being connected to an SAP system.

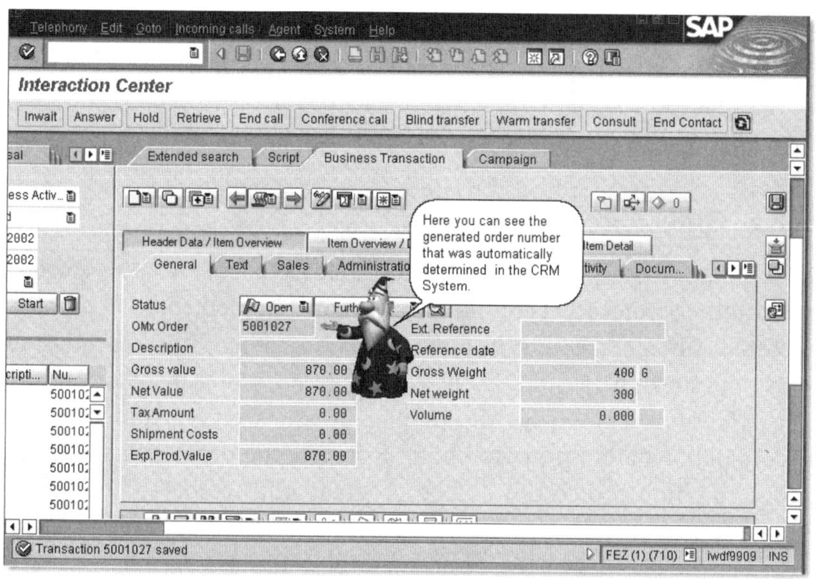

Figure 18.48 Recorded Transaction and Playback Using SAP Tutor

The tutorials you create can also be run in different modes: demo mode, where the entire sequence is run without user entries; practice mode, where the end user is guided through the entries via help texts; and exam mode, where there is no additional help available after an initial task description and where the rate of correct user actions can be evaluated. Figure 18.48 shows a sample training sequence. More information and sample tutorials are available in the SAP Service Marketplace at *http://service.sap.com/saptutor*.

Technical upgrade

The technical upgrade is an expense factor both directly and indirectly. On the one hand, you need to consider the time and the resources necessary to perform the upgrade throughout the entire system landscape. On the other hand, every hour of downtime for the production system means a loss in business activity, which can also be measured in monetary terms.

Upgrade Weekend Support

To minimize the risk of downtime, a service offer exists that aims to provide better support in the event of errors. The Upgrade Weekend Support supports the most critical portion of the upgrade project, that is, the weekend during which the production system is upgraded. For this purpose you are assigned a direct contact from SAP Support. Its task is to accelerate the process of handling messages and finding solutions by forwarding them directly to the correct contact person and by monitoring and returning processing results until the task is completed.

18.8.2 Other Recommendations

Upgrade project

To summarize the previous chapters, a release change can be considered another project that continues the original implementation project. Therefore, an upgrade must be handled like any other project, beginning with roles and responsibilities up to the creation of a detailed project plan. The more knowledge the individual teams retain from working with implementation projects—both regarding the project plan and the implementation and corresponding program adjustments—the easier it will be to perform the upgrade. Note that you have the best chance of ensuring the success of the project during the planning phase of the release change. Aside from the usual planning activities such as defining the desired organization structure or work, resource, and budget plans, the project volume should be accurate from the get go—for example, by executing a parallel archiving project. Such a project would result in a smaller database that can positively affect downtime during the upgrade. On the other hand, as mentioned, an archiving project would be a parallel project, requiring resources and coordination. Furthermore, a new release often provides more comprehensive archiving objects that would ease such work after the upgrade. The decision whether to carry out only a technical upgrade, implement new functionality to the greatest extent possible, or go with something in between these two options has to be weighed carefully.

Unlike with other implementation projects, you have to consider other ancillary conditions during a release change, for example, that you should build up an additional project system landscape for the release change, particularly if the project will span several months. For this purpose, you need to check whether the existing resources in the system administration and development areas are sufficient to ensure both the maintenance of the existing system and that of the new release, or, if you need to include additional consultants in the project. In general, you should assign external resources to the maintenance tasks because after completion of the upgrade project, the related knowledge is often lost when consultants leave. The timing of the development freeze for the upgrade project must be coordinated as thoroughly as possible with other potentially planned projects. The longer the development can be frozen, the easier the project planning for adjustments and tests will be, as well as the project planning for the required landscape.

This duration and the aforementioned planning for the project should be observed because design changes affect the landscape and time and costs increase at a higher rate if short-term adjustments need to be carried out during the implementation if a large team is occupied with the project. Therefore, it is preferable if corrections such as these are incorporated during a small project after the upgrade has been completed.

This also applies to integrating additional Support Packages. Even though the latest version might seem to bring advantages, the changes they introduce into the system landscape can result in new adaptations and tests. Therefore, additional SAP Support Packages or SAP Enhancement Packages should be imported into the upgrade project landscape only if the rest of the project plan (that is, modification adjustment and tests) is matched accordingly. Overall, the upgrade project is easier to perform if fewer requirements were defined and if a minimum of other parallel projects need to be coordinated. But, if these recommendations cannot be adhered to—due to comprehensive modifications that should be reverted to the standard SAP version, or due to many complex interfaces—you should plan project milestones, including time buffers, even more carefully and observe the critical transport route to avoid falling behind schedule.

Especially if you do not perform upgrades on a regular basis, it will almost be inevitable that errors will occur both in the technical execution and in the subsequent tests. It will also be almost inevitable that the adaptation of previous modifications will take longer than scheduled, or that key personnel will not be available due to illness or vacation. If no time buffers exist, the schedule can easily slip. You should also check at the very beginning of the project what steps you can take proactively, irrespective of the actual release change, such as replacing frontend PCs, distributing the SAP GUI, or making other adaptations to the hardware because the hardware delivery could be delayed.

Upgrade tests During the tests, you should ensure that you can work with real data, if possible. Although this is often not required for module tests, the more complex the changes are to the business processes and the more critical the application is, the more you should pay attention to the quality of the test data, and to the volume and level of detail of the test cases. This applies to the tests of business processes and interfaces and, if necessary, also to the downtime test for the upgrade. This is because the QAS system cannot always be compared to the PRD system in a way that allows the tests to provide meaningful results. In addition, it is advisable to prepare test cases for validation after the release change to quickly find out whether the upgrade was successful. During the execution of the production upgrade, you can no longer run extensive test series; these tests must have been completed successfully beforehand.

Upgrade method On the technical side, it is recommended that you read both the upgrade guide and the relevant upgrade notes. The latter should also be checked for changes on a regular basis during the project. Usually, there is a note for every SAP product that refers to the database platform, the underlying system basis, and the product itself. If other software is installed in the system, such as SAP add-ons or third-party products, you need to look for additional documentation on how to proceed with these during an upgrade. Check in the SAP Service Marketplace or with software partners. You should note, however, that these upgrade notes are often only an entry area for related notes, which must all be checked for their relevance to the current project.

In most cases, to reduce the upgrade downtime, you should use the downtime-minimized method. This procedure also enables you to use the incremental table conversion ICNV to schedule certain adaptations in the upgrade uptime. Especially when processing objects that are subject to changes during the upgrade, implementing an archiving project has a positive effect on the runtime.

For selecting the ideal point in time to start the upgrade, we would like to point out the following behavior of the system switch upgrade— the copying of data from technical tables to "shadow tables," done to further reduce downtime. For data consistency reasons, a database trigger is created after the copy process. It is triggered when the data is changed during normal operation, after it has been copied. If a long time passes between the MODPROF_TRANS phase and the start of downtime, the probability increases that these triggers become active and that the data needs to be copied again during downtime. If the schedule is not observed during the upgrade duration test, but user actions similar to those planned later are not carried out and the test upgrade is instead resumed immediately, it is possible that these effects were not detected and that the downtime might be extended accordingly. Depending on the affected table, this can be a matter of minutes or can take up to several hours.

The activities that should be processed prior to the MODPROF_TRANS phase are additional factors that affect the duration of downtime. Primarily, these include the controlled completion of the interfaces and business processes, as well as the strategy for the backup implementation.

After the actual upgrade, you must schedule additional time before you can start live operations again. For this, you must take into account the transport import time, the runtime of mass generations using Transaction SGEN, the latest user department tests, and the final backup.

If downtime is a critical aspect, you should consider it carefully during testing. In fact, the upgrade of the production system should be rather "boring." This can be accomplished with frequent upgrade tests and using an upgrade script created in the tests. You can, for example, base this upgrade script on the upgrade phase list delivered by SAP, where relevant instructions are stored for every required action. Ideally, you should provide screenshots, detailed descriptions, and schedules so that anyone can perform the upgrade if the person responsible for upgrades is sick. Even for the administrator, actions to the production system are not routine, and a system query can easily be confirmed inadvertently at the wrong time, or a high availability solution that had not been previously implemented might not behave as expected.

Therefore, you should have an appropriate emergency plan in place should insurmountable difficulties arise. The "point of no return" at which the upgrade should be completed at the latest—that is, before you have to start a system restore to resume operation on time using the old release—should become just as familiar to all involved as should the telephone numbers of all relevant people or, if necessary, the passwords of the superusers for SAP, the operating system, and the database. The restore operation should also have been tested beforehand to avoid a backup error from being detected during the restore.

SAP provides several services to support you in the various stages of an upgrade project—from planning to execution. They can be found in the SAP Service Marketplace at *http://service.sap.com/upgradeservices*.

18.9 Questions

1. **Which of the following statements are true of the SAP release strategy?**

   A. The 5-1-2 maintenance strategy applies to all SAP products.

   B. New products first go through the ramp-up phase.

   C. During the ramp-up phase, the product is already generally available.

   D. No SAP Support Packages are delivered during the ramp-up phase.

2. **Which of the following statements are correct with regard to release changes?**

   A. The objects in the customer namespace are not overwritten.

   B. A Repository switch replaces your current Repository with the Repository in the new release.

   C. All customer modifications to ABAP Dictionary objects are lost.

   D. The customer modifications to SAP objects that you want to keep must be transferred to the new release using the modification adjustment.

3. **Which of the following statements are true of the modification adjustment?**

   A. Transaction SPAU is used for most of the ABAP Dictionary objects.

   B. Transaction SPDD is used for most of the ABAP Dictionary objects.

C. If Transaction SPDD is not used although it is required, this can lead to data losses.

D. During the modification adjustment, you must revert to the standard SAP version.

4. **Which benefits are provided by the system switch upgrade?**

   A. The system switch upgrade makes a modification adjustment redundant.

   B. The system switch upgrade makes the creation of a backup before the upgrade redundant.

   C. The system switch upgrade shortens the time during which the system cannot be used productively.

   D. The SPDD adjustment can be carried out before the beginning of downtime.

5. **Which of the following statements are true of SAP Enhancement Packages?**

   A. SAP provides Enhancement Packages for all ERP releases, such as SAP R/3 4.6C, SAP R/3 Enterprise, or SAP ERP 6.0.

   B. SAP Enhancement Packages use the switch mechanism of the SAP Enhancement and Switch Framework.

   C. If an SAP Enhancement Package has been imported, you must also update it in further EhP updates.

   D. The delivery of the SAP Enhancement Packages is cumulative, that is, an EhP X+1 package also automatically contains the content of EhP X.

6. **Which of the following statements are true of Unicode and SAP release changes?**

   A. For upgrades to SAP products that are based on SAP NetWeaver 7.0, a change to Unicode is only mandatory for systems with multiple installed code pages.

   B. Transports between different SAP releases are generally not possible if only one release has been converted to Unicode.

C. Using the combined upgrade and Unicode conversion procedures, CU&UC and TU&UC, reduces system downtime considerably.

D. In contrast to upgrades, for Unicode conversions system downtime is directly linked to the database size.

7. **How is an SAP system that uses a J2EE Engine upgraded?**

A. A combination with the ABAP stack installed in parallel is possible and is synchronized by the upgrade tools.

B. The screens to control both the ABAP and the Java upgrade are set up in a similar way and use the same method to communicate with the upgrade tools.

C. In contrast to the ABAP upgrade, you cannot integrate additional software packages or patches.

D. The structure of the J2EE upgrade phase sequence is much simpler than that of the ABAP upgrade because primarily, the J2EE upgrade includes only deployments, not modification adjustments.

SAP Solution Manager is the platform recommended by SAP that supports you in all phases of the product lifecycle to perform different tasks, such as system implementation, maintenance, and release upgrade. This chapter focuses on the areas in which you receive support for transport-related activities.

19 SAP Solution Manager

SAP Solution Manager is a central system for managing and documenting a complex and distributed solution landscape. It supports the entire lifecycle of a software solution—from business blueprint to implementation projects to productive operation. SAP Solution Manager provides access to tools, methods, and preconfigured content. The individual functions of SAP Solution Manager are as follows:

Functions

- **Implementation projects**
  - Creating the business blueprint.
  - Central storage of project documentation, training documents, test cases, and so on.
  - Access to implementation roadmaps and best-practice documents.
- **Customizing Distribution**
  - The Customizing Scout lets you compare Customizing in different SAP components, for example, SAP ERP and SAP Customer Relationship Management (SAP CRM).
  - Customizing Distribution lets you transfer Customizing settings from a source system to a target system and therefore keep the settings consistent.
- **Global rollout**
  - Creating project templates that can be used in a rollout, for example, from the corporate headquarters to the subsidiaries.

- **Test Management**
  - Environment for organizing and performing unit tests subsequent to software changes. Tools to automate test procedures are also available (extended Computer Aided Test Tool, eCATT).
- **E-Learning Management**
  - Creating training materials using SAP Tutor.
  - Distribution of the learning materials in learning maps (computer-aided self-paced trainings) to train end users after software changes, or after a new functionality has been implemented.
- **Solution Monitoring**
  - Monitoring of all connected SAP systems from a central system.
  - Business process-related monitoring. In particular, the transactions, interfaces, and protocols of a specific business process are monitored.
  - Service level reporting.
- **Root cause analysis**
  - The root cause analysis describes how to—in the event of an error—proceed to find and remove disruptions as fast as possible. SAP Solution Manager comprises various tools that are helpful for root cause analysis.
  - These tools are particularly useful in complex landscapes to isolate the component responsible for the problem, for example, the Portal, network, SAP ERP backend, or database. Another important factor is the analysis of performance problems in the Java environment.
  - The following analysis procedures are available: Workload analysis, trace analysis, change analysis, and exception analysis.
  - The Root Cause Analysis application runs on the Java stack of SAP Solution Manager. It is only available if Solution Manager is installed as a dual-stack system.
- **Service Delivery**
  - Access to programs and services that help you optimize your system landscape's performance and availability, and minimize the risks during system operation.

- **Service Desk**
  Workflow for creating and editing problem notifications.
- **Change Management**
  This tool provides a workflow for managing software changes. All changes are clearly documented and Transport Management System (TMS) functions are called in the background. In addition to the organizational procedures of change management, bundling changes in projects and releases is supported in particular.
- **Maintenance Optimizer**
  The Maintenance Optimizer guides you through planning, downloading, and implementing SAP Support Packages and patches for your systems. Moreover, the Maintenance Optimizer allows you to install Enhancement Packages or integrate them in an upgrade to SAP ERP 6.0.

In this chapter, we will describe the SAP Solution Manager functions that are specific to change management. They include the following:

- Customizing Synchronization
- Change Management
- Maintenance Optimizer
- Change Analysis
- Upgrade Support

Before we begin, however, we have to clarify certain central concepts used in SAP Solution Manager.

System landscape

SAP Solution Manager provides a repository for the central storage of your SAP system landscape information. In that repository, you can store all of the required information such as hardware, and OS and database version information, as well as details on systems, software components, and patch statuses. The data can be read from the system landscape directory (SLD), provided the SLD has been configured in your system landscape.

A properly maintained system landscape is an essential prerequisite for the other functions of SAP Solution Manager, such as implementation and template projects, change management, Customizing synchronization, solution monitoring, services, and Service Desk.

You can maintain the system landscape in SAP Solution Manager using Transaction SMSY.

Business processes

You can use the business process function to document the company business processes you want to map in the systems. During the creation of a business blueprint for projects, you set up a project structure in which all relevant business scenarios, processes, and process steps are hierarchically structured. Moreover, you can create project documentation to assign to individual scenarios, processes, or process steps. Furthermore, you can assign transactions to each process step and thus determine the flow of your business processes in the SAP systems.

The business process is a central concept within SAP Solution Manager. Many other functions such as business process monitoring or testing, for example, are based on this concept. You can maintain business processes in Transactions SOLAR01 or SOLAR02.

Projects

In the project management component of SAP Solution Manager (Transaction SOLAR_PROJECT_ADMIN), you can create Solution Manager projects and perform all central administrative project tasks. You can manage several types of projects in SAP Solution Manager, as follows:

- **Implementation project**
  Project for implementing business processes in an SAP landscape.
- **Template project**
  Project for using a template to make your project structure—or parts of it—including assigned objects (documentation, test cases, and IMG activities) available to other projects. You can lock templates—either completely or partially—against changes when they are used in other projects.
- **Upgrade project**
  Project for upgrading existing systems.
- **Optimization project**
  Project for optimizing an existing system. For example, optimization projects can be used in combination with SAP Services.
- **Safeguarding project**
  Project for eliminating a critical state during the implementation or operation of an SAP solution.

- **Maintenance project**
  Project for maintaining a system or system landscape. This project type plays an important role in change management.

Solution

In a solution, you can bundle systems and the appropriate business processes according to your requirements, to monitor your production business processes in live operation using the appropriate systems, and to improve the lifecycle of your most critical business processes. All production systems that constitute the most important core business processes should be included in the same solution. All Solution Manager scenarios relating to the operation of a production solution are assigned to a solution. These scenarios include the following:

- Services and Support
- Solution Monitoring
- Solution Reporting
- Service Desk
- Root Cause Analysis

19.1 Customizing Synchronization

If you operate several SAP components simultaneously in a solution landscape, for example, SAP ERP and SAP CRM, it is often necessary that specific Customizing settings are identical for all systems involved. You can ensure that this is the case using Customizing Synchronization. Areas to be synchronized, among others, can be customer and product groups, sales districts, terms of payment, terms of delivery, picking groups, currencies, countries, regions, and units of measurement.

SAP provides the following two tools that support Customizing Synchronization: Customizing Distribution and the Customizing Scout.

Customizing Distribution

- *Customizing Distribution* transfers Customizing from a source system to a target system. A distinction is made between initial distribution and delta distribution. Delta distribution is used to keep the two systems in a continuously consistent state. Customizing Distribution is a tool that performs various tasks, such as the following:

  - Configuring training, demo, and test systems using the initial distribution of Customizing.
  - Keeping SAP ERP, SAP CRM, and SAP Supply Chain Management (SAP SCM) systems in a synchronous state by using the delta distribution so that cross-component processes can run smoothly.
  - Synchronizing Customizing in different SAP ERP systems to prepare an Application Link Enabling (ALE) distribution of master data.

Customizing Scout

- The *Customizing Scout* is a tool that allows you to perform Customizing comparisons between different systems.

You can use several predefined synchronization objects for both Customizing Distribution and the Customizing Scout. They are Customizing objects that must be stored simultaneously in different components. Furthermore, you can select any transportable Customizing object of the types, *table, view, table including text table, view cluster, individual transaction*, and *logical transport object* for Customizing Synchronization. The Customizing objects, however, must meet several requirements that are described in great detail in the online help.

19.1.1 Customizing Distribution

Customizing Distribution transfers Customizing from a source system (e.g., SAP ERP) to a target system (e.g., SAP CRM). It always takes place between development systems. When the distribution is completed, the changes can be transferred via transport request into the downstream systems of the transport landscape. Customizing Distribution is an enhanced functionality, used primarily for comparisons and distributing Customizing changes with extensive logging options.

In a development landscape, Customizing Distribution enables you to:

- Download Customizing from a source system into a target system for the first time (initial distribution)
- Distribute Customizing in a time-controlled manner
- Distribute Customizing automatically with each transport release or Customizing change (from Release 4.6C)
- Distribute Customizing manually

[+] There can be only one type of distribution active per Solution Manager project and source client, which means that you must decide which type of Customizing Distribution you want to use. The same applies to Customizing Distributions that do not pertain to a particular project.

Predefined Customizing objects

Specific Customizing objects that need to be synchronized frequently are already predefined in the system. These are known as *Synchronization objects*. You can edit these objects and create additional Customizing objects for the distribution in the editor for synchronization groups.

Locking Customizing objects in the target system

Customizing settings that must be changed via Customizing Distribution can be locked against manual changes in the target system. The lock may apply to the entire Customizing object, or you can use filters to restrict it to individual key areas. This allows you to accept additional settings in the target system that differ from those in the source system.

Requirements for Customizing Distribution

Before you can configure the Customizing Distribution, you have to do some preliminary work, which is illustrated in Figure 19.1.

1. First, you must maintain the involved systems in the Solution Manager system landscape (Transaction SMSY).
2. Next, you must maintain RFC connections between SAP Solution Manager and the involved systems.
3. Then, you must create a Solution Manager project of the implementation project type. The systems to be synchronized must be assigned to that project. You can do this in Solution Manager Transaction SOLAR_PROJECT_ADMIN.
4. In the development systems to be synchronized, you must generate IMGs that have the same name as the Solution Manager project.
5. Finally, you can load the synchronization objects.

Refer to the online help for detailed instructions on how to configure Customizing Distribution.

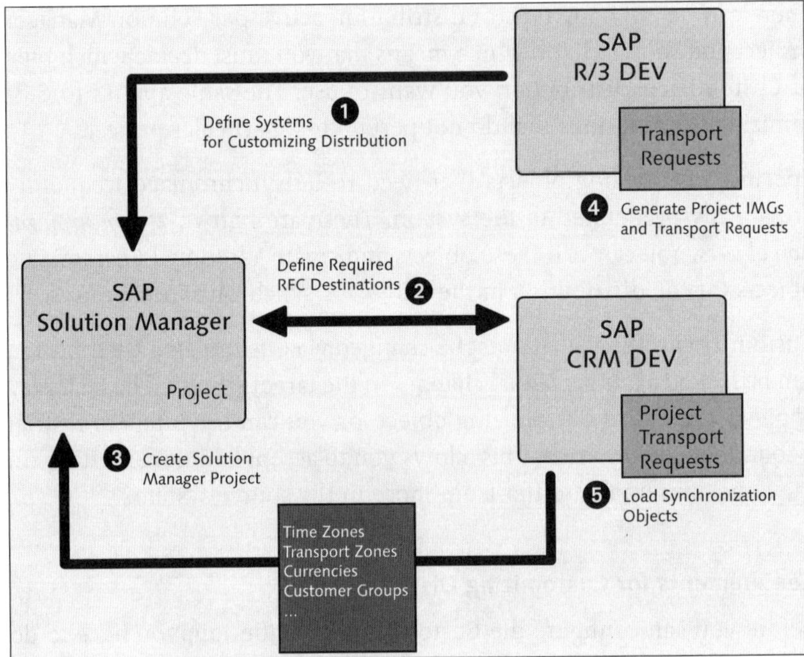

Figure 19.1 Configuring Customizing Distribution

You can now set up the Customizing Distribution using predefined or custom synchronization groups (Transaction SCDT_SETUP):

1. Select the Customizing objects or IMG activities you want to distribute. To do so, you must create a synchronization group in the synchronization group editor. The synchronization group should contain all Customizing objects you want to consider for the distribution of a source component to a target component.
2. Start the *Initial Distribution* to synchronize selected Customizing in a source system with Customizing in target systems only once. When doing so, you must specify the following settings:
   - The synchronization group that should be activated for the Customizing Distribution.
   - The development system from which you want to distribute changes (source system).
   - The development systems to which you want to distribute changes (target systems).

3. To enable the transfer of selected Customizing changes from a source system into target systems, you must set up automatic Customizing Distribution. In this context, you can also define whether Customizing Distribution should take place during Customizing, at the time of a transport release, or at fixed time intervals.

Customizing Distribution Procedure

The procedure in Customizing Distribution is as follows (see Figure 19.2):

1. Perform Customizing changes in the Customizing Distribution source system.
2. The source system then notifies the SAP Solution Manager system about the changes. The SAP Solution Manager system checks the following:
   - Whether the Customizing changes are part of a synchronization group for which the Customizing Distribution is active.
   - To which target systems the changes should be transferred.
3. The SAP Solution Manager system converts Customizing data that must be distributed into Customizing data for the target system.
4. The SAP Solution Manager system transfers the Customizing changes to the target systems.
5. Due to the Customizing Distribution, changes are written to the transport requests in the target systems. These changes let you transport the new Customizing settings into the downstream systems of the transport flow.

The target systems notify the SAP Solution Manager system about possible errors during the Customizing Distribution. You should then check the logs of the Customizing Distribution in SAP Solution Manager. Next, you can use the Customizing Scout to verify whether the Customizing was actually synchronized with the Customizing Distribution.

Customizing Distribution takes place between development systems. If data should be transported to a QA system, and later on to a production system, you must release the relevant transport requests. This ensures that the Customizing settings are synchronized not only in the development system, but in all other downstream systems as well.

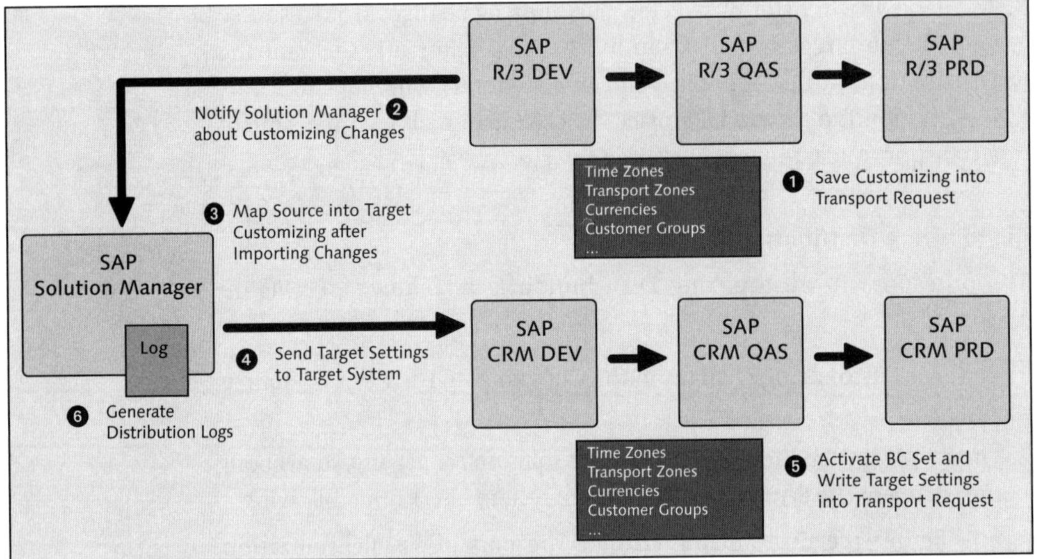

Figure 19.2 Automatic Customizing Distribution Flow with Transport Control

You can change or copy Customizing Distributions at any time using the menu. After copying, you can change the distribution option or the distribution project, for example.

Figure 19.3 shows the initial screen for the Customizing Distribution.

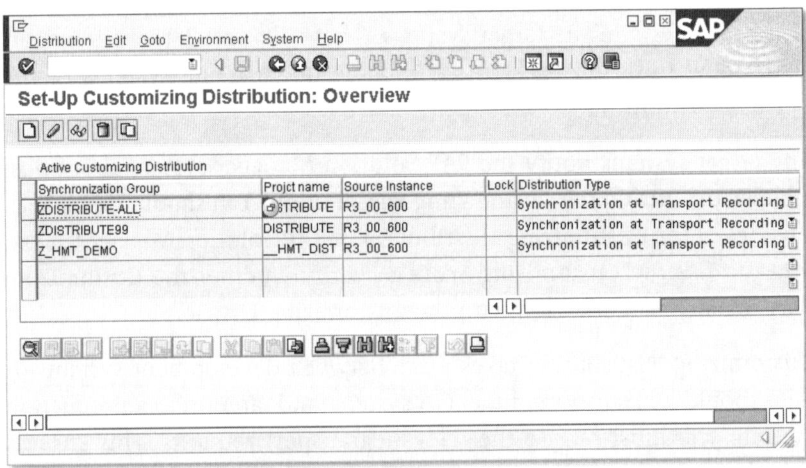

Figure 19.3 Customizing Distribution, Initial Screen—Transaction SCDT_SETUP

Figure 19.4 shows the initial screen to change a Customizing Distribution.

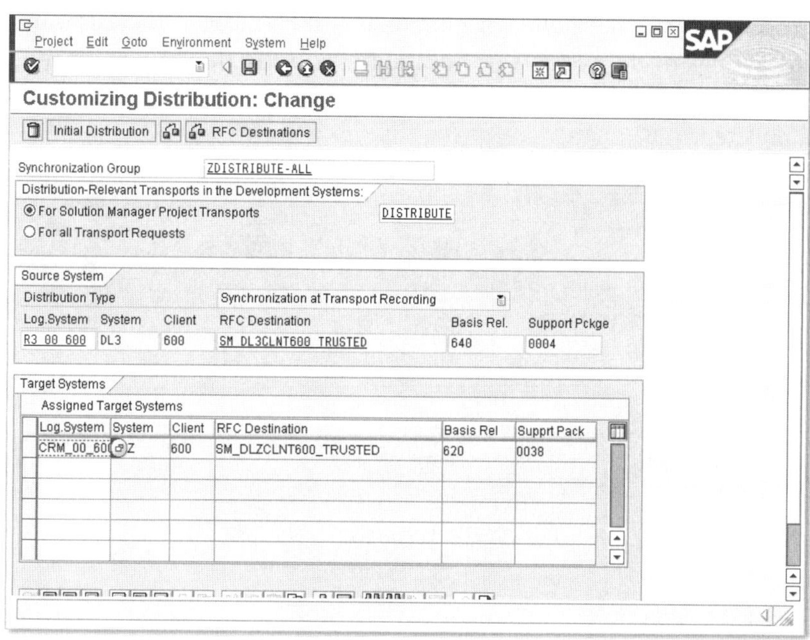

Figure 19.4 Configuring Customizing Distribution

19.1.2 The Customizing Scout

To compare the Customizing settings of different SAP systems, you can use the Customizing Scout. The comparison always occurs between two SAP systems, for instance, between an SAP ERP and an SAP CRM system.

Synchronization objects

Customizing objects that must be frequently synchronized are predefined for selected components in the system. They are referred to as *synchronization objects*. The synchronization group editor lets you edit existing synchronization objects and create new ones.

[+]

In the following sections, the system that is used as a comparison reference is also referred to as the source system in an SAP system landscape and it will be an SAP ERP system. All other systems in the SAP system landscape are referred to as target systems and will be compared only with the source system.

The comparison is used to synchronize the Customizing settings during an implementation or system landscape change. You can use the comparison as a starting point for eliminating differences in the Customizing settings of the systems, for example, by using the Implementation Guide (IMG) or the Customizing Distribution after the comparison is completed.

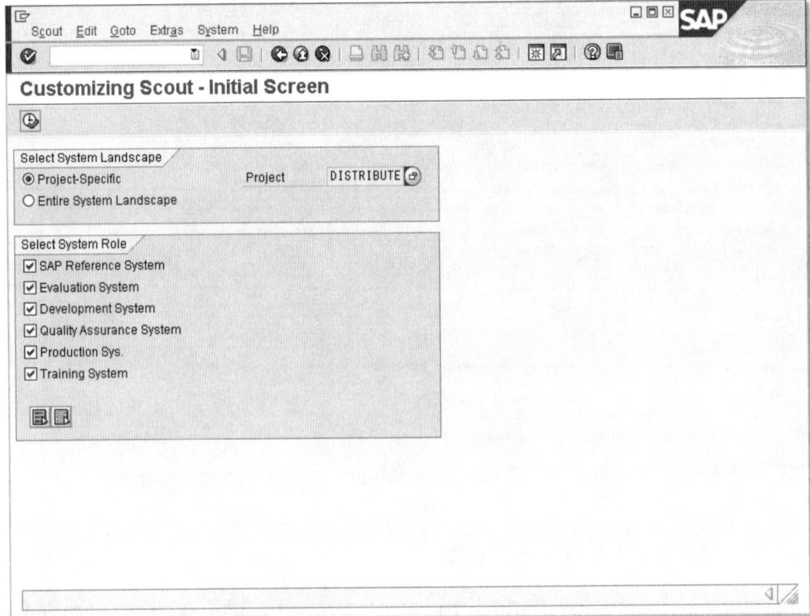

Figure 19.5 Customizing Scout, Initial Screen—Transaction SCOUT

Selecting the System Landscape

Before you run a comparison, you should select the system landscape you want to use, for example:

- A system landscape that was defined in SAP Solution Manager in the context of a specific project
- The entire system landscape

Comparison Runs

All comparison runs within a Solution Manager project are always based on the same source system. The source system serves as a reference for Customizing settings. The target system can be selected from the existing system landscape.

Figure 19.6 shows an overview of available comparison runs for a specific Solution Manager project. You can display or delete existing comparison runs. New comparison runs can be performed in the dialog box or in the background. Moreover, you can schedule periodic background comparison runs.

You can also create specific comparison runs for only those systems whose Customizing must be synchronized with the Customizing Distribution.

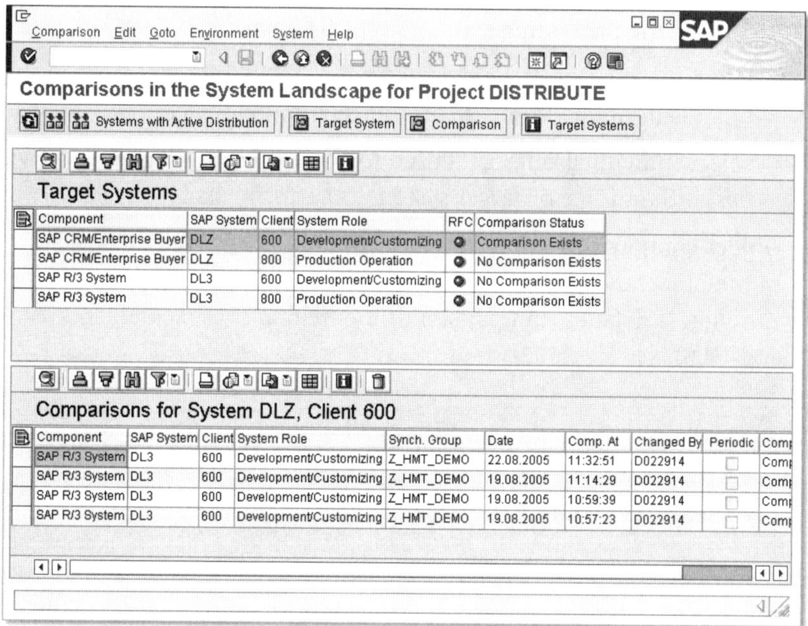

Component	SAP System	Client	System Role	RFC	Comparison Status
SAP CRM/Enterprise Buyer	DLZ	600	Development/Customizing		Comparison Exists
SAP CRM/Enterprise Buyer	DLZ	800	Production Operation		No Comparison Exists
SAP R/3 System	DL3	600	Development/Customizing		No Comparison Exists
SAP R/3 System	DL3	800	Production Operation		No Comparison Exists

Component	SAP System	Client	System Role	Synch. Group	Date	Comp. At	Changed By	Periodic	Comp
SAP R/3 System	DL3	600	Development/Customizing	Z_HMT_DEMO	22.08.2005	11:32:51	D022914		Comp
SAP R/3 System	DL3	600	Development/Customizing	Z_HMT_DEMO	19.08.2005	11:14:29	D022914		Comp
SAP R/3 System	DL3	600	Development/Customizing	Z_HMT_DEMO	19.08.2005	10:59:39	D022914		Comp
SAP R/3 System	DL3	600	Development/Customizing	Z_HMT_DEMO	19.08.2005	10:57:23	D022914		Comp

Figure 19.6 Existing Comparison Runs in the Customizing Scout

Displaying the Comparison Result

The comparison result can be displayed in levels of detail, as follows:

- **Comparison runs in the system landscape**
  You'll get an overview of all of the systems you have selected for the comparison runs. Furthermore, you can get a list of all existing comparison runs for each system (see Figure 19.6).
- **Object overview**
  For each system, you can display a list of all compared objects, including their comparison and processing statuses (see Figure 19.7). Utilities and other functions allow you to perform the following tasks in the object overview:
  - Display a comparison log for erroneous comparison runs that have been cancelled.
  - Change the processing status of specific objects.
  - Filter the display of objects according to various criteria for the processing status, comparison status, and the object type.
  - Select individual objects and go to the corresponding IMG activities in the source or target system to perform changes.
- **Object comparison**
  In the object overview, you can select a Customizing object and start and view a detailed comparison of the field entries (see Figures 19.7 and 19.8).

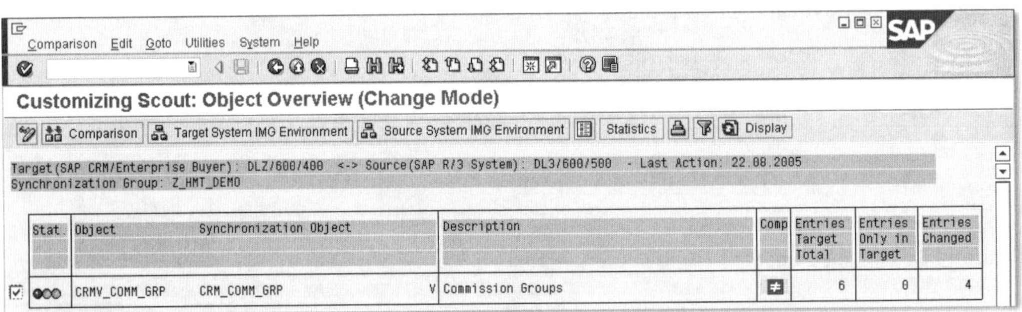

Figure 19.7 Result of a Comparison Run for a Synchronization Object

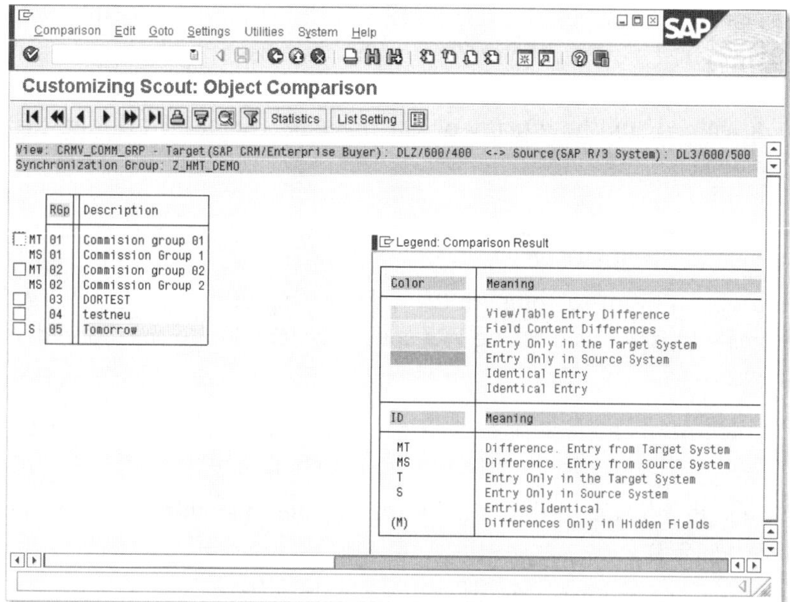

Figure 19.8 Display of the Different Table Contents

Loading Object Lists

Before you can start a comparison run between an application component such as SAP CRM and an SAP ERP system, you must provide the Customizing Scout with the list of Customizing objects that should be synchronized in your landscape. These object lists are contained in the standard versions of several application components. After you have downloaded the object lists from the application component into the SAP Solution Manager system, the Customizing Scout has access to them.

1. To launch the Customizing Scout, select Tools • Customizing • Distribution • Customizing Scout from the SAP menu or enter Transaction SCOUT.
2. Select Extras • Load Object Lists.
3. Specify a system from which you want to download the object lists.

   If you have already downloaded an object list, you can set the New objects only flag so that only new objects are downloaded that are not yet contained in your object lists.
4. Select Next.

The system downloads the respective object list and then displays an overview. In the overview you can see the systems for which object lists have been downloaded, how many objects have been added during the last download, and how many objects have been modified during that download.

Customizing Comparison

You probably want to compare the Customizing of one or more target systems with the Customizing in a source system. To do so, proceed as follows:

1. In the SAP menu, select TOOLS • CUSTOMIZING • DISTRIBUTION • CUSTOMIZING SCOUT, or enter Transaction SCOUT.

   The system displays the initial screen of the Customizing Scout (see Figure 19.5).
2. Select a system landscape and one or more system roles.

   You can use the input help to select a project from SAP Solution Manager. The system then also includes the corresponding system landscape in the comparison run.
3. Select DISPLAY SELECTION.

   The system now displays a list of all systems that belong to the system landscape you selected or to your transport domain. You can view all existing comparison runs by double-clicking on a system (see Figure 19.6).
4. To compare the Customizing objects of one or more target systems with Customizing objects in a source system, select one or more target systems in the list and click COMPARISON.

   The subsequent dialog box displays all selected logical systems. A check is run in the background to determine whether an RFC destination exists. A log is displayed if there is an error.
5. Specify a synchronization group, or select all synchronization objects for the component.
6. Enter a source system and a source client.
7. If you compare only one system with an SAP ERP reference system, you should decide whether you want to run the comparison in the

currently active dialog box or in the background. If you want to compare more than one system with an SAP ERP reference system, the comparison will always run in the background.

8. If you have started a background comparison, proceed as follows:
   - If necessary, in the dialog box that pops up, specify a server for running the background job.
   - Specify your start date values for background processing and save your entries.

   The system now checks whether you have the authorization to run the comparison and whether an RFC destination exists. A log is displayed if there is an error.

Single comparison in dialog

If you select the SINGLE COMPARISON IN DIALOG option, the system displays a list of the objects that were compared. This list provides information on the processing status and the comparison result for each object.

Total comparison in background

After the the comparison has been completed, you can select a system and click REFRESH. After that, you can display the most recently completed comparison run.

Object overview

In the OBJECT OVERVIEW, the system displays the technical name and the description from the target system for each Customizing object. If a synchronization object exists for a Customizing object, the technical name of that synchronization object will also be displayed.

There are two possible status indicators for each Customizing object:

- COMPARISON STATUS
  This status indicates the existence and type of differences. It is automatically assigned.
- PROCESSING STATUS
  This status lets you differentiate between objects that have already been processed and those that are yet to be processed.

Processing status

You can assign the processing status manually. However, if you run a new comparison, the processing status of objects that no longer differ automatically changes from OPEN (red traffic light) to CLOSED (green traffic light). You can view a list of these settings using the legend (see Figure 19.9).

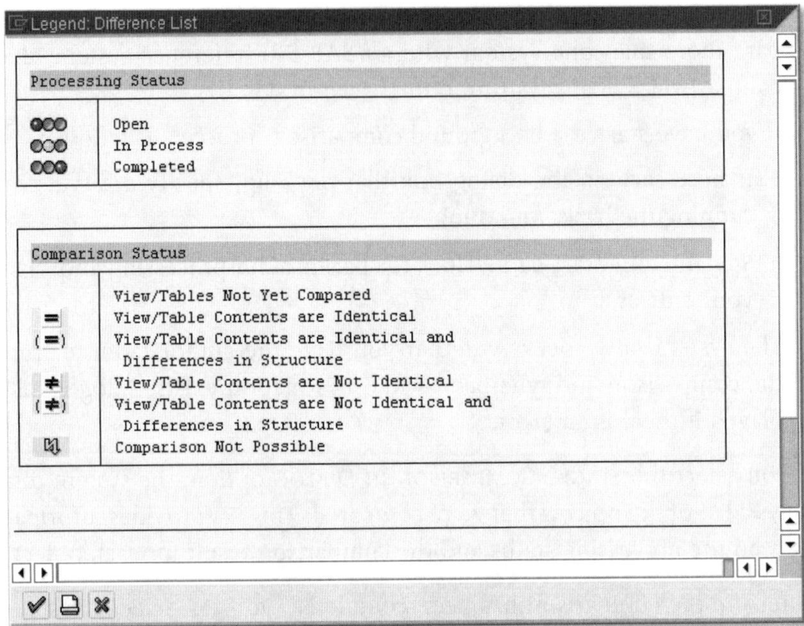

Figure 19.9 Possible Values for the Comparison and Processing Statuses

Changing the Processing Status of a Comparison Object

You compared one or more systems with a source system and based on this comparison, you made a few changes to Customizing objects. Therefore, you now want to change the processing status of individual Customizing objects.

To do so, search for the relevant object in the list and click the processing status. If you click it several times, you'll see that the status changes again.

[+] The processing status is recalculated after each comparison run. In particular, all processing statuses are reset to OPEN for objects that still contain differences, even if you have changed the processing status in the last comparison run. If your list contains objects that show differences which are not relevant for your Customizing, you can use the synchronization group editor to restrict the selection to relevant objects only.

19.1.3 Creating and Loading Synchronization Objects

The comparison of Customizing settings and Customizing distribution are based on synchronization objects. These objects must first be created in SAP Solution Manager or loaded from the SAP systems to be synchronized. Synchronization objects are required if Customizing objects in different systems contain identical content but different structures; for example, if they contain different table and field names.

Creating synchronization objects

To create synchronization objects, proceed as follows:

1. Log on to the target system for Customizing Distribution.
2. Start the tool for creating synchronization objects (Transaction SCDT_MAPPING).
3. Create a synchronization object and observe the following rules:
   - If a table is used in several Customizing objects, you must create a synchronization object for each Customizing object.
   - Summarize the tables or views that must be transported together into a synchronization object. For example, you should summarize all of the tables in the target system that correspond to subobjects of a view or view cluster in the source system.
4. If necessary, you should assign table and field names to each other when creating the synchronization object. When doing so, note the following:
   - The data types of the fields do not need to be identical, just assignment-compatible.
   - The ends of fields get truncated if they are longer in one component than in another.
   - Data fields that do not exist in one component will be ignored.
   - For the target system, all key fields of the involved tables and views must be defined for a Customizing object. For the source system, you can use any field of the tables and views involved.
   - If you use several tables or views for the source system, the system links the records of the individual tables or views with each other according to the following algorithm:

     a) One of the tables is labeled as the primary table.

b) For secondary tables, an inner join is performed for the key fields and the fields of the same name in the primary table to link the two tables.

c) Additional key fields of the secondary table may exist and be mapped to fields in the target structure.

d) If you use a table with a text field, the text field is automatically identified as such by the system.

- If you assign a table with a text field in a source system to a view in the target system, you must specify filtering rules for the source object. To do so, create a filter for the language field with the value $SPRAS or $SLANGU.
- If you assign a table or view to another table or view without mapping all source object fields to the target objects' fields, you must specify the filtering rules for the source object. Create a filter for the key fields that have not been considered and contain a fixed or generic value.

5. Check all created and existing synchronization objects you want to use.

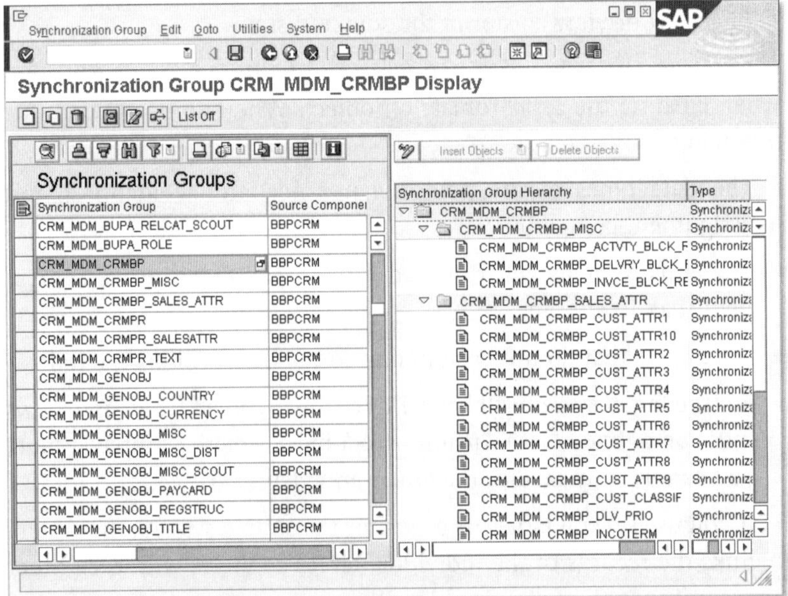

Figure 19.10 Synchronization Group Editor, Initial Screen—Transaction SCDT_GROUPS

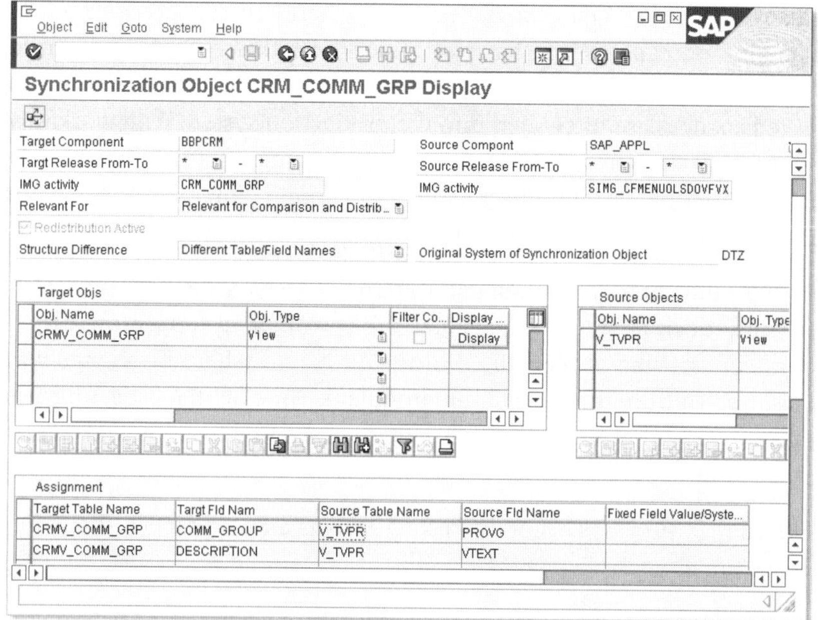

Figure 19.11 Changing Synchronization Objects

Loading synchronization objects

To load synchronization objects, proceed as follows:

1. Log on to the SAP Solution Manager system.
2. Start the Synchronization Group Editor (Transaction SCDT_GROUPS, see Figure 19.10) and load the synchronization objects from the system in which you previously created them into the SAP Solution Manager system.

The synchronization objects are then available to you for use in Customizing Distribution and in the Customizing Scout. You can now use Customizing Distribution for your work or run a cross-component Customizing comparison.

19.2 Change Request Management

Continuous changes, frequently changing requirements from user departments, and increasingly complex system landscapes represent a growing challenge for the system operation.

Workflow

Change Request Management lets you perform all changes to the SAP system landscape on the basis of a workflow that can be customized to your individual requirements. This ensures that your approved and tested changes are integrated into the production system. The workflow contains all steps from the creation of a change request to the import into the production system. Optionally, you can also integrate the Service Desk functionality of SAP Solution Manager.

Retraceability

At the same time, all actions and approval steps are clearly and consistently documented. This enables the customer to retrace the origin of a request, who implemented the request, and when the change was imported into the production environment. An essential aspect here is that all relevant information is provided at a central location and can be called at any time.

Types of changes

The change process preconfigured by SAP as a best practice that comprises three types of changes:

- Urgent correction
- Regular correction as part of a project cycle
- Implementation project

Urgent correction

The urgent correction is a single change that must be quickly implemented into the production system to immediately solve an urgent problem. Less urgent changes can be bundled and imported into the production system at the end of a maintenance cycle.

Projects

Large changes are treated as implementation projects. They have their own project cycle that is independent of the maintenance cycle. The project cycle includes several project phases (development, test, go live) during which specific transport activities are possible. The project phases are controlled centrally from SAP Solution Manager and provide basic conditions for developers they cannot bypass. This ensures a higher quality development process. Optionally, you can use the project planning system *cProjects*. It enables resource planning and a connection to the backend, for example, to CATS (*Cross Application Time Sheet*) for activity recording.

Import Project All

Change Request Management uses the technical import strategy IMPORT PROJECT ALL. This allows you to develop one or more projects at the same time. The projects can be imported into the test or production system at different points in time.

Connection to transport management

However, Change Request Management is unique in that you can not only manage the changes, but that you are also provided with a connection to transport management. Transport requests are created centrally from SAP Solution Manager, released there, and imported into the downstream systems. This way, SAP Solution Manager always knows which transport request belongs to which functional requirement and which transport request was imported into which system. A tedious and error-prone manual transfer of transport request number and transport status into the change management tool is thus omitted. Furthermore, comprehensive reporting provides flexible views of the data.

Also, the transport request's short text contains the ID and the change request's short text. This way, you can always retrace why a change to the system was carried out and whether this change is still required. This is very useful, for example, for a modification adjustment after an upgrade.

Changes that do not require any transport connection can be recorded using Change Request Management. Here, a change request is made for all changes and this request passes all approval steps. All steps required for implementation are documented.

Statutory requirements

Change Request Management provides functions that are indispensable to guarantee transparent solution implementation and operation. In many areas, this transparency is required by statutory guidelines and is checked regularly during audits. Examples are the requirements of the Sarbanes-Oxley Act (SOX) or the specifications of the Food and Drug Administration (FDA).

Figure 19.12 shows the different areas that are covered by Change Request Management.

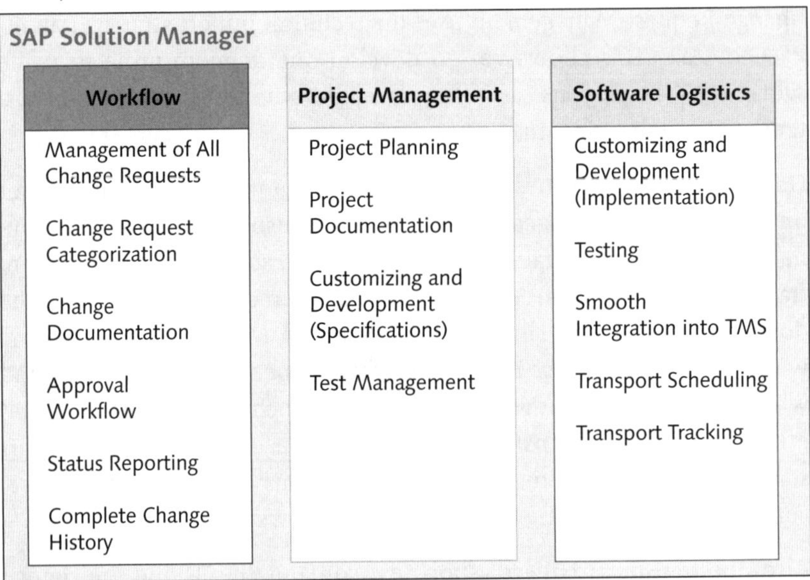

Figure 19.12 Areas of Change Request Management

19.2.1 Change Request Management Workflow

SAP provides a standard workflow for Change Request Management (see Figure 19.13) that can be customized to your individual requirements. The workflow is adapted to the description of the change management process in the IT Infrastructure Library (ITIL).

IT Infrastructure Library

ITIL is a collection of publications that describe a possible implementation of an IT service management (ITSM) and have become an internationally acknowledged de-facto standard (see also *http://www.itil.org*). The roles participating in the Change Request Management are also taken from the ITIL process.

An end user works with a transaction and detects an error. He can now create a support message—in which he describes the error—directly from the transaction. The message then appears in the worklist (Transaction CRM_DNO_MONITOR) of a Service Desk employee who processes the message. He checks whether this error was due to incorrect operation or whether the system must be changed. If a change is necessary, he documents his results in a support message and automatically creates a change request as a follow-on document. The Service Desk message and change request are connected via the document flow and the assignment is transparent all of the time.

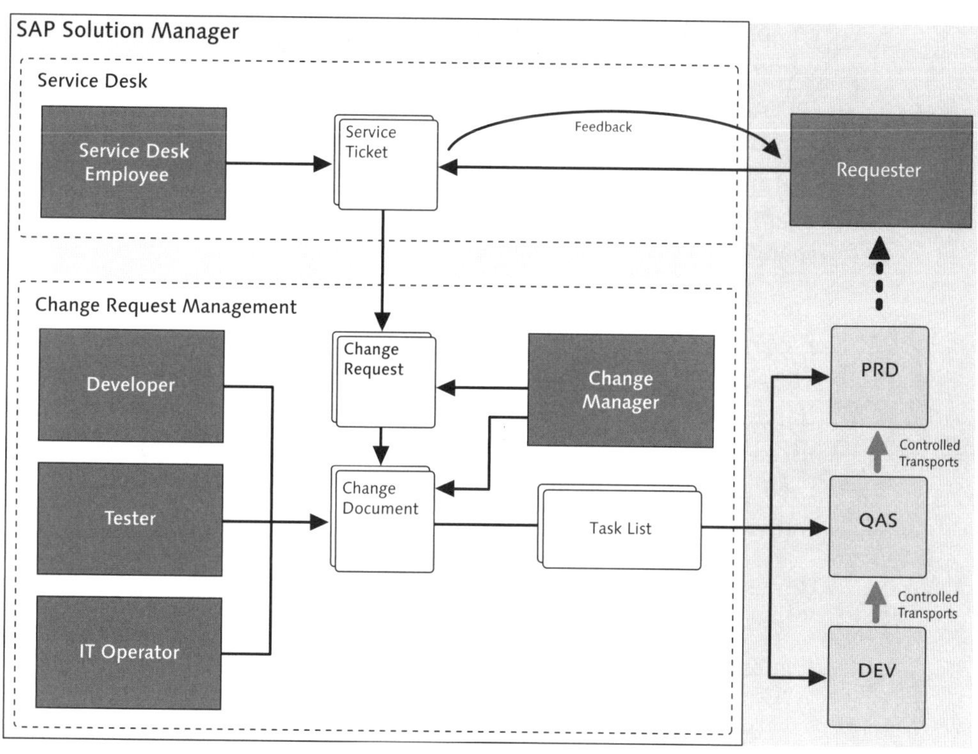

Figure 19.13 Change Request Management Workflow

Change manager

The change request then appears in the worklist of the change manager who is responsible for evaluating the request. He must determine whether the change makes sense, what side effects could occur and what risks could arise during the implementation, how tedious the implementation is, and what resources are available. Possibly, the change manager must consult other experts to obtain the necessary information.

Change Advisory Board

Many organizations have a board that regularly meets to decide on planned changes. In the ITIL process, this board is called the *Change Advisory Board*. The role of the Change Advisory Board is also defined in the Change Request Management workflow. The change request is approved or rejected. If the request is approved, a priority and category must be assigned, and the change must be allocated to a project or maintenance cycle.

Developers and testers

After a change request has been approved, another ticket is created: the *change document*. This can be an urgent or regular correction, depending on the classification set by the change manager. The change document comprises the workflow for implementing the change. It appears in the worklist of the developer who implements the change and releases it for testing. Then, the document is transferred to the tester. After a successful test, the changes can be transported to the production system. The standard workflow also includes a final check after the import into the production system. If this change was implemented successfully, the change process can be completed.

The change request and change documents are preconfigured service processes. From a technical perspective, these are CRM transaction types. They have a status profile and an action profile. The process passes the different statuses step by step. In each status, you can implement specific user actions. Both the status profile and the action profile can be configured using the CRM Customizing activities. This allows you to specify individual transaction types.

19.2.2 Architecture

Figure 19.14 shows the objects used in Change Request Management.

Solution Manager project

The central part of Change Request Management is the Solution-Manager project. It must contain satellite systems for which transports should be implemented.

Logical component

These are stored in the logical component. The logical component contains the system landscape and the transport routes to be used by Change Request Management.

IMG project

The IMG project is created in the connected development systems from the project management component of SAP Solution Manager (Transaction SOLAR_PROJECT_ADMIN) to bundle the settings—configured for an SAP Solution Manager project using the SAP Implementation Guide (IMG)—in one system.

The CTS project is a container within a logical system (a combination of a system and a client) that combines transport requests belonging to the IMG project.

CTS project

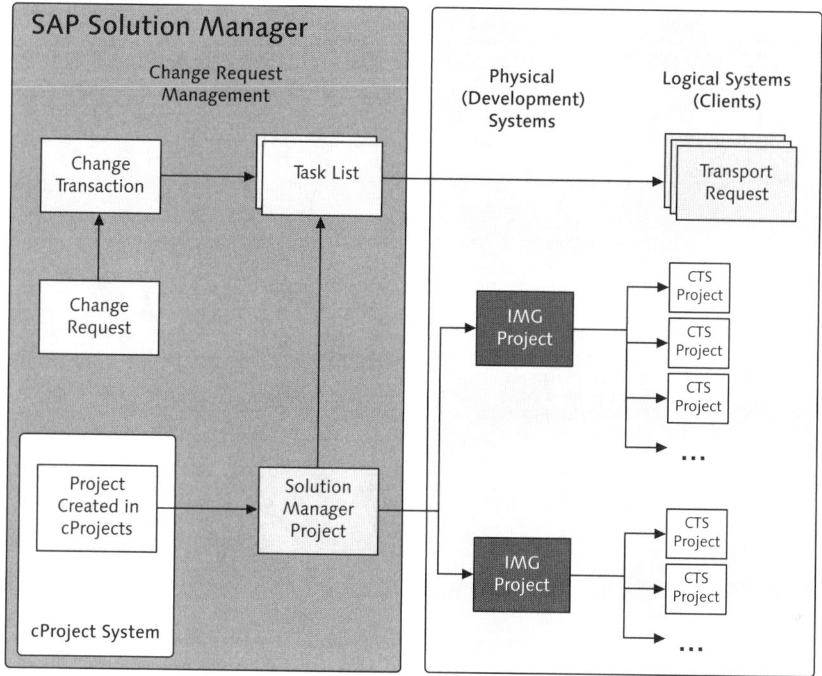

Figure 19.14 Projects in Change Request Management

Use Transaction /TMWFLOW/PROJ (Project Logistics) to obtain an overview of all objects contained in the project (see Figure 19.15). On the PROJECT STRUCTURE tab you can see the interrelationships at a glance:

- Solution Manager project
- Project or maintenance cycle
- Task list
- Assigned cProjects project
- IMG project
- CTS project and the transport requests recorded for it

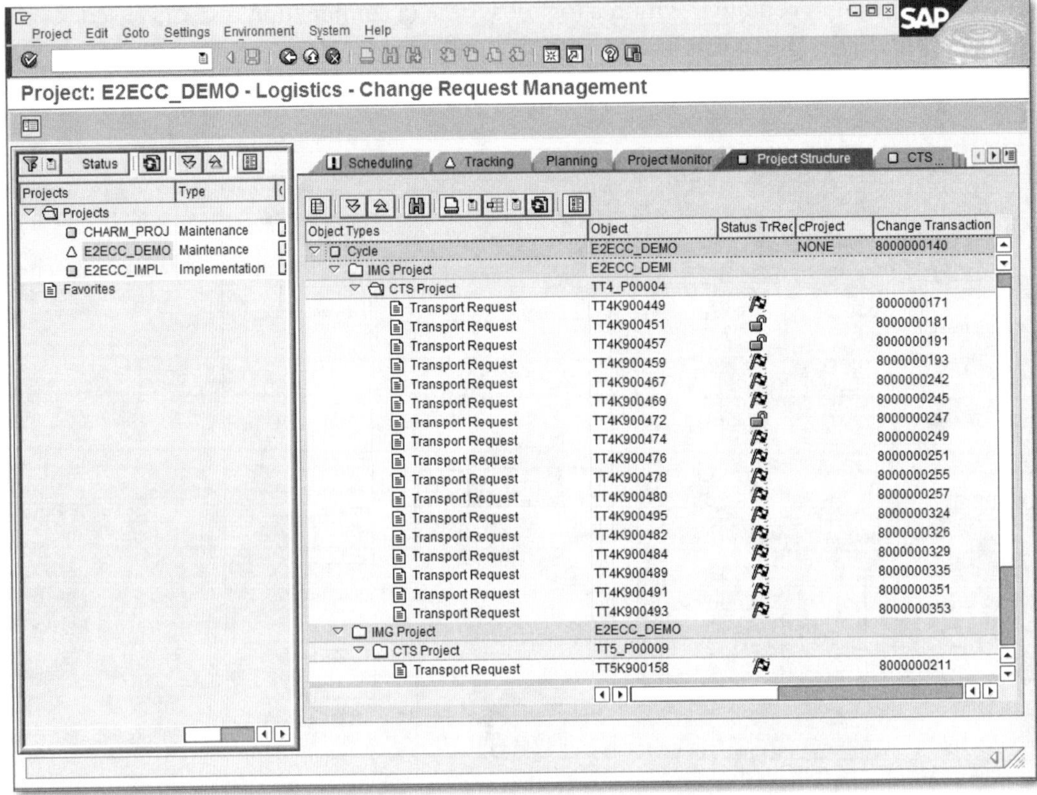

Figure 19.15 Transaction Project Logistics (/TMWFLOW/PROJ)

19.2.3 Project Cycles

Release Management

SAP recommends that you collect changes for a certain period of time and then import them as bundles into the production systems, rather than import individual changes on a continuous basis. These maintenance cycles are highly advisable because you can then test all changes simultaneously and avoid adverse side effects that might occur with individual transport requests. Furthermore, you can test the potential for problems for business processes that already exist in the system (regression testing). The strategy to import changes as a bundle into the production system is also referred to as the *release strategy*. Change Request Management supports Release Management. For this purpose, the SAP Solution Manager project was extended by another object: the project cycle. A project that has been activated for Change Request Management always contains a project cycle. The project cycle and its phase structure provide an operative supplement to the project plan. An individual project cycle includes the following phases (see Figure 19.16):

- Development without Release
- Development with Release
- Test
- Preparation for go live (Emergency Correction)
- Go-Live

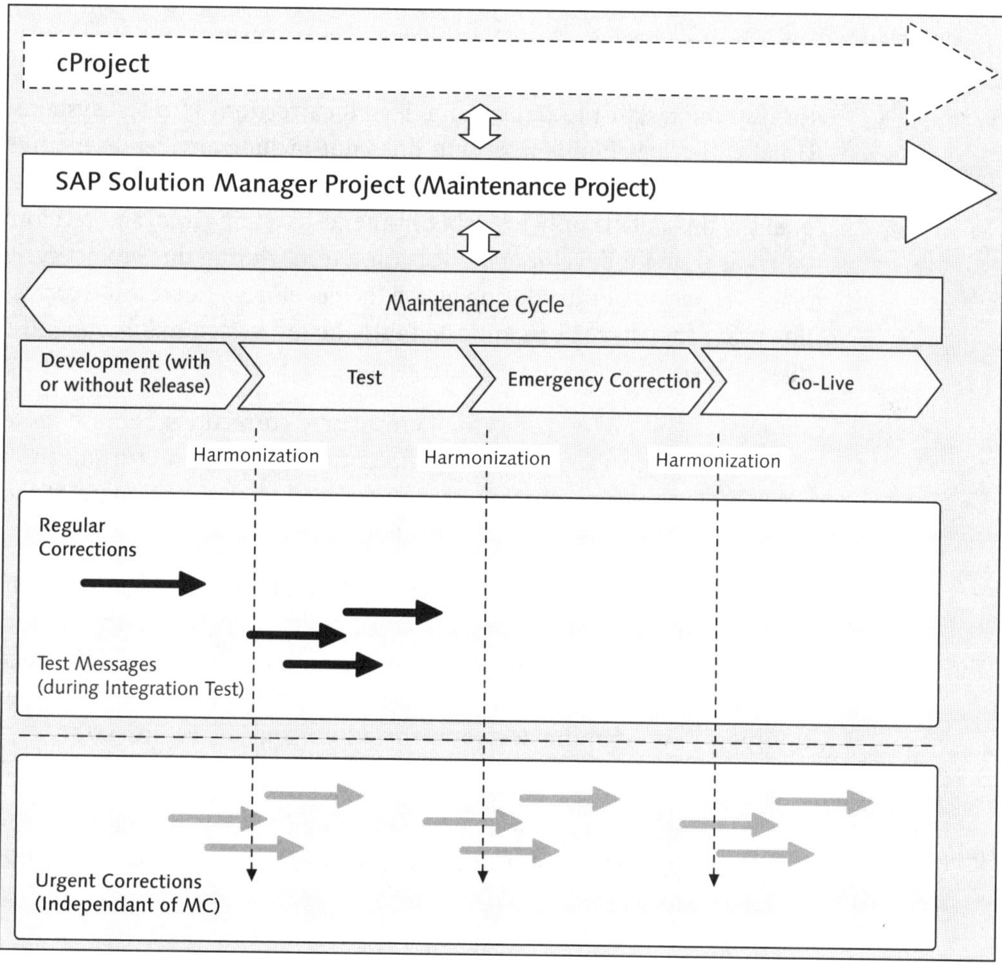

Figure 19.16 Phases of a Project Cycle

The phases are controlled centrally from SAP Solution Manager and provide basic conditions for developers that cannot be bypassed.

Development without Release

During the *Development without Release* phase you cannot export any transport requests from the development system. As a result, the test system is not changed, for example, if another project is tested there. Moreover, the transport requests remain open in the development system so that the Workbench lock persists for a long time for the changed objects and the transport requests already have a certain quality at the time of release.

Development with Release

If the change manager changes the project cycle status from DEVELOPMENT WITHOUT RELEASE to DEVELOPMENT WITH RELEASE, the developers can release transport requests from a correction. The system administrator uses the task list to import all released corrections into test systems. Usually, the development system does not include any representative test data that enables developers to test the developed corrections. Frequently, this data is only available in the test system. You can therefore schedule time for development tests (unit tests) during this project cycle phase—a period of time during which the developers can test the corrections after they have been imported into the test systems. Subsequently, they can set the status to DEVELOPMENT COMPLETED.

During the test phase, you cannot create new corrections because these would constitute an expansion of the project scope in the current project. If a new correction is necessary, you need to reset the phase of the project cycle to DEVELOPMENT WITH RELEASE.

Test

During the test phase, testers can test the corrections with regard to their functional and technical correctness. If a tester detects an error, he can document it using a test message and inform the appropriate developer about the error. Using the test message, the developer can create a new transport request in the development system and correct the error.

Emergency Correction (Preparation for Go-Live)

If changes have to be performed upon completion of the test phase, transport requests and jobs may be created and released during the *Emergency Correction* phase, but this is possible only via the task list of the schedule manager.

During the *Go-Live* phase, the entire transport buffer of the CTS project is imported into the production systems in the order of release. During all other project phases, the production systems are locked against imports to prevent accidental imports. During this phase, you cannot create or release any transport requests. After the import into the production system environment, no open transport requests exist and the transport buffer is empty. You can now complete the project cycle by setting the status to CONFIRMED. The project is now completed.

Go-Live

The project cycle is a preconfigured service process (Transaction type SDDV). It is saved in the system as a CRM document and can be displayed using Transaction CRMD_ORDER (see Figure 19.17). This transaction also allows you to switch the phases and save additional information about the project cycle.

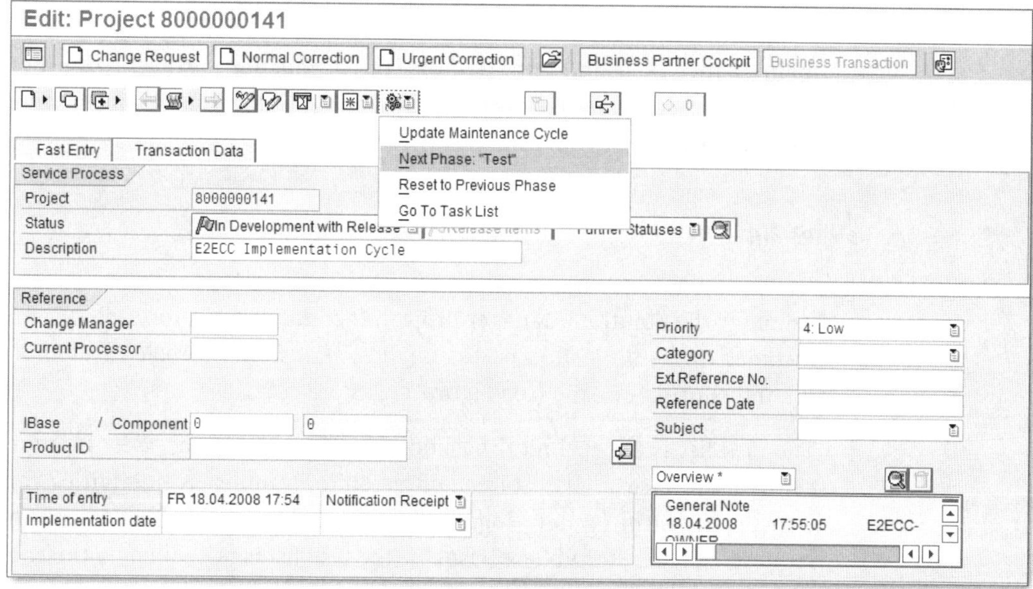

Figure 19.17 Displaying a Project Cycle in Transaction CRMD_ORDER

The maintenance cycle is a special project cycle (Transaction type SDMN). It is used to extend and maintain solutions that are already used in the production system. A maintenance cycle is automatically created

Maintenance Cycle

if the corresponding Solution Manager project is of the *maintenance* type. This project cycle has certain specific features. The maintenance cycle includes an additional correction type, *urgent correction*, which enables you to flexibly implement urgent corrections in the form of preliminary transports. This is not required for implementation projects because the implementation is not yet used in the production system. The maintenance cycle is also a periodically occurring procedure. This means that the maintenance is carried out at predefined intervals, for example, every month. During this time, the maintenance cycle passes through all project phases from Development without Release to Go-Live. At the end of the Go-Live phase, you do not conclude the cycle, but instead reset its status to DEVELOPMENT WITHOUT RELEASE to start a new cycle. From a technical perspective, this same maintenance cycle is implemented several times. The advantage of this procedure is that changes whose development has not been completed when the test is started can be further developed and can be tested during the next maintenance cycle and imported into the production system. This is not possible in implementation projects where all developments must be completed when the test starts.

19.2.4 Task List

The task list is generated when Change Request Management is activated for the Solution Manager project. It contains tasks for each system included in the project. In particular, it contains tasks for each system in the transport landscape (see Figure 19.18).

The task list is the technical backbone of all change processes. It is the central interface to the connected satellite systems. All activities for transport control (system logon, create, release, and import transport request, etc.) are stored here. Usually, the task list is not called by the end user directly, but is called in the background by the service processes the user applies. The project import (IMPORT PROJECT ALL) is an exception that can only be started in the task list.

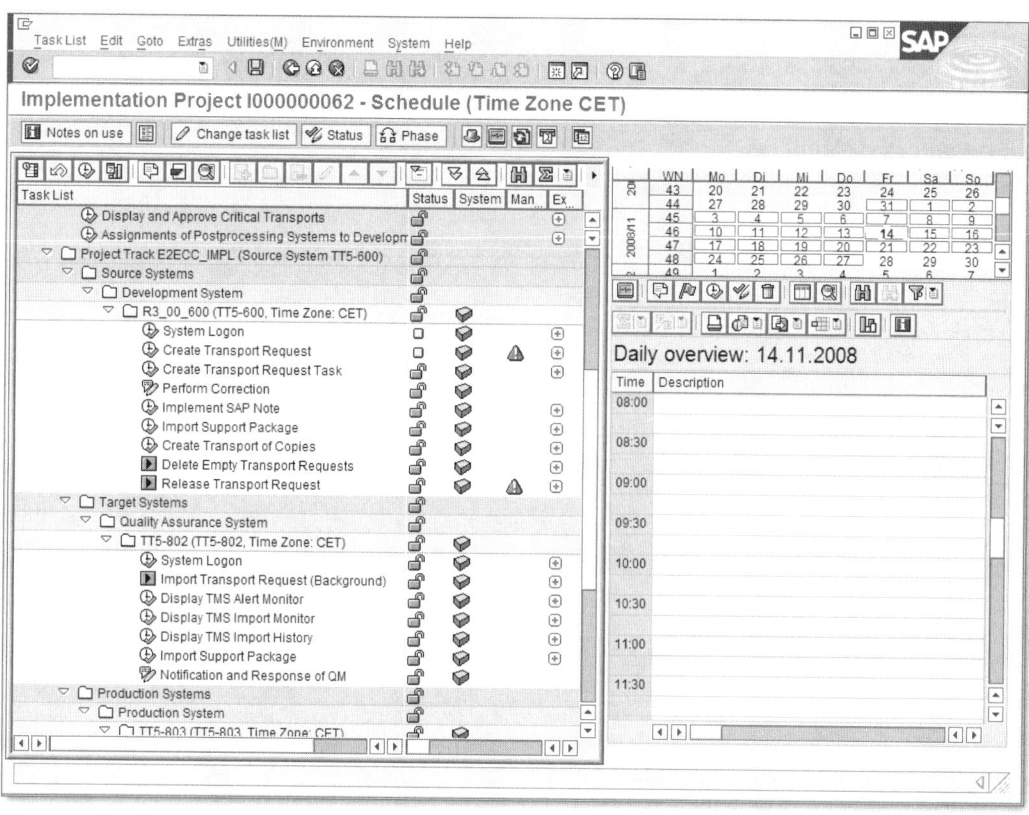

Figure 19.18 Change Request Management Task List

19.2.5 Change Management Work Center

The concept of work centers was introduced with Support Package 15 of SAP Solution Manager 7.0. A work center comprises an overview of the most critical information about an activity area and includes jumps to other transactions that are necessary to carry out the activity. The work center is role-based, that is, a user can view only information that is relevant for his work and for which he has corresponding authorizations.

Work center

Work centers exist for different parts of IT Service Management. The Change Management work center shows an overview of all change processes relevant for the user (see Figure 19.19). From here, he can navigate to the change processes or he can create a new change process using the appropriate buttons.

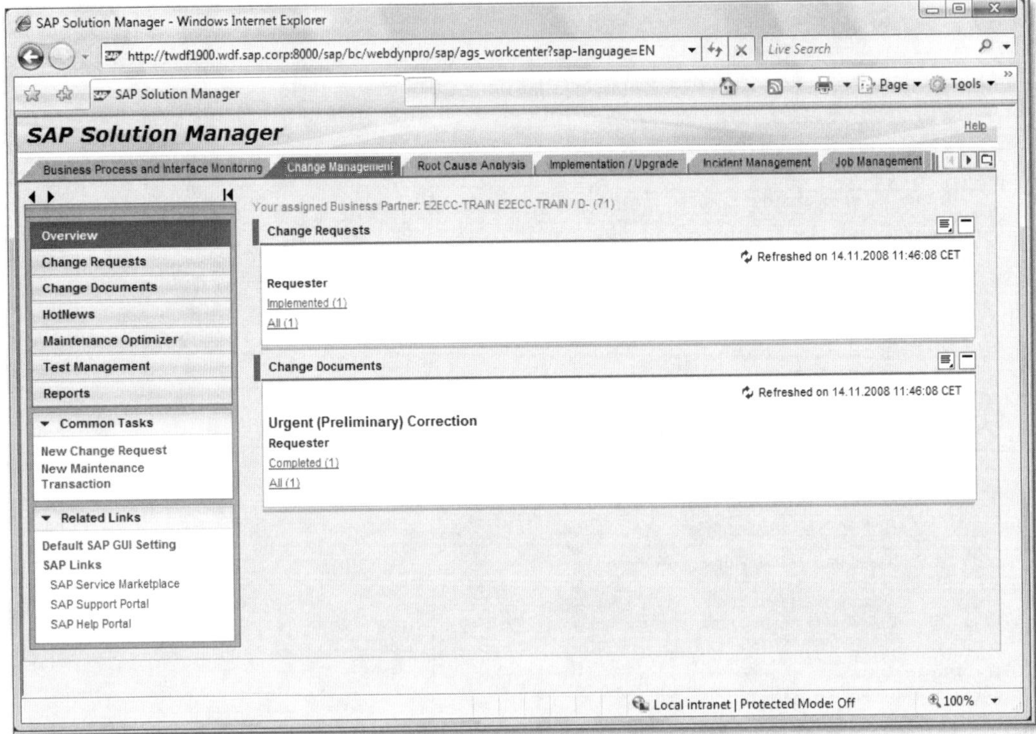

Figure 19.19 Change Management Work Center

19.2.6 Change Request

After Change Request Management has been activated for a Solution Manager project, you can apply or process change requests. These tasks can be handled using the Change Management work center (see Figure 19.20).

The change request (Transaction type SDCR) is a preconfigured service process that contains all of the important information about the planned change, including the following:

- Change request: unique transaction number for the change request.
- Description: Short text for the change request.
- Sold-to Party: department that requested the change.
- Requester: the person who requested the change.

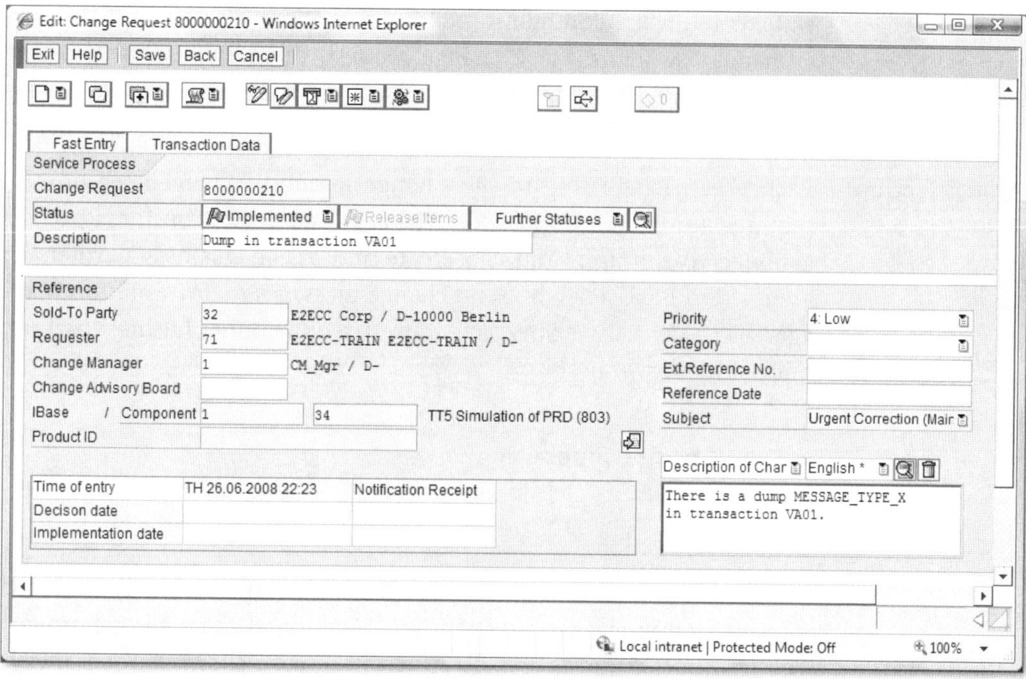

Figure 19.20 Change Request

- Change Manager: person who is responsible for evaluation and approval of the change request.
- Change Advisory Board: the board that is responsible for evaluation and approval of the change request.
- Installation/Component: the production system in which the change should be implemented.
- Priority: priorities available by default (four in total).
- Category: customer-specific categorization of changes.
- External Reference Number: reference to a transaction number in another system, for example, in an external Service Desk system.
- Reference Date: desired change date.
- Subject: type of correction that should be implemented, as decided by the change manager, for example, an urgent correction or a regular correction. The different types of changes are described in the following section.

- Texts to ensure communication: texts that can also be configured as mandatory fields. For a change request, these are: DESCRIPTION OF CHANGE, REASON FOR CHANGE, EFFECT ON BUSINESS PARTNER, EFFECT ON SYSTEM(S), CHANGE REQUEST - INTERNAL, CHANGE REQUEST - REPLY.

Business partner

Each user participating in the Change Request Management process requires a user in SAP Solution Manager and a CRM business partner assigned to the user. You can create and assign business partners in Transaction BP. Users who send change messages to SAP Solution Manager via HELP • CREATE SUPPORT MESSAGE require only a business partner, but not their own user.

19.2.7 Change Types

Regular Correction

Change requests that require a transport request are usually classified as *regular corrections* (Transaction type SDMJ) and assigned to a project. The transport requests associated with the correction are then always imported into the downstream systems together with all of the other project transport requests. A preliminary transport of the regular correction outside of the project import is not possible. The regular correction has the following status profile:

- Created
- In Development
- To be Tested
- Consolidated
- Production
- Withdrawn

The following section describes the process of a regular correction in detail.

The change manager approves the change request as a regular correction. Solution Manager then automatically creates a change process of the *regular correction* type. It appears in the developer's worklist (Transaction CRM_DNO_MONITOR). If an email notification was configured, the developer receives a message stating that a correction is available. As an alternative, he can also check his worklist regularly. He then processes the correction and enters his name. The status changes to *In Development*. Next, he creates a transport request, logs on to the development system, and implements the requested change. Subsequently, he releases his transport tasks in the development system (Transaction SE09) and logs off again. He then sets the correction's status to *To be Tested* and transfers it to the tester. Change Request Management offers the dual control principle; that is, you can specify that the developer and tester must be two different people.

Transport of copies

At the same time, Solution Manager automatically transfers the developer's changes into the import buffer of the test system using a transport of copies. After the next project import into the test system, the correction can be tested. The tester tests the change and sets the correction's status to *Consolidated* if the test was successful. The developer's original transport request is now automatically released and sent to the import buffer of the test system. In the event of an error, the tester can reset the status back to *In Development*. The process would then have to be repeated until the test completes successfully.

[+]

The regular correction works with transports of copies. This has two advantages. First, the original transport request remains open in the development system for a longer period of time so that the changed objects remain locked. Second, only transport requests that have been tested are released. This reduces the number of errant transport requests that must be imported into the production systems because the transports of copies are not forwarded to the import buffer of the production systems. This, in turn, reduces the time required for the import.

The change manager now waits until all regular corrections of the project have been tested successfully. He then imports the project into the test system for the last time and switches the project to the TEST phase. Next, the integration test of the entire project is initiated. If this test also completes successfully, the project can be imported into the production system. For this purpose, the project phase must be switched to GO-LIVE. After all transport requests have been imported successfully, you can set the status of the corrections to PRODUCTION.

[+] You can set this status for all regular corrections of a project at the end of a project cycle by carrying out the report CRM_SOCM_SERVICE_REPORT.

Urgent Correction

Urgent corrections (Transaction type SDHF) can only be created within maintenance projects. They have their own task list and can be imported as preliminary transports into the test and production systems independent of the maintenance cycle. However, they remain in the buffer after the import. In a regular import using the task list of the maintenance cycle, the entire transport buffer of the project is imported in a consolidated manner using the method IMPORT PROJECT ALL. Here, urgent corrections are re-imported in the correct sequence. This ensures that sequence problems do not occur between transport requests.

Test Message

Test messages (Transaction type SDTM) were introduced so that errors are sent to developers and fixed during the test phase. In this phase, you can no longer release regular corrections. However, you can release transport requests belonging to test messages and import them into the test system. Test messages are not related to a correction because the integration test usually relates to the entire project. A separate approval step is not required for a test message. It has the following status profile:

- Created
- In Process
- To be retested
- Confirmed
- Withdrawn

Administrative Change

The *administrative change* (Transaction type SDAD) is used to implement and track changes that do not require any transport requests, for example, number range changes or user data. Using administrative changes allows you to also manage changes to non-SAP systems. They have the following status profile:

- Created
- In Process
- Completed
- Confirmed
- Confirmed
- Withdrawn

19.2.8 Change Tracking

In addition to Change Management, SAP Solution Manager allows you to analyze changes that have been performed. You can trace all actions that are connected to changes within a Solution Manager project. You can also trace all transport requests from the system in which they have been created, through to the systems into which they were imported for a specific project, across all systems of a project landscape. You can also navigate to the transport logs and to the import queue, as well as to the corresponding service processes or task lists. Furthermore, you can navigate to the Solution Manager project, the IMG project in the component system, or the CTS project.

Options for analysis

The following analysis options are available:

- **Project analysis**
  With a project analysis, you can trace all changes to a project that has been defined in Solution Manager.
- **System analysis**
  The system analysis lets you compare transport requests between two SAP systems. You can identify missing transport requests and differences in the processing sequence.
- **Analysis of change request**
  With the analysis of change requests, you can trace change requests from systems in which they were created, through to all systems into which transports are imported.

Comparing Transport Requests in Two Systems

You want to compare two systems with each other (e.g., a development system and a consolidation system) to determine which transport requests have been imported or exported. Proceed as follows:

1. Access Transaction /TMWFLOW/CMSCONF.
2. Select the SEARCH tab in the CHANGE MANAGEMENT – CHANGE TRACKING screen.
3. Use the F4 help in the SYSTEM ANALYSIS group box to select the two systems you want to compare with each other (and optionally also their clients).

[+] The data you enter in the PROJECT, DATA, and TIME fields refers to both systems.

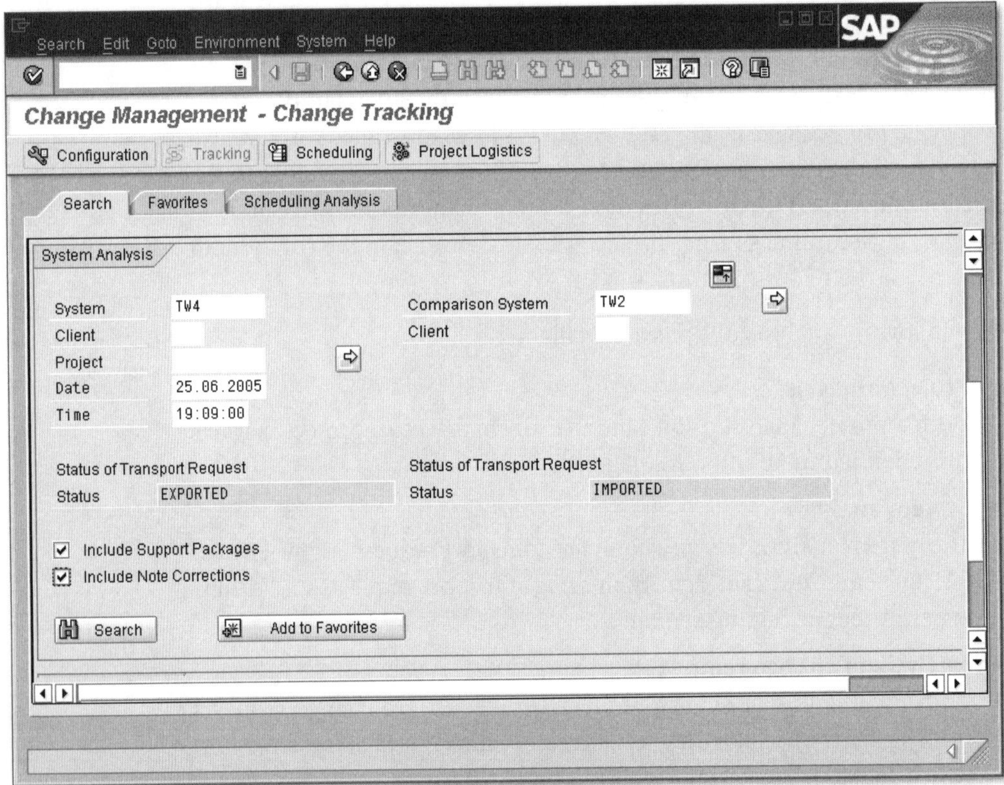

Figure 19.21 Comparing Transport Requests Between Two Systems: Selection Screen

4. Use the [F4] help in the STATUS OF TRANSPORT REQUEST field to select the statuses you want to compare with each other.
5. The default selection is EXPORTED for the first system and IMPORTED for the system with which you want to compare it. Note that you can also change these entries.
6. If you want to display information on the Support Packages and SAP Notes that have been imported into the system, check the INCLUDE SUPPORT PACKAGES and INCLUDE NOTE CORRECTIONS fields.
7. Click the SEARCH button.

A new screen that displays all of the information about the two systems reflects the criteria you selected (see Figure 19.22). In this screen, you can display the data used in the last run of the data collector by clicking on the REFRESH DATA button.

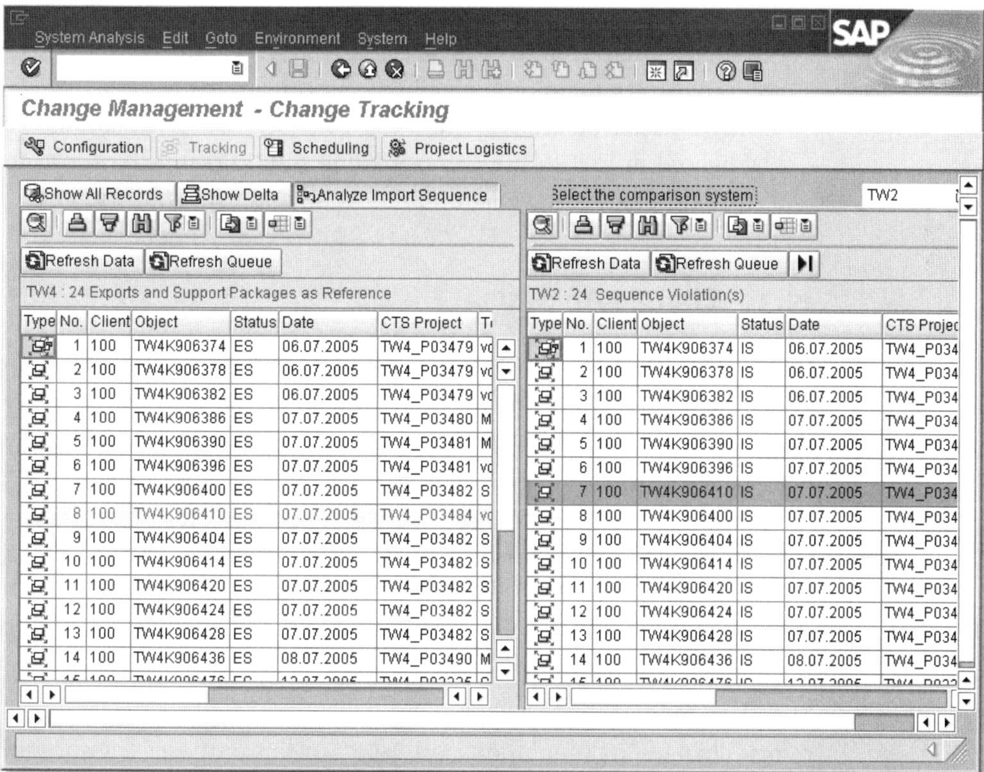

Figure 19.22 Comparing Transport Requests Between Two Systems: Results List

The comparison screen provides the following functions:

- **Show all records**
  This is the default setting used when two systems are compared with each other.
- **Show Delta**
  You can use this function only if you have selected EXPORTED and IMPORTED as the STATUS OF TRANSPORT REQUEST in the previous dialog box. This function allows you to identify changes that were exported from the first, but not imported into the second system. Alternatively, you can identify changes that were imported into the second, but not exported from the first system.
- **Analyze Import Sequence**
  Use this function to find out whether there are differences in the sequence in which the changes were exported from the first and imported into the second system. The number of sequence violations is displayed in the top right-hand area of the screen. If violations exist, you can display them individually by clicking on the NEXT SEQUENCE VIOLATION icon (next to the REFRESH DATA icon). The violations are highlighted in red. In the corresponding row, click the TYPE icon to display the respective violation in the left-hand pane of the screen.

19.3 Change Analysis

Until now, we have primarily focused on how to transport changes from system A to system B. However, the system administrator frequently needs to know later which changes were implemented when. Especially if there is an error, you will want to know what has been changed. In many areas this transparency is required by statutory guidelines and is checked regularly during audits. However, not only the changes to the SAP system are important. Infrastructure changes to hardware and software within the SAP system environment also frequently impact the production operation.

The Change Analysis application in SAP Solution Manager allows you to retrace changes in the solution landscape. For this purpose, snapshots of the system configuration are stored at regular intervals. This information lets you identify changes and compare different configuration settings. These changes are determined automatically; that is, the administrator does not have to manually log the changes.

Root cause analysis

The Change Analysis runs on the Java stack of SAP Solution Manager and is part of the *root cause analysis* scenario. Like all other applications of the root cause analysis, the *Change Analysis* application is available only in English.

19.3.1 Features

The Change Analysis allows you to track changes to an SAP solution. For this purpose, both technical configuration parameters and changes contained in the transport requests are considered, as follows:

- Operating system parameters
- Database parameters
- ABAP parameters
- Java parameters
- Software releases
- SAP Notes
- Transport requests

Drilldown functionality

The data is displayed in a comprehensive user interface. Initially, you are shown the number of changes per system, day, and change type. This way, the system administrator can quickly determine whether changes have been made to the system. The drilldown functionality of SAP NetWeaver BI can be used to see additional details for the relevant changes. For parameter changes, you can display a list of the parameters that were changed on a specific day. If the change was recorded in a transport request, you can find the transport request number and continue with the analysis in the corresponding satellite system.

19.3.2 Performing an Analysis

To perform a Change Analysis, start SAP Solution Manager. Select Transaction SOLUTION_MANAGER. Choose GoTo • Solution Manager

DIAGNOSTICS. The logon screen of Solution Manager Diagnostics displays. Enter your user name and password.

- At the highest navigation level, select ROOT CAUSE ANALYSIS • CONFIGURATION.
- In the LANDSCAPE SELECTION area, select the solution and the system role.
- In the APPLICATION SELECTION area, select the E2E CHANGE ANALYSIS application.
- UnderE2E CHANGE ANALYSIS – DETAILED SELECTION, select the system you want to analyze.
- Click START.

The system automatically creates the OVERVIEW tab (see Figure 19.23) as well as an additional tab for each product instance of the selected systems. The descriptions of the tabs contain the system ID and the product instance.

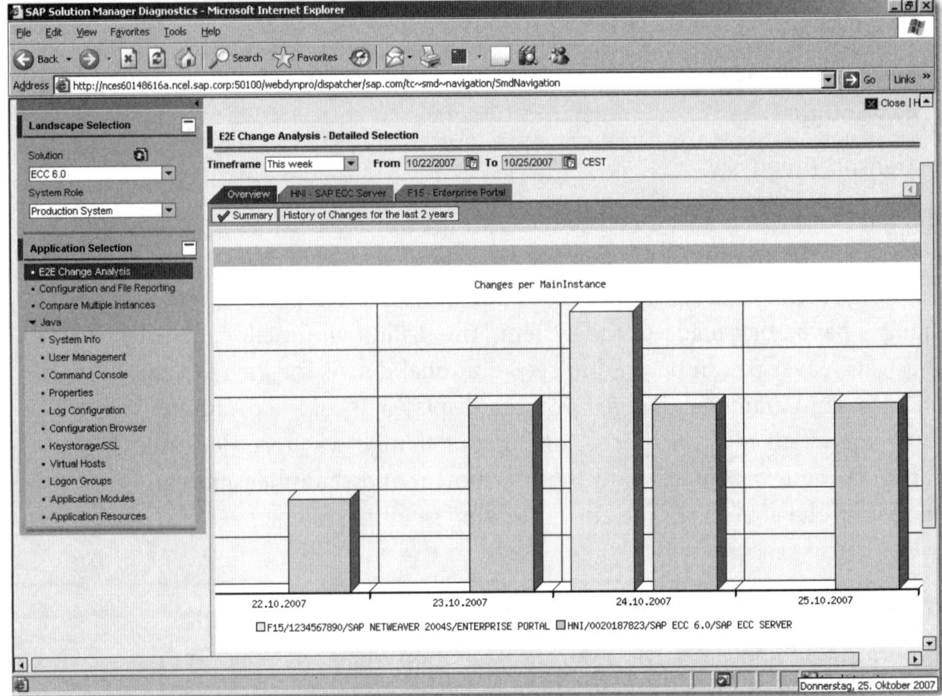

Figure 19.23 Change Analysis—Overview

Analysis period

The default analysis period is one week. To change it, use the pulldown menu in the TIMEFRAME field. Using the CUSTOM SELECTION option, you can select any period. The data is read from SAP NetWeaver BI in accordance with the selected period.

In this example, the solution comprises an SAP ECC Server and SAP NetWeaver Portal. The changes are sorted by individual days. The legend at the bottom edge of the diagram shows the system to which the respective bar belongs. The overview lets you quickly determine the system in which changes have been made. In this example, changes were made to the SAP ECC Server which now should be analyzed in more detail. Select the SAP ECC SERVER tab (see Figure 19.24).

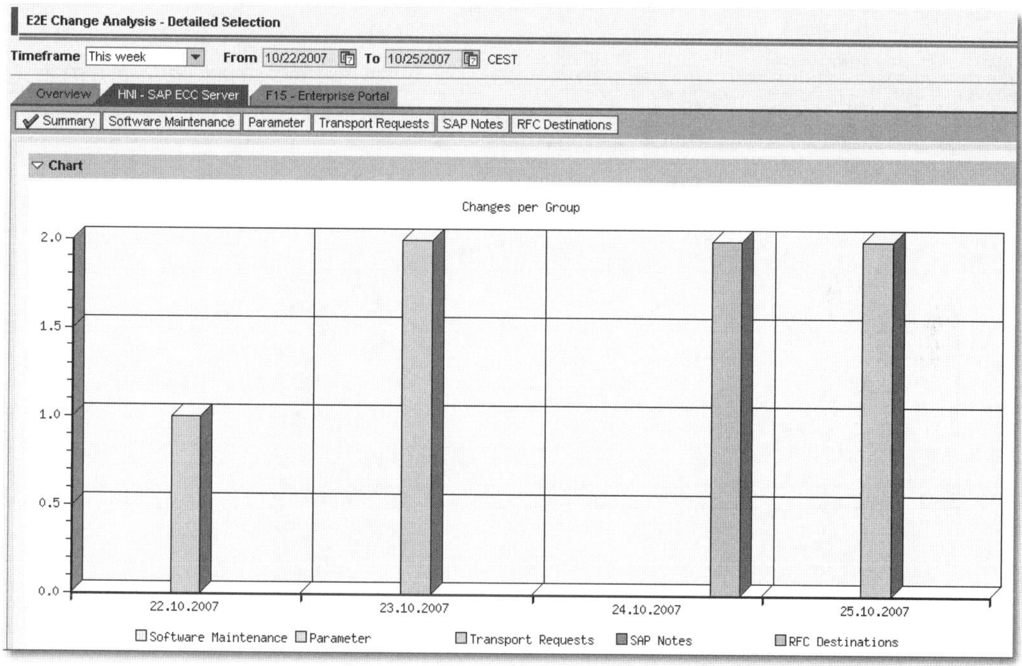

Figure 19.24 Overview of the SAP ECC Server

Change types and change groups

The summary of the SAP ECC Server shows which types of changes have been implemented. These are classified in change types and summarized in change groups. The SOFTWARE MAINTENANCE group contains software versions and imported Support Packages. The PARAMETER group comprises changed ABAP instance and database parameters. The groups TRANSPORT REQUESTS and SAP NOTES provide the number of transport requests and SAP Notes that were imported per day. RFC DESTINATIONS contains new or changed RFC connections.

The summary of SAP NetWeaver Portal (see Figure 19.25) shows the various change groups for Java-based systems. The categories are: APPLICATION, DISPATCHER, SERVER, NODE TYPE INDEPENDENT CONFIGURATION, and SOFTWARE RELEASE. During the analysis period, three parameter changes of the NODE TYPE INDEPENDENT CONFIGURATION type were performed, which now should be examined in greater detail. To do so, click the corresponding button for this change group.

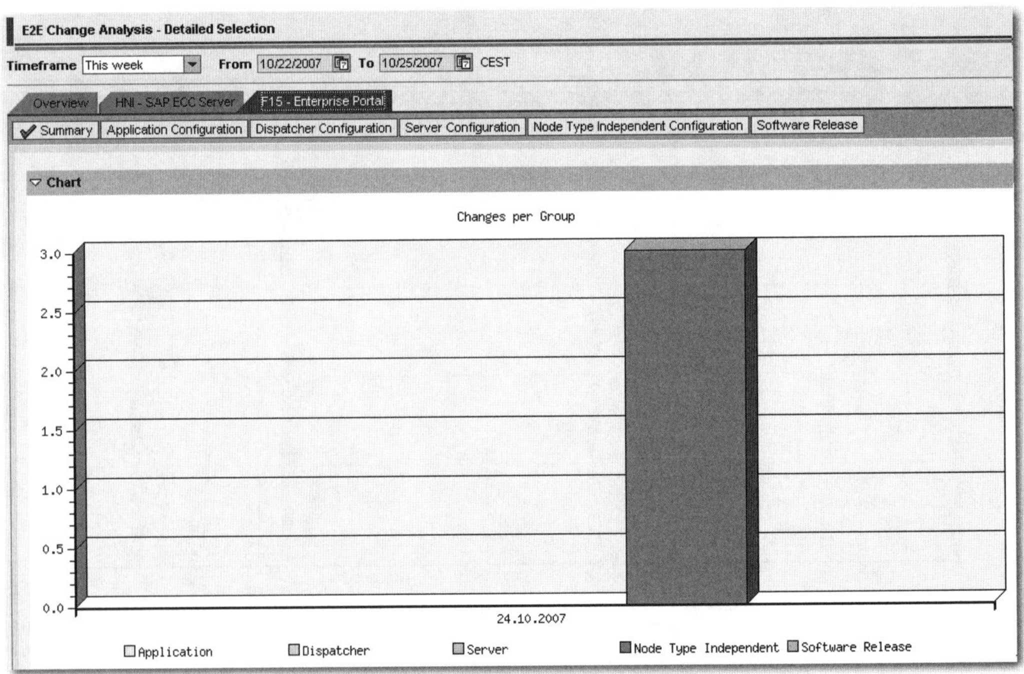

Figure 19.25 Overview of SAP NetWeaver Portal

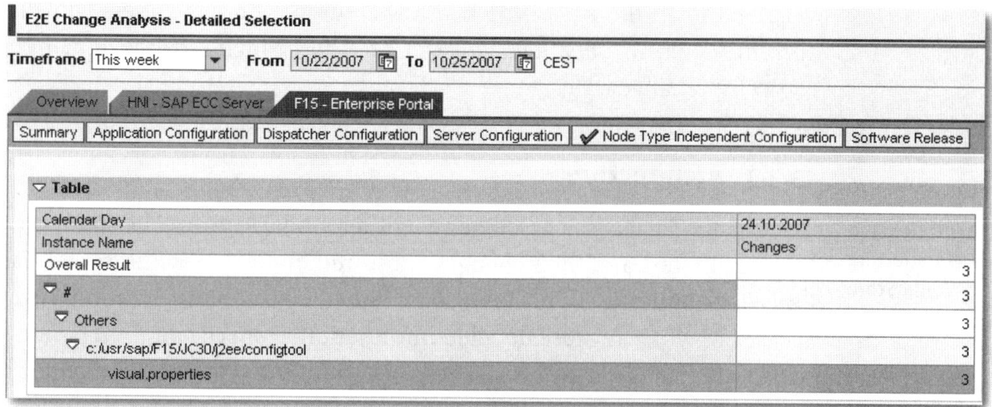

Figure 19.26 Parameter Changes for SAP NetWeaver Portal

The three changes were performed on October 24 (see Figure 19.26). The row including the parameter changes is highlighted green. This means that an additional drilldown is possible. This drilldown displays the detailed configuration parameters which are stored in Solution Manager. They can be displayed using the Detail Viewer (see Figure 19.27).

E2E CA DetailViewer

Name	Value	Change date	Add. Information
JC30/j2ee/			
configtool/visual.properties			Type properties
split	238	10.24.2007 23:06:56	Current value
x.coord	126	10.24.2007 23:06:56	Current value
x.coord	4	03.13.2007 17:08:47	Old initial value
x.coord	0	04.13.2007 13:58:19	Old updated value
x.coord	126	10.24.2007 23:06:56	Current value
y.coord	51	10.24.2007 23:06:56	Current value

Row 1 of 8

Figure 19.27 Detail Viewer

Detail Viewer

The Detail Viewer displays the changed parameters, including their change history. In this case, this is the ConfigStore `configtool/ visual.properties`. The parameters `split`, `x.coord`, and `y.coord` were changed. The current value and the date of the last change are displayed. For each parameter, you can display the history, including previous values and change timestamps. The history starts with the initial value (OLD INITIAL

VALUE entry in the ADD INFORMATION column) and concludes with the current value. In between, you can see the changed values and their respective change date.

19.3.3 Architecture

Configuration and File Reporting ConfigStore

The Change Analysis is based on two different data stores. The configuration parameters and their changes are stored in the *Configuration and File Reporting* application which is also an integral part of SAP Solution Manager. Here, you can store detailed information in special data containers, which are called *ConfigStore*. There are different types of ConfigStores for the various types of configuration information. The most important types are `xml`, `txt`, `ini`, and `properties`. They include two columns, PARAMETER and VALUE.

Top-down view

ConfigStores are summarized in change types and change groups for the Change Analysis. Change types are the smallest unit for which changes are counted and displayed. A change type contains the changes of one or more related ConfigStores. Changes types are combined in change groups. The Change Analysis provides a top-down view you can use to navigate from the change groups to the change types. Detailed changes in the ConfigStores can be displayed using the *Detail Viewer*.

Change groups and change types are defined for ABAP-based systems. For Java, the change group corresponds to the location of the ConfigStore (file system or database). For the change type, you use the alias of the ConfigStore definition. This allows for a useful grouping of data.

Table 19.1 contains the ABAP change types and change groups.

Change Group	Change Type
ABAP Basis Configuration	ABAP Instance Parameter
ABAP Software Version	Component Release Implemented Packages SAP Kernel SAP Notes Support Package Level

Table 19.1 Change Groups and Change Types

Transports	Customizing Workbench
Others	RFC Destinations
BI Parameter	RSADMIN RSADMINA RSADMINC RSADMINS
BIA Parameter	RSDDTREXADMIN
Database DB6	DB DB6 DBMCONFIG DB DB6 LEVEL DB DB6 PAHI DB DB6 REGISTRY
Database MAXDB	DB MAXDB LEVEL DB MAXDB PARAMETER
Database MSSQL	DB MSSQL LEVEL DB MSSQL OPTIONS DB MSSQL PARAMETER
Database ORA	DB ORA LEVEL DB ORA PARAMETER DB ORA RACPARAMETER
OS (Operating System)	Others

Table 19.1 Change Groups and Change Types (Cont.)

The number of changes per change type is transferred to SAP NetWeaver BI on a daily basis and is based on the information in the ConfigStores. These are the two different data stores that are used in the Change Analysis. The aggregated number of changes per day is stored in SAP NetWeaver BI to enable top-down analysis. The detailed configuration information and the change history of the configuration parameters are retained as basic information in the ConfigStores of the *Configuration and File Reporting* application.

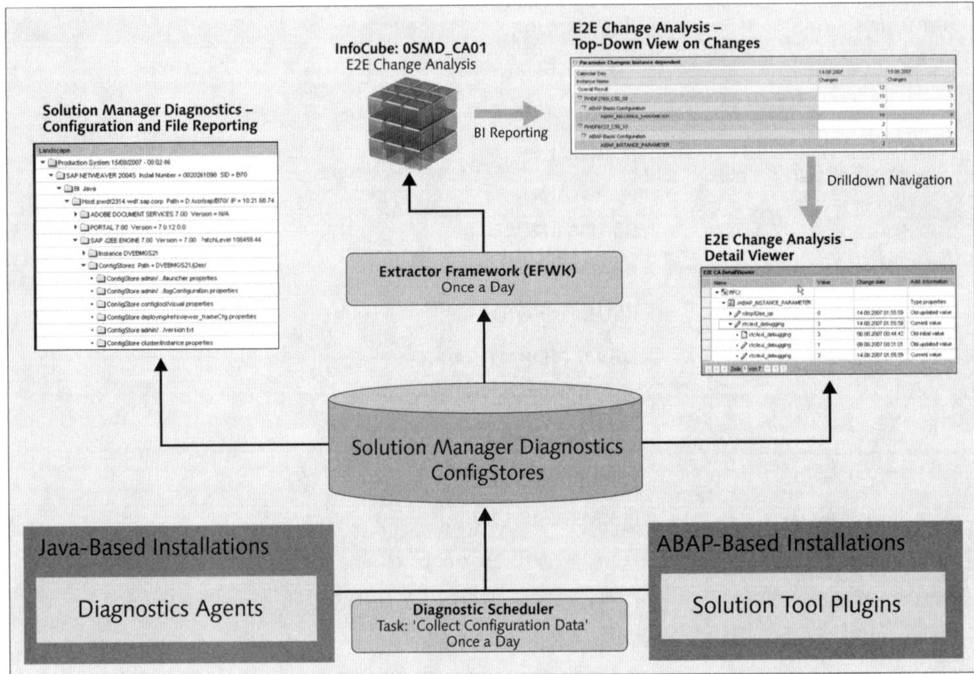

Figure 19.28 Data Collection for the Change Analysis

The ConfigStores are filled using Solution Manager Scheduler, which collects data from the connected satellite systems once a day. In Java-based systems, the data is collected using Diagnostics agents; in ABAP-based systems this is accomplished using plug-in extractors.

Extractor Framework

Subsequently, the data is transferred from the ConfigStores to an SAP NetWeaver BI InfoCube. The Extractor Framework of SAP Solution Manager is used for this purpose. Using SAP NetWeaver BI provides a top-down view of collected data. You can navigate from the aggregated data (number of changes per day) to the detailed data.

Data sources

The change analysis accesses different data sources. Some data is stored directly in the file system; some is read from the database tables. Most configuration data does not have a timestamp and change history. For this data, a snapshot of the current parameter values is stored and compared to the values of the previous day. If a deviation exists for a parameter, the change time of the last snapshot is assigned to this parameter. This way, you can create a complete change history for all configuration parameters. However, the change timestamp of a parameter is the point of time when the system determined the change, not the actual time when the parameter was changed in the system. Exceptions are SAP Notes, RFC connections, and transport requests for which you can determine the exact change time from the system.

19.4 SAP Maintenance Optimizer

Importing and testing Support Packages and patches are tasks performed on a regular basis by SAP administrators. In particular, the increasing number of SAP solutions and software components, and the newly added Java and web applications have, in the last few years, multiplied the effort required for software maintenance. SAP Maintenance Optimizer considerably facilitates the maintenance process. It is an important tool for managing software releases and for planning and implementing maintenance activities in the SAP landscape.

19.4.1 Features

SAP Maintenance Optimizer guides you through the planning, downloading, and implementation of SAP Support Packages. Moreover, the Maintenance Optimizer lets you install Enhancement Packages or integrate them in an upgrade to SAP ERP 6.0.

Maintenance Optimizer is part of SAP Solution Manager 7.0, with which you can find information about the existing systems, software components, and Support Package releases. On the basis of this data, Maintenance Optimizer calculates the Support Packages to be imported to obtain the required Support Package stack. A *guided procedure* guides you through the process of Support Package selection and download.

Approval of Support Packages in the download basket

If you select Support Packages manually, you are directly guided to the appropriate download area of the SAP Software Distribution Center for the required product. This includes the approval of Support Packages in the download basket, a step that is necessary for all products based on SAP NetWeaver 7.0. For these products, you cannot directly download the Support Packages from the SAP Service Marketplace. All actions are logged and can subsequently be retraced in reporting.

Enhancement Packages

When importing Enhancement Packages, Maintenance Optimizer calculates the required software components that need to be enhanced to get a specific functionality. Moreover, the necessary Support Packages of the enhanced and non-enhanced software components are calculated.

Release upgrade

Using Maintenance Optimizer, you can integrate the installation of Enhancement Packages (EhP) in the upgrade to *SAP ERP 6.0* for product versions that support an upgrade to SAP ERP 6.0. Maintenance Optimizer calculates all of the files you have to download from the SAP Service Marketplace in addition to the files provided on the upgrade DVD.

19.4.2 Integration with other Tools

Maintenance Optimizer is integrated with the following tools:

- **SAP Solution Manager**
  If you start a new product maintenance procedure, Maintenance Optimizer reads the imported Support Packages from your solution and calculates the necessary Support Packages to obtain the desired Support Package level.
- **SAP Service Marketplace**
  Maintenance Optimizer directly guides you to the corresponding area of the SAP Software Distribution Center for the product you want to maintain. It reads the download basket of the S-User assigned to you and approves the selected items in the basket so that they can be downloaded. Log on to the SAP Service Marketplace as the S-User assigned to you. The S-User is the user ID for the SAP Service Marketplace.
- **Software Lifecycle Manager**
  Maintenance Optimizer uses the Software Lifecycle Manager to automatically download manually selected or automatically calculated files into a central directory. The Software Lifecycle Manager is optional. As an alternative, you can use the SAP Download Manager to download Support Packages, or download the Support Packages individually from the SAP Service Marketplace.
- **SAP Upgrade Tools**
  Maintenance Optimizer creates a stack configuration file in XML format that contains a list of all downloaded Support Packages. This list

can be evaluated by the SAP Upgrade Tools SPAM, SAINT, JSPM, and SAPJup. All Support Packages that are listed in the package configuration file are then automatically integrated. This automates the definition of the import queue.

19.4.3 Setting up Maintenance Optimizer

Basic Solution Manager settings

To be able to use Maintenance Optimizer, you must install or set up SAP Solution Manager 7.0. All satellite systems to be supplied with Support Packages must be connected and included in a solution. The RFC connection SAP-OSS to the SAP Service Marketplace must exist to be able to download Support Packages.

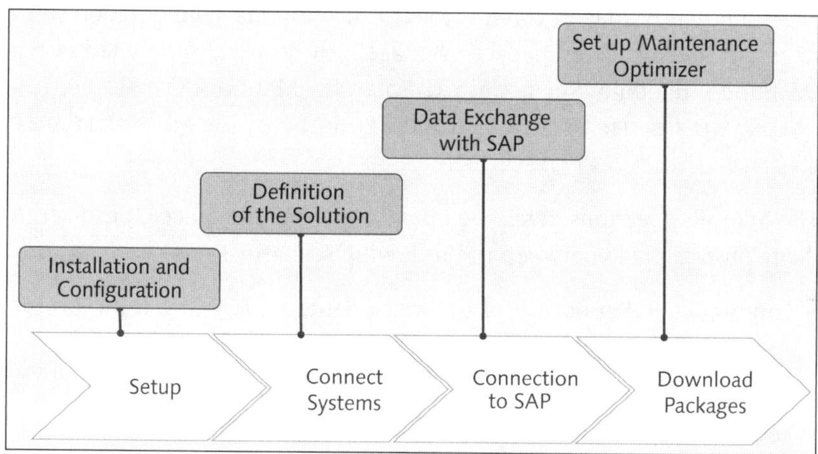

Figure 19.29 Prerequisites for Maintenance Optimizer

Activate Maintenance Optimizer BC Set

The special configuration steps for Maintenance Optimizer are defined in the SAP Solution Manager Implementation Guide (IMG). You can find the IMG in Transaction SPRO. Navigate to IMG Node SAP SOLUTION MANAGER • CONFIGURATION • BASIC SETTINGS • STANDARD CONFIGURATION OF BASIC SETTINGS • SOLUTION MANAGER • BASIC BC SETS FOR CONFIGURATION • ACTIVATE MAINTENANCE OPTIMIZER BC SET.

Assign S-User

Next, you have to assign a user in the SAP Service Marketplace to each user of SAP Solution Manager. This is done using Transaction AISUSER. A table is displayed in which you can create an entry for each user who needs to work with Maintenance Optimizer. In the SAP Service Marketplace, enter the respective user ID of SAP Solution Manager and the appropriate S-User. You do not have to enter the prefix S000 because it is automatically added. The assignment of an S-User is necessary because SAP Solution Manager logs on to the SAP Service Marketplace in the background to download Support Packages.

[+] The S-User must be authorized to download software in the SAP Service Marketplace.

The user in SAP Solution Manager requires the authorization object SAP_MAINT_OPT_ADMIN to have all authorizations in Maintenance Optimizer.

Configuration of the Software Lifecycle Manager

If you want to download Support Packages automatically using the Software Lifecycle Manager, you must perform additional configuration steps to set up the Software Lifecycle Manager. These are also detailed in the IMG under the following node: SAP SOLUTION MANAGER CONFIGURATION • SCENARIO-SPECIFIC SETTINGS • CHANGE MANAGEMENT • MAINTENANCE OPTIMIZER (SOFTWARE LIFECYCLE MANAGER).

Scenarios

The following sections detail the operation of Maintenance Optimizer. A distinction is made between the following scenarios:

- Import of a Support Package stack (automatic calculation of the required Support Packages)
- Import of an individual Support Package (manual selection of the required Support Packages)
- Import of Enhancement Packages

19.4.4 Import of Support Packages

There are many reasons to import Support Packages at regular intervals; for example, to import new bug fixes proactively or to benefit from enhanced functionality. Moreover, statutory changes are provided via Support Packages.

For proactive software maintenance, SAP recommends using Support Package stacks. These are Support Package combinations that are coordinated with and tested for a specific product. Maintenance Optimizer calculates the delta between the Support Package level currently imported in the system and the desired Support Package level and downloads the missing Support Packages.

To start Maintenance Optimizer, call Transaction SOLUTION_MANAGER and navigate to CHANGE MANAGEMENT • MAINTENANCE OPTIMIZER. Select the solution into which you want to import the Support Packages and create a new maintenance procedure (CREATE NEW MAINTENANCE TRANSACTION button).

Maintenance transaction

The new maintenance transaction comprises five steps:

1. Plan Maintenance: Select the systems into which the Support Packages should be imported.
2. Select Files: Select the Support Packages to be imported. Depending on the download option, this step involves five single steps.
3. Download Files: In this step, the selected Support Packages are downloaded from the SAP Service Marketplace.
4. Perform Implementation: Import the Support Packages into the satellite systems.
5. End Maintenance: After all Support Packages are imported, the maintenance procedure ends.

When you create a new maintenance procedure, you automatically enter the first of these five steps, which are described in more detail in the following sections.

1. Plan Maintenance

In the upper part of the input screen, you have to enter a priority and a short text for the maintenance procedure to be able to identify the maintenance procedure in the list of all maintenance procedures later on. You can also store documents in the procedure, for instance, project documentation. If required, you can also specify the persons responsible for this procedure. By default, the roles *Sold-to-Party* (of the maintenance procedure) and *Message Processor* (the current processor) are available. This is particularly useful if the sold-to party and the processor are different people; for example, if the user department requests the import of Support Packages and the IT department performs the import.

[+] The roles *Sold-to-Party* and *Message Processor* are stored as business partners. A Solution Manager user must be assigned to a business partner in Transaction BP before he can assume one of the roles.

In the lower part of the input screen, you first select the product version for which you want to import Support Packages. All systems are displayed that belong to the product version. Select the desired system and click CONTINUE. A transaction number is generated that uniquely identifies the maintenance procedure.

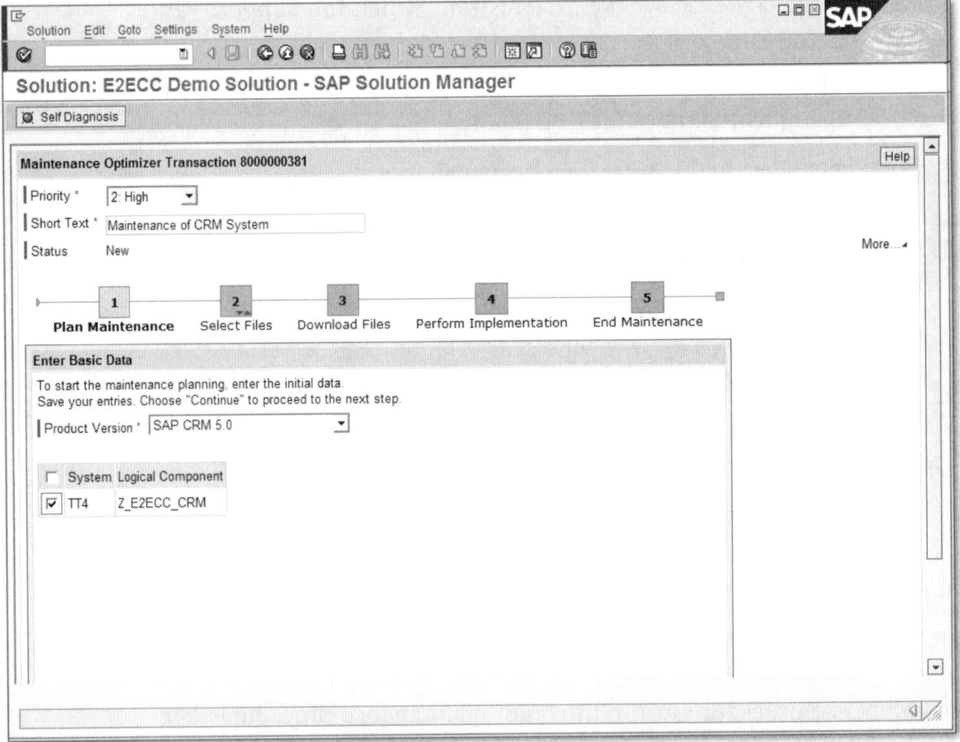

Figure 19.30 Plan Maintenance

2. Select Files

In the second step, you need to select the required Support Packages. As already mentioned, there are two options to select Support Packages: CALCULATE DOWNLOAD FILES AUTOMATICALLY or FILL DOWNLOAD BASKET MANUALLY.

Calculate download files automatically

If Maintenance Optimizer is supposed to determine the required files, select the FIND DOWNLOAD FILES option. Five substeps display.

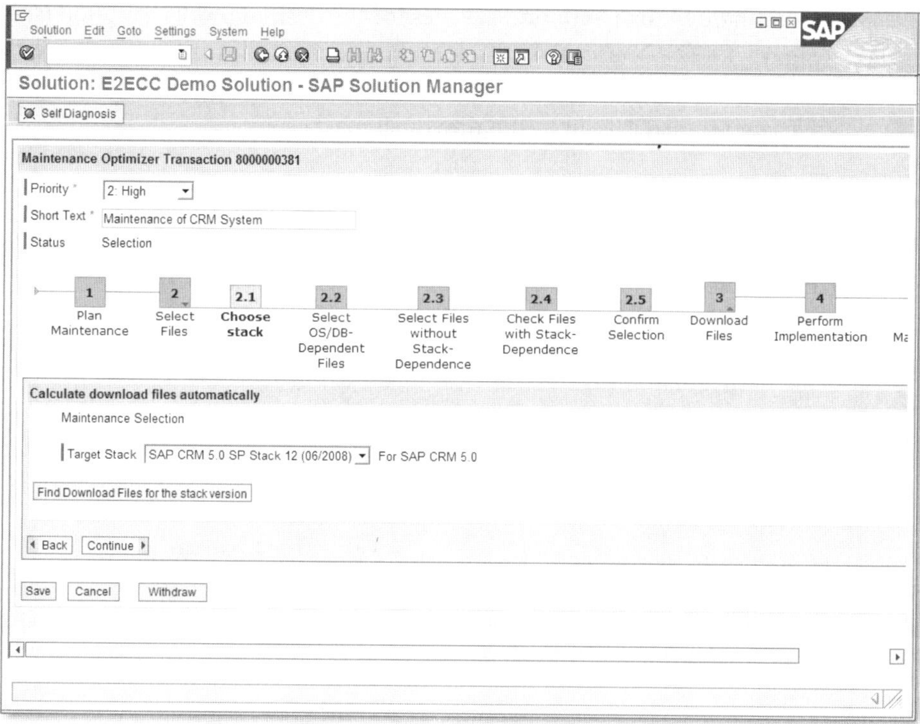

Figure 19.31 Select Files with Substeps

First, you choose the desired Support Package stack and click the FIND DOWNLOAD FILES FOR THE STACK VERSION button (see Figure 19.31)

The next substep lists the required operating system and database files. Select the files that match your environment and click CONTINUE.

In the next screen, you will see a list of files that are independent of the selected stack (for example, kernel updates). All files are selected by default. Deselect the files you do not need and click CONTINUE.

The next screen shows all files belonging to the stack. Again, deselect the files you do not need and click CONTINUE.

The last substep transfers the selected files to the download basket of the S-User assigned to your Solution Manager User.

Manually select Support Packages

If you want to select the required Support Packages manually, click the SELECT FILES FOR <PRODUCT VERSION> button. A browser with the SAP Service Marketplace opens and you can directly jump to the page where you can download Support Packages for the desired product version (see Figure 19.32). You can then select the required files from the Support Package stack or navigate to the relevant software component. Select the files and transfer them to the download basket.

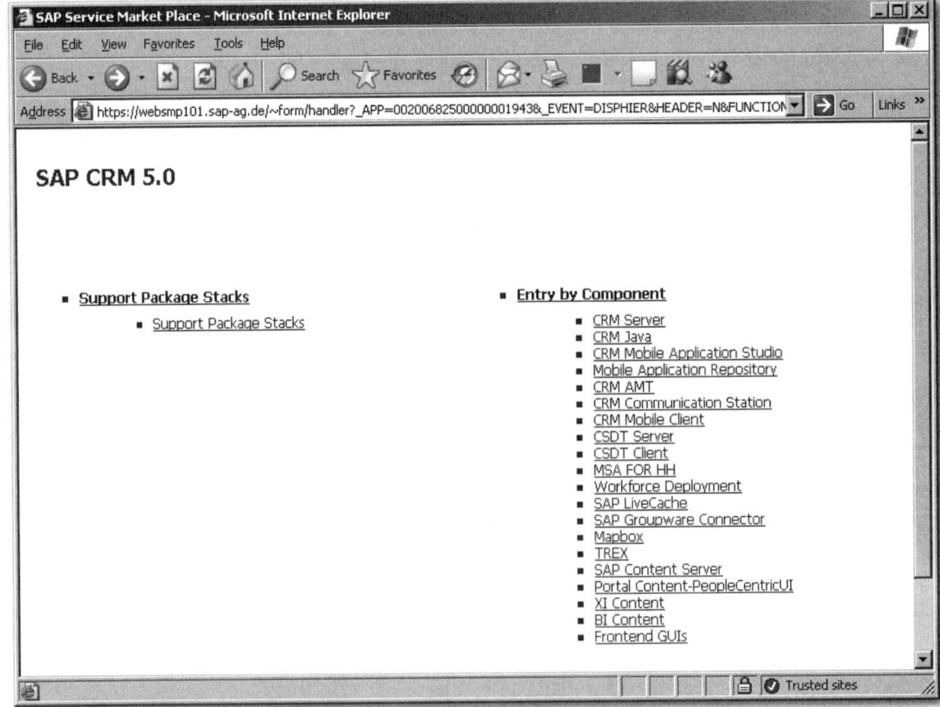

Figure 19.32 Manually Filling the Download Basket

When you have selected the required files and added them to the download basket—either automatically or manually—click CONTINUE to go to the next step.

3. Download Files

Confirm files

In the next step, you must first confirm the files before they can be downloaded. Click CONFIRM FILES IN DOWNLOAD BASKET. An overview of all files in the download basket is displayed (see Figure 19.33). Review the files and click Confirm Download. After you have confirmed the selection, the files are downloaded using the SAP Download Manager. As an alternative, you can go to the download basket in the SAP Service Marketplace and download the files directly with a right-click. When the download is completed click Continue (see Figure 19.34).

SAP Solution Manager

Maintenance Optimizer: Confirm Files for Download (User: S0004360953)

	File	Description	Download Status	Size [kb]	Date	Time
☑	SAPKB70012	Basis Support Package 12 for 7.00	Awaiting Confirmation	102097	14.11.2008	13:11:59
☑	SAPJEE12_0-10003469.SCA	SP12 for SAP J2EE Engine 7.00	Awaiting Confirmation	55725	14.11.2008	13:13:02

Confirm Download | Exit | Refresh

Figure 19.33 Confirm Files

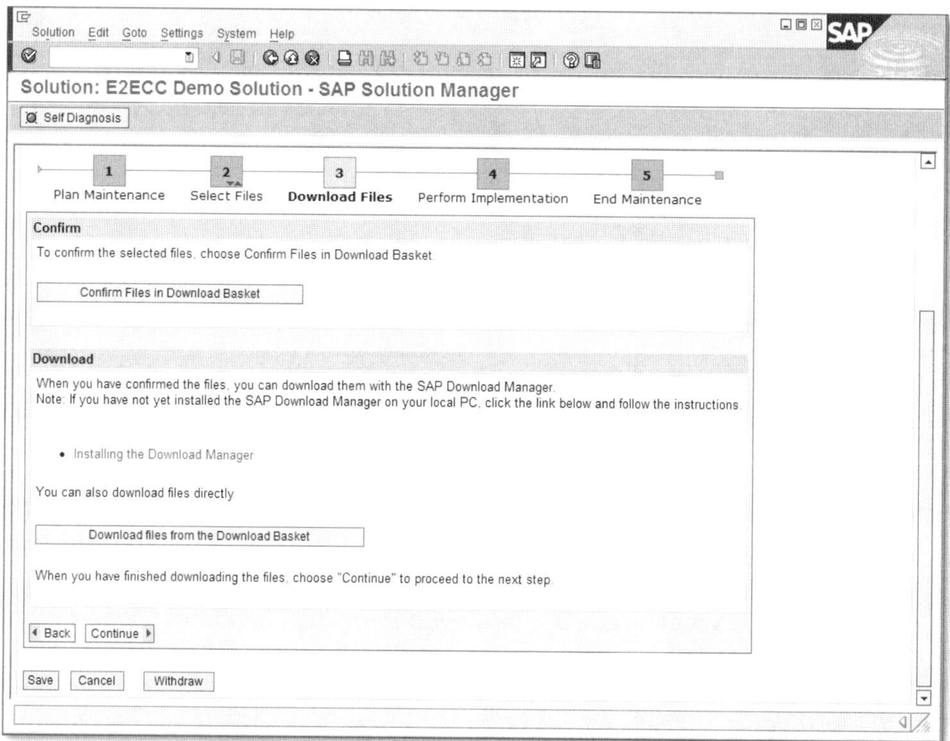

Figure 19.34 Download Files

4. Perform Implementation

In the next step, you see the list of Support Packages you downloaded in the previous step. You can directly see the Support Packages to be imported in this maintenance procedure. Moreover, you can call detailed information and side effects for each Support Package. (See Figure 19.35.)

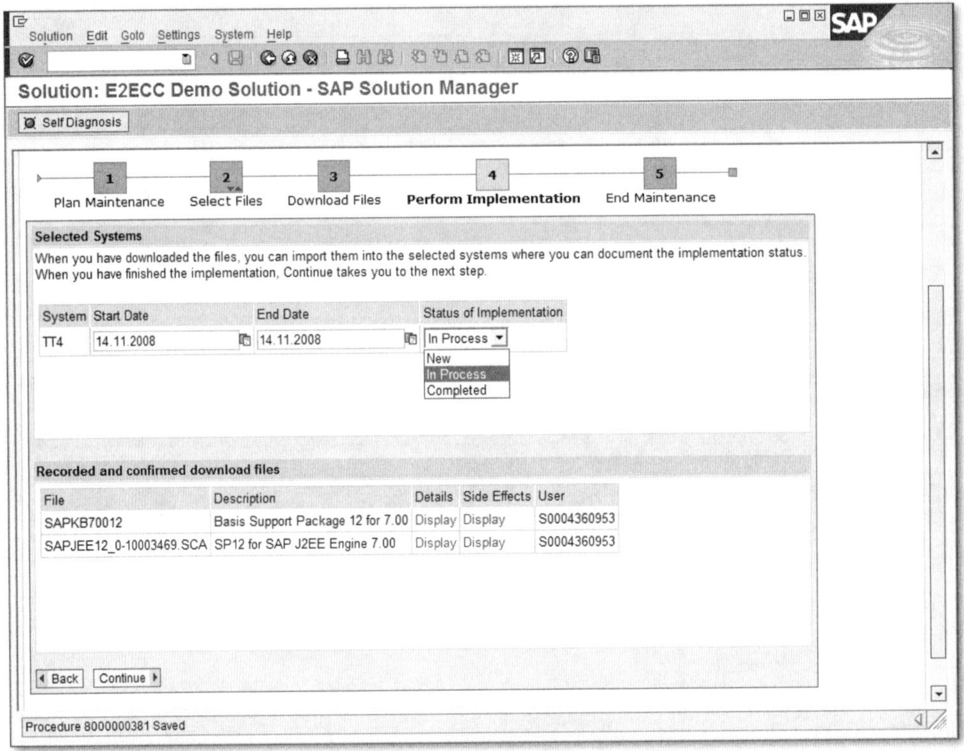

Figure 19.35 Perform Implementation

The implementation of Support Packages is performed by SAP Support Package tools. For ABAP stacks these tools are the SAP Support Package Manager (SPAM) or the SAP Add-on Installation Tool (SAINT). For Java stacks it is the Java Support Package Manager (JSPM). In future extension phases, Maintenance Optimizer will control the import of Support Packages to a larger extent, and in connection with the Software Lifecycle Manager. Currently, you can only document the progress of the Support Package implementation in this step. For each system, you can set the status to NEW, IN PROCESS, or COMPLETED.

After the Support Packages are imported into all systems, you can conclude the maintenance procedure. Set the implementation status of all systems to COMPLETED and click CONTINUE.

5. End Maintenance

When you have successfully completed the maintenance of your systems, complete the product maintenance procedure. After you have set the status to COMPLETED you can no longer change the maintenance transaction.

19.4.5 Import of Enhancement Packages

Enhancement Packages and business functions

As of SAP ERP 6.0 you can import Enhancement Packages. This allows you to upgrade individual software components to a higher release to obtain new functionality. The new functionality is inactive initially and must be switched on using business functions. Enhancement Packages are frequently imported together with Support Packages and the required business functions activated in the subsequent implementation project. The new concept of Enhancement Packages lets you avoid an elaborate release upgrade project.

Technical usage

A business function is new functionality, for example, the Enterprise Asset Management. To use this functionality, you must upgrade specific software components to a higher version. In the case of Enterprise Asset Management, these are SAP_APPL and EA-APPL. The number of software components whose version must be upgraded is called *technical usage*. For the example of Enterprise Asset Management you require the technical usage *Central Applications*, which consist of the software components SAP_APPL and EA-APPL. SAP Note 1083576 includes a list of business functions for Enhancement Package 3 along with information on the technical usages that must be imported respectively.

If you create a maintenance procedure for SAP ERP 6.0 in Maintenance Optimizer, you can either perform pure software maintenance or, in addition, import Enhancement Packages. If you choose the ENHANCEMENT PACKAGE INSTALLATION option, you must select the version of the Enhancement Package, Support Package stack, and the technical usage in the next step.

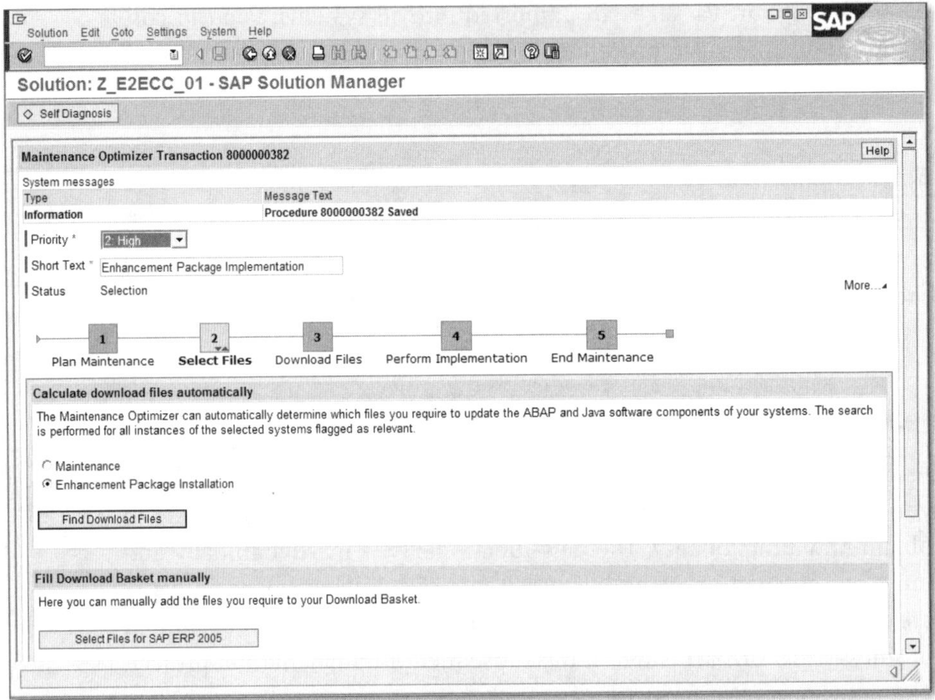

Figure 19.36 Enhancement Package Download with Maintenance Optimizer

SAP Maintenance Optimizer calculates all required Support Packages and Enhancement Packages to upgrade the current system status to the desired Enhancement Package version and Support Package level. You must download the following packages:

- Support Packages that are prerequisites for the Enhancement Package import
- Support Packages for enhanced software components
- Support Packages for non-enhanced software components

Equivalencies exist between the Support Packages for enhanced software components and for non-enhanced software components. For example, Support Package Stack 13 for ERP 6.00 is equivalent to Support Package Stack 2 for ERP 6.03. This means that the packages have the same maintenance level and are synchronized in chronological order. All corrections contained in Support Package 13 for ERP 6.00 are also contained in Support Package 2 for ERP 6.03.

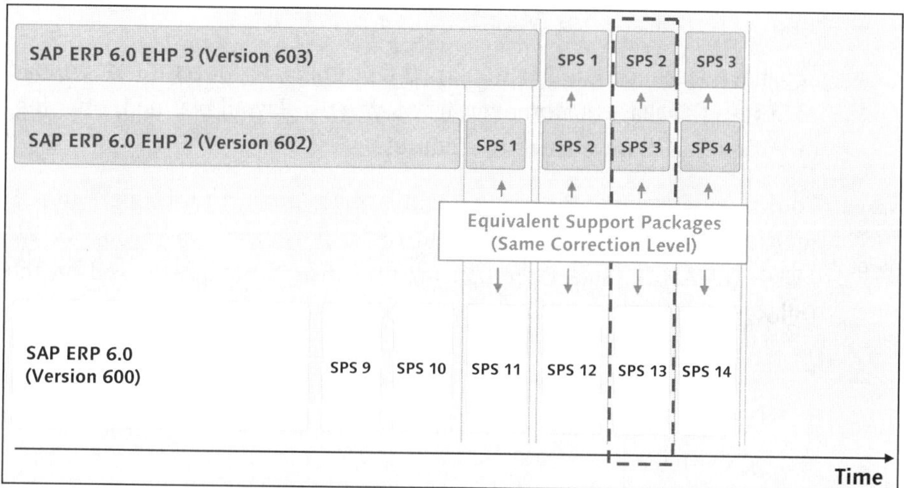

Figure 19.37 Equivalent Support Package Levels for Enhanced and Non-Enhanced Software Components

For the example shown in Figure 19.37, Support Package Stack 2 for Enhancement Package 3 was selected. This means that Support Package 2 is downloaded for all enhanced software components and Support Package 13 for all non-enhanced components.

At the end of the download process, Maintenance Optimizer creates a stack configuration file in XML format. This file comprises a list of all downloaded Support Packages. The stack configuration file can be read using the import tools JSPM and SAINT (see Figure 19.38). Thereby, the tools are made known which Support Packages should be imported. The definition of the import queue is implemented automatically.

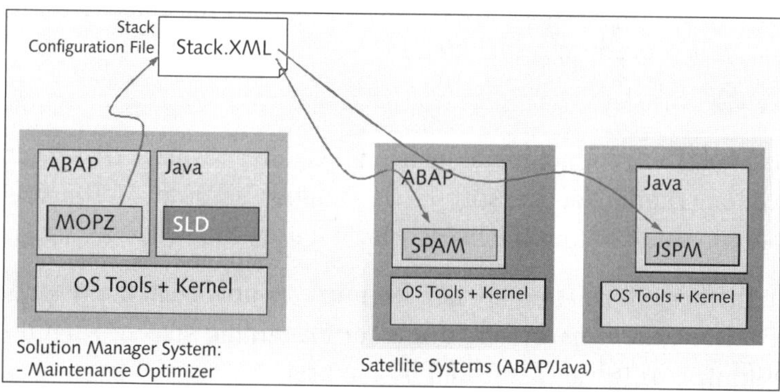

Figure 19.38 Stack Configuration File in XML Format

19.4.6 Reporting for Maintenance Procedures

You have learned how Maintenance Optimizer supports the download of Support Packages. Moreover, it lets you display all planned, ongoing, or completed maintenance procedures.

Display maintenance procedures

To display an overview of the product maintenance procedures implemented using Maintenance Optimizer, call Transaction /TMWFLOW/MAINTENANCE. Select product maintenance procedures based on the following criteria:

- SYSTEM STATUS:
  - Open
  - Completed
- PRIORITY: Priority selected by the user for this procedure
- USER STATUS: Corresponds to the current step of a procedure
- CREATED/CHANGED ON: Date on which the procedure was created or last changed
- CREATED/CHANGED BY: User who created the procedure or made the last change
- SOLUTION: Solution Manager solution in which the procedure was created
- SAP PRODUCT: Product version selected in the maintenance transaction
- SYSTEM: The system entered in the procedure
- SYSTEM STATUS: Implementation status of the systems in the procedure. If at least one system in the procedure meets the status criteria selected, this procedure is included in the report.
- Choose EXECUTE.

As a result, a list of product maintenance procedures displays that meet your selection criteria. You can sort the information according to the different columns and/or store the list as a local file for further processing.

To obtain further information about a list entry, double-click the respective entry. The system navigates to the corresponding step in Maintenance Optimizer as it was last stored by the user.

19.5 Upgrade Support

For a release upgrade, you have to face many challenges, particularly in the areas of project planning and management, application adaptation, testing, and user training. SAP Solution Manager provides various functions that can help you to save costs, increase efficiency, and reduce risks.

Solution Manager work center

In addition to the use of different functions in SAP Solution Manager by calling individual transactions, as of Support Package level SPS15, different tasks are combined in work centers. These can be activated using Customizing settings. From a work center, you can access the relevant messages, alerts, evaluations, and documents, perform tasks for which you have authorization, and perform the corresponding role assignments. For an upgrade project, you select the IMPLEMENTATION AND UPGRADE work center (see Figure 19.39) after you have called this view using Transaction SOLMAN_WORK CENTER.

Upgrade project support

The application of the functions described here can be performed via the work center, directly via the transactions listed, and also if you start an upgrade project. You will benefit especially if you have already carried out an implementation project using SAP Solution Manager that by copying you can use as the starting point for your upgrade project. To create an upgrade project, start Transaction SOLAR_PROJECT_ADMIN. When you create a new project, you create it as an upgrade project. If projects already exist in your system, you can use an implementation project, a template project, or another upgrade project as the basis for the copy. You can simply copy this reference project into a new upgrade project and check the data that was copied. If there is doubt, you should copy all data, including all documents and test plans, because you can easily delete any unneccessary data later on. If the copy is changed, the data of the original project is retained for documentation reasons.

[+]

When you copy documents from an existing project, you should create a new knowledge warehouse context (documentation enhancement) for the upgrade project. This way, the original document remains unchanged.

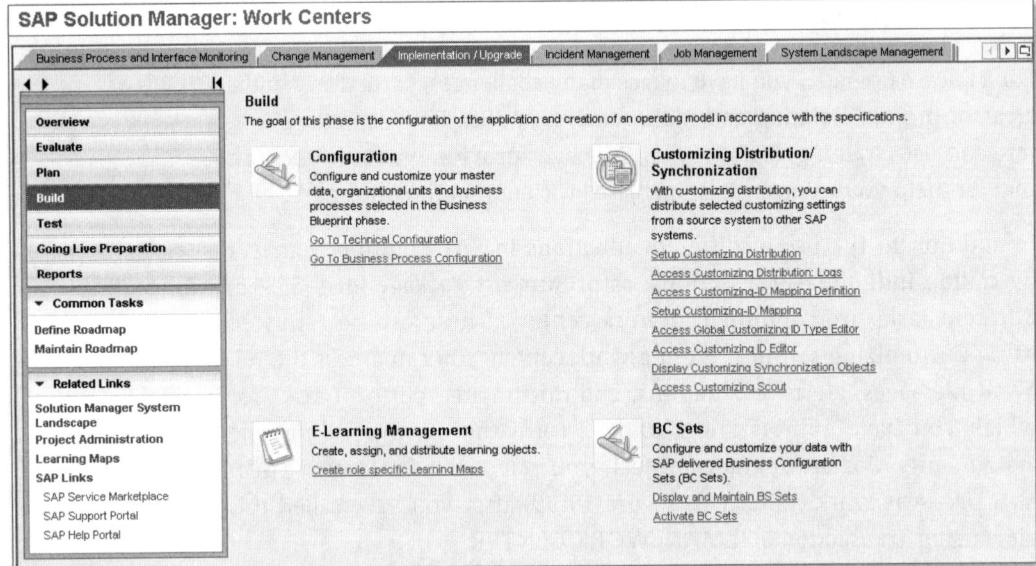

Figure 19.39 Upgrade Work Center

Upgrade Roadmap

Roadmaps include the standard SAP implementation method and cover the most important aspects and phases of an SAP implementation. The SAP Upgrade Roadmap provides a guide that is structured by phases for implementing an upgrade project. Its contents incorporate the experience from numerous projects and describe all tasks required for a successful upgrade of an SAP solution.

[+] The content of the roadmap is an integral part of the software component ST-ICO. This is why you should have installed the latest version on your system.

After you have created a project as described previously, assign it to an Upgrade Roadmap. To do so, select the GENERIC ROADMAP variant for the desired upgrade path. Thus, using accelerators and tools in the roadmap, you can easily access the corresponding transactions used for implementing the project tasks.

Phases

The phases of the Upgrade Roadmap are as follows:

- Project preparation
- Creation of an upgrade blueprint
- Upgrade realization
- Production preparation
- Production implementation and continuous support

Aside from these phases, there is an additional hierarchical classification within the roadmap. The phases contain several work packages which, in turn, include activities and tasks. Aside from their general description, the results to be achieved, and other tasks possibly required, the task area also includes interesting notes for the execution, as well as accelerators that are often available for this purpose. Accelerators are transactions for system information or hyperlinks directly referencing Best Practices in the SAP Service Marketplace. Because both tasks and accelerators are provided with attributes, you can easily filter the tasks for the project manager or the system administrator, by using the SAP Solution Manager filter functions, for example. Another interesting filter option lets you filter by one of the solution-specific upgrade paths—of which more than 60 currently exist—to only display information relevant for a CRM upgrade, for example. You can also centrally store your own information about the individual tasks such as the current task status, the project members involved, or extended documentation. In addition to further personalization options, from the Upgrade Roadmap of SAP Solution Manager, you can export tasks to Microsoft Project.

If you want to get an overview of the Upgrade Roadmap contents without using SAP Solution Manager, you can load the HTML version from the SAP Service Marketplace to your PC and view it locally using a web browser. You will still have the complete contents with all accelerators at hand; only the extended functions, such as further processing or filtering, are not available in this variant. You can download both the HTML version and the transport for SAP Solution Manager as of Version 3.1 from the SAP Service Marketplace at *http://service.sap.com/upgraderoadmap*. The Upgrade Roadmap (see Figure 19.40) is available in German and English.

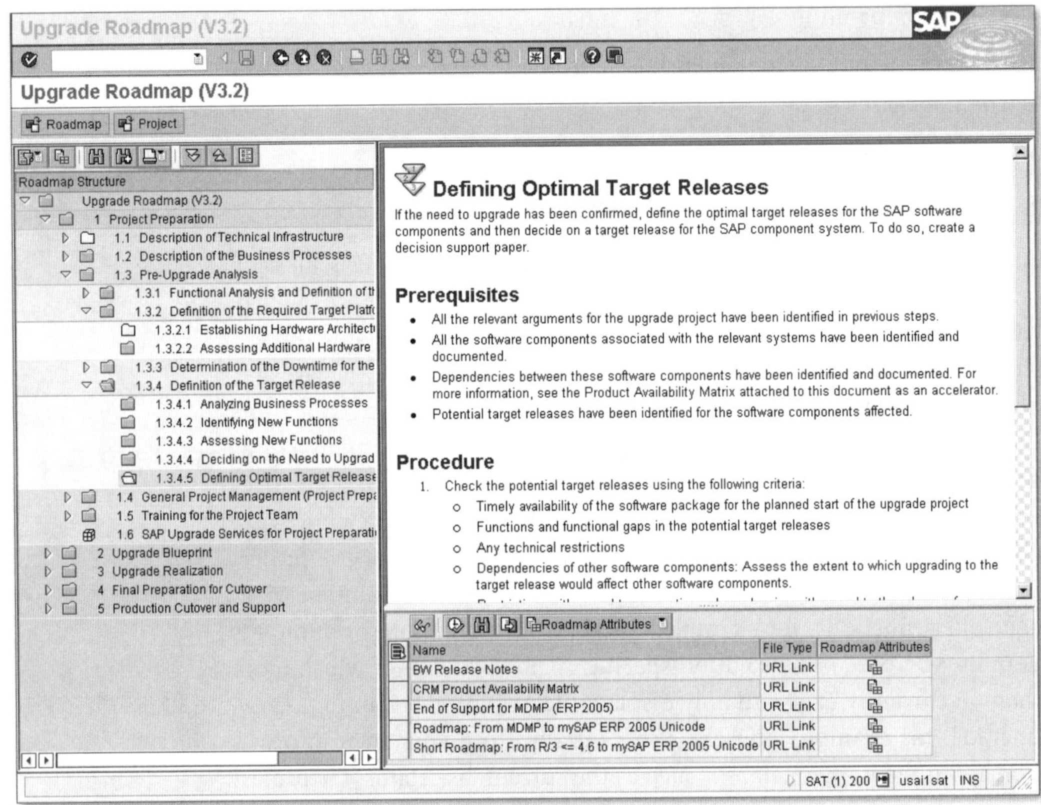

Figure 19.40 Upgrade Roadmap

Project preparation

If you follow the phases of an Upgrade Roadmap, the *project preparation* provides you with the tasks for reviewing the current situation, including the existing system landscape. You can use the system landscape reporting in Transaction SMSY to evaluate the data according to product, software component, and Support Package level. In SMSY, you can centrally maintain the data manually and adapt it automatically using additional tools, for example, the System Landscape Directory (SLD) or the Landscape Infrastructure Server (LIS). This product version and logical system data is combined in logical components that are relevant for upgradeable technical units and business process description.

Example: Using Information about Technical Units

In your analysis, you have identified the following technical units as the initial status:

SAP R/3 4.6C with operating system HP-UX 11.23/IA64 and database Oracle 9.2. You selected SAP ERP 6.0 ECC 6.0 as the target release. Using the information from the Product Availability Matrix (PAM), which you can find in the SAP Service Marketplace at http://service.sap.com/PAM, you determine that SAP ERP 6.0 ECC 6.0 is released with the technical units shown in Figure 19.41.

> Releases SAP ECC Server Database Platforms SAP KERNEL 7.00 64-BIT ORACLE...

Released Database Version	Operating System Version	Date (Internal)	Status (Internal)	Date (External)	Status (External)	System Status	Remarks
ORACLE 10.1 64-BIT	HP-UX 11.11/PA-RISC	24.10.2005	Released	24.10.2005	Released		
ORACLE 10.1 64-BIT	HP-UX 11.23/IA64 64BIT	24.10.2005	Released	24.10.2005	Released		
ORACLE 10.1 64-BIT	HP-UX 11.23/PA-RISC	24.10.2005	Released	24.10.2005	Released		
ORACLE 10.2 64-BIT	HP-UX 11.11/PA-RISC	31.03.2006	Released	31.03.2006	Released		
ORACLE 10.2 64-BIT	HP-UX 11.23/IA64 64BIT	22.05.2006	Released	22.05.2006	Released		
ORACLE 10.2 64-BIT	HP-UX 11.23/PA-RISC	31.03.2006	Released	31.03.2006	Released		
ORACLE 10.2 64-BIT	HP-UX 11.31/IA64 64BIT	11.04.2007	Released	11.04.2007	Released		
ORACLE 10.2 64-BIT	HP-UX 11.31/PA-RISC	12.12.2007	Released	12.12.2007	Released		

Figure 19.41 Product Availability Matrix, ERP 6.00/HPUX/Oracle

It is obvious that the operation of the OS and DB combination used under SAP ERP 6.0 ECC 6.0 with SAP Kernel 700 is released only with a 64-bit version for HP-UX and Oracle Version 10.x. To reduce the downtime during the upgrade, it is recommended to first upgrade the operating system or the database. A check of the released kernels for the start Release 4.6C reveals that for 4.6C, a kernel is released for the corresponding OS and DB combination (see Figure 19.42): HP-UX 11.23/IA64 and Oracle 10.2 with the 4.6D EX2 kernel. You can therefore already upgrade the database during a maintenance window prior to the SAP upgrade and schedule it accordingly in milestone planning.

> Releases R/3 Server Database Platforms SAP KERNEL 4.6D_EX2 64-BIT ORACLE...

Released Database Version	Operating System Version	Date (Internal)	Status (Internal)	Date (External)	Status (External)	System Status	Remarks
ORACLE 10.2 64-BIT	HP-UX 11.11/PA-RISC	14.11.2007	Released	14.11.2007	Released		
ORACLE 10.2 64-BIT	HP-UX 11.23/IA64 64BIT	14.11.2007	Released	14.11.2007	Released		
ORACLE 10.2 64-BIT	HP-UX 11.23/PA-RISC	14.11.2007	Released	14.11.2007	Released		
ORACLE 10.2 64-BIT	HP-UX 11.31/IA64 64BIT	14.11.2007	Released	14.11.2007	Released		
ORACLE 10.2 64-BIT	HP-UX 11.31/PA-RISC	14.11.2007	Released	14.11.2007	Released		

Figure 19.42 Product Availability Matrix, 4.6C/HPUX/Oracle

For the description of the business processes you will only include the definition of future process requirements if no project exists as a basis. After you have processed all work packages of the first phase, you can export the roadmap to an external project software package in which you maintain the project-specific activities. This can then be imported into the documentation tabulator project to maintain details, such as resources and budget, and to make it available centrally to the project team.

Blueprint

In the blueprint phase, you create either new processes for the new release or adapt the existing processes accordingly. If you used a copy of an existing project, and if the original project was built via the default Business Process Repository (BPR), you can determine the changes between the releases using the comparison functions. To do so, use Transaction SA_PROJECT_UPGRADE; the differences are later displayed in Transaction SOLAR01 for the business blueprint and in Transaction SOLAR02 for the configuration. The determination of the upgrade-relevant IMG activities is also facilitated if you can build on an existing project; these can be used in an initial upgrade project if the IMG activities have been assigned to the project during the first step. In both cases, for unused IMG objects within projects, the important new activities can be found without any problem. The information for the business blueprint is maintained using Transaction SOLAR01. In addition to the business processes, you must also plan the system landscape for the target release. You can maintain the possible changes in Transaction SOLAR_EVAL, but you might have to create new logical components for the new software component. Moreover, you must plan the test activities during this phase and implement a rough analysis of the test cases that were transferred from the existing project and that now have to be adapted to the new release. Next, you should plan the training of end users. If documentation exists, you must check its usability in the upgrade; otherwise you will have to create a requirements catalog for delta trainings along the process structure of the business processes in the documentation tabulator.

Realization

In the upgrade realization phase, SAP Solution Manager supports you in the implementation of the upgrade or the delta configuration; you do not have to individually check all configurations of the SAP Implementation Guide (IMG) for changes. The upgrade-relevant IMG changes as well as all upgrade-independent configuration adaptations are automatically determined based on the release information of the SAP components. You can start this comparison via SOLAR_PROJECT_ADMIN – SYSTEM LANDSCAPE tab, DISTRIBUTE UPGRADE FLAG on the IMG PROJECTS tab (see Figure 19.43); the results are copied automatically. The system indicates the upgrade-relevant IMG activities in the configuration on the CONFIGURATION tab in the UPGRADE FLAG column. Using Transaction SOLAR_EVAL • ANALYSIS • PROJECT • CONFIGURATION • PROJECT VIEWS • ASSIGN IMG OBJECTS IN PROJECT VIEWS you can determine this information using the reports of the project views. Upgrade-relevant IMG activities that are not part of your upgrade project already can also be determined via SOLAR_EVAL by using the option COMPARE WITH VIEWS. Missing IMG activities should be assigned to the corresponding processes using Transaction SOLAR02.

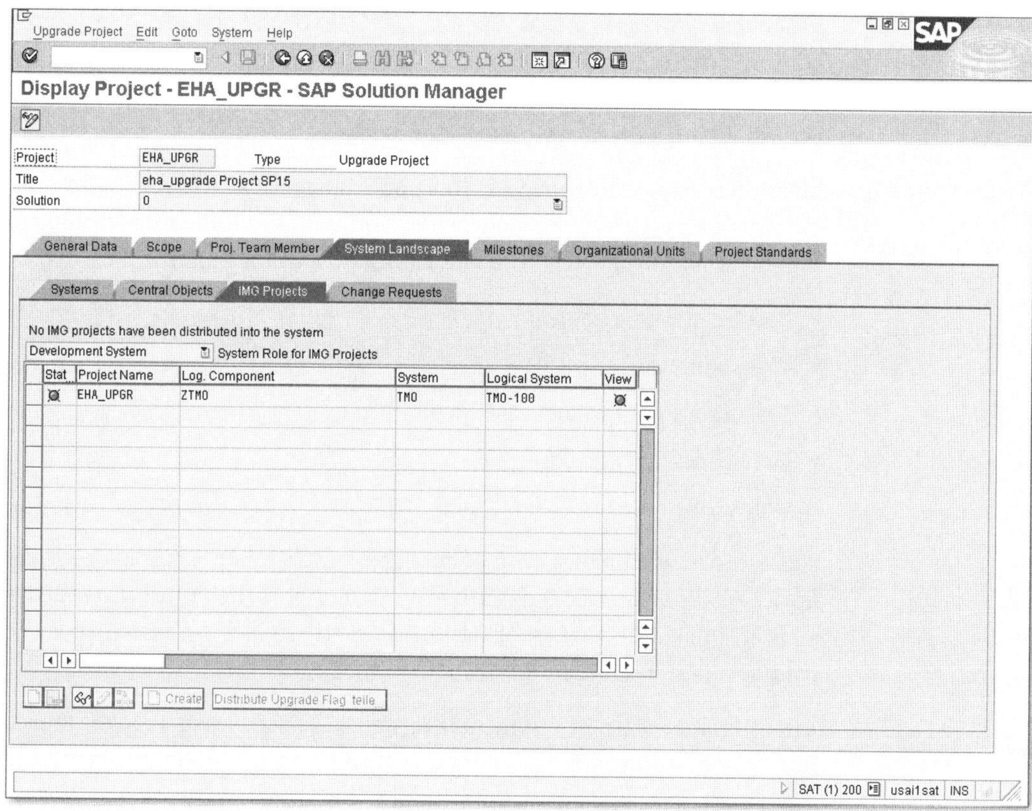

Figure 19.43 Transaction SOLAR_PROJECT_ADMIN

When the upgrade configuration is completed, you can perform the first tests. You can use SAP Solution Manager to organize and implement the tests. Based on the test cases that were assigned during the blueprint phase you can now generate process-oriented test plans. These are created using the test plan administration in Transaction STWB_2. In the Test Workbench integrated with SAP Solution Manager, you can create small test packages and assign them to testers who perform the acceptance tests. The testers can refer to the documentation of the manual test packages to find out what needs to be tested or they can execute an automated test using eCATT. If, in the project administration SOLAR_PROJECT_ADMIN, you assign the logical systems to the test systems, which are now located in the new release, the testers can directly navigate from SAP Solution Manager to these systems to perform the tests. For the tests, you can set status information such as *successfully tested* or *subsequent test required*; you can also navigate to the Service Desk to create error messages. Finally, you can track the progress of the tests via the reporting of the Test Workbench. The analysis can be called using SOLAR_EVAL • ANALYSIS • PROJECT • TEST • PROJECT STATUS ANALYSES.

[+] The enterprise edition of SAP Solution Manager, which you must purchase and activate explicitly, provides you with the following additional functions within the Test Workbench for Test Management:

- Release status scheme
- Test sequence
- Test assignment at test case level
- User check in test plan
- Workflow

You can use all functions independent of each other, except for workflow. SAP Note 1109650 describes how to import the enterprise edition add-on. For additional information refer to *http://www.service.sap.com/solutionmanager* • ENTERPRISE EDITION.

Production preparation

After you have carried out the various tests, such as the user acceptance, integration, and regression tests using SAP Solution Manager, you can now implement another action: training end users.

[+] Using SAP Solution Manager, and based on the existing project structure, you can create learning maps for the respective end user task areas as well as for the new functions with which, for example, purchasers or accountants of your enterprise, will work. A learning map is a comprehensive documentation provided as a computer-aided self-paced training that presents, in HTML format, brief information about lessons and links to the training materials. Figure 19.44 shows an example of a Learning Map. You can integrate e-learning materials in self-paced trainings, such as SAP Tutors, presentations, or test cases. To create learning maps on a role-specific basis, you must first create the end user roles in the HR-Org model.

If you have a central HR system, you should create the roles in the central HR system and distribute them in your Solution Manager system.

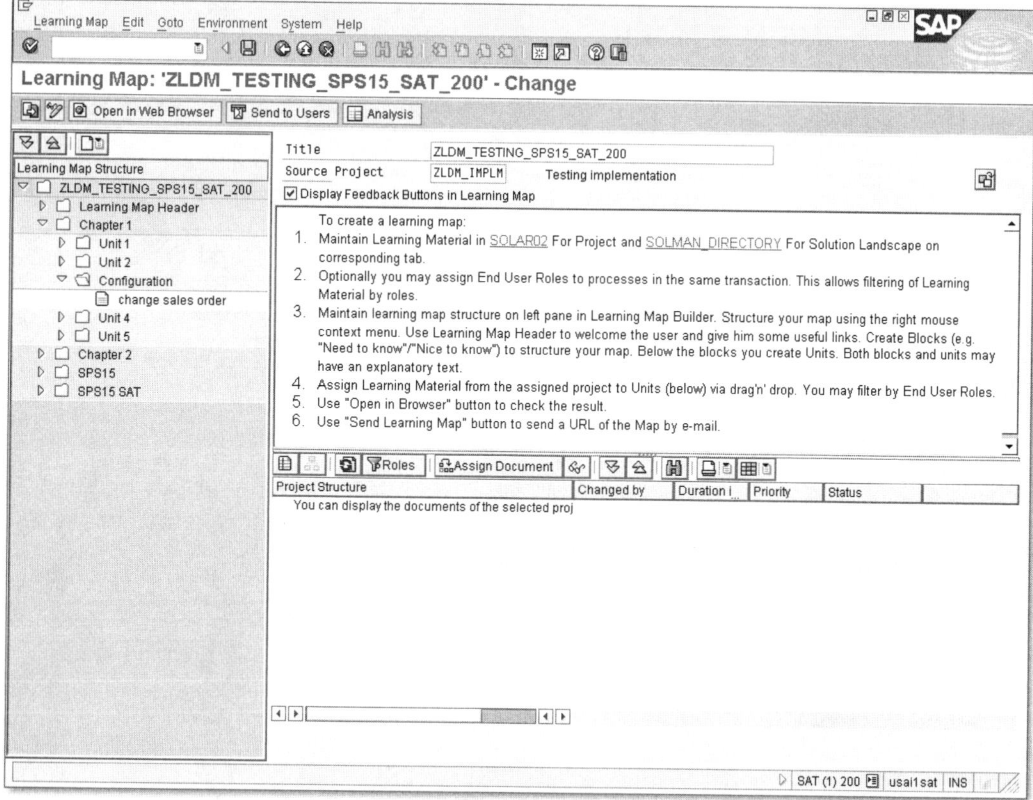

Figure 19.44 Learning Map

Create or enhance the training material in the Configuration Transaction SOLAR02, LEARNING MATERIAL tab, along the business process structure and assign the user roles to several individual positions or organizational units via the END USER ROLES tab, for example. You generate a learning map from Transaction SOLAR_LEARNING_MAP • CREATE. Using OPEN IN WEB BROWSER, you can display the learning map directly in HTML format. Using SEND TO USERS, you can select the end user role to which the learning map should be sent. If you use the EMAIL option, you create a text template that includes the link to the learning map. You then open your local email client to compose an email with the template text and send it to end users. After end users have processed the learning material, they can appraise the material anonymously. The results, such as individual or average evaluations, number of calls of the learning maps, as well as feedback comments can be displayed in the SOLAR_LEARNING_MAP analysis.

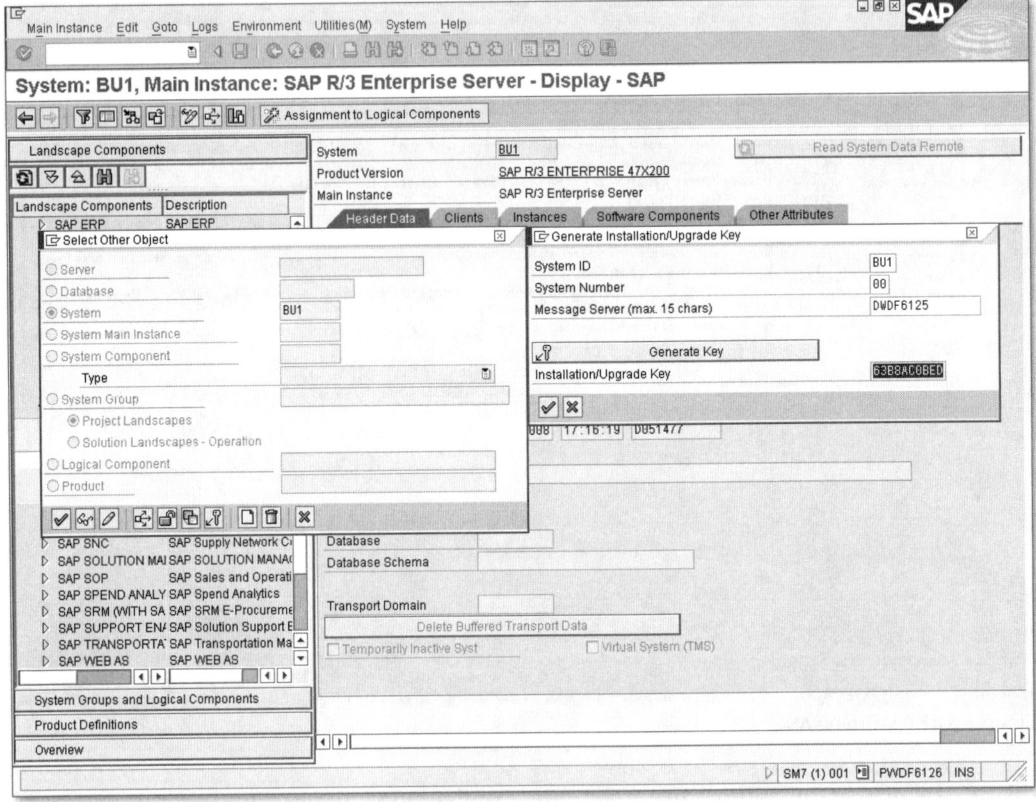

Figure 19.45 Requesting the Solution Manager Key

Solution Manager Key

Because of these and many other benefits for the implementation and upgrade, using SAP Solution Manager has become mandatory for technical upgrades of SAP solutions based on SAP NetWeaver 04.

This becomes obvious when running the upgrade control program SAPup, because you are prompted for a key that can only be generated using SAP Solution Manager. Proceed as follows:

1. In SAP Solution Manager, call Transaction SMSY.
2. To create the system for which you want to generate the key in the system landscape, select SYSTEMS • CREATE NEW SYSTEM and using LANDSCAPE COMPONENT, enter the SYSTEM ID, product, and product version. Save your entries.
3. Generate the key using the menu entry SYSTEM LANDSCAPE • OTHER OBJECT • SYSTEM. Select the desired system. Next, choose GENERATE INSTALLATION /UPGRADE KEY (see Figure 19.45) enter the required data, and select GENERATE KEY.
4. Enter the key in the UPGRADE TOOL SAPUP.

19.6 Questions

1. **Which of the following statements are true of Customizing Distribution?**

   A. Customizing Distribution synchronizes Customizing settings in different systems.

   B. Customizing Distribution only works for systems with identical release statuses.

   C. Customizing Distribution can also be set up without SAP Solution Manager.

   D. Customizing Distribution usually takes place between development systems. The QA and production systems are provided with transport requests.

2. **Which of the following statements are true of the Customizing Scout?**

   A. The Customizing Scout can only be used for systems with identical release statuses.

   B. Comparison runs can be saved and displayed at a later point in time.

   C. Synchronization objects can be compared.

   D. Comparison runs cannot be performed in the background.

3. **Which of the following statements are true of Maintenance Projects?**

   A. Urgent corrections can be created even if no maintenance project exists.

   B. Regular corrections can be released in any phase of a maintenance cycle.

   C. A maintenance project is created in Transaction SOLAR_PROJECT_ADMIN.

   D. Regular corrections can be released in phase Development with Release.

4. **Which of the following statements are true of urgent corrections?**

   A. Urgent corrections can be part of a maintenance project or implementation project.

   B. Urgent corrections are not documented in SAP Solution Manager.

   C. Urgent corrections must be approved by the Change Manager.

   D. Urgent corrections can be released in any phase of a maintenance cycle.

5. **Which functions are provided in the change analysis?**

   A. Configuration data can be distributed from a master system to all other systems.

   B. You can display the configuration parameters that were changed on a specific day.

C. You can set up email notifications for system administrators if specific parameter values are changed.

D. You can determine how many transport requests were imported on a specific day.

6. **How does the change analysis support the error search in an SAP solution? The change analysis....**

   A. ... identifies the system and the software component responsible for the error.

   B. ... provides a central entry point for determining changes to a solution.

   C. ... contains the values of the configuration parameter and the entire change history.

   D. ... enables you to send error messages to the SAP Solution Manager Service Desk.

7. **Which benefits does Maintenance Optimizer offer?**

   A. It reduces the import times for Support Packages and Enhancement Packages.

   B. It simplifies the download of Support Packages.

   C. It provides an overview of current and past maintenance activities.

   D. It helps to evaluate the functional effects of a Support Package.

8. **What are the prerequisites for using Maintenance Optimizer?**

   A. Change Request Management must be set up.

   B. An RFC connection to the SAP Support Portal must be set up.

   C. The reporting about side effects must be configured.

   D. An S-User for the SAP Service Marketplace must be assigned to the user in SAP Solution Manager.

   E. The system to be maintained must be integrated with a solution in SAP Solution Manager.

9. **Which activities of an upgrade project does SAP Solution Manager support?**

   A. Generating the upgrade key

   B. Reviewing the system landscape situation

   C. Evaluation of PREPARE

   D. Determining upgrade-relevant IMG activities

10. **Which phases does the Upgrade Roadmap include?**

   A. Project preparation

   B. Creation of an upgrade blueprint

   C. Production preparation

   D. Production implementation and support

Appendices

A Transport Profile Parameters

This section provides information on the different transport profile parameters used to support the delivery of change requests to import buffers and the import of change requests into SAP ERP systems. The transport profile therefore configures the transport control program `tp`. Chapter 7 describes the configuration of the transport profile. This section lists useful transport parameters and provides the following information for each:

- Name of the parameter
- Possible values
- The default value
- SAP releases for which the parameter is valid
- A description of the parameter

abapntfmode

Values: t or b
Default value: t
SAP release information: As of SAP Basis Release 4.5
Description: This parameter is meaningful only if the transport control program `tp` is running on Windows platforms. The value of the parameter determines whether text files are opened in Unix compatibility mode. This mode is necessary if a transport directory is shared between Unix and Windows NT application servers. When `abapntfmode` is set to "t", all text files are opened in normal Windows text mode. When it is set to "b", all text files are opened in binary mode, which is compatible with Unix file formats.

alllog

Value: Text
Default value: ALOG$(syear)$(yweek)
SAP release information: All
Description: The name of the log file in the transport directory `log` that lists all of the individual `tp` steps.

allow_rc4

Value: Boolean
Default value: TRUE
SAP release information: As of SAP Basis Release 4.6A
Description: This parameter changes a return code of 4 (warning) to return code 0 when it is set to FALSE. This parameter is applied so that batch jobs that call `tp` as an external command interpret each return code that is not 0 as an error and cancel the job.

buffreset

Value: Boolean
Default value: TRUE
SAP release information: All
Description: The transport control program `tp` and `R3trans` reset all of the SAP system buffers so that all application servers can react to changes in the database. Buffer synchronization takes several seconds until all application servers have read the request to reset all buffers. You can set the repetition period for reading the synchronization requests with profile parameters for the SAP system (`rdisp/bufreftime`). Although this buffer reset is turned on by default, you can disable the buffer reset by `tp` by setting `buffreset` to FALSE.

bufreftime

Value: Integer
Default value: 180
SAP release information: All
Description: The value of this parameter specifies how long the transport control program `tp` should wait, in seconds, until it can assume that all of the SAP system buffers have been synchronized. The value of this parameter should correspond to the `rdisp/bufreftime` profile parameter of the SAP system in question.

c_import

Value: Boolean
Default value: FALSE
SAP release information: All
Description: Allows or disallows the import of change requests that are the result of a relocation transport (change requests of type "c"). By default, all types of change requests can be imported. However, you can disallow the import of relocation transports (created using Transaction SE01) by setting the parameter `c_import` to TRUE.

Communication_system

Value: Text
Default value: None
SAP release information: As of SAP Basis Release 7.0
Description: When the parameter `non_abap_system` is set, the corresponding communication system must also receive a value. `Communication_system`, which manages the meta information of transports, receives the SID value of the corresponding system.

cofilelifetime

Value: Integer
Default value: 365
SAP release information: All
Description: The number of days since a control file has been touched. A file in the transport directory `cofiles` is considered to be not needed if the corresponding change request is not in the import buffer of any SAP system and has a time stamp that is older than the value set by the parameter `cofilelifetime`. If the file is no longer needed based on the criteria, a combination of the commands `tp check` and `tp clearold` will delete the file. Using this parameter, you can set the minimum age of a control file, in days. Because a data file requires a control file for import, the value set by `cofilelifetime` should correspond to the value for `olddatalifetime`.

ctc

Value: Boolean
Default value: FALSE
SAP release information: As of SAP Basis Release 4.5
Description: `ctc` stands for Client Transport Control, and when set to TRUE, activates extended transport control, allowing you to specify client and system combinations in transport routes. Extended transport control requires a new import buffer format (the transport parameter `nbufform` is set to TRUE implicitly). This new buffer format is only supported beginning with `tp` version 264. As a result, you can set the new parameter `ctc` only if all transport control programs that work with a specific SAP system have at least version 264. Older tp versions destroy this new import buffer. To protect the new import buffer from being destroyed by older `tp` versions, set the value for transport parameter `tp_version` to at least 264.

datalifetime

Value: Integer
Default value: 200
SAP release information: All
Description: The number of days since a data file has been touched. A file in the transport directory `data` is considered to be not needed if the corresponding change request is not in the import buffer of any SAP system and has a time stamp that is older than the value set by the parameter `datalifetime`. The file is moved to the transport directory `olddata` using a combination of the commands `tp check` and `tp clearold`. Using this parameter, you can set the minimum age of a data file, in days.

dbcodepage

Values: american_america.us7ascii or american_america.we8dec
Default value: None
SAP release information: As of R/3 Release 4.0 (no longer supported as of SAP Basis Release 6.40)

Description: The code page of the Oracle database instance. The Oracle databases are installed with the code page american_america.we8dec. In this case, you must enter the value american_america.we8dec in the transport profile. When the value is set, `tp` will set the environment variable `NLS_LANG` accordingly.

dbconfpath

Value: Text
Default value: $transdir
SAP release information: All (no longer supported as of SAP Basis Release 6.40)
Description: You can use this parameter to inform the transport control program `tp` where the configuration files for Oracle SQL*NET V2 are located. The default value $transdir indicates that SAP has already stored these files centrally in the transport directory. `tp` derives the value of the environment variable TNS_ADMIN from this parameter. However, if the transport parameter `dbswpath` is set, the parameter `dbconfpath` is ignored.

dbhost

Value: Text
Default value: None
SAP release information: All (no longer supported as of SAP Basis Release 6.40)
Description: This parameter specifies the host name—the computer on which the database runs or (valid for Oracle and DB2 on AIX) on which the database processes run. For an Informix database, the host name is case sensitive. For MS SQL, the TCP/IP host name on which the database runs is used.

dblibpath

Value: Text
Default value: /usr/sap/$(system)/SYS/exe/run/ for Unix
SAP release information: As of SAP Basis Release 4.5 (no longer supported as of SAP Basis Release 6.40)

Description: The directory in which the dynamic SAP database interface is located. In the standard system, these files are always in the executable directory of the application server. Therefore, you do not have to change the default value. `tp` derives the value of the environment variable `dir_Library` from the value of this parameter.

Under Windows, you have to enter the path to the dynamic SAP interface only if it is not located in the environment variable path set under Windows. Otherwise, the DLL is searched for in the default path.

As of SAP Basis Release 4.5, `tp` sets this variable according to the value of the transport profile parameter `dbtype`.

dblogicalname

Value: Text
Default value: $dbname
SAP release information: All (no longer supported as of SAP Basis Release 6.40)
Description: Sets the logical name that identifies the database instance in an Oracle network.

dbname

Value: Text
Default value: $(system)
SAP release information: All (no longer supported as of SAP Basis Release 6.40)
Description: The name of the database instance. The standard installation uses the name of the SAP system for the name of the database instance or for the logical name of the database.

dbswpath

Value: Text
Default value: None
SAP release information: As of R/3 Release 4.0

Description: The value of the directory in which the Oracle client software is installed. If the parameter is set, the transport control program `tp` derives the following environment variables in a Unix environment:

- Oracle_HOME = $(dbswpath)
- TNS_ADMIN = $(dbswpath)/network/admin (on Unix)
- ORA_NLS = $(dbswpath)/ocommon/nls/admin/data (on Unix)
- ORA_NLS32 = $(dbswpath)/ocommon/nls32/admin/data (on Unix)
- ORA_NLS33 = $(dbswpath)/ocommon/nls33/admin/data (on Unix)

Note that the environment variables ORA_NLS, ORA_NLS32 and ORA_NLS33 are no longer set as of SAP Basis Release 4.6.

dbtype

Values: ora, ada, db2, db4, db6, inf, or mss
Default value: The SAP system's database type
SAP release information: All (no longer supported as of SAP Basis Release 6.40)
Description: Indicates the type of the deployed database. As of SAP Basis Release 4.5, used to set the environment variable `dbms_type`. This variable has to be set correctly to be able to load the correct shared dbsl-library.

dummy

Value: Boolean
Default value: FALSE
SAP release information: All
Description: You can use this parameter to make a dummy system, such as a virtual system, known in the transport profile. Imports are not performed for an SAP system with the parameter `dummy` set to TRUE, but an import buffer for the system will be maintained. When creating a virtual system in the TMS, the value of `dummy` is automatically set to TRUE in the transport profile.

exporttoascii

Value: Boolean
Default value: FALSE
SAP release information: As of SAP Basis Release 6.40
Description: This parameter is transferred to `R3trans` during an export from a Unicode system if the value is set to TRUE. As a result, `R3trans` exports all character data as ASCII bytes. To a certain extent, this allows for an import in older releases. Refer to SAP Note 638357 for additional details.

impmon_mode

Value: Text
Default value: DEFAULT
SAP release information: As of SAP Basis Release 6.10
Description: With IMPMON_MODE you can control how detailed imports are monitored. Using the value NORMAL, you can enter the information about start and end of the various transport steps in table TPSTAT. No steps are logged if you use the value OFF. When you set the value to DETAILED, `tp` enters additional information about the current steps and their return code in table TPSTAT after they have been completed. A high degree of detail may result in performance problems and you should therefore keep this value set to NORMAL.

informix_server

Value: Text
Default value: $(dbhost)$(dbname)shm
SAP release information: All (no longer supported as of SAP Basis Release 6.40)
Description: The Informix database server name for a local connection.

informix_serveralias

Value: Text
Default value: $(dbhost)$(dbname)tcp
SAP release information: All (no longer supported as of SAP Basis Release 6.40)

Description: The Informix database server name for a remote connection.

informixdir

Value: Text
Default value: /informix/<SID>
SAP release information: All
Description: The directory name where the Informix database software is located.

informixsqlhost

Value: Text
Default value: $(informixdir)/etc/sqlhosts[.tli|.soc]
SAP release information: All
Description: This parameter is used to specify the complete path and name of the SQL host's file for an Informix database.

k_import

Value: Boolean
Default value: FALSE
SAP release information: All
Description: Allows or disallows the import of Workbench change requests (change requests of type "k"). By default, all types of change requests can be imported. However, you can disallow the import of Workbench change requests by setting parameter `k_import` to TRUE.

language

Value: Text
Default value: None
SAP release information: All
Description: The value passed to `R3trans` to indicate what languages should be exported. By default, this parameter is empty; therefore, R3trans exports language-dependent data from all languages it can find—in other words, all languages installed in the SAP system. If the param-

eter `language` is transferred, `R3trans` tries to export the languages specified in this text. A single letter identifies each language. You can specify several languages by entering a sequence of letters. Note that the transport parameter `lsm` is used with the parameter `language`.

loglifetime

Value: Integer
Default value: 200
SAP release information: All
Description: The number of days since a log file has been touched. A file in the transport directory `log` is considered to be not needed if the corresponding change request is not in the import buffer of any SAP system and has a time stamp that is older than the value set by the parameter `loglifetime`. If the file is no longer needed based on the criteria, a combination of the commands `tp check` and `tp clearold` will delete the log file. Using this parameter, you can set the minimum age of a log file, in days.

mssql_passwd

Value: Text
Default value: None
SAP release information: All
Description: The password for a user in the MS SQL database. This is used together with parameter `mssql_user`.

mssql_user

Value: Text
Default value: None
SAP release information: All
Description: The username for a connection to the MS SQL database. This information, in combination with `mssql_passwd`, allows for access to an MS SQL database using a unique user and password rather than the default user and password.

nbufform

Value: Boolean
Default value: FALSE
SAP release information: As of SAP Basis Release 4.5
Description: Transport request names in newer SAP Basis releases may have a length of 20 characters. However, these transport requests cannot be processed in the previous import buffer format. The parameter nbufform is set to TRUE implicitly when you set the parameter ctc to TRUE. As with parameter ctc, you have to protect this change to the import buffer format from transport control programs that use the old import buffer format. The new import buffer format requires at least a tp version of 264. Older tp versions destroy this new import buffer. Therefore, when parameter nbufform is activated, set the value for the transport profile parameter tp_version to at least 264.

new_sapnames

Value: Boolean
Default value: FALSE
SAP Basis release information: All
Description: A file is created in the transport directory sapnames for every user of an SAP system in the transport group. By default, the file corresponds to the user's name. However, usernames in the SAP system may not be valid filenames at the operating system level. For example, a certain username length or using special characters such as a space or a period may not be permissible as filenames and could cause problems. To address this issue, usernames can be modified to create filenames that are valid in all operating systems. The real username is stored in the corresponding file. Setting the parameter new_sapnames to TRUE activates this function. Once this parameter has been set to TRUE, you should not set it back to FALSE (unless you also delete all of the files in the transport directory sapnames).

non_abap_system

Value: Boolean
Default value: FALSE
SAP release information: As of SAP Basis Release 7.0

Description: If this parameter is set for a specific system, the system is marked as a system that does not import or export ABAP content, only files. This complies with the new R3trans functionality of only including files in a transport request. If the parameter `non_abap_system` is set, the corresponding parameter `communication_system` must also be set.

olddatalifetime

Value: Integer
Default value: 365
SAP Basis release information: All
Description: A combination of the commands `tp check` and `tp clearold` move data files from the transport directory `data` to the transport directory `olddata` based on the parameter `datalifetime`. These commands also delete any data files in the `olddata` transport directory whose time stamp is older than the value set by `olddatalifetime`. Using this parameter, you can set the minimum age of a data file, in days. Note that the minimum age refers to the date the file was created, not to the date on which the file was copied to the directory `olddata`. Therefore, the value of `olddatalifetime` should be greater than the value of `datalifetime`.

opticonnect

Value: Boolean
Default value: FALSE
SAP Basis release information: All
Description: Must be TRUE for a DB2 database environment when `opticonnect` is installed.

r3transpath

Value: Text
Default value: R3trans for Unix and AS/400 and R3trans.exe for Windows
SAP Basis release information: All
Description: This parameter is used to pass the complete name of the program `R3trans` to the transport control program `tp`. The default value is not a complete path specification. The operating system and the set-

tings of the operating system are used to find the correct value. If this does not work, you can provide the complete path to `R3trans`.

recclient

Values: ALL, OFF, or list of client values, separated by a comma
Default value: OFF
SAP Basis release information: All
Description: Activates the recording of changes to Customizing settings during import for either all clients or the clients listed. By default, recording of imported Customizing settings does not take place. The value of this parameter should correspond to the `rec/client` profile parameter of the SAP system in question.

repeatonerror

Values: 0, 8, or 9
Default value: 9
SAP Basis release information: All
Description: After successful import, a change request is typically removed from the import buffer (unless a special import option is used to keep the change request in the buffer after import). The parameter `repeatonerror` defines the criteria for a successful import. It specifies the return code up to which a change request is considered successfully processed. Return codes less than the value defined for `repeatonerror` are accepted as successful. Change requests that result in a return code greater than or equal to the value of `repeatonerror` are not removed from the import buffer because they have not been successfully processed.

setunicodeflag

Value: Boolean
Default value: FALSE
SAP Basis release information: As of SAP Basis Release 6.10
Description: If this parameter is set, the option setunicodeflag=yes is transferred to R3trans. As a result, objects receive the attribute unicode checks=active during imports from a release version < 6.10. Refer to SAP Note 330267 for additional details.

sourcesystems

Value: Text
Default value: None
SAP Basis release information: All
Description: A list of SAP system names, separated by a common. This list defines the SAP system from which change requests have originated that can then be imported. By default, this value is empty; therefore, change requests from any SAP system can be imported. However, if the transport parameter has been defined, only change requests whose source system is listed can be imported. This parameter is useful for protecting an SAP system's import process.

stopimmediately

Value: Boolean
Default value: FALSE (as of SAP Basis Release 4.6, the default value will be TRUE)
SAP release information: As of SAP Basis Release 4.5
Description: By default, the transport control program `tp` stops at the end of an import step if an error occurred during that step. When this parameter is set to TRUE, `tp` reacts to errors immediately following the error rather than at the end of the import step. For example, if `stoponerror` is set to 9 and a change request gets an error 12, with `stopimmediately` set to TRUE, the import process stops immediately after the errant change request. If `stopimmediately` is set to FALSE, the main import step is completed for all change requests before `tp` reports an error from the change request that experienced the error.

stoponerror

Values: 0, 8, and 9
Default value: 9
SAP release information: All
Description: The maximum return code for which `tp` checks at the completion of every transport step. If the return code is equal to or greater than the value set, the import process is stopped. For example, if the

DDIC transport step results in return code 8 (indicating an error), the default value of `stoponerror` will not cause `tp` to end the import process. However, if `stoponerror` is set to a value of 8, a return code of 8 will cause the import process to stop. If `stoponerror` is set to zero, `tp` is never stopped.

syslog

Value: Text
Default value: SLOG$(syear)$(yweek).$(system)
SAP release information: All
Description: The name of the log file in the transport directory `log` that lists all of the `tp` import activities for a specific SAP system.

t_import

Value: Boolean
Default value: FALSE
SAP release information: All
Description: Allows or disallows the import of change requests that result from a transport of copies (change requests of type "t"). By default, all types of change requests can be imported. However, you can disallow the import of the transport of copies (created using Transaction SE01) by setting the parameter `t_import` to TRUE.

targetsystems

Value: Text
Default value: None
SAP release information: All
Description: You can define a list of SAP target system names (up to 50). Commas separate the names in the list. An import using `tp` is allowed only for systems included in the list. Other transport request are removed from the import buffer. If no `targetsystem` is defined, you can import all requests independent of the target system.

testimport

Value: Boolean
Default value: TRUE (as of SAP Basis Release 4.6, the default value is FALSE and as of SAP Basis Release 6.10, the parameter is not longer supported)
SAP release information: All
Description: By default, after export of a change request, the transport control program `tp` performs a test import to see whether the Repository objects in the change request might generate errors upon import into the target system. From time to time, the test import into the target system is not possible—for example, when the planned target system is not running an SAP system or is nonexistent, as in the case of a virtual system. Setting `testimport` to FALSE for the source system lets you turn off the test import. For example, to turn off test imports for all change requests exported from the development system, you must set `testimport` to FALSE for the development system.

testsystems

Value: Text
Default value: None
SAP release information: All
Description: You can define a list of SAP test system names (up to 50). Commas separate the names in the list. If the export of a change request is successful, the transport control program `tp` adds the change request to the import buffer of the change request's defined target system as well as any SAP systems defined by `testsystems` for that target system. For example, typically, all change requests released from the development system have a target system defined as the quality assurance system. Release and export of such a change request causes the change request to be added to the import buffer of QAS. If the parameter `testsystems` is set to TST, the change request is also added to the import buffer of the SAP system TST.

tp_version

Value: Integer
Default value: None
SAP release information: All
Description: This parameter sets the oldest version of `tp` that can be used to perform `tp` commands on an import buffer. Any `tp` version equal to or greater than this version can be used. This parameter does not usually need to be set—except when the parameter `ctc` or `nbufform` is set to TRUE. In that case, `tp_version` needs to be set to at least 264. This ensures that older tp versions do not destroy import buffers that use a new import buffer format.

transdir

Value: Text
Default value: None
SAP release information: All
Description: The path to the root of the transport directory. This parameter is required and therefore must be set. For a Unix environment, for example, `transdir` is often set to /usr/sap/trans/.

vers_at_imp

Values: NEVER, C_ONLY, or ALWAYS
Default value: NEVER
SAP release information: As of SAP Basis Release 4.5
Description: Typically, versions for Repository objects exist only on the source system—that is, where the object is changed. During the transport of a new source, no version is created in the import system. However, customers often need to have detailed storage of all versions in either their quality assurance or production systems so that if these systems are copied or upgraded, version history can be maintained. If you set the parameter to either C_ONLY or ALWAYS, additional steps take place during the import that generate versions of the imported objects in the target system. Prior to the import of the ABAP Dictionary objects, the change request's command file is imported, and a version of all objects listed in the command file is added to the target system's version database.

Versions are created only if the current version of the object is not the same as the latest version in the database, or if a version does not yet exist for the object in the version database. Although the value ALWAYS activates versions at import for all objects, the value C_ONLY creates versions of objects only when the change request to be imported is a relocation transport (with or without development class and transport layer change). Relocation transports are created and released using the Transport Organizer (Transaction SE01).

w_import

Value: Boolean
Default value: FALSE
SAP release information: All
Description: Allows or disallows the import of Customizing change requests (change requests of type "w"). By default, all types of change requests can be imported. However, you can disallow the import of Customizing change requests by setting the parameter `w_import` to TRUE.

B Selected Transaction Codes

Table B.1 lists the most important SAP transaction codes for the support of change and transport management in the SAP system. You can enter SAP transaction codes in the command field of an SAP screen in the following ways:

Entering transaction codes

- **/n<transaction code>**
  Entering the transaction code this way exits the current SAP screen and displays the initial screen of the transaction.
- **/o<transaction code>**
  Entering the transaction code this way sends the current user session to the background and creates a new user session to display the initial transaction screen.

Code	Description
AL11	Display SAP Directories
AL12	Buffer Synchronization
ASU/ UPGRADE	Starting Application-Specific Upgrade Support
BALE	ALE Administration and Monitoring
DB02	Analyze Tables and Indexes (Missing Database Objects and Space Requirements)
OSS1	Log on to SAPNet—R/3 Frontend Services (formerly known as SAP's Online Service System)
PFCG	Profile Generator: Maintain Activity Groups
RZ01	Job Scheduling Monitor
RZ10	Maintain Profile Parameters
RZ20	Alert Monitor

Table B.1 Transaction Codes Used for Change and Transport Management

Code	Description
RZ21	Customizing the Alert Monitor
S001	ABAP Workbench
SADJ	Customizing Transfer Assistant
SALE	ALE IMG Activities
SARA	Archive Administration
SB09	Business Navigator
SCAT	CATT
SCC1	Client Copy Per Transport Request
SCC3	Client Copy Logs
SCC4	Client Administration
SCC5	Client Delete
SCC7	Client Import—Post-Processing
SCC8	Client Export
SCC9	Remote Client Copy
SCCL	Local Client Copy
SCMP	Individual View/Table Comparison
SCPR3	Business Configuration Sets: Maintenance
SCPR20	Business Configuration Sets: Activation
SCPR20PR	Business Configuration Sets: Activation Logs
SCU0	Customizing Cross-System Viewer
SCU3	Table History
SCUM	Central User Administration
SE01	Transport Organizer
SE03	Workbench Organizer: Tools
SE06	Processing After Installation for CTO
SE09	Workbench Organizer

Table B.1 Transaction Codes Used for Change and Transport Management (Cont.)

Code	Description
SE10	Customizing Organizer
SE11	ABAP Data Dictionary Maintenance
SE12	ABAP Data Dictionary Display
SE13	Maintain Technical Settings for Tables
SE14	Utilities for Dictionary Tables
SE15	Repository Information System
SE16	Display Table Content
SE17	General Table Display
SE37	Function Builder
SE38	ABAP Editor
SE41	Menu Painter
SE51	Screen Painter
SE71	SAPscript Forms
SE72	SAPscript Styles
SE80	Repository Browser
SE93	Maintain Transaction Codes
SE95	Modification Browser
SECATT	extended Computer Aided Test Tool (eCATT)
SFW1	Definition of Switches for the Switch Framework
SFW2	Define a Business Function
SFW3	Define Business Function Sets
SFW5	Activate Switches of the Switch Framework
SLIN	ABAP Extended Program Check
SM02	System Messages
SM04	User Overview
SM12	Display and Delete SAP Enqueues

Table B.1 Transaction Codes Used for Change and Transport Management (Cont.)

Code	Description
SM13	Display Update Requests and Resolve Errors
SM21	System Log
SM28	Installation Check
SM30	Table/View Maintenance
SM31	Table Maintenance
SM35	Batch Input Monitoring
SM36	Schedule Background Jobs
SM37	Background Job Overview
SM39	Job Analysis
SM49	Execute External Operating System Commands
SM50	Work Process Overview
SM51	Instance Overview
SM56	Reset or Check the Number Range Buffer
SM58	Error Log for Asynchronous RFC
SM59	Display or Maintain RFC Destinations
SM63	Display and Maintain Operation Modes
SM64	Trigger an Event
SM65	Analysis Tool for Background Processing
SM66	Global Work Process Overview
SM69	Maintain External Operating System Commands
SMLG	Maintain Assignments of Logon Groups to Instances
SMLI	Language Import Utility
SMLT	Language Transport Utility
SMOD	SAP Enhancement Management
SNRO	Maintain Number Range Objects
SO99	Upgrade Information System

Table B.1 Transaction Codes Used for Change and Transport Management (Cont.)

Code	Description
SOBJ	Attribute Maintenance Objects
SPAM	SAP Package Manager (SPAM)
SPAU	Display Modified Objects in the Runtime Environment
SPAU_ENH	Display Modified Enhancement Framework Objects
SPDD	Display Modified DDIC Objects
SPRO	Customizing from within the IMG
SPRP	Start IMG Project Administration
ST02	Statistics of the SAP Buffer
ST03	Workload Monitor
ST04	Database Performance Monitor
ST06	Operating System Monitor
ST08	Network Monitor
ST09	Network Alert Monitor
STEM	CATT Utilities
STMS	Transport Management System
STWB_1	Test Catalog Management
STWB_2	Test Plan Management
STWB_WORK	Tester Worklist
STWB_INFO	Status Info System for Test Workbench
SU01	Maintain Users
SU01D	Display Users
SU02	Maintain Authorization Profiles
SU03	Maintain Authorizations
SU05	Maintain Internet Users
SU10	Mass Changes to User Master Records

Table B.1 Transaction Codes Used for Change and Transport Management (Cont.)

Code	Description
SU12	Mass Delete of User Master Records
SU20	Maintain Authorization Fields
SU21	Maintain Authorization Objects
SU22	Authorization Object Usage in Transactions
SU26	Adjust Authorization Checks
SU3	Maintain Own User Data
SU30	Full Authorization Check
SU56	Analyze User Buffer
SUPC	Profiles for Activity Groups
SUPF	Integrated User Maintenance
SUPO	Maintain Organization Levels

Table B.1 Transaction Codes Used for Change and Transport Management (Cont.)

C Glossary

ABAP Advanced Business Application Programming. Programming language of the SAP system.

ABAP Dictionary Central storage facility that contains metadata (data about data) for all objects in the SAP system. The ABAP Dictionary describes the logical structure of application development objects and their representation in the structures of the underlying relational database. All runtime environment components such as application programs or the database interface get information about these objects from the ABAP Dictionary. The ABAP Dictionary is an active data dictionary and is fully integrated into the ABAP Workbench.

ABAP Editor ABAP Workbench tool for developing and maintaining ABAP programs, function modules, screen flow logic, type groups, and logical databases. Aside from normal text operations (such as insert, search, and replace), the ABAP Editor provides several special functions to support program development.

ABAP Workbench SAP's integrated graphical programming environment. The ABAP Workbench supports the development of and changes to SAP client/server applications written in ABAP. You can use the tools of the ABAP Workbench to write ABAP code, design screens, create user interfaces, use predefined functions, get access to database information, control access to development objects, test applications for efficiency, and debug applications.

Activation Process that makes a runtime object available. The effect of activation is to generate runtime objects, which are accessed by application programs and screen templates.

Activity Changes to version made by users, and stored in a workspace. Users log the changes to the workspace resources that correspond to individual logical changes. These changes are hidden from other users until they are made available via check-in.

Activity group Subset of actions from the set of actions that were defined in the Enterprise IMG. From the activity group, you can use the Profile Generator to generate the authorizations needed by SAP users for these actions.

Add-on patch Support Packages that are component patches for add-on installations. They are specific for an add-on of a particular SAP release. They contain corrections only for the specific add-on.

ADO Application defined objects.

ALE Application Link Enabling. ALE is a technology used for building and operating distributed applications. The main purpose of ALE is to ensure a distributed but integrated SAP installation. It comprises a controlled business message exchange with consistent data storage in nonpermanently connected SAP applications. Applications are integrated through synchronous and asynchronous communication rather than through a central database.

ALE consist of three layers:

- Application services
- Distribution services
- Communication services

ALE Customizing Distribution Process that lets you ensure that the Customizing settings related to ALE scenarios are identical in the different SAP systems of the system landscape.

Alert Monitor A tool that enables you to monitor all actions that have been performed with TMS and that draws your attention to critical information.

API Application Programming Interface. Software package used by an application program to call a service provided by the operating system—for example, to open a file.

Application data Client-specific data that comprises master data and business transactional data.

Application server A computer on which at least one SAP instance runs.

ArchiveLink A communications interface between SAP applications and external components, integrated into the Basis component of the SAP system. ArchiveLink has the following interfaces: user interface, interface to the SAP applications, and interface to the external components (archive systems, viewer systems, and scan systems).

Archiving object A logical object comprising related business data in the database that is read from the database using an archiving program. After it has been successfully archived, a logical object can be deleted by a specially generated deletion program.

ASU Application Specific Upgrade. Collection of programs and notes to process application-specific aspects of an upgrade.

Automatic recording of changes Client change option that permits changes to the Customizing settings of the client and requires these change to be automatically recorded to change requests.

Background processing Processing that does not take place on the screen. Data is processed in the background, while other functions can be executed in parallel on the screen. Although background processes are not visible to users and run without user intervention (no dialog box is involved), they have the same priority as online processes.

Backup domain controller SAP system that can assume the functions of the transport domain controller if it fails.

BAPI Business Application Programming Interface. Standardized programming interface that provides external access to business processes and data in the SAP system.

Batch input Method and tools for rapid import of data from sequential files into the SAP database.

Build space Area in CBS that exactly describes a development configuration. If a new track is created in Change Management Service (CMS), build spaces are automatically created for the development and consolidation.

Business Configuration Sets A saved snapshot of Customizing settings that can be used for comparison with the Customizing Cross-System Viewer.

Business process A business process is a predefined workflow in an enterprise. In SAP Solution Manager, you can document the business processes. Predefined sample processes (templates) are available for specific scenarios.

Button Element of the graphical user interface. Click a button to execute the button's function. You can select buttons using a keyboard or a mouse.

CATT Computer Aided Test Tool. You can use this tool to generate test data and automate and test business processes.

CCMS Computing Center Management System. Tools for monitoring, controlling, and configuring the SAP system. The CCMS supports 24-hour system administration functions from within the SAP system. You can analyze system load and monitor distributed resource usage of system components.

Change analysis Scenario in SAP Solution Manager used to track the automatic recording of software and configuration parameters of a solution. It is part of the root cause analysis scenario.

Change and transport management The handling of changes to software and their distribution to different environments. These changes may be required by changes in how an enterprise does business. From a technical perspective, change and transport management is the process by which changes made to on SAP system are distributed to one or more SAP systems in a consistent and timely manner after appropriate testing and verification to ensure a stable and predictable production environment.

Change and Transport Organizers (CTO) The Organizers in the SAP system used to manage change requests as a result of development effort in the ABAP Workbench and Customizing activities in the IMG. It comprises the Workbench Organizer, the Customizing Organizer, and the Transport Organizer.

Change and Transport System (CTS) Tools used to manage changes and development in the SAP system and their transport to other SAP systems. It comprises the Change and Transport Organizers, the Transport Management System, and the operating system level programs `tp` and `R3trans`.

Change Management Service The SAP Change Management Service (CMS) controls the transports and deployments in the development environment by carrying out the appropriate installation, distribution, or deployment in the SAP J2EE server environment for the archives that resulted from the build processes of the SAP CBS. In addition, the CMS is responsible for configuring the transport landscape.

Change Manager The Change Manager is a role in the ITIL change process responsible for all types of changes in the system landscape. He is responsible for approving and rejecting change requests in particular.

Change request Electronic document in Change Request Management that contains a request for a software change.
Information source in the Workbench Organizer and Customizing Organizer that records and manages all changes made to SAP Repository objects and Customiz-

ing settings during an SAP implementation project.

Change Request Management Change Request Management is a scenario in SAP Solution Manager, comprising the management of change requests. It includes workflows for the approval and implementation processes of software changes. Furthermore, it assumes control of transport requests in connected satellite systems.

Client From a commercial law, organizational, and technical perspective, a closed unit within an SAP system with separate master records within a table.

Client compare Determining the differences in Customizing settings between two SAP clients.

Client copy according to a transport request Functionality with which you can transport client-dependent objects of either a change request or a task between clients in the same SAP system.

Client copy Function that allows you to copy a client in the same SAP system (local client copy) or to another SAP system (remote client copy) Client copy profiles determine the data to be copied: Customizing data, application data, and/or user master data.

Client copy profile A profile that enables you to copy certain data (for instance, Customizing data, application data, or user master data) from one client into another client. SAP provides all possible profiles from which you must select the appropriate profile for your copy requirements.

Client settings During client maintenance, options are available to determine whether client-dependent and client-independent changes can occur, and whether recording these changes is automatic. You can also define the client's role, and set additional restrictions and protections for the client. The system administrator should consciously decide the appropriate client settings for all clients in the system landscape.

Client transport Functionality with which you can copy the contents of one client to another client in a different SAP system by first performing a client export and then a client import.

Client-dependent Specific only to one client. Settings in client-dependent tables relate only to the client that was accessed during the logon process. Such tables contain the client number in the client's primary key.

Client-independent Relevant for all clients in an SAP System.

Client-specific transport route A transport route that consolidates or delivers to an SAP system and client combination rather than just an SAP system.

Close coupling Close coupling allows you to attach developments from within a development environment directly to the transport request of the ABAP transport system.

Component Build Service The Component Build Service (CBS) is part of SAP NWDI and is used to centrally build archives from sources. The CBS is responsible for creating runtime objects such as Java archives, which can later be deployed in the J2EE Engine. The CBS allows for incremental builds, as well as an automated rebuild of dependent software components, by reading the necessary resources from the DTR. Component builds are based on the SAP component model.

Conflict Resolution Transport (CRT) A type of Support Package used exclusively for SAP ERP add-ons such as industry solutions—for example, IS-OIL. They are designed to resolve conflicts that can occur between either a Hot Package or a Legal Change Patch and the add-on.

Consolidation route Regular transport route of an SAP Repository object from the integration system to the consolidation system. The consolidation route is specified for each SAP Repository object by the transport layer for the object's development class.

Consolidation system System in the system landscape to which change requests are exported according to a consolidation route. The consolidation system in a three-system landscape is the quality assurance system; in a two-system landscape, it is the production system.

Control file A list of required import steps for each released and exported change request. All control files are saved to the transport directory `cofiles`.

Correction (Regular correction.) Electronic document that describes a software change process in Change Request Management and contains a workflow for the implementation of a software change.

CPI-C Common Programming Interface-Communication. Programming interface—the basis for synchronous, system-to-system, program-to-program communication.

CTS+ The enhanced Change and Transport System (CTS+) allows you to attach non-ABAP objects to transport requests. The Change and Transport System (CTS), which has been known in the ABAP world for many years, is used as the infrastructure.

CTS project A CTS project is a collective container for transport requests in an SAP system. All transport requests belonging to the same CTS project can be imported collectively. CTS projects were implemented for Release 4.6B and support the process used by many customers to import transport requests into the production system by project.

CU&UC Combined Unicode & Upgrade Conversion. The combined upgrade and Unicode conversion procedure provides an optimized sequence of the relevant steps to enable reduced system downtime, especially for the combination of an SAP R/3 4.6C upgrade to SAP ERP 6.0 and Unicode conversion.

Current settings Allow for certain kinds of Customizing changes, known as data-only Customizing changes, to be carried out in a production client without being saved as change requests.

Customer development Additions to the standard software delivered by SAP using the ABAP Workbench. Customer developments involve creating customer-specific objects using the customer's name range and namespace.

Customizing Adjusting the SAP system to specific customer requirements by selecting variants, parameter settings, etc.

Customizing change requests Change request for recording and transporting changed system settings in client-dependent tables.

Customizing Cross-System Viewer The client comparison tool. In addition to determining the differences in Customizing settings, the Customizing Cross-System Viewer provides for the correction/adjustment of differences. It is often simply referred to as the Cross-System Viewer.

Customizing Distribution The Customizing Distribution enables you to transfer the Customizing from one system to another system using SAP Solution Manager, or you can update Customizing in multiple systems at the same time.

Customizing Organizer (CO) Tool to manage change requests of all types in an SAP system. The Customizing Organizer is part of the Change and Transport Organizer.

Customizing Scout The Customizing Scout is a tool in SAP Solution Manager that allows you to perform Customizing comparisons between different systems.

Customizing Transfer Assistant Tool for the comparison and adjustment of client-dependent changes imported into an SAP system.

Data archiving Removing data that is currently not needed from the SAP database and storing it in archives (see also Archiving object).

Data file Exported SAP Repository objects and/or table data residing at the operating system level in the transport directory `data` for each released and exported change request.

Database Set of data (organized, for example, in files) for permanent storage on the hard disk. Each SAP system has only one database.

Database copy Also known as "system copy". If you create an SAP system using a database copy, the SAP installation is not set up with the standard SAP database whose content is supplied by an existing SAP system using SAP migration tools specific to your platform and SAP release.

Database instance An administrative unit that allows access to a database. A database instance consists of database processes with a common set of database buffers in shared memory. Normally, there is only one database instance for each database. DB2/390 and Oracle Parallel Server are database systems for which a database can be made up of multiple database instances. In an SAP system, a database instance can either be alone on a single computer or together with one or possibly more SAP instances.

Database server A computer with at least one database instance.

DBA Database Administration.

Delivery class Classification attribute for ABAP Dictionary tables. The delivery class determines who (SAP or the customer) is responsible for maintaining the contents of a table. It also controls how a table behaves during a client copy, a client transport, and an SAP release upgrade.

Delivery route Continuation of the transport route after the consolidation route or after any other delivery route for developments in the ABAP Workbench and Customizing. After import into the consolidation system or another recipient system (the source system of the delivery route) change requests are identified for the import into the target system of the delivery route.

Delta Customizing Customizing activities the customer needs to perform to be able to use new functionality in the business application components after an SAP release upgrade. While upgrade Customizing is mandatory for existing functionality, delta Customizing is only necessary to make use of new functionality.

Design Time Repository The central storage and versioning of the Java sources and other resources required for development is taken over by the SAP Design Time Repository (DTR). To enable development in a team, automated conflict detection and the corresponding conflict resolution for different versions is provided. Together with the SAP NetWeaver Developer Studio, the DTR allows for the support of all projects, such as Web Dynpro or Enterprise Java Beans.

Development class A grouping of SAP Repository objects belonging to a common area. Unlike the objects in a change request, the grouping is logical rather than temporal. The development class is assigned a transport layer to ensure that all objects have the same consolidation route.

Development component Container for development objects in Java that can be used for both the structuring of the application and simplified reusability.

Development Configuration The Development Configuration (DC) determines the view of the developer of the development infrastructure. It specifies the software components to be developed and controls access to objects in SAP NWDI. All developers using the same DC work with the same consistent objects.

Development system System in a system landscape where development and Customizing work is performed.

Dialog box Box that is called from a primary window and is displayed there.

Dialog work process SAP work process to process request from users working online.

Dispatcher Process that coordinates the work processes of an SAP instance.

Dual stack system SAP system that consists of an ABAP stack and a Java stack.

eCATT extended Computer Aided Test Tool. You can use this tool to automate tests for business processes. Unlike CATT, you can also record Dynpros with controls and business processes that span multiple systems.

ECC ERP Central Component. ECC is the successor of SAP R/3 and the central system of an SAP ERP solution.

Eclipse Open source development platform for Java programs on which the SAP NetWeaver Developer Studio (NWDS) is based.

EDI Electronic Data Interchange. Electronic interchange of structured data (e.g., business documents) between business partners in different countries who may be using different hardware, software, and communication services.

End mark An end mark is a marker placed in import queues to indicate that only the requests before the marker should be imported. If you look at an import queue, an end mark is indicated with the statement "End of Import Queue." Only one end mark is possible per import queue. The terms *end mark* and *stopmark* are often used interchangeably.

Enhanced Change and Transport System The enhanced Change and Transport System (CTS+) allows you to attach non-ABAP objects to transport requests. The Change and Transport System (CTS), which has been known in the ABAP world for many years, is used as the infrastructure.

Enhancement Package Package for the delivery of new functions, by software component; comparable to Support Packages. Innovations can be activated individually based on the Switch and Enhancement Framework.

Enhancement Enhancements generally consist of user exits provided by SAP in the program code to call up external, customer-developed programs. The source code of the SAP release of the SAP standard does not need to be changed, because the connected customer objects also lie in the customer name range. The advantage of using enhancements is that during a subsequent upgrade, you do not need to perform a modification adjustment. Enhancements are not affected by upgrading to a new SAP Release.

Enqueue SAP enqueues help to ensure data consistency by prohibiting the changing of data by more than one user at a time. An SAP enqueue is set explicitly within an ABAP program by an enqueue function module and is explicitly released by a dequeue function module. SAP enqueues are in effect over several steps within an SAP transaction. Remaining SAP enqueues are released at the end of the SAP transaction.

Enterprise IMG Company-specific Implementation Guide.

Export The processes by which all objects of a change request are extracted from the database of the source SAP system. The extracted data is saved to a data file at the operating system level. In addition, a command file is created that indicates how the data should be imported into an SAP system.

Extended Transport Control With extended transport control, transport routes can include client specifications or groups of client and system combinations.

Extension Sets Extension Sets were introduced with Release 4.7 Enterprise. These are software components with their own Support Packages. New functionality is delivered primarily in Extension Sets so that the core remains stable. Extension Sets are inactive by default and can be activated if required.

External system An SAP system defined from within TMS for which no physical system exists in the transport domain. As with virtual systems, an import queue is maintained for external systems if defined as part of a transport layer. Unlike virtual systems, external systems have their own transport directory that may be explicitly defined.

Firewall Software for protecting a local network against unauthorized access from outside.

General Availability (GA) A phase in the SAP release strategy in which a new release is available to all customers.

GUI Graphical User Interface. The medium through which a user can exchange information with the computer. You use the GUI to select commands, start programs, display files, and perform other operations by selecting function keys or buttons, menu options, and icons with the mouse.

High availability Property of a service or system that remains in production operation most of the time. High availability for an SAP system means that unplanned and planned downtimes are reduced to a minimum. Good system administration is important here. You can reduce unplanned downtime by using preventive hardware and software solutions that are designed to reduce single points of failure in the services that support the system. You can reduce planned downtime by optimizing the scheduling of necessary maintenance activities.

HotNews SAP Notes with Priority 1 that describe critical errors. New HotNews should be checked regularly and, if relevant, imported proactively.

IDoc type Internal document in SAP format into which the data of a business process is transferred. An IDoc is a real business process formatted in the IDoc type. An IDoc type is described by the following components:

- A control record: Its format is identical for all IDoc types.
- One or more records: A record consists of a fixed administration segment and a data segment. The number and format of the segments differ for different IDoc types.
- Status records: These records describe stages of processing an IDOC can go through. The status records have the same format for all IDoc types.

IMG view Part of a project IMG that, for example, contains all mandatory activities of a project.

Implementation Guide (IMG)) A tool for making customer-specific adjustments to the SAP system. For each application component, the Implementation Guide contains:

- All steps to implement the SAP system
- All default settings and all activities to configure the SAP system.
- A hierarchical structure that maps the structure of the SAP application component
- Lists of all documentation relevant to the implementation of the SAP system

Import The process by which all objects of previously released and exported change requests are transported into a target SAP system using either the TMS or the transport control program tp.

Import buffer A file at the operating system level containing the list of change request to be imported into a specific SAP system. This file resides in the transport directory buffer. The terms import buffer and import queue are often used interchangeably.

Import options Import options that can be assigned either from within TMS import functionality or when using the `tp` command. They are used to cause specific rules of the Change and Transport System (CTS) to be ignored. Traditionally, these options are also known as unconditional modes.

Import queue The import queue in the SAP system reflects the operating system level import buffer and contains the list of requests that will be imported during the next import. The terms import buffer and import queue are often used interchangeably.

Industry Solution (IS) Industry-specific SAP ERP applications. For example, IS-H (IS Hospital) or IS-RE (IS Real Estate).

Instance Group of resources such as memory and work processes, usually in support of a single application or database server in the SAP client/server environment. Instance processes share a common set of buffers and are controlled by the same dispatcher process. An SAP system can consist of one or more instances.

Integration system System in the system landscape where developments and Customizing are carried out and then transported to the consolidation system. Each SAP Repository object is assigned to an integration system through its development class and transport layer.

Integration testing Testing a sequence of business processes of the same workflow and of the relevant cross-function boundaries. Integration testing includes outputs, interfaces, procedures, organizational structures, and security profiles. The focus is on likely business events or exceptions with extensive consequences.

Internet Transaction Server (ITS) Gateway between the SAP ERP system and the World Wide Web.

ITIL ITIL (IT Infrastructure Library) is a global de-facto standard describing IT service processes.

J2EE Engine The SAP J2EE Engine is part of the SAP

NetWeaver Application Server. It is a platform for Java programs that are based on the J2EE standard.

Java Support Package Manager The Java Support Package Manager (JSPM) is a central coordination tool that controls the import of Support Packages and Enhancement Packages into Java-based systems.

LAN Local Area Network.

Legacy system Typically, refers to a customer's previous system (for example, a mainframe system). The data in this system has to be reformatted before it is imported into a new system (e.g., into a client/server system such as SAP).

Local change request Change request that cannot be transported to other SAP systems.

Local object Repository object that is assigned to a local development class, such as $TMP. Local objects are local to the SAP system in which they were created and cannot be transported.

Locks The locking of data during transaction processing and the locking of SAP Repository objects during development work.
If a user changes a data record with a transaction or changes a Repository object, the same record or object cannot be accessed simultaneously by a second user. The record or object is locked for the duration of processing (ENQUEUE). It is it released or unlocked afterwards (DEQUEUE).
Repository objects are locked in Workbench change requests until the change request is released.

Logging of Customizing activities Functionality for analyzing table logs of Customizing activities. Table logs are only generated if table logging has been activated for the client.

Logical system A way of representing a client in an SAP system without having to define the SAP system. Logical systems allow applications to run with a common data basis. In SAP terms, a logical system is a client defined in a database. Logical systems can exchange messages and can be used, for example, by ALE.

Loose coupling Loose coupling allows you to add software archive files to transport requests of the ABAP transport system. In contrast to close coupling, the archive files must first be exported from the development environment to a file system. From there, you can upload a transport request.

Maintenance cycle A maintenance cycle is a period of time in which corrections are made to the system landscape and then imported collectively into the production system.

Maintenance Optimizer Maintenance Optimizer is part of SAP Solution Manager. It controls the download and implementation of Support Packages and Enhancement Packages.

Manual transport The recording of Customizing changes to a change request using a manual rather than an automatic method. Some IMG activities can only be transported using a manual transport option.

Master data Master data is a type of application data that changes infrequently, but is required for the completion of most business transactions. Examples of master data include lists of customers, vendors, and materials, and even the company's chart of accounts.

MDMP Multi-Display Multi-Processing Codepages. An MDMP system uses more than one code page. Depending on the logon language you can dynamically switch between the installed code pages. MDMP is a proprietary SAP implementation to use languages from different code pages in one system.

Mode User mode in an SAP GUI window.

Modification adjustment Adjustment of SAP Repository objects that have been modified by the customer during an SAP release upgrade or when importing Support Packages. This is based on a comparison of Repository objects of the SAP standard as they were before the release upgrade (old state) and the same objects as they will be after the upgrade (new state).

Modification Assistant Functionality designed to help manage the repair of a Repository object using the ABAP Workbench tools. The Modification Assistant guides the change process to ensure that changes are well documented, original forms of the objects are preserved, and the change request to which the changes are recorded is indicated.

Modification Browser Detailed documentation of all repairs made in an SAP System.

Modifications Changes made by a customer to SAP Repository objects of the SAP standard. During an SAP release upgrade, modifications may require the new SAP standard to be adjusted.

Name range An interval in a namespace. The name range for customer programs is the set of program names beginning with Y or Z. Customer name ranges can be reserved in view V_TRESN.

Name server Part of the SAP System Landscape Directory (SLD). The name server allows reserving globally unique names for Java development objects.

Namespace Set of all names that satisfy the specific properties of the namespace. A namespace is defined by a prefix SAP provides to the customer or software partner.

Nametab Runtime object of a table. The runtime object contains all of the information stored in the ABAP Dictionary in a format that is optimized for the application programs.

Non-ABAP system A non-ABAP system is a system that does not include an ABAP stack. In the CTS+ environment, systems that contain only a Java stack are referred to as non--ABAP systems.

Object checks When activated, object checks subject Repository objects in a change request to checks, such as a syntax check for ABAP programs, prior to the release of the change request.

Object Directory Catalog of SAP Repository objects that contains the following information: object type, object name, original system, person responsible, and development class.

Object list List of SAP Repository objects and/or Customizing objects in change requests or tasks. Whenever changes are made, objects are added to the object list of a task. When a task is released, its object list is placed in the object list of the request to which it is assigned.

OCS Online Correction Support. OCS is a global term comprising multiple tools designed to help you support your production environment by supplying Support Packages.

Original object The original of an object is usually the version maintained in the development system. Because all changes and developments are made using the original, it may never be overwritten by a transport.

Package A grouping of Repository objects belonging to a common area. Unlike the objects in a change request, the grouping is logical rather than temporal. The package is assigned a transport layer to ensure that all objects have the same consolidation route. Objects in packages can only be called from the outside via defined interfaces.

Performance Measurement of the efficiency of a computer system.

Preliminary import Import of a single change request. Preliminary imports allow you to expedite an individual request through the defined transport routes. A preliminary import imports the request and adds it to the next import queue defined by the transport route. To minimize the risks associated with preliminary imports, the request remains in the original import queue after the import, and is reimported the next time the entire import queue is imported. This ensures that the order in which groups of objects are imported is always the same as the order in which they were exported.

PREPARE Program preparing an SAP system for an upgrade. This includes implementing system checks as well as copying tools required for the upgrade. The control is implemented sequentially, according to phases that are grouped in modules.

Presentation server A computer providing GUI services.

Production system System that contains an enterprise's active business processes. This is where "live" production data is entered.

Profile Generator Automatically generates an authorization profile based on the activities in an activity group.

Project IMG Subset of the Enterprise IMG, containing only the components of the Enterprise IMG that are required in a particular Customizing project.

Quality assurance procedure A procedure in transport management introduced with Release 4.6B to improve the quality of transports into the production system. Transports must be checked and approved in the quality assurance system before they can be imported into the production system.

Quality assurance system System in which final testing is carried out. Tested, stable development objects and Customizing settings are transported into the quality assurance system at times defined for final testing. After verification and sign-off, the development objects and Customizing settings are delivered to the production system.

R/3 Runtime system 3.

R/3 System Consists of a central instance offering the services DVEBMGS (Dialog, Update, Enqueue, Batch, Message, Gateway, Spool), a database instance, optional dialog instances offering mainly the service D and B, and optional PC frontends. The successor of R/3 was renamed to SAP ERP due to enhanced functionality.

R/3 system service Logical function required to support the R/3 system, such as the database service and the application services, which may include the services Dialog, Update, Enqueue, Batch, Message, Gateway, and Spool.

R3trans A transport utility at the operating system level for transport of data between SAP systems. `R3trans` is also used for the installation of new SAP systems, for migration to other SAP releases, and for logical backups. Other programs usually call `R3trans`, in particular the transport control program `tp` and the upgrade control program `R3up`.

Ramp-Up Ramp-up is a process of SAP to launch new products.

RDBMS Relational Database Management System.

RDDIMPDP Background job that is scheduled event-periodic. It starts background jobs required for transports. `RDDIMPDP` is triggered by `tp`, which uses the executable `sapevt` at the operating system level to send event SAP_TRIGGER_RDDIMPDP. `RDDIMPDP` is also known as the transport dispatcher.

Recipient system SAP system in a system landscape, connected to the consolidation system via a transport route. Through this connection, the recipient system always receives the copies of change requests that have been imported into the consolidation system. The production system is an example of a recipient system in a default three-system landscape.

Release The process by which the owner of a change request or task indicates that the contents of the change request or task have been unit tested. Release of a change request of either type Transportable Change Request or Customizing Change request initiates the export process.

Release Customizing Only IMG activities affected by a given SAP release upgrade in the business application components concerned are presented for processing. SAP distinguishes between Upgrade Customizing (corrected or amended functionality) and Delta Customizing (new functionality) for SAP release upgrades.

Relocation transports The transport of Repository objects for the purpose of changing the ownership, development class, and/or transport layer for those objects. Relocation transports are possible using the Transport Organizer.

Repair An SAP Repository object that is not changed in the original system. All modifications of standard SAP objects are repairs because the customer's system is not the original system of SAP objects.

Repair flag A flag that protects an object changed in a system other than the original system from being overwritten by an import.

Repository Central storage facility for all development objects in the ABAP Workbench. These include ABAP programs, screens, and documentation.

Repository Browser ABAP Workbench navigation tool for managing development objects. The user interface of the Repository Browser resembles a file manager where development objects are grouped together in object lists in a hierarchical structure.

Repository object Object in the SAP Repository. Repository objects are development objects of the ABAP Workbench.

Repository switch A procedure during an SAP release upgrade that replaces an existing SAP Repository with a new SAP Repository.

Return code Value that indicates whether a tool (either within the SAP system or at the operating system level) ran successfully, with warnings, or with errors.

RFC Remote Function Call. RFC is an SAP interface protocol based on CPI-C. It allows the programming of communication processes between systems to be simplified considerably. Using RFCs, predefined functions can be called and executed in a remote system or within the same system. RFCs are used for communication control, parameter passing, and error handling.

Roadmap Roadmaps are guidelines of how to proceed in SAP implementation or upgrade projects. They replace the previously used ASAP guidelines, are contained in SAP Solution Manager, and can be integrated with the SAP Solution Manager projects.

Runtime environment Total of all programs that must be available for execution at runtime. The ABAP Interpreter in the runtime environment does not use the original of an ABAP program. Instead, you use a copy that is generated once during the runtime (early binding). Runtime objects such as programs and screens are automatically regenerated (late binding) if a timestamp comparison between the object and the ABAP dictionary determines a difference.

SAINT The SAP Add-on Installation Tool (SAINT) is a transaction to install and update add-ons.

SAP GUI SAP Graphical User Interface.

SAP NetWeaver Developer Studio The SAP NetWeaver Developer Studio (NWDS) is the SAP development environment for creating a variety of different SAP J2EE applications. The NWDS is based on the Eclipse open source development platform.

SAP NetWeaver Development Infrastructure The SAP NetWeaver Development Infrastructure (NWDI) consists of local development environments, the SAP NetWeaver Developer Studio (NWDS), and additional server-based software components and services that can provide a development team with a consistent central environment and thereby support the entire lifecycle of a product.

SAP Note Assistant The SAP Note Assistant is a tool to automatically import SAP Notes using Coding corrections.

SAP Notes SAP's announcements of corrections or enhancements to SAP systems. Often, an SAP Note provides a solution, or a solution will be provided with the next Support Package.

SAP Patch Manager (SPAM) Customer side of the OCS. The SAP Patch Manager enables you to import Support Packages provided by SAP into the customer system. It is also known as SAP Package Manager.

SAP Reference IMG Complete Implementation Guide containing all Customizing activities supplied by SAP. It is organized according to business application components.

SAP Service Marketplace Support and information services of SAP from where you can access

SAP Notes and Support Packages, for example.

SAP Software Change Registration (SSCR) A procedure for registering users who change Repository objects using the tools of the ABAP Workbench and for registering changes to SAP sources and SAP Repository objects.

SAP System Landscape Directory Strictly speaking, the SAP System Landscape Directory (SLD) does not belong to the SAP NetWeaver Development Infrastructure because it can be used for many other purposes without even using the development environment. However, the NWDI builds on the SLD as a central server application to access information about the existing system landscape, the software components contained in it, and the name range reservation (name server).

SAPjup Central coordination program for controlling the upgrade of an SAP system based on Java.

SAProuter A software module that functions as part of the firewall system. The SAProuter simplifies the configuration of network security and the control of traffic to and from the SAP system. It establishes an indirect connection between the SAP network and the external network. It provides limited access at the application level between the client software and the SAP application server.

SAPup Central coordination program for controlling the entire upgrade of an SAP system based on ABAP. This control occurs sequentially, according to phases.

Server The term server has multiple meanings in the SAP environment. It should therefore be used only if it is clear whether it means a logical unit, such as an SAP instance, or a physical unit, such as a computer.

Session Manager The tool used for central control of SAP applications. The Session Manager is a graphical navigation interface used to manage sessions and start application transactions. It can generate both company-specific and user-specific menus.

Shared memory Main memory area that can be accessed by all work processes in an instance. The term shared memory is also used to mean the main memory area shared by the RDBMS-processes.

Side effects In rare cases, an SAP Note causes an unwanted side effect at another location of the SAP software. Side effects are recorded in Note attributes and can thus be easily found and evaluated.

SID SAP System Identification. Placeholder for the three-character name of an SAP system.

SMSY Solution Manager System Landscape. This is a transaction in SAP Solution Manager for maintaining the SAP system landscape.

Software Deployment Manager The SAP Software Deployment Manager (SDM) is the tool called by the Change Management Service to perform the actual deployment of a new or changed software component version.

Software logistics Procedures and tools required for the creation, documentation, and distribution of development and Customizing changes throughout the SAP-recommended system landscape.

Solution Group of systems that are managed in SAP Solution Manager—for example, all systems that are operated by the same subsidiary.

Solution Manager project The Solution Manager project is used to plan and implement SAP implementation, maintenance, upgrade, or global rollout projects. Among others, system landscapes, business processes, or roadmaps are assigned to the Solution Manager project.

SPAM Update Support Package that contains improvements and extensions to the SAP Patch Manager.

SQL Structured Query Language. A database language for accessing relational databases.

Standard request A default change request automatically used to record changes without prompting for a request number. A standard request must be manually set and is valid for a specified period of time.

Standard transport layer The default transport layer for an SAP system and the transport layer used by all Customizing change requests released from that system.

Stopmark A stop mark is a marker placed in import queues to indicate that only the requests before the marker should be imported. Often, the words *end mark* and *stopmark* are used interchangeably.

Support Package A generic term for the different collections of general improvements and changes to the standard SAP software that SAP provides through the SAP Service Marketplace.

Support Package Collection Support Packages are grouped into Support Package Collections at regular intervals. These are stored on CD-ROMs and delivered automatically to all customers. Support Package Collections are available for Support Packages of types Hot Package and Legal Change Patches.

Support Package stack A Support Package stack is a combination of Support Packages that has been tested and recommended by SAP.

Switch and Enhancement Framework The Switch and Enhancement Framework is used to integrate different concepts for modification-free enhancement of Repository objects such as programs or BAdIs. It therefore serves as the basis for using SAP Enhancement Packages.

Synchronization objects Synchronization objects are objects that can be compared to or synchronized with the Customizing Scout or Customizing Distribution. You create synchronization objects if Customizing objects in different systems contain identical content but have different structures, for example, if they contain different table and field names.

System change option Global setting to permit changes to SAP Repository objects based on the object's namespace and type.

System copy Also known as a database copy. If you create an SAP system using a database copy, the SAP system is not installed with the standard SAP database, but with a database whose content is supplied by an existing SAP system using SAP migration tools specific to your platform and SAP Release.

System landscape The SAP systems and clients required for a company's implementation and maintenance of SAP software. The recommended standard SAP system landscape consists of a development system, a quality assurance system, and a production system.

System switch upgrade The system switch upgrade procedure was introduced with the upgrades to systems with SAP Basis Release 6.10 and higher. It replaces the previously used repository switch procedure and reduces the downtime required for the upgrade.

Table logging Activating the logging of all changes to SAP-selected

Customizing tables to provide an audit history with information about who made what changes to the data.

Target group A group of SAP system and client combinations to which transport routes can consolidate or deliver.

Task User-specific information carrier in the Change and Transport Organizers for entering and managing all changes to SAP Repository objects and Customizing settings. When an object is changed, it is recorded to a task. Tasks are assigned to a change request.

TCP/IP Transmission Control Protocol/Internet Protocol.

Track A track contains all development configurations (DC) and all parts of the runtime environment that are necessary for the development, testing, and creation of one or more software components. A track is therefore a separate production line for a specific release of a Java software component.

Transaction code Succession of alphanumeric characters used to name a transaction—that is, a particular ABAP program in the SAP ERP system. For example Transaction VA01 (CREATE SALES ORDER).

Transaction data Data collected during standard business activities/transactions; typically related to specific master data. For example, data relating to a specific sale is considered transaction data and can be assigned to the master data of the purchaser.

Transport The movement (export and import) of changes recorded in change requests between different SAP systems.

Transport control program (tp) An operation system level utility for controlling the transport of change requests between SAP systems and for SAP release upgrades.

Transport directory Operating system disk space that provides the management facility for all data to be transported between SAP systems.

Transport domain All SAP systems to be managed in the Transport Management System (TMS) belong to a transport domain. In this domain, system settings such as transport route settings are identical for all SAP systems. To have consistent settings in the transport domain, one SAP system (the transport domain controller) has the reference configuration, and all the other SAP systems in the transport domain receive copies of this reference configuration.

Transport domain controller An SAP system in the transport domain from which transport configuration activities for the entire transport domain are controlled. These activities include accepting SAP systems into the transport domain, creating virtual SAP systems, and establishing transport routes between different SAP systems.

Transport group All SAP systems within a transport group share the same transport directory.

Transport layer Used to determine the integration and consolidation system for SAP Repository objects. A transport layer is assigned to each development class and thus to all SAP Repository objects in that development class. It determines the SAP system in which developments or changes are performed, and whether objects will be transported to other systems when development work has been completed.

Transport log Record of the transfer of the objects in a particular change request from a source system to a target system. A transport log contains the following:

- A summary of transport activities
- A log detailing the export of objects from a source system
- 'The results of the import check
- A log detailing the import of objects into a target system

Transport Management System (TMS) The tool in the SAP system that enables centralized transport configuration, and the execution and monitoring of exports and imports between SAP systems in a single transport domain.

Transport Organizer (TO) Tool for preparing and managing transports that supplements the more commonly used Workbench Organizer and Customizing Organizer. The Transport Organizer is part of the Change and Transport Organizer.

Transport Organizer Web UI The Transport Organizer Web UI is a Web Dynpro ABAP application that provides functions similar to the Transport Organizer. It provides enhanced functions for the management of transport request in non-ABAP systems.

Transport profile The parameter settings for the operating system transport command program `tp`. This file resides at the operating system level in the transport directory `bin`.

Transport request A released and exported change request. This term and the term change request are often used interchangeably.

Transport route Transport routes are used to define both the target system in which you want to consolidate change requests and the SAP system to which change requests are delivered after verification and testing. Transport routes are either of type Consolidation or type Delivery.

Transportable change request Change request that will be exported to a defined consolidation system when released.

TU&UC Twin Unicode & Upgrade Conversion. In contrast to the CU&UC procedure, this requires an additional system—a copy of the production system (twin)—to reduce system downtime. However, this procedure is not limited to the combination of an SAP R/3 4.6C upgrade to SAP ERP 6.0 with Unicode conversion.

Unicode Cross-language character set for international data processing (www.unicode.org). Subset of the UCS character set according to ISO-10646.

Unit testing Lowest level of testing, where the program or transaction is tested and evaluated for faults (in contrast to business integration testing). Unit testing is the first test that is completed, usually during the Customizing and development effort, while business integration testing usually occurs in the quality assurance system. With unit testing, the focus is on the program's internal functions rather than on system integration.

Upgrade Assistant Tool that is used to support SAP release upgrades. The Upgrade Assistant provides one or more graphical user interfaces for the upgrade control program. It also allows you to execute an SAP upgrade remotely and monitor its status.

Upgrade Customizing Customizing activities that are required if you want to continue to use the same functions in your application components as before after an SAP release upgrade. Upgrade Customizing covers changes to functions already used in live systems.

Urgent correction Transaction type for managing change requests—using SAP Solution Manager—that must be quickly implemented into the production system. From a technical perspective, urgent corrections are implemented through a single transport.

User master data Logon and authorization information for SAP users. Only users who have a user master record can log on to a client in an SAP system and use specific transactions.

Version database Storage location for versions of SAP Repository objects that are created when a change request is released.

View "Virtual table," simultaneously displaying data from several "real" tables in the ABAP Dictionary. When you create a table, you assign a key to it. However, the fields in the key may be inadequate for solving certain problems. Thus, you can generate a view from several tables or parts of a table.

Virtual system SAP system configured as a placeholder for an SAP system that has not yet been set up. Transport routes can be defined for virtual systems, and the import queue can be maintained and displayed.

WAN Wide Area Network

Work center Central initial transaction in SAP Solution Manager for carrying out specific tasks. It comprises an overview of the most critical information about an activity area and includes jumps to other transactions that are necessary to carry out this activity.

Work process (WP) Process for processing a specific SAP ERP request. The following work processes are available:

- Dialog
- Update
- Background
- Spool
- Enqueue

Work processes can be assigned to dedicated application servers.

Workbench change request Change request for recording and transporting SAP Repository objects and changed system settings from cross-client tables (client-dependent Customizing).

Workbench Organizer (WBO) Tools for managing Workbench change requests required to record changes as a result of development efforts using the tools of the ABAP Workbench. The Workbench Organizer is part of the Change and Transport Organizer.

D Questions and Answers

D.1 Chapter 1: SAP ERP Architecture and Data Components

1. **Which of the following components indicate that SAP ERP is a client/server system?**

   A. Multiple databases.

   B. A database server.

   C. Three separate hardware servers: a database server, an application server, and a presentation server.

   D. A database service, an application service, and a presentation service.

   Answer: D

2. **Which of the following is NOT contained in the SAP ERP database?**

   A. The Repository

   B. Kernel

   C. Customer data

   D. Transaction data

   E. Customizing data

   F. ABAP Dictionary

   Answer: B

3. **Which of the following statements is correct with regard to SAP clients?**

   A. An SAP client has its own customer data and programs, which are not accessible to other clients within the same SAP system.

   B. An SAP client shares Customizing and application data with other clients in the same SAP system.

C. An SAP client shares all Repository objects and client-independent Customizing with all other clients in the same SAP system.

D. An SAP client enables you to separate application data from Customizing data.

Answer: C

4. **Which of the following statements is correct with regard to SAP's client concept?**

   A. All Customizing settings are client-independent.

   B. A client has a unique set of application data.

   C. A client has its own Repository objects.

   D. All Customizing settings are client-dependent.

   Answer: B

D.2 Chapter 2: Realizing Business Processes in SAP ERP

1. **Which of the following strategies enables SAP customers to avoid making modifications to standard SAP objects?**

   A. Using enhancement technologies such as program exits and menu exits.

   B. Modifying SAP-delivered programs.

   C. Changing standard SAP functionality using the IMG.

   D. Performing Customizing to provide the required functionality.

   Answer: A, D

2. **Which of the following statements are correct with regard to the IMG?**

   A. The IMG consists of a series of Customizing activities for defining a company's business processes.

   B. The IMG is an online resource providing the necessary information and steps to help you implement SAP application modules.

C. The IMG is client-independent.

D. All of the above.

Answer: D

3. **Which of the following strategies enables an enterprise to meet its business needs by changing or enhancing SAP functionality?**

   A. Maintaining application data using the various SAP business transactions in the SAP standard.

   B. Using the ABAP Workbench to create the required Repository objects.

   C. Using Customizing to modify programs after obtaining an access key from the SAP Service Marketplace.

   D. Using customer exits to enhance the functionality of existing standard SAP objects.

   Answer: B, D

4. **Which of the following statements are correct with regard to modifications?**

   A. A modification is a change to a standard SAP object.

   B. A modification must be registered through SSCR.

   C. SAP recommends modifications only if the customer's business needs cannot be met by Customizing, enhancement technologies, or customer development.

   D. All of the above.

   Answer: D

5. **Which of the following statements is correct with regard to Customizing?**

   A. Customizing enables SAP application processes to be set to reflect a company's business needs.

   B. Customizing can be performed only from within a Project IMG.

   C. Customizing is necessary because SAP ERP, for example, is delivered without business processes.

   D. None of the above.

   Answer: A

6. **Which of the following statements are correct with regard to Repository objects?**

   A. Customers can develop new Repository objects using the tools in the ABAP Workbench.

   B. Customer-developed Repository objects reside in the Repository alongside SAP-standard objects.

   C. Customers can create and assign new Repository objects to a development class.

   D. All of the above.

   Answer: D

D.3 Chapter 3: The SAP ERP System Landscape

1. **Which of the following statements is correct with regard to critical client roles as recommended by SAP?**

   A. Customizing changes can be made in any client.

   B. All Customizing and development changes should be made in a single client.

   C. Repository objects should be created and changed in the quality assurance client.

   D. Unit testing should take place in the Customizing-and-development client.

   Answer: B

2. **Which of the following activities should not be performed within a system landscape?**

   A. Customizing and development changes are transported to a quality assurance client before being delivered to production.

   B. The SAP ERP system is upgraded to new releases.

   C. Development changes are made directly in the production client.

   D. Clients are assigned a specific role.

   Answer: C

3. **Which of the following benefits does the three-system landscape recommended by SAP have?**

   A. Customizing and development, testing, and production activities take place in separate database environments and do not affect one another.

   B. Changes are tested in the quality assurance system and imported into the production system only after verification.

   C. Client-independent changes can be made in the development system without immediately affecting the production client.

   D. All of the above.

   Answer: D

4. **Which of the following statements is correct with regard to multiple SAP clients?**

   A. All clients in the same SAP system share the same Repository and client-independent Customizing settings.

   B. No more than one client in the same SAP system should allow changes to client-independent Customizing objects.

   C. If a client allows for changes to client-dependent Customizing, the client should also allow for changes to client-independent Customizing objects.

   D. All of the above.

   Answer: D

5. **Which of the following statements is correct with regard to the setup of a three-system landscape?**

   A. There is only one database for the system landscape.

   B. One client should allow for the automatic recording of client-dependent Customizing and for client-independent changes.

   C. All SAP systems have the same system ID.

   D. All clients must have unique client numbers.

   Answer: B

6. **Which of the following statements is correct with regard to the CUST client?**

   A. It should allow changes to client-independent Customizing, but not Repository objects.

   B. It should automatically record all changes to Customizing settings.

   C. It should not allow changes to client-dependent and client-independent Customizing settings.

   D. It should allow for all changes, but not require recording of changes to change requests.

   Answer: B

7. **Which of the following statements is correct with regard to a two-system landscape?**

   A. It is not optimal because opportunity to test the transport of changes from the development system to the production system is limited.

   B. It allows for changes to Customizing in the production system.

   C. It is recommended by SAP because Customizing and development do not impact quality assurance testing.

   D. All of the above.

   Answer: A

8. **Which of the following statements are correct with regard to a phased implementation?**

   A. All Customizing changes made in the production support system must also be made in the development system.

   B. The system landscape requires five SAP systems.

   C. Changes in the production support system do not have to be made in the development environment.

   D. The system landscape needs an environment that supports the production system with any required changes.

   Answer: A, D

9. **Which of the following statements is not valid with regard to a global system landscape?**

   A. A global template can be used for the rollout of corporate Customizing settings and development efforts.

   B. Management of different Repository objects (those developed by the corporate office versus those developed locally) can be managed using namespaces and name ranges for the Repository objects.

   C. Merging the Customizing settings delivered by the corporate office with local Customizing efforts can be accomplished easily using change requests.

   D. SAP provides different tools to aid in the rollout of a global template.

   Answer: D

D.4 Chapter 4: Managing Changes and Data in an SAP ERP System Landscape

1. **Which of the following statements is correct with regard to Customizing and development changes?**

   A. All changes are recorded to tasks in Customizing change requests.

   B. The changes should be recorded to tasks in change requests for transport to other clients and systems.

   C. The changes must be manually performed in every SAP system.

   D. The changes can easily be made simultaneously in multiple clients.

   Answer: B

2. **Which of the following statements with regard to change requests is FALSE?**

   A. The Customizing Organizer and the Workbench Organizer are tools used to view, create, and manage change requests.

B. A change request is a collection of tasks where developers and people performing Customizing record the changes they make.

C. All changes made as a result of IMG activities are recorded to Customizing change requests.

D. SAP recommends setting your SAP system so that Customizing changes made in the Customizing-and-development client are automatically recorded to change requests.

Answer: C

3. **For which of the following activities is the TMS (Transaction STMS)** *not* **designed?**

A. Releasing change requests

B. Viewing import queues

C. Viewing log files generated by both the export process and the import process

D. Initiating the import process

Answer: A

4. **Which of the following statements is correct after you have successfully imported change requests into the quality assurance system?**

A. The change requests must be released again to be exported to the production system.

B. The data files containing the changed objects are deleted from the transport directory.

C. The change requests need to be manually added to the import queue of the production system.

D. The change requests are automatically added to the import queue of the production system.

Answer: D

5. **Which of the following statements is correct with regard to the change requests in an import queue?**

A. They are sequenced according to their change request number.

B. They are sequenced in the order in which they were exported from the development system.

C. They are sequenced according to the name of the user who released the requests.

D. They are not sequenced by default, but arranged in a variety of ways using the TMS.

Answer: B

6. **Which of the following techniques can be used to transfer application data between two production systems?**

   A. Recording transaction data to change requests

   B. Using ALE to transfer application data

   C. Using the client copy tool

   D. All of the above.

   Answer: B

7. **Which of the following types of data transfer are possible with an appropriate use of interface technologies?**

   A. Transferring legacy data to an SAP system

   B. Transferring data between clients

   C. Transferring data to non-SAP systems

   D. Transporting change requests to multiple SAP systems

   Answer: A, B, C

8. **Which of the following statements is correct with regard to user master data?**

   A. User master data can be transported in a change request.

   B. User master data is unique to each SAP system, but is shared across clients in the same SAP system.

   C. A specific client copy option enables you to distribute user master data together with authorization profile data.

   D. User master data includes all user logon information, including the definition of authorizations and profiles.

   Answer: C

D.5 Chapter 5: Setting Up a System Landscape

1. **Which of the following clients should you copy to create new clients and ensure that all data from post-installation processing is also copied?**

   A. Client 001

   B. Client 000

   C. Client 066

   Answer: B

2. **Which of the following is *not* an SAP-recommended strategy for setting up a system landscape?**

   A. Using a client copy from the development system to set up your quality assurance and production systems when the change request strategy is not an option

   B. Creating the production system as a combination of a client copy from the quality assurance system and change requests from the development system

   C. Using the same setup strategy to establish both the quality assurance and production systems

   D. Setting up the quality assurance and production systems by importing change requests transported from the development system

   Answer: B

3. **Which of the following are correct with regard to the setup of the TMS?**

   A. The TMS should be set up when the development system is installed.

   B. The TMS should include all SAP systems in the system landscape, even if the SAP systems do not physically exist.

   C. The TMS is critical in establishing the transport route between the development and quality assurance systems.

   D. The TMS should be set up before change requests are created in the Customizing-and-development client.

   Answer: A, B, C, D

4. **Which of the following is correct with regard to the system copy strategy?**

   A. SAP recommends the system copy strategy because all Customizing and development objects are transferred.

   B. SAP does not recommend the system copy strategy because there is no easy way to eliminate unwanted application data.

   C. A system copy is the easiest setup strategy recommended by SAP.

   D. A system copy eliminates the need for change requests for your entire SAP implementation.

   Answer: B

D.6 Chapter 6: Maintaining a System Landscape

1. **Which of the following activities is NOT necessary for releasing and exporting a change request?**

   A. Documenting every task in the change request

   B. Releasing every task in the change request

   C. Verification of the contents of the change request by the system administrator

   D. Unit testing the change request

   Answer: C

2. **Which of the following statements is correct with regard to the tasks used in change requests that record Customizing and development changes?**

   A. Tasks belong to a change request.

   B. Tasks can be used by several SAP users.

   C. Tasks are the direct responsibility of a project lead.

   D. Tasks record only client-specific changes.

   Answer: A

3. **Which of the following indicates that a change request has been signed off after quality assurance testing?**

   A. The change request is released after unit testing.

   B. The change request is successfully imported into the quality assurance system.

   C. The change request is added to the import queue of all other SAP systems in the system landscape.

   D. The project lead communicates their approval of the change request.

   Answer: D

4. **Which of the following is NOT an SAP recommendation?**

   A. Imports into the quality assurance and production systems should occur in the same sequence.

   B. Even if the import process is automatically scripted, a technical consultant or system administrator should review the results of the import.

   C. Project leads should manually add change requests to the import queue of the quality assurance system.

   D. Change requests are imported in the same sequence in which they were exported from the development system.

   Answer: C

5. **Which of the following is SAP's recommendation on how to rush an emergency correction into the production system?**

   A. Make the change directly in the production system.

   B. Transport the change from the development system to the quality assurance system and production system using a preliminary import.

   C. Make the change and use a client copy with a change request to distribute the change to production.

   D. Make the change in the quality assurance system and transport the change using a preliminary import.

   Answer: B

6. **Which of the following transport activities is NOT typically the responsibility of the system administrator?**
   A. Importing change requests into all clients within the system landscape
   B. Verifying the success of the import process
   C. Releasing change requests
   D. Assisting in solving either export or import errors
   Answer: C
7. **Which of the following does SAP provide as customer support?**
   A. Release upgrades to provide new functionality.
   B. Support Packages to correct identified problems in a specific release.
   C. SAP Notes to announce errors and corrections for the reported problems.
   D. All of the above.
   Answer: D

D.7 Chapter 7: Transport Setup Activities at Installation

1. **The SAP system ID (SID):**
   A. Must be unique for each system sharing the same transport directory
   B. Must be unique for each system in the system landscape
   C. Can start with a number
   D. Can consist of any three-character combination
   Answer: A, B
2. **Which of the following statements is correct with regard to the transport directory?**
   A. There can be only one transport directory in a system landscape.
   B. All SAP systems within a transport group share a common transport directory.

C. In system landscapes using heterogeneous platforms, it is not possible to have a common transport directory.

D. Only the production system can contain the transport directory.

Answer: B

3. **Which of the following statements are correct with regard to the transport control program `tp`?**

   A. It is stored in subdirectory `bin` of the transport directory.

   B. It uses program `R3trans` to access the databases when transporting changes.

   C. It cannot be used directly at the operating system level.

   D. It depends on the settings of the transport profile.

   Answer: B, D

4. **The transport profile:**

   A. Is stored in subdirectory `bin` of the transport directory

   B. Contains comments and parameter settings that configure the transport control program `tp`

   C. Is managed from within TMS as of R/3 Release 4.5, but is modified with operating system text editors in earlier releases

   D. Contains only settings that are valid for all SAP systems in the system landscape

   Answer: A, B, C

5. **The initialization procedure of the CTO:**

   A. Is especially required after a system copy

   B. Establishes the initial value for change request IDs

   C. Is not mandatory to enable transports

   D. Is performed automatically during SAP installation by program `R3setup`

   Answer: A, B

6. **Which of the following statements is correct with regard to the settings governing changes to Repository objects?**

   A. Only the customer name range should be modifiable in production systems.

B. Developments are possible in an SAP system only if you have applied for a development namespace.

C. If the global change option is set to NOT MODIFIABLE, it is nevertheless possible to make changes in certain name spaces or clients that have their change option set to MODIFIABLE.

D. The global change option should always be set to NOT MODIFIABLE for the quality assurance system and the production system.

Answer: D

D.8 Chapter 8: Setting Up the TMS

1. **Which of the following statements is correct with regard to the SAP systems belonging to a transport domain?**

   A. They all share the same transport directory.

   B. They are managed centrally using TMS.

   C. They belong to the same transport group.

   D. They must run on the same operating system and database platform.

   Answer: B

2. **Which of the following statements is correct with regard to the domain controller?**

   A. It must be the production system.

   B. It occurs once in a transport domain.

   C. It occurs in each transport group.

   D. It can only be the SAP system that was originally designated as the transport domain controller.

   E. It should never be the production system due to the high system load caused by the domain controller.

   Answer: B

3. **Which of the following statements are correct with regard to the TMS?**

   A. It needs to be initialized only on the transport domain controller.

   B. It needs to be initialized only on the transport domain controller and the backup domain controller.

   C. It must be initialized on every SAP system.

   D. It must be set up before you can set up transport routes.

   Answer: C, D

4. **Which of the following statements are correct with regard to the RFC destinations for TMS connections?**

   A. They are generated automatically when a transport route is created.

   B. They are generated between the domain controller and each SAP system in the transport domain.

   C. They must be established manually before you can use the TMS.

   D. They are generated during the TMS initialization process.

   E. They are only needed for importing change requests.

   Answer: B, D

5. **How is the actual system landscape, including SAP system roles and relationships, defined using the TMS?**

   A. By including all SAP systems in the transport domain

   B. By configuring transport routes

   C. By assigning a role to each SAP system during the TMS initialization process

   D. By designating real, virtual, and external SAP systems

   Answer: B

6. **Which of the following statements is correct with regard to a consolidation route?**

   A. It is defined by an integration system and a consolidation system, and is associated with a transport layer.

B. It is created in the TMS by defining only an integration system and a consolidation system.

C. It is not necessarily required in a two-system landscape.

D. It can be defined only once in a transport group.

Answer: A

7. **Which of the following statements are correct with regard to client-specific transport routes?**

A. For security reasons, client-independent objects such as programs can no longer be transported.

B. They can only be used if the extended transport control is activated and `tp` includes a minimum version status.

C. They are only allowed for target groups.

D. They may not be used in conjunction with client-independent transport routes.

Answer: B, D

D.9 Chapter 9: Client Tools

1. **After you create a new client entry in table T000, which of the following activities lets you provide the client with data?**

A. A remote client copy to populate the client with data from a client in another SAP system

B. A client transport to import data from a client in another SAP system

C. A local client copy to import data from a client within the same SAP system

D. All of the above

Answer: D

2. **Which of the following *cannot* be used to restrict a client from certain activities?**

A. The client role

B. The client-dependent change option

C. The client ID-number

D. A client restriction

E. The client-independent change option

Answer: C

3. **Which of the following tasks can be performed using the client copy tools?**

   A. Merging application data from one client into another

   B. Copying only application data from one client to another

   C. Copying only Customizing data from one client to another

   D. All of the above

   Answer: C

4. **Which of the following tasks can be performed using client copy profiles?**

   A. Scheduling a client copy to occur at a time when system use is low

   B. Selecting the subset of application data that will be copied when a client copy is executed

   C. Providing required user authorization for the use of client tools

   D. Determining the data that will be copied when a client copy is executed

   Answer: D

5. **Which of the following statements is correct with regard to table logging?**

   A. Table logging should be used instead of change requests whenever possible.

   B. Table logging provides an audit history of who made what changes and when.

   C. Table logging does not negatively impact system resources.

   D. All of the above.

   Answer: B

D.10 Chapter 10: Managing Development Changes

1. **Which of the following statements is *false* with regard to development classes?**

   A. Development classes facilitate project management by grouping similar Repository objects.

   B. All Repository objects are assigned to a development class.

   C. A development class determines the transport route a changed Repository object will follow.

   D. A local object does not need a development class.

   Answer: D

2. **Which of the following kinds of changes are transported using Workbench change requests?**

   A. Client-independent changes.

   B. Modifications to SAP-delivered objects.

   C. Changes made using the ABAP Editor and ABAP Dictionary.

   D. Repairs to Repository objects that originated in another SAP ERP system.

   D. All of the above.

   Answer: E

3. **Which of the following data is *not* contained in the object list of a task?**

   A.The actual change made to the objects listed in the task

   B.The list of changed objects recorded to the task

   C.Whether the objects recorded to the task are locked

   D. The complete Object Directory entry for the object

   Answer: A, D

4. **Which of the following statements are correct with regard to repairs and modifications?**

   A. Repairs are changes to SAP-delivered objects; modifications are changes to any object that originated in an SAP system other than the current SAP system.

B. A repair flag protects a Repository object against being overwritten by an import.

C. All repairs are saved to Workbench change requests.

D. A modification is a change to a standard SAP object.

D. All of the above.

Answer: B, C, D

5. **Which additional enhancement options does the Enhancement Framework provide as of SAP NetWeaver 7.0?**

   A. Implicit enhancement points

   B. Implicit enhancement sections

   C. Explicit enhancement points

   D. Explicit enhancement sections

   Answer: A, C, D

6. **Which of the following statements are correct in regard to the Switch Framework?**

   A. The Switch Framework is only available for the activation of SAP industry solutions.

   B. Business functions can be switched on and off.

   C. Business function sets group several business functions into semantic units to enable switching the business functions together.

   D. All of the above.

   Answer: B, C

D.11 Chapter 11: Managing Customizing Changes

1. **Which of the following requirements must be met before you can change both client-dependent and client-independent Customizing settings in a client?**

   A. The client settings must allow for changes to client-independent Customizing objects.

   B. The client role must be PRODUCTION.

C. The system change option must be set to MODIFIABLE.

D. The client settings must allow for changes to client-dependent Customizing.

Answer: A, C, D

2. **Which of the following statements are correct when project leads and project team members receive only the recommended authorizations?**

A. Only developers can create change requests.

B. Only project leads can create change requests and are therefore responsible for assigning project team members to change requests.

C. Project team members can create and release change requests.

D. Project leads can release change requests.

Answer: B, D

3. **Which of the following statements are correct with regard to Project IMGs?**

A. The Project IMG provides access to the Customizing activities defined for a particular project.

B. Customizing is performed in the Project IMG tree structure.

C. The Project IMG lets you display project status information and document Customizing activities.

D. All of the above.

Answer: D

4. **Which of the following activities are performed using the Customizing Organizer?**

A. Viewing all Customizing change requests related to a particular user

B. Viewing all Workbench change requests related to a particular user

C. Viewing all change requests related to a particular user

D. Managing change requests you own or reviewing change requests in which you have assigned tasks

Answer: A, B, C, D

5. **Which of the following statements is correct in regard to Customizing?**

   A. All Customizing activities in the IMG are client-dependent.

   B. All changes resulting from IMG activities can be transported.

   C. All Customizing changes are automatically recorded to a change request if the client change option is set to AUTOMATIC RECORDING OF CHANGES.

   D. A Customizing activity may involve the creation of client-independent objects and therefore requires a Workbench change request.

   Answer: D

6. **Which of the following activities are performed using client comparison tools?**

   A. Comparing the Customizing settings of two SAP clients in the same SAP system or in a different SAP system

   B. Adjusting the Customizing differences between two different SAP clients

   C. Transporting Customizing settings into the production client

   D. Comparing the objects listed in the object list of a change request with an SAP client

   Answer: A, B, D

D.12 Chapter 12: Releasing and Exporting Change Requests

1. **Which of the following is a prerequisite for copying client-dependent changes to a unit test client using** CLIENT COPY BY TRANSPORT REQUEST **(Transaction SCC1)?**

   A. The change request has been released.

   B. The tasks have been released, but the change request has not.

C. The tasks have been released after successful unit testing by the owner of the task.

D. The change request has not been released.

Answer: D

2. **Which of the following are the result of releasing a task?**

A. A data file is created in the transport directory and contains the objects recorded in the change request.

B. The object list and documentation for the task are copied to the change request.

C. All objects recorded in the task are locked.

D. You can no longer save changes to that task.

Answer: B, D

3. **Which of the following are the result of releasing and exporting a change request?**

A. A data file is created in the transport directory to contain copies of the objects recorded in the change request.

B. Versions are created in the version database for all SAP Repository objects in the object list of the change request.

C. All repairs recorded in the change request are confirmed.

D. You can no longer save changes to that change request.

Answer: A, B, D

4. **When you release a Customizing change request, you can do which of the following?**

A. Release the change request to another Customizing change request.

B. Schedule the release of the change request for a later time.

C. Release the change request to a transportable change request.

D. Initiate immediate release and export.

Answer: C, D

5. **Which of the following is a prerequisite for releasing a transportable change request?**

   A. There are no syntax errors in the ABAP programs recorded to the change request.

   B. You must own the tasks in the change request.

   C. All Repository objects in the change request are locked by the change request.

   D. The change request has documentation.

   Answer: C

6. **The export process initiates which of the following activities?**

   A. The creation of files in the transport directory

   B. The automatic import of change requests into the target system—for example, the quality assurance system

   C. The addition of the exported change request to the import buffer of the target system

   D. The deletion of the change request within the SAP system

   Answer: A, C

7. **Which of the following activities result in a version history for all Repository objects?**

   A. A Repository object is recorded to a change request.

   B. Change requests are imported into an SAP system, and the transport parameter `vers_at_imp` is activated.

   C. A task containing a Repository object is released.

   D. A change request containing a Repository object is released.

   Answer: B, D

D.13 Chapter 13: Importing Change Requests

1. **Which of the following statements are correct with regard to import queues?**

   A. Import queues are the TMS representation of the import buffer at the operating system level.

B. You have to manipulate import queues to transport change requests.

C. Import queues should be closed before starting an import using TMS.

D. You can import only an entire import queue.

Answer: A, C

2. **Which of the following statements are correct with regard to preliminary imports?**

   A. SAP recommends using preliminary imports rather than imports of entire queues.

   B. Preliminary imports should be performed only in exceptional cases.

   C. Change requests imported as preliminary imports remain in the import queue.

   D. Change requests are deleted from the import queue after preliminary imports. This prevents them from being imported again with the next import of the entire import queue.

   Answer: B, C

3. **Which of the following statements is correct with regard to imports into an SAP system?**

   A. Imports can be performed only by using the START IMPORT functionality in the TMS.

   B. Imports can be performed only by using `tp` commands at the operating system level to prepare the import queue and then using the START IMPORT functionality in the TMS.

   C. Imports can be performed only by using `tp` commands at the operating system level.

   D. Imports can be performed by using either a `tp` command at the operating system level or the TMS import functionality.

   Answer: D

4. **Which of the following statements is correct with regard to transports between different transport groups?**

   A. They are not possible.

B. They can be performed only by using `tp` at the operating system level with special options.

C. They can be performed using the TMS with special options provided by the expert mode.

D. They require you to adjust the corresponding import queues.

Answer: D

5. **Which of the following statements are correct with regard to transports between different transport domains?**

A. They are not possible.

B. They require you to create a virtual system and a virtual transport directory.

C. They require you to configure identical transport groups within the different transport domains.

D. They require you to create an external system and an external transport directory.

E. They require you to adjust the corresponding import queues.

Answer: D, E

D.14 Chapter 14: Technical Insight—the Import Process

1. **Which of the following statements are correct with regard to the transport control program `tp`?**

A. To perform imports, `tp` must always be used directly on the operating system level.

B. SAP recommends that you use the TMS instead of `tp` to perform imports.

C. `tp` is responsible for exporting and importing objects from and to SAP systems.

D. `tp` does not observe the sequence of change requests in the import queue when performing imports.

Answer: B, C

2. **Which of the following statements are correct with regard to import queues and import buffers?**

   A. Import queues are the TMS representation in SAP systems of the import buffer files on the operating system level.

   B. Import queues and import buffers are completely independent of each other.

   C. Import buffers have to be manipulated before imports can be performed on the operating system level.

   D. Manipulating import buffers may cause serious inconsistencies and should be performed only in exceptional cases.

   Answer: A, D

3. **Which of the following statements are correct with regard to the import options formerly known as *unconditional modes*?**

   A. Import options cannot be used when imports are performed on the operating system level using `tp`.

   B. Import options are used to cause specific rules of the Change and Transport System (CTS) to be ignored.

   C. Import options must be used when importing into multiple clients using `tp`.

   D. Import options can be selected in the TMS using the expert mode.

   Answer: B, C, D

4. **Which of the following statements are correct with regard to the sequence of processing steps** `tp` **follows when performing imports?**

   A. `tp` collectively processes each import step for all change requests in an import queue before proceeding with the next import step.

   B. `tp` processes all import steps for a single request before proceeding to the next change request.

   C. The processing sequence followed by `tp` ensures that when a change request with a faulty object is followed in the import queue by a change request with the corrected object, the faulty object will not affect the runtime environment of the target system.

D. `tp` imports and activates ABAP Dictionary structures prior to the main import phase to ensure that the current structures can receive new data during the main import phase.

Answer: A, C, D

5. **Which of the following statements are correct with regard to troubleshooting imports?**

A. In the SAP ERP system, you cannot display log files that do not depend on a specific request. For example, you cannot display log files related to generic import steps, such as structure conversion.

B. SAP recommends that you check the SLOG file and the ALOG file before checking the single step log files.

C. By default, all return codes greater than 8 cause `tp` to abort a running import.

D. `tp` is the only transport tool that uses return codes.

Answer: A, B, C

6. **Which of the following statements are correct in regard to buffer synchronization?**

A. Transport activities do not affect buffer synchronization.

B. Imports affect buffer synchronization even in central SAP systems.

C. `R3trans` can invalidate buffer content.

D. Importing data into a production system can significantly impact performance because some buffer content may be invalidated and reloaded. This causes high system load.

E. Importing programs and ABAP Dictionary data cannot cause inconsistencies in the target system, even if the programs or data affect running programs and their environment.

Answer: B, C, D

7. **Which of the following statements are correct with regard to the interaction between transport tools?**

   A. During exports, `tp` calls `R3trans` to access the database of the source system and extract the objects to be transported.

   B. `tp` triggers the transport daemon `RDDIMPDP` in the SAP system using the operating system tool `sapevt`.

   C. Using the tables TRBAT and TRJOB, `tp` communicates with ABAP programs involved in the transport process.

   D. `tp` communicates with only `RDDIMPD`.

   Answer: A, B, C

D.15 Chapter 15: SAP NetWeaver Development Infrastructure

1. **Which of the following statements about the NetWeaver Development Infrastructure (NWDI) are correct?**

   A. It consists of several coordinated tools for designing, developing, and testing Java programs.

   B. It can be used as both a local and central development environment.

   C. It is not suitable for teams with several developers.

   D. It is not suitable for transporting ABAP and Java components.

   Answer: A, B

2. **Which functions are fulfilled by the SAP Design Time Repository (DTR)?**

   A. The DTR takes care of the central storage, versioning, and management of Java sources.

   B. The DTR provides automated conflict verifications.

   C. The DTR can also store Word files.

   D. The DTR manages archives that are required for software development.

   Answer: A, B, C

3. **Which functions are fulfilled by the SAP System Landscape Directory (SLD)?**

   A. It is a tool for central user management.

   B. It stores information about the system landscape.

   C. It works like a central data cache.

   D. It stores version information about the installed software components.

   Answer: B, D

4. **Which of the following services are required for Java transports?**

   A. Java Activation Framework (JAF)

   B. Design Time Repository (DTR)

   C. Component Build Service (CBS)

   D. Change Management Service (CMS)

   E. Enterprise Information System (EIS)

   Answer: B, C, D

5. **Which of the following statements are correct with regard to tracks, systems, and development configurations?**

   A. A track always contains exactly one development configuration.

   B. A track contains multiple systems.

   C. A system consists of a development configuration and a runtime environment.

   D. A track serves to develop various software components in different releases.

   E. A track serves to develop only one release of a specific software component.

   Answer: B, C, E

6. **Which of the following statements are correct with regard to Design Time Repository (DTR) and Central Build Service (CBS)?**

   A. The DTR consists of one active and one inactive workspace.

B. The development components can be used by other developers by checking in at the DTR.

C. The development components can be used by other developers through activation in the CBS.

D. If the central build fails, the elements of the active workspace enter the inactive workspace.

Answer: A, C

7. **Which of the following statements are correct with regard to the transport of Java objects?**

   A. The objects are automatically activated when requests are imported into the consolidation system.

   B. Like in the ABAP environment, only individual development objects and (generally) not entire software components are imported into the production system.

   C. During the assembly step, only references to required software components are created.

   D. During the assembly step, all required software components are included in the archive to be created.

   Answer: A, C

D.16 Chapter 16: Enhanced Change and Transport System

1. **Which objects can be imported with the Software Deployment Manager?**

   A. Software Deployment archives

   B. Software Component archives

   C. Java patches

   D. ABAP Support Packages

   Answer: A, B, C

2. **Which are advantages of the enhanced Change and Transport System?**

   A. Tracking parameter changes in heterogeneous environments

   B. Software distribution of non-ABAP objects

   C. Simultaneous distribution of changes in dual-stack systems

   D. A shared user interface to distribute software changes in different development environments

   Answer: B, C, D

3. **What effects does the WBO_REL_REQ_STRATEGY = AUTO transport parameter setting have?**

   A. A new transport request is created in the Domain Controller if a default transport request is not available for the user.

   B. The system releases the transport requests automatically when an object is attached.

   C. The application displays an error message if a standard transport request is not available for the user.

   Answer: B

4. **Where is the enhanced Change and Transport System configured?**

   A. In the Configuration of the Transport Management System (TMS)

   B. In the Instance profile of the Java stack

   C. In the Instance profile of the ABAP stack

   Answer: A

5. **How can you simultaneously distribute changes in business processes that run in ABAP and Java systems, for example, in the ESS/MSS scenario?**

   A. The enhanced Change and Transport System enables you to create transport requests that contain ABAP and Java objects.

   B. The enhanced Change and Transport System enables you to define dependencies between transport requests in the ABAP and Java stack.

C. The SAP NetWeaver Development Infrastructure (NWDI) enables you to define dependencies between transport requests in the ABAP and Java stack.

Answer: A

D.17 Chapter 17: Maintaining SAP Software

1. **What are the benefits of importing SAP Support Packages?**

   A. Proactive solution of known problems

   B. Functional extensions to SAP software

   C. Improved ease of maintenance and reduced time and effort for repairs and maintenance

   Answer: A, C

2. **Which of the following statements are true with regard to the SAP Note Assistant?**

   A. It simplifies the maintenance of programs in the customer namespace.

   B. It enables you to import Notes that contain code corrections.

   C. It simplifies the process of making changes to Data Dictionary objects.

   D. It identifies dependencies between SAP Notes.

   E. It can replace the process of importing Support Packages.

   Answer: B, D

3. **Which of the following statements are true with regard to Support Packages?**

   A. They change the SAP standard of your SAP system before the next release upgrade.

   B. You can import all types of Support Packages into all SAP systems, regardless of the components installed in the target system.

   C. Support Packages are available only to customers who are taking part in the ramp-up.

D. Different types of Support Packages may be required for SAP systems with different components.

Answer: A, D

4. **Which of the following statements are true with regard to the SAP Patch Manager?**

   A. The Patch Manager ensures that Support Packages are imported in the correct order.

   B. The SAP Patch Manager does not check whether the type of Support Package you want to import is suitable for your SAP ERP installation. You have to determine whether you need a particular Conflict Resolution Transport, for example.

   C. The SAP Patch Manager does not allow you to protect SAP objects you have modified. These objects are automatically overwritten.

   D. The SAP Patch Manager automatically opens Transactions SPDD and SPAU for the modification adjustment process, if required.

   Answer: A, D

5. **Which of the following statements are true with regard to Support Package stacks?**

   A. Support Package stacks are combinations of Support Packages that are recommended by SAP.

   B. Support Package stacks should be imported only if an urgent problem is preventing an import from being carried out.

   C. Support Package stacks are Support Package combinations that have been particularly well tested by SAP.

   D. The SAPGUI version also must be upgraded to the latest level with every Support Package stack upgrade.

   Answer: A, C

6. **Which of the following statements are true with regard to ABAP and Java corrections?**

   A. An ABAP Support Package always overwrites all objects of a software component.

B. A Java Support Package always overwrites all objects of a software component.

C. An individual ABAP program can be changed using an SAP Note that contains a correction instruction.

D. An individual Java program can be changed using the Software Deployment Archive (SDA).

Answer: B, C

7. **Where can you find version information about a Java system?**

   A. Under *http://<hostname>:<port>/sap/monitoring/ComponentInfo*

   B. In the SAP System Landscape Directory (SLD)

   C. In the system status information of the ABAP stack (only for dual-stack systems)

   C. In Transaction SPAM of the ABAP stack (only for dual-stack systems)

   Answer: A, B

D.18 Chapter 18: SAP Software Release Upgrade

1. **Which of the following statements are true of the SAP release strategy?**

   A. The 5-1-2 maintenance strategy applies to all SAP products.

   B. New products first go through the ramp-up phase.

   C. During the ramp-up phase, the product is already generally available.

   D. No SAP Support Packages are delivered during the ramp-up phase.

   Answer: B

2. **Which of the following statements are correct with regard to release changes?**

   A. The objects in the customer namespace are not overwritten.

   B. A repository switch replaces your current repository with the repository in the new release.

C. All customer modifications to ABAP Dictionary objects are lost.

D. The customer modifications to SAP objects that you want to keep must be transferred to the new release using the modification adjustment.

Answer: A, B, D

3. **Which of the following statements are true of the modification adjustment?**

   A. Transaction SPAU is used for most of the ABAP Dictionary objects.

   B. Transaction SPDD is used for most of the ABAP Dictionary objects.

   C. If Transaction SPDD is not used although it is required, this can lead to data losses.

   D. During the modification adjustment, you must revert to the SAP standard version.

   Answer: B, C

4. **Which benefits are provided by the system switch upgrade?**

   A. The system switch upgrade makes a modification adjustment redundant.

   B. The system switch upgrade makes the creation of a backup before the upgrade redundant.

   C. The system switch upgrade shortens the time during which the system cannot be used productively.

   D. The SPDD adjustment can be carried out before the beginning of downtime.

   Answer: C, D

5. **Which of the following statements are true of SAP Enhancement Packages?**

   A. SAP provides Enhancement Packages for all ERP releases, such as SAP R/3 4.6C, SAP R/3 Enterprise, or SAP ERP 6.0.

   B. SAP Enhancement Packages use the switch mechanism of the SAP Enhancement and Switch Framework.

C. If an SAP Enhancement Package has been imported, you must also update it in further EhP updates.

D. The delivery of the SAP Enhancement Packages is cumulative, that is, an EhP X+1 package also automatically contains the content of EhP X.

Answer: B, C, D

6. **Which of the following statements are true of Unicode and SAP release changes?**

   A. For upgrades to SAP products that are based on SAP NetWeaver 7.0, a change to Unicode is only mandatory for systems with multiple installed code pages.

   B. Transports between different SAP releases are generally not possible when only one release has been converted to Unicode.

   C. Using the combined upgrade and Unicode conversion procedures, CU&UC and TU&UC, reduces system downtime considerably.

   D. In contrast to upgrades, for Unicode conversions system downtime is directly linked to the database size.

   Answer: A, C, D

7. **How is an SAP system that uses a J2EE Engine upgraded?**

   A. A combination with the ABAP stack installed in parallel is possible and is synchronized by the upgrade tools.

   B. The screens to control both the ABAP and the Java upgrade are set up in a similar way and use the same method to communicate with the upgrade tools.

   C. In contrast to the ABAP upgrade, you cannot integrate additional software packages or patches.

   D. The structure of the J2EE upgrade phase sequence is much simpler than that of the ABAP upgrade, because primarily, the J2EE upgrade includes only deployments, not modification adjustments.

   Answer: A, B, D

D.19 Chapter 19: SAP Solution Manager

1. **Which of the following statements are true of Customizing Distribution?**

   A. Customizing Distribution synchronizcs Customizing scttings in different systems.

   B. Customizing Distribution only works for systems with identical release statuses.

   C. Customizing Distribution can also be set up without SAP Solution Manager.

   D. Customizing Distribution usually takes place between development systems. The QA and production systems are provided with transport requests.

   Answer: A, D

2. **Which of the following statements are true of the Customizing Scout?**

   A. The Customizing Scout can only be used for systems with identical release statuses.

   B. Comparison runs can be saved and displayed at a later point in time.

   C. Synchronization objects can be compared.

   D. Comparison runs cannot be performed in the background.

   Answer: B, C

3. **Which of the following statements are true of Maintenance Projects?**

   A. Urgent corrections can be created even if no maintenance project exists.

   B. Regular corrections can be released in any phase of a maintenance cycle.

   C. A maintenance project is created in Transaction SOLAR_PROJECT_ADMIN.

   D. Regular corrections can be released in phase Development with Release.

   Answer: C, D

4. **Which of the following statements are true of urgent corrections?**

   A. Urgent corrections can be part of a maintenance project or implementation project.

   B. Urgent corrections are not documented in SAP Solution Manager.

   C. Urgent corrections must be approved by the Change Manager.

   D. Urgent corrections can be released in any phase of a maintenance cycle.

   Answer: C

5. **Which functions are provided in the change analysis?**

   A. Configuration data can be distributed from a master system to all other systems.

   B. You can display the configuration parameters that were changed on a specific day.

   C. You can set up email notifications for system administrators if specific parameter values are changed.

   D. You can determine how many transport requests were imported on a specific day.

   Answer: B, D

6. **How does the change analysis support the error search in an SAP solution? The change analysis....**

   A. ... identifies the system and the software component responsible for the error.

   B. ... provides a central entry point for determining changes to a solution.

   C. ... contains the values of the configuration parameter and the entire change history.

   D. ... enables you to send error messages to the SAP Solution Manager Service Desk.

   Answer: B, C

7. **Which benefits does Maintenance Optimizer offer?**

   A. It reduces the import times for Support Packages and Enhancement Packages.

   B. It simplifies the download of Support Packages.

   C. It provides an overview of current and past maintenance activities.

   D. It helps to evaluate the functional effects of a Support Package.

   Answer: B, C

8. **What are the prerequisites for using Maintenance Optimizer?**

   A. Change Request Management must be set up.

   B. An RFC connection to the SAP Support Portal must be set up.

   C. An S-User for the SAP Service Marketplace must be assigned to the user in SAP Solution Manager.

   E. The system to be maintained must be integrated with a solution in SAP Solution Manager.

   Answer: B, D, E

9. **Which activities of an upgrade project does SAP Solution Manager support?**

   A. Generating the upgrade key

   B. Reviewing the system landscape situation

   C. Evaluation of PREPARE

   D. Determining upgrade-relevant IMG activities

   Answer: A, B, D

10. **Which phases does the Upgrade Roadmap include?**

    A. Project preparation

    B. Creation of an upgrade blueprint

    C. Production preparation

    D. Production implementation and support

    Answer: A, B, C, D

E Literature

E.1 SAP Online Help

To access the SAP online documentation of an SAP NetWeaver system, on the initial screen, select HELP • SAP LIBRARY. Then, choose the following path:

- SAP NETWEAVER LIBRARY • ADMINISTRATOR'S GUIDE • TECHNICAL OPERATIONS MANUAL • GENERAL ADMINISTRATION TASKS • SOFTWARE LOGISTICS
- Here, you can find a description of the change and transport management system for ABAP as well as for Java.

SAP Solution Manager has its own online help. You can access it if you are logged on to an SAP Solution Manager system. In the initial screen, select HELP • SAP LIBRARY.

The SAP online help is also available under *http://help.sap.com*.

E.2 SAP Training Courses

Currently, SAP provides the following training course for the change and transport management area:

- **ADM325**
  Software Logistics
- **ADM326**
  Upgrade
- **ADM200**
  SAP NetWeaver Application Server Java Administration
- **ADM225**
  SAP Software Logistics for Java
- **E2E200**
  E2E Change Control Management

E.3 SAP Developer Network (SDN)

The SAP Developer Network is an online platform for SAP developers and system administrators. Here, you can find technical articles, documentations, and how-to guides. Online forums are also provided to discuss current questions, and areas exist where experts answer questions on current topics. The software change management area can be accessed via the link

https://www.sdn.sap.com/irj/sdn/swchangemgmt

E.4 SAP Service Marketplace

The SAP Service Marketplace is separate from the public SAP website, *http://www.sap.com*. Customers, partners, SAP employees, and potential customers require corresponding authorizations to access the SAP Service Marketplace at *http://service.sap.com*. Using quick links, which are simply appended to the address of the SAP Service Marketplace, you can quickly access the relevant information, for example, *http://service.sap.com/solutionmanager*.

Other important quick links include the following: */upgrade*, */testing*, */swdc* (Software Distribution Center).

E.5 Bibliography

- Föse, Frank, Hagemann, Sigrid, and Will, Liane. *SAP NetWeaver ABAP System Administration*. 3rd edition. SAP PRESS, 2008.
- Barzewski, Alfred, et al. *Java Programming with SAP NetWeaver*. 2nd edition. SAP PRESS, 2008.
- Vanstechelman, Bert, Mergaerts, Mark, and Matthys, Dirk. *SAP NetWeaver Application Server Upgrade Guide*. 2nd edition. SAP PRESS, 2007.
- Schäfer, Marc O., and Melich, Matthias. *SAP Solution Manager Enterprise Edition*. SAP PRESS, 2009.

- Helfen, Markus, Lauer, Michael, and Trauthwein, Hans Martin. *Testing SAP Solutions*. SAP PRESS, 2007.
- Bürckel, Nils, Davidenkoff, Alexander, and Werner, Detlef. *Unicode in SAP Systems.* SAP PRESS, 2007.

F Authors

Armin Kösegi, Support Architect

Armin Kösegi studied process engineering at the Mannheim University of Applied Sciences, focusing on process control engineering and control technology. After graduating, he worked for a medium-sized process control enterprise in the areas of support, training, and consulting. In 1998, he joined SAP's product support division where he specialized in the handling of problem tickets for SAP NetWeaver Application Server. He later assumed management of the topics upgrade and transport system in the service area of SAP Active Global Support. In this area, he made significant contributions to projects for upgrade safeguarding and optimization activities at upgrade runtime. Within the framework of IT planning services, Armin currently supports customers in strategic decisions with regard to upgrade and software change management. If you have questions, you are welcome to contact Armin at armin.koesegi@sap.com.

Rainer Nerding, Service Architect

After finishing his studies of physics, Rainer Nerding worked in application support within the client/server environment and later the SAP environment of a medium-sized enterprise in the automotive supply industry. Since 2000, Rainer Nerding has been working in the area of software change management at SAP Active Global Support. In the beginning, he was responsible for handling problem tickets. Today, he focuses on development and delivery of services and consulting offerings, primarily in the areas of software change management and Support Packages. Rainer is responsible for the development of different services for the analysis and optimization of transport processes in customer systems and he has project experience from numerous customer applications and service deliveries. Feel free to contact Rainer at rainer.nerding@sap.com.

Index

D

E

F

G

H

I

J

K

L

M

N

O

P

Q

R

S

SAP PRESS

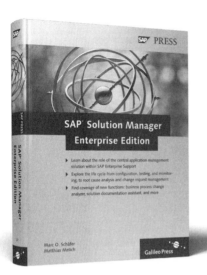

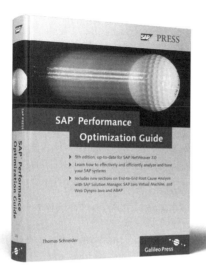

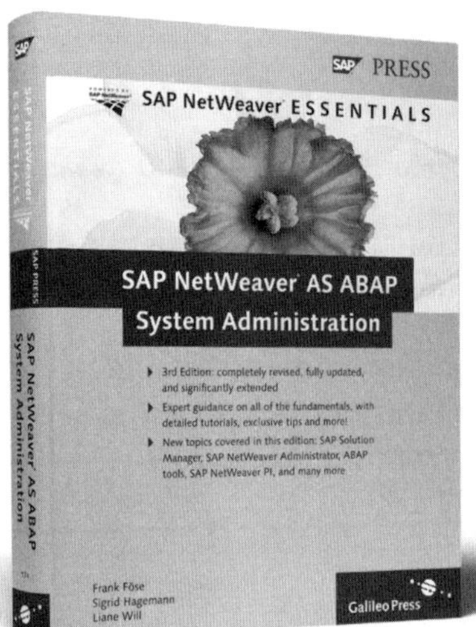

3rd Edition: completely revised, fully updated and significantly extended

Expert guidance on all of the fundamentals, with detailed tutorials, exclusive tips and more!

New topics covered in this edition: SAP Solution Manager, SAP NetWeaver Administrator, ABAP tools, SAP NetWeaver PI, and many more

Frank Föse, Sigrid Hagemann, Liane Will

SAP NetWeaver ABAP System Administration

This completely revised, updated and extended edition of our best-selling SAP System Administration book provides administrators and SAP Basis consultants with the core knowledge needed for effective and efficient system maintenance of SAP NetWeaver Application Server ABAP 7.0 and 7.1. With the help of this book, you'll master fundamental concepts such as architecture, processes, client administration, authorizations, and many others, while you learn how to optimize your use of the system's key administration tools. You'll profit from step-by-step tutorials as well as proven tips and tricks with this comprehensive book, which is also suitable to help you prepare for the certified SAP Technical Consultant exam.

646 pp., 3. edition 2008, 69,95 Euro / US$ 69.95
ISBN 978-1-59229-174-8

>> www.sap-press.de/1643

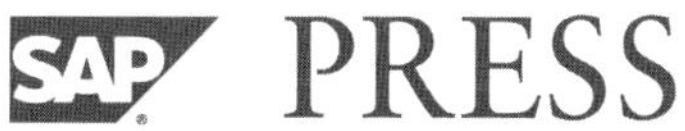

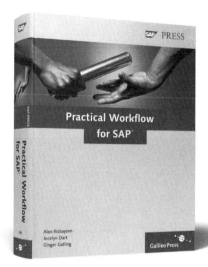